GW00792365

GA

3 PAPER BLDGS

TEMPLE

LONDON EC4

Gabriel Moss Esq.
3, Paper Buildings,
Temple London E.C.4.
01-353-3721

THE LAW AND PRACTICE AS TO RECEIVERS

AUSTRALIA
The Law Book Company Ltd.
Sydney : Melbourne : Brisbane

CANADA AND U.S.A.
The Carswell Company Ltd.
Agincourt, Ontario

INDIA
N. M. Tripathi Private Ltd.
Bombay

ISRAEL
Steimatzky's Agency Ltd.
Jerusalem : Tel Aviv : Haifa

MALAYSIA : SINGAPORE : BRUNEI
Malayan Law Journal (Pte.) Ltd.
Singapore

NEW ZEALAND
Sweet & Maxwell (N.Z.) Ltd.
Wellington

PAKISTAN
Pakistan Law House
Karachi

KERR

ON THE LAW AND PRACTICE AS TO

RECEIVERS

FIFTEENTH EDITION

BY

RAYMOND WALTON, M.A., B.C.L.

One of Her Majesty's Justices;
Hon. Fellow of the College of Estate Management;
A Bencher of Lincoln's Inn

With
a
Chapter on Extra-territoriality
and
Associated Appendices
by

MUIR HUNTER, M.A.

One of Her Majesty's Counsel
A Bencher of Gray's Inn

LONDON

SWEET & MAXWELL

1978

First Edition	(1869)	By W. W. Kerr
Second Edition	(1882)	By W. W. Kerr
Third Edition	(1891)	By W. W. Kerr
Fourth Edition	(1900)	By P. F. Wheeler
Fifth Edition	(1905)	By W. D. Rawlins
Sixth Edition	(1912)	By F. C. Watmough
Seventh Edition	(1921)	By F. C. Watmough
Eighth Edition	(1924)	By F. C. Watmough
Ninth Edition	(1930)	By F. C. Watmough
Tenth Edition	(1935)	By F. C. Watmough
Eleventh Edition	(1946)	By F. C. Watmough
Twelfth Edition	(1952)	By R. Walton and A. W. Sanson
Thirteenth Edition	(1963)	By R. Walton
Fourteenth Edition	(1972)	By R. Walton
Fifteenth Edition	(1978)	By R. Walton

Published in 1978 by
Sweet & Maxwell Limited of
11 New Fetter Lane, London,
and printed in Great Britain
by The Eastern Press Limited
of London and Reading

ISBN 0 421 229101

PREFACE

IT has become almost a ritual to note in successive Prefaces to successive editions of *Kerr on Receivers* that the space devoted to the problems facing receivers appointed out of court has been greatly expanded since the last edition. This is as equally true of the present edition as of its immediate predecessor. Indeed, the law relating to the appointment of receivers by the court is reasonably well settled in all its aspects, and the task of an Editor is basically to attempt to note the changes effected by legislation and the alterations in the Rules of the Supreme Court.

It is far otherwise with receivers appointed out of court, where the law is, and has now for some time been, in a continual state of development. In view of this country's membership of the European Economic Community, it appears highly likely that that development will soon include many more international aspects than hitherto. With this in mind, it has fortunately proved possible to persuade Mr. Muir Hunter, Q.C., who has unrivalled practical experience of the law of bankruptcy in an international setting, to contribute an important entirely new Chapter on Extra-territoriality, and two related Appendices on " The Paulian Action " and " Securities comparable to floating charges in other jurisdictions."

It is accordingly hoped that the much expanded second Part of *Kerr on Receivers* will afford receivers appointed out of court as much guidance in the changed conditions of the times as its predecessors have done. The law is attempted to be stated as at December 1, 1977.

RAYMOND WALTON

PUBLISHER'S NOTE

As at the date of going to press, the Employment Protection (Consolidation) Bill had not received the Royal Assent. The book, however, has taken account of the Bill as if it were an Act, with the section number being those of the Bill as printed on July 19, 1977. It is hoped that the reader will find this approach more helpful than references to the old legislation.

TABLE OF CONTENTS

PART ONE—RECEIVERS APPOINTED BY THE COURT

TABLE OF CASES

ix

TABLE OF CASES

PAGE

xliii

TABLE OF STATUTES

TABLE OF STATUTORY RULES AND ORDERS

RULES OF THE SUPREME COURT

Part I

RECEIVERS APPOINTED BY THE COURT

CHAPTER 1

PRINCIPLES ON WHICH A RECEIVER IS APPOINTED BY THE HIGH COURT OF JUSTICE

Nature of the office. A receiver in an action is an impartial person appointed by the court to collect and receive, pending the proceedings, the rents, issues and profits of land, or personal estate, which it does not seem reasonable to the court that either party should collect or receive, or for enabling the same to be distributed among the persons entitled.

Jurisdiction. The jurisdiction of the Court of Chancery to appoint a receiver was founded on the inadequacy of the remedy to be obtained in the courts of ordinary jurisdiction; where that remedy was inadequate for the purposes of justice, the Court of Chancery would, on a proper case being made out, appoint a receiver.[1]

The courts of common law had not, under the former procedure, jurisdiction to appoint a receiver. But under the Supreme Court of Judicature Act 1873, s. 16 (now Supreme Court of Judicature Act 1925, s. 18 (2) (*a*)), all the jurisdiction of the Court of Chancery became vested in the High Court of Justice; and under section 25 (8) of that Act (now s. 45 of the Act of 1925) a receiver may be appointed by interlocutory order in all cases in which it appears to the court to be just and convenient that such order should be made; and any such order may be made either unconditionally or upon such terms and conditions as the court thinks fit.

A receiver may now, therefore, be appointed in any division of the High Court. In one sense the jurisdiction to appoint a receiver is enlarged [2]; certain inconvenient rules are relaxed and there is no longer any limit to the jurisdiction to appoint a receiver upon interlocutory application.[3] But the principles upon which the jurisdiction is exercised are still those upon which the Court of Chancery proceeded.[4] Thus a receiver may be appointed in any

---

[1] *Hopkins* v. *Worcester, etc., Canal Co.* (1868) 6 Eq. 437, 447, *per* Giffard L.J.; *Cupit* v. *Jackson* (1824) 13 Price 721, 734, *per* Alexander C.B.

[2] *Anglo-Italian Bank* v. *Davies* (1878) 9 Ch.D. 286, 293.

[3] *Gawthorpe* v. *Gawthorpe* [1878] W.N. 91, *per* Jessel M.R.; *Coney* v. *Bennett* 29 Ch.D. 993.

[4] *Holmes* v. *Millage* [1893] 1 Q.B. 551; *Harris* v. *Beauchamp* [1894] 1 Q.B. 801 *Edwards* v. *Picard* [1909] 2 K.B. 903; *cf. Smith* v. *Tsakyris* [1929] W.N. 39.

proceedings without the commencement of special proceedings being necessary; and although it is no longer necessary for a judgment creditor to commence proceedings in the Chancery Division before obtaining a receiver over an equitable interest,[5] a receiver will not be appointed in cases where the Court of Chancery would have had no jurisdiction to make the appointment after the special proceedings had been instituted.[6] The court will not now, any more than it would formerly, appoint a receiver by way of equitable execution, over property the title to which is legal, merely because it affords a more convenient method of obtaining payment,[7] save under its statutory powers in this regard.[8] Nor will it appoint a receiver merely because the property is not amenable to legal execution for reasons other than the equitable nature of the debtor's title [9]; nor will the court appoint a receiver except in aid of existing rights.[10]

The words " interlocutory order " in the Judicature Act 1925, s. 45, are not confined in their meaning to an order between writ and final judgment, but mean an order other than an order made by way of final judgment in an action, whether such order be made before judgment or after.[11] The court cannot properly order discovery on a motion for a receiver, after judgment, though it may order production of documents necessary for working out the judgment.[12]

The court has the same power of appointing a receiver at the trial of the action as it has on interlocutory application.[13]

The jurisdiction of the court relative to the appointment of receivers and the authority to be given them has been further enlarged by the provisions of R.S.C., Order 29, rule 2, where it is necessary to preserve property which is in dispute in a pending action,[14] or where it is the subject-matter of an arbitration.[15]

---

[5] *Smith* v. *Cowell* (1880) 6 Q.B.D. 75.

[6] *Holmes* v. *Millage, supra*; *Morgan* v. *Hart* [1914] 2 K.B. 183.

[7] *Morgan* v. *Hart, supra*; and p. 94, *post*.

[8] See Administration of Justice Act 1956, s. 36, and p. 94, *post*

[9] *Edwards* v. *Picard, supra*.

[10] *Philips* v. *Jones* (1884) 28 S.J. 360.

[11] *Smith* v. *Cowell* (1880) 6 Q.B.D. 75, 78.

[12] *Korkis* v. *Andrew Weir & Co.* [1914] W.N. 99; if accounts have been referred to a special referee, application should be made to him.

[13] *Re Prytherch* (1889) 42 Ch.D. 590.

[14] *Per* Farwell L.J. in *Leney & Sons* v. *Callingham* [1908] 1 K.B. 79; and see *Chaplin* v. *Barnett* (1912) 28 T.L.R. 256.

[15] Arbitration Act 1950, s. 12 (6) (*h*).

The court has also an express power under certain statutes to appoint a receiver.[16]

The court will not in general [17] entertain an action by an encumbrancer in which a receiver only is claimed; there must be a claim for foreclosure or sale.[18] In other cases substantive relief, in addition to a receiver, must also be claimed, save in a few exceptional cases, *e.g.* where the appointment is made under the express provisions of a statute, or *semble* where the appointment is sought to preserve the assets of a deceased person and the nominal defendant has not intermeddled with the assets.[19]

Object of appointment. A receiver can only be properly appointed for the purpose of getting in and holding or securing funds or other property, which the court at the trial, or in the course of the action, will have the means of distributing amongst, or making over to, the persons or person entitled thereto.[20] The object sought by such appointment is therefore the safeguarding of property for the benefit of those entitled to it.[21] There are two main classes of cases in which the appointment is made: (1) to enable persons who possess rights over property to obtain the benefit of those rights and to preserve the property pending realisation, where ordinary legal remedies are defective [22]; and (2) to preserve property from some danger which threatens it.

Appointment to enforce rights. In the first class of cases are included those in which the court appoints a receiver at the instance of a mortgagee whose principal is immediately payable or whose interest is in arrear [23]; cases of equitable execution, *i.e.* where the appointment is made to enable a judgment creditor to obtain payment out of property which cannot be reached by legal execution,[24] are within this class. In such cases the appointment is made as a matter of course as soon as the applicant's right is established, and it is unnecessary to allege any danger to the

---

[16] *e.g.* Railway Companies Act 1867, s. 4: see p. 52, *post.*

[17] See *Re Newport Construction Co. Ltd.* [1948] Ch. 217.

[18] *Gasson and Hallagan* v. *Jell* [1940] Ch. 248; *Re Newport, etc., Co., supra.*

[19] This exception is more apparent than real; for in most cases accounts should be asked for in the first instance.

[20] *Evans* v. *Coventry* (1855) 3 Drew. 80; see, too, *Wright* v. *Vernon, ibid.* 112.

[21] *Tullett* v. *Armstrong* (1836) 1 Keen 428; *Owen* v. *Homan* (1853) 4 H.L.C. 997, 1032.

[22] *Cummins* v. *Perkins* [1899] 1 Ch. 16, 19.

[23] *Re Crompton & Co. Ltd.* [1914] 1 Ch. 954.

[24] The court has always had jurisdiction to protect a fund for a person entitled to be paid out of it: *Cummins* v. *Perkins* [1899] 1 Ch. 16, 19.

property [25]; for the appointment of a receiver is necessary to enable the applicant to obtain that to which he is entitled. Cases in which the appointment is made under a statutory provision also fall within this class: so do cases where a receiver is appointed over the assets of a dissolved partnership. Where there is an alternative legal remedy, as in the case of legal mortgages,[26] the court has a discretion, but the appointment is now frequently made without proof of jeopardy.

Appointment to preserve property. The second class of cases includes those in which the appointment is made to preserve property pending litigation to decide the rights of the parties,[27] or to prevent a scramble among those entitled, as where a receiver is appointed pending a grant of probate or administration,[28] or to preserve property of persons under disability,[29] or where there is danger of the property being damaged or dissipated by those with the legal title, such as executors or trustees,[30] or tenants for life,[31] or by persons with a partial interest, such as partners,[32] or by the persons in control, as where directors of a company with equal powers are at variance.[33] In all cases within this second class it is necessary to allege and prove some peril to the property; the appointment then rests on the sound discretion of the court.[34] In exercising its discretion the court proceeds with caution, and is governed by a view of all the circumstances. No positive or unvarying rule can be laid down as to whether the court will or will not interfere by this kind of interim protection of the property. Where, indeed, the property is as it were *in medio*, in the enjoyment of no one, it is the common interest of all parties that the court should prevent a scramble, and a receiver will readily be appointed: as, for instance, over the property of a deceased person pending a litigation as to the right to probate or administration. But where the object of the plaintiff is to assert a right to property of which the defendant is in enjoyment, the case presents more difficulty. The court by taking possession at the instance of the plaintiff may

---

[25] *Re Crompton & Co., supra*; and p. 29, *post.*
[26] *Pratchett* v. *Drew* [1924] 1 Ch. 280; and p. 27, *post.*
[27] *Tullett* v. *Armstrong* (1836) 1 Keen 428; *Owen* v. *Homan* (1853) 4 H.L.C. 997, 1032.
[28] See p. 19, *post.*   [29] See p. 73, *post.*   [30] Chap. 2, Section 2.
[31] See p. 17, *post.*   [32] See pp. 64 *et seq.*
[33] *Stanfield* v. *Gibbon* [1925] W.N. 11. See also *Featherstone* v. *Cooke* (1873) 16 Eq. 298; *Trade Auxiliary Co.* v. *Vickers* (1873) 16 Eq. 303.
[34] *Greville* v. *Fleming* (1845) 2 J. & L. 339; *Re Prytherch* (1889) 42 Ch.D. 590; *Re Henry Pound, Son & Hutchins* (1889) 42 Ch.D. 402.

be doing a wrong to the defendant; in some cases an irreparable wrong. If the plaintiff should eventually fail in establishing his right against the defendant, the court may by its interim interference have caused mischief to the defendant for which the subsequent restoration of the property may afford no adequate compensation.[35] Where the evidence on which the court is to act is very clearly in favour of the plaintiff, then the risk of eventual injury to the defendant is very small, and the court does not hesitate to interfere. Where there is more doubt, there is, of course, more difficulty. The question is one of degree, as to which, therefore, it is impossible to lay down any precise or unvarying rule.[36]

If the court is satisfied upon the materials it has before it that the party who makes the application has established a good prima facie title, and that the property the subject-matter of the proceedings will be in danger if left until the trial in the possession or under the control [37] of the party against whom the receiver is asked for,[38] or, at least, that there is reason to apprehend that the party who makes the application will be in a worse situation if the appointment of a receiver be delayed,[39] the appointment of a receiver is almost a matter of course.[40] If there is no danger to the property, and no fact is in evidence to show the necessity or expediency of appointing a receiver, a receiver will not be appointed.[41]

The duty of the court upon a motion for a receiver is merely to protect the property for the benefit of the person or persons to whom the court, when it has all the materials necessary for a determination, shall think it properly belongs.[42] On a motion for a receiver the court will not prejudice the action,[43] or say what view it will take at the trial.[44] Indeed, the court will not appoint a receiver at the instance of a person whose right is disputed, where the effect of the order would be to establish the right, even if the

---

[35] See *Marshall* v. *Charteris* [1920] 1 Ch. 520.

[36] *Owen* v. *Homan* (1853) 4 H.L.C. 997, 1032, *per* Lord Cranworth and *cf.* text to note 63 p. 66, *post*.

[37] *Cummins* v. *Perkins* [1899] 1 Ch. 16; *Leney & Sons Ltd.* v. *Callingham* [1908] 1 K.B. 79.

[38] *Evans* v. *Coventry* (1854) 5 D.M. & G. 918.

[39] *Aberdeen* v. *Chitty* (1839) 3 Y. & C. 382; *Thomas* v. *Davies* (1847) 11 Beav. 29.

[40] See *Middleton* v. *Dodswell* (1806) 13 Ves. 266; *Oldfield* v. *Cobbett* (1835) 4 L.J.Ch. 272; *Real and Personal Advance Co.* v. *Macarthy* (1879) 27 W.R. 706.

[41] See *Whitworth* v. *Whyddon* (1850) 2 Mac. & G. 52; *Wright* v. *Vernon* (1855) 3 Drew. 112; *Micklethwait* v. *Micklethwait* (1857) 1 De G. & J. 504.

[42] *Blakeney* v. *Dufaur* (1851) 15 Beav. 42.

[43] *Huguenin* v. *Baseley* (1808) 13 Ves. 107.

[44] *Fripp* v. *Chard Ry.* (1853) 11 Ha. 264; *Skinners' Company* v. *Irish Society* (1836) 1 My. & Cr. 164.

court be satisfied that the person against whom the demand is made is fencing off the claim.[45] Nor will the appointment be made where it might affect legal rights: formerly a receiver would not, for instance, have been appointed merely to prevent an executor exercising his right of retainer.[46]

Postponed operation of appointment. In an appropriate case, an appointment of a receiver may be made immediately, but with directions that the receiver shall not give security or take possession of the assets until the expiration of a limited time.[47] Normally, however, the appointment will not be made until there are moneys for him to receive.[48]

Conduct of applicant. The court, on the application for a receiver, always looks to the conduct of the party who makes the application, and will usually refuse to interfere unless his conduct has been free from blame.[49] Parties who have acquiesced in property being enjoyed against their own alleged rights cannot, except in special circumstances, come to the court for a receiver.[50]

Defendant submitting to order. The court may abstain from appointing a receiver on the submission of the defendant to an order to pay money into court [51] or to the plaintiff,[52] to deal with moneys as the court shall direct,[53] or to pay an occupation rent.[54]

Pleading and practice. Provided the proper parties were before the court,[55] technical objections as to parties were never an answer on the application for a receiver, if a case for the appointment of a receiver was shown [56]: and if the objection is a

[45] *Greville* v. *Fleming* (1845) 2 J. & L. 335: see *Marshall* v. *Charteris* [1920] 1 Ch. 520.
[46] *Re Wells* (1890) 45 Ch.D. 569. The right of retainer has now been abolished by Administration of Estates Act 1971, s. 10.
[47] *Re Crompton & Co. Ltd.* [1914] 1 Ch. 954, *per* Warrington J. at p. 967.
[48] *Re Knott End Railway Act 1898* [1901] 2 Ch. 8 (railway not yet open for public traffic).
[49] See *Baxter* v. *West* (1858) 28 L.J.Ch. 160. *Cf. Wood* v. *Hitchings* (1840) 2 Beav. 297.
[50] *Gray* v. *Chaplin* (1826) 2 Russ. 147; *Skinners' Company* v. *Irish Society* (1836) 1 My. & Cr. 162.
[51] *Curling* v. *Lord Townshend* (1816) 19 Ves. 633; *Palmer* v. *Vaughan* (1818) 3 Sw. 173.
[52] *Pritchard* v. *Fleetwood* (1815) 1 Mer. 54.
[53] *Talbot* v. *Hope Scott* (1858) 4 K. & J. 141.
[54] *Porter* v. *Lopes* (1877) 7 Ch.D. 358; *Real and Personal Advance Co.* v. *Macarthy* (1879) 27 W.R. 707.
[55] See p. 112, *post*, note 22; *Mukherjee* v. *Giri* (1927) 55 L.R.Ind.App. 131.
[56] *Evans* v. *Coventry* (1854) 5 D.M. & G. 918; *Hamp* v. *Robinson* (1865) 3 D.J. & S. 109; *Re Johnson* (1866) L.R. 1 Ch. 325.

formal one, and such as may be removed by amendment,[57] the court will not stay its hand.

The evidence should show that all parties with an interest in the property are before the court [58]; but if a sufficient case is made out the appointment may be made in the absence of some of the persons interested.

If the subject of the action in respect of which a receiver is sought is a matter of public interest, the Attorney-General should be made a party.[59]

If a receiver is claimed generally, the court may grant the claim as far as is proper, or in a limited form.[60]

Where a receiver has been appointed generally in an action, it is unnecessary, when the action comes on upon further consideration, to insert in the minutes a direction to continue the receiver.[61] So, also, a receiver appointed on an interlocutory application before judgment need not be continued by the judgment,[62] unless the appointment was in the first instance an interim appointment only.[63] If the judgment continues a receiver who has been appointed until judgment or further order, this is virtually a new appointment, and further security must be given.[64]

The practice on the appointment, the effect of the order and other topics are dealt with at length in subsequent chapters. The procedure of the Queen's Bench Division in relation to the appointment of a receiver is, as far as possible, analogous to the procedure in like circumstances of the Chancery Division.[65]

Concurrent actions. The High Court has jurisdiction to appoint a receiver in a proper case, although another court has already appointed a receiver over the same property in a concurrent action,[66] and will stay further proceedings in such concurrent action if in the circumstances of the case they are vexatious.[67]

---

[57] Under R.S.C., Ord. 15, r. 6.
[58] *Gray* v. *Chaplin* (1826) 2 Russ. 147.
[59] *Gray* v. *Chaplin* (1826) 2 Russ. 147; *Skinners' Company* v. *Irish Society* (1836) 1 My. & Cr. 162: see *Re Chamberlain's Settlement* [1921] 1 Ch. 533.
[60] *Major* v. *Major* (1844) 8 Jur. 797.
[61] *Re Underwood* (1889) 37 W.R. 428; but if the further consideration disposes of the matter, provision should be made for discharge of the receiver.
[62] *Davies* v. *Vale of Evesham Preserves* [1895] W.N. 105; 73 L.T. 150; 43 W.R. 646.
[63] *Cruse* v. *Smith* (1879) 24 S.J. 121.
[64] *Brinsley* v. *Lynton Hotel Co.* [1895] W.N. 53.
[65] *Walmsley* v. *Mundy* (1884) 13 Q.B.D. 807. As to appointment in divorce, see p. 42, *post.*
[66] *Nothard* v. *Proctor* (1875) 1 Ch.D. 4.
[67] *Re Connolly Bros. Ltd.* [1911] 1 Ch. 731.

Thus an equitable mortgagee had commenced an action in the Palatine Court and obtained a receiver therein *ex parte*, after a writ had, to his knowledge, been issued in a debenture holders' action in the Chancery Division relative to the same, amongst other, property; Parker J., who had appointed a receiver in the Chancery action without knowledge of the order made in the Palatine action, restrained the plaintiff in the latter action from further proceeding therewith, on the ground that all matters in dispute could be adjusted in the Chancery action, whereas some only of them could be dealt with in the Palatine action, and that the conduct of the plaintiff in the latter action was in the circumstances vexatious: this decision was affirmed by the Court of Appeal.[68]

The Crown. No receiver by way of equitable execution can be appointed against the Crown.[69] For relief analogous to attachment which may be obtained against the Crown, see Chapter 2, p. 39, *post*.

Foreign Sovereigns. The submission to arbitration of a foreign Sovereign does not enable the court to appoint a receiver over property of the Sovereign within the jurisdiction to enforce payment of money or costs, but it is submitted that a receiver might be appointed over property which is the subject of litigation to which he is a party [70]; or which is the subject-matter of the arbitration.

Costs. The court, at its discretion, may either (i) deal with the costs of a motion for a receiver at the time of the application,[71] or (ii) order the costs of the application to be costs in the action,[72] or (iii) reserve the costs,[73] even although the application is refused.[74] The former practice was that where no direction as to costs was given the party making a successful motion was entitled to his costs as costs in the action, but the party opposing was not; where the motion failed the party moving was not, in the absence of express direction, but the party opposing was, entitled to his

---

[68] *Re Connolly Bros. Ltd.* [1911] 1 Ch. 731; the proper course where such an order has been made is to apply in the concurrent action for the discharge of the receiver appointed therein.

[69] Crown Proceedings Act 1947, s. 25 (4).

[70] See *Duff Development Co.* v. *Kelantan Government* [1923] 1 Ch. 385; on appeal [1924] A.C. 797; *cf. Re Suarez* [1917] 2 Ch. 131.

[71] *Goodman* v. *Whitcomb* (1820) 1 J. & W. 593; *Wilson* v. *Wilson* (1837) 2 Keen 249; *Wood* v. *Hitchings* (1840) 4 Jur. 858.

[72] *Hewett* v. *Murray* (1885) 54 L.J.Ch. 572; *Tillett* v. *Nixon* (1883) 25 Ch.D. 238.

[73] *Chaplin* v. *Young* (1862) 6 L.T. 97.

[74] *Baxter* v. *West* (1858) 28 L.J.Ch. 169; *Coope* v. *Creswell* (1863) 12 W.R. 299.

costs as costs in the action; where the motion was not opposed the costs of both parties were costs in the action.[75] Although an express Order of the Court is now necessary in every case,[76] these principles are still usually followed.

The respondent to an abandoned motion is entitled to his costs thereof, although he has given no notice of his claim to such costs.[77]

Where at the trial an application for a receiver was unsuccessful, but the plaintiff was successful on another claim, he was ordered to pay the costs so far as increased by the application for a receiver.[78]

Where a plaintiff proceeds by writ instead of originating summons in a case where he might have proceeded by originating summons, he will be allowed such costs only as he would have been entitled to if he had proceeded by originating summons.[79] A mortgagee can now, under R.S.C., Order 88, rule 1, obtain all relief to which he is entitled in a proceeding [80] commenced by originating summons. But as pointed out above,[81] he cannot in general ask for a receiver only. Proceedings by a mortgagee in which there is a claim for payment of principal money or possession of property forming security for money or for delivery of possession of the mortgaged property are assigned to the Chancery Division.[82]

Appeal. An appeal lies to the Court of Appeal without leave from an order granting or refusing a receiver.[83] For an Order of the Court of Appeal appointing a receiver see *Hyde* v. *Warden* [84]: and for an Order of the House of Lords see *Houlditch* v. *Donegal (Marquis).*[85] An appeal will equally lie if it is the personality of the receiver which is in question, but it requires a very strong case before the court will interfere with the discretion of the judge in this respect.[86]

---

[75] See *Corcoran* v. *Witt* (1872) L.R. 13 Eq. 53; *cf. Grimston* v. *Timms* (1870) 18 W.R. 747, 781. And see Morgan and Wurzburg, *Law of Costs in Chancery Division,* pp. 47–55; *Supreme Court Practice* (1976), Vol. 1, note to Ord. 62, r. 9, paras. 62/9/16 *et seq.* As to county court practice, see *Friis* v. *Paramount Bagwash Co.* (*No.* 2) [1940] 2 K.B. 654, 657.

[76] R.S.C., Ord. 62, r. 3 (1).

[77] *Hinde* v. *Power* [1913] W.N. 184.

[78] *Re New York Taxicab Co.* [1913] 1 Ch. 1.

[79] *Barr* v. *Harding* (1887) 36 W.R. 216; *Re Francke* [1888] W.N. 69; 57 L.J.Ch. 437.

[80] The decision in *Wallis* v. *Griffiths* [1921] 2 Ch. 301 is now obsolete since the alteration of the above rule. See *Alliance Building Society* v. *Varma* [1949] Ch. 724.

[81] *Ante,* p. 5.   [82] R.S.C., Ord. 88, r. 2.

[83] Judicature Act 1925, s. 31 (1) (*i*) (ii).

[84] (1876) 1 Ex.D. 309.   [85] (1834) 2 Cl. & F. 470.

[86] *Re New Zealand Midland Ry. Co.* (1897) 13 T.L.R. 212.

CHAPTER 2

IN WHAT CASES A RECEIVER WILL BE APPOINTED

SECTION 1. IN THE CASE OF MINORS [1]

Receiver of minor's estate. A legal estate in land can in no case be vested in a minor [2]; it will be vested either in trustees for sale [3] or in Settled Land Act trustees as statutory owners [4] or remain vested in the grantor.[5] The principles and practice relating to the appointment of a receiver against trustees and executors [6] will, therefore, apply where the protection of an infant's property is necessary.

Where a minor is beneficially entitled to any property the court, with a view to the application of the capital or income for his maintenance, may appoint a person to convey, or vest the right to transfer stock or shares or things in action or to receive dividends or recover a thing in action.[7] Application should be made under this section and not for a receiver generally.

SECTION 2. IN THE CASE OF EXECUTORS AND TRUSTEES

Grounds of appointment. The court will, upon a proper case being made out, dispossess an executor or trustee of the trust estate by appointing a receiver, but it will not do so upon slight grounds. It is for the testator or creator of the trust, and not for the court, to say in whom the trust for the administration of the property shall be reposed. A strong case must be made out to

---

[1] That is to say, a person who has not attained the age of 18: Family Law Reform Act 1969, s. 1.

[2] Law of Property Act 1925, s. 1 (6).

[3] See Law of Property Act 1925, s. 19 and Sched. 1, Pt. 3.

[4] Settled Land Act 1925, ss. 1 (1) (*d*), (2), 26 and Sched. 2, para. 3.

[5] A conveyance to an infant operates as an agreement for a settlement: Law of Property Act 1925, s. 19 (1); Settled Land Act 1925, s. 27 (1). In such a case a receiver would be readily appointed, against a grantor retaining rents.

[6] See *post*, pp. 13–19.

[7] Trustee Act 1925, s. 53. It applies to enable a disentailing assurance to be executed for enabling money to be raised for the benefit of the minor tenant in tail: *Re Gower's Settlement* [1934] Ch. 365 and *cf. Re Meux* [1958] Ch. 154. Where there is capital money, an order may be made for its application for advancement or education of a minor tenant in tail under s. 64, Settled Land Act 1925; *cf. Re Scarisbrick's Resettled Estates* [1944] Ch. 229.

induce the court to dispossess a trustee or executor who is willing to act.[8] It must clearly be shown that the nature and position of the property is such as to warrant the interference of the court.[9] Thus the court will not, at the instance of one of several parties interested in an estate, displace a competent trustee, or take the possession from him, unless he has wilfully or ignorantly permitted the property to be placed in a state of insecurity, which due care or conduct would have prevented. It is not enough that the estate may have depreciated in value, and that the incumbrances thereon may have been increasing, if the management of the trustees does not appear to have been improper.[10]

It is no sufficient cause for the appointment of a receiver that one of several trustees has disclaimed, unless the remaining trustees consent to such appointment [11]; nor that the trustees or executors are poor or in mean circumstances [12]; nor that, being trustees for sale, they have let the purchaser into possession before they received the purchase-moneys, for the court will not necessarily infer this to be misconduct.[13]

Nor is it a sufficient cause for the appointment of a receiver that one of several trustees is inactive,[14] or has gone abroad, though where a sole executor or trustee or all the trustees are out of the jurisdiction a receiver may be appointed where there is default by the agent here in rendering accounts.[15] Where a sole trustee or one of several trustees is an enemy or in enemy territory, a receiver can be appointed in case of urgency to protect the property: but this is rarely necessary; the proper course is to appoint or apply for the appointment of a new trustee and for a vesting order. This jurisdiction has been exercised in the case of a foreign testator even if the trustees who are in enemy territory have been appointed by a foreign court where there are assets within the jurisdiction.

---

[8] *Middleton* v. *Dodswell* (1806) 13 Ves. 268; *Smith* v. *Smith* (1836) 2 Y. & C. 361; *Bainbridge* v. *Blair* (1841) 4 L.J.Ch. 207.

[9] *Whitworth* v. *Whyddon* (1850) 2 Mac. & G. 52.

[10] *Barkley* v. *Lord Reay* (1843) 2 Ha. 308.

[11] *Browell* v. *Reed* (1843) 1 Ha. 434.

[12] *Anon.*, 12 Ves. 4; *Howard* v. *Papera* (1815) 1 Madd.142.

[13] *Browell* v. *Reed* (1842) 1 Ha. 434.

[14] *Ibid.* but *cf. Tait* v. *Jenkins* (1842) 1 Y. & C.C.C. 492. If he is absent from the U.K. for 12 months, a new trustee may be appointed: see Trustee Act 1925, s. 36.

[15] *Noad* v. *Backhouse* (1843) 2 Y. & C.C.C. 529; *Smith* v. *Smith* (1853) 10 Ha.App. 71; *Westby* v. *Westby* (1847) 2 Coop.C.C. 210; *Dickins* v. *Harris* [1866] W.N. 93; 14 L.T. 98.

Misconduct, etc., a ground for a receiver. If any misconduct, waste, or improper disposition of the assets can be shown,[16] or if it appear that the trust property has been improperly managed, or is in danger of being lost [17]—*e.g.* owing to the insolvency of the executor [18]—or if it can be satisfactorily established that parties in a fiduciary position have been guilty of a breach of duty, there is a sufficient foundation for the appointment of a receiver.[19]

Similarly, a receiver may be appointed at the instance of sureties to an administration bond where the administrator threatens to distribute the estate without providing for a contingent liability.[20]

The appointment of a receiver pending a grant of probate or letters of administration is dealt with in the next section.[21]

Where a portion of a trust fund has been lost, that loss is prima facie evidence of a breach of duty on the part of the trustees, sufficient to authorise the interference of the court by the appointment of a receiver.[22] So, also, it has been held to be a good ground for the appointment of a receiver that an executor or trustee has omitted to raise a certain sum as, according to the will of his testator, he should have done for the maintenance and education of infant legatees,[23] or that he has left a considerable portion of it outstanding on improper securities [24]; though in all these cases the matter may be dealt with by the appointment of new trustees, or in a proper case by a vesting order under various statutory provisions.[25] So, also, a receiver will be appointed if it appears that the trustee has an undue bias towards one of the contending parties,[26] or where, in consequence of disputes among the trustees,

---

[16] *Anon.* (1806) 12 Ves. 4, *per* Sir W. Grant; see, too, *Oldfield* v. *Cobbett* (1835) 4 L.J.Ch. 272. Query whether this would include distribution of the estate in accordance with the terms of the will within six months from the grant without making provision for a possible claim under the Inheritance (Provision for Family and Dependants) Act 1975 (see *Re Simson* [1950] Ch. 38); s. 26 of the Matrimonial Causes Act 1965 or s. 31 of the Matrimonial Causes Act 1973.

[17] *Middleton* v. *Dodswell* (1806) 13 Ves. 266, 276; *Colebourne* v. *Colebourne* (1876) 1 Ch.D. 690.

[18] *Gawthorpe* v. *Gawthorpe* [1878] W.N. 91; *Re H.'s Estate, H.* v. *H.* (1876) 1 Ch.D. 276.

[19] *Evans* v. *Coventry* (1854) 5 D.M. & G. 918; *Bainbrigge* v. *Blair* (1841) 3 Beav. 421; *Nothard* v. *Proctor* (1875) 1 Ch.D. 4; *Hamilton* v. *Girdlestone* [1876] W.N. 202.

[20] *Re Anderson-Berry, Harris* v. *Griffith* [1928] Ch. 290.

[21] *Post*, p. 20.

[22] *Evans* v. *Coventry* (1854) 5 D.M. & G. 918.

[23] *Richards* v. *Perkins* (1839) 3 Y. & C. 307; *Hart* v. *Tulk* (1849) 6 Ha. 611.

[24] *Ibid.*

[25] *e.g.* Settled Land Act 1925, ss. 12 (1), 16 (7): Administration of Estates Act 1925, s. 43 (2). [26] *Earl Talbot* v. *Hope Scott*, 4 K. & J. 139.

the payment of rents has been permitted to fall into arrear,[27] or where a trustee, in spite of repeated applications, with no proper excuse refuses or neglects to render an account to the beneficiaries.[28]

Where a man, who had accepted and held moneys for particular persons upon certain trusts, afterwards denied the legality of the trusts on which he held the moneys, the court appointed a receiver.[29]

A creditor in an administration action cannot, unless a case of waste of assets be shown or some other special case be made out, have a receiver appointed merely because the administrator will not admit assets, or, formerly, had been paying debts and preferring creditors when the estate was insolvent,[30] though the case would have been otherwise if any preferential debts [31] were being disregarded. Nor would the court formerly have interfered with an executor's legal right of retainer by the appointment of a receiver, in cases where it was not shown that the assets are being wasted.[32] It is only in cases of improper conduct or danger to the assets reasonably proved that the court will interfere by appointing a receiver.[33]

Bankruptcy, etc., of trustee. If a sole executor or trustee becomes bankrupt, there is a case for the appointment of a receiver.[34] But if a testator has selected an insolvent debtor as his executor, with full knowledge of his insolvency, the court will not, on the bare fact of the insolvency alone, interfere by appointing a receiver [35]: though the fact that a testator has not altered a will made before the insolvency, after knowledge of the insolvency, is

---

[27] *Wilson* v. *Wilson* (1837) 2 Keen 249.

[28] See also R.S.C., Ord. 85, r. 5 (2).

[29] *Sheppard* v. *Oxenford* (1855) 1 K. & J. 492.

[30] *Philips* v. *Jones* (1884) 28 S.J. 360; *Re Harris* (1887) 35 W.R. 710; 56 L.J.Ch. 754. The dictum of Jessel M.R. to the contrary in *Re Radcliffe* (1876) 7 Ch.D. 733, cannot be regarded as law: *Re Wells* (1890) 45 Ch.D. 569, 574. The right of preference has now been abolished by Administration of Estates Act 1971, s. 10. An order for administration can now be speedily obtained under R.S.C., Ord. 85, r. 2, or in bankruptcy under Bankruptcy Act 1914, s. 130. As to effect of transfer on claim of a trustee in an earlier bankruptcy, see Bankruptcy (Amendment) Act 1926, s. 3.

[31] See Administration of Estates Act 1925, s. 34 (1), and Sched. 1, Pt. 1.

[32] *Re Wells* (1890) 45 Ch.D. 569, approved *Re Stevens* [1898] 1 Ch. 162, 173. The right of retainer has now been abolished by Administration of Estates Act 1971, s. 10.

[33] *Baird* v. *Walker* (1890) 35 S.J. 56; 90 L.T. 56.

[34] *Re Johnson* (1866) L.R. 1 Ch. 325; *Re Hopkins*, 19 Ch.D. 61; or an injunction may be granted: *Bowen* v. *Phillips* [1897] 1 Ch. 174. The court may, if it considers it expedient, appoint a receiver instead of directing the return of effects alleged to be vested in an executor which have been taken possession of by a trustee in bankruptcy.

[35] *Gladdon* v. *Stoneman* (1808) 1 Madd. 143n.; *Stainton* v. *Carron Co*. (1864) 18 Beav. 146, 161.

not sufficient to deter the court from appointing a receiver [36]; and the court may make the appointment where the estate is barely sufficient for creditors.[37] An interim order may be refused where some parties refuse to join in the application, although the personal representative was not nominated by the testator, but is the administrator of an executrix.[38]

Poverty, etc., of trustee. Although it is not a sufficient cause for the appointment of a receiver that an executor or trustee is poor or in mean circumstances,[39] the case is different if an executor or administrator be proved to be of bad character and drunken habits, as well as in poverty.[40]

Inasmuch as a married woman has for many years been in all respects competent to act as executrix,[41] the earlier cases in which a receiver was appointed on the sole ground that an executrix was married to a man who was insolvent or out of the jurisdiction [42] must now be considered obsolete; but as in any other case of undue influence, if either an executor or an executrix is under the influence of a fraudulent, or possibly even a necessitous, spouse this would presumably be a factor influencing the court on an application to appoint a receiver on the ground of jeopardy.

Receiver appointed by consent. If all the *cestuis que trust*, or parties beneficially interested in an estate, concur in the application for a receiver, and the trustee consents, the court will make the order [43]; or if the only acting trustee consents, the others being abroad [44] or guilty of misconduct.[45] Similarly, where, of two trustees, one had died and the survivor refused to act, a receiver was appointed in spite of the opposition of the representative of the deceased trustee, who had advanced money out of his own pocket to an annuitant under the will, in expectation of repayment out of the assets.[46]

---

[36] *Langley* v. *Hawke* (1820) 5 Madd. 46.
[37] *Oldfield* v. *Cobbett* (1835) 4 L.J.Ch. 272.
[38] *Smith* v. *Smith* (1836) 2 Y. & C. 361.
[39] *Supra*, p. 13.
[40] *Everett* v. *Prythergch* (1841) 12 Sim. 368; and see *Dillon* v. *Lord Mountcashell* (1727) 4 Bro.P.C. 306.
[41] Law Reform (Married Women and Tortfeasors) Act 1935, Pt. 1; Law of Property Act 1925, s. 170.
[42] *Taylor* v. *Allen* (1741) 2 Atk. 213; see *Bathe* v. *Bank of England* (1858) 4 K. & J. 564.
[43] *Brodie* v. *Barry* (1811) 3 Mer. 696.
[44] *Tidd* v. *Lister* (1854) 5 Madd. 433.
[45] *Middleton* v. *Dodswell* (1806) 13 Ves. 268.
[46] *Palmer* v. *Wright* (1846) 10 Beav. 237.

Other cases. In a case where two out of three trustees chose to act separately, and took securities in their own names, omitting that of the third trustee, a *cestui que trust* was held entitled to a receiver.[47] A receiver may also be appointed where the co-trustees cannot act through disagreement among themselves.[48] So, too, where the trustees had to manage a business and were themselves not qualified to do so, but could not agree in appointing some person as manager, a receiver was appointed.[49]

Settled land. Land which is subject to a settlement within the meaning of the Settled Land Act 1925 is vested in the tenant for life upon the trusts of the settlement, or if there is no tenant for life of full age in the trustees as statutory owners; or on the death of a tenant for life, where the settlement continues to exist, in his special personal representatives. The appointment of a receiver against a tenant for life will, as under the old law, be made where he does not apply the income in keeping down incumbrances [50] or omits to keep leaseholds in repair according to the covenants in the leases.[51] In cases where a tenant for life does not fulfil his obligations to maintain and insure improvements under section 88 of the Settled Land Act 1925, it is conceived that a receiver will be appointed.[52] A receiver has been refused where a tenant for life pulled down houses, but was rebuilding them.[53]

Under the old law a receiver was appointed where a tenant for life refused to produce deeds to enable a term for raising portions to be created. A vesting order can now be obtained where the tenant for life refuses or neglects to create a legal estate required for giving effect to any provision of the settlement,[54] and a similar provision applies in the case of personal representatives [55]; similarly, where a tenant for life or other person refuses to execute any instrument required for vesting the land in the person entitled

---

[47] *Swale* v. *Swale* (1856) 22 Beav. 584.

[48] *Bagot* v. *Bagot* (1841) 10 L.J.Ch. 116; *Day* v. *Croft* (1839) *Lewin on Trusts*, 16th ed., p. 646; as to power of majority (who may be assisted by injunction) see *Re Whiteley* [1910] 1 Ch. 600.

[49] *Hart* v. *Denham* [1871] W.N. 2.

[50] See note (a) to *Giffard* v. *Hort* (1804) 1 Sch. & Lef. 386, 407. See *Gresley* v. *Adderley* (1818) 1 Sw. 579; *Bertie* v. *Abingdon* (1817) 3 Mer. 560; *Shore* v. *Shore* (1859) 4 Dr. 501.

[51] *Re Fowler* (1881) 16 Ch.D. 723.

[52] An injunction and damages would be an alternative remedy.

[53] *Micklethwait* v. *Micklethwait* (1857) 1 De G. & J. 504.

[54] Or if he is outside the U.K. or cannot be found; Settled Land Act 1925, s. 16 (7).

[55] Administration of Estates Act 1925, s. 43 (2).

to have the land vested in him [56]; and where a tenant for life has ceased by bankruptcy, assignment or otherwise to have a sub-stantial interest, the trustees can be authorised to exercise his powers.[57] These provisions usually enable an application for a receiver to be dispensed with, but pending the making of a vesting order a receiver may be appointed in urgent cases.

Trust for sale. Land can no longer be held in undivided shares either at law or in equity, and the interests of tenants in common take effect behind a trust for sale. Partition actions are abolished, but in addition to the power of trustees under section 28 (3) of the Law of Property Act 1925, which is exercisable where the shares have vested in the trustees whether or not subject to a further settlement,[58] the court has jurisdiction under section 30 to order a partition or sale.[59] On an application under this section a receiver can be appointed in a proper case, either on interlocutory applica-tion or at the hearing.

Where the trustees for sale are also the beneficiaries, and one is in possession and retaining the whole of the rents, a receiver may be appointed as under the old law [60]; or the trustee in occupation might presumably be ordered to pay an occupation rent [61] or give security.[62] Similarly with joint tenants both in law and equity, whose equitable interests are subject to a trust for sale.

Where land is held for the purposes of trade, a receiver is appointed on the same principle as in partnership cases.[63] There may be a partnership in the trade though not in land vested in one or more of the partners. Where the land is the subject-matter of the action, a receiver may be appointed over both the land and the business, when that is the convenient course.[64]

Deed of arrangement. A receiver will be appointed when the property of a debtor has been vested in trustees for the benefit of

---

[56] Settled Land Act 1925, s. 12: *e.g.* where a tenant for life whose life interest has been surrendered by himself, or his trustee in bankruptcy to the next remainder-man refuses to convey: see *Re Shawdon Estates* [1930] 2 Ch. 1.

[57] *Ibid.* s. 24. *Cf. Re Thornhill's Settlement* [1941] Ch. 24.

[58] *Re Brooker* [1934] Ch. 610; *cf. Re Thomas* [1930] 1 Ch. 194.

[59] Or the trustees for sale can be authorised to partition under Trustee Act 1925, s. 57: see *Re Thomas* [1930] 1 Ch. 194.

[60] *Norway* v. *Rowe* (1816) 19 Ves. 159; *Sandford* v. *Ballard* (1861) 30 Beav. 109.

[61] *Porter* v. *Lopes* (1877) 7 Ch.D. 359.

[62] *Street* v. *Anderton* (1793) 4 Bro.C.C. 414; *Murray* v. *Cockerell* [1866] W.N. 223.

[63] *Jeffreys* v. *Smith* (1820) 1 J. & W. 298, 302.

[64] See *Roberts* v. *Eberhardt* (1853) Kay 148, 159.

his creditors, and the appointment is necessary for the protection of the property.[65] Application is made to the court having jurisdiction in bankruptcy.[66]

Implied trusts. In the case of misconduct by trustees, the court will appoint a receiver as well where the trust arises by implication as where it is expressed.[67] An order for the appointment of a receiver of the rents and profits of an estate for the purpose of accumulating a fund was made where the tenant for life had fraudulently obtained a sum of stock to which the trustees of the settlement were entitled.[68]

In a case where on proof of a secret trust the court was satisfied that real and personal estate had been bequeathed on the faith of a promise made by the legatee that she would dispose of the property in favour of the plaintiffs, a receiver was appointed.[69]

Pending proceedings abroad. If one of the next-of-kin of a foreigner obtains administration here, pending proceedings abroad to ascertain who are entitled, an action for a receiver can be maintained by a person claiming as next-of-kin.[70]

SECTION 3. PENDING A GRANT OF PROBATE OR LETTERS OF ADMINISTRATION

During litigation in the Ecclesiastical Court as to probate or administration, the Court of Chancery would entertain a bill for the mere preservation of the property of the deceased till the litigation was determined, and would appoint a receiver, although the Ecclesiastical Court might, by appointing an administrator, have provided for the collection of the effects *pendente lite*.[71] It was, indeed, a matter of course, where no probate or administration had been granted, for the Court of Chancery to appoint a receiver, pending bona fide litigation in the Ecclesiastical Court to determine the right to probate or administration, unless a special

---

[65] *Waterlow* v. *Sharp* [1867] W.N. 64.

[66] See Deeds of Arrangement Act 1914; *Re Wilson* [1916] 1 K.B. 382.

[67] See *Re One and All Sickness Association, The Times*, December 12, 18, 1908, where a receiver of the property of an unregistered friendly society was appointed, it being held that the relationship of trustee and beneficiary existed. As to winding up, see *Re Victoria Society* [1913] 1 Ch. 167.

[68] *Woodyatt* v. *Gresley* (1836) 8 Sim. 180.

[69] *Podmore* v. *Gunning* (1836) 7 Sim. 644.

[70] *Transatlantic Co.* v. *Pietroni* (1860) John. 604. This would now be in proceedings for administration.

[71] *Watkins* v. *Brent* (1835) 1 Myl. & Cr. 97; *Wood* v. *Hitchings* (1840) 2 Beav. 289; on appeal 4 Jur. 858; *De Feucheres* v. *Dawes* (1842) 5 Beav. 110.

case was made out for not doing so.[72] In cases where the representation was in contest and no person had been appointed executor or administrator, the court would interfere, not because of the contest, but because there was no proper person to receive the assets.[73] But the appointment was refused where the property was of trifling value or where no sufficient ground had been shown to warrant the interference of the court.[74]

Appointment of receiver before probate. Under the present practice contentious probate proceedings are assigned to the Chancery Division of the High Court.[75] However, in order to protect the assets, the Chancery Division will, in an action by a beneficiary or creditor against the persons named as executors in the will or entitled to a grant of letters of administration,[76] claiming a receiver, appoint one pending the grant.[77] The writ may claim administration after the grant has been made,[78] or accounts; though of course no order for administration can be made before a grant has been obtained by the defendant. Where there is already a *lis pendens* [79] the application should, prima facie, be made in that action for an administrator *pendente lite* [80]; but the existence of such proceedings does not displace the jurisdiction to appoint a receiver [81]; but after an administrator *pendente lite* has been appointed, a receiver will only be appointed in special circumstances.[82] The appointment is an interim appointment

---

[72] *Watkins* v. *Brent* (1835) 1 Myl. & Cr. 97; *Grimston* v. *Turner* (1870) 18 W.R. 724; [1870] W.N. 93. Before the grant of administration a receiver and manager may be appointed to carry on the business of an intestate: *Blackett* v. *Blackett* (1871) 19 W.R. 559; *Re Wright* (1888) 32 S.J. 721.

[73] *Rendall* v. *Rendall* (1841) 1 Ha. 154, *per* Wigram V.-C.; *Parkin* v. *Seddons* (1873) 16 Eq. 36.   [74] *Whitworth* v. *Whyddon* (1850) 2 Mac. & G. 55.

[75] Administration of Justice Act 1970, s. 1 (4) (*b*); R.S.C., Ord. 76.

[76] See further p. 21, *post.*

[77] *Re Oakes* [1917] 1 Ch. 230; *Re Wenge* [1911] W.N. 129; and see *Re Shephard* (1889) 43 Ch.D. 131; *Macleod* v. *Lane* (1886) 2 T.L.R. 322; *Re Dawson* (1906) 75 L.J.Ch. 201; *In the goods of Pryse* [1904] P. 304; *Re Clark* [1910] W.N. 234. Under the old practice it was held that an action to protect and also to administer the estate was irregular: *Overington* v. *Ward* (1865) 34 Beav. 175.

[78] *Per* Eve J. in *Re Wenge* [1911] W.N. 129. But *semble* this only applies where the defendant is an executor: *cf. Ingall* v. *Moran* [1944] K.B. 160 (C.A.).

[79] A caveat though warned is not a *lis pendens* for this purpose: *Salter* v. *Salter* [1896] P. 291.

[80] *Re Parker* (1885) 54 L.J.Ch. 694; and see *Re Moore* (1888) 13 P.D. 36; *Re Green* [1895] W.N. 69.   [81] *Re Oakes* [1917] 1 Ch. 230.

[82] *Veret* v. *Duprez* (1868) L.R. 6 Eq. 330; *Parkin* v. *Seddons* (1873) L.R. 16 Eq. 34. Both these cases were decided when the administrator *pendente lite* was appointed by the Probate Division of the High Court of Justice. The practice may well now harden against the appointment of a receiver in such circumstances. As to practice where the receiver was appointed before the administrator *pendente lite*, see *post*, p. 24.

only, and is usually made to expire within a few days of a grant being obtained.[83] In order to found jurisdiction to make the appointment, an action must have been commenced, and the writ must specifically claim a receiver [84]; the person named in the will as executor [85] or the person entitled to take out administration[86] and any other person who has intermeddled with the estate should be made defendant. Where no will is known to exist and no successor on intestacy is known, a person who has intermeddled with the estate would, it seems, be a sufficient defendant.[87]

Death of executor sole defendant. Upon the death of a sole executor against whom an action has been commenced for the administration of the estate of his testator, an interim receiver will be appointed in such action pending a fresh grant being obtained, if the assets are in peril.[88] In such cases a receiver will be appointed before [89] or after [90] judgment, and although there is no living defendant on the record.[91]

Pending proceedings to recall probate. If probate or administration has been granted, the circumstance that a suit is pending to recall or revoke probate or administration, is not of itself a sufficient ground for the court, as of course, to interfere to prevent the parties to whom probate or administration has been granted, from using their powers. In such a case it is only in special circumstances that the court will make the appointment [92]; for where there is a legal title to receive, the court ought not to interfere, unless the legal title is abused, or there is evidence of intention to abuse it [93]: as, for instance, where a prima facie case of fraud is made out,[94] or where peril to the assets is shown, whether

---

[83] *Re Clark* [1910] W.N. 234; but even under the old practice a bill was not demurrable in such a case because it asked for a receiver generally (*Major* v. *Major* (1844) 8 Jur. 797); the appointment may be extended if there is jeopardy, on the proper parties being added.

[84] *Re Wenge* [1911] W.N. 129; *Re Oakes, supra.*

[85] *Re Sutcliffe* [1942] Ch. 453.

[86] *Re Leask* (1891) 65 L.T. 199.

[87] *Cf. Re Chalmers* [1921] W.N. 129.

[88] *Re Clark* [1910] W.N. 131, 234, following *Cash* v. *Parker* (1879) 12 Ch.D. 293; *Re Shephard* (1889) 43 Ch.D. 131; and see *Mullane* v. *Ahern* (1891) 28 L.R.Ir. 105.

[89] *Re Clark* [1910] W.N. 234.

[90] *Cash* v. *Parker* (1897) 12 Ch.D. 293.

[91] *Re Clark, supra.*

[92] *Watkins* v. *Brent* (1835) 1 Myl. & Cr. 97; *Newton* v. *Ricketts* (1847) 11 Jur. 662; *Rendall* v. *Rendall* (1841) 1 Ha. 154.

[93] *Devey* v. *Thornton* (1851) 9 Ha. 229.

[94] *Rutherford* v. *Douglas* (1822) 1 Sim. & St. 111n.; *Watkins* v. *Brent* (1835) 1 Myl. & Cr. 102; *Dimes* v. *Steinberg* (1854) 2 Sm. & G. 75.

from insolvency or otherwise.[95] A grant is neither impounded nor withheld on the ground of jeopardy; in such cases, therefore, application should be made for a receiver.[96] Such application was therefore successfully made where it appeared that there was no executor or administrator in existence with power to act as such, notwithstanding there was no ground laid for interference in respect of any improper conduct of the parties.[97] Where, accordingly, an executor, by agreeing with his opponents that the question as to the validity of the supposed testamentary papers should be tried in the suit to recall probate, had treated himself as not being complete executor, a receiver was appointed [98]: " If," said Wigram V.-C. in *Rendall* v. *Rendall*,[99] " the question be whether the party claiming to be executor is so *de jure* or not, a receiver will be appointed." And a receiver has been appointed upon the application of the actual executor, pending a suit to annul probate, upon the ground that the opposing party, by having given notice to the debtors to the estate not to pay to the applicant, had produced by his own act an incapacity on the part of the executor to collect and preserve the assets.[1]

Upon these principles a receiver would be granted pending an application to revoke a grant of probate or administration to the estate of a tenant for life as regards land continuing to be settled after his death,[2] where the grant has been obtained for an improper purpose or is being improperly employed. This will, however, rarely be necessary as the revocation is speedily obtained. Alternatively a special or additional personal representative may be appointed under section 23 of the Administration of Estates Act 1925.

Administrator " pendente lite." Under section 163 of the Judicature Act 1925,[3] where any legal proceedings touching the validity of a will or for obtaining, recalling or revoking any grant are pending, the High Court [4] may grant administration to an

---

[95] *Ball* v. *Oliver* (1813) 2 V. & B. 96; *Newton* v. *Ricketts* (1847) 11 Jur. 662; *Devey* v. *Thornton* (1851) 9 Ha. 229.

[96] *In the goods of Moxley* [1916] 1 I.R. 145.

[97] *Watkins* v. *Brent* (1835) 1 Myl. & Cr. 97.

[98] *Ibid.*

[99] (1841) 1 Ha. 155.

[1] *Marr* v. *Littlewood* (1837) 2 Myl. & Cr. 454.

[2] See *Bridgett and Hayes' Contract* [1928] Ch. 163.

[3] Replacing ss. 70 and 71 of the Court of Probate Act 1857.

[4] This jurisdiction is exercised by the Chancery Division. See Administration of Justice Act 1970, s. 1 and R.S.C., Ord. 76, r. 15.

administrator who has all the powers of a general administrator [5] other than the right of distributing the residue, and every such administrator is to be subject to the immediate control of the court and act under its direction. Remuneration may be allowed.[6] Even if there is a life interest in the estate, it is not necessary to appoint more than one administrator *pendente lite*.[7] In order that the Chancery Division may have jurisdiction under this Act, there must be an actual *lis pendens* before it: the entering of a *caveat*, through warned by the executor, is not sufficient.[8] The practical difference is however, minimal: if there is a pending action, the application will be made by summons, and, if not, by originating summons.[9]

The appointment may be made on the application of a person not a party, *e.g.* a creditor where the proceedings are likely to be prolonged,[10] or where the parties to the testamentary suit take no steps to bring it to trial.[11] In a case where there was a contest as to the validity of several wills made by a tenant for life, none of which affected the beneficial interest in the settled land, and the litigation was likely to be prolonged, the Settled Land Act trustees were appointed administrators *pendente lite* of the settled land without security and with liberty to exercise all powers without leave of the court.[12]

The court has jurisdiction under the section to appoint the same person administrator and receiver *pendente lite* of the estates of a person whose sole executor has died, and of such executor, where an action is pending as to the testamentary dispositions of such executor, although there is no litigation pending relative to the estate of the original testator.[13]

---

[5] As to such powers, see Administration of Estates Act 1925, ss. 2, 32–34. When such jurisdiction was exercised by the Probate Division, it followed the settled practice of the Chancery Division in appointing receivers: *Re Bevan, Bevan* v. *Houldsworth* [1948] 1 All E.R. 271.

[6] See *Neale* v. *Bailey* (1875) 23 W.R. 418; and, as to costs of administrator and receiver, *Taylor* v. *Taylor* (1881) 6 P.D. 29.

[7] *Re Price* (1931) 75 S.J. 295 (s. 163 is not controlled by s. 160).

[8] *Salter* v. *Salter* [1896] P. 291.

[9] R.S.C., Ord. 76, r. 15 (1). The summons or other document by which the order is sought attracts a fee of £5 unless the administrator *pendente lite* is to be excused from passing his accounts: Supreme Court Fees Order 1975 (S.I. 1975 No. 1343), Fee No. 22.

[10] *Tichborne* v. *Tichborne* (1869) L.R. 1 P. & D. 730.

[11] *In the goods of Evans* (1891) 5 P.D. 215; *In the estate of Cleaver* [1905] P. 319.

[12] *Re St. Germans* (1943) unreported. It is submitted that in such a case a special grant of administration limited to the settled land might have been made to the trustees under s. 162 of the Judicature Act 1925.

[13] *Shorter* v. *Shorter* [1911] P. 184: see, however, *Salter* v. *Salter* [1896] P. 291.

If the deceased died since 1897 a grant *pendente lite* normally includes both real and personal estate; but if the deceased died before 1926, only on notice to the heir, unless his citation is dispensed with.[14] The grant terminates with the decree,[15] or the decision of an appeal therefrom, before the actual grant of probate or letters of administration.[16]

A party to the litigation will not in general be appointed except by consent [17] though there is no absolute rule to this effect.[18] If the parties to the litigation do not agree upon a nominee, the court may refer it to the Master to nominate a person to act.

As soon as the Chancery Court clothes anybody with the character of an administrator, even although he is only appointed *pendente lite*, it will usually discharge the order for a receiver, and will allow the administrator to receive the estate, but will hold its hand over his dealings with it, and make such orders upon him as it may think proper.[19] Where the appointment of an administrator *pendente lite* is made, the provisions of R.S.C., Ord. 30, rr. 2 (relating to security),[20] 4 (relating to accounts),[21] and 6 (relating to default) [22] and (subject to subsection (2) of s. 163 of the Judicature Act 1925, which empowers the court to fix such reasonable remuneration as it thinks fit for the administrator) 3 (relating to remuneration) [23] will apply.[24] Where the probate litigation may be prolonged and it is necessary to deal by sale, lease or mortgage with the property, the appointment of an administrator *pendente lite* is essential: the receiver cannot make title. The receiver appointed will sometimes be appointed administrator *pendente lite* [25]; and a grant outright may be made to him, *e.g.* where the next-of-kin though cited are unable to find security,[26] or do not apply for a grant.[27]

---

[14] *Wiggins* v. *Hudson* (1890) 80 L.T. 296; *Re Messiter Terry* (1908) 24 T.L.R. 465.
[15] *Wieland* v. *Bird* [1894] P. 262.
[16] *Taylor* v. *Taylor* (1881) 6 P.D. 29.
[17] *De Chatelain* v. *Pontigny* (1858) 1 Sw. & Tr. 34.
[18] *Re Griffin* [1925] P. 38.
[19] *Tichborne* v. *Tichborne* (1869) 1 P. & D. 730 *per* Lord Penzance at p. 733.
[20] See p. 117, *post.*
[21] See p. 255, *post.*
[22] See p. 261, *post.*
[23] See p. 246, *post.*
[24] R.S.C., Ord. 76, r. 15 (2).
[25] *In the goods of Evans* (1891) 15 P.D. 215; *In the estate of Cleaver* [1905] P. 319.
[26] *In the goods of G. Moore* [1892] P. 145.
[27] *In the goods of Mayer* (1873) 3 P. & M. 39.

Pleading. The court, though it may appoint a receiver to get in a testator's estate in aid of an administrator *pendente lite*, will not appoint a receiver over property of a testator claimed by a party independently of the will, even though that person's title may be impeached on the ground of fraud. Where, pending a contest between the plaintiff and the defendant, as to the validity of two wills, the plaintiff filed a bill for a receiver of the testatrix's estate, and to set aside an assignment made by her to the defendant, the court refused to appoint a receiver of the property comprised in the assignment, that being claimed by the defendant independently of either will.[28]

Though a receiver has been appointed during a litigation in the proper court respecting the validity of a will, the court will not, on that account alone, order the person named as executor to pay into court money in his hands belonging to the testator's estate received previously to the appointment of the receiver.[29]

Practice. It has been said that an action to appoint a receiver pending litigation as to probate or administration should not be brought to a hearing.[30] A motion, therefore, to dismiss such action for want of prosecution will be refused with costs.[31] But where the grant of probate or administration has been made to the defendant and the writ claims administration or is amended so as to claim administration after grant, there appears to be no reason why an order for administration should not be made in the action. The court will after grant make an order by consent for the continuance of the receiver, and for payment of costs, and the investment of the fund in court.[32] Normally after the probate litigation is over, it is the practice to discharge the receiver and dispose of the costs; and, if it appears that there was no reasonable ground for instituting the action at all, the court may order the plaintiff to pay all the costs although a receiver has been appointed.[33]

Estate of a British subject dying abroad. If a foreign personal representative brings assets of the estate into this country, the court may appoint a receiver at the instance of the personal

---

[28] *Jones* v. *Goodrich* (1840) 10 Sim. 327; on appeal, 4 Jur. 98.

[29] *Reed* v. *Harris* (1836) 7 Sim. 639; *Edwards* v. *Edwards* (1852) 10 Ha.App. 63.

[30] *Anderson* v. *Guichard* (1851) 9 Ha. 275; but see *Carrow* v. *Ferrior* (1868) 16 W.R. 841, 1072.

[31] *Edwards* v. *Edwards* (1853) 7 Jur. 826.

[32] *Anderson* v. *Guichard* (1851) 9 Ha. 275.

[33] *Barton* v. *Rock* (1856) 22 Beav. 81, 376.

representative instituted here to prevent those assets being
removed elsewhere.[34] If the foreign personal representative
collects English assets, such as debts due in England, he
is apparently executor *de son tort*, and a receiver would be appointed at the instance of a beneficiary or English personal
representative.

SECTION 4. IN CASES BETWEEN MORTGAGOR AND
MORTGAGEE

Legal mortgagee. Before the Judicature Acts, a mortgagee
having the legal estate could not, except under special circumstances, obtain from the Court of Chancery the appointment of a
receiver over the mortgaged property, because he could take
possession under his legal title.[35] But since the Judicature Acts
the court [36] will appoint a receiver at the instance of a legal
mortgagee after default in payment of principal or interest.[37]
The court does this, not because the mortagee has in fact less
power than he formerly had to take possession,[38] but because there
is an obvious convenience in appointing a receiver, so as to
prevent a mortgagee from being in the unpleasant position of a
mortgagee in possession.[39] Since 1925 a mortgagor always retains a
legal estate if he had one when the mortgage was created [40]; and a
mortgagee under a charge by way of legal mortgage is to be
treated as in the same position as a mortgagee by demise.[41]

The appointment of a receiver at the instance of a legal mortgagee is not a matter of course, and the court has a discretion
in the matter [42]; but under the present practice where an action
for foreclosure is pending the court will usually appoint a receiver
at the instance of a legal mortgagee, and will do so on interlocutory motion where the mortgagor is in possession; possession

---

[34] *Hervey* v. *Fitzpatrick* (1854) Kay 421. As to position of an administrator
attorney for a foreign principal, see *Re Achillopoulos* [1928] Ch. 433.
   [35] *Berney* v. *Sewell* (1820) 1 J. & W. 648; *Pease* v. *Fletcher* (1875) 1 Ch.D. 273.
   [36] As to mortgages of metalliferous mines in Cornwall, see statutes referred to at
pp. 71, 72, *post.*
   [37] *Tillett* v. *Nixon* (1883) 25 Ch.D. 238.
   [38] As to the exclusive jurisdiction of the county court in certain mortgage actions
for possession, see Administration of Justice Act 1970, s. 37, and *Manchester Unity
Trustees* v. *Sadler* [1974] 1 W.L.R. 770.
   [39] *Re Pope* (1886) 17 Q.B.D. 749; *Re Prytherch* (1889) 42 Ch.D. 590.
   [40] See *Smith* v. *Tsakyris* [1929] W.N. 39.
   [41] Law of Property Act 1925, s. 87.
   [42] *Mason* v. *Westoby* (1886) 32 Ch.D. 206; *Re Prytherch, supra.*

is usually directed to be given to the receiver, but the mortgagor may be allowed to attorn tenant at a rent.[43]

All actions by a mortgagee in which payment or possession is claimed, as well as actions to enforce the security, are now assigned to the Chancery Division [44]; and all such actions may be commenced by originating summons.[45] In actions claiming foreclosure or sale so commenced, the appointment may be made at the hearing by the master; in cases of urgency application may be made to the court on motion.

The fact that the legal mortgagee has taken possession does not prevent the court from appointing a receiver at his instance,[46] though in such a case the mortgagee may be required to show some special circumstances to induce the court to relieve him from the position in which he has placed himself.[47] The fact that a mortgagee has an express power to appoint a receiver under his security or by statute [48] will not deter the court from making the appointment [49]: nor will the fact that the mortgagee has exercised the power, at all events where the mortgagor is himself in possession. Where more than one mortgagee is interested, if the power of appointing a receiver is not exercised by the mortgagee to whom it is confided bona fide the court will appoint its own receiver.[50]

Rentcharge. Before the Judicature Act of 1873, it was held that, where an annuity was charged on land, with a power of distress superadded by the Landlord and Tenant Act 1730, the annuitant could help himself, and was not entitled to the appointment of a receiver.[51] The remedies of the owner of a rentcharge or other yearly sum charged on land or the income of land created since 1881 are, subject to any contrary intention contained in the instrument creating it,[52] contained in section 121 of the Law of Property Act 1925 and include distress under subsection (2), and possession and the creation of a term under subsections (3)

---

[43] *Pratchett* v. *Drew* [1924] 1 Ch. 280.

[44] R.S.C., Ord. 88, r. 2.

[45] R.S.C., Ord. 88. See notes to that rule in *Supreme Court Practice* (1976), Vol. 1, as to practice before the master.

[46] *County of Gloucester Bank* v. *Rudry Merthyr Co.* [1895] 1 Ch. 629.

[47] *Ibid.*

[48] See Chap. 15, *post.*

[49] *Tillett* v. *Nixon* (1883) 25 Ch.D. 238.

[50] See *Re Maskelyne British Typewriter* [1898] 1 Ch. 133; and *post*, Chap. 15; see also *Re Slogger Automatic Feeder Co.* [1915] 1 Ch. 478.

[51] *Sollory* v. *Leaver* (1869) L.R. 9 Eq. 22; and see *Kelsey* v. *Kelsey* (1874) L.R. 17 Eq. 495.

[52] Law of Property Act 1925, s. 121 (5).

and (4).[53] It is conceived that the court has jurisdiction to appoint a receiver to enforce payment of arrears,[54] except where the rentcharge is created under the Improvement of Land Act 1864 or any special Improvement Act [55]; but there appears to be no reported case where this has been done. Where a rentcharge is charged upon another rentcharge, and is in arrear, the owner of the former may appoint a receiver of the latter under section 122.

After foreclosure. After judgment for foreclosure absolute, the action being at an end, the plaintiff cannot obtain an order for a receiver, even though the conveyance of the foreclosed property has not been settled. In a proper case, however, the court may open a foreclosure, where special circumstances are shown for the reconsideration of the judgment.[56]

Mortgagee of tolls, etc. Receivers have been appointed at the instance of mortgagees of turnpike and other tolls.[57] The Turnpike Roads Act 1822 provided that there should be no priority between mortgages of such tolls. So, when a mortgagee took possession upon not being paid, and retained the whole proceeds in discharge of his own demand, a receiver was appointed at the instance of another mortgagee.[58] " Under an ordinary mortgage," said Turner L.J.,[59] " the mortgagee when he enters into possession holds for his own benefit. Under a mortgage of this description he becomes, when he enters into possession, liable to the other mortgagees to the extent of their interest. This liability would entitle him, upon possession taken, to come to the court to have it ascertained what is due upon the other mortgages, and for a receiver to aid him in the due application of the tolls; and if this court can be called upon to appoint a receiver immediately after the possession recovered at law, it can hardly be necessary that the proceedings at law should first be taken."

---

[53] A legal term can only be created if the rentcharge is held for a legal estate, *i.e.* it must be perpetual or for a term of years absolute.

[54] Under Judicature Act 1925, s. 45. *Cf. Pease* v. *Fletcher* (1875) 1 Ch.D. 273; *Mason* v. *Westoby* (1886) 32 Ch.D. 206; *Re Prytherch* (1889) 42 Ch.D. 590; *Re Tucker* [1893] 2 Ch. 323; *Hambro* v. *Hambro* [1894] 2 Ch. 364.

[55] See Improvement of Land Act 1899, s. 3 (which limits the remedy to s. 121 of the Law of Property Act 1925), and Law of Property Act 1925, s. 207 (c).

[56] *Wills* v. *Luff* (1888) 38 Ch.D. 197.

[57] *Lord Crewe* v. *Edleston* (1857) 1 De G. & J. 93.

[58] *Dumville* v. *Ashbrooke* (1829) 3 Russ. 99n.

[59] *Lord Crewe* v. *Edleston* (1857) 1 De G. & J. 93, 109.

Equitable mortgagee. The right to the appointment of a receiver is one of the rights which accrue to an equitable mortgagee [60] whose security has become enforceable as one of the steps in realisation.[61] An equitable mortgagee has, in the absence of express agreement, no means of taking possession [62]: he cannot by notice to tenants enforce payment of their rents to him.[63] If, therefore, there is no prior legal incumbrancer in possession the court as a matter of right appoints a receiver upon the application of an equitable mortgagee whose security has become enforceable either under its express terms or by operation of law.[64]

A receiver will be appointed at the instance of an equitable incumbrancer if the principal has become payable,[65] or if the payment of interest is in arrear though the principal is not payable,[66] or if there is reason to apprehend that the property is in peril or insufficient to pay the charges on it.[67]

The existence of a prior legal mortgage forms no bar to the appointment of a receiver at the instance of a subsequent incumbrancer, unless the legal mortgagee is in possession.[68] The court will not allow a prior legal incumbrancer to object to the appointment by anything short of an assertion of his legal right of taking possession or appointing a receiver [69]; and the fact that the legal mortgagee has a right to appoint a receiver by the express

---

[60] A second or subsequent mortgagee is no longer necessarily an equitable mortgagee: see Law of Property Act 1925, ss. 85 (2), 86 (2).

[61] See *Re Crompton & Co. Ltd.* [1914] 1 Ch. 967; as to debenture holders, see Section 7, p. 55, *post*.

[62] Although it appears that the court can order the mortgagor to give up possession to him: *Barclays Bank* v. *Bird* [1954] Ch. 274.

[63] *Vacuum Oil Co.* v. *Ellis* [1914] 1 K.B. 703; though if his mortgage is by deed he may appoint a receiver under Law of Property Act 1925, s. 101 (1) (iii). See pp. 284 *et seq., post*.

[64] See *Re Crompton & Co. Ltd., supra*; *Dalmer* v. *Dashwood* (1793) 2 Cox 383; *Davis* v. *Duke of Marlborough* (1818) 2 Swans. 108, 137; *Hopkins* v. *Worcester, etc., Canal Co.* (1868) L.R. 6 Eq. 437, *per* Gifford V.-C. at p. 447.

[65] Where there is an express provision that the principal is not to be called in as long as interest is punctually paid, punctually means on the day fixed for payments: *Maclaine* v. *Gatty* [1921] A.C. 376.

[66] *Burrowes* v. *Molloy* (1845) 2 Jo. & Lat. 521; *Wilson* v. *Wilson* (1837) 2 Keen 249; *Hopkins* v. *Worcester and Birmingham Canal Co.* (1868) L.R. 6 Eq. 447. In mortgage transactions prima facie month means calendar month: *Schiller* v. *Peterson & Co. Ltd.* [1924] 1 Ch. 394.

[67] See p. 59, *post*, and *Herbert* v. *Greene* (1889) 3 Ir.Ch. 273; *Moore* v. *Malyon* (1889) 33 S.J. 699.

[68] *Post*, p. 30; and see *Norway* v. *Rowe* (1816) 19 Ves. 158.

[69] *Silver* v. *Bishop of Norwich* (1816) 3 Sw. 114n.; *Re Metropolitan Amalgamated Estates* [1912] 2 Ch. 497.

terms of his security makes no difference to this rule.[70] Except in
the case of debentures second mortgagees in most cases have a
legal estate.[71]

If a subsequent incumbrancer or judgment creditor was in
possession of the estate, the Court of Chancery would appoint a
receiver at the instance of a prior incumbrancer, if by reason of
a prior legal estate the latter could not recover in ejectment [72]; but
a prior incumbrancer, having the legal estate and a right in law to
recover possession, was left to his remedy in ejectment.[73] Under
the present practice receivers are freely appointed at the instance
of legal mortgagees and possession ordered to be given to such
receivers.[74]

Parties. Where second or third incumbrancers apply for a
receiver in foreclosure proceedings it is not essential to make the
prior mortgagee or mortgagees parties, though the court will see
their rights are not prejudiced [75]: subsequent incumbrancers,
including judgment creditors who have obtained a charge,[76] as
well as the mortgagor, must be made defendants.[77] In orders for
the appointment of a receiver at the instance of a second or later
incumbrancer there should be inserted the words " without
prejudice to the rights of prior incumbrancers who may think fit
to take possession by virtue of their respective securities." [78] If
these words are inserted a prior incumbrancer who has taken
possession or a receiver appointed by him is not displaced and it
appears that a legal mortgagee could take possession without
applying for leave to the court.[79] If the above words are omitted
the rights of a prior legal mortgagee to take possession or appoint

---

[70] *Bord* v. *Tollemache* (1862) 1 New Rep. 177; *Re Metropolitan Amalgamated
Estates, supra.*
[71] See note 60, p. 29, *ante.*
[72] *White* v. *Bishop of Peterborough* (1818) 3 Sw. 109; *Silver* v. *Bishop of Norwich*
(1816) 3 Sw. 116n.
[73] *Silver* v. *Bishop of Norwich, supra.*   [74] See p. 26, *ante.*
[75] *Norway* v. *Rowe* (1816) 19 Ves. 144, 152. See article by Master Mosse in *Law
Notes,* 1934, p. 917.
[76] See p. 137, *post.*
[77] *Dalmer* v. *Dashwood* (1793) 2 Cox 378; *Rose* v. *Page* (1829) 2 Sim. 471; but see
Price v. *Williams* (1806) Coop. 31; a receiver may, however, be appointed in the
absence of some of the subsequent incumbrancers: see *Re Crigglestone Coal Co.*
[1906] 1 Ch. 523.
[78] Seton, *Forms of Judgments and Orders* (7th ed.), pp. 765, 798; *Lewis* v. *Zouche*
(1828) 2 Sim. 388; *Smith* v. *Lord Effingham* (1839) 2 Beav. 232; *Underhay* v. *Read*
(1887) 20 Q.B.D. 209.
[79] *Underhay* v. *Read, supra*; see *Re Metropolitan Amalgamated Estates, infra,*
where the point was raised, but *Underhay* v. *Read* was not referred to.

a receiver remain unaffected,[80] but he must obtain the leave of the court before enforcing those rights,[81] and where his security is deficient or nearly so, he has in effect to bear the costs of such an application. Though a legal mortgagee may have appointed a receiver at the date when the court in ignorance of that fact appoints a receiver at the instance of a subsequent incumbrancer, the latter appointment is effective, though the court's receiver will be at once displaced upon the application of the legal mortgagee, as from the date of service of such application.[82]

If a receiver has already been appointed at the instance of a subsequent incumbrancer, the prior incumbrancer may apply for a receiver, but if the security of the subsequent incumbrancer includes other property, the receiver already appointed will be treated as receiver for the prior incumbrancer as to the property included in his security, in order to avoid the expense of two receivers. If the security of the prior incumbrancer includes property other than that included in the security of the subsequent incumbrancer, a fresh action by the former is necessary [83]; but if it does not he can apply to be added as a defendant in the subsequent incumbrancer's action and apply in the action. Similarly, if a receiver has been appointed in a partnership action, an incumbrancer who intervenes should commence a fresh action if his security contains property additional to the assets of the partnership.

Instances of exercise of jurisdiction. A receiver may be appointed on the application of an equitable mortgagee of leasehold property, against a person in possession under an agreement with the mortgagor for an assignment of the latter's interest in the property.[84] And though the security of the applicant may be one which gave him no right to be considered a mortgagee of the estate, but only made the rents a fund for payment of interest and of premiums upon a policy of insurance, out of the produce of which the principal was to be paid, a receiver will be appointed.[85]

---

[80] See *Davis* v. *Duke of Marlborough* (1818) 2 Swans. 108, 137, 138.

[81] *Re Metropolitan Amalgamated Estates* [1912] 2 Ch. 497.

[82] *Re Metropolitan Amalgamated Estates* [1912] 2 Ch. 497, and see *post*, p. 143.

[83] Leave should be obtained to assign it to the same group as the existing action: see R.S.C., Ord. 4, r. 1 (6).

[84] *Reid* v. *Middleton* (1823) T. & R. 455; but only if the equitable mortgagee has registered his mortgage as a land charge, unless he holds the deeds.

[85] *Taylor* v. *Emerson* (1843) 4 Dr. & War. 122; see also *Cummins* v. *Perkins* [1899] 1 Ch. 16; as to right of creditor of a building society, see *Baker* v. *Landport, etc., Building Society* (1912) 56 S.J. 224.

Undivided shares in land can no longer exist. A mortgage of the interest of a tenant in common in possession is a mortgage of an interest under a trust for sale.[86] Although, therefore, a receiver will be appointed at the instance of a mortgagee of an undivided share of the interest of the tenant in common in the proceeds of sale, and rents and profits until sale, a receiver of the rents and profits of the land will only be appointed in case of such misconduct by the trustees in whom the legal estate is vested as justifies such appointment [87]; *e.g.* where the trustees for sale omit to hand over the mortgaged share of the rents or proceeds of sale to the mortgagee after notice requiring them to do so.[88] In cases where mortgages of all the undivided shares made before 1926 for securing the same mortgage money are vested in the same mortgagees,[89] the mortgage becomes a legal mortgage; but in the case of mortgages made after the Act this is not so. Where, however, all the undivided shares are not mortgaged to the same mortgagee, and the mortgagors are themselves the trustees in whom the legal estate is vested, it is possible that a receiver might be appointed of the rents and profits of the estate, at all events where there are no subsequent mortgagees; in such a case the mortgagee has not the legal estate.[90]

Prior legal mortgagee in possession. The court will not appoint a receiver, at the instance of a subsequent incumbrancer, against a prior [91] legal mortgagee in possession,[92] as long as anything remains due to the latter on the mortgage security, for he is entitled to retain that possession until he is fully paid. In the absence of misconduct [93] a receiver will not be appointed against him except

---

[86] Except the unusual case where the case falls within para. 4 of Pt. 4 of Sched. I to Law of Property Act 1925, as amended by Law of Property (Amendment) Act 1926, as to which see *Re Barratt* [1929] 1 Ch. 336. In such cases the beneficial interest of the tenant in common is an equitable interest in the land, which is vested in the tenants in common as joint tenants.

[87] See Section 2 of this chapter.

[88] See *Re Pawson's Settlement* [1917] 1 Ch. 541. As to power of sale and to appoint receiver, see Law of Property Act 1925, s. 102.

[89] Law of Property Act 1925, Sched. I, Pt. 4, para. 1 (7).

[90] For a case under the old law, where a receiver was appointed over the estate at the instance of a mortgagee of an undivided share, see *Sumsion* v. *Crutwell* (1833) 31 W.R. 399. In *Holmes* v. *Bell* (1840) 2 Beav. 398, a receiver of the rents and profits of an estate belonging to mortgagors as tenants in common was appointed where one of them was out of the jurisdiction.

[91] See as to the restrictions upon obtaining priority by tacking under the new law, Law of Property Act 1925, s. 94.

[92] *Richards* v. *Gould* (1827) 1 Mol. 22.

[93] See p. 34, *post*.

on his own confession that he has been paid off, or on his refusal to accept what is due to him.[94] If he swears that something is due to him on his mortgage security, no receiver will be appointed against him,[95] and the only course is to pay him off according to his own statement of the debt.[96] It is not necessary, in order to preserve his possession, that he should be able to state with great precision what sum is due to him. It is enough if he can swear that something is due to him (however small it may be) on the security [97]; the court will not try the truth of the statement by affidavits against it.[98] If, however, he will not state that something is due to him, the court will appoint a receiver.[99] The statement must be a distinct and positive statement, not a vague assertion,[1] such as of belief that, when the accounts are taken, some particular sum will be found due.[2] Nor can the incomplete state of his accounts be admitted as an excuse for his not being able to say that something is due. If a mortgagee in possession keeps his accounts so negligently that neither he, nor a subsequent incumbrancer, nor the owner of the estate can ascertain what is due, the court may assume that nothing is due.[3] Time, however, may be given him to make an affidavit of the debt.[4]

The rule, as to not appointing a receiver against a prior legal mortgagee in possession, has been held to apply in favour of persons in possession entitled to a mortgage and prior charges on the estate, though they had applied part of the rents in payment of the interest on those charges, instead of discharging the principal of the mortgage; it being the proper course, as between the tenant for life and the owners of the inheritance, to keep down such interest out of the rents and not to treat the surplus rents, after payment of the interest on the unpaid part of the principal, as applicable to the discharge of such unpaid principal.[5]

In order to deprive an equitable mortgagee of his right to a

---

[94] *Berney* v. *Sewell* (1820) 1 J. & W. 649.
[95] *Quarrell* v. *Beckford* (1807) 13 Ves. 377.
[96] *Berney* v. *Sewell*, *supra*.
[97] *Quarrell* v. *Beckford*, *supra*.
[98] *Rowe* v. *Wood* (1822) 2 Jac. & W. 553.
[99] *Quarrell* v. *Beckford*, *supra*; *Rowe* v. *Wood*, *supra*.
[1] *Hiles* v. *Moore* (1852) 15 Beav. 181
[2] *Ibid.*
[3] *Codrington* v. *Parker* (1810) 16 Ves. 469; *Hiles* v. *Moore* (1852) 15 Beav. 181.
[4] *Codrington* v. *Parker*, *supra*.
[5] *Faulkner* v. *Daniel* (1843) 3 Ha. 104n.; 10 L.J.Ch. 34. The old cases must be read in the light of the present law which enables a second mortgagee under a legal mortgage to take a legal estate.

receiver, the possession of the party must be such a possession as invests him with a title to receive the rents and profits in his capacity of mortgagee. A mere possession as tenant is not sufficient.[6]

Exceptional case. Still, although a receiver will not, as a general rule, be appointed against a prior legal mortgagee in possession, the court may, if a case of gross mismanagement of the estate be made to appear, deprive a mortgagee of possession by appointing a receiver; but to warrant such an interference the mismanagement must be of a clear and specific nature.[7]

Manager. If a mortgagee's security includes (either expressly or by implication) not only land, but a business carried on upon the land, the court may, upon his application, appoint a manager as well as a receiver.[8]

In such cases, if the mortgagee elects to have the receiver also appointed manager, the goodwill of the business forms part of the property entrusted to the receiver, who must, therefore, do all acts necessary to preserve it: he cannot, therefore, without the express permission of the court,[9] disregard contracts entered into by the mortgagor, because to do so would result in the destruction of the goodwill.[10] If, however, the mortgagee elects to have a receiver only, and possession is taken by the receiver, the latter may disregard contracts entered into by the mortgagor, because he is under no obligation to preserve the goodwill.[11] It is, as a rule, useless to appoint a manager unless he can utilise or acquire the chattels employed in the business. It must be remembered that, except in the case of incorporated companies and certain statutory bodies, a charge on chattels is void, unless registered as a bill of sale, though it may be valid as to the remainder of the property comprised therein.[12]

It seems that, although the court will not appoint a manager of

---

[6] *Archdeacon* v. *Bowes* (1796) 3 Anst. 752. Where an equitable mortgagee had taken possession under the mistaken impression that he was the owner, payment of interest was presumed to prevent the charge becoming barred by the Statute of Limitations: *Re Battersby* [1911] 1 I.R. 453.

[7] *Rowe* v. *Wood* (1822) 2 Jac. & W. 553.

[8] *County of Gloucester Bank* v. *Rudry, etc., Colliery Co.* [1895] 1 Ch. 629; and see Chap. 9.

[9] *Post*, pp. 220, 231 *et seq.*

[10] See *Re Newdigate Colliery Co.* [1912] 1 Ch. 468; *post*, pp. 231 *et seq.*

[11] See *Re Newdigate Colliery Co.* [1912] 1 Ch. 468, *per* Cozens-Hardy M.R. and Moulton L.J.

[12] *Re North Wales Produce Co.* [1922] 2 Ch. 340.

licensed premises at the instance of a mortgagee whose security does not include the goodwill,[13] it may, where the licences are in jeopardy, authorise the receiver to keep the house open as licensed premises and to do all acts necessary to preserve the licences.[14]

Rent Restriction Acts, etc. In the case of controlled mortgages on dwelling-houses to which the Rent Restriction Acts [15] apply,[16] no step can be taken to enforce the security as long as certain conditions, including the payment of interest within the period limited by the Act of 1977, are observed.[17] The restrictions do not apply to equitable charges by deposit or otherwise.[18]

In the case of regulated mortgages, the court has certain powers to mitigate hardship caused by the taking of steps to enforce the security.[19]

Reserve and auxiliary forces. See Reserve and Auxiliary Forces (Protection of Civil Interests) Act 1951, s. 2, as amended by the Guardianship of Minors Act 1971, Sched. 1.

SECTION 5. IN CASES BETWEEN DEBTOR AND CREDITOR

General creditors. General creditors may, like specific incumbrancers, have a receiver of the property of their debtor,[20] provided they can show to the court the existence of circumstances creating the equity on which alone the jurisdiction arises.[21] Thus, where it is made to appear that an executor or devisee is wasting the personal or real estate, a receiver may be appointed in administration proceedings commenced by simple contract creditors,[22] who may also obtain the appointment of a receiver of real and personal estate pending a grant of probate.[23]

---

[13] *Whitley* v. *Challis* [1892] 1 Ch. 64.

[14] See *Charrington* v. *Camp* [1902] 1 Ch. 386; *Leney & Sons Ltd.* v. *Callingham* [1908] 1 K.B. 79, where such an order was made on the application of lessors seeking to recover possession.

[15] Now Rent Act 1977.

[16] See Rent Act 1977, ss. 129 and 130 and Counter-Inflation Act 1973, s. 14. No mortgage created after August 14, 1974 comes within the scope of these provisions.

[17] After proceedings are commenced when interest is in arrear, the protection of the Acts cannot be recovered by payment of arrears: *Evans* v. *Horner* [1925] Ch. 177.

[18] See p. 307, *post.*

[19] Rent Act 1977, s. 132: see p. 308, *post.*

[20] *Owen* v. *Homan* (1853) 4 H.L.C. 997; *Oldfield* v. *Cobbett* (1835) 4 L.J.Ch. 272.

[21] See *Re Shephard* (1889) 43 Ch.D. 131, 138.

[22] As to order for administration in bankruptcy, see Bankruptcy Act 1914, s. 130; the order cannot be made unless the personal representative is a party: *Re a Debtor* [1939] Ch. 594.

[23] Sect. 3, p. 19, *ante.*

Independently of the Judicature Act 1925, where a plaintiff has a right to be paid out of a particular fund, the court will appoint a receiver in order to prevent that fund from being dissipated so as to defeat his rights. The appointment of a receiver in such a case is not by way of equitable execution, but analogous to it.[24] Another remedy is applied by the court in divorce, which will interfere by injunction to restrain a husband from disposing of his property so as to defeat an order for payment of alimony or maintenance accrued due.[25]

The fact that the real estate over which a receiver is sought is in mortgage, will not prevent the appointment of a receiver unless the mortgagee is in possession.[26]

Still, although general creditors may have a receiver of the property of the debtor, a strong case must be made out to warrant the interference of the court. The court will not, unless a clear case is established, deprive a person of property on which the claimant has no specific claim, in order that if he establishes his claim as a creditor, there may be assets wherewith to satisfy it.[27] The provisions applied in the case of a creditor seeking payment out of a married woman's separate estate are now obsolete.

Judgment creditors. Before the Judicature Acts, the Court of Chancery exercised a jurisdiction in aid of judgments at law. A judgment creditor who had sued out a writ of *elegit* or *fi. fa.* on his judgment, but found himself precluded from obtaining execution at law on the ground that the debtor had no lands, goods, or chattels out of which the judgment could be satisfied at law, had a right to come to the Court of Chancery for the appointment of a receiver of the proceeds of the estate of the debtor which could be reached in equity.[28] The Court of Chancery,

---

[24] *Cummins* v. *Perkins* [1899] 1 Ch. 16, 19, *per* Lindley M.R. Where persons against whom the plaintiff has a money demand have an equitable interest in property the persons with the legal title may be joined as defendants, though no substantive relief is claimed against them other than payment out of the property of sums recovered from their co-defendant; but where inconvenience would be caused by the joinder, the trustees will be struck out: *Ideal Films* v. *Richards* [1927] 2 K.B. 374.

[25] *Fanshawe* v. *Fanshawe* [1927] P. 238. See also Matrimonial Proceedings and Property Act 1970, s. 16.

[26] *Rhodes* v. *Mostyn* (1853) 17 Jur. 1007; *Bryan* v. *Cormick* (1788) 1 Cox 422; *Berney* v. *Sewell* (1820) 1 Jac. & W. 648; *Cadogan* v. *Lyric Theatre* [1894] 3 Ch. 338, 340.

[27] *Owen* v. *Homan* (1853) 4 H.L.C. 997, 1036.

[28] *Smith* v. *Hurst* (1845) 1 Coll. 705; 10 Ha. 48; *Smith* v. *Cowell* (1880) 6 Q.B.D. 75; *Ex p. Charrington* (1888) 22 Q.B.D. 191; see, as to form of order, *Wells* v. *Kilpin* (1874) L.R. 18 Eq. 299.

before exercising the jurisdiction, required to be satisfied of two things; first, that the plaintiff in the action had tried all he could to get satisfaction at law; and then, that the debtor was possessed of a particular interest which could not be attached at law.[29] Since the Judicature Act 1873, the first of these conditions has ceased to apply: but the second still holds good as a general principle, although modified in relation to legal interests in land.[30] It is no longer necessary to the judgment creditor before obtaining an order for equitable execution to issue a *fi. fa.*[31]

But neither the Judicature Acts nor subsequent legislation, such as the conversion of the equitable interest of a mortgagor into a legal estate,[32] affected the practice of the Court of Chancery by which a receiver was only appointed in aid of a judgment at law where there was a legal impediment to ordinary execution.[33] Special provision has, however, now been made by statute for the enforcement of judgments against the debtor's land or interests in land.[34]

Equitable relief distinguished from equitable execution. In appointing a receiver in aid of a legal judgment for a legal debt, the Court of Chancery, it has been very commonly said, granted equitable execution; but the expression is not correct.[35] The appointment of a receiver is not execution, but equitable relief granted under circumstances which make it right that legal difficulties should be removed out of the creditor's way. What a judgment creditor gets by the appointment of a receiver is not execution but equitable relief, which is granted on the ground that there is no remedy by execution at law.[36]

This distinction between equitable relief and execution is of importance, because the creditor who applies to have a receiver

---

[29] *Per* Jessel M.R. in *Salt* v. *Cooper* (1880) 16 Ch.D. 544, 552; *Re Pope* (1886) 17 Q.B.D. 749.

[30] Administration of Justice Act 1956, s. 34. See p. 94, *post.*

[31] *Re Whiteley* (1887) 56 L.T. 846; see, too, *Coney* v. *Bennett* (1885) 29 Ch.D. 993; *Manchester and Liverpool, etc., Banking Co.* v. *Parkinson* (1888) 22 Q.B.D. 173; and *post*, p. 228. Nor was it necessary, under the old practice to sue out an *elegit: Ex p. Evans* (1879) 13 Ch.D. 260; *Re Pope* (1886) 17 Q.B.D. 749; see, too, *Hills* v. *Webber* (1901) 17 T.L.R. 513.

[32] *Smith* v. *Tsakyris* [1929] W.N. 39.

[33] *Ante*, p. 4.

[34] Administration of Justice Act 1956, s. 36; see pp. 94 *et seq., post.*

[35] *Morgan* v. *Hart* [1914] 2 K.B. 183; *Re a Company* [1915] 1 Ch. 526.

[36] *Re Shephard* (1889) 43 Ch.D. 131, 135; *Levasseur* v. *Mason & Barry* [1891] 2 Q.B. 79. See, too, *Re Marquis of Anglesey* [1903] 2 Ch. 727, 731; *Thompson* v. *Gill* [1903] 1 K.B. 760, 765; *Re Bond* [1911] 2 K.B. 988.

appointed stands in many respects in a very different position from a creditor who issues execution.[37] Thus, an order cannot be made appointing a receiver by way of equitable execution after the death of the judgment debtor, even though he was alive when the application was first made,[38] for this would amount to preferring one creditor of a deceased person to another [39]; and the executors of a deceased judgment creditor are not entitled to apply for a receiver under R.S.C., Ord. 46, r. 4, because this does not amount to asking for leave to issue execution within that rule.[40]

A judgment creditor who has obtained equitable execution subject to existing incumbrances does not obtain priority by giving notice to trustees of the debtor.[41]

The cases in which the court will appoint a receiver at the instance of a judgment creditor depend mainly upon the nature of the property and of the judgment debtor's interest in it: this matter and the principles which guide the court in the exercise of its jurisdiction are dealt with in Chapter 3,[42] and the practice on appointment in Chapter 5.[43]

The powers of equitable execution should not be exercised except in cases where the judgment debt is sufficiently large to justify this expensive procedure,[44] and the property sought to be charged in execution is not only of a fitting character, but likely to satisfy a reasonable proportion of the debt.[45] In some cases, receivership orders have been granted over contingent and reversionary interests, whereas the sounder practice would have been to grant orders over that class of property by way of charge only, so as to avoid costs being incurred in settling security, etc., for what is at the moment, if granted, a mere dry receivership.[46] The following rule of court has accordingly been made, for the purpose of limiting the cases in which a receiver can be appointed:

---

[37] See, further, *post*, p. 137.   [38] *Re Shephard* (1889) 43 Ch.D. 131.

[39] *Re Cave* [1892] W.N. 142. The appointment of a receiver in *Waddell* v. *Waddell* [1892] P. 226, over the estate of a deceased co-respondent at the instance of a petitioner in a divorce suit to enforce payment of costs, appears to have been made without jurisdiction, as the suit had lapsed by the death and there was no power to add the legal personal representatives: *Brydges* v. *Brydges* [1909] P. 187; *Coleman* v. *Coleman* [1920] P. 71.

[40] *Norburn* v. *Norburn* [1894] 1 Q.B. 448. It appears that the proper course is for the executors to apply to be added as parties under R.S.C., Ord. 15, r. 7.

[41] *Arden* v. *Arden* (1885) 29 Ch.D. 702; and see *Re Ind Coope & Co.* [1911] 2 Ch. 223.   [42] p. 92, *post*.   [43] p. 123, *post*.

[44] *I.* v. *K.* [1884] W.N. 63.   [45] *Walls Ltd.* v. *Legge* [1923] 2 K.B. 240.

[46] The appointment will not be made at all if it will certainly prove ineffective: *Harper* v. *McIntyre* (1907) 51 S.J. 701.

" Where an application is made for the appointment of a receiver by way of equitable execution, the Court, in determining whether it is just or convenient that the appointment should be made shall have regard to the amount claimed by the judgment creditor, to the amount likely to be obtained by the receiver and to the probable costs of his appointment and may direct an inquiry on any of these matters or any other matter before making the appointment." [47]

Courts of Bankruptcy have jurisdiction to appoint a receiver by way of equitable execution, for the purpose of enforcing orders for the payment of money to the trustee in bankruptcy.[48] But such an order will not, as a general rule, be made upon an *ex parte* application.[49]

The Bankruptcy Court may, if it is necessary for the protection of the estate, at any time after the presentation of a petition and before a receiving order is made, appoint the official receiver interim receiver of the property of the debtor or any part of it.[50]

Attachment of moneys payable by the Crown. No order for the attachment of debts, or for the appointment of a sequestrator or for the appointment of a receiver can be made in respect of any money due or accruing or alleged to be due or accruing to a judgment debtor from the Crown.[51] But where such an order could have been obtained in respect of such money if it had been due or accruing from a subject, the court may on the application by summons of the judgment creditor make an order restraining the judgment debtor from receiving such money, and directing payment by the Crown to the judgment creditor or to a sequestrator or receiver; and the court or a judge may appoint a sequestrator or receiver for that purpose.[52] Wages or salaries payable to officers of the Crown as such, moneys subject to the provisions of any enactment prohibiting or restricting assigning or charging or taking in execution [53] and the National Savings Bank deposits are exempt from this jurisdiction.[54]

---

[47] R.S.C., Ord. 51, r. 1 (1).   [48] *Re Goudie* [1896] 2 Q.B. 481.   [49] *Ibid.*
[50] Bankruptcy Act 1914, s. 8; for practice, Bankruptcy Rules 1952, rr. 157–161. The official receiver acts till a trustee is appointed, s. 74 (1). As to power to appoint a manager, s. 10.
[51] Crown Proceedings Act 1947, s. 27; R.S.C., Ord. 77, r. 16 (1).
[52] Crown Proceedings Act 1947, s. 27; R.S.C., Ord. 77, r. 16 (2). For details of procedure see *ibid.* r. 16 (3).
[53] See note 32 to Ord. 49, r. 1, in the *Supreme Court Practice* (1976), Vol. 1, para. 49/1/28 and at pp. 86–88, *post.*
[54] Crown Proceedings Act 1947, s. 27 (1) proviso; Post Office Act 1969, s. 94 and Sched. 6, Pt. 3.

Debt not ascertained. The court will not necessarily refuse to appoint a receiver until the amount of the applicant's debt has been ascertained. Therefore, where an action by a married woman was dismissed with costs to be paid out of her separate property, and the only separate property of the plaintiff consisted of a share under a will which the trustees were about to pay over to the plaintiff, the court appointed a receiver to receive the share before the costs had been taxed.[55] This is, however, a very special decision: normally no receiver will be affected in respect of untaxed costs.[56]

Assignee of part of debt. The same principle which prevents the assignee of part of a judgment debt from issuing execution at law, namely, because the assignor can only issue execution for the whole debt and cannot put the assignee in any better position than himself,[57] appears to apply to prevent such assignee from obtaining a receiver by way of equitable execution.[58]

A creditor who has obtained an order for payment of costs, and has endeavoured to obtain a sequestration, but has failed to do so from the conduct of the debtor, is entitled to apply for a receiver in lieu of sequestration.[59] So also a judgment for the payment of money into court may be enforced by the appointment of a receiver, where service of the writ of attachment cannot be effected.[60]

Partnership Act 1890, s. 23. By virtue of section 23 (2) of the Partnership Act 1890,[61] the High Court or a judge thereof, or a county court, may, on the application by summons of any judgment creditor of a partner, make an order charging that partner's interest in the partnership property and profits with payment of the amount of the judgment debt and interest thereon, and may by the same or a subsequent order appoint a receiver of that partner's share of profits (whether already declared or accruing), and of any other money which may be coming to him in respect of the partnership, and direct all accounts and inquiries and give all

---

[55] *Cummins* v. *Perkins* [1899] 1 Ch. 16.

[56] *Willis* v. *Cooper* (1900) 40 S.J. 698.

[57] *Forster* v. *Baker* [1910] 2 K.B. 636; though part of a debt can be assigned in equity: *Re Steel Wing Co.* [1921] 1 Ch. 349.

[58] See *Rothschild* v. *Fisher* [1920] 2 K.B. 243.

[59] *Bryant* v. *Bull* (1878) 10 Ch.D. 153.

[60] *Stanger Leathes* v. *Stanger Leathes* [1882] W.N. 71; *Coney* v. *Bennett* (1885) 29 Ch.D. 993; *Re Pemberton* [1907] W.N. 118.

[61] As amended by the Courts Act 1971, Sched. 2, Pt. 2.

other orders and directions which might have been directed or given if the charge had been made in favour of the judgment creditor by the partner, or which the circumstances of the case may require.

By section 23 (4) it is provided that the section shall apply in the case of a cost-book company as if the company were a partnership within the meaning of the Act; and by section 7 of the Limited Partnerships Act 1907, section 23 (2) of the Act of 1890 applies to the limited partnership.

By R.S.C., Ord. 81, r. 10, every application under this section must be made by summons which must be served, in the case of partnership other than a cost-book company, on the judgment debtor and on his partners or such of them as are within the jurisdiction, or, in the case of a cost-book company, on the judgment debtor and the purser (*i.e.* the principal manager of the mine) of the company.

The summons is supported by an affidavit which need not, as in the case of an ordinary debtor, state that the defendant has no other property available for execution, and usually asks for a named receiver in addition to a charging order: if it is apprehended that the debtor may deal with his interest an injunction should be applied for *ex parte* on affidavit. The smallness of the amount due constitutes no objection to the order.[62] The order can be made by a Master or District Registrar.[63]

The section has been held to apply to a foreign firm having a branch house in England.[64]

A charging order under the section does not make the judgment creditor of the partner a secured creditor under the Bankruptcy Act 1914.[65] After the appointment of a receiver the court may give a creditor leave to issue execution: but this is inconvenient and it is preferable either (a) to direct the receiver to pay the execution creditor out of money come to his hands [66]: or (b) to give the creditor a charge on the net assets.[67] The order

---

[62] See *Summers* v. *Simpson* (1902) unrep., cited in *Supreme Court Practice* (1976), Vol. 1, para. 81/10/2.

[63] R.S.C., Ord. 81, r. 10 (2).

[64] *Brown, Jansen & Co.* v. *Hutchinson & Co.* [1895] 1 Q.B. 737. See the judgment of Lindley L.J. for some valuable observations on the effect of appointing a receiver under the section.

[65] *Wild* v. *Southwood* [1897] 1 Q.B. 317.

[66] *Mitchell* v. *Weise* [1892] W.N. 129.

[67] For form see *Kewney* v. *Attrill* (1887) 34 Ch.D. 345; Seton, *Forms of Judgments and Orders*, p. 471.

should include an undertaking not to deal with the charge except subject to an order of the court: this enables priority to be given to the receiver's remuneration and expenses: and the creditor obtains priority over other creditors.[68]

Rates. A receiver will not be appointed at the instance of a judgment creditor over rates.[69]

Matrimonial causes. A judge of the Family Division sitting in Divorce, has jurisdiction to enforce orders by the appointment of a receiver under section 45 of the Judicature Act 1925[70]; unless an application for a variation order is pending, *fi. fa.* to enforce an order for payment issues as of course,[71] and it is a common practice to enforce orders by sequestration.[72] It has been said [73] that receivers are sometimes appointed to administer sequestered property. A receiver has been appointed by the Court of Chancery on the application of a divorced wife who had obtained an order for maintenance [74]; but though a judge of the Chancery or Queen's Bench Division may have jurisdiction to make such an order under section 45 of the Judicature Act 1925, in view of the exclusive jurisdiction of the Family Division to enforce its own orders,[75] it is submitted that the application ought to be made to a judge of the Family Division, and that a receiver would not be appointed by any other court. It appears that the only remedy for non-payment of alimony is still in the Family Division.[76] After the death of a co-respondent [77] or petitioner,[78]

---

[68] *Newport* v. *Pougher* [1937] Ch. 214; see further notes in *Supreme Court Practice* (1976), Vol. 1, to Ord. 81, r. 10. A charging order can only be enforced by sale; not by foreclosure: *Daponte* v. *Shubert* [1939] Ch. 958.

[69] See p. 54; there is a remedy by mandamus.

[70] See p. 4. The practice laid down in R.S.C., Ord. 30 (*post*, p. 112), is followed.

[71] Matrimonial Causes Rules 1973 (S.I. 1973 No. 2016 (L.29)), r. 86. They can also be enforced by committal: *Leavis* v. *Leavis* [1921] P. 299. Orders in the county court with divorce jurisdiction are enforceable by warrant of execution (r. 86). As to enforcement by attachment of earnings, see Attachment of Earnings Act 1971, s. 5.

[72] See *Capron* v. *Capron* [1927] P. 243.   [73] *Dixon on Divorce* (1908), p. 288.

[74] *Oliver* v. *Lowther* (1880) 28 W.R. 381.

[75] See *Ivimey* v. *Ivimey* [1908] 2 K.B. 260; *Robins* v. *Robins* [1907] 2 K.B. 13; *Re Hedderwick* [1933] Ch. 669.

[76] It has been suggested (see *Bailey* v. *Bailey* (1884) 13 Q.B.D. 860; *Morse* v. *Muir* [1939] 2 K.B. 106, *per* Goddard L.J.) that the effect of r. 81 of the Matrimonial Causes Rules 1937 (now r. 3 of the Matrimonial Causes Rules 1973 (S.I. 1973 No. 2016 (L.29)), was to bring R.S.C., Ord. 45, r. 1, into operation and to nullify the above decisions, but it appears that the effect of r. 62 (of the Rules of 1937: now r. 86 of the Rules of 1973) is to retain the exclusive right of the Family Division to enforce orders for maintenance and alimony. See *Re Woolgar, Woolgar* v. *Hopkins* [1942] Ch. 318 but *cf. W.* v. *W.* [1961] P. 113 as to the mode of enforcement.

[77] *Brydges* v. *Brydges* [1909] P. 187.   [78] *Coleman* v. *Coleman* [1920] P. 71.

the Family Division has no jurisdiction to enforce an order for payment of damages or costs or, *semble*, arrears of alimony or maintenance, since the legal personal representative cannot be added.[79] Although in one case [80] it was held that the wife could prove against the estate of a deceased husband for one year's alimony, this decision has not been followed and proof or administration has been refused on the ground that no debt in respect of alimony or maintenance exists.[81]

Foreign judgments. The effect of the Judgments Extension Act 1868 is that a decree of the Court of Session in Scotland is, when a certificate of it has been registered under that Act, to be treated as if it had been originally an English judgment; and, therefore, the appointment of a receiver by way of equitable execution may be made upon such a certificate.[82] The registration of a judgment of a colonial court under Part II of the Administration of Justice Act 1920 [83] or of a foreign judgment under section 2 of the Foreign Judgments (Reciprocal Enforcement) Act 1933 [84] presumably has the same effect.

Equitable creditors. The case of equitable incumbrancers is dealt with in the preceding section. There may, however, be cases in which an equitable creditor may not be an incumbrancer in the ordinary sense of the word, but he may have a right to be paid out of a particular fund or a right to the protection of certain property. The court will not appoint a receiver at the suit of an equitable creditor without an enforceable charge, however clear his claim may be, unless it is satisfied that the property is in danger, or unless there be some other equity upon which to found the application. In a case where a testator had devised his estate to a man for life without impeachment of waste " except voluntary waste in pulling down houses and not rebuilding the same, or others of equal or greater degree," the tenant for life pulled down the mansion house with the intention of forthwith building a better one on the site, and was proceeding with all reasonable dispatch to

---

[79] *Ibid.*; *quaere Waddell* v. *Waddell* [1892] P. 226.

[80] *Re Stillwell* [1916] 1 Ch. 365.

[81] *Re Hedderwick* [1933] Ch. 669; *Re Woolgar* [1942] Ch. 318; *Re Bidie* [1948] Ch. 697.

[82] *Thompson* v. *Gill* [1903] 1 K.B. 760, 771.

[83] See R.S.C., Ord. 71, as to procedure, and notes in *Supreme Court Practice* (1976) as to the parts of the British Dominions to which the Act now applies. It does not apply to the Republic of Ireland.

[84] R.S.C., Ord. 71, and notes in *Supreme Court Practice* (1976).

carry such intention into effect; and it was contended that he was an equitable debtor for the value of the house pulled down, by virtue of the obligation imposed on him by the will to rebuild. There being no pretence for saying that he was not proceeding to fulfil his obligation, the party entitled to the next vested remainder was held not entitled to have a receiver of the rents appointed, in order to secure the rebuilding of the mansion.[85]

SECTION 6. IN THE CASE OF STATUTORY UNDERTAKINGS AND CORPORATIONS

Mortgagee's right to receiver. Where a mortgage has been made by a statutory company or body of its " undertaking," or the tolls and dues arising therefrom, the mortgagee may, for the protection of his security, come to the court for a receiver.[86] The appointment of a receiver is the only remedy open to secured creditors under the Companies Clauses Acts: the right to fore-closure or sale is not open to them.[87]

So mortgagees of turnpike,[88] dock,[89] or market[90] tolls have been held to have a right to come to the court to have a receiver appointed. And a person who has sold land to a statutory company in consideration of a rentcharge has a right to come to the court for a receiver.[91]

The court has jurisdiction to appoint a receiver at the instance of a mortgagee of tolls, independently of any statute.[92] When a

---

[85] *Micklethwait* v. *Micklethwait* (1857) 1 De G. & J. 504.

[86] *Fripp* v. *Chard Ry.* (1853) 11 Ha. 241; *Potts* v. *Warwick and Birmingham Canal Co.* (1853) Kay 146; *Gardner* v. *London, Chatham & Dover Ry.* (1867) L.R. 2 Ch. 201; *Blaker* v. *Herts and Essex Waterworks Co.* (1889) 41 Ch.D. 399; see, as to form of order, Seton (7th ed.), p. 736; *Postlethwaite* v. *Maryport Harbour Trustees* [1869] W.N. 37. In *Att.-Gen.* v. *Mersey Docks and Harbour Board* (unreported; *Financial Times*, December 11, 1970) the order provided that the receiver should only apply his receipts in discharge of the operating costs of the Board, which had other revenues available, to the extent to which such revenues were insufficient. The receiver is of the tolls, not the profits only: *Griffin* v. *Bishop's Castle Ry.* (1867) 15 W.R. 1058.

[87] *Blaker* v. *Herts and Essex Waterworks Co.* (1889) 41 Ch.D. 399. This principle also applied to the holders of debentures of a tramway company governed by the Tramways Act 1870: *Marshall* v. *South Staffordshire Tramways Co.* [1895] 2 Ch. 36.

[88] *Knapp* v. *Williams* (1798) 4 Ves. 430n., *per* Lord Loughborough; *Lord Crewe* v. *Edleston* (1857) 1 De G. & J. 109.

[89] *Ames* v. *Birkenhead Docks* (1855) 20 Beav. 342; *Att.-Gen.* v. *Mersey Docks and Harbour Board, supra.*

[90] *De Winton* v. *Mayor of Brecon* (1859) 26 Beav. 533.

[91] *Eyton* v. *Denbigh, etc., Ry.* (1868) L.R. 6 Eq. 14, 488.

[92] *De Winton* v. *Mayor of Brecon, supra*; *Hopkins* v. *Worcester and Birmingham Canal Co.* (1868) L.R. 6 Eq. 437.

statute authorises a mortgage, it authorises, as incidental to it, all necessary remedies to compel payment, and in the case of tolls a power to appoint a receiver.[93] But no mortgage or assignment by a company incorporated by statute for a specific purpose with statutory privileges and obligations is valid except to the extent and in the manner permitted by Parliament.[94]

The fact that a precise and specific remedy may be pointed out by the act of incorporation does not deprive a party of his right to a receiver; as, for instance, the fact that there is a provision by statute [95] for the appointment of a receiver through the medium of two justices of the peace. Nor is it any objection to the appointment of a receiver that the company has duties to perform, the neglect of which might subject it to indictment; for the order of the court always gives the parties liberty to apply, whereby such consequences may be averted.[96]

The court will appoint a receiver at the instance of mortgagees or debenture holders of a company formed for the conduct of a public undertaking,[97] when the interest is in arrear,[98] or when the principal is in arrear although all interest has been paid [99]; in this connection it is to be observed that in the cases of debentures created under the Companies Clauses Acts, the principal becomes payable only on the final winding up of the affairs of the company,[1] though redeemable debenture stock, and debentures in the case of public utility companies,[2] may now be issued. Where neither principal nor interest is in arrear, the court will appoint a receiver

---

[93] *De Winton* v. *Mayor of Brecon, supra,* at p. 541. The Mortgage Debenture Acts 1865 (ss. 41, 42, 44–47) and 1870 (repealed) contained express provisions for the appointment of a receiver by the Chancery Division in the case of companies to which the Acts applied.

[94] See *post,* p. 234.

[95] *e.g.* Companies Clauses Consolidation Act 1845, ss. 53, 54; Commissioners Clauses Act 1847, ss. 86, 87, and many private Acts; as to powers of such a receiver, see *Carmichael* v. *Greenock Harbour Trustees* [1910] A.C. 274.

[96] *Fripp* v. *Chard Ry.* (1853) 11 Ha. 259; and see cases cited note 5 on p. 46, *post.*

[97] As to what companies fall within this category, see *Re Crystal Palace Co.* (1911) 104 L.T. 898, affd. *sub nom. Saunders* v. *Bevan* (1912) 28 T.L.R. 518. As to the powers of such a receiver, see *Carmichael* v. *Greenock Harbour Trustees* [1910] A.C. 274.

[98] *Bissill* v. *Bradford Tramways Co.* [1891] W.N. 51. For form of appointment over undertaking of a gas and water company, see *Re Ticehurst Gas and Water Co.* (1910) 128 L.T. 516.

[99] *Hopkins* v. *Worcester and Birmingham Canal Co.* (1868) L.R. 6 Eq. 437. As to validity of a charge by a statutory company, see *Re Glyn Valley Tramway Co.* [1937] Ch. 465.

[1] See *Attree* v. *Hawe* (1878) 9 Ch.D. 337; *Cross* v. *Imp. Continental Gas Assocn.* [1923] 2 Ch. 553.

[2] Statutory Companies (Redeemable Stock) Act 1915.

where the whole security is in jeopardy.[3] But where the interest is not in arrear, a statutory debenture stockholder, who is an annuitant with no enforceable charge, cannot maintain an action to restrain the company from making an application of its money which is *intra vires*; though there may be cases in which the court will interfere to restrain acts manifestly to his injury.[4]

Pleading. A mortgagee or debenture holder seeking to obtain the appointment of a receiver, must sue on behalf of himself and all other mortgagees who have an interest identical with his own, or are in the same class as himself.[5]

Form of order. The court will not, at the suit of mortgagees, appoint a receiver of a public company, established by the legislature for a particular object, without providing as far as possible for the future working and continuance of the undertaking.[6] A receiver so appointed [7] has, however, no powers of management, nor will a manager be appointed except under the express provisions of a statute.[8] The order will also be without prejudice to the rights of prior incumbrancers.

Receiver of chattel property. Even after a receiver of the tolls had been appointed, the Court of Chancery appointed a receiver of the chattel property of a railway company on a motion by a debenture holder, when the company had by a deed assigned its rolling stock and chattels to trustees for the general benefit of creditors.[9]

Judgment creditor. An ordinary judgment creditor of a statutory undertaking has the right (except when, as in the case of railway companies, there is a statutory prohibition [10]), to obtain execution

---

[3] *Legg* v. *Mathieson* (1860) 29 L.J.Ch. 385; *Wildy* v. *Mid-Hants Ry.* (1868) 16 W.R. 409; where the creditors were proceeding by way of *elegit* (now abolished: see note 11, p. 47, *post*) *cf.* cases cited p. 47, *post*.

[4] *Lawrence* v. *West Somerset Mineral Ry.* [1918] 2 Ch. 250; see *Yorkshire Railway Waggon Co.* v. *Maclure* (1882) 21 Ch.D. 309, 314; *Re Liskeard and Caradon Ry.* [1903] 2 Ch. 681, 686, 687; *Cross* v. *Imp. Cont. Gas Assocn.* [1923] 2 Ch. 553.

[5] *Potts* v. *Warwick and Birmingham Canal Co.* (1853) Kay 142; *Fripp* v. *Chard Ry.* (1853) 11 Ha. 241; *Hope* v. *Croydon Tramways Co.* (1887) 34 Ch.D. 730.

[6] *Fripp* v. *Chard Ry.* (1853) 11 Ha. 241, 265; *q.v.* as to the form of the order; also Seton (7th ed.), pp. 736, 755; *Potts* v. *Warwick and Birmingham Canal Co.* (1853) Kay 143 and note 86, p. 44, *ante*.

[7] Or under the specific powers of the Commissioners Clauses Acts, see *Carmichael* v. *Greenock Harbour Trustees* [1910] A.C. 274.

[8] See *post*, p. 242.

[9] *Waterlow* v. *Sharp* [1867] W.N. 64.

[10] See *post*, p. 52.

by means of a *fi. fa.* against the chattels; and he had (before the abolition of this writ [11]) the right by means of an *elegit* to obtain possession of the lands of the company or undertakers.[12] But he must not interfere with the working or management of the undertaking,[13] with the result that in many cases possession is useless to him, and therefore the court may, it seems, subject to the rights of mortgagees, appoint a receiver to enable him to obtain payment from the receipts of the company.[14] A judgment creditor might formerly, under and in accordance with the provisions of the Judgments Act 1864, s. 4, as amended by the Land Charges Act 1900 (since repealed), have had an order for sale of superfluous lands of a statutory company.[15] In accordance with the modern practice introduced by the Administration of Justice Act 1956, which abolished these provisions, the judgment creditor's remedy is now by means of the imposition of a charge and the appointment of a receiver.[16]

When the unpaid vendor of land taken by a railway company commenced an action against the company to enforce his lien, the court refused to appoint a receiver before judgment had been obtained in the action, even though the company admitted liability.[17]

Where the security of the debenture holders did not extend to the whole of the property, and the debenture holders had also obtained a personal judgment, the court appointed the receiver in the debenture holders' action to be receiver of all the property not included in the previous order.[18]

Priorities between mortgagee and judgment creditor. As between a judgment creditor and a mortgagee of the undertaking, who had obtained his mortgage before the recovery of the judgment,

---

[11] By s. 34 (1) of the Administration of Justice Act 1956.

[12] *Russell* v. *East Anglian Ry.* (1850) 3 Mac. & G. 104; *Potts* v. *Warwick, etc., Canal Co.* (1853) Kay 142.

[13] *Potts* v. *Warwick, etc., Canal Co., supra. Cf. Contract Corpn.* v. *Tottenham, etc., Ry.* [1868] W.N. 242.

[14] See *Hope* v. *Croydon Tramways* (1887) 34 Ch.D. 730; *Contract Corpn.* v. *Tottenham, etc., Ry.* [1868] W.N. 242; *Kingston* v. *Cowbridge Ry.* (1872) 41 L.J.Ch. 152.

[15] See *Re Bishop's Waltham Ry.* (1866) L.R. 2 Ch. 382, 384; *Gardner* v. *L.C. & D. Ry., ex p. Grissell* (1867) 2 Ch.App. 385; *Re Calne Ry.* (1870) L.R. 9 Eq. 658; *Re Ogilvie* (1872) L.R. 7 Ch. 174; *Re Hull, Barnsley, etc., Ry.* (1888) 40 Ch.D. 119, 120; *Stagg* v. *Medway Upper Navigation Co.* [1903] 1 Ch. 169, 174.

[16] See Chap. 3, p. 85, *post.*

[17] *Latimer* v. *Aylesbury and Buckingham Ry.* (1878) 9 Ch.D. 385.

[18] *Hope* v. *Croydon Tramways Co.* (1887) 34 Ch.D. 730.

the right of the mortgagee is paramount.[19] Accordingly, when a receiver has been appointed at the instance of a mortgagee, his right is prior to the claim of a judgment creditor, whose whole interest in the land can be that only which subsists subject to the right of the receiver and the provisions of the statutes. Notwithstanding that a receiver may have been appointed at the instance of a mortgagee, a judgment creditor may also have a receiver appointed; but the receiver who has been appointed at the instance of a judgment creditor takes without prejudice to the right of a receiver appointed at the instance of a mortgagee.[20] The fact that judgment may have been obtained before the appointment of a receiver at the instance of the mortgagee does not vary the rule. If the mortgagee is not in possession by his receiver at the time when execution is issued, the judgment creditor's receiver may take the rates and tolls then due; but, as to the rates and tolls thereafter to become due, he will be stopped at any time by the mortgagee entering into possession by his receiver.[21]

In determining the respective rights of a mortgagee of a public undertaking, and a judgment creditor, it is necessary to bear in mind that the effect of a mortgage or debentures secured on a company's undertaking and tolls in accordance with the provisions of the Companies Clauses Consolidation Act 1845 is to create a lien on the tolls, the unpaid calls, and undertaking as a whole. No specific charge is created on the assets, nor on the proceeds of any sold in the course of the company's business, nor on surplus lands of the company nor their proceeds, for it is contemplated that the company will dispose of these in the course of its business.[22] But where the company obtains statutory authority to sell its assets in bulk, the debentures constitute such a charge on the proceeds as to entitle the debenture holders to payment thereout

---

[19] *Legg* v. *Mathieson* (1860) 2 Giff. 71; *Wildy* v. *Mid-Hants Ry.* (1868) 16 W.R. 409; and see p. 45, *ante*.

[20] See *Ames* v. *Birkenhead Docks* (1855) 20 Beav. 332; *Hopkins* v. *Worcester and Birmingham Canal Co.* (1868) L.R. 6 Eq. 437. Under the former practice a judgment creditor in possession might be given liberty, though not a party to the cause, to appear at the hearing of the motion, or to give a notice of motion to discharge or vary the order: *De Winton* v. *Mayor, etc., of Brecon* (1859) 26 Beav. 539.

[21] See *Ames* v. *Birkenhead Docks* (1855) 20 Beav. 332, 348, 352, referring to provisions of the Common Law Procedure Act 1854, now replaced by R.S.C., Ord. 49.

[22] *Gardner* v. *London, Chatham and Dover Ry.* (1867) L.R. 2 Ch. 201; and see *Attree* v. *Hawe* (1878) 9 Ch.D. 337; also *Hart* v. *Eastern Union Ry.* (1852) 7 Exch. 265; *Eastern Union Ry.* v. *Hart* (1852) 8 Exch. 116.

in priority to judgment creditors [23]; and the same would appear to be the case with the land on which the undertaking is carried on, the debenture constituting a charge in the nature of a floating charge till the property is disposed of.[24] According to these principles, where a railway company, being indebted to contractors for work done, had granted to them, as a security for the debt, a specific charge upon the money to arise from the sale of the company's surplus lands, it was held that the holders of mortgage debentures of the company, made in the form given in Schedule C to the above Act of 1845, had no charge upon those lands or the proceeds of the sale of them, but that the assignees of the contractors were entitled to have a receiver of those proceeds appointed.[25] In an earlier case it had been held that the mortgagee of the tolls arising from a company's undertaking could not have an injunction and receiver against judgment creditors who were about to take under an *elegit* [26] the lands of the company [27]; but it appears that the court will interfere to protect the debenture holders where the action of the creditors would result in destroying the substratum of the company; thus a judgment creditor has been restrained, at the instance of a mortgagee, from taking under a writ of *elegit* [28] the works, rails, etc., incidental to the working of the railway,[29] and though chattels may be seized under a *fi. fa.*,[30] yet where the seizure would destroy the power of the company to carry on its business, it is apprehended that the court would appoint a receiver. But a mortgagee with a specific charge on the proceeds of sale of lands sold by the company (not on the lands themselves), was held not entitled to a charge on the proceeds of a sale effected by judgment creditors.[31]

No mortgage or assignment by a company incorporated for a specific purpose with statutory privileges and obligations is valid except to the extent and in the manner permitted by Parliament.[32]

---

[23] *Re Liskeard and Caradon Ry.* [1903] 2 Ch. 681; see *Yorks. Waggon Co.* v. *Maclure* (1882) 21 Ch.D. 309, 314–315.

[24] See *Legg* v. *Mathieson* (1860) 2 Giff. 71.

[25] *Gardner* v. *London, Chatham and Dover Ry.* (1867) L.R. 2 Ch. 201.

[26] Now abolished; see Administration of Justice Act 1956, s. 34.

[27] *Perkins* v. *Deptford Pier Co.* (1843) 13 Sim. 277.

[28] See *supra*, n. 26.

[29] *Legg* v. *Mathieson* (1860) 2 Giff. 71; see now Railway Companies Act 1867, p. 52, *post.*

[30] *Russell* v. *East Anglian Ry.* (1850) 3 Mac. & G. 104; though now in the case of railways the creditor can only obtain a receiver: see p. 52, *post.*

[31] *Wickham* v. *New Brunswick, etc. Ry.* (1865) L.R. 1 P.C. 64.

[32] See *Re Woking U.D.C.* (*Basingstoke Canal Act*) [1914] 1 Ch. 300.

But a company incorporated by statute, although it has exhausted its borrowing power in creating mortgages of its undertaking, may still create a valid security for an existing debt over all its property that may be taken in execution; and such security will be valid if given to mortgagees who are pressing for payment. A judgment creditor will not therefore be allowed to levy execution on surplus lands or chattels which are included in such a security and of which a receiver is in possession.[33]

Statutory bond holder as distinguished from a mortgagee. The position of a statutory bond holder of a company governed by the Companies Clauses Act [34] must be carefully distinguished from the position of mortgagee. A statutory bond holder is not entitled to an equitable charge on the tolls and traffic receipts of the undertaking, or to have a receiver appointed over such tolls and receipts, for the purpose of paying his claim.[35] Thus, where a receiver had been appointed by consent at the suit of a bond holder of a railway company, it was held that the order for a receiver ought not to have been made,[36] and the execution creditor was allowed to levy under his writ of *fi. fa.* against the goods of the company, notwithstanding the possession of the receiver [37]; the reasoning on which the creditor was held entitled to this writ would have entitled him to a writ of *elegit* [38] (now the appointment of a receiver [39]) against the lands of the company as well.[40]

Receiver appointed at instance of statutory bond holder. A statutory bond or debenture holder, who has obtained judgment and execution against the company, may bring an action on behalf of himself and all other bond holders for a receiver,[41] but he is not bound to bring his action in that form. A statutory bond or debenture holder, who has recovered judgment and issued execution against the company, is not a trustee of the money he may recover under the execution for himself and all

---

[33] *Stagg* v. *Medway Upper Navigation Co.* [1903] 1 Ch. 169; *Reeve* v. *Medway Upper Navigation Co.* (1905) 21 T.L.R. 400.

[34] As to railway companies, see p. 52, *post.*

[35] *Imperial Mercantile Credit Assocn.* v. *Newry & Armagh Ry., etc.* (1868) I.L.R. 2 Eq. 524; see *Lawrence* v. *West Somerset Ry.* [1918] 2 Ch. 250; *Cross* v. *Imperial Continental Gas Assocn.* [1923] 2 Ch. 553.

[36] *Russell* v. *East Anglian Ry.* (1850) 3 Mac. & G. 151.

[37] See *Bowen* v. *Brecon Ry.* (1867) L.R. 3 Eq. 541, 548.

[38] See n. 26, p. 49, *ante.*

[39] Administration of Justice Act 1956, s. 36.

[40] *Imperial Mercantile Credit Assocn.* v. *Newry & Armagh Ry., etc.* (1868) I.L.R. 2 Eq. 539, *per* Christian L.J.   [41] *Ibid.* 526, *per* Christian L.J.

other bond or debenture holders. If he gets paid by the company under his execution before any of the other holders intervene or come into competition with him, he may keep what he has got.[42] The proper mode of giving effect to the provisions with respect to non-priority as between bond holders which are contained in the Companies Clauses Consolidation Act 1845, s. 44, is conceived to be to let them operate after the bond holders come into competition with each other, but not so as to undo past transactions. The priority there spoken of is not a priority existing by virtue of some or one of the bonds, but a priority to be acquired by execution; in other words, a priority not as between bonds which are not charges at all but as between executions.[43]

Priority of mortgagees " inter se." Section 42 of the Companies Clauses Consolidation Act 1845 limits and diminishes the intrinsic rights of mortgagees, imposing on them the principle of non-priority.[44] After an action has been brought by a mortgage debenture holder suing on behalf of himself and all other mortgage debenture holders, against a company governed by that Act, and a receiver has been appointed, a single mortgage debenture holder, who has recovered judgment against the company on his debenture, is not entitled to issue execution on his judgment otherwise than as a trustee for himself and all other mortgage debenture holders entitled to be paid *pari passu* with himself.[45] The intent of the Act being that parity of possession shall be given to those who have parity of security, one mortgage debenture holder is not entitled, as soon as he can recover judgment, to acquire an advantage for himself over the other mortgage debenture holders.[46] Accordingly, where a receiver had been appointed in a suit instituted on behalf of all the mortgage debenture holders of a railway company, and a judgment was afterwards recovered against the company by one of the mortgage debenture holders, an inquiry was directed whether it would be for the benefit of the debenture holders generally that any proceedings should be taken by the receiver for the purpose of making the judgment available for them.[47]

---

[42] *Imperial Mercantile Credit Assocn.* v. *Newry, etc., Ry.* (1868) I.L.R. 2 Eq. 524, 543; see, too, *Fountaine* v. *Carmarthen Ry.* (1868) L.R. 5 Eq. 324, *per* Lord Hatherley.
[43] See I.L.R. 2 Eq. 543, *per* Christian L.J.
[44] I.L.R. 2 Eq. 524, 534, *per* Christian L.J.
[45] *Bowen* v. *Brecon Ry.* (1867) L.R. 3 Eq. 541.
[46] *Ibid.* p. 550.
[47] *Ibid.*; see, too, *Hope* v. *Croydon Tramways Co.* (1887) 34 Ch.D. 730.

Right of judgment creditor to the chattels of a company. Section 4 of the Railway Companies Act 1867 made perpetual by 38 & 39 Vict. c. 31, protects the plant and rolling stock of a railway company from being taken in execution.[48] By the Carriage by Railway Act 1972, this protection was extended to any railway undertaking carrying passengers or their luggage in accordance with the International Convention concerning the Carriage of Passengers and Luggage by Rail (CIV) of February 25, 1961, or carrying goods in accordance with the International Convention concerning the Carriage of Goods by Rail (CIM) of February 25, 1961, if the judgment on which the execution issues is given by a court in the United Kingdom in an action arising on a contract which incorporates the provisions of the relevant convention.[49] But a person who has recovered judgment against a railway company for a sum of money may obtain the appointment of a receiver, and also, if necessary, of a manager of the undertaking of the company, on application by petition in a summary way to the Chancery Division [50]; and the section further provides that " all money received by such receiver or manager shall, after due provision for the working expenses of the railway and other proper outgoings in respect of the undertaking,[51] be applied and distributed under the direction of the court in payment of the debts of the company and otherwise according to the rights and priorities of the persons for the time being interested therein; and on payment of the amount due to every such judgment creditor as aforesaid the court may, if it think fit, discharge such receiver or such receiver and manager." [52]

A judgment creditor of a railway company who obtains a receivership order under section 4 of the Act of 1867 does not thereby obtain priority over other creditors.[53]

In a case in which, after a receiver of the undertaking of a

---

[48] *Re Manchester & Milford Ry.* (1880) 14 Ch.D. 645. The vesting, by the Transport Act 1947, of practically the whole of the railway undertakings of the country in the British Transport Commission, greatly diminished the practical importance of these special provisions. See now the Transport Acts 1962 and 1968.

[49] Carriage by Railway Act 1972, s. 6 (3).

[50] *Re Manchester & Milford Ry.* (1880) 14 Ch.D. 645. Applications under the Act are regulated by rules contained in Part II of an Order of Court, dated January 24, 1868, and printed in L.R. 3 Ch. at p. xlii.

[51] *Re Eastern & Midlands Ry.* (1890) 45 Ch.D. 367; *Re Wrexham, Mold and Connah's Quay Ry.* [1900] 1 Ch. 261; *G.E. Ry.* v. *East London Ry.* (1881) 44 L.T. 903.

[52] *Re Manchester & Milford Ry.* (1880) 14 Ch.D. 645; *Re Mersey Ry.* (1888) 37 Ch.D. 610.

[53] *Re Mersey Ry.* (1888) 37 Ch.D. 610.

railway company had been appointed under the above section 4, the company's rolling stock and other chattels were sold to another company under an agreement, confirmed by statute, which directed the purchasing company to pay the purchase-money to the receiver, it was held that the purchase-money constituted money received by the receiver within the meaning of the section; and, further, that the holders of mortgage debentures charging the undertaking of the railway company were entitled, by virtue of section 23 of the same Act of 1867, to a fund representing that money, in priority to unsecured creditors.[54]

Section 4 of the Act of 1867, though prohibiting execution against the rolling stock of a railway company, does not interfere with the right of a creditor who has recovered judgment against a railway company to apply under section 36 of the Companies Clauses Consolidation Act 1845 for leave to issue execution against a shareholder of the company who has been appointed receiver, to the extent of any moneys remaining due in respect of his share.[55]

Priority of mortgagees and bond holders of railway company. The priority of mortgagees and bond and debenture stock holders of a railway company against the company, and the property from time to time of the company, over all other claims on account of any debts incurred or engagements entered into by the company after August 20, 1867, was declared by section 23 of the Railway Companies Act 1867.[56] The section gives no priority which the mortgagees and bond and debenture holders did not previously possess, except when a receiver has been appointed under section 4, or on a winding up or scheme.[57] It does not entitle them to priority of payment out of the proceeds of surplus lands sold on the application of judgment creditors.[58] The section, moreover provides that this priority shall not affect any claim against the company in respect of any rentcharge granted or to be granted by the company in pursuance of the Lands Clauses Consolidation Act 1845, or the Lands Clauses Consolidation Acts Amendment Act 1860, or in respect of any rent or sum, reserved by or payable

---

[54] *Re Liskeard & Caradon Ry.* [1903] 2 Ch. 681.
[55] *Re West Lancashire Ry.* [1890] W.N. 165; 63 L.T. 56.
[56] *Re Cornwall Minerals Ry.* (1882) 48 L.T. 41; *Re Eastern & Midlands Ry.* (1890) 45 Ch.D. 367.
[57] *Re Hull, Barnsley, etc. Ry.* (1888) 40 Ch.D. 119.
[58] *Ibid.*; *Gardner v. L.C. & D. Ry.* (1867) 2 Ch.App. 201.

under any lease granted or made to the company by any person in pursuance of any Act relating to the company, which is entitled to rank in priority to, or *pari passu* with, the interest on the company's mortgages, bonds or debenture stock.

Local authorities. Whatever the date of the borrowing, all money borrowed by a local authority is charged indifferently on all its revenues.[59] And, subject to any priority existing at, or any right to priority conferred by a security created before June 1, 1934,[60] all securities created under any enactment or instrument under an enactment rank *pari passu*.[61]

Local authorities may raise money by mortgage, by the issue of stock of debentures or annuity certificates under the Local Loans Act 1875; of bonds, of bills, by agreement with the Public Works Loan Commissioners; or by any other means approved by the Secretary of State with the consent of the Treasury.[62] The form of any mortgage deed and the terms of the issue of stocks and bonds are subject to regulation by statutory instrument.[63] Apart from express statutory provision a receiver is not appointed over rates.[64] However, under the relevant statutory instrument,[65] if any principal money or interest due on any mortgage [66] or stocks or bonds made by a local authority is unpaid for two months after demand in writing is made by the mortgagee for payment, the mortgagee may without prejudice to any other remedies apply to the High Court for a receiver: there must be £500 due to the applicant or applicants, more than one mortgagee being entitled to join in the application.[67] The court may confer on the receiver such powers of making, collecting, receiving, and recovering rates and of issuing and enforcing precepts as are possessed by the local authority or its officers.

Where a local authority borrows on the security of debentures under the provisions of the Local Loans Act 1875, and makes default in payment of a sum or sums of not less than £500 for a

---

[59] Local Government Act 1972, Sched. 13, para. 11 (1).
[60] *Ibid.* para. 11 (3).
[61] *Ibid.* para. 11 (2).
[62] Local Government Act 1972, s. 172 and Sched. 13, para. 2 (1).
[63] *Ibid.* Sched. 13, para. 4 (1).
[64] *Preston* v. *Yarmouth* (1872) 7 Ch.App. 655.
[65] The Local Authority (Mortgages) Regulations 1974 (S.I. 1974 No. 518), para. 9, in the case of mortgages and the Local Authority (Stocks and Bonds) Regulations 1974 (S.I. 1974 No. 519), para. 22, in the case of stocks and bonds.
[66] Other than one secured on sewage land and plant: Highways Act 1959, s. 244 (3).
[67] The application will be by originating summons: R.S.C., Ord. 5, r. 3.

period of twenty-one days, the creditors may apply to a county court for appointment of a receiver [68] over the local rate subject to the security.[69] These provisions were by section 13 of the Rating and Valuation Act 1925 (now s. 15 of the General Rate Act 1967) applied to enable a precepting authority to obtain the appointment of a receiver where a rating authority failed to meet a precept under that Act. Section 15 of the General Rate Act 1967 applies to Greater London as it applies elsewhere.[70]

In addition to the remedies provided by these statutes, a judgment creditor may also proceed by mandamus.

SECTION 7. COMPANIES INCORPORATED UNDER THE COMPANIES ACTS

The appointment of a receiver over the undertaking and assets of a company incorporated under the Companies Act 1948, or the Acts which it replaces, is usually made upon the application of mortgagees or debenture holders.[71] The appointment may, in cases of jeopardy, be made at the instance of contributories or the company: thus a receiver and manager was appointed for a limited time where disputes between directors had led to a dereliction in the management [72]; similarly where there was no governing body a receiver was appointed pending a general meeting.[73] The appointment will not be made where winding up is a more appropriate remedy.

---

[68] See the section referred to in the next note as to his powers.

[69] Local Loans Act 1875, s. 12. The section is without prejudice to other remedies. These provisions of the Act are incorporated into various local statutes. As to when money becomes due on a debenture issued hereunder, see *Edinburgh Corpn.* v. *British Linen Bank* [1913] A.C. 133.

[70] s. 13 of the 1925 Act was extended (with the necessary modifications) to the Administrative County of London by s. 43 of the London County Council (General Powers) Act 1949, repealing s. 2 of the Local Authorities (Financial Provisions) Act 1921. S. 43 came into operation on April 1, 1951. It continued to apply after the London Government Act 1963 (establishing Greater London) until replaced by s. 15 of the 1967 Act.

[71] Foreclosure may be obtained: see *Re Corporate Equitable, etc., Society* [1940] Ch. 654, if all debenture holders are parties.

[72] *Stanfield* v. *Gibbon* [1925] W.N. 11: application by contributories and the company: a receiver who had been previously appointed in a mortgagee's foreclosure action was appointed in the action. See also *Featherstone* v. *Cooke* (1873) L.R. 16 Eq. 298.

[73] *Trade Auxiliary Co.* v. *Vickers* (1873) L.R. 16 Eq. 303; Seton, *Forms of Judgments and Orders*, pp. 694, 695. Except in very urgent cases, a meeting will be directed under Companies Act 1948, s. 135, in lieu of the appointment. Application is by originating summons: R.S.C., Ord. 102, r. 2 (1).

Debenture holders and mortgagees. These, however, are exceptional cases, and the appointment is usually made at the instance of holders of debentures or trustees of a trust deed for securing debenture stock or the holders of debenture stock [74] or of a mortgagee with a fixed charge. In these cases the general principles applicable to mortgages, equitable or legal as the case may be, apply.

A receiver will be appointed at the instance of a holder of debentures or of debenture stock which constitutes a charge [75] in the following cases:

1. When the principal is in arrear, [76] or when the interest is in arrear, even though, in accordance with the terms of the debenture or trust deed, the principal has not thereby been rendered payable, [77] or when any other event has happened by which, under the terms of the debenture or trust deed, the security has become enforceable. It is sufficient if the principal has become due at the date of the application, though it was not in arrear when the writ was issued. [78]

2. When the security has crystallised into a specific charge by reason of a winding-up order or resolution, and that though the winding up is for purposes of reconstruction or amalgamation, and the debenture specifically provides that the security is to be enforceable in the case of a winding up otherwise than for purposes of reconstruction or amalgamation; since it is a characteristic of a floating security that it crystallises into a specific charge when the company has become incapable of carrying on its business, and an

---

[74] A debenture stock holder who has no direct contract with the company is not therefore a creditor who can petition for the compulsory winding up of the company (*Re Dunderland Ore Co.* [1909] 1 Ch. 446); but as a *cestui que trust* entitled to the benefit of the trust deed, he can apply for a receiver if the trustees do not (see *Re Empress Engineering Co.* (1880) 16 Ch.D. 125).

[75] If the debenture is a mere bond without a charge (see *Wylie* v. *Carlyon* [1922] 1 Ch. 51) there is no security, and the remedy is by personal judgment against the company for payment only: a receiver can only be obtained by way of equitable execution to enforce the judgment over property amenable to that remedy. The extension of the definition of debentures in s. 455 of the Companies Act 1948 to include securities not creating a charge does not affect this principle.

[76] Even if no interest is in arrear: see *Hopkins* v. *Worcester, etc., Canal Co.* (1868) L.R. 6 Eq. 437. As to when principal becomes payable when payment cannot be enforced so long as interest is punctually paid, see *Maclaine* v. *Gatty* [1921] 1 A.C. 376.

[77] *Strong* v. *Carlyle Press* [1893] 1 Ch. 268; as to power to issue irredeemable debentures, see s. 89, and to reissue debentures, Companies Act 1948, s. 90. A different date for redemption cannot be fixed by the reissued debenture, *Re Antofagasta Ry.* [1939] Ch. 732. See *Bissill* v. *Bradford Tramways Co.* [1891] W.N. 51.

[78] *Hodson* v. *Tea Co.*, 14 Ch.D. 859; *Wallace* v. *Universal Co.* [1894] 2 Ch. 547; *Re Victoria Steamboats* [1897] 1 Ch. 158; *Re Carshalton Park Estate* [1908] 2 Ch. 62.

equitable incumbrancer with a specific charge is entitled to a receiver.[79]

3. Where the security is in jeopardy,[80] as, for instance, where creditors are pressing and a winding up is imminent,[81] or where the company's funds and credit are exhausted and creditors are threatening,[82] or where the company is threatening to dispose of its whole undertaking,[83] or to distribute among shareholders a reserve fund which is its sole asset.[84] But the mere fact that the security is for the time being insufficient is not of itself enough to establish a case of jeopardy where no creditors are pressing [85]; and where the debenture holders had a specific charge which was sufficient to answer their claim, as well as floating charge, the appointment was limited to the property specifically charged, though a case of jeopardy was made out.[86]

Validity of debenture.[87] The memorandum of association almost invariably confers an express power to mortgage the undertaking,[88] but even in the absence of an express power a commercial or trading company has an implied power to borrow on security,[89] and such a power may be implied in other companies as incidental to the purposes for which they were formed. A power to borrow money can, however, only be a power properly so called. Thus, no matter how the matter is dealt with in the memorandum, it cannot be an independent object; and hence borrowing which, to

---

[79] *Re Crompton & Co. Ltd.* [1914] 1 Ch. 954.

[80] *Macmahon* v. *North Kent Co.* [1891] 2 Ch. 148; *Edwards* v. *Standard Rolling Stock Syndicate* [1893] 1 Ch. 574; *Thorn* v. *Nine Reefs* (1892) 67 L.T. 93; *Re Victoria Steamboats* [1897] 1 Ch. 158; and cases *infra*, notes 81 to 85.

[81] *Re London Pressed Hinge Co.* [1905] 1 Ch. 576.

[82] *Re Braunstein and Marjolaine* [1914] W.N. 335. For a case where a receiver was appointed against a company in a state of suspended animation (club of enemy members), see *Higginson* v. *German Athenaeum Ltd.* (1916) 32 T.L.R. 277.

[83] *Hubbuck* v. *Helms* (1887) 56 L.J.Ch. 536; but not where only one of several businesses is to be disposed of: see *Foster* v. *Borax Co.* [1899] 2 Ch. 130.

[84] *Re Tilt Cove Copper Co. Ltd.* [1913] 2 Ch. 588.

[85] *Re New York Taxicab Co. Ltd.* [1913] 1 Ch. 1.

[86] *Gregson* v. *George Taplin & Co.* (1916) 112 L.T. 985.

[87] See generally Palmer, *Company Precedents* (16th ed.), Vol. III, Chap. 5.

[88] As to the possibility of borrowing formally in order being *ultra vires* see, *Charterbridge Corporation Ltd.* v. *Lloyds Bank Ltd.* [1970] Ch. 62; *Re Introductions Ltd.* [1970] Ch. 199. The position in this latter case would not have been affected by s. 9 of the European Communities Act 1972 (see p. 58 *post*) as the lender was in possession of a copy of the memorandum.

[89] See *Re Badger* [1905] 1 Ch. 568, 573; *Re Patent File Co.* (1870) L.R. 6 Ch. 83. In the case of industrial assurance companies the industrial assurance fund cannot be charged: see s. 13 of the Industrial Assurance Act 1923.

the knowledge of the lender, is made for a purpose not authorised by the memorandum, cannot but be *ultra vires*.[90]

But in the case of a non-commercial company such as a club, it has been held that even a power to create debentures does not necessarily imply a power to charge the assets.[91] Uncalled capital may be charged only under an express power in the memorandum.[92]

However, in favour of a person dealing with the company in good faith, any borrowing, like any other transaction decided upon by the directors, is now deemed to be within the power both of the company and its directors, whatever the contents of the memorandum or articles of association.[93] The lender is presumed to have acted in good faith unless the contrary is proved, and he is not bound to make any inquiries as to the power of either the directors or of the company itself.[93]

Mortgages or charges,[94] except charges on chattels which, if made by an individual, would not require registration as a bill of sale,[95] are void against the liquidator and creditors so far as they purport to create a security,[96] unless particulars are registered pursuant to Part 3 of the Companies Act 1948 [97] within 21 days,[98] or the time for registration is extended under section 101. The date of a trust deed to secure notes, not that of the issue of the notes, is the relevant date.[99] An out-and-out assignment of part of a book debt is not registrable under section 95.[1] A floating charge created within 12 [2] months of the commencement of a winding up will

---

[90] *Re Introductions Ltd.* [1970] Ch. 199, C.A.

[91] *Wylie* v. *Carlyon* [1922] 1 Ch. 51; nor does the fact that the advance was employed in paying off a prior charge necessarily create a charge: *ibid*. See now the definition of debenture in s. 455 (1) of the Companies Act 1948.

[92] *Re Pyle Works* (1890) 44 Ch.D. 534; *Newton* v. *Debentureholders' Co.* [1895] A.C. 244.

[93] European Communities Act 1972, s. 9 (1).

[94] See, as to what amounts to a charge, *Re David Allester Ltd.* [1922] 2 Ch. 211 (deposit of bills of lading for collection). *Re Kent and Sussex Sawmills* [1947] Ch. 177 (assignment absolute in form).

[95] See *Dublin Distillery* v. *Doherty* [1914] A.C. 823; *Wrightson* v. *MacArthur* [1921] 2 K.B. 807.

[96] Even against a subsequent mortgagee with notice: *Re Monolithic Building Co. Ltd.* [1915] 1 Ch. 643.

[97] Or s. 93 of the Act of 1908 or s. 79 of the Act of 1929.

[98] In the case of a charge created out of the U.K. and comprising property situate outside, see Companies Act 1948, s. 95 (3), as to date from which the 21 days run.

[99] *Transport and General Corpn.* v. *Morgan* [1939] Ch. 531.

[1] *Ashby Warner & Co.* v. *Simmons* [1936] W.N. 212; 155 L.T. 371 (C.A.). As to hire-purchase agreements, see *Re Inglefield Ltd.* [1933] Ch. 483; *Transport & General Corpn.* v. *Morgan, supra.*

[2] Under the 1929 Act it was six (s. 266) and this applies to all charges created before January 1, 1948: Companies Act 1948, s. 322 (1).

then become invalid under section 322 of the same Act, unless it is proved that the company was solvent [3] immediately after the creation of the charge except to the extent to which it is a security for cash paid to the company at the time of, or subsequently to, and in consideration of the charge.[4] The charge only is invalidated, and money paid in discharge of the secured debt cannot be recovered by the liquidator except on the ground of fraudulent preference.[5] The fact that the money is applied in discharge of a debt owing to a firm in which the lender is a partner does not prevent the money being " cash paid to the company." [6] A debenture of a registered industrial and provident society is void as to chattels unless registered as a bill of sale, but valid as to other property.[7]

Any conveyance or assignment, including an equitable charge,[8] by a company of all its property to trustees for the benefit of all its creditors is void under section 320 (2) of the Companies Act 1948.[9] Any mortgage or debenture which would in the case of an individual be void as a fraudulent preference in bankruptcy is likewise void.[10] The debentures create no enforceable charge on property the assignment of which to the company has been set aside as fraudulent on the bankruptcy of the assignor.[11]

The right of debenture holders whose equitable charge has become enforceable is absolute, and does not rest in the discretion of the court [12]; thus a receiver will be appointed though a liquidator has before been appointed [13]; in such a case the liquidator is sometimes appointed to be the receiver.[14] And although, where the appointment is asked for on the ground of jeopardy, the court has a

[3] *i.e.* able to pay its debts as they arise: *Re Patrick & Lyon Ltd.* [1933] Ch. 786.
[4] *Re Columbian Fireproofing Co.* [1910] 2 Ch. 120; *Re Orleans Motor Co.* [1911] 2 Ch. 41; *Re Stanton Ltd.* [1929] 1 Ch. 180; *Re Matthew Ellis Ltd.* [1933] Ch. 458 (C.A.); *Re Destone Fabrics Ltd.* [1941] Ch. 319; *Re Ambassadors (Bournemouth) Ltd.*, 105 S.J. 969; *Re Yeovil Glove Co. Ltd.* [1965] Ch. 148. Interest at the rate of 5 per cent. per annum on such a cash advance is also a valid charge: Companies Act 1948, s. 322 (1) and S.I. 1952 No. 1865.
[5] *Re Parkes Garage* [1929] 1 Ch. 129.
[6] *Re Matthew Ellis Ltd. supra.*
[7] *Re North Wales Produce Co.* [1922] 2 Ch. 340.
[8] *London City & Midland Bank* v. *H. Dickenson Ltd.* [1922] W.N. 13.
[9] Replacing s. 210 (3) of the Act of 1908 and s. 265 (3) of the Act of 1929.
[10] Companies Act 1948, s. 320 (1).
[11] *Re Simms* [1934] 1 Ch. 1: *q.v.* as to position of receiver.
[12] See *Strong* v. *Carlyle Press Ltd.* [1893] 1 Ch. 268; *Re Crompton & Co. Ltd.* [1914] 1 Ch. 954 and *ante*, p. 6.
[13] *Strong* v. *Carlyle Press Ltd., supra.*
[14] See p. 108, *post.*

discretion, yet if a case of real jeopardy is made out the application
cannot be refused.[15]

The decision of the question whether the principal is in arrear
depends upon the terms of the debentures: where no place is fixed
for payment it is the duty of the company to seek the debenture
holder and tender the money [16]: but where payment is to be made
at the company's office there is no default unless the debenture
holder attends and gives the company an opportunity to pay.[17]
Where the principal is payable on demand, the debtor is not
entitled to more time than would be required to produce the
money from safe keeping, for example at a bank.[18] The debtor is
not entitled to time in which to negotiate a deal which might
produce the money.[18] Where the principal is payable on demand
at a certain place, but there is no such provision as to interest, and
the company makes default in payment of interest, the principal
becomes due though no demand is made at the specified place.[19]
If the covenant is to pay on or before a date fixed, the effect is to
make the money payable on that day with an option to the company to pay on an earlier date [20]; if the covenant is to pay on or
after a date fixed, the money becomes payable on or after that date
on demand by the covenantee.[21] A provision that a covenant to
pay is only to be enforced at the option of the covenantor is void
for repugnancy [22]; but where there is no covenant to pay, but
stock is made redeemable at the option of the covenantor, there is
no obligation to pay until the covenantor has assumed it.[23]

Where receiver appointed by debenture holders. The fact that
debenture holders have, under a power contained in the debentures,
appointed their own receiver does not preclude the court from
appointing its own receiver in a proper case.[24]

---

[15] See *Re London Pressed Hinge Co.* [1905] 1 Ch. 576.
[16] *Fowler* v. *Midland Electric Corporation* [1917] 1 Ch. 656.
[17] *Re Escalera Silver Lead Mining Co.* (1908) 25 T.L.R. 87.
[18] *Cripps Ltd.* v. *Wickenden* [1973] 1 W.L.R. 944.
[19] *Re Harris Calculating Machine Co.* [1914] 1 Ch. 920.
[20] *Re Tewkesbury Gas Co.* [1911] 2 Ch. 279, affirmed [1912] 1 Ch. 1; see also
Central Printing Works v. *Walker* (1907) 24 T.L.R. 88.
[21] *Re Tewkesbury Gas Co.*, *supra*. As to currency in which the money is payable,
see *Adelaide Electric Supply Co.* v. *Prudential Assurance Co.* [1934] A.C. 122 (over-
ruling *Broken Hill Co.* v. *Latham* [1933] Ch. 333); *Feist* v. *Societe Intercommunale
Belge* [1934] A.C. 161; *New Brunswick Ry.* v. *British, etc., Trust Corporation* [1939]
A.C. 1.
[22] *Watling* v. *Lewis* [1911] 1 Ch. 414; *Re Tewkesbury Gas Co.* [1911] 2 Ch. 279, 285.
[23] See *Edinburgh Corporation* v. *British Linen Bank* [1913] A.C. 133.
[24] *Re Slogger Automatic Feeder Co. Ltd.* [1915] 1 Ch. 478; see *post*, p. 109, as to
practice.

The holder of a floating security cannot enforce his claim to any specific item of property over which the charge exists until the security has crystallised.[25] A receiver should usually be asked for over the whole of the property to which the charge extends, though an item of property which is considered valueless may be excluded from the appointment.[26] But it is submitted that the court has a discretion and if on the application to enforce the floating charge by the appointment of a receiver certain items are excluded, it may be that the court would refuse a subsequent application to include them.

If the charge extends to the goodwill, as it usually does in the case of debentures, the receiver will also be appointed manager: this topic is fully dealt with in Chapter 13. The debenture holder may, however, elect whether he will have a receiver simply, who would be unable to fulfil the company's contracts, so destroying the goodwill, besides rendering the company liable in damages, or a receiver and manager whose duty it would be to carry out contracts.[27] It is submitted that if debenture holders of a prior series elect for a receiver only, being satisfied that the assets apart from the goodwill are sufficient to pay them in full, or, if they have no charge on the goodwill, the receiver would be appointed manager on the application of subsequent incumbrancers whose security includes the goodwill, or of the company, where this can be effected without damage to the prior incumbrancers. In similar circumstances it appears that the only remedy of unsecured creditors would be to obtain a winding-up order and apply to have the liquidator appointed manager.

Registration of appointment. A person who obtains an order for the appointment of a receiver or manager of the property of a company, or appoints such receiver or manager under the powers of any instrument, must under section 102 (1) of the Companies Act 1948 within seven days give notice to the Registrar of Companies who thereupon enters the fact on the register of charges.

Statutory duties. Any receiver so appointed is subject to numerous statutory obligations, which are dealt with in Chapter 8, *post*.

---

[25] *Evans* v. *Rival Granite Quarries* [1910] 2 K.B. 979.
[26] See *Re Griffin Hotel* [1941] Ch. 129, where an hotel subject to a prior mortgage was excluded.
[27] See *Re Newdigate Colliery Co.* [1912] 1 Ch. 468.

SECTION 8. IN CASES BETWEEN VENDOR AND PURCHASER

Actions for rescission. The court will, upon a proper case being made out, interfere upon motion, and appoint a receiver, in cases between vendor and purchaser. Accordingly, where, on a bill impeaching a sale of land on the ground of fraud, and alleging gross inadequacy of consideration and undue advantage taken of the ignorance of the vendor, the court was of opinion, from the materials before it, that it was hardly possible the transaction could stand at the hearing, a receiver was appointed in a suit instituted against the devisees of the party charged with fraud.[28] So also, where it appeared that the defendants had obtained the conveyance of the legal estate from the plaintiff upon a strong suspicion of abused confidence, a receiver was appointed.[29] But where there is no clear evidence of danger to the property from neglect or misconduct, the court will not usually appoint a receiver in an action to set aside a conveyance [30]; but a receiver and manager will be appointed where necessary to preserve the property, for instance, in order to keep a coal mine in working order.[31]

Specific performance. If a fair prima facie case for the specific performance of a contract is made to appear, the court may interfere upon motion and appoint a receiver.[32]

On application of purchaser. Thus in a case where completion was postponed for five years upon condition that the purchaser paid interest on his purchase-money out of the rents and profits punctually, a receiver was appointed at the instance of a mortgagee of the purchaser's interest when the vendor had re-entered upon the property in breach of the contract.[33] So also a receiver was appointed where it was alleged that an estate under a voluntary settlement was being utilised to defeat the claim of a purchaser for value.[34] Similarly a receiver has been appointed in an action to enforce specific performance of a bill of sale of chattels where

---

[28] *Stillwell* v. *Wilkins* (1821) Jac. 282.

[29] *Huguenin* v. *Baseley* (1808) 13 Ves. 107.

[30] *George* v. *Evans* (1840) 4 Y. & C. 211, a case of a purchase by a trustee.

[31] *Gibbs* v. *David* (1875) L.R. 20 Eq. 373.

[32] See *Kennedy* v. *Lee* (1817) 3 Mer. 441; *M'Cleod* v. *Phelps* (1838) 2 Jur. 962. The appointment may be made in special circumstances before the order for sale is made absolute: *Re Stafford* (1892) 31 L.R.Ir. 195.

[33] *Dawson* v. *Yates* (1839) 1 Beav. 301.

[34] *Metcalfe* v. *Pulvertoft* (1813) 1 V. & B. 180.

there was evidence of immediate danger to the chattels.[35] It is submitted that a receiver would be appointed against a vendor who, after payment of the whole of the purchase-money, has refused to execute a conveyance. Where no good title was made, and there was no fund in court, a receiver was appointed and ordered to apply the rents in discharge of the purchaser's interests and costs.[36]

On vendor's motion. A receiver has been appointed at the instance of a vendor against a purchaser in possession, who was insolvent and endeavouring to dispose of the estate [37]; against a railway company at the instance of an unpaid vendor [38]; when considerable expenditure was necessary, for which the vendor did not wish to be responsible, where the title had been referred to the master [39]; where a purchaser in possession was dealing with the land contrary to the usual course of husbandry [40]; where, in order to avoid forfeiture, a vendor of leaseholds was obliged to pay rent by reason of default on the part of the purchaser.[41] A receiver and manager has been appointed of a farm, pending an appeal by a plaintiff, in an action for specific performance of an agreement for a lease.[42]

Indemnity of vendor. A vendor of a business is entitled to be indemnified against losses in carrying it on where delay in completion is due to the purchaser's default [43]; it is apprehended that, if he so desires, the vendor might, for his own protection, obtain the appointment of a receiver in such a case.[44]

SECTION 9. IN CASES BETWEEN COVENANTOR AND COVENANTEE

Where a covenantor refuses to perform his covenant, with the result that the covenantee is being deprived of his right to payment

---

[35] *Taylor* v. *Eckersley* (1876) 2 Ch.D. 302; (1877) 5 Ch.D. 741.
[36] *Hill* v. *Kirwan* (1826) 1 Hog. 175.
[37] *Hall* v. *Jenkinson* (1813) 2 V. & B. 125.
[38] *Munns* v. *Isle of Wight Ry.* (1870) L.R. 5 Ch. 414; see *Williams* v. *Aylesbury Ry.* (1873) 21 W.R. 819; *Ware* v. *Same, ibid.*
[39] *Boehm* v. *Wood* (1820) 2 Jac. & W. 236; and see 1 Jac. & W. 441.
[40] *Osborne* v. *Harvey* (1842) 1 Y. & C.C.C. 116.
[41] *Cook* v. *Andrews* [1897] 1 Ch. 266.
[42] *Hyde* v. *Warden* (1876) 1 Ex.D. 309.
[43] See *Golden Bread Co.* v. *Hemmings* [1922] 1 Ch. 162.
[44] See *Hyde* v. *Warden* (1876) 1 Ex.D. 309.

out of, or to an effective charge upon, particular property, a receiver may be appointed; such cases are equivalent to cases of relief given to an equitable mortgagee. Thus a receiver has been appointed against a tenant in tail [45] refusing to fulfil a covenant to bar his estate tail in order to secure an advance [46]; against the owner of property who refused to carry out his covenant to secure an advance by a mortgage [47]; and against a person who refused to secure an annuity on subsequently acquired property pursuant to a covenant to do so. [48]

The court will interfere, when necessary, to prevent irreparable mischief from breach of covenant, although the property may have to be distributed in bankruptcy, and though the Court of Bankruptcy may be able to give the same relief. [49]

SECTION 10. IN PARTNERSHIP CASES

When dissolution has taken place. The readiness of the court to appoint a receiver in partnership cases depends upon whether the partnership has been dissolved at the time when the application is made. If a dissolution has clearly been effected by the service of the writ, [50] or if the partnership has expired by effluxion of time, a receiver will readily be appointed, though the appointment is not a matter of course [51]; it will be enough to show that one of the former partners is delaying the winding up and realisation of the business. [52] Conversely, if all that is shown is that a partner has retired from the partnership, leaving the remaining partners to carry on the former business, he will not be entitled to such an appointment. [53]

---

[45] If the legal estate is not in the tenant in tail in possession, the person in whom it is vested might, *semble*, be added.

[46] *Free* v. *Hind* (1827) 2 Sim. 7.

[47] *Shakel* v. *Marlborough* (1819) 4 Madd. 463.

[48] *Metcalf* v. *Archbishop of York* (1833) 6 Sim. 225; 1 M. & C. 553. This case was decided when a charge on a benefice could be effected.

[49] *Riches* v. *Owen* (1868) L.R. 3 Ch. 821.

[50] As is the case in partnership at will.

[51] *Pini* v. *Roncoroni* [1892] 1 Ch. 633. A receiver and manager can be appointed though the partnership has expired: *Taylor* v. *Neate* (1888) 39 Ch.D. 538. The appointment was made notwithstanding a provision in the articles for distribution of the assets with a view to the sale of the business as a going concern. The receiver was directed not to enter into contracts involving liability of more than £200 without the consent of the partners or the direction of the judge.

[52] The notice of motion itself may in an urgent case ask leave for the receiver to accept a pending offer for a specific asset, but proper evidence must be contained in the affidavits. By consent, an immediate dissolution and accounts are often ordered on the motion.   [53] *Sobell* v. *Boston* [1975] 1 W.L.R. 1587.

Principles on which a receiver is appointed. If, however, the partnership is a continuing one, and may continue, the court is always placed in a position of very great difficulty: if it grants the motion, the effect of it is to put an end to the partnership, which one of the parties claims a right to have continued; while if it refuses the motion, it leaves the defendant at liberty to go on with the partnership business at the risk, and probably to the great loss and prejudice, of the dissenting party. Between these difficulties it is not very easy to select the course which is best to be taken, but the court is under the necessity of adopting some mode of proceeding to protect, according to the best view it can take of the matter, the interests of both parties.[54]

Where dissolution would be ordered at trial. The court does not therefore appoint a receiver unless it is reasonably clear that a dissolution will be ordered at the trial.[55] If it is not, the court will sometimes grant an injunction to restrain a partner from doing the acts which are complained of, although it will not grant a receiver [56]; for the latter course has the effect of taking the business out of the hands of the partners altogether.[57] Where complaints are made of breaches of partnership articles, it must be seen whether the complaints are urged with a view to making them the foundation of a dissolution, or of a judgment enforcing and carrying on the partnership according to the original terms, and preventing, by proper means, the recurrence of those breaches which have happened before by reason of the conduct of one of the parties.[58]

All the partners, or their representatives, must be before the court before accounts can be ordered [59]; or, *semble*, before a receiver can be appointed, except in cases of extreme jeopardy where a partner cannot be speedily served.

As the appointment is made for the purpose of preserving the assets pending realisation and of effecting that realisation, the writ should claim a dissolution, but it is not absolutely necessary

---

[54] *Madgwick* v. *Wimble* (1843) 6 Beav. 500, *per* Lord Langdale; see, too, *Blakeney* v. *Dufaur* (1851) 15 Beav. 42; *Sargant* v. *Read* (1876) 1 Ch.D. 600.

[55] *Goodman* v. *Whitcomb* (1820) 1 Jac. & W. 589; *Smith* v. *Jeyes* (1841) 4 Beav. 503; *Roberts* v. *Eberhardt* (1853) Kay 148.

[56] *Hall* v. *Hall* (1850) 3 Mac. & G. 79, 86.

[57] See *Hartz* v. *Shrader* (1803) 8 Ves. 317; *Hall* v. *Hall* (1850) 3 Mac. & G. 79.

[58] *Hall* v. *Hall* (1850) 3 Mac. & G. 79, 87.

[59] *Public Trustee* v. *Elder* [1936] Ch. 776.

that it should expressly do so. It is enough if it is plain that it is
necessary to put an end to the concern.[60] If this be proved, the
case stands upon precisely the same basis as if the action had been
brought exclusively for the purpose of the dissolution.[61] The
court will, in all cases, entertain an application for a receiver, if the
object of the action is to wind up the partnership affairs, and the
appointment of the receiver is sought with that view.[62]

If, however, it is doubtful whether there is or is not an unexpired term, a receiver will, having regard to the possible consequences of the appointment if there is in truth no partnership,
not normally [63] be appointed, unless, of course, there is danger to
the assets [64]: so where a partnership is alleged on one side and
denied on the other,[65] unless the person in possession of the assets
consents.

Where dissolution not claimed. In certain cases a receiver will
be appointed even where a dissolution is not expressly or impliedly
claimed, as, for instance, to receive money, where there is reason
to fear that, if received by the parties, it might be misapplied, and
thus justice could not be done at the trial [66]; thus a receiver has
been appointed over the takings of a theatre to secure their
application in accordance with an agreement between the partners [67]; and a receiver has been appointed to secure property until
a dispute between the partners has been determined, though
dissolution was not claimed.[68] In such cases the duties of a receiver
are purely administrative.

Receiver not ordered as of course. The court will not, as a matter
of course, appoint a receiver of the partnership assets, even where
a case for dissolution is made.[69] The very basis of a partnership
contract being the mutual confidence reposed in each other by the

---

[60] *Wallworth* v. *Holt* (1836) 4 M. & C. 619. In limited partnership cases the remedy
is by winding up: see *Re Hughes & Co.* [1911] 1 Ch. 342.
[61] *Hall* v. *Hall* (1850) 3 Mac. & G. 79, 89.
[62] *Sheppard* v. *Oxenford* (1855) 1 K. & J. 491.
[63] See *Floydd* v. *Cheney* [1970] Ch. 602; *Tate* v. *Barry* (1928) 28 S.R. (N.S.W.) 380.
[64] *Baxter* v. *West* (1858) 28 L.J.Ch. 169; *Longbottom* v. *Woodhead* (1887) 31 S.J.
796.
[65] *Peacock* v. *Peacock* (1809) 16 Ves. 49; *Fairburn* v. *Pearson* (1850) 2 Mac. & G.
144; *Tucker* v. *Prior* (1889) 31 S.J. 784; *cf. Re Beard* [1915] H.B.R. 191.
[66] *Hall* v. *Hall* (1850) 3 Mac. & G. 79, 90.
[67] *Coust* v. *Harris* (1824) T. & R. 496.
[68] *Medwin* v. *Ditchman* [1882] W.N. 121; 47 L.T. 250.
[69] *Harding* v. *Glover* (1810) 18 Ves. 281; *Fairburn* v. *Pearson* (1850) 2 Mac. & G.
145. *Cf. Sobell* v. *Boston* [1975] 1 W.L.R. 1587.

parties,[70] the court will not appoint a receiver, unless some special ground for its interference is established.[71] It must appear that the member of the firm against whom the appointment of a receiver is sought has done acts which are inconsistent with the duty of a partner, and are of a nature to destroy the mutual confidence which ought to subsist between the parties.[72]

In the case of a professional firm, since the appointment of a receiver and manager may easily do far more harm than good, the court will be reluctant to make the appointment in such cases unless it is unavoidable.[73]

Misconduct of partner. The ground on which the court is most commonly asked to appoint a receiver is where, by the misconduct of a partner, his right of personal intervention in the partnership affairs has been forfeited, and the partnership funds are in danger of being lost. Mere quarrels and disagreements between the partners arising from infirmities of temper are not a sufficient ground for the interference of the court.[74] The due winding up of the affairs of the concern must be endangered, to induce the court to appoint a receiver.[75] The non-co-operation of one partner, whereby the whole responsibility of management is thrown on his co-partner, is not sufficient.[76] But if the quarrels between the partners are such as to occasion a complete deadlock in carrying on the business, a receiver will be appointed.[77]

The appointment will be made where a partner has so misconducted himself as to show that he is no longer to be trusted; as, for example, if one partner colludes with the debtors of the firm, and allows them to delay paying their debts,[78] or if he is carrying on a separate trade on his own account with the partnership property,[79] or if a surviving partner insists on carrying on the

---

[70] *Philips* v. *Atkinson* (1787) 2 Bro.C.C. 272; see too, *Peacock* v. *Peacock* (1809) 16 Ves. 51.

[71] *Harding* v. *Glover* (1810) 18 Ves. 281.

[72] *Smith* v. *Jeyes* (1841) 4 Beav. 503.

[73] *Floydd* v. *Cheney* [1970] Ch. 602, 610; *Sobell* v. *Boston* [1975] 1 W.L.R. 1587, at pp. 1593–1594.

[74] See *Goodman* v. *Whitcomb* (1820) 1 Jac. & W. 593; *Marshall* v. *Colman* (1820) 2 Jac. & W. 266; *Smith* v. *Jeyes* (1841) 4 Beav. 504.

[75] See *Goodman* v. *Whitcomb* (1820) 1 Jac. & W. 593; *Smith* v. *Jeyes* (1841) 4 Beav. 504.

[76] *Roberts* v. *Eberhardt* (1853) Kay 148; see, too, *Rowe* v. *Wood* (1822) 2 Jac. & W. 556, where one partner declined to advance more money to work a mine.

[77] See *Re Yenidje Tobacco Co.* [1916] 2 Ch. 426.

[78] *Estwick* v. *Conningsby* (1682) 1 Vern. 118.

[79] *Harding* v. *Glover* (1810) 18 Ves. 281.

business and employing therein the assets of his deceased partner [80]; or if, in the opinion of the court, a case has arisen for the inter- position of the court to secure the estate of a deceased partner against loss [81]; or if, the partnership property being abroad, one of the partners goes off in order to do what he likes with it [82]; or if the persons having the control of the partnership assets have already made away with some of them [83]; or if there has been such mismanagement as to endanger the whole concern [84]; or if one of the partners has acted in a manner inconsistent with the duties and obligations which are implied in every partnership contract. [85]

The unwillingness of the court to appoint a receiver at the suit of one member of a firm against another being based on the con- fidence originally reposed in each other by the parties, the ground of the rule has no longer any place if it appears that the confidence has been misplaced, [86] as, for instance, where a prima facie case is made that the plaintiff has been induced to enter into partnership with the defendant by the fraudulent misrepresenta- tions of the latter. [87]

Partner excluded from management. There is a case for a receiver, even although there be no misconduct endangering the partnership assets, if one partner excludes another partner from the manage- ment of the partnership affairs. [88] This doctrine is acted on where the defendant contends that the plaintiff is not a partner, [89] or that he has no interest in the partnership assets, [90] or where the

---

[80] *Madgwick* v. *Wimble* (1843) 6 Beav. 495.

[81] *Baldwin* v. *Booth* [1872] W.N. 229; *Young* v. *Buckett* (1882) 30 W.R. 511; 46 L.T. 269.

[82] *Sheppard* v. *Oxenford* (1855) 1 K. & J. 491.

[83] *Evans* v. *Coventry* (1854) 5 De G.M. & G. 911.

[84] See *De Tastet* v. *Bordieu* (1805) cited 2 Bro.C.C. 272; *Jeffreys* v. *Smith* (1820) 1 Jac. & W. 298; *Hall* v. *Hall* (1850) 3 Mac. & G. 79; *Chaplin* v. *Young* (1862) 6 L.T. 97.

[85] *Smith* v. *Jeyes* (1841) 4 Beav. 505; *Young* v. *Buckett* (1882) 30 W.R. 511; 46 L.T. 269.

[86] See *Chapman* v. *Beach* (1820) 1 Jac. & W. 594n.

[87] See *Ex p. Broome* (1811) 1 Rose 69.

[88] See *Wilson* v. *Greenwood* (1818) 1 Sw. 481; *Goodman* v. *Whitcomb* (1820) 1 Jac. & W. 592; *Rowe* v. *Wood* (1822) 2 Jac. & W. 558; *Const* v. *Harris* (1824) T. & R. 496. A dissolution which takes place on the refusal of an appointee under a will to become a partner is not a dissolution arising from the exclusion of the appointee by the surviving partner, and therefore will not be a foundation for a receiver: *Kershaw* v. *Matthews* (1826) 2 Russ. 62.

[89] *Peacock* v. *Peacock* (1809) 16 Ves. 49; *Blakeney* v. *Dufaur* (1851) 15 Beav. 40.

[90] *Wilson* v. *Greenwood* (1818) 1 Sw. 471, where the plaintiffs were the assignees of a bankrupt partner. See, too, *Clegg* v. *Fishwick* (1849) 1 Mac. & G. 294, where the plaintiff was the administratrix of a deceased partner.

partnership is disputed by the defendant on the ground of illegality[91]—as, for instance, where its object is contrary to public policy.[92]

Inasmuch as the court will not appoint a receiver against a partner unless some special ground for doing so can be shown, it follows that, in the case of a firm consisting of three or four members, there is more difficulty in obtaining a receiver than in a firm consisting of two. For, the appointment of a receiver operating as an injunction against the members, there must be some ground for excluding all who oppose the application. If the object is to exclude some or one only from intermeddling, the appropriate remedy is rather by injunction than by the appointment of a receiver.[93]

Partners without power of dissolution. Another case, in which the court may be called upon to appoint a receiver, is where the partners have by agreement divested themselves more or less of their right to wind up the affairs of the concern. In one case,[94] for instance, the plaintiff and defendant, on dissolving partnership, appointed a third person to get in the assets of the partnership, and agreed not to interfere with him. After the agreement had been partially acted on, one of the partners died, and disputes arising between the executors of the deceased partner and the surviving partner, the latter got in some of the debts of the firm in violation of the agreement. A bill having been filed by the executors of the deceased partner for an injunction and a receiver, the court on motion appointed a receiver, but declined to grant an injunction, on the ground that there was no sufficient impropriety of conduct on the part of the defendant to render such an order necessary.[95]

Death, bankruptcy, etc., of a partner. The reasoning on which the court proceeds, in refusing to appoint a receiver at the instance of one member of a firm against another, does not apply to the

---

[91] *Hale* v. *Hale* (1841) 4 Beav. 369. A partnership between bookmakers has been held not to be, *per se*, illegal (*Thwaites* v. *Coulthwaite* [1896] 1 Ch. 496; *Keen* v. *Price* [1914] 2 Ch. 98; *Jeffrey* v. *Bamford* [1921] 2 K.B. 351), notwithstanding the dictum of Fletcher Moulton L.J. in *Hyams* v. *Stuart-King* [1908] 2 K.B. 696, 718; and see now Betting, Gaming and Lotteries Act 1963; but a receiver would not be appointed to get in gaming debts.

[92] *Quaere*, whether a partnership to carry on a business, which would involve breach of the law of a friendly state, is illegal.

[93] *Hall* v. *Hall* (1850) 3 Mac. & G. 79.

[94] *Davis* v. *Amer* (1854) 3 Drew. 64.

[95] See also *Turner* v. *Major* (1836) 3 Giff. 442.

case of persons who acquire an interest in the partnership assets by events over which the parties have no control. If a member of a firm dies, or becomes bankrupt, the partnership is determined, as far as his personal representatives or trustee in bankruptcy are or is concerned. The personal representatives of a deceased partner are not strictly partners, nor is the trustee of a bankrupt partner strictly a partner, with the surviving or solvent partners or partner. They (or he) are (or is) only tenants (or tenant) in common with the surviving or solvent partners or partner to the extent of the interest which the deceased or bankrupt partner had in the partnership assets at the time of his death or bankruptcy as the case may be.[96] It is, consequently, a matter of course to appoint a receiver when all the partners are dead, and an action is pending between their representatives [97]; or when such appointment is sought by a partner against the personal representatives or trustee in bankruptcy of his deceased or bankrupt co-partner.[98] *Fraser* v. *Kershaw* [99] is a good illustration of the doctrine. There one partner had become bankrupt; the share of the other partner had been taken in execution under *fi. fa.* for a separate debt, and had been assigned to the judgment creditor by the sheriff. The creditor, as the assignee from the sheriff of the share and interest of the non-bankrupt partner, claimed the right of winding up the affairs of the partnership, and to exclude the assignees of the bankrupt partner from interfering. But, on bill filed by the assignees in bankruptcy against the judgment creditor, the court granted an injunction and appointed a receiver, holding that the right of the non-bankrupt partner to wind up the affairs was personal to himself and not transferable, and, therefore, did not pass with his share and interest in the partnership assets.[1]

The death or bankruptcy of one of the members of a firm is not itself a ground for the appointment of a receiver, as against the surviving or solvent partner or partners.[2] If a partner dies,[3] or becomes bankrupt,[4] a right to wind up the partnership concern

---

[96] *Ex p. Williams* (1805) 11 Ves. 5, 6; *Wilson* v. *Greenwood* (1818) 1 Sw. 480; *Fraser* v. *Kershaw* (1856) 2 K. & J. 499.

[97] *Philips* v. *Atkinson* (1787) 2 Bro.C.C. 272.

[98] *Freeland* v. *Stansfield* (1854) 16 Jur. 792; 2 Sm. & G. 479.

[99] (1856) 2 K. & J. 496.

[1] For the procedure against partnership property for a partner's separate judgment debt, see the Partnership Act 1890, s. 23, *ante*, p. 40.

[2] See *Philips* v. *Atkinson* (1787) 2 Bro.C.C. 272.

[3] *Collins* v. *Young* (1853) 1 Macq. 385.

[4] *Fraser* v. *Kershaw* (1856) 2 K. & J. 499

and collect the assets is by law vested in the surviving [5] or solvent [6] partner or partners, as the case may be. Before the court will interfere and appoint a receiver, some breach or neglect of duty on their part must be established.[7]

If it is more convenient that the affairs of the partnership should be wound up in bankruptcy, the court will not appoint a receiver: thus, where one partner had died and the other had been adjudicated bankrupt, the court, on the application of the trustee in bankruptcy, discharged an order for a receiver made in a partnership action commenced by the executors of the dead partner, on proof that the solvency of the partnership and of the dead partner's estate was very doubtful.[8]

Disputes referable to arbitration. A receiver may be appointed in an action for dissolution, notwithstanding a reference of disputes to arbitration [9]; but it may now be more convenient to apply in the arbitration for the appointment of a receiver under the Arbitration Act 1950.[10] The court will, by one and the same order, appoint a receiver and stay all proceedings in the action except for the purpose of carrying out the order for a receiver.[11]

County court jurisdiction. Where the value of the whole property, stock and credits of the partnership does not exceed in value £15,000 the county court can exercise all the powers and authority of the High Court in actions for dissolution or winding up.[12]

A partnership formed to work metalliferous mines in Cornwall is a " company " within the meaning of that term in sections 2 and 28 of the Stannaries Act 1887 and is by section 1 (2) of the Partnership Act 1890 excluded from the provisions of the latter Act; and by virtue of section 1 of the Stannaries Court (Abolition) Act 1896

---

[5] *Collins* v. *Young* (1853) 1 Macq. 385.

[6] *Freeland* v. *Stansfield* (1854) 2 Sm. & G. 487; *Fraser* v. *Kershaw* (1856) 2 K. & J. 499.

[7] *Collins* v. *Young* (1853) 1 Macq. 385; see *Baldwin* v. *Booth* [1872] W.N. 229. The court will not appoint an administrator *pendente lite* against a surviving partner, unless under very special circumstances: *Horrell* v. *Witts* (1866) L.R. 1 P. & M. 103.

[8] *Hulme* v. *Rowbotham* [1907] W.N. 162, 189; most of the assets were situate in the jurisdiction of the county court which was the tribunal in the bankruptcy proceedings. Executors carrying on a testator's business cannot be made bankrupt as partners: *Re Fisher* [1912] 2 K.B. 491.

[9] *Halsey* v. *Windham* [1882] W.N. 108; *Compagnie du Sénégal* v. *Woods* [1883] W.N. 180; 53 L.J.Ch. 166.

[10] s. 12 (6) (*h*).   [11] *Pini* v. *Roncoroni* [1892] 1 Ch. 633.

[12] County Courts Act 1959, s. 52. Administration of Justice Act 1969, s. 5.; County Courts Jurisdiction Order 1977 (S.I. 1977 No. 600). As to transfers, see Act of 1959, ss. 54, 76, 77.

and section 218 (5) of the Companies Act 1948, the county court of Cornwall has exclusive jurisdiction to wind up such a partnership, and an application for a receiver should be made to that court.[13]

Enemy partner. The outbreak of war causes the dissolution of a partnership, one of the partners in which is an enemy,[14] though the enemy partner is entitled to his share of profits made in winding up the business.[15] In such cases a receiver will be appointed in an action in which the English partner is plaintiff[16]; the enemy partner can be made defendant, but cannot be a plaintiff.[17] After a vesting order has been made under the Trading with the Enemy Act 1939, and rules thereunder, the Custodian of Enemy Property will be defendant in place of the enemy. Enemy character for this purpose does not depend upon nationality but upon residence in an enemy territory.[18]

Pending action in foreign tribunal. Where partners have agreed to refer disputes to a foreign tribunal, the court will not appoint a receiver during the liquidation of the partnership affairs, unless it is shown that the rights of the partners cannot be sufficiently protected by the foreign tribunal.[19]

Mining partnerships. In cases of mining partnerships a receiver will be appointed or refused upon the same principles as in other cases of partnership. Accordingly, if a dissolution or winding up is not sought, a receiver will not be appointed[20]; but, where a dissolution or winding up is sought, a receiver and manager will be appointed, if there are any such grounds for the appointment as are sufficient in other cases,[21] or if the partners

---

[13] *Dunbar* v. *Harvey* [1913] 2 Ch. 530. The court sits at Truro. In the case of a company formed under the Companies Acts the High Court has concurrent jurisdiction to wind up: Companies Act 1948, s. 218 (4).

[14] See *Kupfer* v. *Kupfer* [1915] W.N. 397.

[15] See *Hugh Stevenson & Sons Ltd.* v. *Aktiegesellschaft für Cartonnagen Industrie* [1918] A.C. 239; as to consideration determining enemy character, *post*, p. 81.

[16] *Rombach* v. *Rombach* [1910] W.N. 423. See *Armitage* v. *Borgman* (1915) 84 L.J.Ch. 784, where a receiver was appointed in a case where the enemy partners retired immediately before the war.

[17] *Porter* v. *Freudenberg* [1915] 1 K.B. 857. An alien enemy was allowed to be joined as a formal plaintiff in actions to recover debts due to the partnership: *Rodriguez* v. *Speyer Bros.* [1919] A.C. 59. But this part of the decision will not be followed (see *Sovfracht (V/O)* v. *Van Udens Scheepvaart en Agentuur Maatschappij (N.V. Gebr.)* [1943] A.C. 203).

[18] See p. 82, *post*.

[19] *Law* v. *Garrett* (1878) 8 Ch.D. 26.   [20] *Roberts* v. *Eberhardt* (1853) Kay 148.

[21] *Ibid.*; *Sheppard* v. *Oxenford* (1855) 1 K. & J. 491.

cannot agree as to the proper mode of working the mines until they are sold.[22]

Thus in one case [23] a receiver was refused, although one of the partners excluded the other from interfering in the concern; but the case was a peculiar one, for the partner complained of was not only a partner but also a mortgagee in possession, and his mortgage debt was unsatisfied. Again, in another,[24] although the plaintiff had been excluded, a receiver of a mining concern was refused on the ground of his laches; for he had been excluded for some time, and had taken no steps to assert his right until the mines proved profitable.[25]

Again, where one of the partners in a mining concern had become mentally infirm, the court would not appoint a manager to carry on the business, but ordered a sale, and appointed an interim manager only.[26]

Form of order. In cases where a receiver of partnership property is appointed, the order should direct all partners and other parties to deliver over to the receiver all securities in their hands for such estate or property, and also the stock-in-trade and effects of the partnership, together with all books and papers relating thereto.[27] The court may abstain from making an order for the delivery of partnership books and papers, if there is no necessity for it, and if it would occasion inconvenience.[28]

By section 23 of the Partnership Act 1890, a judgment creditor of a partner may obtain an order appointing a receiver of that partner's share of profits, and of any other moneys which may be coming to him in respect of the partnership.[29]

SECTION 11. IN CASES OF MENTAL INFIRMITY

In cases of mental infirmity the court has always exercised a jurisdiction to appoint a receiver though no action is pending,[30]

---

[22] *Jeffreys* v. *Smith* (1820) 1 Jac. & W. 298; *Roberts* v. *Eberhardt* (1853); Kay 148; *Lees* v. *Jones* (1857) 3 Jur.(N.S.) 954; as to mines in Cornwall, see p. 71, *ante*.

[23] *Rowe* v. *Wood* (1822) 2 Jac. & W. 553.

[24] *Norway* v. *Rowe* (1812) 19 Ves. 144, 158, 159.

[25] See *Clegg* v. *Edmondson* (1857) 8 De G.M. & G. 808.

[26] *Rowlands* v. *Williams* (1861) 30 Beav. 310.

[27] Seton (7th ed.), p. 728.

[28] *Dacie* v. *John* (1824) M'Clell. 206.

[29] See *ante*, p. 40, also *Brand* v. *Sandground* (1901) 85 L.T. 517.

[30] *Ex p. Whitfield* (1742) 2 Atk. 315.

but under the present practice [31] the application is made to the
Court of Protection in proceedings under the Mental Health Act
1959 and the appointment is not now made by the Chancery
Division [32] except in the case of trustees. [33]

Receivers under the Mental Health Act 1959. By section 105
of the Mental Health Act 1959, the judge [34]—in practice the master
of the Court of Protection [35]—is authorised to appoint receivers,
to exercise large powers of administration and management over
the property of persons incapable, by reason of mental disorder of
managing and administering their property and affairs who are
comprehensively called " patients." [36] The receiver is to do all
such things in relation to the property and affairs of the patient as
the judge [37] orders or directs him to do and may do any such
thing in relation thereto as the judge [37] may authorise him to do. [38]
The powers of the judge [39] in this respect are very wide. [40]

Wide as are the powers which may be conferred upon a receiver, [41]
he has no powers over the person of the patient. The jurisdiction
extends to patients resident abroad with property here: and under
section 106 stocks registered here in the name of any person in
respect of whom a person has been appointed to exercise powers
with respect to his property or affairs on grounds which would
render him a patient if resident here, may be ordered to be transferred to the foreign curator. [42] Where an English patient has
property in a foreign country it is usually necessary for the English
receiver to appoint an attorney under the direction of the master.
The practice of the Court of Protection with regard to the appointment of so-called receivers is entirely distinct from that in the case
of ordinary receivers and is not therefore dealt with in this work. [43]

---

[31] As to the practice prior to the Act of 1959, see Heywood and Massey's *Court of
Protection Practice* (10th ed.), Chap. 1.
[32] As to appointment of receivers under the practice prior to the Lunacy Act 1890,
see *Ex p. Radcliffe* (1820) 1 Jac. & W. 639; *Re Birch, Shelford on Lunacy* 187.
[33] See p. 76, *post.*
[34] For definition see Mental Health Act 1959, ss. 100 (4) and 119.
[35] See *ibid.* s. 101 (4).
[36] *Ibid.* s. 101. Formerly under s. 116 of the Lunacy Act 1890, the jurisdiction
related only to specified categories of patients.
[37] *Supra*, n. 34.   [38] Mental Health Act 1959, s. 105 (1).
[39] *Supra*, n. 34.   [40] *Ibid.* ss. 102 and 103.
[41] *Supra*, n. 34.
[42] Mental Health Act 1959, s. 106. Formerly under the Lunacy Act 1891, s. 134,
the judge only had jurisdiction where a declaration of lunacy had been made in the
country of residence. If not, the Chancery Division would assume jurisdiction.
[43] See Heywood & Massey's *Court of Protection Practice* (10th ed.).

Effect of orders. When the property of a patient becomes subject to the control of the Court of Protection by the appointment of a receiver, and the receiver is in physical possession, it cannot be seized under a writ of *fi. fa.* by an execution creditor of the patient, the patient's right to maintenance having priority over the claims of the execution creditor.[44] But where a judgment creditor, having notice of the pendency of a summons in the Court of Protection for the appointment of a receiver, issued a *fi. fa.* under which the goods of the patient were seized before any order was made on the summons, and a receiver was afterwards appointed while the goods were in the possession of the sheriff, it was held that the creditor's claim must be satisfied before anything could be allowed for the maintenance of the patient.[45] For a receiver so appointed is only authorised to take possession of the patient's equitable interest in his property; and accordingly an order under section 105 of the Mental Health Act 1959 appointing such a receiver does not affect any previously acquired rights of third persons against the property of the patient, which are of such a nature that effect can be given to them at law or in equity, as, for instance, a vendor's lien for unpaid purchase-money.[46] The receiver cannot be authorised to sell the patient's estate tail, but he can be authorised to sell the land so as to bar the estate tail.[47]

The existence of an order appointing a receiver of certain specified property of a debtor does not prevent a receiving order in bankruptcy being made against such a debtor after he has recovered his faculties.[48]

A direction in the order for the receiver to pay debts incurred after the date of the receivership order creates no charge in favour of the creditors, and the judge[49] cannot make it a term of the order for payment out to the executor of the patient that the debts shall be discharged.[50]

Where an order authorised the receiver to receive and give a discharge for all dividends accrued due before lodgment, it was held that the bank must pay these dividends to the receiver.[51]

---

[44] *Re Winkle* [1894] 2 Ch. 519.
[45] *Re Clarke* [1898] 1 Ch. 336.
[46] *Davies* v. *Thomas* [1900] 2 Ch. 462, 472, 473, explaining *Re Winkle, supra.*
[47] *Re E. D. S.* [1914] 1 Ch. 618; the proceeds being resettled on analogous trusts.
[48] *Re Belton (a debtor)* [1913] W.N. 63; 108 L.T. 344.
[49] See n. 32, p. 74, *ante.*
[50] *Re Wheater* [1928] Ch. 223.
[51] *Re Spurling* [1909] 1 Ch. 199; see p. 201 for form of order. It was formerly usual to order transfer into court, *Re Browne* [1894] 3 Ch. 412.

The receiver is the statutory agent of the patient [52]; a solicitor employed by the receiver therefore has an independent right against the patient's estate, and the Statute of Limitations cannot be pleaded by the receiver, unless the judge [53] in his discretion so orders.[54]

The mere appointment does not cause a forfeiture of a protected life interest, as the receiver is a statutory agent for the patient,[55] nor does the fact that certain costs, fees and percentages are by statute [56] charged on the patient's estate cause such a forfeiture [57]; and the appointment prevents a subsequent document purporting to be a charge operating as a forfeiture since it is wholly void.[58]

The appointment of a receiver by the Court of Protection does not prevent the court in divorce from securing payment of an annual sum for the divorced wife. Where by an order in the Court of Protection provision has been made for the wife the proper course is to apply in the Family Division for permanent maintenance and for an order that it be secured at the same rate as that so ordered by the Court of Protection (if that be considered proper) without prejudice to any further order of the Court of Protection, the security not to be enforceable while the order of the Court of Protection is subsisting or till the death of the husband.[59]

The High Court still retains its jurisdiction in the case of trustees who are patients [60]; but there is concurrent jurisdiction in the Court of Protection to make orders for appointment of new trustees and vesting orders under section 54 of the Trustee Act 1925 [61] in the cases specified in that section, including cases where the patient-trustee has any beneficial interest.[62] Where the appointment of a receiver of the trust property is required, there must be administration proceedings in the Chancery Division.

---

[52] *Plumpton* v. *Burkinshaw* [1908] 2 K.B. 572; *Re Oppenheim's Will Trust* [1950] Ch. 633.

[53] See n. 34, p. 74, *ante.*

[54] *Re E. G.* [1914] 1 Ch. 927.

[55] *Re Marshall* [1920] 1 Ch. 284. *Cf. Re Silverston* [1949] Ch. 270 (legacy to person if in patient's employment).

[56] Mental Health Act 1959, s. 112 (5).

[57] *Ibid.* s. 112 (6), replacing Law Reform (Miscellaneous Provisions) Act 1949, s. 8, which nullified the effect of *Re Custance's Settlements* [1946] Ch. 42, which was, however, wrongly decided: *Re Westby's Settlement* [1950] Ch. 296.

[58] *Re Marshall* [1920] 1 Ch. 284.

[59] *C. L.* v. *C. F. W.* [1928] P. 223.

[60] See also Court of Protection Rules 1960, rr. 18–20.   [61] *Ibid.*

[62] See generally note "Appointment of New Trustees" in *Supreme Court Practice* (1976), Vol. II, paras. 2124 *et seq.* The concurrent jurisdiction extends to cases where an order of the Court of Protection has authorised exercise of a power of appointing a trustee.

Interim receiver. In a proper case, the judge [63] will appoint an interim receiver of the estate of the supposed patient and, if the case is urgent, will do so upon an *ex parte* application; but unless the person appointed is the Official Solicitor, he must not, in default of a direction to the contrary, act as such until he has given security.[64] And in such a case, if actions are pending against the supposed patient, the receiver's proper course is to apply to be appointed guardian *ad litem* in the several actions.[65] Where under the old practice a petition had been presented, but, pending the hearing, a coroner's jury had found a verdict of murder while of unsound mind against the supposed patient, a receiver was appointed till further order, the expression " interim " receiver being inappropriate to such a case.[66]

Documents belonging to alleged patient in possession of receiver. In *Re Cathcart*,[67] pending an inquiry as to the state of mind of an alleged patient, the Official Solicitor had been appointed receiver of her estate, and in that capacity had in his possession a mass of documents belonging to her. Upon an application made on her behalf for liberty to inspect and take copies of such of the documents as she might require for her defence on the inquiry, the Court of Appeal held that the proper course would be for the master, who had charge of the inquiry, to look through the documents and ascertain which of them were relevant to the inquiry; but that the parties were not at liberty to go before the master for the purpose.

Where there are no proceedings in the Court of Protection the High Court will not now, it seems, exercise its jurisdiction to order rents and profits of property belonging to a patient to be paid to a person for the benefit of the patient, if the latter is within the jurisdiction[68]; application should be made to the Court of Protection for a receiver. The High Court may, however, make such an order where the patient is out of the jurisdiction,[69] and if a foreign court of competent jurisdiction has appointed an

---

[63] See n. 34, p. 74, *ante*.
[64] Court of Protection Rules 1960, r. 65 (1); *Re Pountain* (1888) 37 Ch.D. 609, 610, application made to the Lords Justices, *ex parte*.
[65] *Ibid. per* Cotton L.J. at p. 610.
[66] *Re A. G.* (1909) 53 S.J. 615.
[67] [1902] W.N. 80.
[68] *Re Barker's Trusts* [1904] W.N. 13.
[69] *Re Carr's Trusts* [1904] 1 Ch. 792; see also *Didisheim* v. *London and Westminster Bank* [1900] 2 Ch. 15.

administrator with authority to receive specified property of the
patient in this country, the persons, in whose hands such property
is, should hand it over to the administrator; if they insist on an
action being brought in this country they may not be allowed
costs.[70] Such an action is brought by the foreign administrator
in his own name and as next friend of the patient. In the case of
property to which the title of the person of unsound mind is
equitable the court has a discretion to limit the order to sums
required for maintenance.

Discharge of a receiver. The receiver must be discharged if
the judge [71] is satisfied that the former patient has become capable
of managing and administering his property and affairs, and may
be discharged at any time if the judge [71] considers it expedient to
do so. And the receiver will also be discharged (without any order)
on the death of the patient.[72] It follows that he cannot, therefore,
take credit for payments made,[73] nor can his sureties be made
liable for rents and profits received by him after that date although,
of course, he and they remain liable in respect of all moneys
received before the death.[74]

SECTION 12. IN THE CASE OF PERSONS IN POSSESSION
OF REAL ESTATE UNDER A LEGAL TITLE

Practice of the Court of Chancery. The Court of Chancery
would not, at the instance of a person alleging a mere legal title
against another party who was in possession of real estate, and
who also claimed to hold by a legal title, disturb that possession
by appointing a receiver. There being open to the plaintiff a full
and adequate remedy at common law, he had no equity to come
to the Court of Chancery for relief. The court would not interfere
with a legal title, unless there was some equity by which it could
affect the conscience of the party in possession. There might be
cases in which the court would interfere to prevent absolute
destructive waste, where the value of the property would be

---

[70] *Pélégrin* v. *Coutts & Co.* [1915] 1 Ch. 696, and see Mental Health Act 1959, s.
106, and p. 74, *ante*, as to stock in the name of the patient.

[71] See n. 34, p. 74, *ante*.

[72] Mental Health Act 1959, s. 105 (2).

[73] See *Re Bennett* [1913] 2 Ch. 318.

[74] *Re Walker* [1907] 2 Ch. 120. The receiver himself, it seems, could not be made
liable in the existing, though he could be in properly constituted, proceedings:
see also *Re Seager Hunt* [1906] 2 Ch. 295. See r. 74 of the Court of Protection Rules
1960 as to jurisdiction after the death.

destroyed if steps were not taken, or where the contest lay between a person having a well-established pedigree and a person without any reasonable appearance of title; but, as a general rule, where one person was in possession of the rents and profits of an estate, claiming to be the holder by a legal title, and another person also claimed to hold by a legal title, the former could not be ousted in the Court of Chancery until the true ownership of the legal title had been finally determined at law.[75]

The court would not, however, be deterred from appointing a receiver by the fact that the defendant held under a legal title, where the plaintiff could show a sufficient equity in his favour [76]: as, for instance, where a case of fraud [77] or undue influence [78] was made out.

The fact that a defendant partner was in possession under a legal title did not deter the court from appointing a receiver if a proper case was made out [79]; and similarly in the case of trustees.[80] A receiver, moreover, would be appointed at the instance of an equitable incumbrancer against a mortgagor with the legal estate,[81] or of owners of a rentcharge against a mortgagee who neglected to pay it.[82] The appointment was also made against vendors in specific performance actions in suitable cases.[83]

The rule, that a receiver would not be appointed when the person having the legal estate was in actual possession of the property, did not apply where the person in possession was in possession merely upon execution under a judgment. In such a case, a creditor who had taken out execution (now a receiver for such a creditor [84]) could not hold property against an estate created prior to his debt.[85]

Cases where the appointment is made pending probate or a grant of administration are dealt with in section 3.[86]

---

[75] *Earl Talbot* v. *Hope Scott* (1858) 4 K. & J. 96, 112; *Carrow* v. *Ferrior* (1868) L.R. 3 Ch. 719.

[76] *Mordaunt* v. *Hooper* (1756) Amb. 311; *Clark* v. *Dew* (1829) 1 R. & M. 103; *Bainbrigge* v. *Baddeley* (1851) 3 Mac. & G. 420.

[77] *Huguenin* v. *Baseley* (1807) 13 Ves. 105; *Lloyd* v. *Passingham* (1809) 16 Ves. 50; *Mordaunt* v. *Hooper* (1756) Amb. 311; *Woodyatt* v. *Gresley* (1836) 8 Sim. 187.

[78] *Stillwell* v. *Wilkins* (1821) Jac. 82.   [79] Section 10, *ante*, p. 64.

[80] Section 2, *ante*, p. 12.   [81] Section 4, *ante*, p. 26.

[82] *Pritchard* v. *Fleetwood* (1895) 1 Mer. 54; *Shee* v. *Harris* (1844) J. & L. 92.

[83] *Ante*, p. 62.

[84] Administration of Justice Act 1956, ss. 34 and 36.

[85] *Whitworth* v. *Gaugain* (1841) Cr. & Ph. 325; 3 Ha. 416; 1 Ph. 728; *Anderson* v. *Kemshead* (1852) 16 Beav. 344; and see *ante*, p. 29.

[86] *Ante*, p. 19.

Judicature Act 1873. The Judicature Act 1873 did not affect
the principles upon which the jurisdiction of the court to appoint
a receiver is exercised.[87] Though in an action for the recovery of
land, the High Court has jurisdiction [88] upon interim application
to appoint a receiver against a person in possession even under a
legal title,[89] that jurisdiction will be exercised with the utmost care,
since it operates to prejudice the right of a defendant in possession
to plead his possession as a statutory defence and put the plaintiff
to proof of his paramount title, while the application compels the
defendant to disclose his title: more, it puts the court in the
difficulty that the substantial issue in the action may be determined,
in effect, on evidence admissible on interlocutory application, but
not at the trial.[90] If the defendant is actually in occupation the
appointment will not be made, except in very special circumstances [91]: it is not enough to show that the defendant is a married
woman without means, and only discloses a shadowy title.[92]
Where there was vacant possession the appointment has been
made in the absence of the owner of the legal estate.[93] The occupation of tenants is an important factor, as, if the defendant were
found to have no title they might not get a good discharge for
their rents, and yet might be open to distress.[94] In such cases if
the plaintiff makes out a good prima facie title, and the defendant
discloses only a very shadowy title, the appointment may be
made [95]; and when the defendant lessee has been admittedly
guilty of a breach of a covenant to carry on business on the
premises, the appointment has been made even where the defendant
was in occupation: thus in an action by a lessor for recovery of
possession of an hotel where the licences were in jeopardy and
there appeared to be a strong prima facie probability of the
plaintiff succeeding in recovering possession at the trial, the court
on interlocutory motion appointed a receiver of the licences (which
were ordered to be handed over to him) as well as of the rents and

---

[87] *Ante*, p. 4. See also Ord. 29, r. 2, p. 4, *ante.*

[88] See now Judicature Act 1925, s. 45.

[89] *Foxwell* v. *Van Grutten* [1897] 1 Ch. 64.

[90] *Marshall* v. *Charteris* [1920] 1 Ch. 520, 523, 524.

[91] For an example of an appointment made against a plaintiff in unusual circumstances see *Porter* v. *Lopes* (1877) 7 Ch.D. 358, 359.

[92] *Marshall* v. *Charteris* [1920] 1 Ch. 520.

[93] *Berry* v. *Keen* (1882) 51 L.J.Ch. 912.

[94] *John* v. *John* [1898] 2 Ch. 573; see *Marshall* v. *Charteris* [1920] 1 Ch. 520; and
Gwatkin v. *Bird*, 52 L.J.Q.B. 263; *Percy* v. *Thomas*, 28 S.J. 533.

[95] *Ibid.*

profits, and directed that the receiver should be at liberty to keep the premises open as an hotel and to do all acts necessary to preserve the licences.[96]

In all such cases, the court has to consider whether special interference with the possession of a defendant is required, on the basis that there is a well founded fear that the property in question will be dissipated, or that other irreparable mischief may be done unless the court gives its protection.[97]

SECTION 13. IN OTHER CASES

Enemies. Under the Trading with the Enemy Act 1939 (which repeals the former Trading with the Enemy Acts), the Board of Trade after report by an inspector appointed under section 3 (1) has power to appoint a supervisor of any business carried on by the person named in the order, to secure compliance with the prohibition against trading with the enemy in section 1.[98] Such an appointment would displace a receiver appointed in an action from the control of the business. The Board has also power under section 7 of the Rules made under the Act by order to vest any property of an enemy in an official called " the Custodian of Enemy Property." After such an order has been made, but not previously, the Custodian is the assign of the enemy for the purpose of initiating or being a defendant in any proceedings relating to the property comprised in the order including proceedings in which a receiver is sought. A person who is an enemy cannot sue but may be sued here.[99] There are many cases in which an enemy may be a necessary defendant if no vesting order has been made. In a partnership order, for instance, in which accounts are claimed all the partners must be represented.[1] If one partner is an enemy, he must be made a defendant but a receiver would be appointed without service or before an order dispensing with service. The test of enemy character, with regard to a right to sue

---

[96] *Leney & Sons Ltd.* v. *Callingham* [1908] 1 K.B. 79, correcting form of order drawn up in *Charrington & Co.* v. *Camp* [1902] 1 Ch. 386. See further for addition to order, Seton, *Forms of Judgments and Orders* (7th ed.), p. 732.

[97] *Mukherjee* v. *Giri* (1927) 55 L.R.Ind.App. 131.

[98] For definitions of " enemy " and " enemy territory " see ss. 2 and 15. S. 3A of the Act contains a power which was widely used in the 1939–45 War, for the Board to make a restriction order or winding-up order in respect of any such business, and to appoint a controller to carry out the order.

[99] See *ante*, n. 17, p. 72.

[1] *Public Trustee* v. *Elder* [1926] Ch. 776.

in the Queen's courts, is residence or carrying on business in an enemy country or a country under the control of the enemy.[2] An English national or other person in a country controlled by the enemy is an enemy for the purpose of this rule.

Apart from the above legislation the appointment of a receiver at the instance of a manager here of an enemy's business was refused.[3]

Bailee. An interim receiver may be appointed of a chattel in an action in which the owner sues for its return from a bailee, who claims a lien, and the receiver may be authorised to allow the owner to use the chattel.[4] In an action for return of a piano let on hire-purchase, the plaintiff has been appointed receiver on his *ex parte* application until hearing of a summons for delivery up.

Lien. The normal remedy of a person entitled to an equitable lien over the property of another who cannot obtain satisfaction of his demand is a judicial sale.[5] Pending sale, a receiver may of course be appointed.[6] There may also be cases—for example where the lien is an unpaid vendor's lien over real property which has now become part of a railway system [7] where the appointment of a receiver can be obtained over the property subject to the lien as being the only practicable means of enforcement.

Interpleader. The court or a judge may, in an interpleader under R.S.C., Ord. 17, r. 6, to try the right to goods seized in execution, order under rule 8 that, instead of a sale by the sheriff, a receiver and manager of the property be appointed.[8]

Pending reference to arbitration. The court has jurisdiction to appoint a receiver pending a reference to arbitration, if a proper

---

[2] *Porter* v. *Freudenberg* [1915] 1 K.B. 857; *Sovfracht* v. *Van Udens* [1943] A.C. 203. See as to companies and incorporated bodies, *Daimler Co.* v. *Continental Tyre Co.* [1916] 2 A.C. 307; *The Pamia* (1943) 112 L.J.P. 34.

[3] *Maxwell* v. *Grunhut* (1914) 31 T.L.R. 79; *Re Gaudig and Blum* (1915) 31 T.L.R. 315.

[4] *Hatton* v. *Car Maintenance Co.* [1915] 1 Ch. 621. As to extent and relinquishment of such a lien, see *Green* v. *All Motors Ltd.* [1917] 1 K.B. 625; *Reliance Motor Works* v. *Pennington* [1923] 1 K.B. 127.

[5] *Hope* v. *Booth* (1830) 1 B. & Ad. 498.

[6] *Bishop of Winchester* v. *Mid-Hants Ry.* (1867) L.R. 5 Eq. 17. *Cf. Ponoka-Calmar Oils* v. *Earl F. Wakefield Co.* [1960] A.C. 18 (receiver appointed as part of statutory machinery for enforcement of lien could not prejudice claim of lien holder).

[7] *Munns* v. *Isle of Wight Ry.* (1870) 5 Ch.App. 414.

[8] *Howell* v. *Dawson* (1884) 13 Q.B.D. 67.

case is made out for doing so.[9] Where there is an agreement to refer all matters in dispute under a contract to arbitration, and an action is subsequently brought on the contract, in which it is found to be desirable, for the protection of the property which is the subject of the contract, that a receiver should be appointed, it is competent for the court to appoint a receiver, and by the same order to stay all further proceedings in the action, except for the purpose of carrying out the order for a receiver. This is certainly the case as regards domestic arbitration agreements [10]—those which provide for arbitration in the United Kingdom between parties neither of whom is an individual who is a national of or habitually resident in any state other than the U.K. nor a body corporate which is incorporated in or whose central management and control is exercised in any state other than the U.K. [11]—and probably the situation as regards non domestic arbitration agreements, although the occasions for the appointment of a receiver may be fewer.[12] After a reference to arbitration a receiver can be appointed.[13]

Pending foreign litigation. The court has jurisdiction to appoin a receiver pending litigation in a foreign court.[14]

Foreign bankruptcy. The court will appoint the *curateur*, in a foreign bankruptcy, receiver of the land of the debtor in England with power to sell.[15]

Tithe redemption annuity.[15a] By subsection (3) of section 2 of the Tithe Act 1891 (applied by section 16 (3) of the Tithe Act 1936 to tithe redemption annuity), tithe redemption annuity which was three months in arrear could be recovered by the appointment of a receiver

---

[9] *Law* v. *Garrett* (1878) 8 Ch.D. 26; *Halsey* v. *Windham* [1882] W.N. 108. The arbitrator cannot appoint a receiver. There would be no means of controlling his actions short of the commencement of another action. See *Re Mackey* (1834) 2 A. & E. 356.   [10] See the definition in Arbitration Act 1975, s. 1 (4).

[11] *Compagnie du Sénégal* v. *Wood* (1883) 53 L.J.Ch. 167; [1883] W.N. 180; *Pini* v. *Roncoroni* [1892] 1 Ch. 633.

[12] Arbitration Act 1975, s. 1 (1), (2) and Arbitration Act 1970, s. 28.

[13] Arbitration Act 1950, s. 12 (6) (*h*). Having regard to the machinery for taking the receiver's account, the application is conveniently made in the Chancery Division.

[14] *Transatlantic Co.* v. *Pietroni* (1860) John. 607; see, too, *Evans* v. *Puleston* [1880] W.N. 89, 127; *Law* v. *Garrett* (1878) 8 Ch.D. 27.

[15] *Re Kooperman* [1928] W.N. 101. The report is silent as to the means of carrying out the conveyance, but it seems that a vesting order could be obtained under Trustee Act 1925, s. 44, without the necessity of proceeding under Judicature Act 1925, s. 47.

[15a] Now abolished, see Finance Act, 1977, s. 56.

by the county court,[16] except in cases covered by subsection (2), *i.e.* where the owner of the lands was in occupation, in which case the remedy was by distress; subsection (2) only applied where the owner was in occupation of the whole of the lands.[17] The owner was deemed to be in occupation unless anyone else is proved to be so.[18] Where land was let at ground rents the order contained a declaration that the receiver was only to receive the rack-rents paid by occupiers.[19] The order had to be registered under section 6 (1) (*b*) of the Land Charges Act 1972, otherwise it was void against a purchaser under section 6 (4).[20]

Trade unions. Prior to the Industrial Relations Act 1971, as the court could not enforce any agreement for the application of trade union funds in provision of benefits,[21] a receiver could not be appointed over the general funds, or funds collected for a special purpose, to prevent their application contrary to agreement.[22] The Trade Union Act 1871 was repealed by the 1971 Act, but it, in its turn was repealed by the Trade Union and Labour Relations Act 1974, without, however, re-enacting the provisions of the 1871 Act, s. 4. It therefore appears that in such cases a receiver could now be appointed.

---

[16] For forms, see Tithe Rentcharge Recovery Rules 1891, Form 8. These Rules have been amended by the Tithe (Amendment) Rules 1959 (S.I. 1959 No. 1984). As to procedure by distress: *Swaffer* v. *Mulcahy* [1934] 1 K.B. 608; *Queen Anne's Bounty* v. *Blacklock's Exors.* [1934] 1 K.B. 399; *Same* v. *Thorne* [1934] 2 K.B. 175.

[17] *Ecclesiastical Commissioners* v. *Upjohn* [1913] 1 K.B. 501.

[18] *Franklin* v. *M'Creagh* [1923] W.N. 132.

[19] *Peed* v. *King* (1894) 11 T.L.R. 18.

[20] After satisfaction of the arrears the registration should be vacated. If this is not done application can be made to the county court: see definition of court in Land Charges Act 1972, s. 17 (1).

[21] Trade Union Act 1871, s. 4.

[22] *Sansom* v. *London Vehicle Workers' Union* (1920) 36 T.L.R. 666; as to when an injunction could be granted, see *Amalgamated Society of Carpenters* v. *Braithwaite* [1922] 2 A.C. 440.

CHAPTER 3

OVER WHAT PROPERTY A RECEIVER MAY BE APPOINTED

IN determining whether or not the property is of such a nature that the court will appoint a receiver of it, it is necessary to consider the nature of the applicant's title.

There is considerable difference according to whether the appointment is made to preserve the subject-matter of a suit or by way of equitable execution. In the former case the appointment extends over the whole subject-matter of the suit, real and personal, including both legal and equitable interests [1]; in the latter case there are certain well-defined restrictions as to the property which will be subjected to the appointment, and these are discussed in the latter part of this chapter. [2]

Where the application is made for the purpose of preserving the subject-matter of the suit, it is most frequently made at the instance of an incumbrancer seeking to enforce his charge. In such cases it must be shown that the property is capable of assignment, and that prima facie a valid assignment or charge has been made, for otherwise the applicant has no title to maintain the action.

Property which is assignable. It is not proposed to attempt to specify every description of property which is, or is not, assignable. Present and future earnings, [3] present and future debts, possibilities and expectancies [4] are assignable: so are rights to indemnity. In some cases, however, though the property is assignable, the instrument of assignment may contain provisions, invalid as offensive to public policy or otherwise, which invalidate the assignment. [6]

---

[1] See *Davis* v. *Duke of Marlborough* (1818) 1 Swans. 74, 83; 2 Swans. 108, 132.

[2] See pp. 92–96, *post.*

[3] *Holmes* v. *Millage* [1893] 1 Q.B. 554, 559; *Horwood* v. *Millar's Timber and Trading Co. Ltd.* [1917] 1 K.B. 305. But an assignment by a member of a profession of his future earnings is void against a trustee in bankruptcy in respect of receipts after commencement of the bankruptcy: *Re de Marney* [1943] Ch. 126. The remedy of a judgment creditor is *semble* by attachment of the debt.

[4] *Tailby* v. *Official Receiver* (1888) 13 App.Cas. 542; *Re Lind* [1915] 1 Ch. 744 [1915] 2 Ch. 345.

[5] Even before anything is due: *British Union Co.* v. *Rawson* [1916] 2 Ch. 476.

[6] *Horwood* v. *Millar's Trading and Timber Co. Ltd.* [1917] 1 K.B. 305; *A. Schroeder Music Publishing Co. Ltd.* v. *Macauley* [1974] 1 W.L.R. 1308.

Assignments contrary to public policy. The assignment of
certain forms of property is void in some cases as contrary to
public policy, in others as forbidden by statute.[7] Thus assignments
of the following are void as contrary to public policy: the pay or
half-pay of an officer in the army, navy, or air force,[8] or the
salary of a person holding a civil office in the public service[9];
the salary of a clerk of the peace, a freehold office connected with
the administration of justice[10]; of a clerk of petty sessions in
Ireland, as he is a public and judicial officer[11]; sums payable to an
assistant parliamentary counsel to the Treasury.[12]

Pensions or half-pay involving any liability to future service
are inalienable[13]; but where they are granted wholly in consideration of past services they are alienable[14] unless alienation
is prohibited by statute.[15] The following have been held assignable:
salary of a chaplain to a workhouse[16]; of the office of Master
Forester to a royal forest[17]; unascertained sums due from an
insurance committee to a panel doctor[18]; a retiring annuity or
pension payable to a covenanted member of the Indian Civil
Service[19]; a pension payable to a member of the Royal Irish
Constabulary without liability to serve again.[20] In an Irish case[21]
it was held in effect that arrears of a salary, though possibly future
payments were not assignable, might be assigned; but even if this

---

[7] As to immunity from attachment whilst in the hands of the Crown, see p. 39,
ante, and R.S.C., Ord. 77.

[8] See *Apthorpe* v. *Apthorpe* (1887) 12 P.D. 192; *Ex p. Huggins* (1882) 21 Ch.D. 85;
Re Mirams [1891] 1 Q.B. 594.

[9] *Cooper* v. *Reilly* (1829) 2 Sim. 560, append. (1830) 1 Russ. & M. 560, and cases
cited in preceding note. *Quaere* as to the salary of a Member of Parliament: see
Hollinshead v. *Hazleton* [1916] 1 A.C. 428.

[10] *Palmer* v. *Bate* (1821) 6 Moo. 28; see *Palmer* v. *Vaughan* (1818) 3 Swa. 173. The
office was abolished by the Courts Act 1971, s. 44.

[11] *M'Creery* v. *Bennett* [1904] 2 I.R. 69.

[12] *Cooper* v. *Reilly, supra*; these fees were irrecoverable at law.

[13] *Wells* v. *Foster* (1841) 8 M. & W. 152; *Macdonald* v. *O'Toole* [1908] 2 I.R. 386;
and see *Knill* v. *Dumergue* [1911] 2 Ch. 199. As to how far pensions and allowances
under the Superannuation Act 1972 involve liability to future services, see *Macdonald*
v. *O'Toole* [1908] 2 I.R. 386.

[14] See *Davis* v. *Duke of Marlborough* (1818) 1 Swans. 74, 79; *Dent* v. *Dent* (1867)
L.R. 1 P. 366; *Willcock* v. *Terrell* (1878) 3 Ex.D. 323; *Manning* v. *Mullins* [1898] 2
I.R. 34; *Knill* v. *Dumergue* [1911] 2 Ch. 199.

[15] See pp. 87, 88, *post* as to statutory prohibitions.

[16] *Re Mirams* [1891] 1 Q.B. 594.

[17] *Blanchard* v. *Cawthorne* (1833) 4 Sim. 566.

[18] *O'Driscoll* v. *Manchester Insurance Committee* [1915] 3 K.B. 499.

[19] *Knill* v. *Dumergue, supra*.

[20] See *Manning* v. *Mullins* [1898] 2 I.R. 34.

[21] *Picton* v. *Cullen* [1900] 2 I.R. 612. See *Price* v. *Lovett* (1851) 20 L.J.Ch. 270.

decision be correct, arrears of a pension inalienable by statute cannot be assigned before they are actually paid over.[22]

Pensions, etc., unassignable by statute. The following are unassignable by statute: any benefit payable to civil servants and other comparable public employees under a scheme made under section 1 of the Superannuation Act 1972 [23]; pensions and allowances granted to officers or men, or to widows or dependants of officers and men who have been in the naval,[24] military,[25] or air [26] service of the Crown; parliamentary pensions [27]; pensions payable to members of the police force or their dependants [28]; to officers employed in the National Health Service [29]; superannuation allowance or gratuity to school teachers [30]; to officers and employees of local authorities [31]; to members of fire brigades [32]; naval prize money [33]; all benefits under the Social Security Act 1975 [34]; or Social Security Pensions Act 1975 [35]; non-contributory benefits [36]; child benefit [37]; pension payable to a retiring incumbent [38]; pension payable to an Irish town clerk.[39] A lump sum payable as compensation under the Superannuation Acts, is in the same position as a pension.[40] Sums payable as compensation under the

---

[22] *Crowe* v. *Price* (1889) 22 Q.B.D. 429; *Jones* v. *Coventry* [1909] 2 K.B. 1029.

[23] *Ibid.* s. 5 (1). The main current scheme is the Principal Civil Service Pension Scheme 1972.

[24] Naval and Marine Pay and Pensions Act 1865, s. 4.

[25] Army Act 1955, s. 203.

[26] Air Force Act 1955, s. 203.

[27] Parliamentary and other Pensions Act 1972, s. 20.

[28] Police Pensions Act 1976, s. 9.

[29] National Health Service (Superannuation) Regulations 1961 (S.I. 1961 No. 1441), reg. 54.

[30] Superannuation Act, s. 9, Sched. 3, para. 9; Teachers (Superannuation) Regulations 1976 (S.I. 1976 No. 1987), art. 95 (1).

[31] Superannuation Act 1972, Sched. 7, para. 5, preserving the effect of Local Government Superannuation Act 1953, s. 20 (repealed) as if it were a provision of a statutory scheme under the 1972 Act.

[32] Fire Services Act 1947, s. 26; Fire Services Act 1951, s. 1; Firemen's Pension Scheme Order 1973 (S.I. 1973 No. 966), Appendix 2, art. 70.

[33] Naval Agency and Distribution Act 1864, s. 15. Now abolished: see Prize Act 1948, s. 9.

[34] *Ibid.* s. 87.

[35] *Ibid.* s. 48.

[36] Supplementary Benefit Act 1966 (Ministry of Social Security Act), s. 20.

[37] Child Benefit Act 1975, s. 12 (1).

[38] Clergy Pensions Measure 1961, s. 35 (2).

[39] Under Local Officers' Superannuation (Ireland) Act 1869; *Brenan* v. *Morrissey* (1890) 26 L.R.Ir. 618.

[40] See *Re Lupton* [1912] 1 K.B. 107; see also *Macdonald* v. *O'Toole* [1908] 2 I.R. 386.

War Damage Act 1943 could be assigned or charged only with the permission in writing of the War Damage Commission.[41]

Money received for commutation of a pension does not come within the prohibition against alienation in section 203 of the Army Act 1955.[42] After money has been actually paid over as an instalment of a pension by the paymaster it loses the protection and may be assigned or attached, but this does not include money credited to a pensioner's account at a bank, in respect of a warrant which has not been paid by the paymaster.[43] Post War Credits could only be assigned under certain special conditions.[44]

Private unassignable pensions. Sums payable under pension trust deeds are usually made wholly or partly unassignable by the terms of the deed. But if a private pension is unassignable, it may be possible for the court to order the mortgagor to execute an irrevocable power of attorney enabling the receiver to receive the same.[45]

Fellowship. Though in one case [46] a receiver over the profits of a fellowship was refused, it was subsequently held that there might be a receiver of past and future appropriations in respect of the profits of a fellowship, the duties being so light that no questions of public policy could interfere with the validity of the assignment.[47] Similarly, a receiver has been appointed of the profits of a canonry of a collegiate church, to which no cure of souls belonged, but only the duty of a certain residence and of attendance on divine service, the performance of which duty by the canon was of no benefit to the public.[48]

Ecclesiastical benefices. Formerly there could not have been a receiver of the profits of an ecclesiastical benefice, either at the instance of an assignee or a judgment creditor; for a beneficed clergyman was prohibited by the Benefices Act 1571 from charging the fruits of his living.[49] This Act was repealed by the Benefices

---

[41] War Damage Act 1943, s. 23.

[42] *Crowe* v. *Price* (1889) 22 Q.B.D. 429; see *Price* v. *Lovett* (1851) 20 L.J.Ch. 270.

[43] *Jones & Co.* v. *Coventry* [1909] 2 K.B. 1029; in the former case the remedy is attachment, not equitable execution.

[44] Finance Act 1941, s. 7 (4); Finance Act 1954, s. 15 (2).

[45] *James* v. *Ellis* (1870) referred to in *Ambler* v. *Bolton* (1872) L.R. 14 Eq. 427, 429.

[46] *Berkeley* v. *King's College* (1830) 10 Beav. 602.

[47] *Feistel* v. *King's College* (1847) 10 Beav. 491. Most fellowships now involve considerable duties.

[48] *Grenfell* v. *Dean and Canons of Windsor* (1840) 2 Beav. 544.

[49] *Hawkins* v. *Gathercole* (1855) 6 De G.M. & G. 1; see *Long* v. *Storie* (1849) 3 De G. & Sm. 309.

Act, passed in the year 1803, and so the law remained until the year 1817, when, by the Benefices Act 1817, the charging of ecclesiastical benefices was again prohibited, and the statute of Elizabeth was revived: so that between the years 1803 and 1817 there was no law prohibiting a clergyman from charging his ecclesiastical benefice [50]; and a receiver was accordingly on several occasions, in cases arising between those years, appointed over an ecclesiastical benefice.[51] The policy of the Benefices Act 1571, revived by the Benefices Act 1817, was not in any way affected by the Judgments Act 1838, but the statute was repealed by the Statute Law Revision Act 1948, Sched. Consequently the law appears to have been restored to the pre-1817 position.

Maintenance, etc. Sums ordered to be paid for the following purposes are unassignable and consequently a receiver cannot be appointed over them, *viz.* maintenance pending suit ordered to be paid to a wife judicially separated [52]; a weekly sum ordered by a court of summary jurisdiction to be paid by a husband to a wife for her maintenance under the Matrimonial Proceedings (Magistrates' Courts) Act 1960 [53]; maintenance ordered to be paid by a husband for the support of his divorced wife [54]; a voluntary allowance by the husband, which is taken into account in fixing the amount of maintenance [55]; a sum payable under a bastardy order.[56]

The following are assignable, *viz.*: sums payable to a wife under a separation deed,[57] and, *semble*, an annuity secured for a divorced wife under section 23 of the Matrimonial Proceedings and Property Act 1973.[58]

Arrears of maintenance are, it seems, assignable [59]; but it is submitted that a receiver would not be appointed over them, at all events during the life of the husband, since the enforcement of

---

[50] *Metcalfe* v. *Archbishop of York* (1833) 1 M. & C. 553.

[51] *Silver* v. *Bishop of Norwich* (1816) 3 Sw. 112n.; *White* v. *Bishop of Peterborough* (1818) 3 Sw. 109; *Metcalfe* v. *Archbishop of York* (1833) 1 M. & C. 553.

[52] *Re Robinson* (1884) 27 Ch.D. 160; see *Linton* v. *Linton* (1885) 15 Q.B.D. 239; *Smith* v. *Smith, infra.*

[53] *Paquine* v. *Snary* [1909] 1 K.B. 688; the order here was under the Summary Jurisdiction (Married Women) Act 1895.

[54] *Watkins* v. *Watkins* [1896] P. 222; *Smith* v. *Smith* [1923] P. 191.

[55] *Walls Ltd.* v. *Legge* [1923] 2 K.B. 240.

[56] *Re Harrington* [1908] 2 Ch. 687.

[57] *Victor* v. *Victor* [1912] 1 K.B. 247; and see *Clark* v. *Clark* [1906] P. 131.

[58] Replacing s. 2 of the Matrimonial Proceedings and Property Act 1965, s. 19 (2) of the Matrimonial Causes Act 1950, s. 190 (1) of the Judicature Act 1925, s. 22 of the Matrimonial Causes Act 1857; see *Harrison* v. *Harrison*, 13 P.D. 180.

[59] *Per* Lindley L.J. in *Watkins* v. *Watkins* [1896] P. 228.

payment of such arrears is wholly in the discretion of the court in divorce,[60] the relationship of debtor and creditor not being created,[61] and it is presumed that payment would only be enforced in favour of that person for whose support the maintenance was ordered to be paid. The same appears to be the case with arrears of maintenance pending suit.[62]

Other descriptions of property. Many descriptions of property over which a receiver will be appointed for purposes of preservation or to enforce a charge, are mentioned in the various sections of Chapter 2; there is practically no limit in respect of the property in such cases: thus, a receiver has been appointed over public-house licences,[63] heirlooms,[64] a motor car,[65] a newspaper,[66] profits of a solicitor's business.[67] *Semble,* a receiver may be appointed over a patent, whether being worked or not, at the instance of an assignee.[68] In some cases certain property, *e.g.* uncalled capital,[69] will be excluded from the order appointing a receiver where the applicant's charge can be made effective by other means; in other cases special powers are given to the receiver [70] in accordance with the nature of the property.[71]

Ships. A receiver has been appointed of a ship,[72] of a ship and her gear,[73] of the freight of a ship [74] and of the machinery of a steam vessel.[75] So, also, a receiver may be appointed when an action of co-ownership is brought by the owner of one moiety of a vessel against the owner of the other moiety.[76]

---

[60] See *Robins* v. *Robins* [1907] 2 K.B. 13; *Ivimey* v. *Ivimey* [1908] 2 K.B. 260; *Brydges* v. *Brydges* [1909] P. 187; *ante,* pp. 42, 43.

[61] *Campbell* v. *Campbell* [1922] P. 187; and see note 80, p. 43, *ante.*

[62] See *Smith* v. *Smith* [1923] P. 191. As to claims against the estate of the deceased husband, see *ante,* p. 43.

[63] *Charrington* v. *Camp* [1902] 1 Ch. 386; *Leney* v. *Callingham* [1908] 1 K.B. 79.

[64] *Earl of Shaftesbury* v. *Duke of Marlborough* (1820) Seton, *Forms of Judgments and Orders* (7th ed.), p. 734.

[65] *Hatton* v. *Car Maintenance Co.* [1915] 1 Ch. 621.

[66] *Kelly* v. *Hutton* (1869) 17 W.R. 425; *Chaplin* v. *Young* (1862) 6 L.T. 97.

[67] *Candler* v. *Candler* (1821) Jac. 225.

[68] See *Edwards & Co.* v. *Picard* [1909] 2 K.B. 903.

[69] See *post,* p. 100.

[70] See especially Chap. 9.

[71] *e.g. Leney* v. *Callingham, supra.*

[72] *Re Edderside* (1887) 31 S.J. 744.

[73] *Compagnie du Sénégal* v. *Woods & Co.* [1883] W.N. 180; 53 L.J.Ch. 166.

[74] *Roberts* v. *Roberts* (1854) Seton (7th ed.), p. 772; *Burn* v. *Herlofson* (1887) 56 L.T. 722.

[75] *Brenan* v. *Preston* (1852) 2 De G.M. & G. 831; 10 Ha. 334.

[76] *The Ampthill* (1880) 5 P.D. 224.

In a case where the legal title to a ship was in question, and the plaintiff had no equitable as distinct from a legal title, a receiver was refused, but an order was made by which the legal proceedings for ascertaining the title were accelerated, and the court took possession of the ship, giving each party liberty to apply for the possession and use upon giving security to deal with her as the court should direct.[77]

Rates and tolls. A receiver was refused of rates which were to be assessed by commissioners at a future period, for until the assessment there was nothing to collect.[78] There may be a receiver of the tolls of turnpike roads, or of canal or railway, dock or market companies.[79] The extent to which a receiver may be appointed over a statutory undertaking has been already dealt with.[80]

Property in foreign parts. It is not necessary, in order that the court may have jurisdiction to appoint a receiver, that the property in respect of which he is to be appointed should be in England, or indeed, in any part of Her Majesty's dominions,[81] though the extent to which the receiver may be able to obtain possession of the property depends on the *lex loci*. Persons have been appointed to receive the rents and profits of real estates and to convert, get in and remit the proceeds of property and assets, in cases in which the estate or property in question has been in Ireland [82]; in the West Indies [83]; in India [84]; in Canada [85]; in China [86]; in Italy [87]; in America [88]; in New South Wales [89]; in Jersey [90]; in Brazil [91] and in Peru.[92] But the court will not make such an order if it would be useless.[93] Although the court has no

---

[77] *Ridgway* v. *Roberts* (1844) 4 Hare 106.

[78] *Drewry* v. *Barnes* (1826) 3 Russ. 94, 105; but see *Gibbons* v. *Fletcher* (1853) 11 Ha. 251.

[79] Chap. 2, Section 6, *ante*.   [80] *Ante*, p. 44.

[81] *Houlditch* v. *Lord Donegal* (1834) 8 Bligh 344.

[82] *Ibid.*; *Bolton* v. *Curre* [1894] W.N. 122; Seton (7th ed.), p. 776.

[83] *Bunbury* v. *Bunbury* (1839) 1 Beav. 336; *Barkley* v. *Lord Reay* (1843) 2 Ha. 308.

[84] *Logan* v. *Princess of Coorg*, Seton, *Forms of Judgments and Orders* (7th ed.), p. 776; *Keys* v. *Keys* (1839) *ibid.*; 1 Beav. 425.

[85] *Tylee* v. *Tylee* (1853) Seton (7th ed.), p. 777.

[86] *Hodson* v. *Watson* (1788) Seton (7th ed.), p. 776.

[87] *Hinton* v. *Galli* (1854) 24 L.J.Ch. 121; *Drewry* v. *Darwin* (1765) Seton (7th ed.), p. 777.

[88] *Hanson* v. *Walker* (1829) 7 L.J.Ch. 135.

[89] *Underwood* v. *Frost* (1857) Seton (7th ed.), p. 776.

[90] *Smith* v. *Smith* (1853) 10 Ha.App. 71.

[91] *Duder* v. *Amsterdamsch Trustees Kantoor* [1902] 2 Ch. 132.

[92] *Re Huinac Copper Mines* [1910] W.N. 218.

[93] *Mercantile Investment Co.* v. *River Plate Trust* [1892] 2 Ch. 303.

power of enforcing its orders and decrees in places beyond the jurisdiction, the receiver may be authorised to proceed abroad,[94] or to appoint an attorney, and a party to the cause who resists him or his attorney will be guilty of contempt.[95] A man will not, however, be appointed receiver of an estate which is out of the jurisdiction, unless he is within the reach of the court, or has submitted himself, or is amenable to, its jurisdiction.[96]

The course which the court usually adopts, where an estate is in a foreign country or out of the jurisdiction, is to appoint a receiver in this country, with power, if it be found expedient, to appoint an agent, with the approbation of the judge, in the country where the estate is situate, to collect the estate and remit the same to the receiver in this country.[97] The receiver or his agent will recover possession of the estate according to the laws of the country in which it is found.[98] The receiver will, when necessary, be empowered to sell lands abroad, according to a scheme approved by the judge.[99] Where a receiver in a debenture holder's action was unable to obtain possession of the property, because the courts of the country (Peru) in which it was situate refused to recognise any title other than that of the company, the court ordered the company to appoint attorneys to take possession on behalf of the receiver.[1]

Equitable execution. Where the appointment is sought by way of equitable execution, the property over which a receiver will be appointed is more restricted. It is first essential to show that the property, over which the appointment is required, is capable of assignment.[2] In addition, apart from execution against land, as to which there are special statutory provisions [3] and from cases of fraudulent conduct on the part of the judgment

---

[94] See Palmer's *Company Precedents* (16th ed.), Vol. 3, Chap. 61, p. 647. The debenture holders consented.

[95] *Langford* v. *Langford* (1835) 5 L.J.Ch. 60.

[96] See *Houlditch* v. *Lord Donegal* (1834) 8 Bligh 344; *Carron Iron Co.* v. *Maclaren* (1855) 5 H.L.C. 416.

[97] *Anon.* v. *Lindsay* (1808) 15 Ves. 91; *Keys* v. *Keys* (1839) 1 Beav. 425; *Smith* v. *Smith* (1853) 10 Ha.App. 71; *Hinton* v. *Galli* (1854) 24 L.J.Ch. 211; Seton, *Forms of Judgments and Orders* (7th ed.), p. 777.

[98] *Smith* v. *Smith* (1853) 10 Ha.App. 71. Consider *Re Maudslay, Sons & Field* [1900] 1 Ch. 602, 611; and *Re Derwent Rolling Mills Co.* (1905) 21 T.L.R. 81, 701.

[99] *Tylee* v. *Tylee* (1853) Seton, *Forms of Judgments and Orders* (7th ed.), p. 777.

[1] *Re Huinac Copper Mines* [1910] W.N. 218: security is not required from the attorney.

[2] See *ante*, pp. 87 *et seq.* as to pensions and other property which are incapable of assignment.

[3] Administration of Justice Act 1956, ss. 34–36. See pp. 94–96, *post.*

debtor or other very special circumstances, it must also be shown that legal execution is impossible owing to some impediment arising from the character in law of the judgment debtor's interest.[4] It is not sufficient to show that the property is inaccessible to legal execution [5]: the judgment creditor must go further and show that there are certain difficulties arising from the nature of the interest of the debtor in the property which make legal execution impossible, but which if removed would enable legal execution to issue.[6] The Judicature Acts made no difference in this respect: the court still applies the principles upon which the Court of Chancery formerly acted, in determining whether equitable execution can issue.[7] If, however, it is proved that the judgment debtor is threatening or intending to deal with the property in such a manner as to amount to a fraudulent attempt to defeat the rights of creditors, or in some other analogous circumstances, a receiver may be granted even over property susceptible to legal execution,[8] as, for instance, where the debtor, a German company, was endeavouring to collect debts due to it and remove the proceeds from the jurisdiction.[9]

In accordance with these principles the court will not, except in the very special circumstances mentioned, appoint a receiver by way of equitable execution over property which can be reached by *fi. fa.*, or attachment of debts [10]; nor over present or future earnings [11]; nor over money paid for admission at a theatre [12]; nor over debts merely because a security is about to be created over them,[13]

---

[4] *Holmes* v. *Millage* [1893] 1 Q.B. 551; *Morgan* v. *Hart* [1914] 2 K.B. 183, where the prior cases are reviewed. This principle is not always strictly observed in the Queen's Bench Division. For a case where, even before the Administration of Justice Act 1956, a receiver was appointed over the judgment debtor's leasehold premises in which his interest was legal, and comments of Clauson J., see *Re Bueb* [1927] W.N. 298; *cf. Smith* v. *Tsakyris* [1929] W.N. 39. The rule was recognised in s. 325 (2) of the Companies Act 1948, now amended by the Administration of Justice Act 1956, s. 36 (4).

[5] *Holmes* v. *Millage, supra.*

[6] *Per* Cotton L.J., *Re Shephard* (1889) 43 Ch.D. 135; *per* Bowen L.J., *ibid.* at p. 137; *Holmes* v. *Millage* [1893] 1 Q.B. 555; *Harris* v. *Beauchamp* [1894] 1 Q.B. 801.

[7] *Holmes* v. *Millage, supra*; *Edwards & Co.* v. *Picard* [1909] 2 K.B. 903; *Morgan* v. *Hart, supra.*

[8] See *Manchester and Liverpool District Banking Co.* v. *Parkinson* (1888) 22 Q.B.D. 173; *Harris* v. *Beauchamp Bros.* [1894] 1 Q.B. 801, 806, 810, 811.

[9] *Goldschmidt* v. *Oberrheinische Metallwerke* [1906] 1 K.B. 373.

[10] See *Holmes* v. *Millage, Morgan* v. *Hart, supra.*

[11] *Holmes* v. *Millage, supra*, including directors' fees not earned; see *Hamilton* v. *Brogden* [1891] W.N. 36.

[12] *Cadogan* v. *Lyric Theatres Ltd.* [1894] 3 Ch. 338.

[13] *Harris* v. *Beauchamp Bros.* [1894] 1 Q.B. 801. For a case involving a remarkable disregard of this principle see *Re Swallow Footwear Ltd.*, *The Times*, October 23, 1956.

nor over furniture of the debtor stored with that of other persons so as to be indistinguishable by the judgment creditor [14]; nor over a patent not being worked.[15]

Estates and interests in land. Prior to the coming into force of the Administration of Justice Act 1956, equitable execution was in general only available against equitable interests in land, because execution could be levied against legal estates under the writ of *elegit*.[16] This distinction is now obsolete.

The Administration of Justice Act 1956 abolished the writ of *elegit* [17] and also the provisions of the Law of Property Act 1925 under which judgments entered up in the Supreme Court operated as charges on land of the judgment debtor [18] and substituted a fresh system of execution against land and interest in land, legal or equitable.[19]

It is now provided that the High Court [20] and any county court [21] may, for the purpose of enforcing a judgment or order for the payment of money by order, impose on any land or interest in land (which does not include an interest in the proceeds of sale) [22] of the debtor specified in the order a charge for securing the payment of any moneys due or to become due [23] under the judgment or order. The order may be made by a master.[24] Any such order may be made either absolutely or conditionally.[25]

Any such order is, in the first instance, an order to show cause (or *nisi*) specifying the time and place for further consideration

---

[14] *Morgan* v. *Hart* [1914] 2 K.B. 183. In *Hills* v. *Webber* (1901) 17 T.L.R. 513, a receiver was appointed over the interest of the debtor, who was joint tenant of three houses, two of which only were subject to a mortgage but the circumstances were special.

[15] *Edwards & Co.* v. *Picard* [1909] 2 K.B. 903; the proceeds of a patent being worked by a licensee could be reached by legal execution.

[16] As to what could be seized under the writ of *eligit* see Judgments Act 1838, s. 11; Bankruptcy Act 1883, s. 144.

[17] Administration of Justice Act 1956, s. 34 (1).

[18] *Ibid.* s. 34 (2).

[19] *Ibid.* ss. 35, 36.

[20] *Ibid.* s. 35 (1). See generally *Re Overseas Aviation Engineering (G.B.) Ltd.* [1963] Ch. 24.

[21] County Courts Act 1959, s. 141 (1).

[22] *Irani Finance Ltd.* v. *Singh* [1971] Ch. 59 (land held by legal and beneficial joint tenants). *Cf. National Westminster Bank Ltd.* v. *Allen* [1971] 3 W.L.R. 495 (property held legally and beneficially by joint tenants jointly liable on judgment debt).

[23] This expression does not cover untaxed costs: *A. & M. Records Inc.* v. *Darakdjian* [1975] 1 W.L.R. 1610.

[24] *Barclays Bank Ltd.* v. *Moore* [1967] 1 W.L.R. 1201; R.S.C., Ord. 32, r. 11 (1) (*d*).

[25] Administration of Justice Act 1956, s. 35 (2); County Courts Act 1959, s. 141 (2). As to costs, see R.S.C., Ord. 62, App. III, para. 5 (*c*).

and imposing the charge until that time in any event.[26] On further consideration, the court will, unless it appears that there is sufficient contrary reason, make the order absolute with or without notification.[27] Appeal from a final order lies direct to the Court of Appeal.[28]

The power, however, is a discretionary power, and before the court imposes the charge, it must be satisfied that it is proper to place the judgment creditor at an advantage over other creditors. So that, for example, if the court is aware that the debtor is in liquidation and is, or is likely to turn out to be, insolvent, the order should not be made.[29]

A charging order under these provisions is a form of execution, and in order to be valid as against a trustee in bankruptcy [30] or a liquidator [31] it must be completed by seizure or the appointment of a receiver before bankruptcy or liquidation as the case may be.[32]

The provisions of the Land Charges Act 1972 (as regards unregistered land) and the Land Registration Act 1925 (as regards registered land) apply in relation to any such order as they apply to other writs or orders affecting land issued or made for the purposes of enforcing judgments. Save as aforesaid, they have the like effect and are enforceable in the same manner as an equitable charge created by the debtor in writing under his hand.[33] The ultimate remedy of the creditors will therefore be an order for sale.[34]

These provisions apply in relation to a judgment, order, decree or award (however called) of any court or arbitrator (including any foreign court or foreign arbitrator) which is or has become enforceable (whether wholly or to a limited extent) as if it were a judgment or order of the High Court or any county court as they apply in relation to a judgment or order of the High Court or the county court.[35]

---

[26] R.S.C., Ord. 50, r. 1 (2). See the Order generally as to the procedure.

[27] R.S.C., Ord. 50, r. 1 (6).

[28] *Rainbow* v. *Moorgate Properties Ltd.* [1975] 1 W.L.R. 788.

[29] *Rainbow* v. *Moorgate Properties Ltd.* [1975] 1 W.L.R. 788; but see *Glass (Cardiff) Ltd.* v. *Jardean Properties Ltd.* (1976) 120 S.J. 167, C.A.

[30] Bankruptcy Act 1914, s. 40.

[31] Companies Act 1948, s. 325.

[32] *Re Overseas Aviation Engineering (G.B.) Ltd.*, *supra*; *Barclays Bank Ltd.* v. *Moore, supra, per* Danckwerts L.J. at p. 1207.

[33] Administration of Justice Act 1956, s. 35 (3); County Courts Act 1959, s. 141 (3). The judgment creditor would therefore be entitled to be added as a party to any foreclosure action by a mortgagee of the land, but must take the action as he finds it: *Re Parbola Ltd.* [1909] 2 Ch. 437.

[34] *Matthews* v. *Goodday* (1861) 31 L.J.Ch. 282.

[35] Administration of Justice Act 1956, s. 35 (4); County Courts Act 1959, s. 141 (4).

Whether or not a charge has been imposed on land by any such order,[36] the power of the High Court [37] or the county court [38] to appoint a receiver by way of equitable execution is extended to all legal as well as equitable estates and interests in land. This power is in addition to and not in derogation of any power of the court to appoint a receiver in any proceedings for enforcing any charge imposed under the foregoing provisions.[39] Where an order has been made and is duly registered under the Land Charges Act 1972,[40] the provisions of that Act which provide that an order appointing a receiver and any proceedings pursuant to the order or in obedience thereto shall be void against a purchaser unless the order is registered [41] do not apply to an order appointing a receiver made either in proceedings for enforcing the charge or by way of equitable execution.[42]

Mortgagor. Receivers by way of equitable execution were prior to 1926 appointed against a mortgagor over an equity of redemption.[43] Since 1925 a mortgagor of land retains the legal estate he had prior to the mortgage.[44] Therefore, after 1925 and prior to the coming into force of the 1956 Act, the judgment creditor had a remedy by *elegit* [45]; and in accordance with the principles stated above, could not obtain the appointment of a receiver. Since the coming into force of the Administration of Justice Act 1956, there is statutory warrant for the appointment of a receiver in such a case.[46] It seems also that a receiver could be appointed over the balance of proceeds of sale in the hands of a mortgagee after satisfying his own incumbrance at the instance of a judgment creditor of the mortgagor seeing that the mortgagee is

---

[36] Administration of Justice Act 1956, s. 36 (2); County Courts Act 1959, s. 142 (2).
[37] Administration of Justice Act 1956, s. 36 (1); County Courts Act 1959, s. 142 (1).
[38] County Courts Act 1959, s. 142 (1).
[39] See *supra*, n. 36.
[40] s. 6. As registration can only be made against the " estate owner " (see *ibid*. s. 6 (2) and definition of land in s. 17 (1)) it would appear that registration is only possible in the case of execution against a legal interest. Presumably in the cases of equitable interests notice will simply be given to the trustees, as in the case of any other charge by a beneficiary. For a form of Order for the appointment of a receiver to enforce a charging order in land see Queen's Bench Masters' Practice Form No. PF 105A; *Supreme Court Practice* (1976), Vol. II, para. 245A.
[41] s. 6 (4).
[42] Administration of Justice Act 1956, s. 36 (3); County Courts Act 1959, s. 142 (3).
[43] *Ex p. Evans* (1879) 13 Ch.D. 253; *Anglo-Italian Bank* v. *Davies* (1878) 9 Ch.D. 275; *Smith* v. *Cowell* (1880) 6 Q.B.D. 75.
[44] Law of Property Act 1925, ss. 85–87.
[45] *Smith* v. *Tsakyris* [1929] W.N. 39.
[46] See s. 36.

in the position of a trustee [47]; or over proceeds of sale under a pending contract at the instance of a judgment creditor of the vendor. The remedy by attachment is defective as there is usually no ascertained debt due to the vendor before completion.

Settled land. Where land is the subject-matter of a settlement within the meaning of the Settled Land Act 1925, the interests of the beneficiaries as such are equitable, and the proper remedy of a judgment creditor has since 1925 been by way of equitable execution, even against the tenant for life; for the legal estate is vested in him as trustee [48] and is not therefore subject to his judgment debt.

Trust for sale. The interests of persons under a trust for sale are equitable and a receiver has always been the appropriate remedy.[49]

Miscellaneous. A receiver may be appointed over the interest of a mortgagee in a theatre [50]; where a legal estate is outstanding [51]; where a fund in another court is payable to a judgment debtor [52]; over the income of a trust fund [53]; over a judgment debtor's interest in an outstanding charge upon land and subsisting policies of insurance.[54] Again a receiver may be appointed of a reversionary interest [55]; of a sufficient portion of a reversionary legacy to satisfy plaintiff's debt [56]; but not over the debtor's share in an intestate's estate before a grant of administration.[57] The appointment over interests in partnership property is discussed in the previous chapter.[58]

The receivership can only affect the interest of the debtor.[59]

Cases in which a receiver will not be appointed. A receiver

---

[47] See Law of Property Act 1925, s. 105; *Thorne* v. *Heard* [1895] A.C. 495.

[48] Settled Land Act 1925, s. 107.

[49] As in *Stevens* v. *Hutchinson* [1953] Ch. 299. Such appointment does not make the receiver a " person interested " in the proceeds of sale within Law of Property Act 1925, s. 30, *ibid*.

[50] *Cadogan* v. *Lyric Theatres Ltd.* [1894] 3 Ch. 338.

[51] *Wells* v. *Kilpin* (1874) L.R. 18 Eq. 298.

[52] *Westhead* v. *Reilly* (1883) 25 Ch.D. 413. Where the fund is in court a charging order is the appropriate remedy; see *Fahey* v. *Tobin* [1901] 1 I.R. 516, 517.

[53] *Oliver* v. *Lowther* (1880) 28 W.R. 381; *Webb* v. *Stenton* (1883) 11 Q.B.D. 530.

[54] *Beamish* v. *Stevenson* (1886) 18 L.R.Ir. 319; see *Orr* v. *Grierson* (1895) 28 L.R.Ir. 20.

[55] *Fuggle* v. *Bland* (1883) 11 Q.B.D. 711; *Tyrrell* v. *Painton* [1895] 1 Q.B. 202; *Ideal Bedding Co.* v. *Holland* [1907] 2 Ch. 157.

[56] *Macnicoll* v. *Parnell* (1887) 35 W.R. 773.

[57] *Mullane* v. *Ahern* (1891) 28 L.R.Ir. 105: *sed quaere*.

[58] *Ante*, p. 40.

[59] *Wills* v. *Luff* (1888) 38 Ch.D. 200.

cannot be appointed to receive the interest of a fund, the disposal
of which is in the absolute discretion of trustees or others. It
must be clearly shown that there is something payable to the
defendant in such a way as to make his interest assignable.[60] But
where the judgment debtor is the sole object of a discretionary
trust, it is apprehended that a receiver may be appointed.[61] A
receiver will not be appointed over property of no appreciable
value.[62]

It has been held in Ireland that a receiver will not be appointed
over a gratuity which has been awarded to a public servant before
it is paid over [63]; and the same would be the case with a gratuity
which a private employer had expressed an intention to pay.[64]
A receiver will not be appointed where the effect of the appointment might be to destroy the property,[65] though the appointment
of a receiver, without powers of management, may be obtained by
the incumbrancer of a business, and the goodwill thus destroyed.[66]

Property of married women. As a result of the policy inaugurated
by the Law Reform (Married Women and Tortfeasors) Act
1935, and carried to its logical conclusion by the Married Women
(Restraint upon Anticipation) Act 1949, a married woman as
regards her property, and as regards the law of bankruptcy and
the enforcement of judgments and orders is in the same position
as a *feme sole*: property can no longer be held for her separate use.[67]
It is, however, provided by section 4 (1) (*b*) of the 1935 Act that
nothing in that Act shall enable any judgment or order against a
married woman in respect of a contract or obligation incurred
before August 2, 1935,[68] to be enforced in bankruptcy. Equitable
execution against a married woman is therefore now obtained in
all cases on the same principles as against a man.

---

[60] *R.* v. *Lincolnshire County Court Judge* (1887) 20 Q.B.D. 167; and see *Willis* v.
Cooper (1900) 44 S.J. 698, where the appointment of a receiver to secure the payment
of untaxed costs was refused.
[61] See *Re Smith* [1928] Ch. 915; so where two joint judgment debtors are the only
objects.
[62] *Walls Ltd.* v. *Legge* [1923] 2 K.B. 240.
[63] *Timothy* v. *Day* [1908] 2 I.R. 26; but see *Re Lupton* [1912] 1 K.B. 107. See also
Wells v. *Wells* [1914] P. 157 (barrister's fees).
[64] *Timothy* v. *Day, supra,* at p. 31 of the report.
[65] *Hamilton* v. *Brogden* [1891] W.N. 14.   [66] *Ante,* p. 34.
[67] s. 1 of the 1935 Act; s. 1 of the 1949 Act. The result of these provisions is that in
a great many instruments the life interest of a married woman is directed to be held
on protective trusts, which are a bar to legal or equitable execution.
[68] This applies to an obligation partly incurred before the specified date: *Re a
Debtor* [1938] Ch. 694.

Form of order. Both the summons and order, in cases where the appointment is sought by way of equitable execution, should specify the property over which the receiver is sought, for the receiver will not be appointed over the debtor's property generally.[69] It appears that the debtor may be examined under the provisions of R.S.C., Ord. 48, rr. 1 and 2, in order to ascertain the nature of the property.[70] This does not amount to the enforcement of a judgment or order for which leave is required under the Reserve and Auxiliary Forces, etc., Act 1951.[71] Any special directions as to keeping accounts of different property should be inserted in the order. Where the debtor was entitled to rent of furniture and a house let together, of which the house was in mortgage, the receiver was as against the mortgagee held entitled to rent apportioned to the furniture.[72]

Creditor resident outside scheduled territories. Where the judgment creditor resides outside the scheduled territories, as defined by the Exchange Control Act 1947, or is acting by order or on behalf of a person so resident, and there is no effective Treasury permission under the Act, any order for the appointment of a receiver by way of equitable execution must direct him to pay into court to the credit of the cause or matter in which he is appointed any balance due from him after deduction of his proper salary or allowance.[73]

COMPANIES

In the case of ordinary limited companies questions can rarely, if ever, arise as to whether the property is or is not assignable. In the case of statutory undertakings, the extent to which a receiver can be appointed over the assets has been discussed in a previous section.[74]

In the case of ordinary limited companies, the conditions necessary to the creation of a valid charge are mentioned on a previous page.[75] The accidental omission of an item from the particulars registered under section 95 of the Companies Act 1948 [76] does not affect the security over, nor the receiver's right to take possession of, that item.[77]

---

[69] *Hamilton* v. *Brogden* [1891] W.N. 14.
[70] *Ibid.* See also *Morgan* v. *Hart, per* Phillimore L.J. [1914] 2 K.B. 183 at p. 191.
[71] *Cf.* s. 3 (9) proviso and *Fagot* v. *Gaches* [1943] 1 K.B. 10 (a decision under the Courts (Emergency Powers) Act 1943).
[72] *Hoare* v. *Hove Bungalows* (1912) 56 S.J. 686 (C.A.).
[73] R.S.C., Ord. 51, r. 1 (2).   [74] Chap. 2, p. 44, *ante.*
[75] pp. 57 *et seq., ante.*   [76] Replacing s. 79 of the Companies Act 1929.
[77] *National Provincial Bank* v. *Charnley* [1924] 1 K.B. 341.

The title of debenture holders is not good against the trustee in bankruptcy in respect of assets the assignment of which to the company was void as fraudulent or an act of bankruptcy.[78] A receiver is a trespasser as regards such assets.[79]

Where the liquidator recovered money which had been paid to an unsecured creditor on the ground of fraudulent preference, it was held that the debenture holder's charge, which had crystallised by the appointment of a receiver before the liquidation, did not extend to this money, as at the date of crystallisation the company had no right whatever in respect of it.[80]

If certain specific assets are excluded from the debenture holder's charge, they must be excluded from the order appointing a receiver.[81] In a case in which different sets of debentures specifically charged certain items and all sets included a floating charge over the undertaking, different receivers were appointed over the respective specifically charged assets and one of them was appointed manager.[82] The practice where foreign property is included has already been discussed.[83]

It is the practice to exclude uncalled capital from a receivership order, even though it is included in the charge given by the debentures.[84]

If there is a doubt as to the property over which the debenture holder's charge extends, a summons may be issued for an inquiry to bring out the relevant facts [85]; in the meantime the receiver may be ordered to carry to a separate account property as to which the doubt exists. The fact that some things included in a general assignment cannot be ascertained does not affect the assignee's right to the remainder [86]; nor does the fact that the security is invalid as to certain items.[87]

Books and papers. When debentures charge all the property and assets of a company, including its uncalled capital, the order

[78] *Re Dombrowski* (1923) 92 L.J.Ch. 415; see *Re Gunsbourg* [1920] 2 K.B. 426.
[79] *Re Simms* [1934] 1 Ch. 1.
[80] *Re Yagerphone Ltd.* [1935] Ch. 392.
[81] In such a case as *Lemon* v. *Austin Friars Investment Trust* [1926] Ch. 1 (C.A.), the security though operating as a debenture would not have enabled a receiver to be appointed over the assets.
[82] See *Re Ind, Coope & Co.* [1911] 2 Ch. 223.
[83] See p. 91, *ante.*
[84] See pp. 109 and 218, *post*, as to duties of receiver in such a case.
[85] *Re Gregory, Love & Co.* [1916] 1 Ch. 203.
[86] See *Imperial Paper Mills* v. *Quebec Bank* (1913) 110 L.T. 91.
[87] See *Re North Wales Produce Co.* [1922] 2 Ch. 340.

appointing a receiver usually directs that all books and documents relating to such property and assets be handed over to the receiver. But if the company is being wound up, the liquidator is entitled to the custody of such books and documents as relate to the management and business of the company and are not necessary to support the title of the holders of the debentures, and the court will order the delivery of these books and documents to the liquidator, on an undertaking by him to produce them to the receiver.[88] The court has no power to order instruments which have been deposited in the Land Registry to be delivered up to a receiver in a debenture holder's action unless the property has been redeemed or sold.[89] Where title deeds are in the custody of trustees for debenture holders the court may, for reasons of convenience, order them to be handed over to a receiver for the debenture holders on his undertaking to re-deliver them; there is no hard-and-fast rule, the matter being one for the discretion of the court in each case.[90]

[88] *Engel* v. *South Metropolitan Brewing Co.* [1892] 1 Ch. 442.
[89] *Somerset* v. *Lands Securities Co.* [1894] 3 Ch. 464.
[90] *Re Ind, Coope & Co.* (1909) 26 T.L.R. 11.

CHAPTER 4

WHO MAY BE APPOINTED RECEIVER

Disinterested person: exceptions. A receiver appointed in an action should, as a general rule, be a person wholly disinterested in the subject-matter [1]; but it is competent to the court, upon the consent of the parties, and in a proper case without such consent,[2] to appoint as receiver a person who is interested in the subject-matter of the action, if it is satisfied that the appointment will be attended with benefit to the estate.[3] Accordingly, in an action to dissolve a partnership, one of the partners is often appointed receiver.[4] In an urgent case the plaintiff has been appointed on his *ex parte* application.[5] So, also, a mortgagee in possession has been appointed receiver [6]; and, in an Irish case, the owner of incumbered lands which had been directed to be sold was appointed, the incumbrancers consenting, but no receiver's fees were allowed him.[7] Where the appointment is by way of equitable execution it is not unusual to appoint the judgment creditor without salary.[8]

A party to the action will not usually be appointed receiver unless he undertakes to act without salary,[9] though in partnership cases salary is sometimes allowed.[10]

When a party to the action is appointed receiver, he does not thereby lose any privilege belonging to him as such party,[11] nor are his rights as receiver affected by his liabilities as a party.[12]

The appointment of a party as receiver without the consent of the other parties is most frequently made in partnership cases,

---

[1] See *Re Lloyd* (1879) 12 Ch.D. 451.

[2] See p. 103, *post.*

[3] See *Boyle* v. *Bettws Llantwit Colliery Co.* (1876) 2 Ch.D. 726; unpaid vendor appointed.

[4] See p. 103, *post.*

[5] *Taylor* v. *Eckersley* (1876) 2 Ch.D. 302; *Hyde* v. *Warden* (1876) 1 Ex.D. 309; *Fuggle* v. *Bland* (1883) 11 Q.B.D. 711.

[6] *Re Prytherch* (1889) 42 Ch.D. 590; and see *Davis* v. *Barrett* (1844) 13 L.J.Ch. 304.

[7] *Re Golding* (1888) 21 L.R.Ir. 194.

[8] See *Supreme Court Practice* (1976), Vol. I, note to R.S.C., Ord. 30, r. 3; and *Pawley* v. *Pawley* [1905] 1 Ch. 593.

[9] *Re Prytherch* (1889) 42 Ch.D. 590; *Wilson* v. *Greenwood* (1818) 1 Swa. 471, 483; *Hoffman* v. *Duncan* (1853) 18 Jur. 69; *Sargant* v. *Read* (1876) 1 Ch.D. 600.

[10] See *Davy* v. *Scarth* [1906] 1 Ch. 55.

[11] *Scott* v. *Platel* (1847) 2 Ph. 229, 230.

[12] *Davy* v. *Scarth* [1906] 1 Ch. 55.

because in such cases it is likely to be for the benefit of the estate: if the partner actually carrying on the business has not been guilty of such misconduct as to have rendered it unsafe to trust him, the court sometimes appoints him receiver and manager with or without salary according to circumstances.[13] It is usual, however, to require him to give security duly to manage the partnership affairs, and to account for moneys received by him.[14] And where the appointment of a receiver is referred by the judge to the master, leave is sometimes given for each partner to propose himself. If an independent person is appointed he may be authorised to appoint a working partner as manager at remuneration.

Trustee. It is not according to the usual course of the court to appoint a trustee to be receiver, though a trustee with no active duties to perform, or with powers not yet exercisable, is sometimes appointed.[15] The court, on appointing a receiver of a trust estate, looks to the trustee to see that the receiver is doing his duty.[16] The two characters of trustee and receiver are rarely compatible, and, in addition to this, the appointment of a trustee to act as receiver is, unless he undertakes to act without remuneration, a violation of the rule of equity that a trustee cannot derive any benefit from the discharge of his duty as trustee. The court will even remove a receiver whose private interests are in conflict with his duties, notwithstanding that his acts may for the most part have been for the general good of the property, and that a majority in number and value of the incumbrancers on it may desire that he be retained.[17] The rule against appointing a trustee to be a receiver applies whether he is a sole trustee or is acting jointly with others.[18]

In special cases, however, where the appointment of a trustee to be receiver will be beneficial to the estate, as, for instance, where he has a peculiar knowledge of the estate, or no one else can be found who will act with the same benefit to the estate, the

---

[13] *Wilson* v. *Greenwood* (1818) 1 Sw. 483; see *Maund* v. *Allies* (1839) 4 Myl. & Cr. 507; *Sheppard* v. *Oxenford* (1855) 1 K. & J. 501; *Hoffman* v. *Duncan* (1853) 18 Jur. 69 (retired partner liable for debts); *Sargant* v. *Read* (1876) 1 Ch.D. 600.
[14] *Wilson* v. *Greenwood* (1818) 1 Sw. 471; *Blakeney* v. *Dufaur* (1851) 15 Beav. 44; *Sargant* v. *Read* (1876) 1 Ch.D. 600; *Collins* v. *Barker* [1893] 1 Ch. 578.
[15] *Sutton* v. *Jones* (1809) 15 Ves. 584, 587, 588. *Cf. Tait* v. *Jenkins* (1842) 1 Y. & C.C.C. 492.
[16] *Sykes* v. *Hastings* (1805) 11 Ves. 363; *Sutton* v. *Jones* (1809) 15 Ves. 587; *cf. Craig* v. *Att.-Gen.* [1926] N.I. 218.
[17] *Fripp* v. *Chard Ry.* (1853) 11 Ha. 241, 260; *cf. Cookes* v. *Cookes* (1865) 2 De G. J. & S. 526, 530.
[18] *Anon* v. *Jolland* (1802) 8 Ves. 72.

court will make the appointment.[19] He may be required to undertake to act without remuneration. Remuneration is not usually allowed to a trustee acting as receiver,[20] but there is no inflexible rule against the allowance of remuneration.[21]

Under special circumstances a trustee may be appointed receiver with a salary. Where, for instance, a testator had appointed as trustee of his estates a person who for many years had been the paid receiver and manager of them, he was continued as receiver with salary, the tenant for life being an infant.[22] There appears to be less objection than in other cases to appoint a trustee for the purposes of the Settled Land Act 1925 to be receiver of an estate or to allow him remuneration so long as there is a tenant for life of full age: for as trustee he has no duties as regards the management of the land.

Where a trustee is willing to act as receiver without salary, he will be allowed to propose himself, but the judge is not bound to accept him.[23]

Party in a fiduciary position, etc. The rule, that the court will not sanction the appointment as receiver of a person whose duty it is to check and control the receiver, is extended to other persons besides trustees [24]; *e.g.* the next friend of a minor whose duty it is to watch the accounts and check the conduct of a receiver of the minor's estate [25]; or the solicitor of a party having the conduct of an action because it will be his duty to check the receiver's accounts.[26]

Nor will a man be appointed receiver whose position may cause difficulty in administering justice: thus a master in Chancery, whose duty it was to pass the accounts and check the conduct of a receiver, was held to be disqualified.[27]

Although a solicitor in an action [28] cannot be appointed receiver of the estate in relation to which he is acting as solicitor,

---

[19] *Gardner* v. *Blane* (1842) 1 Ha. 381; *Powys* v. *Blagrave* (1853) 18 Jur. 463.

[20] *Re Bignell, Bignell* v. *Chapman* [1892] 1 Ch. 59.

[21] *Sutton* v. *Jones* (1809) 15 Ves. 584; *Pilkington* v. *Baker* (1876) 24 W.R. 234.

[22] *Bury* v. *Newport* (1856) 23 Beav. 30.

[23] *Banks* v. *Banks* (1850) 14 Jur. 659.

[24] See *Cookes* v. *Cookes* (1865) 2 De G.J. & S. 526, 530.

[25] *Stone* v. *Wishart* (1817) 2 Madd. 64. Lord Eldon refused to appoint the son of a next friend: *Taylor* v. *Oldham* (1822) Jac. 529.

[26] *Garland* v. *Garland* (1793) 2 Ves.Jr. 137; *Wilson* v. *Poe* (1825) 1 Hog. 322; *cf.* *Grundy* v. *Buckeridge* (1853) 22 L.J.Ch. 1007; *Craig* v. *Att.-Gen.* [1926] N.I. 218.

[27] *Ex p. Fletcher* (1801) 6 Ves. 427.

[28] *Garland* v. *Garland, supra*; *Re Lloyd* (1879) 12 Ch.D. 449.

there is no general objection to the appointment of a solicitor to be receiver.[29] In one case,[30] the solicitor of a married woman was, on her application, appointed receiver of her separate estate, although a strong affidavit was made by her husband, seeking to show the unfitness of the solicitor for the office.

Considerations looked to in making the appointment. The person appointed ought to be one who, consistently with his professional and other pursuits, can spare sufficient time for the duties of his office.[31] Accordingly, in a case where a man proposed as receiver was a Member of Parliament and a practising barrister, and also resided at a very considerable distance from the estate, the court held that these circumstances, though not amounting to an absolute disqualification, formed sufficient grounds to render further consideration advisable.[32]

The court will not appoint as receiver a person whose privileges protect him from the ordinary remedies which it may become proper to enforce,[33] such as a peer [34]; or probably a Member of the House of Commons [35]; or a person under security to the Crown having regard to the Crown's prerogative rights.[36]

Any party interested in the proceedings [37] may propose that some person other than the person proposed be appointed. A stranger to the action cannot propose a receiver.[38] The most suitable person should be appointed, without regard to the party by whom he has been proposed.[39] In making the selection the circumstances of the case and the interests of all parties must be taken into consideration [40] but, other things being equal, that is, if the parties are equally interested, and the persons proposed

---

[29] See *Wilson* v. *Poe* (1825) 1 Hog. 322; *Della Cainea* v. *Hayward* (1825) M'Clell. & Y. 272.

[30] *Bagot* v. *Bagot* (1838) 2 Jur. 1063.

[31] *Wynne* v. *Lord Newborough* (1808) 15 Ves. 283.

[32] *Ibid.* Distance is of less consideration nowadays.

[33] *Att.-Gen.* v. *Gee* (1813) 2 V. & B. 208.

[34] *Ibid.*

[35] See *Lord Wellesley's Case* (1831) 2 R. & M. 639; *Lechmere Charlton's Case* (1837) 2 Myl. & G. 316; *Re Armstrong, ex p. Lindsay* [1892] 1 Q.B. 327; *cf. Re Gent* (1888) 40 Ch.D. 190.

[36] *Att.-Gen.* v. *Day* (1817) 2 Madd. 246, 254; Daniell's *Chancery Practice* (8th ed., 1470–1472). These rights do not apply in bankruptcy: see Bankruptcy Act 1914, s. 151.

[37] *Att.-Gen.* v. *Day* (1817) 2 Madd. 246; *Bagot* v. *Bagot* (1838) 2 Jur. 1063.

[38] *Att.-Gen.* v. *Day, supra.*

[39] *Lespinasse* v. *Bell* (1821) 2 Jac. & W. 436. *Cf. Att.-Gen.* v. *Dyson* (1826) 2 Sim. & St. 528.

[40] *Wood* v. *Hitchings* (1840) 4 Jur. 858.

on both sides are unobjectionable, the person proposed by the party having the conduct of the proceedings is usually preferred.[41] In the appointment of a receiver, considerable attention will be given to the recommendations of a testator.[42]

If an estate over which a receiver is to be appointed is in mortgage, preference will be given to the person proposed by the mortgagee, unless there is some substantial objection to him, although a person proposed by the mortgagor may be more experienced in the duties of the office.[43]

A party to the action may propose himself as receiver, if leave to that effect is given and embodied in the judgment or order[44]; but not otherwise,[45] unless leave be subsequently obtained on summons at chambers.[46]

Under the old practice of the Court of Chancery, when the appointment of a receiver rested with the masters in Chancery, it was a settled rule not to entertain any objection to the report of the master which was not founded on principle.[47] Under the present practice the Court of Appeal acts on the same principles, and accordingly, will not entertain an application bringing in question the decision of the judge as to the most suitable person to be appointed receiver, unless the appointment is open to some overwhelming objection in point of choice, or some objection fatal in point of principle.[48]

It is a substantial objection to the appointment of a receiver that he has an undue partiality for one of the parties[49]; but if an order has been made, without any objection on the part of any of the parties, giving liberty to one of the parties to propose himself

---

[41] *Wilson* v. *Poe* (1825) 1 Hog. 322; see *Baylies* v. *Baylies* (1844) 1 Coll. 548; *Bord* v. *Tollemache* (1862) 1 New Rep. 177. Where a receiver had been appointed in two administration suits, the carriage of the order was given to the plaintiff who first gave notice of motion: *Hart* v. *Tuok* (1849) 6 Ha. 611.

[42] *Wynne* v. *Lord Newborough* (1808) 15 Ves. 283.

[43] *Wilkins* v. *Williams* (1798) 3 Ves. 588; *Tillett* v. *Nixon* (1883) 25 Ch.D. 239; see, too, *Bord* v. *Tollemache* (1862) 1 New Rep. 177, where the deed contained a provision for the appointment of a receiver by the first mortgagee, and the suit for the appointment of a receiver was instituted by a second mortgagee.

[44] *Meaden* v. *Sealey* (1849) 6 Ha. 620; *Cookes* v. *Cookes* (1865) 2 De G.J. & S. 526; Seton (7th ed.), pp. 729, 739.

[45] *Davis* v. *Duke of Marlborough* (1818) 2 Swans. 108.

[46] See, for a form of summons, Atkin's *Court Forms* (2nd ed.), Vol. 33, p. 185; see Daniell's *Chancery Practice* (8th ed.), p. 1470.

[47] *Cookes* v. *Cookes* (1865) 2 De G.J. & S. 530; *Tharp* v. *Tharp* (1857) 12 Ves. 317.

[48] *Cookes* v. *Cookes* (1865) 2 De G.J. & S. 530; *Perry* v. *Oriental Hotels Co.* (1870) L.R. 5 Ch. 421; *Nothard* v. *Proctor* (1875) 1 Ch.D. 4.

[49] *Blakeway* v. *Blakeway* (1833) 2 L.J.(N.S.)Ch. 75.

as receiver, the question is one not of principle, but of judicial discretion with regard had to all the circumstances of the case; and, if the judge appoints the party proposing himself, the Court of Appeal will not interfere with that selection.[50] The mere fact of the existence of disputes or differences between the parties to an action does not debar the judge from appointing a party to the action.[51]

Where a receiver has been appointed, the court will not remove him on the mere ground of his being an illiterate person, in the absence of some weightier reason, such as mismanagement, dishonesty, or incompetency to manage the estate.[52]

IN COMPANY CASES

A body corporate is not qualified for appointment as receiver of the property of a company [53] formed and registered under the Companies Act 1948 or preceding Companies Acts.[54] Any such purported appointment is a nullity.[55] If, after July 1, 1948, an undischarged bankrupt acts as receiver or manager of the property of a company on behalf of debenture holders otherwise than under an appointment by the court, he becomes liable to imprisonment or a fine or both.[56]

In the case of companies an accountant is very frequently appointed. It is only in special circumstances that the court will appoint the plaintiff in a debenture holders' action receiver, and then only, as a rule, subject to production of an affidavit that all the other debenture holders consent.[57] A director will not as a rule be appointed. Thus a chartered accountant resident near Birmingham has been appointed receiver and manager of a company, the assets of which were a building estate near London,

---

[50] *Cookes* v. *Cookes* (1865) 2 De G.J. & S. 526, 532.

[51] *Ibid.* at p. 531.

[52] *Chaytor* v. *Maclean* (1848) 11 L.T.(o.s.) 2.

[53] This expression, by s. 376 (*a*) of the Companies Act 1948, includes a receiver of part only of the company's property, and a receiver only of the income arising from its property or from part thereof; and similarly in the case of a manager.

[54] Companies Act 1948, s. 366. There is a penalty of £100. " Body corporate " includes corporations not companies for the purpose of the Act. In the application of the section to Scotland, body corporate does not include a firm.

[55] *Portman Building Society* v. *Gallwey* [1955] 1 W.L.R. 96.

[56] Companies Act 1948, s. 367. The section does not apply where both the apportionment and the bankruptcy were before the commencement of the Act. The marginal note to the section refers to disqualification from acting as receiver or manager, but the section itself provides only for penalties.

[57] See *Budgett* v. *Improved Furnace Syndicate* [1901] W.N. 23.

though the appointment of the managing director was desired by another debenture holder [58]: but the receiver may be authorised to appoint a director as manager. One of the persons entrusted with powers of management over a statutory undertaking will sometimes be appointed.[59]

Liquidator. Where there is a winding up it has been said to be a rule of convenience that the court will take care, in order to avoid trouble and expense, that the receiver and the liquidator shall be one and the same person in every case where that can properly be done [60]: though some judges have considered it undesirable that one person should fill both posts, as the interests represented may conflict.[61] Where, after the making of an order to wind up a company and the appointment of a liquidator, the appointment of a receiver is applied for by the plaintiffs in a debenture holders' action, the liquidator has frequently been appointed receiver,[62] but not if special circumstances rendered his appointment undesirable, *e.g.* if he has assumed a position of hostility to the debenture holders [63]; the discretion of the judge of first instance will seldom be interfered with by the Court of Appeal.[64] Where a liquidator in a voluntary winding up is also receiver, this fact may be sufficient ground for removing him from the former position on the application of creditors.[65]

A receiver who has been appointed before the commencement of the winding up of a company is not displaced by the appointment of a liquidator; but the court may remove a receiver appointed before the commencement of the winding-up proceedings, or after a winding-up order has been obtained, and appoint the liquidator to act as receiver as well as liquidator.[66] This, however, is " only a prima facie rule of practice; if justice or convenience

---

[58] *Re Carshalton Park Estate Ltd.* [1908] 2 Ch. 62, 66.

[59] *Ames* v. *Birkenhead Docks* (1855) 20 Beav. 332; *Potts* v. *Warwick and Birmingham Canal Co.* (1853) Kay 143.

[60] *Re Joshua Stubbs* [1891] 1 Ch. 475, 482.

[61] *Re Karamelli & Barnett Ltd.* [1917] 1 Ch. 203, *per* Neville J. " The liquidator acts for and in the interests of the company whereas, the receiver and manager acts for and in the interests of the debenture-holders and not for the company ": *per* Lawrence J. in *Stead Hazel & Co.* v. *Cooper* [1933] 1 K.B. 840, 843.

[62] *Perry* v. *Oriental Hotels Co.* (1870) L.R. 5 Ch. 420; *Tottenham* v. *Swansea Zinc Ore Co.* [1884] W.N. 54; 53 L.J.Ch. 776.

[63] *Giles* v. *Nuthall* [1885] W.N. 51; see, too, *Boyle* v. *Bettws, etc., Colliery Co.* (1876) 2 Ch.D. 726; and *Strong* v. *Carlyle Press* [1893] 1 Ch. 268.

[64] *Giles* v. *Nuthall* [1885] W.N. 51.

[65] *Re Karamelli & Barnett Ltd.* [1917] 1 Ch. 203.

[66] See *supra*; *Campbell* v. *Compagnie Générale* (1876) 2 Ch.D. 181.

require it, the rule will be displaced." [67] And it will be displaced if there is only (as is, in fact, now normally the case) a small amount of unpaid capital to be got in. In such a case the court will generally abstain from substituting the liquidator for a receiver, and will allow the receiver to continue to act [68]; or the appointment may be split, the receiver being only displaced as to uncalled capital. [69] And if the assets of the company are not enough to pay the debenture holders, the court will not remove the receiver in favour of a liquidator who wishes to question the validity of the debentures. [70]

Where debenture holders have a right under their security to appoint a receiver, a winding-up order coupled with the appointment of a liquidator does not interfere with this right, though it may prevent the receiver from doing various things which he was authorised to do by the debenture deed, for instance, carrying on the business or making a call. There is no case in which the court has appointed the liquidator to act as receiver for debenture holders, except where the debenture holders have themselves come to the court and asked for a receiver. In that case the court, in the exercise of its discretion, will generally appoint the liquidator, as being the most suitable person. But where, under the terms of their security, the debenture holders have a right to appoint their own receiver, and they come to the court insisting on their right, they are entitled to an order giving their receiver liberty to take possession. [71] In such a case the court has no discretion. A power of appointing a receiver conferred by a company's debentures must be exercised bona fide in the interest of the debenture holders only, and accordingly, in a case in which it had been exercised by the donee of the power, a debenture holder who was also a shareholder, in the interest of the shareholders the court interfered and appointed its own receiver [72]; and so also where the appoint-

---

[67] *British Linen Co.* v. *South American and Mexican Co.* [1894] 1 Ch. 108, *per* Vaughan Williams J. at p. 119; *Bartlett* v. *Northumberland Avenue Hotel Co.*, 53 L.T. 611. In the former case the receiver was allowed to continue to act in respect of certain assets particularly difficult to realise.

[68] *Re Joshua Stubbs* [1891] 1 Ch. 475, 483. See, too, *Re Vimbos Ltd.* [1900] 1 Ch. 470, where all the assets, which were of considerable amount, were realised by a receiver appointed by debenture holders shortly before the company went into liquidation.

[69] *British Linen Co.* v. *South American and Mexican Co.*, *supra*.

[70] *Strong* v. *Carlyle Press* [1893] 1 Ch. 268.

[71] See *Re Henry Pound, Son and Hutchins* (1889) 42 Ch.D. 402.

[72] *Re Maskelyne British Typewriter* [1898] 1 Ch. 133.

ment was made by means of the vote of a person who had assigned his debenture to the plaintiff and against the wishes of the latter.[73]

Where a receiver has been appointed out of court, the court often appoints the same person. In such cases the order should include a direction to the receiver to include in the accounts to be brought in by him all receipts, payments and liabilities incurred before his appointment in the action. If another person is appointed, liberty should be given by the order to the original receiver to apply to have his accounts taken in the action: in such a case if the receiver is not agent for the company he has a right of indemnity against the debenture holders.[74]

Appeal. Where a judge of first instance has, in the exercise of his discretion, refused to displace a receiver by a liquidator the Court of Appeal will not, in the absence of special circumstances to justify their so doing, interfere with the exercise of that discretion.[75]

Custody of books. Where the receiver is not displaced, a question may arise between him and the liquidator as to the custody of the books of the company. In general the liquidator is entitled to the custody of such of the books and documents of the company as relate to its management and business and are not necessary to support the title of the debenture holders.[76]

Official Receiver. Where an application is made to the court to appoint a receiver on behalf of the debenture holders or other creditors of a company which is being wound up by the court in England the official receiver may be so appointed.[77]

---

[73] *Re Slogger Automatic Feeder Co.* [1915] 1 Ch. 478.
[74] *Re Arctic Supplies* [1932] W.N. 79.
[75] *Re Joshua Stubbs* [1891] 1 Ch. 475; *Bartlett* v. *Northumberland Avenue Hotel Co.* (1886) 53 L.T. 611.
[76] See *Engel* v. *South Metropolitan Brewing Co.* [1892] 1 Ch. 442, cited *ante*, p. 101.
[77] Companies Act 1948, s. 368.

CHAPTER 5

MODE OF APPOINTMENT OF A RECEIVER

Receiver not appointed unless in an action. Except in relation to and for the purposes of any reference to arbitration,[1] in certain statutory cases,[2] and in cases under the jurisdiction in cases of mental infirmity,[3] the court has no jurisdiction to appoint a receiver unless an action is pending.[4]

A proceeding by originating summons, originating motion or petition, is in general an action for this purpose.[5]

Form of application. The appointment of a receiver should be expressly claimed in the originating process,[6] but a receiver may be appointed in the absence of express claim [7] or the originating process may be amended.[8]

In the Chancery Division where, as is usually the case, the appointment is required before trial, or hearing of an originating summons, the application is made by motion [9] in open court: but where the judge to whom the application should be made is sitting in chambers an *ex parte* application may be made to him in very urgent cases.

The application may be made in chambers by summons [9] in the following cases (i) in cases of equitable execution; (ii) to appoint a receiver in place of one retired or deceased [10]; (iii) on the hearing

---

[1] Arbitration Act 1950, s. 12 (6) (*h*).

[2] Under Railway Companies Act 1867 (*ante*, p. 52), the application is by petition.

[3] *Ante*, p. 73.

[4] *Salter* v. *Salter* [1896] P. 291; and see *Gasson and Hallagan* v. *Jell* [1940] Ch. 248.

[5] See Judicature Act 1925, s. 225, for definition of " action," and R.S.C., Ord. 5, r. 1. As to the position prior to the 1965 R.S.C., see *Gee* v. *Bell* (1887) 35 Ch.D. 160; *Weston* v. *Levy* [1887] W.N. 76; *Re Francke* (1888) 57 L.J.Ch. 437. Where the only person interested is the applicant (*e.g.* a sole beneficiary on intestacy requiring an immediate receiver and manager of a business comprised in the estate) the correct mode of application is by *ex parte* originating summons.

[6] *Colebourne* v. *Colebourne* (1876) 1 Ch.D. 690; *Re Wenge* [1911] W.N. 129.

[7] *Norton* v. *Gover* [1877] W.N. 205; *Salt* v. *Cooper* (1880) 16 Ch.D. 544; *Osborne* v. *Harvey* (1842) 1 Y. & C.C.C. 116.

[8] *Colebourne* v. *Colebourne, supra.*

[9] Exceptionally, the document by which the appointment is sought requires a £5 fee except in a case where the receiver is absolved from passing his accounts: Supreme Court Fees Order 1970 (S.I. 1975 No. 1343), Fee No. 22.

[10] *Grote* v. *Bing* (1852) 20 L.T. 124; 9 Ha. 50; *Booth* v. *Colton* (1868 16 W.R. 683; Seton (7th ed.), p. 729

of an originating summons in chambers, *e.g.* for sale or fore-closure [11]; (iv) by consent.[12]

In the Queen's Bench Division receivers are seldom appointed, except in cases of equitable execution: if the action is one in which a receiver is required it should not as a rule be commenced in that Division, and if so commenced should be transferred to the Chancery Division,[13] and must be so transferred where the proceeding is to enforce a security, except in the case of actions assigned to the Family Division.[14] The practice in the Family Division follows that in the Chancery Division.[15]

By whom application made. An application for a receiver may be made by any party.[16] It is provided by R.S.C., Ord. 30, r. 1, that the application may be made either *ex parte* or on notice. It is conceived that, in a very urgent case, a defendant may obtain the appointment of a receiver on such an application.[17] Under the old practice a defendant could not apply before decree,[18] but he may now apply at any stage,[19] even if the plaintiff has applied. In such a case one order is made on both motions, the conduct being usually given to the plaintiff.[20] The relief sought by the defendant must be incidental to, or arise out of, the relief claimed by the plaintiff, or the defendant must counterclaim or issue a writ before he can obtain a receiver.[21]

Parties. The appointment of a receiver is subject to the ordinary rule that equitable relief can only be granted when the proper parties are before the court.[22] If the application is by incumbrancers, prior incumbrancers need not, but all subsequent incumbrancers and the person entitled to the ultimate equity of redemption should be made parties, though the order for a receiver in case of

---

[11] In normal cases proceedings by a mortgagee, except debenture holders' actions, are commenced by originating summons; see R.S.C., Ord. 88.

[12] See *Blackburn* v. *Ravenhill* (1852) 20 L.T.O.S. 88.

[13] See *Russian Bank* v. *British Bank for Foreign Trade* [1921] 2 A.C. 438. For a form of order for the appointment of a receiver in a pending action in the Queen's Bench Division, see Queen's Bench Master's Practice Form No. PF 65; *Supreme Court Practice* (1976), Vol. II, para. 205.

[14] R.S.C., Ord. 88, r. 2.

[15] See also p. 125, *post*.

[16] See *Carter* v. *Fey* [1894] 2 Ch. 541, for instances in which the application may be made by a defendant.

[17] See *Hick* v. *Lockwood* [1883] W.N. 48.

[18] *Robinson* v. *Hadley* (1849) 11 Beav. 614.

[19] *Porter* v. *Lopes* (1877) 7 Ch.D. 358.

[20] *Sargant* v. *Read* (1876) 1 Ch.D. 600.

[21] *Carter* v. *Fey* [1894] 2 Ch. 541.   [22] *Re Shephard* (1889) 43 Ch.D. 131.

urgency may be made in the absence of some of the subsequent incumbrancers.[23] A creditor who has obtained judgment against a debtor in an action against the debtor and another cannot after the death of the debtor, obtain an order appointing a receiver of the interest of the deceased debtor in real estate for the purpose of satisfying the judgment debt.[24] In cases of emergency, however, a receiver may sometimes be appointed after the death of a sole defendant; thus where in a creditor's action against an executrix for administration, judgment had been pronounced, and a summons for the appointment of a receiver had been taken out, but pending the summons the executrix died, and there was evidence that the estate needed immediate protection, the court, on the application of the plaintiff, appointed a receiver, with powers limited in duration until ten days after the appointment of an administrator *de bonis non*, the plaintiff undertaking to use all possible speed in obtaining the appointment of himself or some other person as such administrator, and to accept short notice of motion to discharge the receiver.[25] In a similar case the order was made where the death of the sole executor occurred after judgment.[26]

The executors of a deceased plaintiff who has recovered judgment cannot apply for the appointment of a receiver under R.S.C., Order 46, rules 2, 4, as such an appointment is not execution within the meaning of those rules and rule 1.[27]

Application made at any stage. The appointment may be made at any stage of an action according as the urgency of the case may require[28] without formal application if necessary. A receiver may be appointed *ex parte* even after judgment[29] where there is risk of the defendant making away with the property[30]: but an injunction is preferred in such cases if it will be effective.

---

[23] See p. 126, *post*.
[24] *Re Cave* [1892] W.N. 142; *Re Shephard, supra; quaere Waddell* v. *Waddell* [1892] P. 226.
[25] *Cash* v. *Parker* (1879) 12 Ch.D. 294. See, too, *Taylor* v. *Eckersley* (1876) 2 Ch.D. 302; *Evans* v. *Lloyd* [1889] W.N. 171; *Piperno* v. *Harmston* (1886) 3 T.L.R. 219, and see R.S.C., Ord. 15, r. 15.
[26] *Re Clark* [1910] W.N. 234; see p. 21, *ante*.
[27] *Norburn* v. *Norburn* [1894] 1 Q.B. 448; see *Thompson* v. *Gill* [1903] 1 K.B. 770. *Semble*, they should apply to be added as parties under R.S.C., Ord. 15, r. 7.
[28] *Anglo-Italian Bank* v. *Davies* (1878) 9 Ch.D. 287; *Bryant* v. *Bull* (1878) 10 Ch.D. 153.
[29] *Lucas* v. *Harris* (1886) 18 Q.B.D. 127, 134; *Re Potts* [1893] 1 Q.B. 648; *Re Connolly Bros.* [1911] 1 Ch. 742.
[30] *Evans* v. *Lloyd* [1889] W.N. 171; *Minter* v. *Kent Land Society* (1895) 72 L.T. 186.

Practice on application. In general there must be at least two clear days between the service of the notice of motion for a receiver and the day named in the notice for hearing the motion.[31] " Clear days " means working days, excluding Saturdays and Sundays.[32] Short notice of motion cannot be given without express leave,[33] and it must appear upon the face of the notice of motion that leave has been obtained to serve it as short.[34] In ordinary cases of urgency leave is obtained to serve the defendant with short notice of motion for a receiver along with the writ; otherwise service can be effected on two days' notice at any time after the issue of the writ.[35] The fact of such leave having been obtained must also be mentioned in the notice of motion. In cases of great urgency a receiver may be appointed even before service of the writ [36]; leave is given to serve short notice of motion with the writ, and the appointment is made in the first instance, only until the day for which notice is given. Where leave to serve short notice is required, application must be made to the judge. In such cases, in the interests of fairness, copies of affidavits proposed to be used on the motion should, if possible, be served with the notice of motion or as soon as possible after service.[37]

Exceptionally, a notice of motion attracts a fee of £5, unless the receiver is to be absolved from passing his accounts, when no fee will be payable, as in the case with an ordinary notice of motion.[38] The original notice of motion (together with a clean copy for the judge) is handed to the registrar in court and filed.[39] The notice of the motion must be served on the defendant personally or upon his solicitor.[40] The order may be made on affidavit of service of the notice of motion.[41]

---

[31] R.S.C., Ord. 8, r. 2 (2).
[32] R.S.C., Ord. 3, r. 2 (5). *Brammall* v. *Mutual Ins. Corpn.* [1915] W.N. 78.
[33] R.S.C., Ord. 8, r. 2 (2); and see *Hart* v. *Tulk* (1849) 6 Hare 611.
[34] *Dawson* v. *Beeson* (1883) 22 Ch.D. 504.   [35] See R.S.C., Ord. 8, r. 4.
[36] *Re H.'s Estate* (1876) 1 Ch.D. 276; Seton (7th ed.), p. 737.
[37] *Paravicini* v. *L. C. R. Gunner* [1919] W.N. 173.
[38] Supreme Court Funds Order (S.C.F.O.) 1975 (S.I. 1975 No. 1343), Fee No. 22.
[39] Order of the Lord Chancellor, January 20, 1922.
[40] *i.e.* the solicitor on the record: see *Bayley* v. *Maple* (1911) 27 T.L.R. 284. Under the former practice whereunder documents could in certain cases be filed in the Central Office in default of appearance, this procedure was nevertheless not applicable in such cases as the present. *Tilling* v. *Blythe* [1899] 1 Q.B. 557. *Cf.* R.S.C., Ord. 65, r. 9. If a notice of motion is served before appearance, Ord. 65, r. 2, does not apply; where service on one of two defendants, who resided together and who entered appearances shortly after (both having been served personally with the writ), sufficient service on the latter: *Jarvis* v. *Hemmings* [1912] W.N. 33.
[41] *Meaden* v. *Sealey* (1849) 6 Ha. 620.

A notice of motion stating it is to be moved before the judge of the Chancery Division before whom it would in the normal course of events come, has been held good, though, owing to the system of linked judges, or for any other reason, it is moved before another judge and respondent does not appear.[42]

The rule which requires previous notice to be served on a defendant who has not appeared is subject to an exception, where the defendant has absconded to avoid service and his residence is unknown.[43] Under the old practice it was held to be also subject to an exception where the defendant was out of the jurisdiction and could not be served.[44] This practice will still be applied in cases where a defendant is in territory controlled by an enemy: and in normal times, although there are now facilities for service out of the jurisdiction,[45] in cases of urgency a receiver will be appointed before service where service is delayed by the defendant's absence abroad: but the appointment may be made for a limited time or leave reserved to the defendant on appearing to move on short notice to discharge the order.

If a defendant has made an affidavit in the action, he may be considered to have appeared for the purpose of the appointment of a receiver, although no formal appearance has been entered for him.[46]

A company[47] or an unincorporated association[48] can only appear in court by counsel or *semble* in chambers by its solicitor. A defendant who is served with a notice of motion cannot claim to be heard either personally or by counsel, until he has entered an appearance: but he or counsel on his behalf will usually be heard on a personal undertaking by such defendant or his solicitor to enter an appearance forthwith. It is the duty of counsel for defendant to ascertain and inform the court if appearance has

---

[42] *Re Madame Romney Ltd.* [1915] W.N. 389. Under modern practice the judge is not named, except in the case of a motion for judgment. Service of an amended notice was ordered in such a case in *Jackson* v. *Webster* [1920] W.N. 295.

[43] *Dowling* v. *Hudson* (1851) 14 Beav. 423; *London and South-Western Bank* v. *Facey* (1871) 19 W.R. 676. *Cf.* R.S.C., Ord. 65, r. 9.

[44] *Tanfield* v. *Irvine* (1826) 2 Russ. 149; *Gibbins* v. *Mainwaring* (1837) 9 Sim. 77.

[45] R.S.C., Ord. 11, rr. 1 and 9.

[46] *Vann* v. *Barnett* (1787) 2 Bro.C.C. 158.

[47] See *Frinton U.D.C.* v. *Walton Land Co.* [1938] W.N. 31, and *cf. Tritonia Ltd.* v. *Equity and Law Life Assurance Society* [1943] A.C. 584. A company or other corporate body can only sue and enter appearance by a solicitor: see *Re London County Council and London Tramways Co.'s Arbitration* (1897) 13 T.L.R. 254. As to the position in the county court, see *Kinnell* v. *Harding* [1918] 1 K.B. 405.

[48] *Aminal Defence, etc., Society* v. *I.R.C.* [1950] W.N. 276.

been entered and to impress on the defendant or his solicitor the necessity of complying with the undertaking.[49]

At the trial or after judgment. The court has the same power of appointing a receiver at the trial as on interlocutory application,[50] and also after judgment.[51]

In addition to the cases of equitable execution,[52] the court appoints a receiver after judgment in cases of urgency [53]: though if the action is spent fresh proceedings are necessary [54]: for instance, where a person, not a party to the cause, had been so long in possession without accounting that there was danger of his acquiring an absolute title to adverse possession [55]; where a mortgagee of the *corpus* in possession had not shown clearly that anything was due upon his mortgage, and the next mortgage estate, being only on a life estate, was in danger of being lost by the delay and the possible inability of the first mortgagee to refund if he should be ordered to do so [56]; where the application could not have been made at the hearing [57]; in a case where it appeared by the report that the circumstances would, at the hearing, have entitled the applicant to a receiver [58]; and where, after a decree for sale of land, the defendant, by neglecting to bring in the title deeds, was preventing the plaintiff from obtaining the benefit of the decree.[59]

Affidavits. An application for a receiver must be supported by evidence showing that the appointment is necessary or expedient,[60] and if, as is usually the case, the appointment of a named person is sought, by an affidavit of fitness,[61] which must not be made by the solicitor to the applicant or to the proposed receiver. If an affidavit of fitness is misleading, the receiver will

---

[49] Practice Note [1934] W.N. 228; repeated [1950] W.N. 279.

[50] *Re Prytherch* (1889) 42 Ch.D. 590.

[51] *Anglo-Italian Bank* v. *Davies* (1878) 9 Ch.D. 286; and see *Bryant* v. *Bull* (1878) 10 Ch.D. 153.

[52] See p. 123, *post*.

[53] *Wright* v. *Vernon* (1855) 3 Drew. 112; *Smith* v. *Cowell* (1880) 6 Q.B.D. 75.

[54] *Re Hearn* [1913] W.N. 103.

[55] *Thomas* v. *Davies* (1847) 11 Beav. 29.

[56] *Hiles* v. *Moore* (1852) 15 Beav. 175.

[57] *Bainbridge* v. *Blair* (1841) 4 L.J.Ch. 207.

[58] *Att.-Gen.* v. *Mayor of Galway* (1829) 1 Moll. 94, 104.

[59] *Shee* v. *Harris* (1844) 1 J. & L. 91; see, too, *Hacket* v. *Snow* (1847) 10 Ir.Eq. 220.

[60] See *Middleton* v. *Dodswell* (1806) 13 Ves. 269. As to form of affidavit where the appointment is sought by way of equitable execution, see p. 123, *post*.

[61] Form, Atkin's *Court Forms* (2nd ed.), Vol. 33, p. 181.

be discharged.[62] If a statement of claim has been served and the application is made before judgment, the affidavits ought to be founded on the allegations in the statement of claim, and, if statements not so founded are introduced into the affidavits, the court may decline to attend to them.[63] Affidavits filed in proceedings in the Chancery Division must express dates and sums of money in figures not words [64] and must not use the expression and/or.[65]

Security to be given. A person appointed to act as receiver must, unless otherwise ordered, first give security, to be allowed by the court or a judge, duly to account for what he shall receive as such receiver, and to pay the same as the court shall direct.[66] If the security is not given, the appointment will lapse.

Practice on appointment. If the applicant makes out a case for the appointment of a receiver, and the applicant satisfies the court of the fitness of his nominee, the court will either (1) appoint such nominee by name upon his first giving security, or (2) appoint such nominee with liberty to act at once and ordering him to give security by a fixed day,[67] the applicant undertaking to be responsible for what he may receive or become liable for in the meantime [68]; the order in this case provides that, if security is not given within the time limited, or such time as the court or judge may allow, the appointment as receiver (and manager) is to determine on the expiration of such period [69]: or (3) appoint such

---

[62] *Re Church Press Ltd.* [1917] W.N. 39; see this case as to necessity for correctly describing deponent.

[63] See *Dawson* v. *Yates* (1839) 1 Beav. 306; *cf. Cremen* v. *Hawkes* (1845) 2 J. & L. 674.

[64] [1940] W.N. 41. See generally as to affidavits, R.S.C., Ord. 41, and in *Supreme Court Practice* (1976).

[65] [1940] W.N. 188.

[66] R.S.C., Ord. 30, r. 2; *Re Pountain* (1888) 37 Ch.D. 609; see, as to receivers in cases of mental infirmity, the Court of Protection Rules 1960, rr. 47–51, 53, 65–69. A receiver appointed in an action in the Chancery Division commenced in a district registry (other than the registries of Leeds, Liverpool, Manchester, Newcastle-upon-Tyne, and Preston, as to which see Ord. 32, r. 26) must give security in London. In Queen's Bench actions the receiver gives security in the registry. As to the security to be given by a special manager, see Companies Act 1948, s. 263 (2).

[67] Usually within three weeks.

[68] See p. 127, *post.* Such an undertaking is not normally accepted from a limited company, but must be given by a director or other responsible person.

[69] See resolution of Chancery judges, note to *Re Sims and Woods* [1916] W.N. 233; *Rowley* v. *Desborough* [1916] W.N. 152; *Taylor* v. *Eckersley* (1876) 2 Ch.D. 302; 5 Ch.D. 741. See Practice Note [1943] W.N. 71, as to form of order confirming a receiver who has acted after the lapse of an interim appointment in his office.

nominee without security.[70] If the applicant does not ask for the appointment of a named person, or alternatively does not satisfy the court of the fitness of his nominee, the court will order that a proper person be appointed receiver, and refer the nomination to chambers.[71]

Practice on giving security. In case (1) the cause or matter is adjourned to chambers, in order that such person may give security, and the registrar sends a note to the master that the person named has been appointed on giving security to receive the specified property, and that the order will be completed on the master furnishing a note of the security having been given and of the times fixed to bring in the accounts. In case (2) a copy order is left in chambers, and in either case a summons is issued to proceed on the order. On the return of the summons the party having the conduct of the proceedings brings into chambers evidence showing the nature and value of the property over which the receivership is to extend,[72] and the master in either case fixes the amount of the security to be given by the receiver.

If the amount of the security exceeds £1,000 it is now given by guarantee in Chancery Masters' Practice Form 37,[73] under which joint and several covenants are entered into by the receiver and a guarantee society.[74] Where security in respect of additional liability is required it is given by indorsement on the guarantee.[75] If the security required is substantial—say in excess of £50,000— the master may, in the exercise of his discretion, require it to be spread over more than one society. The matter is, however, entirely one of discretion. If not exceeding £1,000 the security may be given by an undertaking signed by the receiver and his sureties or surety, or in the case of a guarantee society or company sealed with its seal or otherwise duly executed.[76] The secretary of the guarantee society or company makes an affidavit showing the assets and liabilities of the society or company, and that it is empowered to guarantee and that all proper claims and demands

---

[70] *Post*, p. 120.
[71] See *Anderson* v. *Kemshead* (1852) 16 Beav. 345; *Lane* v. *Lane* (1883) 25 Ch.D. 66; *Tillett* v. *Nixon* (1883), *ibid.* 238.
[72] Form of affidavit, Atkin's *Court Forms* (2nd ed.), Vol. 33, p. 196.
[73] See *Supreme Court Practice* (1976), Vol. II, para. 379.
[74] See R.S.C., Ord. 30, r. 2 (3).
[75] See *Supreme Court Practice* (1976), Vol. II, para. 379.
[76] R.S.C., Ord. 30, r. 2. For form of undertaking see Chancery Masters' Practice Form 38, *Supreme Court Practice* (1976), Vol. II, para. 380.

have been duly satisfied. An undertaking from a society or company whose guarantee is usually taken, is accepted without any such affidavit.

Under the present practice the form of guarantee or undertaking is not settled by the master, but is brought into chambers completed. Although the usual stamp duty falls to be paid in respect of the documents, there are no fees now payable in respect of the approval of the guarantee or undertaking.[77]

If further security is required the guarantee is indorsed in the form at the end of Chancery Masters' Practice Form 37.[78]

The guarantee or undertaking must be filed in the Central Office.[79]

Thereupon in case (1) the master sends a note to the registrar that the receiver has given security, specifying the mode thereof, and the periods fixed for the passing of the receiver's accounts and payment into court of the balance due thereon, and the registrar enters in the order the evidence of the security having been given and completes the order.

The master will then make a certificate of the completion of the security and of the periods fixed for the passing of the receiver's accounts and payments into court of the balance due thereon. The certificate is indorsed on the order. There is now no fee [80] on the certificate of completion of security.

If a named person is not appointed on the application for a receiver, but it is referred to chambers to appoint a proper person, a summons to proceed on the order is taken out and the party having the carriage of the order asks in the summons for the appointment of a named person, and other names may be proposed by other parties: evidence of fitness is produced and the master makes the appointment, adjourning the matter to the judge if required: times for passing the accounts and the amount of the security are settled and the security completed as above; a separate order is drawn up appointing the receiver by name.

If any doubt is alleged to exist as to the solvency of the sureties, the opposing solicitor may attend at the time for settling the security and examine the sureties on these points.[81]

---

[77] See Supreme Court Fees Order 1975 (S.I. 1975 No. 1343).
[78] See *Supreme Court Practice* (1976), Vol. II, para. 379.
[79] R.S.C., Ord. 30, r. 2 (4).
[80] See Supreme Court Fees Order 1975 (S.I. 1975 No. 1343).
[81] *Smith on Receivers* 18. The partner of the receiver, or persons in trade together, or the solicitor in the action, are usually rejected.

The security of a Scottish guarantee company may be accepted, if the company submits to the jurisdiction and signs an address for service within the jurisdiction.[82] Inquiry should be made to the chief master's chambers to ascertain whether the requisite resolutions have been passed and lodged with the chief master. If this has not been done the applicant should obtain instructions at the chambers as to procedure: the company may be accepted in the same way as an English company subject to evidence of solvency and execution of the guarantee. There is no rule of practice prohibiting the acceptance of the bond of a foreign company in a proper case.[83]

Where the property over which a receiver has been appointed has increased in value during the receivership, additional security may be required to be given by him.[84] Upon any event, such as death, winding up, or bankruptcy, happening which would prevent the guarantee or bankruptcy being effectually put in force against the sureties, an order will be made at chambers, on summons, directing the receiver to give a new security.

Dispensing with security. The court will not in ordinary cases dispense with the usual security, even with the consent of the parties interested.[85] But if all the parties interested are competent, and agree to appoint a receiver of their own authority and not by the authority of the court, the court may allow him to act without security.[86] In a case where a testator had by his will directed that a named person should be appointed receiver of his real and personal estates, stating that he intended by the appointment to give him a pecuniary benefit, the court appointed that person to be receiver and agent of the estates (the testator's only real estate being in the West Indies) on his own personal recognisance only [87]; and even in a case where all the parties were not competent to consent, the circumstance that the person proposed for receiver had been employed by the testator to manage his estates was held to be a reason for dispensing with sureties, and appointing him receiver of the estates on his own personal recognisance only.[88]

---

[82] Resolution of Judges of Chancery Division, July 5, 1909.
[83] *Aldrich v. British Griffin Chilled Iron and Steel Co.* [1904] 2 K.B. 850.
[84] Seton (7th ed.), p. 742.
[85] *Manners v. Furze* (1847) 11 Beav. 30.
[86] *Manners v. Furze* (1847) 11 Beav. 30, 31.
[87] *Hibbert v. Hibbert* (1808) 3 Mer. 681.
[88] *Carlisle v. Berkeley* (1759) Amb. 699; see, too, *Wilson v. Wilson* (1847) 11 Jur. 793.

But where some of the parties were not *sui juris*, and, therefore, incapable of giving consent, the court declined to dispense with the usual security.[89]

It is not unusual, where no salary is given to the receiver, to dispense with the security.[90] So, security may be dispensed with where the party appointed receiver will only have to incur expenditure.[91] So, also, security was dispensed with where the order appointing a receiver was made merely for the purpose of creating a charge upon the debtor's property subject to prior incumbrances, and the receiver was not to go into possession or receive anything.[92] However, unless specific moneys received by the receiver are ordered to be paid by him to a named person, which is not the usual case, the appointment of a receiver does not create a charge.[93]

Practice in the Queen's Bench Division. The practice of the Queen's Bench Division on giving security is fully stated in the *Supreme Court Practice*[94] and it is not thought necessary to set out the practice here.

Form of order as to property. The order appointing a receiver should either state on the face of it the property over which the appointment is to extend or refer to the pleadings or some document in the proceedings which describes the property.[95] In the case of mortgaged property, the description will follow the terms of the mortgage, and if the latter is in general terms the order will be so likewise. In the case of a receiver by way of equitable execution, the property should be specified; the appointment will not be made over the debtor's equitable interests in general terms. The order usually directs the receiver to pass his accounts from time to time, and to pay the balances found due from him, as the judge shall direct, or directions to this effect may be given in chambers.

If the appointment of a receiver is over real or leasehold property, the order usually directs the parties to the record who

---

[89] *Tylee* v. *Tylee* (1853) 17 Beav. 583.

[90] *Gardner* v. *Blane* (1842) 1 Hare 381; *Re Prytherch* (1889) 42 Ch.D. 590; see, too, *Pilkington* v. *Baker* (1876) 24 W.R. 234.

[91] *Hyde* v. *Warden* (1876) 1 Ex.D. 309, 310; *Boyle* v. *Bettws Llantwit Colliery Co.* (1876) 2 Ch.D. 726; *Fuggle* v. *Bland* (1883) 11 Q.B.D. 711.

[92] *Hewett* v. *Murray* [1885] W.N. 53; 54 L.J.Ch. 573. For form of order appointing a receiver by way of equitable execution without security, see also 52 L.T. 380.

[93] *Re Whiteheart* (1971) 116 S.J. 75. See further p. 137, *post*.

[94] See notes to R.S.C., Ord, 30, r. 2, in the *Supreme Court Practice* (1976).

[95] Seton (7th ed.), p. 738.

are in possession, not as tenants but as owners, to deliver up to him in possession,[96] or to attorn tenant to the receiver at an occupation rent [97]; and an order directing possession to be given to the receiver may, in a proper case, be obtained even upon an interlocutory application.[98] In a mortgagee's action where the mortgagor is in possession, prima facie the proper order on interlocutory motion for a receiver is to order possession to be given to the receiver, though the court has a discretion and may allow the mortgagor to attorn tenant at an occupation rent.[99]

The mortgagor is entitled to remain in occupation without payment of rent until such an order is made.[1]

Directions in order. If tenants are in possession of real or leasehold property over which a receiver is appointed, the order should direct them to attorn and pay their rents in arrear and the growing rents to the receiver [2]; but this direction should be omitted where the estates are out of England or Wales.[3]

If the property over which a receiver is appointed is outstanding personal estate, the order should direct parties in possession of such estate to deliver over to the receiver all such estate, and also all securities in their hands for such estate or property together with all books and papers relating thereto.[4]

The costs incurred with reference to the completion of the security of the receiver, and subsequent thereto, are in the first instance paid by the receiver, and will be allowed him in passing his first account.[5] Premiums paid by the receiver to a guarantee

---

[96] *Griffith* v. *Griffith* (1751) 2 Ves.Sen. 401; *Everett* v. *Belding* (1852) 22 L.J.Ch. 75; 1 W.R. 44; *Hawkes* v. *Holland* [1881] W.N. 128; see, as to form of order, *Davis* v. *Duke of Marlborough* (1818) 2 Swans. 108, 116; *Baylies* v. *Baylies* (1844) 1 Coll. 548; *Edgell* v. *Wilson* [1893] W.N. 145.

[97] *Re Burchnall, Walker* v. *Burchnall* [1893] W.N. 171. For form of Order see Atkin's *Court Forms* (2nd ed.), Vol. 33, p. 214.

[98] *Ind, Coope & Co.* v. *Mee* [1895] W.N. 8; *Charrington & Co.* v. *Camp* [1902] 1 Ch. 386. In *Taylor* v. *Soper* [1890] W.N. 121; 62 L.T. 828, North J. refused in special circumstances to make an order for delivery up of possession before trial.

[99] *Pratchett* v. *Drew* [1924] 1 Ch. 280; *Masters* v. *Crouch* (1927) 63 L.J.N.C. 557; plaintiff second mortgagee.

[1] See *Yorkshire Banking Co.* v. *Mullan* (1887) 25 Ch.D. 12; *Re Burchnall* [1893] W.N. 17.

[2] Seton (7th ed.), p. 762.   [3] *Ibid.* p. 776.

[4] Seton (7th ed.), p. 725; *Truman* v. *Redgrave* (1881) 18 Ch.D. 547; *Leney & Sons Ltd.* v. *Callingham* [1908] 1 K.B. 79. If necessary, a receiver will be ordered to keep separate accounts of real and personal estates: *Hill* v. *Hibbitt* (1868) 18 L.T. 553.

[5] Daniell's *Chancery Practice* (8th ed.), p. 1492. As to costs where an ignorant person had been induced by the misrepresentations of the plaintiff to consent to act as receiver, and afterwards, on discovering the nature of the office, refused to enter into the recognisance, see *Hunter* v. *Pring* (1845) 8 Ir.Eq. 102.

society which had become his surety were formerly not allowed, unless he was acting without salary [6]; under modern practice they are usually allowed in all cases. [7]

A receiver is sometimes appointed until judgment or further order, but very often no limit of time is fixed though a limit is always fixed in the appointment of a manager. Where no limit of time is fixed in the order appointing a receiver, it is not necessary for the judgment to direct that he be continued [8]; but where he is appointed only until judgment or further order, if he is to continue to be receiver the judgment must so direct, and, as this is virtually a new appointment, further security must be given,[9] unless, as is usually the case, the security originally given is made applicable to any continuation of the appointment. Where the appointment is for a limited time, application to extend the appointment can be made by summons before the time limited has expired: if the time has expired an order may be obtained continuing and confirming the appointment.[10]

Practice on application for receiver by way of equitable execution. Where the appointment of a receiver is sought by way of equitable execution (excluding the appointment of a receiver to enforce a charging order on a judgment debtor's land) [11] the application is made both in the Queen's Bench Division and in the Chancery Division by summons in chambers.[12] In the Queen's Bench Division the master can, under R.S.C., Ord. 32, r. 11 (1) (d), make the appointment,[13] and grant an injunction so far as is ancillary or incidental to equitable execution, and the practice in the Chancery Division is similar. In such cases, if the plaintiff does not desire an injunction, he issues a summons without leave. If, for sufficient reason, he requires an interim injunction he applies ex parte to the master for leave to issue the summons, which in that case asks for an interim injunction. The affidavit(s) should state: (1) date and particulars of the judgment, stating that it is unsatisfied, or giving particulars of any partial satisfaction;

---

[6] *Harris* v. *Sleep* [1897] 2 Ch. 80.

[7] See an article by Master Mosse in 101 L.J. 241: the direction of the judges therein mentioned cannot be traced.

[8] *Davies* v. *Vale of Evesham Preserves* [1895] W.N. 105; 43 W.R. 646.

[9] *Brinsley* v. *Lynton Hotel Co.* [1895] W.N. 53; 2 Manson 244.

[10] For a form of order in administration proceedings see [1943] W.N. 71.

[11] *Barclays Bank Ltd.* v. *Moore* [1967] 1 W.L.R. 1201. See p. 94, *ante.*

[12] See *Supreme Court Practice* (1976), notes to R.S.C., Ord. 30, r. 2.

[13] A district registrar has similar powers: R.S.C., Ord. 32, r. 23. In partnership cases the order is made by the judge in person in the Queen's Bench Division.

(2) particulars and result of any execution which has been issued, stating nature of sheriff's return, if any; (3) that defendant has either (i) a legal estate in land, or (ii) no property which can be taken by legal execution, or if he has such property, reasons why legal execution would be futile against such property [14]; (4) particulars of the property over which a receiver is sought; (5) name and address of proposed receiver, and that in deponent's judgment he is a fit and proper person; and (6) that the defendant is in pecuniary difficulties or that the appointment of a receiver without the delay of giving security is of great importance, and that deponent verily believes that the defendant may assign or dispose of his interest in the property unless restrained from so doing by the order of the court.[15] In determining whether it is just or convenient that such appointment should be made, regard must be had to the amount of the judgment debt, the amount may probably be obtained by the receiver,[16] and to the possible costs of his appointment, and the summons may be adjourned for inquiries on these or other matters.[17] If the affidavit is sufficient, leave is given to issue a summons returnable in about seven days, and if the judge or master is satisfied by the affidavit that there is danger of the property being made away with by the judgment debtor an injunction will be granted pending the hearing of the summons [18]; a case of jeopardy must be established by the affidavit.[19] Where the defendant has not appeared it is not sufficient to file the summons at the Central Office; it should be served on the defendant or leave obtained for substituted service.[20]

The practice on giving security and details of the amount allowed for costs and remuneration with Central Office Regulations are fully stated in the *Supreme Court Practice*.[21]

---

[14] It is not necessary to prove that legal execution has been exhausted if it is shown that it would be futile.

[15] For forms see Atkin's *Court Forms* (2nd ed.), Vol. 33, pp. 181, 191.

[16] See *per* Scrutton L.J. in *J. Walls Ltd.* v. *Legge* [1923] 2 K.B. 240, 245, where the sum in question was £3 per annum, and *I.* v. *K.* [1884] W.N. 63.

[17] R.S.C., Ord. 51, r. 1.

[18] For forms of injunction see Atkin's *Court Forms* (2nd ed.), Vol. 33, pp. 192, 193.

[19] *Lloyds Bank* v. *Medway Upper Nav. Co.* [1905] 2 K.B. 359. For an injunction granted in the Chancery Division, see *Westhead* v. *Riley* (1883) 25 Ch.D. 413; and see *Archer* v. *Archer* [1886] W.N. 66. For practice of granting injunctions in the Family Division in lieu of a receiver, see *Bullus* v. *Bullus* (1910) 102 L.T. 399.

[20] *Tilling* v. *Blythe* [1899] 1 Q.B. 557. In practice, however, strict personal service is not insisted on if it is shown that the summons has come to the knowledge of the judgment debtor.

[21] See notes to R.S.C., Ord. 30, r. 2.

A county court judge has jurisdiction to appoint a receiver by way of equitable execution over both equitable [22] and legal estates in land.[23]

An action in the Chancery Division by a creditor who has recovered judgment in the Queen's Bench Division is prima facie so vexatious as to render him liable for the costs of such second action; but if the mere appointment of a receiver will not give the judgment creditor the remedy to which he is entitled, e.g. where there are accounts to be taken between him and the judgment debtor, or if it is necessary to take proceedings in the name of the person having the legal right to sue, the action for a receiver may properly be brought in the Chancery Division.[24]

Divorce. The practice on the appointment of a receiver in the Family Division to enforce payment is similar to that in the other Divisions of the High Court. The application is made on summons before a registrar on affidavit of service of the order for payment and of non-payment: the summons may be served on the respondent's solicitor or service dispensed with and substituted service of the order of appointment by registered letter or advertisement allowed. An injunction may be granted *ex parte* on the applicant's undertaking and the summons adjourned for service. The appointment is made of a named receiver " on his first giving security to the satisfaction of the registrar unless otherwise directed by the court." This is given by an undertaking if the sum is under £1,000 [25] and if over this sum by means of a bond. The bond is prepared by the applicant and left at the registry: if it has not been approved by the respondent an appointment is taken to settle. The registrar then signs his name on the margin of the bond and the order is issued.[26]

COMPANIES

Form of application. In the case of mortgages the practice as to mortgagees generally is applicable.[27] In the case of debentures

---

[22] *R.* v. *Selfe* [1908] 2 K.B. 121.

[23] County Courts Act 1959, s. 142.

[24] *Proskauer* v. *Siebe* [1885] W.N. 159.

[25] *Cf.* R.S.C., Ord. 30, r. 2.

[26] See Matrimonial Causes Rules 1973 (S.I. 1973 No. 2016), r. 86; for practice and forms see *Latey on Divorce* (15th ed.), paras. 4:1498–4:1520.

[27] See *ante*, p. 114. A debenture holder whose security consists of a floating charge ranking subsequent to a legal mortgage is nevertheless a necessary party to an action by the legal mortgagee to enforce his security: *Wallace* v. *Evershed* [1899] 1 Ch. 891.

the application for a receiver is made by notice of motion [28] in a
debenture holders' action [29]: which must include a claim to enforce
the security by sale or foreclosure.[30] Leave to serve short notice
with the writ is usually obtained as the application is urgent.[31]
The action is usually commenced by writ, though an order for
foreclosure could even under the old procedure have been made
on originating summons at the instance of debenture holders.[32]
If the plaintiff's debenture is one of a series, he sues on behalf of
himself and all other debenture holders of the same series and
should specify as accurately as possible the class on behalf of
which he sues [33]; the company and a member of each class of
debenture holders, subsequent to the series of the plaintiff on
behalf of such class, being made defendants.[34] A receiver may,
however, be, and often is, appointed before all the subsequent
debenture holders are parties or represented.[35] If subsequent
debentures are secured by a trust deed, the trustees of that deed,
having regard to R.S.C., Ord. 15, r. 14, sufficiently represent the
debenture holders.[36] Where there is a debenture trust deed to
secure the plaintiff's series, the trustees should be made defendants
if not plaintiffs.[37] If one of several representative plaintiffs with-
draws his retainer he may be added as defendant.[38]

Service on a company is effected by leaving the writ or other
document at, or sending it by post to, its registered office.[39]
If, for whatever reason, there is no registered office, service is
regulated by R.S.C., Ord. 65, r. 3, and is effected by leaving the
document with the secretary or other head officer at the company's

---

[28] For form, see Atkin's *Court Forms* (2nd ed.), Vol. 11; and see n. 42, p. 115, *ante*.

[29] As to practice in such actions, see *Supreme Court Practice* (1976), Vol. II, paras. 2471–2522; Seton (7th ed.), 1953–1973; Palmer's *Precedents* (17th ed., 1960), Vol. III; Atkin's *Court Forms* (2nd ed.), Vol. 11.

[30] See *Gasson and Hallagan* v. *Jell* [1940] Ch. 248; *Re Newport Construction Co. Ltd.* [1948] Ch. 217.

[31] See R.S.C., Ord. 8, r. 2 (2); no leave is now necessary for service with the writ if full notice is given: R.S.C., Ord. 8, r. 4.

[32] *Oldrey* v. *Union Works* (1895) 72 L.T. 627; *Sadler* v. *Worley* [1894] 2 Ch. 170. An order for foreclosure cannot be made unless all the debenture holders are parties: see *Westminster Bank* v. *Residential Properties Co.* [1938] Ch. 639.

[33] *Marshall* v. *South Staffordshire Tramways* [1895] 2 Ch. 36.

[34] Being added if necessary under R.S.C., Ord. 15, r. 6. If any member of the class represented by plaintiff wishes to appear he must apply to be added as a defendant.

[35] *e.g. Re Crigglestone Coal Co.* [1906] 1 Ch. 523.

[36] *Re Wilcox & Co. Ltd.* [1903] W.N. 64.

[37] See *Cox* v. *Dublin City Distillery* [1917] 1 I.R. 203.

[38] *Re Kent Coal Concessions Ltd.* [1923] W.N. 328.

[39] Companies Act 1948, s. 437: see subs. (2) as to a company registered in Scotland.

head office or principal place of business.[40] In the case of an overseas company carrying on business here service is effected on the persons registered under section 407 (1) (c) of the Companies Act 1948, by being addressed to such persons and left at or sent by post to, the address provided.[41] Where this section has not been complied with or the persons so registered are all dead, or have ceased to reside at the addresses given, or refuse to accept service, or cannot be served, service is effected by leaving the document at, or sending it by post to, any place of business established by that company in Great Britain.[42]

Liberty to act before security on the plaintiff's undertaking to be responsible for acts and defaults of the receiver is usually given. Immediate leave for the receiver to borrow and charge the assets to meet necessary expenses may be obtained, if the evidence shows clearly a case of extreme urgency with particulars of the assets and the amount required. But it is only in extreme cases that this leave is given as the matter is more satisfactorily dealt with by the registrar or judge in chambers.

It is a common practice for a motion for a receiver to be, by consent,[43] treated as a motion for judgment where all parties are present, and the order for the usual accounts and inquiries then made. On such a motion the company (or liquidator) ought not to consent to a declaration of charge.[44]

The person on whose application an order for a receiver is made must within seven days of the appointment give notice to the Registrar of Companies.[45]

Form of order. The practice on appointment as to security and generally is dealt with in the earlier part of this chapter.[46] It is essential to complete security within the time fixed, or the appointment lapses.[47]

---

[40] See notes in *Supreme Court Practice* (1976) to R.S.C., Ord. 65, r. 3; the service of a winding-up petition is regulated by the Companies (Winding-Up) Rules 1949 (S.I. 1949 No. 330), r. 29.

[41] Companies Act 1948, s. 412. For form of Affidavit see Queen's Bench Master's Practice, Form No. PF 127; *Supreme Court Practice* (1976) Vol. II, para. 267.

[42] Companies Act 1948, s. 412; the service of a winding-up petition is regulated by the Companies (Winding-Up) Rules 1949 (S.I. 1949 No. 330), r. 29. See *Re Tea Trading Co.* [1933] Ch. 647; *cf. Banque des Marchands de Moscou* v. *Kindersley* [1950] 2 All E.R. 105; affirmed [1951] Ch. 112.

[43] The company can only appear in proceedings before the court by counsel: see *ante*, p. 115.

[44] *Re Gregory, Love & Co. Ltd.* [1916] 1 Ch. 203, 209; unless perhaps in special circumstances the indefeasible nature of the charge is absolutely clear: *ibid.*

[45] Companies Act 1948, s. 102 (1).

[46] As to statutory companies, see *ante*, p. 44.   [47] *Ante*, p. 117.

In a proper case the order may include a direction that the receiver shall not take possession or give security for a specified time.[48]

Effect of winding-up order. After a winding-up order has been made, the action must be assigned to the Group having jurisdiction in winding-up, *viz.* Group A; and if a winding-up order has been made after the commencement of the action, the judge having jurisdiction in winding up may order transfer of the action to that Group.[49] After a winding-up order leave to begin or continue the action must be obtained, but this will be given to incumbrancers as a matter of course.[50]

In March 1900 the judges of the Chancery Division directed that the undertaking by the plaintiff in a debenture holders' action on the appointment of a receiver who was to act at once should extend to all liabilities which would be covered by the completed security, not only to the receipts of the receiver.[51]

Under the above-mentioned direction of March 1900 the order formerly included a direction that the receiver should forthwith pay the preferential debts [52] out of any assets come to his hands which were subject to the floating charge. But having regard to the decision in *Re Glyncorrwg Colliery Co.*[53] the judges of the Chancery Division have decided that the earlier practice is to be resumed and that the order for payment of preferential debts is to be omitted from the order appointing a receiver. There is inserted in the judgment an inquiry as to whether there are any and what creditors entitled to preferential payment under sections 94 and 319 (or 358) of the Companies Act 1948, and what is due to such creditors.[54] The judges also directed that where there were clearly assets available for payment of preferential debts, application should be made to the master for a direction to the receiver to pay them.[55]

---

[48] See *Re Crompton & Sons Ltd.* [1914] 1 Ch. 767.

[49] See generally on practice, Palmer's *Company Precedents* (17th ed., 1960), Vol. III, Chap. 37; Atkin's *Court Forms* (2nd ed.), Vol. 11; and *ante*, p. 108.

[50] s. 231 of the Companies Act 1948. This includes a supervision order: s. 315 (2); *Lloyd* v. *D. Lloyd & Co.*, 6 Ch.D. 339; *Re Wanzer Ltd.* [1891] 1 Ch. 305.

[51] *Re Debenture Holders' Actions* [1900] W.N. 58. As to earlier practice, see *Evans* v. *Lloyd* [1889] W.N. 171; *Re Patrick*, 85 L.T. 398.

[52] See *post*, p. 207.

[53] [1926] Ch. 951; see *post*, p. 216, as to this case.

[54] For form of order, see *Re Burradon Coal Co.* [1929] W.N. 15, stated in *Supreme Court Practice* (1976), Vol. II, para. 2481.

[55] See further, p. 216, *post*.

CHAPTER 6

EFFECT OF APPOINTMENT AND POSSESSION
OF A RECEIVER

IN appointing a receiver the court appoints an officer of its own to take possession of the property over which he is appointed. The appointment, however, does not, without an express direction, effect any change in the possession of land, nor does it create an estate in, or (apart from statutory provisions) charge in favour of, the receiver, or the person obtaining the appointment.[1] A receiver is an officer appointed to collect the rents and profits of real estate, or the income or capital of personal estate, upon the title of the parties to the action; the rights of those parties are not affected by the order, but it operates as an injunction to prevent them from receiving the subject-matter of the order, or from dealing with it to the prejudice of other parties to the action. The rights of persons not parties are not affected by the order, but they cannot exercise those rights without the leave of the court. The above propositions will be illustrated in this chapter.

Date from which appointment operates. A receiver duly appointed by the court is, from the date of his appointment, an officer and representative of the court [2]; but he is not legally clothed with that character, or able to perform the duties of his office, until he has given security and his security has been perfected,[3] except so far as he is expressly authorised to act without security.

When, however, as may be done in urgent cases, an interim receiver is appointed with liberty to act at once with a direction that he give security within a specified time, or if he is appointed without security, he becomes an officer of the court, and is legally clothed with that character from the date of his appointment,[4] though in the former case the appointment lapses unless security is completed within the specified time.[5] So, also, where the order

---

[1] As to when a charge is created, see pp. 137 *et seq., infra.*

[2] *Aston* v. *Heron* (1834) 2 My. & K. 391; *Owen* v. *Homan* (1853) 4 H.L.C. 997, 1032; see *Davy* v. *Scarth* [1906] 1 Ch. 55; *Boehm* v. *Goodall* [1911] 1 Ch. 155.

[3] *Defries* v. *Creed* (1865) 34 L.J.Ch. 607; *Edwards* v. *Edwards* (1876) 2 Ch.D. 291; *Re Sims & Woods Ltd.* [1916] W.N. 233. See, too, *Ridout* v. *Fowler* [1904] 1 Ch. 658; affirmed [1904] 2 Ch. 93.

[4] *Taylor* v. *Eckersley* (1876) 2 Ch.D. 302; (1877) 5 Ch.D. 741.

[5] *Ante,* p. 117.

appointing a receiver with power to take possession does not direct that he shall give security, and the receiver takes possession accordingly, the appointment is complete, even though he is subsequently continued as receiver by an order requiring security to be given.[6]

The appointment of a receiver of the rents of land at the instance of a judgment creditor, though conditional on the receiver's giving security, on registration [7] operates as an immediate delivery of the land in execution; and, when the security is afterwards given, the order relates back accordingly.[8] But as regards personalty, it is settled that, when the order is in the form of appointing a receiver upon his giving security, his appointment is not effectual until the security is given. It is a conditional appointment, and the giving of security is a condition precedent.[9]

Nature of receiver's possession. The appointment of a receiver does not in any way affect the right to the property over which he is appointed. The court takes possession by its receiver, and his possession is that of all parties to the action according to their titles [10]: the receiver does not collect the rents and profits by virtue of any estate vested in him, but by virtue of his position as an officer of the court appointed to collect property upon the title of the parties to the action.[11] In appointing a receiver the court deals with the possession only until the right is determined, if the right be in dispute: or until the property is realised, if the appointment is made for that purpose.[12] If the appointment is made at the instance of incumbrancers, and the incumbrance is cleared off, the possession is restored to him from whom it was taken.[13]

---

[6] *Morrison* v. *Skerne Ironworks Co.* (1889) 60 L.T. 588; 33 S.J. 396.

[7] If an Order imposing a charge on the land to enforce the judgment has been made and registered, further registration of the appointment of the receiver is unnecessary: Administration of Justice Act 1956, s. 36 (3). See generally *Ashburton* v. *Nocton* [1915] 1 Ch. 274. *Cf.* p. 95, *ante*; validity of the charge against a trustee in bankruptcy or a liquidator depends on completion of the execution or the appointment of a receiver before bankruptcy or liquidation.

[8] *Ex p. Evans* (1879) 13 Ch.D. 252; and see *Re Shephard* (1889) 43 Ch.D. 133.

[9] *Per* Farwell J. in *Ridout* v. *Fowler* [1904] 1 Ch. 658, 662; affirmed [1904] 2 Ch. 93; *Edwards* v. *Edwards* (1876) 2 Ch.D. 291; explained in *Ex p. Evans* (1879) 13 Ch.D. 252, 255. See, too, *Re Roundwood Colliery Co.* [1897] 1 Ch. 373, 393.

[10] See *Re Butler* (1863) 13 L.R.Ir. 456; *Bertrand* v. *Davies* (1862) 31 Beav. 436.

[11] *Vine* v. *Raleigh* (1883) 24 Ch.D. 243.

[12] As in the case of partnership, or usually, at the instance of incumbrancers.

[13] *Sharp* v. *Carter* (1735) 3 P.W. 379; *Skip* v. *Harwood* (1747) 3 Atk. 564; *Wells* v. *Kilpin* (1874) L.R. 18 Eq. 298; and see *Moss S.S. Co.* v. *Whinney* [1912] A.C. 254. Where an order for the discharge of a receiver has been made, and he continues in possession after the date of his discharge paying over the rents to the party entitled, his possession is the possession of that party: *Horlock* v. *Smith* (1842) 11 L.J.Ch. 157.

Receiver as officer of the court. Since the receiver is an officer of the court, any property of which he is in possession is strictly in the possession of the court. In a case where there were two claimants to furniture in the possession of the receiver, and the receiver succeeded in displacing the title of the first claimant, he was not thereafter allowed to set up the title of that claimant as an answer to the claim of the second claimant.[14]

Receiver as agent of party entitled. In some cases after the right has been determined, a receiver will be considered as receiver for the person entitled [15]: for instance, in a suit for specific performance where the purchaser was compelled to accept the title [16]; and, conversely, where the appointment was due to the inability of the vendor to make out his title.[17]

Benefit and loss due to acts of receiver. The acts of a receiver are for the benefit of all parties according to their titles: as, for instance, where he is ordered to keep up policies of insurance.[18] Conversely, if a loss arises from the action of a receiver the estate must bear it as between the parties to the action.[19] A plaintiff cannot claim damages for detention of goods while in the hands of a receiver, for the damage is due to the law's delay, not to a wrongful act of the defendant.[20]

Effect as to possession. The appointment of a receiver does not of itself effect a change in the possession of land, nor does a receiver of the rents and profits of land take possession unless the order directs him to do so.[21] If, therefore, one of the parties, for instance, a mortgagor, is in possession, the order should direct him to deliver up possession to the receiver or to attorn tenant at a rent.[22]

Where the order did not direct possession to be given, it was

---

[14] *Re Savoy Estate Ltd.* [1949] Ch. 622. See n. 50, p. 193, *post.*

[15] *Boehm* v. *Wood* (1820) T. & R. 345; *Re Butler* (1863) 13 Ir.Ch. 456; *Rigge* v. *Bowater* (1785) 3 Bro.C.C. 365.

[16] *Boehm* v. *Wood* (1820) T. & R. 345; see, too, *Re Butler* (1863) 13 Ir.Ch. 456.

[17] *McCleod* v. *Phelps* (1838) 2 Jur. 962.

[18] *Seymour* v. *Vernon* (1864) 10 L.T. 58; see *Bertrand* v. *Davies* (1862) 31 Beav. 436; *Frazer* v. *Burgess* (1860) 13 Moo.P.C. 314; *Defries* v. *Creed* (1865) 34 L.J.Ch. 607.

[19] *Hutchinson* v. *Massareene* (1811) 2 Ball. & B. 55; see *Re London United Breweries* [1907] 2 Ch. 511.

[20] *Peruvian Guano Co.* v. *Dreyfus Bros.* [1892] A.C. 166.

[21] *Ex p. Evans* (1879) 13 Ch.D. 252.

[22] See *Pratchett* v. *Drew* [1924] 1 Ch. 280; *cf. Charrington* v. *Camp* [1902] 1 Ch. 386.

held that the entry of a receiver upon the lands of a company did not affect any change in the occupation within section 16 of the Poor Rate Assessment and Collection Act 1869 [23] so as to exempt the property from the obligation to pay arrears of rates,[24] and it appears that the same would be the case where possession is ordered to be given.[25]

The appointment of a receiver of the business of a company and his entry do not create anything in the nature of a fresh occupation under paragraph 14 of Schedule 4 to the Gas Act 1972 so as to enable the receiver to insist on a continued supply of gas without payment of arrears due by the company.[26] Nor, in the like circumstances, can he insist upon a further supply of electricity without payment of the arrears.[27] The Postmaster-General has never claimed payment of the company's telephone account as a condition of continuing the telephone service to the receiver. A receiver appointed by the court was held not an owner within the Public Health Acts.[28]

Income and capital gains tax. A receiver appointed by any court in the United Kingdom which has the direction or control of any property in respect of which income tax [29] or capital gains tax [30] is charged is assessable and chargeable with tax in like manner and to the like amount as would be assessed and charged if the property were not under the direction and control of the court. Where, therefore, a receiver is appointed over a business, he is for income tax purposes deemed to be carrying on the same business, *e.g.* in the case of a receiver of a partnership business or for debenture holders. It is the practice of the revenue to treat

[23] Now replaced by s. 18 of the General Rate Act 1967. In the case of companies priority is now given to arrears of rates up to one year's arrears: see *post*, p. 209.
[24] *Re Marriage, Neave & Co.* [1896] 2 Ch. 663; *National Prov. Bank* v. *United Electric Theatres Ltd.* [1916] 1 Ch. 132; *Gyton* v. *Palmour* [1945] K.B. 426.
[25] See *Husey* v. *London Electric Corpn.* [1902] 1 Ch. 411; but see *Re Marriage, Neave & Co., supra, per* Rigby L.J.
[26] See *Paterson* v. *Gas Light and Coke Co.* [1896] 2 Ch. 476, and *Smith's Case* [1893] 1 Q.B. 323 (decided under s. 18 of the Gas Light and Coke Companies Act 1872, and s. 39 of the Gas Works Clauses Act 1971, respectively). *Cf. Granger* v. *South Wales Electricity Co.* [1931] 1 Ch. 551, decided on the wording of a Special Act.
[27] Cl. 27 of the Sched. to the Electric Lighting (Clauses) Act 1899, adopted by s. 57 of the Electricity Act 1947. *Cf. Granger* v. *South Wales Electricity Co.* [1931] 1 Ch. 551, decided on the wording of a Special Act.
[28] s. 4 of the Public Health Act 1875, now s. 343 of the Public Health Act 1936; *Corporation of Bacup* v. *Smith* (1890) 44 Ch.D. 395.
[29] Taxes Management Act 1970, s. 75 (1).
[30] Taxes Management Act 1970, s. 77 (1).

this as applying to all cases where the receiver has power to carry on the business, even though such powers may be to some extent limited, *e.g.* because he has no right to use the chattels formerly employed therein. A receiver of any person resident in the United Kingdom [31] (other than an incapacitated person [31]) is only required to make the usual return, including the name, address and profits of that person: he is not required to do any other act for the assessment of that person to income tax. [32]

Every such receiver so appointed is answerable for doing all matters and things required to be done under the Income Tax Acts for the purpose of assessment and payment of income tax and capital gains tax. [33]

Executors. Where possession was obtained by a receiver appointed in administration proceedings, the personal liability of the executors for rent was held to be suspended during the term of the receiver's possession. [34]

The appointment of a receiver formerly did not affect the executor's right of retainer, [35] which he might therefore have exercised in respect of existing debts [36] to the extent of assets in his hands when the order was made, though such assets had been handed to the receiver, but not in respect of assets collected by the receiver. [37] The appointment of a receiver in an administration action prevents a return of *nulla bona* to a *fi. fa.* against an executor from operating as a presumption of devastavit. [38] The right of retainer overrides the plaintiff's claim for costs in administration proceedings. [39]

Order removes parties from receipt of rents. Although the order does not necessarily create a charge, nor effect a change in the possession, it removes the parties to the action from the right

---

[31] As to assessment of a non-resident person in the name of a receiver, see ss. 78 and 79; for incapacitated persons including persons of unsound mind, s. 72; as to the duty to make returns in such cases, s. 8.

[32] Taxes Management Act 1970, s. 76 (2).

[33] Taxes Management Act 1970, ss. 75 (2) ad 77 (1).

[34] *Minford* v. *Carse* [1912] 2 I.R. 245.

[35] See also p. 15, *ante.* The right of retainer has now been abolished by Administration of Estates Act 1971, s. 10.

[36] *Re Beavan* [1913] 2 Ch. 595. The right is not affected by an order under s. 130 of the Bankruptcy Act 1914: *Re Broad* (1911) 105 L.T. 719. As to retainer, see Administration of Estates Act 1925, s. 34 (2).

[37] *Re Harrison* (1886) 32 Ch.D. 395; *Re Jones* (1886) 31 Ch.D. 440.

[38] *Batchelar* v. *Evans* [1939] Ch. 1007.

[39] *Re Wester Wemyss* [1940] Ch. 1.

to receive the rents and profits of property bound by the order, or to obtain a transfer to themselves of property to which the order extends: for the order operates as an injunction.[40] It is contempt which will be punished by committal for a judgment debtor to obtain payment of money over which a receiver by way of equitable execution has been appointed after service of the order on him.[41] If a party is himself appointed receiver, he is nonetheless removed from the receipt in his own right of the rents and profits.[42]

Right of receiver to rents. The rents and profits of an estate over which a receiver has been appointed, including unpaid arrears, are, as regards parties to the action, bound from the date of the order [43]; but the appointment does not relate back to the date of the application,[44] though the right of a person, e.g. a first mortgagee whose rights have been interfered with by the appointment, dates back to an application for leave to take possession or appoint a receiver.[45] If a solicitor in the action has received rents without an authority from the court, he must pay them to the receiver, although they were received before the appointment was completed: the solicitor cannot claim a lien for costs.[46] The right of a prior mortgagee is discussed on another page.[47]

If the order directs tenants to pay their rents to the receiver, all rents due and unpaid at the time of the service of the order are bound. The tenants are not answerable in respect of rents which have accrued due and been paid prior to such service [48]; and a person entitled to receive the rents is bound as from the date of the order if he has notice of it.[49] A prepayment by the tenant to the mortgagor, before the due date, is invalid against a receiver who demands it before that date, whether the mortgage is legal or

---

[40] *Tyrrell* v. *Painton* [1895] 1 Q.B. 202; *Ideal Bedding Co.* v. *Holland* [1907] 2 Ch. 157.
[41] *Quaere* whether a person paying the money with notice of the order is not also in contempt: or whether he obtains a valid receipt. See p. 136, *post.*
[42] See *Ames* v. *Birkenhead Docks* (1855) 24 L.J.Ch. 540, where the chairman of a statutory undertaking was appointed; *Davy* v. *Scarth* [1906] 1 Ch. 55.
[43] *Lloyd* v. *Mason* (1837) 2 My. & Cr. 487; *Codrington* v. *Johnstone* (1838) 1 Beav. 520.
[44] *Per* Lindley M.R., *Re Clarke* [1898] 1 Ch. 336, 339.
[45] See p. 142, *post.*
[46] *Wickens* v. *Townsend* (1830) 1 R. & M. 361; *Re Birt* (1883) 22 Ch.D. 604; *Re British Tea Table Co.* (1909) 101 L.T. 707; see also p. 142, *post,* as to lien.
[47] See pp. 142–145, *post.*
[48] See *Ashburton* v. *Nocton* [1915] 1 Ch. 274; *Codrington* v. *Johnstone, supra*; *McDonel* v. *White* (1865) 11 H.L. 570; *Russell* v. *Russell* (1853) 2 Ir.Ch. 574.
[49] *Hollier* v. *Hedges* (1853) 2 Ir.Ch. 376; see *Eastern Trust Co.* v. *McKenzie, Mann & Co.* [1915] A.C. 750.

equitable; the prepayment is only good as to the amount due, not as to the remainder.[50] But a prepayment or release of the rent before the date of the mortgage or charge is valid against a mortgagee or a receiver.[51] The receipt of rent by a receiver appointed in a mortgagee's action does not amount to a recognition of the tenancy so as to prevent the mortgagee subsequently asserting his title paramount.[52]

Effect on third parties. Persons who are not parties to the order are not bound by it in this sense, that no action can be maintained against them, e.g. for rent, until something more has been done to make the order binding on them: a further order that they attorn tenant or pay their arrears to the receiver must be obtained.[53] If, however, after notice of the order, tenants pay their rents to a party bound by the order, they will not obtain a valid receipt, since the order operates as an injunction.[54] The receipt of the receiver will be valid if a receipt could have been given by a party bound by the order, but not otherwise.[55] The same rules will apply where a receiver has been appointed over personal estate at the instance of an incumbrancer, if the property is sufficiently specified in the order.[56] But where the property is not specified, for example where a receiver is appointed against trustees over a trust estate without specifying the investments, the receipt by the trustees of money payable, e.g. on redemption of debentures, will be valid against the receiver; the company being entitled to deal with the persons holding the legal title, and not being affected by virtue that the property is alleged to be trust property.

It is submitted that the same principles apply where a receiver has been appointed over equitable interests in personal estate at

---

[50] *Ashburton* v. *Nocton* [1915] 1 Ch. 274, 290; *Cook* v. *Guerra* (1872) 7 C.P. 132, 136.

[51] See *Green* v. *Rheinberg* (1911) 104 L.T. 149; see *Ashburton* v. *Nocton, supra*; *Wakefield Bank* v. *Yates* [1916] 1 Ch. 452.

[52] *Re O'Rourke's Estate* (1889) 23 L.R.Ir. 497.

[53] See *Seymour* v. *Lucas* (1860) 1 Dr. & Sm. 177; and p. 177, *post*, as to procedure. They may be ordered to pay the costs if they unnecessarily refuse to pay to the receiver: *Re Potts* [1893] 1 Q.B. 648. As to determination of tenancies and raising of rents, see pp. 186, 187, *post*.

[54] See p. 134, *ante*.

[55] For the receiver collects property upon the title of the parties; see p. 130, *ante*, and *Preston* v. *Tunbridge Wells Opera House* [1903] 2 Ch. 323; *Re Metropolitan Amalgamated Estates* [1912] 2 Ch. 497.

[56] For instance, where a receiver is appointed for debenture holders over all the assets, debtors with notice cannot obtain a receipt from the company.

the instance of a judgment creditor, and that after notice of the order and request for payment, the person in whose *dominium* the fund is cannot obtain a valid receipt from the debtor.[57] Such an order, it is submitted, operates as an injunction to prevent the debtor from receiving property to which it relates, or from dealing with it to the prejudice of the judgment creditor [58]; and if a person pays money to one who is to his knowledge restrained from receiving it, he is in contempt and obtains no valid receipt.[59] In one case,[60] it was in effect held that an order appointing a receiver over a debtor's current account at a bank did not prevent the bank, with notice of the order, from honouring cheques drawn by the debtor. It is submitted this decision can only be supported, if at all, on the ground that the order for a receiver was improperly made as there was no bar to legal execution by garnishee proceedings,[61] and that therefore the judgment creditor had no equity to complain of the action of the bank.[62]

No estate in receiver. An order appointing a receiver does not of itself cause any estate to vest in the receiver.[63] Consequently, it does not cause a forfeiture under a clause determining a life interest on the happening of any event, which would cause it to belong to or become vested in any other person than the life tenant, where nothing has been done under the order [64]: and the same would be the case where the gift over is limited to assigning or attempting to assign.[65] But an appointment of a receiver at the instance of a judgment creditor amounts to " a taking in execution by process of law " so as to cause a forfeiture conditioned to occur on the happening of that event.[66] A forfeiture will not be caused where the life tenant merely requests a receiver appointed over the testator's estate to pay a debt out of money due to the life tenant, for this request may refer to money then due.[67]

---

[57] See *Flegg* v. *Prentis* [1892] 2 Ch. 428.

[58] *Tyrrell* v. *Painton* [1895] 1 Q.B. 202; *Ideal Bedding Co.* v. *Holland* [1907] 2 Ch. 157; *Re Anglesey* [1903] 2 Ch. 727; *Singer* v. *Fry*, 84 L.J.K.B. 2025; *Ex p. Peak Hill Goldfield* [1909] 1 K.B. 430.

[59] *Eastern Trust Co.* v. *McKenzie, Mann & Co.* [1915] A.C. 759.

[60] *Giles* v. *Kruyer* [1921] 3 K.B. 23. The reasoning of the judgment appears to conflict with the judgments in *Re Anglesey* and *Ideal Bedding Co.* v. *Holland, supra. Re Pollard* [1903] 2 K.B. 41, on which it is founded, was a case of sequestration.

[61] See R.S.C., Ord. 49.

[62] This ground is not mentioned in the report.

[63] *Vine* v. *Raleigh* (1883) 24 Ch.D. 243.

[64] *Re Beaumont*, 79 L.J.Ch. 744; [1910] W.N. 181; *cf. Re Laye* [1913] 1 Ch. 298.

[65] See *Re Evans* [1920] 2 Ch. 304.   [66] *Blackman* v. *Fysh* [1892] 3 Ch. 209.

[67] *Durran* v. *Durran* [1904] W.N. 184; 91 L.T. 187.

When charge created. The appointment of a receiver does not of itself create a charge, unless specific moneys are ordered to be paid to a specific person.[68] However, as an effect of an agreement between the parties or of the terms of a statute, a charge may be created or rendered enforceable by the appointment. Thus the appointment of a receiver at the instance of debenture holders causes the floating charge created by the debentures to crystallise into a specific enforceable charge.[69]

Charge over land or interest in land. Prior to the coming into force of the Administration of Justice Act 1956, an order appointing a receiver at the instance of a judgment creditor operated, when registered,[70] to create an equitable charge on every interest in land, legal or equitable, to or over which the judgment debtor was beneficially entitled at the date of entry or any time thereafter.[71] Under the present law, having regard to the repeal of the former statutory provisions, the obtaining of an order appointing a receiver in a case where no charging order had been made under section 35 of the 1956 Act,[72] even when registered,[73] would not appear to create any charge on the land.[74] Unless registered, the order would be void as against a purchaser of the land.[75] If the judgment debtor has only an interest in land, no registration is possible,[76] but notice will of course be given to the trustees.

Where an order discharging a receiver over the debtor's interest in leaseholds at the instance of his trustee in bankruptcy contained a provision that the order was not to prejudice the contention of the judgment creditor that he was a secured creditor, it was held that, on the execution being completed, the judgment creditor had no such interest as would entitle him to rank as a secured creditor.[77]

No charge over interests in personalty. There never were any

---

[68] *Re Whiteheart* (1971) 116 S.J. 75.
[69] See p. 161, *post.*
[70] Under Land Charges Act 1972, s. 6 (1).
[71] See Law of Property Act 1925, s. 195; and *Ashburton* v. *Nocton* [1915] 1 Ch. 274, where the previous statutes are considered in great detail.
[72] See p. 94, *ante.*
[73] Under Land Charges Act 1972, s. 6 (1).
[74] Law of Property Act 1925, s. 195 (except subs. (4)), is repealed by Administration of Justice Act 1956, s. 34 (2). It would however appear to complete the execution: *Re Overseas Aviation Engineering (G.B.) Ltd.* [1963] Ch. 24.
[75] Land Charges Act 1972, s. 6 (4).
[76] See the definition of " land " in Land Charges Act 1972, s. 17 (1).
[77] *Re Bueb* [1927] W.N. 298.

statutory provisions applicable to pure personal estate corresponding to section 195 (1) of the Law of Property Act 1925 and
therefore the appointment at the instance of a judgment creditor
of a receiver over the debtor's personal property has never created
a charge [78]; nor could the person who had obtained the order, by
giving notice of it, obtain thereby a charge [79]: nor had or has the
court jurisdiction to make a declaration of charge when making
the appointment. [80] But as has been already stated [81] the order
operates as an injunction to prevent the debtor dealing with the
property over which it extends.

Paramount claims. If the receivership order does not contain a
direction for payment to the judgment creditor, the receiver holds
the property, when it reaches his hands, *in medio*, and it remains
subject to all claims which are paramount to that of the judgment
creditor at the date when the order is obtained; but subject to
these claims, the court will order the receiver to pay the judgment
creditor the amount of his debt in priority to the claims of any
person whose interests in the fund are acquired subsequently
to the date of the order, [82] except those of persons whose claims
may have priority by statute, *e.g.* a trustee in bankruptcy. [83] Thus,
where a judgment creditor had obtained the appointment of a
receiver over certain copper, which was subject to a lien, and the
debtors were subsequently adjudicated to be in judicial liquidation
in France, it was held that the judgment creditor was entitled to
the copper after the lien had been satisfied, in priority to the
liquidator, though nothing had been received at the date of the
liquidation. [84]

---

[78] *Re Potts* [1893] 1 Q.B. 648; *Re Beaumont* [1910] W.N. 181; 79 L.J.Ch. 744;
Ideal Bedding Co. v. *Holland* [1970] 2 Ch. 157; *Stevens* v. *Hutchinson* [1953] Ch. 299.

[79] *Re Potts, supra*; *Re Pearce* [1919] 1 K.B. 354; *Giles* v. *Kruyer* [1921] 3 K.B. 23.

[80] *Flegg* v. *Prentis* [1892] 2 Ch. 428. See *per* Farwell J. in *Ridout* v. *Fowler* [1904]
1 Ch. 662, 663. This case was affirmed by C.A. [1904] 2 Ch. 94.

[81] See p. 134, *ante*, and *de Peyrecave* v. *Nicholson* (1849) 42 W.R. 702; *Westhead*
v. *Riley* (1883) 25 Ch.D. 413.

[82] At all events if they had notice of it.

[83] See *per* Eady J. in *Re Marquis of Anglesey* [1903] 2 Ch. 727, 731, 732; *per* Kekewich J. in *Ideal Bedding Co.* v. *Holland* [1907] 2 Ch. 170; *Ex p. Peak Hill Goldfield
Ltd.* [1909] 1 K.B. 430, 437.

[84] *Levasseur* v. *Mason and Barry* [1891] 2 Q.B. 73. The English Bankruptcy Acts
had no application in this case: see *Re Pearce* [1919] 1 K.B. 354, 364. The case of
Ridout v. *Fowler* [1904] 2 Ch. 93, cited *supra* (claim by judgment creditor of purchaser
in respect of forfeited deposit), was decided against the creditor on the ground that
the forfeiture of the deposit by the vendor was under the contract by virtue of the
purchaser's default, which was prior in date to the receivership order; and that
certain money paid by the vendor was to secure possession of the land, not in part
repayment of the deposit.

Stop orders or charging orders. Further, although a receivership order obtained by a judgment creditor does not create a charge on personal property over which the receiver is appointed, if that property cannot be taken in execution or made available by any other legal process it prevents any subsequent mortgagee or judgment creditor from gaining priority, by means of a stop order or a charging order, over the creditor obtaining the receivership order [85]; the mere omission to obtain a stop order does not postpone a judgment creditor who has obtained a receivership order to a person who subsequently obtains a stop order. [86] But an assignee for value of a debt has priority over a judgment creditor who obtains a receivership order, although the order is made before notice of the assignment has been given. [87]

Cross-claim or set-off. Inasmuch as a receivership order operates as an injunction and prevents the judgment debtor from dealing with the property comprised in it, he cannot utilise such property for purposes of a cross-claim or by way of set-off against a third person. Thus, where the property consists of debentures of a company which have become due, the judgment debtor cannot set them up to defeat a bankruptcy petition by the company, founded on a debt less in amount than the sum secured by the debentures. [88]

Receiver not agent of creditor. A receiver appointed at the instance of a creditor holds the goods of the debtor as agent, not for the creditor but for the court, in order that it may decide the right to them. Moreover, an order appointing a receiver of the goods of a debtor does not make a judgment creditor who has obtained such an order a secured creditor within the meaning of sections 7 and 167 of the Bankruptcy Act 1914. [89] It can only do so if it charges the person in whose hands the money is, not to deal with it except by paying it to, or holding it for, the execution creditor [90]: therefore orders directing the receiver, after making

---

[85] See judgment of Eady J. in *Re Marquis of Anglesey* [1903] 2 Ch. 727, 731. In that case the receivership order was obtained over a judgment debtor's interest in residuary personal estate, partly in court and partly in the hands of an executor to whom notice of the order was at once given; at the date of the order, the residue was unascertained, and the fund in court was insufficient for the payment of the testator's creditors, and therefore the judgment creditor obtaining the order did not obtain either a charging order or a stop order.

[86] See *Re Galland* [1886] W.N. 96; *Fahey* v. *Tobin* [1901] 1 I.R. 516.

[87] *Re Bristow* [1906] 2 I.R. 215.

[88] *Ex p. Peak Hill Goldfield Ltd.* [1909] 1 K.B. 430, 437.

[89] *Re Dickinson* (1888) 22 Q.B.D. 187; *Re Potts* [1893] 1 Q.B. 648; *Re O'Neill* (1888) 21 L.R.Ir. 211.

[90] *Per* Swinfen Eady M.R., *Re Pearce, infra*, p. 363.

such payments as might be ordered, to accumulate the balance to
form a fund for payment of the judgment debt, did not create a
valid charge against the trustee [91]: but an order directing payment
of certain costs out of money in the hands of a receiver does
amount to such a charge, unless the debtors had notice of an act of
bankruptcy at the date of the order, followed by adjudication.[92]

Miscellaneous. The order does not create any charge, so as to
give the creditor priority over other creditors, where the judgment
debtor is a company in liquidation.[93] It is not execution, so as to
entitle the executors of a deceased judgment creditor to apply for
it under R.S.C., Ord. 46, r. 2, in order to enforce a judgment
obtained by their testator.[94] Nor does it amount to a stay of
execution within section 1 (1) (g) of the Bankruptcy Act 1914 so as
to disentitle the judgment creditor's obtaining the order to issue a
bankruptcy notice in respect of the same debt.[95]

The judgment creditor, after obtaining a receiver by way of
equitable execution, has a right under R.S.C., Ord. 48, r. 1, to
examine the debtor as to his means of satisfying judgment, and
also under rule 2 as to the debtor's dealings with property, against
removal of which an injunction had been granted prior to the
appointment.[96]

Bankruptcy of the debtor. The title of the trustee in bankruptcy
prevails over that of a receiver appointed by way of equitable
execution in respect of after-acquired property of the bankrupt,
since section 47 of the Bankruptcy Act 1914 only protects pur-
chasers for value.[97]

Where, in an action to enforce an agreement by the defendant
to give a bill of sale of sundry chattels, an interim receiver of the

[91] *Re Pearce* [1919] 1 K.B. 354.

[92] *Re Gershon and Levy* [1915] 2 K.B. 527, 532; as to effect of a Scottish bankruptcy, see Bankruptcy (Scotland) Act 1913, and *Singer* v. *Fry* (1915) 113 L.T. 552.

[93] *Croshaw* v. *Lyndhurst Ship Co.* [1897] 2 Ch. 154; *Re Lough Neagh Ship Co.*
[1896] 1 I.R. 29.

[94] *Norburn* v. *Norburn* [1894] 1 Q.B. 448; see p. 38, *ante.*

[95] *Re Bond* [1911] 2 K.B. 988; nothing had in fact come into the hands of the
receiver; the court in bankruptcy may inquire whether the receivership order prevented payment of the debt: *ibid.*

[96] *Sturges* v. *Warwick* (1913) 30 T.L.R. 112; see r. 1 as to procedure.

[97] *Hosack* v. *Robins* (*No.* 2) [1918] 2 Ch. 339, a case of a charging order. *Cf. Re
Fox* [1940] N.I. 42. Where the claim of the trustee is made against the assets of a
deceased bankrupt the claim may be defeated by an order for administration in
bankruptcy under Bankruptcy Act 1914, s. 130, the trustee having then only a right
of proof: see Bankruptcy (Amendment) Act 1926, s. 3. Such an order may now be
obtained after judgment in an administration action.

chattels was appointed and took possession, and very soon afterwards the defendant became bankrupt, it was held that the possession of the receiver had taken the chattels out of the order and disposition of the bankrupt at the time of his bankruptcy.[98] But the appointment of a receiver of the book debts of a trader who is afterwards adjudicated bankrupt does not take them out of the order and disposition of the bankrupt, unless the appointment is followed by notice to the debtors before the bankruptcy.[99]

In this connection it is to be observed that by section 43 of the Bankruptcy Act 1914, an assignment, or charge by a trader or person engaged in business on present or future book debts, except debts due from specified debtors, or growing due under specified contracts, or debts included in a bona fide transfer of a business for value, or on an assignment of assets for the benefit of creditors, is void against the trustee in bankruptcy unless registered as a bill of sale.

Since the receiver is not an agent of any party but an officer of the court, a receiver appointed in a partnership action is not a person having " the control or management of the partnership business," upon whom a bankruptcy notice can be served by a creditor of the firm.[1]

Hire-purchase agreement. An ordinary hire-purchase agreement in respect of machinery affixed to the land confers an equitable interest in the land on the hirers-out in priority to the interests of subsequent equitable incumbrancers, such as debenture holders, and entitles them to enter and remove the thing hired after the appointment of a receiver, on leave being obtained.[2]

To whom money in the hands of a receiver belongs on dismissal of action. When money comes into the hands of a receiver appointed in a foreclosure action, and no particular direction has been given

---

[98] *Taylor* v. *Eckersley* (1876) 5 Ch.D. 741.

[99] *Rutter* v. *Everett* [1895] 2 Ch. 872. In *Re Neal* [1914] 2 Ch. 910 Horridge J. expressed disagreement with the dictum of Stirling J. in *Rutter* v. *Everett, supra,* to the effect that, if bankruptcy supervened before notice could reasonably be given, the debts would not be in the order and disposition of the bankrupt, the former judge considering that the assignee of the debt might well have given the notice before the application for a receiver; but this would not apply to an equitable chargee.

[1] *Re Flowers & Co.* [1897] 1 Q.B. 14; and see *Boehm* v. *Goodall* [1911] 1 Ch. 155; *ante,* p. 129.

[2] *Re Morrison, Jones and Taylor Ltd.* [1914] 1 Ch. 50; as to property in chattels, see *Whiteley Ltd.* v. *Hilt* [1918] 2 Ch. 808. See also as to effect of transactions relating to hire-purchase agreements, *Re George Inglefield Ltd.* [1933] Ch. 1; *Transport and General Credit Co.* v. *Morgan* [1939] Ch. 531.

for its application, it belongs prima facie to the plaintiff, who, accordingly, has a right to receive it, in the event of and upon the dismissal of the action.[3] An order for payment of money out of court may be made after the dismissal of an action.[4]

Interpleader. A receiver cannot be compelled to interplead on the ground that his appointment is improper: he can appear for the purpose of asserting his right, and denying the right of any court other than that which appointed him to interfere with his possession.[5]

Charging order. The appointment of a receiver and manager does not necessarily amount to such a preservation of property as to entitle the solicitor to a charging order for his costs; for instance, where the attack, from which the property was preserved, was that of the party whose solicitor asks for the charging order.[6] The solicitor for a plaintiff in a partnership action is, prima facie, entitled to a charging order.[7] In an Irish case the solicitor for a judgment creditor, who had been appointed receiver by way of equitable execution, over so much of a sum due to the defendant as would satisfy the debt and costs, was held entitled to a charge for costs over the amount payable to the judgment creditor.[8]

If a party changes his solicitor in the course of an action in which a receiver has been appointed, the former solicitor cannot assert as against the receiver an unlimited lien.[9]

Persons with paramount rights. If persons with paramount rights, who are not parties to the action, are actually in possession of those rights, the appointment of a receiver does not prejudice them in the enjoyment of those rights.[10] But if they are not actually in possession, then, after a receiver has been appointed, they must come to the court for leave to exercise those rights, in which case their application cannot be refused.[11]

---

[3] *Paynter* v. *Carew* (1854) 18 Jur. 417; but the order should specifically deal with its application.

[4] *Wright* v. *Mitchell* (1811) 18 Ves. 292.

[5] See *Russell* v. *East Anglian Ry.* (1850) 3 Mac. & G. 104, 115, 122, 123.

[6] *Wingfield* v. *Wingfield* [1919] 1 Ch. 462; *secus* where there is collusion, *ibid.* at p. 472.

[7] *Post,* p. 149.

[8] *Duff* v. *Tuite* [1914] 2 I.R. 31: but only after completion of the order, *Wingfield* v. *Wingfield, supra.*

[9] *Dessau* v. *Peters, Rushton & Co.* [1922] 1 Ch. 1, 5, *q.v.* for form of order.

[10] *Evelyn* v. *Lewis* (1844) 3 Hare 472.

[11] See *Re Metropolitan Amalgamated Estates* [1912] 2 Ch. 497.

Receiver for puisne incumbrancer. Thus if a puisne incumbrancer obtains the appointment of a receiver in an action to which a prior mortgagee is not a party, and such prior mortgagee is not actually in possession at the date of the order, the receiver can give a good discharge for rents accrued due, until service by the prior mortgagee of notice of motion for liberty to take possession by himself or a receiver [12]; it makes no difference that the prior mortgagee has previous to the order appointed a receiver who has never given notice to the tenants.[13] The prior mortgagee is entitled to rents paid or accruing after the date of the service of his notice of motion for liberty to take possession.[13] When leave is required under the Reserve and Auxiliary Forces, etc., Act 1951, the right of the prior incumbrancer to the rents dates from service of the originating summons asking for leave.[14]

If the order made on the application of the puisne incumbrancer expressly reserves the rights of prior mortgagees, a prior mortgagee may, without application to the court, give notice to the tenants to pay their rents to him,[15] and a tenant paying to him in obedience to such notice is not guilty of contempt of court and can set up the payment against the receiver. The order appointing a receiver should expressly preserve the rights of prior incumbrancers, but if it does not, the receiver cannot be displaced at the instance of a prior incumbrancer without application to the court, nor is the prior incumbrancer entitled to rents received by the receiver before the date of the application for leave.[16] Thus notice by a mortgagee, not a party, to tenants to pay their rents to him, was held ineffective to give him any title to those rents against the receiver and the parties to the action in a case where the order appointing the receiver did not preserve the rights of mortgagees.[17] For the appointment of a receiver is for the benefit of mortgagees only so far as they avail themselves of it.[18] So if a mortgagee

---

[12] *Thomas* v. *Brigstocke* (1827) 4 Russ. 64; *Preston* v. *Tunbridge Wells Opera House* [1903] 2 Ch. 323, 325. As to dates in this report, see case next cited, p. 501 of report.

[13] *Re Metropolitan Amalgamated Estates* [1912] 2 Ch. 497.

[14] *Re Belbridge Property Trust* [1941] Ch. 304, a decision under the Courts (Emergency Powers) Act 1939.

[15] *Underhay* v. *Read* (1887) 20 Q.B.D. 209: this case appears to cover the query raised in *Re Metropolitan Amalgamated Estates* [1912] 2 Ch. 497 as to the effect of such a reservation. [16] See *Re Metropolitan Amalgamated Estates, supra.*

[17] The suit was for establishing the will of the mortgagor: *Thomas* v. *Brigstocke*, 4 Russ. 65.

[18] *Gresley* v. *Adderley* (1818) 1 Sw. 579; *Salt* v. *Lord Donegal* (1835) Ll. & G. temp.Sug. 91; *Penney* v. *Todd* (1878) 26 W.R. 502; [1878] W.N. 71. *Cf. Piddock* v. *Boultbee* (1867) 16 L.T. 837.

claiming under a title paramount to that under which the receiver has been appointed suffers the receiver to pay away the surplus rents to the beneficial owner, or to apply them for purposes other than the satisfaction of his security, he is not entitled to a retrospective account of rents and profits.[19] Money in the hands of a receiver is not, as in the case of a sequestrator, "*in custodia legis.*"[20]

Though a receiver appointed by an equitable mortgagee is entitled to rents as against a person obtaining a garnishee order, the equitable mortgagee himself obtains no priority by giving notice to tenants to pay their rents to him, nor by appointing a receiver who gives no notice to tenants.[21]

Where a receiver is appointed over an estate, incumbrancers who are not parties may or may not avail themselves of an order appointing a receiver by applying to him. If they apply to him, they will be paid their interest, or, if he refuses or neglects to pay them, they may complain to the court of such neglect or refusal; but if they omit to apply for the interest, it is to be presumed that they are satisfied with the security they have both for interest and also for principal. The court does not enforce payment upon them, nor does it set apart any portion of any rents and profits receivable by the receiver to answer unclaimed interest. The balance is paid in by him, and is carried to the credit of the action without any previous inquiry whether all incumbrancers have or have not been paid their interest.[22] A direction given by the court to the receiver, to keep down the interest on incumbrances, does not have the effect of an appropriation of any rents and profits receivable by him to that specific purpose. It is given partly in justice to the incumbrancers, that they may not be injured by the act of the court in taking possession of rents and profits to which they had a right to resort for payment of their interest, and partly for the benefit of the estate itself, lest the incumbrancers, having their interest stopped, might be induced to take proceedings injurious to those who stand behind them.[23]

---

[19] *Gresley* v. *Adderley* (1818) 1 Sw. 579; *Thomas* v. *Brigstocke* (1827) 4 Russ. 64; *Flight* v. *Camac* (1856) 4 W.R. 664.
[20] *Re Hoare* [1892] 3 Ch. 94; not following. *Delaney* v. *Mansfield* (1825) 1 Hog. 235.
[21] *Vacuum Oil Co.* v. *Ellis* [1914] 1 K.B. 693. But now a second mortgagee may have, and usually has, a legal estate and can give an effective notice to tenants.
[22] *Bertie* v. *Lord Abingdon* (1817) 3 Mer. 567; *Penney* v. *Todd* (1878) 26 W.R.502; [1878] W.N. 71. *Cf. Piddock* v. *Boultbee* (1867) 16 L.T. 837.
[23] *Bertie* v. *Lord Abingdon* (1817) 3 Mer. 567, see, too, *Flight* v. *Camac* (1856) 4 W.R. 664. *Cf. Piddock* v. *Boultbee* (1867) 16 L.T. 837.

Where a receiver has been appointed under an order directing interest on prior incumbrances to be kept down and has received rents with the knowledge of the first mortgagee, that mortgagee, upon afterwards taking possession, is entitled only to the rents in the receiver's hands, after deduction of the receiver's remuneration and expenses.[24]

Interference with the possession of a receiver. When the court has appointed a receiver and the receiver is in possession, his possession is the possession of the court, and may not be disturbed without its leave.[25] If anyone, whoever he be, disturb the possession of the receiver, the court holds that person guilty of contempt of court, and liable to be imprisoned for the contempt.[26] The court will not allow the possession of its receiver to be interfered with or disturbed by anyone, whether claiming by title paramount to or under the right which the receiver was appointed to protect.[27] Libellous statements relating to a business carried on by a receiver and manager are a contempt and may be punished by committal.[28] But unless the receiver comes with clean hands he will not be granted an injunction to restrain any interference with him, for instance, by distress.[29] A man who thinks he has a right paramount to that of the receiver must, before he presumes to take any step of his own motion, apply to the court for leave to assert his right.[30] If the receiver has done anything wrong, the party who has suffered the wrong must apply to the court which appointed the

---

[24] *Davy* v. *Price* [1883] W.N. 226.

[25] *Angel* v. *Smith* (1804) 9 Ves. 335; *Aston* v. *Heron* (1834) 2 My. & K. 391; *Ames* v. *Birkenhead Docks* (1855) 20 Beav. 353; *Defries* v. *Creed* (1865) 34 L.J.Ch. 607. But *cf. Bell* v. *Spereman* (1726) Sel.Cas.Ch. 59.

[26] *Fripp* v. *Bridgewater Canal Co.* (1855) 3 W.R. 356; *Lane* v. *Sterne* (1862) 3 Giff. 629; *Ex p. Hayward* [1881] W.N. 115. See, too, *Dixon* v. *Dixon* [1904] 1 Ch. 161, where an injunction restraining interference with a receiver and manager was applied for and granted. As to form of order for committal for obstructing a receiver, see Seton (7th ed.), p. 454.

[27] *Evelyn* v. *Lewis* (1844) 3 Hare 475; *Russell* v. *East Anglian Ry.* (1850) 3 Mac. & G. 104, 114.

[28] *Helmore* v. *Smith* (1887) 35 Ch.D. 449. The contempt occasioned by abuse of plaintiff in an action in which a receiver is appointed is of a different nature and is due to the fact that his evidence may be affected: see *Re W. Thomas Shipping Co.* [1930] 2 Ch. 368.

[29] *Jarvis* v. *Islington Borough Council* (1909) 73 J.P.J. 323, where the court refused to restrain a distress to recover a fine levied on a company (over the assets of which a receiver had been appointed) for selling adulterated milk, where the offence had been committed by the receiver himself.

[30] *Ibid.*; *Hawkins* v. *Gathercole* (1852) 1 Drew. 12; *Randfield* v. *Randfield* (1860) 1 Dr. & Sm. 314; *Ex p. Cochrane* (1875) L.R. 20 Eq. 282; *Re Botibol* [1947] 1 All E.R. 26; and cases cited in note 26, *supra*.

receiver, and he will get full justice done.[31] But where a claim
cannot be made in the original action,[32] or in any other case
where it is convenient to bring a separate action against the
receiver, leave to bring an action must first be obtained from the
court.[33] In a case in which an action in the Queen's Bench Division
was threatened by the owner of certain plant against a receiver
appointed in a debenture holder's action to enforce a claim in
respect of the user by the receiver of such plant, the court, upon
motion in the debenture holder's action, restrained any proceedings
otherwise than by way of claim therein.[34] And a receiver appointed
to get in property, part of which he finds in the possession of
another receiver, ought not to take proceedings to deprive the
latter of such possession without a direction from the court.[35]

It is not competent for anyone to interfere with the possession
of a receiver on the ground that the order appointing him ought
not to have been made: for persons who feel aggrieved by an
order of the court may question its validity in proper proceedings,
but while it lasts it must be obeyed.[36]

The court requires and insists that application be made to take
possession of any property of which its receiver has taken, or is
directed to take, possession. The rule is not confined to property
actually in the hands of a receiver; for the court will not permit
anyone, without its sanction and authority, to intercept or prevent
payment to the receiver of any property within the territorial
jurisdiction of the court which he has been appointed to receive,
although it may not be actually in his hands.[37]

Foreign property. Where, however, the court appoints a receiver
over property out of the jurisdiction, the receiver is not put in
possession of such foreign property by the mere order of the
court.[38] Something further has to be done, and, until that has
been done in accordance with the foreign law, any person, not a
party to the action, who takes proceedings in the foreign country

---

[31] *Ex p. Day* (1883) 48 L.T. 912; *L. P. Arthur (Insurance) Ltd.* v. *Sisson* [1966] 1
W.L.R. 1384; and p. 159, *post.*

[32] A claim for an injunction against nuisance would be an example.

[33] *Re Botibol* [1947] 1 All E.R. 26.

[34] *Re Maidstone Palace of Varieties* [1909] 2 Ch. 283.

[35] *Ward* v. *Swift* (1848) 6 Hare 309; *Ex p. Cochrane* (1875) L.R. 20 Eq. 282.

[36] *Russell* v. *East Anglian Ry.* (1850) 3 Mac. & G. 104, 117.

[37] *Ames* v. *Birkenhead Docks* (1855) 20 Beav. 353.

[38] See *Re Huinac Copper Mines* [1910] W.N. 218. *Cf.* property in any part of the
U.K. comprised in a floating charge given by a company: see pp. 162 and 313, *post.*

for the purpose of establishing a claim upon the foreign property, is not guilty of a contempt of court, on the ground of interference with the receiver's possession or otherwise. And, in reference to such proceedings, no distinction can be drawn between a foreigner and a British subject.[39] In this connection it is to be observed that the English court will recognise the validity of an equitable charge on foreign property though such charge is not enforceable in the courts of that country.[40]

Acts of interference. Any deliberate act, calculated to destroy property under the management of the court by means of a receiver and manager, is an interference with the receiver, although it may not induce the breaking of any contract. The object of the court is to prevent any undue interference with the administration of justice, and when anyone, whether a partner in a business, a party to the litigation, or a stranger, interferes with an officer of the court, the court will protect that officer.[41]

Receiver not in actual possession. The rule, however, that the possession of a receiver may not be disturbed without leave, does not apply, so far at least as third persons are concerned, until a receiver has been actually appointed, and is in actual possession. Until the appointment has been perfected, and the receiver is actually in possession, a creditor is not debarred from proceeding to execution.[42] An execution creditor may, therefore, seize chattels after an order has been made appointing a receiver on his giving security, but before the security has been given or possession taken.[43] In the case of equitable execution or the appointment of a receiver for debenture holders, the order should if possible be obtained in a form to operate from its date.

Property must be specified. There is no disturbance of a receiver unless the order for the appointment states, on the face of it, the property over which the receiver is appointed, so as to enable the property to be identified.[44]

---

[39] *Re Maudslay, Sons & Field* [1900] 1 Ch. 602, 611.

[40] *Re Anchor Line* [1937] Ch. 483. It can be enforced against property brought within the jurisdiction.

[41] *Per* Swinfen Eady J. in *Dixon* v. *Dixon* [1904] 1 Ch. 161, 163. As to interference with business carried on by a receiver and manager, see p. 145, *ante*, n. 26.

[42] *Defries* v. *Creed* (1865) 34 L.J.Ch. 607; *Edwards* v. *Edwards* (1876) 2 Ch.D. 291.

[43] *Ex p. Evans* (1879) 13 Ch.D. 255, *per* James L.J.

[44] *Crow* v. *Wood* (1850) 13 Beav. 271; *ante*, p. 138.

Execution against shareholder-receiver. Nor, again, was there disturbance of a receiver in a case where, the chairman of a railway company having been appointed receiver, a debenture holder, who had recovered judgment against the company in respect of arrears of interest, applied, under section 36 of the Companies Clauses Consolidation Act 1845, for leave to issue execution against the chairman of the company to the extent of the money remaining due in respect of his shares; the money which would be reached by the execution in such a case being money in the hands of an individual shareholder, and not part of the undertaking or profits of the company, of which a receiver had been appointed.[45]

Receiver in administration action. The appointment of a receiver in an administration action does not prevent trustees, nor parties in whom the property has become vested on the statutory trusts,[46] from selling all or any part of the property without the leave of the court.[47] The same is the case as regards the power of a tenant for life, in whose favour an assent has been made, to sell under the Settled Land Act 1925.[48]

Receiver of life tenancy. Where a receiver had been appointed under the old law over the estate of a tenant for life, the remainder-man was entitled, on the death of the tenant for life, to go into possession without making any application to the court.[49] The special, or, where the land ceases to be settled land, the general, personal representatives who take the legal estates as trustees, would be in the same position; for the appointment would have been only over the equitable interest of the tenant for life.

Permission required for first step. To constitute disturbance of a receiver, it is not necessary that the person complained of should be about to turn the receiver out of possession. The court will not allow the first step to be taken by anyone in an action whether of ejectment[50] or otherwise[51] against a receiver

---

[45] *Re West Lancashire Ry.* [1890] W.N. 165; 63 L.T. 56.

[46] Under Law of Property Act 1925, Sched. I, Part IV.

[47] *Bernhardt* v. *Galsworthy* [1929] 1 Ch. 549; but after an order for administration of an estate or trust, the powers of the executors or trustees can only be exercised with the sanction of the court which may be given generally as to a class of transactions, *e.g.* the creation of tenancies: see *Re Furness* [1943] Ch. 415.

[48] *Ibid.* and *Cardigan* v. *Curzon-Howse* (1885) 30 Ch.D. 531, 538.

[49] *Britton* v. *M'Donnel* (1843) 5 Ir.Eq. 275; *Re Stack* (1862) 13 Ir.Ch. 213.

[50] *Hawkins* v. *Gathercole* (1852) 1 Drew. 12, 18.

[51] *Re Botibol* [1947] 1 All E.R. 26.

without an application having been first made to the court for permission to take it. So, a local authority cannot, without the leave of the court, distrain upon property in the hands of a receiver for money due to it.[52]

Charging order. The form and effect of a charging order obtained by creditors of a partnership after appointment of a receiver in a partnership action has already been discussed.[53] This does not override the right of the solicitor of the plaintiff in the partnership action to a charge for his costs,[54] but it creates a valid charge against the trustees in bankruptcy of the partners, unless the parties in whose favour it is made had notice of an available act of bankruptcy at the date of the order.[55]

Remedies of landlord. It has been already pointed out [56] that persons with paramount rights, unless actually in possession of them at the appointment, must, after a receiver has been appointed, apply to the court for leave to put them in force unless the order preserves their powers: this applies to cases where a receiver has been appointed over the estate of a tenant in possession. The appointment of a receiver as against the estate of a tenant does not affect the rights of the landlord, but he will not be permitted to exercise those rights without first obtaining the leave of the court. Before distraining he should come to the court and ask for authority to distrain, notwithstanding the appointment of a receiver [57]; he acquires no prior claim over other creditors to the proceeds of sale of chattels sold by the receiver after formal notice of his claim to rent.[58]

Similarly, where a partnership was trading in leasehold premises, the reversion to which was acquired by one partner personally, the fact that a receiver of the partnership assets had been appointed did not affect the right of the landlord partner to apply to the court for relief either by way of re-entry, or, if re-entry was refused, for

---

[52] See *Pegge* v. *Neath District Tramways Co.* [1895] 2 Ch. 508; *Reeve* v. *Medway Upper Navigation Co.* (1905) 21 T.L.R. 400: as to a person of unsound mind, see *Winkle* v. *Bailey* [1897] 1 Ch. 123.

[53] p. 40, *ante*.   [54] *Ridd* v. *Thorne* [1902] 2 Ch. 344, 348.

[55] See *Re Gershon and Levy* [1915] 2 K.B. 527, 530.

[56] *Ante*, pp. 143, 145.

[57] *Sutton* v. *Rees* (1863) 9 Jur.(N.S.) 456; see, too, *Walsh* v. *Walsh* (1839) 1 Ir.Eq. 209. Where, however, a receiver is placed over the estate of a superior landlord, and the lands are occupied by under-tenants, the intermediate tenant may distrain upon the occupiers for rent, without any order for the purpose: *Furlong on Landlord and Tenant*, p. 744.

[58] *Sutton* v. *Rees, supra*; see *Re J. W. Abbott & Co.* [1913] W.N. 284.

an order that the receiver should pay the rent.[59] In the event, the receiver was directed to give up possession. The court also held that the fiduciary position of the landlord as a partner did not raise any equity preventing him from exercising his rights as landlord to the full.[60]

So, again, where, after a mortgagee of leasehold land has obtained the appointment by the court of a receiver, the lessor brings an action against the lessee and obtains judgment for recovery of the land, he (the lessor) cannot proceed to enforce the judgment, as against the receiver, by writ of possession, without first getting the leave of the court to do so.[61]

Application for leave to proceed. Persons whose rights are interfered with by having a receiver put in their way may, on making a proper application to the court, obtain all that they can justly require.[62] The court will always take care to give to a party, who applies in a regular manner, protection of his rights, and will even assist him in asserting his rights and having the benefit of them,[63] though the court does not profess to cure every inconvenience arising from its action in appointing a receiver.[64] An instance is the method adopted to enable creditors of a partnership business to obtain payment from the receiver without legal execution, which is discussed on another page.[65]

The proper course for a person to adopt who claims a right paramount to that of the receiver, or rather to that of the party who obtained the receiver, and is prejudiced by having the receiver put in his way, is to apply to the court for leave to proceed,[66] notwithstanding the possession of the receiver, or to come in and be examined *pro interesse suo*.[67] The former course is, usually,

---

[59] *Brenner* v. *Rose* [1973] 1 W.L.R. 443; see also *Hand* v. *Blow* [1901] 2 Ch. 721, 737.

[60] *Brenner* v. *Rose, supra.*

[61] *Morris* v. *Baker* (1903) 73 L.J.Ch. 143. *Cf. Johns* v. *Pink* [1900] 1 Ch. 296; *post,* p. 289.

[62] *Russell* v. *East Anglian Ry.* (1850) 3 Mac. & G. 104, 117.

[63] *Evelyn* v. *Lewis* (1844) 3 Hare 475; *Hawkins* v. *Gathercole* (1852) 1 Drew. 12; *Ex p. Cochrane* (1875) L.R. 20 Eq. 282; *Forster* v. *Manchester and Milford Ry.* (1880) 49 L.J.Ch. 454; [1880] W.N. 63; and see *Re Septimus Parsonage Co.* (1901) 17 T.L.R. 420, where possession was given to trustees for debenture holders, though an action was pending by first debenture holders in which the appointment of a receiver was claimed.

[64] *Hand* v. *Blow* [1901] 2 Ch. 721, 735; see as to rights of lessors, *post,* p. 191.

[65] *Ante,* pp. 40, 149.

[66] See also p. 143 as to incumbrancers.

[67] *Angel* v. *Smith* (1804) 9 Ves. 335; *Russell* v. *East Anglian Ry.* (1850) 3 Mac. & G. 117; *Ex p. Cochrane* (1875) L.R. 20 Eq. 282. In a case where a receiver had been

preferable. The application may be made, as a rule, on summons [68] with notice,[69] or on motion, and may be framed in the alternative, that the receiver may pay the amount of the claimant's demand, or that the latter may be allowed to proceed.[70] The application must be made in the action in which the receiver was appointed, and not, as a rule, in a fresh action against the person who obtained his appointment.[71] In some cases, however, a fresh action may be advisable or even necessary.[72]

Action commenced without leave. If a party who has, without the leave of the court, instituted proceedings at law to recover lands in the possession of a receiver, the court may allow him to continue the action [73]: and may direct an inquiry whether it would be for the benefit of the parties interested that the receiver should defend the ejectment, and charge the expenses in his accounts.[74] Leave may be refused to continue the action.[75]

The court refused to restrain a person from prosecuting an action in a Scottish court, which amounted to interference with a receiver (although it had jurisdiction to do so), where the receiver had been added as a defendant in the Scottish action and his rights and those of the plaintiff could most conveniently be determined in that action.[76]

Inquiry as to interest. Where a person has brought an action against a receiver, or has otherwise interfered with his possession

---

appointed in a suit instituted by incumbrancers, it was held that a judgment creditor might file a bill against the owner and the receiver to have his debt paid out of the surplus; and that the incumbrancers in the former suit need not be made parties to the latter: *Lewis* v. *Lord Zouche* (1828) 2 Sim. 388; but now a garnishee order may be obtained: *post*, p. 153.

[68] *Richards* v. *Richards* (1859) John. 255; *cf. O'Hagan* v. *North Wingfield Colliery Co.* (1882) 26 S.J. 671.

[69] As to form of notice of motion or summons, see Atkin's *Court Forms* (2nd ed.), Vol. 33, p. 209; for form for examination *pro interesse suo*, see Daniell's *Chancery Forms* (7th ed.), p. 778.

[70] *Brooks* v. *Greathed* (1820) 1 J. & W. 178; *Potts* v. *Warwick and Birmingham Canal Co.* (1853) Kay 142; *Russell* v. *East Anglian Ry.* (1850) 3 Mac. & G. 104.

[71] *Searle* v. *Choat* (1884) 25 Ch.D. 723; see, too, *Ames* v. *Richards* (1905) 40 L.J.N.C. 66, where the application (which failed) was made by motion. The receiver is seldom a necessary party: see *Smith* v. *Effingham* (1839) 2 Beav. 232; (1843) 7 Beav. 357.

[72] See p. 31, *ante.*

[73] *Gowar* v. *Bennett* (1847) 9 L.T. 310; see *Aston* v. *Heron* (1834) 2 My. & K. 397.

[74] *Anon.* (1801) 6 Ves. 287.

[75] See *Lees* v. *Waring* (1825) 1 Hog. 216; *cf. Townsend* v. *Somerville* (1824) 1 Hog. 100.

[76] *Re Derwent Rolling Mills* (1905) 21 T.L.R. 81, 701.

without the leave of the court, the order restraining the irregular act may also give leave, or direct, that the author of it be examined *pro interesse suo.*[77]

The inquiry as to interest is conducted in the same manner as that in which it would be conducted if the property were in the possession of sequestrators under a commission of sequestration.[78] If the court, on examining the title, is satisfied that the right of the claimant is clear, it will at once decide the matter in his favour, without directing an inquiry, and order the receiver to pay him what he claims,[79] or give the claimant leave to enforce his legal remedy, notwithstanding the possession of the receiver.[80] Thus, leave was given by the Court of Chancery to a judgment creditor, on his application, to issue legal execution against property in the possession of a receiver.[81] So, also, where a person wishes to distrain on property in the possession of a receiver, the court, on being satisfied that the legal right of distress is paramount to the title of the party for whose benefit the receiver was appointed, will allow the distress to be made, either for rent [82] or for rates or other money due to a local authority,[83] or for money due to a gas board, for which it has obtained a distress warrant under its statutory power.[84] Leave will be given to distrain, notwithstanding the possession of a receiver, for a statutory penalty for breach of a condition in the very constitution of a public company, for instance, neglect by a tramway company to keep rails in repair [85]; but leave was refused to distrain for a penalty under the Highway

---

[77] See *Johnes* v. *Claughton* (1822) Jac. 573.

[78] Daniell's *Chancery Practice* (8th ed.), 801.

[79] *Dixon* v. *Smith* (1818) 1 Sw. 457; *Russell* v. *East Anglian Ry.* (1850) 3 Mac. & G. 104; *Randfield* v. *Randfield*, (1860) 1 Dr. & Sm. 314, *per* Kindersley V.-C.; see, too, *Ex p. Thurgood* (1868) 18 L.T. 18, where damages for injuries sustained by a collision had been recovered against a railway company over which a receiver had been appointed.

[80] Costs will usually be allowed to a successful applicant: *Eyton* v. *Denbigh, etc., Ry.* (1868) L.R. 6 Eq. 14, 488; see *Walsh* v. *Walsh* (1839) 1 Ir.Eq. 209.

[81] *Gooch* v. *Haworth* (1841) 3 Beav. 428; *Potts* v. *Warwick and Birmingham Canal Co.* (1853) Kay 142.

[82] *Cramer* v. *Griffith*, 3 Ir.Eq. 232; *Russell* v. *East Anglian Ry.* (1850) 3 Mac. & G. 104; *Sutton* v. *Rees* (1863) 9 Jur.(N.S.) 456. The right of a landlord to distrain for rent, after the appointment of a receiver in bankruptcy, is limited by the Bankruptcy Act 1914, s. 35, to six months' rent. See *Ex p. Cochrane* (1875) L.R. 20 Eq. 282.

[83] *Pegge* v. *Neath District Tramways Co.* [1895] 2 Ch. 508; and see *Winkle* v. *Bailey* [1897] 1 Ch. 123.

[84] *Re Adolphe Crosbie Ltd.* (1910) 74 J.P. 25.

[85] *Pegge* v. *Neath District Tramways Co.* [1895] 2 Ch. 508; in this case the mortgage did not include the chattels and a receiver ought not to have been appointed over them; see *Reeve* v. *Medway Upper Navigation Co.* (1905) 21 T.L.R. 400.

Acts for failure to pay instalments to a local authority which by agreement had taken over roads which the company was under a statutory liability to repair.[86] Accordingly, where a company's goods had been mortgaged for more than their value to debenture holders, who brought an action to enforce their rights and obtained the appointment of a receiver, and afterwards the company was ordered to be wound up, leave was given to the landlord of the house in which the goods were to distrain, notwithstanding the appointment of the receiver, and notwithstanding the winding-up order, on the ground that, for all practical purposes, the goods were not the goods of the company but of the debenture holders, as against whom the landlord was entitled to distrain.[87] Again, a judgment creditor may obtain a garnishee order, attaching money payable to the judgment debtor which is in the hands of a receiver,[88] but only such money as is actually in his hands when the order is obtained,[89] and not, it seems, money which has by an order been directed to be paid to the judgment debtor.[90] So, where a rent-charge created by a railway company under the Lands Clauses Consolidation Act 1845 had been reserved to a landowner, the court gave him liberty to distrain, notwithstanding that a receiver of the tools of the company had been appointed, in a suit instituted by the owner of a similar rentcharge on behalf of himself and all other owners of similar rentcharges who should come in and contribute to the expenses of the suit.[91] So also, in a case where it was held that a receiver ought not to have been appointed, leave was given to an execution creditor to levy, notwithstanding the appointment.[92]

Practice in Queen's Bench Division. The procedure in equitable

---

[86] *Reeve* v. *Medway Upper Navigation Co., supra.*

[87] *Ex p. Purssell* (1887) 34 Ch.D. 646, 660, 662. See, too, *Re Harpur's Cycle Fittings Co.* [1900] 2 Ch. 731, 734, in which case no receiver had been appointed, but Wright J. considered that that fact made no difference; and distinguished *Re British Fuller's Earth Co.* (1901) 17 T.L.R. 232 (followed in *Re Mayfair, etc., Property Trust* (1945) 174 L.T. 1), where overseers were held to be not entitled to an order directing the receiver appointed in a debenture holder's action to pay to them the amount of a rate out of money in his hands.

[88] *Re Cowan's Estate* (1880) 14 Ch.D. 638.

[89] See *Webb* v. *Stenton* (1883) 11 Q.B.D. 518, criticising some of the dicta in *Re Cowan's Estate, supra.*

[90] *De Winton* v. *Mayor of Brecon* (1859) 28 Beav. 203.

[91] *Eyton* v. *Denbigh, etc., Ry* (1868) L.R. 6 Eq. 14, 488; 16 W.R. 928; *Forster* v. *Manchester and Milford Ry.* (1880) 49 L.J.Ch. 454; [1880] W.N. 63.

[92] *Russell* v. *East Anglian Ry.* (1850) 3 Mac. & G. 104; see *Fowler* v. *Haynes* (1863) 2 N.R. 156.

execution being founded on the equitable and not the common law jurisdiction of the court, the practice in the Queen's Bench Division follows that in the Chancery Division as nearly as circumstances will admit. Thus, where a prior incumbrancer applied to have an order appointing a receiver discharged, and for consequent relief, numerous affidavits were filed upon the application, and the matter was referred to a master of the Queen's Bench Division to report. Upon an application to set aside or vary the report, it was held that the court was bound to consider the objections to the report, and to go into the evidence, and to deal with the report as upon a motion to vary the certificate of a chief clerk [93] in the Chancery Division.[94]

In cases where the court is not satisfied that a receiver ought to have been appointed, the court may, that the execution creditor may not suffer loss by the possession of the receiver, order that the receiver keep within the bailiwick for a certain period sufficient property to answer the demand. Or, in such a case, the court may make an order allowing the creditor to levy, unless the amount of his demand be paid into court to the credit of the action within a week from service of the order, the receiver to be at liberty to pay the amount in, and the money to remain in court subject to further order.[95]

If incumbrancers come in for examination *pro interesse suo* and upon inquiry their claim is made out, they are entitled to have rents and profits received and to be received by the receiver applied in payment of the costs of the application, and then of their incumbrances.[96]

If there is a doubtful question relating to land, and it is purely a matter of title, the court will give the claimant leave to bring ejectment, taking care, however, to protect the possession by giving proper directions.[97] It is not the course of the court, unless it is perfectly clear that there is no foundation for the claim, to refuse leave to try a right which is claimed against its receiver.[98]

In an old case, where a prior incumbrancer had delayed overlong in pursuing his remedies, the Court of Chancery refused his

---

[93] Now a master.
[94] *Walmesley* v. *Mundy* (1884) 13 Q.B.D. 807.
[95] *Russell* v. *East Anglian Ry.* (1850) 3 Mac. & G. 104, 151, 153.
[96] *Walker* v. *Bell* (1816) 2 Madd. 21; *Tatham* v. *Parker* (1853) 1 Sm. & G. 506.
[97] *Empringham* v. *Short* (1844) 3 Hare 470.
[98] *Randfield* v. *Randfield* (1861) 3 De G.F. & J. 772; *Lane* v. *Capsey* [1891] 3 Ch. 411.

application that a receiver, who had been appointed at the instance of a second incumbrancer, should apply the rents according to their priorities; but leave was given to bring ejectment. The ground of the decision was that the prior incumbrancer had no right to come by petition for relief which he had sought in a suit previously commenced by him, but not proceeded with. No costs were given against the prior incumbrancer.[99]

Committal, etc. for disturbance of receiver. A person who disturbs or interferes with the possession of a receiver is guilty of a contempt of court, and is liable to be committed.[1] In extreme or aggravated cases, the court will, for the purpose of vindicating its authority, order a committal[2]; but it does not ordinarily punish by actual committal.[3] The court is generally satisfied with ordering the party in contempt to pay the costs and expenses occasioned by his improper conduct, and also the costs of the application to commit.[4] In some cases an injunction restraining the interference may be an appropriate and sufficient remedy.[5] Thus, where the contempt consists in entering upon land in the possession of a receiver or in bringing an action against a receiver or against a person over whose property a receiver has been appointed, the course of the court is to grant an injunction, restraining the party in contempt from trespassing or prosecuting the action, as the case may be, at the same time ordering him to pay the costs of the application to commit.[6] In such a case, whether the person bringing an action did or did not know that a receiver had been appointed, or however clear his right may be, the court will restrain the prosecution of the action if it was brought without leave.[7] Where the agents of the receiver in the

---

[99] *Brooks* v. *Greathed* (1820) 1 Jac. & W. 178. See also *Wastell* v. *Leslie* (1846) 15 Sim. 453.

[1] *Ante*, pp. 145 *et seq.*

[2] *Ante*, p. 145; *Broad* v. *Wickham* (1831) 4 Sim. 511 (application to commit a person for taking forcible possession against a receiver).

[3] For form of order to commit for interference with a receiver in lunacy, see *Re Seaton* [1928] W.N. 307.

[4] *Russell* v. *East Anglian Ry.* (1850) 3 Mac. & G. 104; *Hawkins* v. *Gathercole* (1852) 1 Drew. 12. A partner who had got in debts adversely to the receiver was ordered within a week to make an affidavit of the amount, and to pay that amount to the receiver, and in default to be committed: *Parker* v. *Pocock* (1874) 30 L.T. 458.

[5] *e.g. Dixon* v. *Dixon* [1904] 1 Ch. 161.

[6] *Johns* v. *Claughton* (1822) Jac. 573; *Aston* v. *Heron* (1834) 2 My. & K. 390; *Tink* v. *Rundle* (1847) 10 Beav. 318; *Evelyn* v. *Lewis* (1844) 3 Hare 473; *Ames* v. *Birkenhead Docks* (1855) 20 Beav. 354; *Bayly* v. *Went* [1884] W.N. 197; 51 L.T. 765.

[7] *Evelyn* v. *Lewis* (1844) 3 Hare 473.

cause, acting upon leave given by the court, took forcible posses-sion of a house occupied by a servant of one of the defendants, an order was made restraining that defendant from prosecuting an indictment against the agents.[8] An action, however, against a person who professes to have acted under the authority of a receiver, will not be restrained unless it is clear that he has really been acting under that authority.[9]

A motion to commit a person for disturbing the possession of a receiver is improper, if made long after the act complained of, and not for the protection of the receiver's possession, but in order indirectly to compel payment of expenses, after settlement of the question relating to the possession. The proper course is to make directly any application for the payment of expenses or costs which may be warranted by the circumstances.[10]

Sheriff may not disturb possession of a receiver. The court will not protect a sheriff who executes process after notice from a receiver that he is in possession.[11]

A sheriff who seizes goods in the possession of a receiver is guilty of a contempt of court,[12] and may be committed, even though the act is really the act of his under-sheriff, and there is no reason to infer that it is the personal act of the sheriff.[13] In a case, however, where an under-sheriff had seized goods in the possession of a receiver, the court, on the submission of the sheriff, abstained from committing him, but ordered him to withdraw from possession, and to pay the costs.[14]

Where a sheriff has taken property, part of which is claimed by a receiver, the latter will be directed to give a list of the property claimed by him to the sheriff, who will be ordered to withdraw from possession of the specified property.[15]

A sheriff may also be restrained, if necessary, from compelling a receiver to interplead, and may be ordered to pay the costs of proceedings for that purpose. If the execution creditor is before the court, he will be restrained from proceeding against the sheriff in relation to the property seized by him, or any property in the

---

[8] *Turner* v. *Turner* (1851) 15 Jur. 218.   [9] *Birch* v. *Oldis* (1837) Sausse & Sc. 146.
[10] *Ward* v. *Swift* (1851) 6 Hare 309.
[11] *Try* v. *Try* (1851) 13 Beav. 422; see, too, *Rock* v. *Cook* (1848) 2 Ph. 691, where the sheriff entered under a *fi. fa.* issued out of Chancery.
[12] *Lane* v. *Sterne* (1862) 3 Giff. 629.
[13] *Russell* v. *East Anglian Ry.* (1850) 3 Mac. & G. 104.
[14] *Russell* v. *East Anglian Ry.* (1850) 3 Mac. & G. 104, 119.
[15] *Willmer* v. *Kidd* (1853) Seton (7th ed.), p. 729.

possession of the receiver. If the execution creditor is not before
the court, this cannot be done, but the sheriff may come to the
court for protection, if necessary.[16]

The court may empower a claimant, who asserts a right against
a receiver, to abate an obstruction. In such a case, the proper
form of order is to give the claimant leave, notwithstanding the
receiver, to pursue any remedies, or do any acts, that he may
lawfully take or do to abate the obstruction.[17]

Person in the position of a receiver appointed abroad. Before the
English courts will recognise the status of a receiver appointed by a
foreign court, they must be satisfied, in accordance with the English
principles of conflict of laws, that the foreign court is one of
competent jurisdiction.[18] They must, therefore, first be satisfied
that there is a sufficient connection between the defendant and the
jurisdiction in which the foreign receiver was appointed. There will
be a sufficient connection if the defendant submitted to the
jurisdiction of the foreign court in the proceedings in which the
receiver was appointed.[19] But, if the defendant is a company, it is
not sufficient that one of its subsidiary companies with assets in
the foreign jurisdiction has appeared in the original action in an
attempt to have the original order set aside, and so submitted to
the jurisdiction.[20] It might, however, be sufficient if the defendant
company had itself been incorporated under the laws of the country
whose courts appointed the receiver, or of any state or territory
thereof [21]; or, perhaps, although more debatably, if it could be
demonstrated that, under the law of the country where it is in fact
incorporated, the title of the foreign receiver would be recognised.[22]
It might be sufficient if the defendant company had itself carried
on business in the foreign country, or that the seat of its central
management and control was located there.[23]

---

[16] *Russell* v. *East Anglian Ry.* (1850) 3 Mac. & G. 104, 120, 122.
[17] *Lane* v. *Capsey* [1891] 3 Ch. 411.
[18] *Schemmer* v. *Property Resources Ltd.* [1975] Ch. 273.
[19] See Dicey's *Conflict of Laws* (9th ed.), Rule 180 (First Case) pp. 993 *et seq.*;
Houlditch v. *Donegall* (1834) 2 Cl. & Fin. 470; *Schemmer* v. *Property Resources Ltd.*
[1975] Ch. 273 at p. 287F, *per* Goulding J.
[20] *Ibid.* at p. 287 F-G, *per* Goulding J.
[21] *Ibid.* at p. 287 G-H, *per* Goulding J.; *Macaulay* v. *Guaranty Trust Co. of New
York* (1927) 44 T.L.R. 99; *North Australian Territory Co.* v. *Goldborough Mort & Co.
Ltd.* (1889) 61 L.T. 716.
[22] *Schemmer* v. *Property Resources Ltd.* at p. 287H, *per* Goulding J.
[23] *Ibid.* at pp. 287–288, *per* Goulding J. *Cf.* Dicey, *op. cit.* Rule 180 (Fourth and
Fifth Cases).

In one case the Securities and Exchange Commission of the United States obtained in proceedings in the American courts the appointment of a receiver over the assets of a holding company. By a further order of the court, the receiver was authorised to take proceedings in the United Kingdom to have himself appointed receiver of the assets of a subsidiary company and its subsidiaries located in the United Kingdom. The receiver issued a writ against the defendant company, the subsidiary of the holding company, claiming the appointment of himself, or some other fit and proper person, as receiver, and suitable injunctions restraining the defendant and its subsidiary companies from parting with their liquid assets. The defendant subsidiary entered a conditional appearance to the writ, and moved for an order setting aside the order giving leave to serve outside the jurisdiction and staying all further proceedings in the action. The court, applying the above principles, granted the defendant company the relief it sought.[24]

If the appointment of the foreign receiver has been made by a court which, according to the principles of English conflict of laws is a court of competent jurisdiction, the court may either recognise his title directly, by allowing him to sue for the assets over which he has been appointed receiver in his own name, or indirectly, by constituting a subsidiary receivership.[25]

The court will also recognise the right of a person, with powers analogous to those of a receiver, appointed by a foreign court of competent jurisdiction over the property of a person resident abroad, to give receipts for dividends on shares in a British company [26] and to sue for a chose in action in his own name [27]: persons who unreasonably refuse to accept such receipts may be disallowed costs if an action is brought.[28] The curateur of a foreign bankrupt will be appointed receiver with power to sell immovables.[29]

Action against receiver. Nobody can bring an action against a receiver in his capacity as such without the leave of the court [30] and if such an action is brought without leave its further prosecution

---

[24] *Schemmer* v. *Property Resources Ltd.* [1975] Ch. 273.
[25] *Ibid.* at p. 287 E-F, *per* Goulding J.
[26] *Lepage* v. *San Paulo Coffee Estates Co.* [1917] W.N. 216 (*mandataire séquestre*).
[27] *Macaulay* v. *Guaranty Trust Co.* [1927] W.N. 308; 44 T.L.R. 99.
[28] *Pélégrin* v. *Coutts & Co.* [1915] 1 Ch. 696.
[29] *Re Kooperman* [1928] W.N. 101.
[30] *Re Maidstone Palace of Varieties Ltd.* [1909] 2 Ch. 283.

will be restrained.[31] In general, a party to an action in which the receiver was appointed may (like any other injured party) obtain any relief to which he is entitled against the receiver by applying in the action,[32] but there may be cases where on such application being made the court decides that the best course for disposing of the issue is for an action to be brought against the receiver. In such cases it will give leave for the action to be brought.[33] In a case in which, at the time when a receiver was appointed, by way of equitable execution, by the High Court, the debtor's property was legally, though not actually, in the possession of a receiver appointed by a county court having jurisdiction in bankruptcy, the equitable execution obtained by the judgment creditor was held to be ineffectual.[34]

A person who is not a party should apply by summons in the action for payment out of a fund in court or by the receiver personally of a debt due to him, where the receiver is personally liable for the debt and where it may be ultimately payable by subrogation out of the fund.[35]

Effect of Limitation Act. The appointment of a receiver in an action will not prevent the operation of the Limitation Act 1939 against a rightful owner who is out of possession and is not a party to the action,[36] nor will it interrupt the possession of a stranger, so as to prevent the statute from conferring a title on him.[37] Nor is a right to damages which has already accrued taken away by the appointment, by consent, of a receiver.[38]

Receiver not acting. Where a receiver had been appointed at the instance of an incumbrancer of a company, and no security

---

[31] *Ibid.*; and see n. 6, p. 155, *ante.*

[32] *Searle* v. *Choat* (1884) 25 Ch.D. 723. This applies to a receiver appointed in bankruptcy proceedings: see *Ex p. Cochrane* (1875) L.R. 20 Eq. 282; *Ex p. Day* (1883) 48 L.T. 912. See as to jurisdiction of High Court and county courts, Bankruptcy Act 1914, ss. 98, 99.

[33] *L. P. Arthur (Insurance) Ltd.* v. *Sisson* [1966] 1 W.L.R. 1384 explaining *Ex p. Day* (1883) 48 L.T. 912; [1883] W.N. 118.

[34] *Salt* v. *Cooper* (1880) 16 Ch.D. 544.

[35] *Re Ernest Hawkins & Co.* (1915) 31 T.L.R. 237: the application was premature as the receiver's account had not been taken. See also *Brocklebank* v. *E. London Ry.* (1879) 12 Ch.D. 839; *Re Rylands Glass Co.* (1905) 118 L.T.Jo. 87 (the report in 49 S.J. is not to be relied upon).

[36] *Harrison* v. *Duignan* (1842) 2 Dr. & War. 295. *Cf. Wrixon* v. *Vize* (1842) 3 Dr. & War. 123.

[37] *Groom* v. *Blake* (1858) 6 Ir.C.L. 401; 8 Ir.C.L. 432. As to payment by a receiver taking the demand out of the Limitation Act, see *post*, Chap. 7, p. 173.

[38] *Dreyfus* v. *Peruvian Guano Co.* (1889) 42 Ch.D. 66; [1892] A.C. 166.

was given and the receiver never acted, the action was stayed on the application of the official solicitor under Ord. 43, r. 7, on production of the company's consent.[39]

When sequestrators are in possession of land in question in an action, the appointment of a receiver of the rents and profits of the land will have the effect of discharging the sequestration.[40] Similarly, the appointment of a receiver in an action has been held to put an end to the power of a trustee appointed for the benefit of creditors to collect the rents.[41]

It is apprehended that if a receiver is appointed over the interest of a tenant for life under the Settled Land Acts, the latter can exercise his statutory powers without the leave of the court.[42]

COMPANIES

The general principles stated in the earlier part of this chapter relative to the possession of a receiver and the effect of the appointment are equally applicable to receivers of the undertaking and property of a company. This section deals only with principles and decisions peculiarly applicable to such last-mentioned receivers: the early part of the chapter should be consulted on any points not mentioned in this section.

Nature of floating charge. The appointment of a receiver with or without powers of management of the undertaking and property of a company is usually made at the instance of debenture holders or other persons having a floating security, with or without a specific charge on part of the property. The nature and effect of a floating security have been discussed at length in many cases [43]: it may be shortly described as an equitable charge on the assets for the time being of a going concern according to their varying condition, which remains dormant until the undertaking charged ceases to be a going concern, or until the person in whose favour the charge exists intervenes; this he may do, unless otherwise agreed, as soon as he pleases after default. As distinct from a specific charge which fastens on definite or ascertained property,

---

[39] *Re Cornish Tin Lands Ltd.* [1918] W.N. 377; costs ordered to be paid by plaintiff.
[40] *Shaw* v. *Wright* (1796) 3 Ves. 22, 24; *Reeves* v. *Cox* (1849) 13 Ir.Eq. 247.
[41] *M'Donnell* v. *White* (1865) 11 H.L.C. 570.
[42] Though this may have been otherwise before 1926: see *Vine* v. *Raleigh*, 24 Ch.D. 243. They are in effect exercisable in right of the legal ownership.
[43] See the cases collected in Palmer's *Company Precedents*, 16th ed., Vol. III, Chap. 7.

or property capable of being defined or ascertained, a floating charge is ambulatory and hovers over the property until some event occurs which causes it to settle and crystallise into a specific charge.[44]

So long as the charge remains floating, the company has a licence to deal with its business and all its assets in the ordinary course.[45] It follows that the complete cessation by the company of its business (as, for example, as the result of a liquidation) will cause the charge to crystallise.[46]

A floating charge need not include all the assets[47]; but it must embrace both present and future property and all property of a particular class,[48] which would in the carrying on of the company's business change from time to time.[49] So long as the charge remains floating, the company can not only deal with its business in the ordinary course, but also, unless otherwise agreed by the terms of the charge, create specific mortgages in priority to it,[50] and even if the creation of specific mortgages is forbidden, the specific mortgagee may have priority if he takes without notice of the prohibition.[51] A charge duly registered under section 95 of the Companies Act 1948, even if taken with notice of an unregistered charge, has priority to the latter.[52]

Crystallisation of floating charge. The appointment of a receiver is one of the events which causes the floating charge to crystallise.[53] The order operates from the date when the appointment becomes

---

[44] See *per* Lord Macnaghten in *Gov. Stock Co.* v. *Manila Ry.* [1897] A.C. 81 at p. 86; *Illingworth* v. *Houldsworth* [1904] A.C. 355; *De Beers Cons. Mines Ltd.* v. *British South Africa Co.* [1912] A.C. 52; *Re Standard Rotary Machine Co.* (1906) 95 L.T. 829. For the extent to which the nature and existence of such a charge will be recognised in foreign jurisdictions, see Chap. 18, *post.*

[45] *Re Standard Manufacturing Co.* [1891] 1 Ch. 627 at p. 641, *per* Fry L.J.; *Robson* v. *Smith* [1895] 1 Ch. 118; *Re Crompton & Co. Ltd.* [1914] 1 Ch. 954; *Brunton* v. *Electrical Engineering Corporation* [1892] 1 Ch. 434; *George Barker (Transport) Ltd.* v. *Eynon* [1974] 1 W.L.R. 462.

[46] *Re Crompton & Co. Ltd., supra.*

[47] *Re Yorkshire Woolcombers' Assocn.* [1903] 2 Ch. 284, affirmed *sub nom. Illingworth* v. *Houldsworth* [1904] A.C. 355.

[48] *Ibid.* [1903] 2 Ch. 284, *per* Cozens-Hardy L.J.

[49] *Ibid.* p. 295, *per* Romer L.J.: see *Nat. Prov. Bank of England* v. *United Electric Theatres Ltd.* [1916] 1 Ch. 132.

[50] *Re Colonial Trusts Corp.* (1879) 15 Ch.D. 465; *Hamer* v. *London City and Midland Bank* (1918) 118 L.T. 571.

[51] *Re Castell and Brown Ltd.* [1898] 1 Ch. 315; *Re Valletort Sanitary Steam Laundry Co. Ltd.* [1903] 2 Ch. 654; see *Cox* v. *Dublin Distillery* [1906] 1 I.R. 446.

[52] *Re Monolithic Building Co.* [1915] 1 Ch. 647. Unless, of course, it is expressly made subject to the unregistered charge.

[53] See *Robson* v. *Smith* [1895] 2 Ch. 118; *Re Crompton & Co. Ltd.* [1914] 1 Ch. 954. As to when appointment is made, *ante,* Chap. 2, Sections 6 and 7.

effective.[54] The receiver becomes entitled to possession of the company's assets, and any interference with his possession is a contempt of court.[55] He takes subject to all specific charges which have been validly created by the company in priority to the floating charge,[56] and to all rights of set-off acquired by debtors to the company in respect of dealings with it.[57] But the title of the receiver prevails over that of execution creditors who have not completed their execution,[58] even though the debentures were not issued at the date of the execution, if there was a valid contract for their issue,[59] and therefore is good against a person who has obtained a garnishee order nisi,[60] or even absolute, if the charge crystallises before actual payment.[61] It was held in one case [62] that the title of the receiver prevailed even over that of a creditor who had obtained a garnishee order absolute, before the debentures were issued to a person with notice of the order, but it is submitted that this case would not be followed.[63] Though the title of the receiver is good against the sheriff, where the execution has not been completed, the receiver cannot claim money paid in discharge or part discharge of the judgment creditor's debt, whether it is paid direct to the judgment creditor or to the sheriff to release the goods; he cannot claim such money in the hands of the sheriff,[64] nor can he claim money paid to the garnishor before crystallisation.[65]

Property in the United Kingdom. A receiver appointed under the law of any part of the United Kingdom in respect of the whole or

---

[54] *Ante*, p. 129.

[55] See the earlier part of the chapter for these topics treated at length.

[56] As to what specific charges have priority, see *supra*: debentures or charges is sued before the appointment may be valid, even if issued after action brought, subject to the provisions of Companies Act 1948, s. 322, as to which see pp. 58, 59, *ante*.

[57] *E. Nelson & Co.* v. *Faber* [1903] 2 K.B. 367; see *Ex p. Peak Hill Goldfield Ltd.* [1909] 1 K.B. 430. As to set-off in relation to transactions arising after the appointment of a manager, see p. 234, *post*.

[58] *Re Opera Ltd.* [1891] 3 Ch. 260; *Davey & Co.* v. *Williamson & Sons* [1898] 2 Q.B. 194; *Evans* v. *Rival Granite Quarries* [1910] 2 K.B. 979.

[59] See *Simultaneous Colour Printing Syn.* v. *Foweraker* [1901] 1 K.B. 771.

[60] *Norton* v. *Yates* [1906] 1 K.B. 112.

[61] *Cairney* v. *Back* [1906] 2 K.B. 746; see *Sinnott* v. *Bowden* [1912] 2 Ch. 414.

[62] *Geisse* v. *Taylor* [1905] 2 K.B. 658.

[63] For though a garnishee order creates no charge, it earmarks a debt to answer a particular claim and prevents the creditor from assigning it, except subject to the garnishee order: *Galbraith* v. *Grimshaw* [1910] A.C. 511; see also *ibid.* [1910] 1 K.B. 339, *per* Kennedy and Farwell L.JJ.; *Goetz* v. *Aders* (1874) 2 Rettie 150.

[64] *Robinson* v. *Burnell's Vienna Bakery Co.* [1904] 2 K.B. 624; *Heaton and Dugard* v. *Cutting Bros.* [1925] 1 K.B. 655. See, however, s. 326 of the Companies Act 1948, *infra.*   [65] *Robson* v. *Smith* [1895] 2 Ch. 118.

part of any property or undertaking of a company in consequence of the company having created a charge which, when created, was a floating charge, is entitled to exercise his powers in any other part of the United Kingdom, so far as their exercise is not inconsistent with the law applicable thereto.[66] Having regard to the wide powers which are automatically conferred upon a receiver under Scottish law (subject to their not being inconsistent with the instrument creating the charge)[67] such inconsistency is unlikely. The appointment will in Scotland be subject to:

(i) the rights of persons who have effectually executed diligence (*i.e.* levied execution) on all or any part of the property of the company prior to the appointment of the receiver; and

(ii) the rights of any person who hold over all, or any part of the property of the company, a fixed security or floating charge having priority over, or ranking *pari passu* with, the floating charge by virtue of which the receiver was appointed.[68]

There are no special problems in Northern Ireland, whose law closely follows English law.

Effect of winding up. By section 326 (1) of the Companies Act 1948, if notice is served on the sheriff that a provisional liquidator has been appointed or resolution for winding up passed, before sale of the goods or completion of the execution by receipt or recovery of the full amount of the levy,[69] the sheriff must deliver the goods or any money seized or received in part satisfaction of the execution to the liquidator, but the costs of the execution are a first charge on the goods or money so delivered. It is apprehended that the receiver's claim to the money or goods, if valid against the sheriff, would be unaffected.

Subsection (2) of the above section, as amended by the Insolvency Act, 1976, s. 1, provides in effect that where under an

---

[66] Administration of Justice Act 1977, s. 7 (1). The 1977 Act repeals Companies (Floating Charges and Receivers) (Scotland) Act 1972, s. 15 (4) which made similar provision, but limited to Scotland. In the 1977 Act the term " receiver " includes a receiver and manager: *ibid.* s. 7 (2).

[67] Companies (Floating Charges and Receivers) (Scotland) Act 1972, s. 15 (1). Floating charges comprising heritable property in Scotland do not require recording in the Register of Sasines; *ibid.* s. 3. As the appointment is made by the court, no question can arise as the valididity of the appointment: *cf. ibid.* s. 15 (3).

[68] *Ibid.* s. 15 (2).

[69] Completion means in the case of goods, seizure and sale; in the case of attachment, payment of the debt; in the case of an equitable interest, appointment of a receiver by way of equitable execution; in the case of land or an interest in land, the appointment of a receiver or seizure: *Re Overseas Aviation Engineering (G.B.) Ltd.* [1963] Ch. 24.

execution in respect of a judgment for more than £250, goods of a company are sold or money paid to avoid sale, the sheriff is to retain the goods or money for fourteen days, less costs of execution: and if within that time notice is served on him for a winding-up petition or resolution for winding up, which is followed by an order, or is passed, the sheriff must pay the money to the liquidator, who may retain it against the execution creditor.[70] The concluding words of the section appear to leave the claim of the receiver for debenture holders unaffected, and the effect of the section may be that the receiver can establish his claim to the money against the liquidator, though he could not have done so against the execution creditor.[71] Finally it is to be noticed that since the coming into force of the Companies Act 1948, the rights conferred by the two subsections already considered upon the liquidator may be set aside by the court in favour of the creditor to such an extent and subject to such terms as the court thinks fit.[72]

The debenture holder's charge does not extend to an asset which does not form part of the company's property when the receiver is appointed, such as money recovered by the liquidator on the ground of fraudulent preference.[73] But it does extend to money recovered from delinquent directors in misfeasance proceedings under section 333 of the Companies Act 1948.[74]

Fraudulent assignment. The holder of a floating charge might assert his claim to the property which the company has disposed of by a fraudulent transaction if the assignee was a party to the fraud, since that would not be a dealing in the ordinary course of business [75]; but he cannot assert his claim to part only of the property comprised in his charge, before the whole security crystallises: he cannot therefore acquire priority by giving notice to a debtor not to pay his debt to a garnishor,[76] nor by giving notice to trustees of a fund not to deal with it [77]; though the appointment of a receiver would have given priority in both these cases by causing the charge to crystallise.

[70] See *Bluston and Bramley Ltd.* v. *Leigh* [1950] 2 K.B. 548 as to the form of notice required.
[71] See *Heaton and Dugard* v. *Cutting Bros.* [1925] 1 K.B. 655.
[72] Companies Act 1948, s. 326 (3).
[73] *Re Yagerphone Ltd.* [1935] Ch. 392. As to fraudulent preference, see ss. 320 and 321 and *Peat* v. *Gresham Trust* [1934] A.C. 252; *Re M. Kushler Ltd.* [1943] Ch. 248.
[74] *Re Anglo-Austrian, etc., Co.* [1895] 2 Ch. 891.
[75] See *Williams* v. *Quebrada Copper Co.* [1895] 2 Ch. 751.
[76] *Evans* v. *Rival Granite Quarries* [1910] 2 K.B. 979.
[77] *Re Ind, Coope & Co.* [1911] 2 Ch. 223.

Where an assignment to the company is set aside as fraudulent, the receiver has no title against the trustee in bankruptcy of the assignor; and the trustee might apply in the action for leave to take possession of the property; but if he elects to treat the receiver as a trespasser, he cannot afterwards obtain an account of profits earned by the receiver.[78]

Nature of possession of a receiver and effect on contracts. The effect of the appointment of a receiver is to paralyse the powers of the company to deal with its property.[79] The legal *persona* of the company, however, still subsists, and its powers in relation to the property comprised in the appointment are delegated to the receiver by his appointment as manager with whatever limitations may be imposed by the order [80]: the powers of the receiver in that event are discussed in Chapter 9. The receiver is not, prima facie, an agent of either the company or the incumbrancers, but an officer of the court exercising the company's powers as such, and as a principal.[81]

Corporation tax. The provisions already noted relating to the liability of a receiver to be assessed to income tax [82] appear only to relate to that tax, and not to extend to corporation tax.[83] There is, therefore, no special provision affecting receivers as such in relation to corporation tax. A receiver appointed by the court is certainly not a " proper officer " of the company within the meaning of the Taxes Management Act 1970, s. 108, nor is he a trustee so as to bring Income and Corporation Taxes Act 1970, s. 243 (2) into play. He does, of course, receive the profits or gains of the company and does occupy its property, but although this might conceivably render him liable to be charged in respect of and to pay the tax relating to the period during which he is in receipt of such income under Schedule B,[84] liability under Schedules A and D appears deliberately to be excluded.[85]

Contracts of service. If the receiver is not also appointed manager, the contracts of the company involving work to be done or goods to be supplied by the company are determined, since there is

---

[78] *Re Simms* [1934] 1 Ch. 1; a case of a receiver appointed out of court.

[79] *Moss S.S. Co.* v. *Whinney* [1912] A.C. 263.

[80] *Parsons* v. *Sovereign Bank of Canada* [1913] A.C. 160.

[81] *Post*, p. 232.   [82] See p. 132, *ante*.

[83] Taxes Management Act 1970, s. 75 refers only to income tax.

[84] See Income and Corporation Taxes Act 1970, s. 92 (1).

[85] See *ibid.* s. 68 (2) in respect of Schedule A; s. 114 (4) in respect of Schedule D. Schedule C income suffers deduction at source: s. 94 (1).

no longer any person in existence with power to carry those contracts into effect [86]: the other parties to such contracts may therefore claim damages for breach.[87] There are certain contracts where the relationship is of a personal nature, such as contracts of service, which are prima facie determined by the appointment of a receiver though he is also appointed manager.[88] It has been suggested that there may be contracts of service, which the change effected by the receiver's appointment is insufficient to determine, as, for instance, in the case of labourers employed on an agricultural estate [89]: but this seems questionable.[90]

The employee whose contract has determined by the appointment can claim damages for wrongful dismissal.[91] But if the receiver has continued to employ him at the same or increased wages for the residue of his term, the continuance in employment might amount to a waiver of the breach by the employee, but mere continuation in the service of the receiver does not necessarily waive the breach.[92] However, from the point of view of redundancy payments, if the employee is immediately re-engaged on the same terms by the receiver, then, for such purposes, the employment is regarded as continuous.[93] Moreover, if the receiver offers to renew the employee's contract of employment, or to re-engage him under a new contract of employment, but the employee refuses the offer, then he will not be entitled to a redundancy payment if he has unreasonably refused that offer.[94] And in considering whether he has unreasonably so refused, the fact that the receiver is now the employer in place of the former employer is not

[86] *Re Newdigate Colliery Co. Ltd.* [1912] 1 Ch. 468.
[87] See *Parsons* v. *Sovereign Bank of Canada* [1913] A.C. 160; as to damages, see *Re Vic Mill Ltd.* [1913] 1 Ch. 465.
[88] *Reid* v. *Explosives Co. Ltd.*, 19 Q.B.D. 264; *Parsons* v. *Sovereign Bank of Canada, supra; Reigate* v. *Union, etc., Co.* [1918] 1 K.B. 592.
[89] *Parsons* v. *Sovereign Bank of Canada* [1913] A.C. 160, 171; see also judgment of Moulton L.J. in *Whinney* v. *Moss S.S. Co.* [1910] 2 K.B. 813: as to position of directors, see *Welstead* v. *Hadley*, 21 T.L.R. 165; *Measures Bros. Ltd.* v. *Measures* [1910] 2 Ch. 248.
[90] See *Nokes* v. *Doncaster Amalgamated Collieries* [1940] A.C. 1014. See, however, 15 *Modern Law Review*, pp. 53–54.
[91] *Measures Bros. Ltd.* v. *Measures* [1910] 1 Ch. 344; and *cf. Re Gramophone Records Ltd.* [1930] W.N. 42. If a new contract on equivalent terms with the receiver is implied, only nominal damages could be recovered: see *Brace* v. *Calder* [1895] 2 Q.B. 261; see *Re English Joint Stock Bank*, 3 Eq. 341; *Re Forster*, 19 L.R.Ir. 240. And *cf. Collier* v. *Sunday Referee Co.* [1940] 2 K.B. 647 as to the necessity for actual employment: as to *quantum, cf. Southern Foundries* v. *Shirlaw* [1940] A.C. 701.
[92] See *Ex p. Pitt*, 40 T.L.R. 5.
[93] Employment Protection (Consolidation) Act 1977, s. 94 (2).
[94] *Ibid.* ss. 94 (3), 82 (3)–(6).

to be taken into account.[95] Unless, at the end of the day, the receiver is able to hand back its business to the company as a going concern, he will, of course, be personally liable in respect of any redundancy payments which then fall to be made in respect of the employees,[96] with the usual right of recoupment of a proportion of such payments from the Secretary of State for Employment.[97] A covenant restricting the employee's employment after the termination of his employment cannot be enforced when the appointment of a receiver has operated as a dismissal.[98]

Deemed insolvency of company for certain purposes. If an employer becomes insolvent, then, under the Employment Protection (Consolidation) Act 1977, the employee himself,[99] and also the persons competent to act in respect of an occupational pension scheme,[1] normally the trustees of such scheme, have rights to be paid various sums by the Secretary of State for Employment out of the Redundancy Fund. For this purpose "insolvency" is defined not only as happening when the company is wound up, whether compulsorily or voluntarily, but also when a receiver or manager of its undertaking is duly appointed, or possession is taken, by or on behalf of the holders of any debentures secured by a floating charge, of any property of the company comprised in or subject to the charge.[2]

As has already been noted, the appointment of the receiver will normally determine contracts of service,[3] and in this case the right of the employee will crystallise on the appointment of the receiver.[4] However, in a large number of cases the employee will be immediately re-engaged by the receiver, and in such cases the practical effect is that the employment will be terminated at some later date, and in such cases the rights of the employee crystallise at that date.[4]

The debts to which these provisions apply are:

(1) Any arrears of pay in respect of a period or periods not exceeding in the aggregate eight weeks;

[95] *Ibid.* s. 94 (4).
[96] *Ibid.* s. 81.
[97] *Ibid.* s. 104.
[98] *Measures Bros. Ltd.* v. *Measures* [1910] 2 Ch. 248; see *General Bill Posting Co.* v. *Atkinson* [1909] A.C. 118.
[99] Employment Protection (Consolidation) Act 1977, s. 122.
[1] *Ibid.* s. 123. For definition of such a scheme, see *ibid.* s. 127 (3).
[2] *Ibid.* s. 127 (1) (*c*).　　　　　　　　　　　　　　　[3] p. 166, *ante.*
[4] Employment Protection (Consolidation) Act 1977, s. 122 (2).

(2) any amount which the employer is liable to pay to the employee for the minimum period of notice required by the 1977 Act,[5] or for any failure of the employer to give the period of notice required by that Act [6];

(3) any holiday pay [7] in respect of a period or periods of holiday, not exceeding six weeks in all, to which the employee became entitled during the 12 months immediately preceding the insolvency or the later termination of his employment;

(4) any basic award of compensation for unfair dismissal [8];

(5) any reasonable sum [9] by way of reimbursement of the whole or part of any fee or premium paid by an apprentice or articled clerk.[10]

Included in (1) above are all the debts expressly included in the scope of "wages" for the purposes of the provisions relating to preferential debts.[11] Claims under the first three heads mentioned above are limited to the rate of £80 per week,[12] but this figure may be varied by order of the Secretary of State for Employment.[13]

Normally of course, a considerable portion of any such claims will, in any event, rank as preferential debts,[14] and will fall to be discharged by the receiver as such; and the Secretary of State will not normally make any such payment until he has applied to the receiver for a statement of the amount of the debt due to the employee on the relevant date and to remain unpaid.[15] The receiver must, on request by the Secretary of State, provide him, as soon as is reasonably practicable, with such a statement.[15] If no such statement is forthcoming within a period of six months from the date when the Secretary of State received an application for payment from an employee, and he is satisfied that there is likely to be further delay before he receives a statement, he may nevertheless make a payment before receiving such statement.[16]

---

[5] *Ibid.* s. 49 (1) or (2).

[6] *Ibid.* s. 51.

[7] For definition see *ibid.* s. 127 (3).

[8] For method of calculation see *ibid.* s. 73.

[9] A sum will be taken to be reasonable if so admitted by the liquidator under Bankruptcy Act 1914, s. 34 as applied to winding up by Companies Act 1948, s. 317. Employment Protection (Consolidation) Act 1977, s. 122 (7).

[10] Employment Protection (Consolidation) Act 1977, s. 122 (3).

[11] *Ibid.* s. 122 (4). For such provisions see pp. 210, 211, *post.*

[12] *Ibid.* s. 122 (5).

[13] *Ibid.* s. 122 (6).

[14] See pp. 207 *et seq., post.*

[15] Employment Protection (Consolidation) Act 1977, s. 122 (10).

[16] *Ibid.* s. 122 (11).

On the making of any such payment by the Secretary of State, he will be subrogated to all the rights of the employee in respect of the payment so made.[17] These rights will include the right to be paid preferentially to the other creditors to the extent to which section 319 of the Companies Act 1948 extends, and he is also entitled to be paid preferentially in priority to any other unsatisfied claims of the employee.[18] For these purposes any sums paid to the Secretary of State are to be treated as if they had been paid by the employee.[18]

Similarly in relation to unpaid contributions to an occupational pension scheme, if there are unpaid contributions which fell to be paid by the company, either on its own account or on behalf of employees—that is to say, because that amount had been deducted from the pay of the employee by way of his contribution—at the time it became insolvent,[19] the Secretary of State must pay into the resources of the scheme out of the Redundancy Fund the sum which in his opinion was payable in respect thereof.[20]

There are, however, elaborate provisions for ascertaining the sum properly payable by the Secretary of State requiring among other matters an actuary's certificate,[21] and he will not normally make a payment until he has received from the receiver a statement of the amount of the relevant contributions which appear to have been unpaid on the date when the company became insolvent.[22] And the receiver must provide him, as before, on request with such a statement as soon as is reasonably practicable.[22] If no such statement or certificate is forthcoming within a period of six months from the date when the Secretary of State received the application for payment, and he is satisfied that there is likely to be further delay before he receives a statement or certificate, he may nevertheless make the payment without first receiving either.[23]

Once again, on making any such payment the Secretary of State will be subrogated to the rights of those competent to act in respect of the scheme, and he will be entitled to the relevant amount of preferential payment.[24]

---

[17] Ibid. s. 125 (1).
[18] Ibid. s. 125 (2).
[19] Ibid. s. 123 (2).
[20] Ibid. s. 123 (1).
[21] Ibid. s. 123 (3), (4), (5).
[22] Ibid. s. 123 (6).
[23] Ibid. s. 123 (7).
[24] Ibid. s. 125 (3). As to preference, see pp. 207 et seq., post.

In addition to the specific duties as to furnishing information placed upon the receiver, and indeed others in the same kind of position such as a liquidator,[25] there is a more general provision under which the Secretary of State may, in relation to the matters mentioned above, require the employer to furnish him with such information as he may reasonably require for the purpose of determining whether any application to him is well founded. He may further require any person having the custody or control of any relevant records, or other documents, to produce for examination on behalf of the Secretary of State any such document in his custody or control which is of such a description as the Secretary of State may require.[26] The requirement is to be made by notice in writing given to the person on whom the requirement is imposed, and may be varied or revoked by a subsequent similar notice.[27] Refusal or wilful neglect to comply attracts a fine not exceeding £100 on summary conviction.[28] If a person, whilst purporting to comply with any such requirement, knowingly or recklessly makes any false statement, he will be liable on summary conviction to a fine not exceeding £400.[29]

It may finally be observed that there is a similar deemed insolvency with regard to redundancy payments,[30] with corresponding rights in the employee to require payment direct from the Secretary of State,[31] and corresponding subrogation of the Secretary of State to his rights.[32] In this case it appears, however, that it is only the employer who can be called upon to provide the Minister with information and to produce documents in its custody or under its control,[33] unless a receiver and manager is held to be comprised in the words " Director, manager, secretary or other similar officer " of the company, all of whom are rendered equally liable with the company if any offence has been committed by it with their consent or connivance, or is attributable to any neglect on their part.[34] If so, then as well as the company, the defaulting receiver would be

---

[25] *Ibid.* ss. 122 (9), 123 (6).
[26] *Ibid.* s. 126 (1).
[27] *Ibid.* s. 126 (2).
[28] *Ibid.* s. 126 (3).
[29] *Ibid.* s. 126 (4).
[30] *Ibid.* s. 106 (5).
[31] *Ibid.* s. 106 (1).
[32] *Ibid.* s. 106 (3) (*a*).
[33] *Ibid.* s. 107 (1).
[34] *Ibid.* s. 120 (1). See *Re B. Johnson & Co.* (*Builders*) *Ltd.* [1955] Ch. 634 (C.A.). (Receiver and manager not normally comprised in this expression.)

liable on summary conviction to a fine not exceeding £100.[35] Any person who, in providing information required by such a notice, makes a statement which he knows to be false in a material particular, or produces for inspection a document which to his knowledge has been wilfully falsified, is liable on summary conviction to a fine not exceeding £100, or to imprisonment for a term not exceeding three months or both, or on conviction on indictment to a fine or to imprisonment for a term not exceeding two years or both.[36]

Third party insurance. If the company is insured against liabilities to third parties and incurs any such liability, whether before or after the happening of any of the events hereinafter mentioned, then on the happening of any such event its rights against the insurers under the contract are automatically transferred to and vested in the third party.[37] The events are (i) a winding-up order being made; (ii) a resolution for voluntary liquidation (otherwise than for the purposes of reconstruction or amalgamation) being passed; (iii) the appointment of a receiver or manager; and (iv) possession being taken by or on behalf of debenture holders of any property comprised in their floating charge. It is correspondingly the duty of the liquidator, receiver or manager or person in possession of the property to give any person who claims that the company is under a liability to him such information as he may reasonably require for the purpose of ascertaining whether any rights have been so transferred to and vested in him, and for enforcing the same.[38] It is impossible to contract out of any of these provisions.[39]

Petition to wind up. A debenture holder who has brought an action to enforce his security, and has obtained the appointment of a receiver, is not thereby precluded from presenting a petition to wind up the company.[40]

---

[35] *Ibid.* s. 107 (2).
[36] *Ibid.* s. 107 (3), (4).
[37] Third Parties (Rights Against Insurers) Act 1930, s. 1 (1). The provisions of this Act are excluded in the case of oil pollution by merchant shipping by the Merchant Shipping (Oil Pollution) Act 1971, s. 12 (5). The Act confers its own system of rights against insurers.
[38] *Ibid.* s. 2 (1). The duty to give information includes a duty to allow all contracts of insurance, receipts for premiums and other relevant documents in his possession or power to be inspected, and copies thereof to be taken: *ibid.* subs. (3).
[39] *Ibid.* ss. 1 (3) and 2 (1).
[40] *Re Borough of Portsmouth Tramways Co.* [1892] 2 Ch. 362.

The appointment of a receiver for debenture holders is not a special circumstance to cause the court to depart from its practice of refusing a winding-up order where the petitioning creditor's debt is under £50.[41]

The appointment of a receiver and payment into court of the proceeds of sale of property subject to the trusts of a debenture trust deed does not necessarily determine the right of the trustees to remuneration and a lien therefor,[42] even though trustees may have a specific power to appoint a receiver and delegate their powers to him.[43] The terms of the trust deed must be considered in each case.[44] The lien of a solicitor for trustees of a debenture trust deed has priority against the debenture holders.[45]

Where two directors of a company, who were entitled to a share in certain sums payable for remuneration to the whole body of directors, had been appointed receivers and managers of the company's business, and had become entitled to remuneration for so acting, it was held that they were nevertheless entitled to their remuneration as directors up to the date of a winding up.[46]

The conduct of a debenture holder's action may be taken from the plaintiff if his interest is adverse in the subject-matter to that of other members of the class represented by him.[47]

---

[41] By analogy with s. 223 of the Act of 1948; now amended by the Insolvency Act 1976, s. 1 and Sched. 1, to £200. So far the increased limit has not been applied by analogy. See *Re Industrial Insurance Co.* [1910] W.N. 245.

[42] *Re Piccadilly Hotel Ltd.* [1911] 2 Ch. 534.

[43] *Re British Cons. Oil Corpn.* [1919] 2 Ch. 81.

[44] *Re Piccadilly Hotel Ltd., supra; Re Anglo-Canadian Lands Ltd.* [1918] 2 Ch. 287, distinguishing *Re Locke and Smith* [1914] 1 Ch. 687; *Re British Cons. Oil Corpn., supra.*

[45] *Re Dee Estates* [1911] 2 Ch. 85.

[46] *Re South-Western of Venezuela Ry.* [1902] 1 Ch. 701.

[47] *Re Services Club Estate Syndicate* [1930] 1 Ch. 78. See *post*, p. 180.

CHAPTER 7

POWERS AND DUTIES OF A RECEIVER

THE general duty of a receiver may be said to be to take possession of the estate, or other property, the subject-matter of dispute in the action, in the room or place of the owner thereof; and, under the sanction of the court, to do, as and when necessary, all such acts of ownership, in relation to the receipts of rents, compelling payment of them, management, letting lands and houses, and otherwise making the property productive, or collecting and realising it, for the parties to be ultimately declared to be entitled thereto, as the owner himself could do if he were in possession.

It is the duty of a receiver as soon as his appointment is effective or he is given leave to act, to require all tenants of freehold or leasehold property to pay their rents to him and where the appointment is over the estate of a deceased person or the assets of a business or undertaking to require all debtors to pay their debts to him. These topics and the obligations of the receiver as to the application of money coming into his hands are treated at length in this chapter.

Parties required to deliver up possession. Where parties to an action are directed by the order appointing a receiver to deliver up to him possession of such parts of the property as are in their holding, the receiver, as soon as his appointment is complete, should apply to them to deliver up possession accordingly. If any of them refuse to do so, the receiver should report the refusal to the solicitor of the party having the conduct of the proceedings, who should then serve the refusing parties or party personally with the order directing possession to be delivered up.[1] A time within which the delivery of possession is to be made must be specified in the order, and the order must be indorsed in the manner prescribed by R.S.C., Ord. 45, r. 7.[2]

If possession is still withheld from the receiver, an application should be made, by motion *ex parte*, for a writ of possession to put the receiver in possession pursuant to the order; and the application should be supported by an affidavit of service of the

[1] *Green* v. *Green* (1829) 2 Sim. 430.
[2] *Savage* v. *Bentley* [1904] W.N. 89; 90 L.T. 641.

order, and of non-compliance.[3] The writ cannot, however, be issued unless the explicit directions of R.S.C., Ord. 45, r. 7, have been complied with.[4] If thought fit, proceedings may be taken for contempt.

Where chattels are concerned a writ of delivery may be obtained.[5] The old Chancery remedy by way of writ of assistance, although in a great measure superseded by the writ of possession (R.S.C., Ord. 45, r. 3), is still available in cases not met by R.S.C., Ord. 45, r. 4, e.g. where chattels, such as documents, are in peril, and a receiver appointed by the court is unable to serve the respondent or to obtain possession, the respondent having absconded and his clerks declining to give up the custody of the documents,[6] or where the respondent was in prison for contempt and the securities required were in his possession or in a locked safe in his office.[7]

If any party to the proceedings who is in possession of the property in question, or any part of it, is not ordered to deliver up possession to the receiver, he is not bound to do so; but he may be charged with an occupation rent for the property in his possession[8]; such occupation rent to be paid only from the date of demand of possession by the receiver, and not from the date of the order appointing the receiver.[9] A person in possession will not be ordered, on interlocutory motion before trial, to pay an occupation rent for a period antecedent to the order fixing the occupation rent.[10] If a party, e.g. a mortgagor, who has been ordered to deliver up possession to the receiver, offers to attorn tenant at an occupation rent with security, the direction of the court should be obtained before proceeding to enforce the order.[11]

Tenants should be required to attorn. If tenants in possession of real or leasehold estates, over which a receiver is appointed, are directed by the order to attorn to the receiver,[12] the receiver should,

---

[3] R.S.C., Ord. 45, r. 3.

[4] *Savage* v. *Bentley* [1904] W.N. 89; 90 L.T. 641. In the case of an order on a company, the company's name must be inserted in the memorandum to be indorsed under that rule, though it is intended to proceed against directors, see *Benabo* v. *Jay* [1941] Ch. 52; and *Iberian Trust* v. *Founders Trust* [1932] 2 K.B. 87, as to form.

[5] R.S.C., Ord. 45, r. 4.

[6] *Wyman* v. *Knight* (1888) 39 Ch.D. 165, *q.v.* for form of order.

[7] *Re Taylor* [1913] W.N. 212.

[8] *Randfield* v. *Randfield* (1861) 31 L.J.Ch. 113.

[9] *Yorkshire Banking Co.* v. *Mullan* (1887) 35 Ch.D. 125.

[10] *Lloyd* v. *Mason* (1837) 2 My. & Cr. 487, 488.

[11] *Pratchett* v. *Drew* [1924] 1 Ch. 280.   [12] *Ante*, p. 173.

as soon as his appointment is complete, call on them to attorn accordingly.[13]

If any tenant refuses to attorn to the receiver, the party prosecuting the order should serve him personally with a copy of the order for the appointment of a receiver, and of the order of certificate completing the appointment,[14] and also with a notice in writing signed by the receiver, requiring him to attorn and pay.[15] If he still refuses to attorn, the tenant should be served with a summons to attorn and pay within a limited time after service of the order to be made on the summons.[16]

The person served may appear to the summons, and inform the court whether he is in possession as tenant or not.[17] If he does not appear, the order will be made upon affidavit of service of the summons, orders, certificate, and notice to attorn, and proof by affidavit of the refusal to attorn.[18] The order will be made without costs in cases where the tenant had reasonable ground for refusing to attorn.[19]

A copy of the order, indorsed in the usual manner, is then served personally upon the person thereby directed to attorn.[20] If the person so served still refuses to attorn, an application should be made for leave to issue a writ of committal against him.[21]

In cases where it does not clearly appear what is the nature of the interest of a person in possession of property over which a receiver has been appointed, it is not necessary to make him a party

[13] The attornment to a receiver appointed by the court constitutes a tenancy by estoppel between the tenant and the receiver, which the court applies to the purposes of collecting and securing the rents till a judgment can be pronounced, taking care that the tenant shall be protected, both while the receiver continues to act, and also when, by the authority of the court, he is withdrawn: *Evans* v. *Mathias* (1857) 7 E. & B. 602. The attornment creates a tenancy between the tenant and the receiver only, and does not enure for the benefit of the person who may ultimately be found to be entitled to the legal estate, so as to enable him to distrain: *ibid.* For a case in which a tenant was not estopped by payment of rent to a receiver appointed under the statutory power, see *Serjeant* v. *Nash, Field & Co.* [1903] 2 K.B. 304.

[14] *Ante*, p. 119.

[15] Daniell's *Chancery Practice* (8th ed.), p. 1481; form of notice to tenant to attorn, and attornment, Atkin's *Court Forms* (2nd ed.), Vol. 33, p. 212.

[16] Form of summons and affidavit, Atkin's *Court Forms* (2nd ed.), Vol. 33, p. 213.

[17] *Reid* v. *Middleton* (1823) Tur. & Rus. 455; *Hobhouse* v. *Hollcombe* (1848) 2 De G. & Sm. 208.

[18] Daniell's *Chancery Practice* (8th ed.), p. 1481; *Hobson* v. *Sherwood* (1854) 19 Beav. 575. Form of affidavit, see Atkin's *Court Forms* (2nd ed.), Vol. 33, p. 213.

[19] *Hobhouse* v. *Hollcombe* (1848) 2 De G. & Sm. 208. *Cf. Hobson* v. *Sherwood* (1854) 19 Beav. 575.

[20] Daniell's *Chancery Practice* (8th ed.), p. 1481.

[21] R.S.C., Ord. 45, rr. 5, 9; Ord. 52; or sequestration may issue under Ord. 45, r. 5.

to the action. The court will, upon allegation that he is a tenant, treat him as a tenant and require him to attorn, unless he can satisfy the court that he holds possession in some other character, and fix him with an occupation rent.[22]

If a judgment creditor is in possession under his judgment, the court cannot order him to attorn.[23]

Delivery of documents by solicitor. A solicitor to a party will be ordered to produce and deliver up to a receiver appointed in an administration action documents over which he has a lien for costs on the ground that he has no higher right than his client to refuse production.[24]

Rents in arrear. The receiver may obtain on summons [25] an order for payment to him of all arrears of rent due at the date of his appointment, though the tenant may not have attorned: the tenant may be ordered to pay the costs of the summons.[26] If the tenant pays rent due to a mortgagor before notice of the order, he will obtain a good receipt.[27]

A person who admits a sum of money to be due from him to the estate cannot dispute the right of the receiver to collect it.[28]

Although a receiver is entitled to all arrears of rent at the date of his appointment, produce not converted into money, which has been separated from the estate before the date of the order, does not belong to the receiver over the land.[29]

Duty of receiver to take proper receipts. When the order directs that the receiver shall keep down the interest of incumbrances, or make any other payments, he must, of course, comply with the order, and the sums so paid by him will be allowed in his accounts. He must, however, take proper receipts from the persons to whom

---

[22] *Reid* v. *Middleton* (1823) Tur. & Rus. 455.

[23] *Davis* v. *Duke of Marlborough* (1818) 2 Swans. 108.

[24] *Re W. Caudery* (1910) 54 S.J. 444; following *Re Hawkes* [1898] 2 Ch. 1; and see *Re Rapid Road Transit Co.* [1909] 1 Ch. 96; *Dessau* v. *Peters, Rushton & Co.* [1922] 1 Ch. 1, 5. As to right of receiver for debenture holders to money in the hands of a solicitor in respect of future costs, see *Re British Tea Table Co.* (1909) 101 L.T. 707. As to position of a director of a company with regard to documents, see *Re Maville Hose* [1939] Ch. 32.

[25] On notice to tenant: form, Atkin's *Court Forms* (2nd ed.), Vol. 33, p. 209.

[26] *Hobson* v. *Sherwood* (1854) 19 Beav. 575; *cf. Re Potts* [1893] 1 Q.B. 648.

[27] See further, p. 134, *ante*.

[28] *Wood* v. *Hitchings* (1840) 2 Beav. 294.

[29] *Codrington* v. *Johnstone* (1838) 1 Beav. 520. But the case is otherwise where the appointment, as in the case of a receiver for debenture holders, includes the whole of the assets.

he makes the payments, and it must be remembered that, in passing his accounts, he will be subject to the rules to which all other accounting parties are subject, and accordingly will be allowed to discharge himself by affidavit only as to payments under £2: for all other payments he must produce proper vouchers [30] unless he can give good reason for their absence.

A receiver is only justified in paying to the person named in an order for payment, or on a power of attorney duly executed by him. Express authority for payment in any other way must be shown by the receiver, on peril of being disallowed credit therefor in vouching his accounts. [31] A solicitor having the carriage of the proceedings has not as such, and in the absence of special authority, power to give a valid receipt for money ordered to be paid by a receiver to his client. [32]

Distress. After a tenant has, by attorning to a receiver, created a tenancy between him and the receiver, [33] the receiver may distrain upon the tenant in his own name, without leave obtained from the court, [34] and may employ a bailiff for this purpose. [35] Before attornment the receiver must distrain in the name of the person having the legal estate. [36] In *Brandon* v. *Brandon* [37] it was stated to be the practice for the receiver not to distrain without an order, for more than one year's arrears of rent. In that case the motion was for leave to distrain in the names of trustees in whom the legal estate was; apparently, if the tenant has attorned, the receiver may distrain without leave for all rent accrued due during the tenancy. [38]

At the instance of a purchaser who had been let into possession a receiver was restrained from distraining for arrears of rent due from a former tenant on the ground that a receiver will not be permitted to utilise the legal estate so as to injure the person having the best title to it. [39]

---

[30] Daniell's *Chancery Practice* (8th ed.), p. 920.   [31] See p. 221, *post.*
[32] *Re Browne* (1886) 19 L.R. Ir. 133.
[33] See *Evans* v. *Mathias* (1857) 7 E. & B. 602.
[34] *Pitt* v. *Snowden* (1752) 3 Atk. 750; *Bennett* v. *Robins* (1832) 5 C. & P. 379; see, too, *Morton* v. *Woods* (1869) L.R. 3 Q.B. 668. A receiver may employ a bailiff to make a distress: *Dancer* v. *Hastings* (1826) 4 Bing. 2. As to distress in cases where a receiver has been appointed by a mortgagee under the power conferred by the Law of Property Act 1925, see p. 293, *post.*
[35] *Birch* v. *Oldis* (1837) Sausse & Sc. 146.
[36] *Hughes* v. *Hughes* (1790) 3 Bro.C.C. 87; 1 Ves.Jun. 161.
[37] (1821) 5 Madd. 473, *per* Leach M.R.
[38] It is, however, conceived that where the arrears are of long standing, the receiver will act properly in obtaining a direction before distraining for the whole.
[39] *Re Powers* (1894) 39 W.R. 185.

Leave that the receiver may distrain in the name of the person
having the legal estate is obtained on summons.[40] If there is any
doubt as to who has the legal right to the rent, the receiver should
make an application to the court for directions; but where there
is no doubt as to who has the legal right to the rent, it is conceived
that the leave of the court to distrain in the name of the person
having the legal estate is not generally necessary.[41] Where, however, the person having the legal estate is a trustee, and objects to
the distress, leave should be obtained, unless the objection is
wholly unreasonable.[42]

Instead of applying that he may have liberty to distrain in the
name of the person having the legal estate, the receiver may
obtain an order on summons, with notice to the tenants, for
payment by the tenants notwithstanding that they may not have
attorned,[43] or he may apply that the tenants do attorn, and that
distresses may afterwards be made in his name. If the tenants
oppose on the ground of the pendency of an action for the same
rent commenced before the appointment of the receiver, the
summons or motion may be ordered to stand over until the action
has been tried.[44]

Where a receiver is appointed without prejudice to the rights of
any prior incumbrancer, and, at the date of the order, a bailiff is
in possession under a distress, the landlord need not apply for leave
to proceed with the distress.[45]

The abatement of an action in which a receiver has been
appointed does not determine the appointment, or suspend the
receiver's authority to proceed against the tenants. His authority
continues until an order is made for his removal.[46]

A receiver appointed at the instance of the mortgagee of an
underlease is the landlord of the premises within the meaning of
that term in section 1 of the Landlord and Tenant Act 1709 and,

---

[40] Form of summons, Atkin's *Court Forms* (2nd ed.), Vol. 33, p. 208. As to form of
order, see Seton (7th ed.), p. 763. The minute of the master is usually considered
sufficient without drawing up an order: Daniell's *Chancery Practice* (8th ed.), p. 1487.
[41] *Pitt* v. *Snowden* (1752) 3 Atk. 750; *Brandon* v. *Brandon* (1821) 5 Madd. 473.
[42] *Della Cainea* v. *Hayward* (1825) M'Clel. & Y. 272.
[43] *Hobson* v. *Sherwood* (1854) 19 Beav. 575, *ante*, p. 169.
[44] *Hobhouse* v. *Hollcombe* (1848) 2 De G. & Sm. 208; as to form of summons for
tenant to attorn, and pay rent, and affidavits, see Atkin's *Court Forms* (2nd ed.),
Vol. 33, p. 213.
[45] *Engel* v. *South Metropolitan, etc., Co.* [1891] W.N. 31.
[46] *Newman* v. *Mills* (1825) 1 Hog. 291; *Brennan* v. *Kenny* (1852) 2 Ir.Ch. 283. For a
case where a distress was rescued by a tenant, see *Fitzpatrick* v. *Eyre* (1824) 1 Hog.
171.

as such, entitled to be paid by an execution creditor,[47] before the latter can proceed with his execution, one year's arrears of rent owing by a tenant: but a yearly sum expressed to be paid for goodwill and fixtures is not rent within the section.[48]

Receiver appointed over personal property. Where a receiver is appointed by the court to get in outstanding personal property, it is his duty to collect all that he can get in [49] and to obtain directions for realisation.[50] If a receiver of book debts is appointed, he must at once give notice of his appointment to the debtors, in order to take the debts out of the order and disposition of the creditor in the event of his becoming bankrupt.[51] A receiver for debenture holders, whose debentures expressly or impliedly confer a power to create a charge in priority to the debentures, cannot obtain priority in respect of a debt due to the company over a person in whose favour a charge thereon has been created, and of whose charge he has knowledge, by giving prior notice to the debtor.[52]

An order appointing a receiver of outstanding personal estate generally contains a direction that the parties in whose possession the same may be shall deliver over to the receiver all securities in their possession for such outstanding personal estate, together with all books and papers relating thereto.[53] If parties in whose hands such securities and papers are, refuse to deliver them up, the receiver should give notice of the refusal to the party conducting the proceedings and the latter must take the necessary steps for enforcing the order.[54]

Trust funds. Where the order does not describe the property, as for instance where the receiver is appointed generally over a trust fund invested in the names of trustees, it may be necessary to obtain a further order expressly referring to the property, to enable

---

[47] *Semble*, neither a receiver appointed over chattels in which the debtor had an equitable interest, nor the creditor would be an execution creditor within the section: see *Norburn* v. *Norburn* [1894] 1 Q.B. 448.

[48] *Cox* v. *Harper* [1910] 1 Ch. 480.

[49] See pp. 173–174, *ante*, as to means of obtaining possession.

[50] As to sales by receiver, see pp. 198 *et seq.*, *post*; and as to the power of a receiver appointed to wind up an Irish Loan Society, to compromise claims, see *O'Reilly* v. *Connor* [1904] 2 I.R. 601.

[51] *Rutter* v. *Everett* [1895] 2 Ch. 872; *Re Neal* [1914] 2 K.B. 910; and see, further, p. 140, *ante*.

[52] *Re Ind, Coope & Co.* [1911] 2 Ch. 223; and see p. 161, *ante*.

[53] Seton (7th ed.), p. 725.

[54] Daniell's *Chancery Practice* (8th ed.), p. 1481.

the receiver to obtain dividends or money payable on redemption of debentures: for a company does not have regard to equitable interests, and, apart from express order, only recognises the legal title of the trustees.

In the performance of his duties and the management of the estate generally, the receiver must have regard to the terms of his appointment. If he requires powers additional to those specifically given or implied thereby, he must obtain from the court leave to exercise such powers, as, for instance, power to carry on a business. Generally speaking, a receiver should not initiate or defend or compromise any proceedings, or do any other act liable to involve the estate in expense, or liability, without obtaining specific authority,[55] which can be obtained on summons supported by an affidavit of the relevant facts.[56] If an agent for sale is appointed by a receiver without leave of the court, the court in its discretion may make him an allowance, even though he is not entitled to commission.[57]

Applications in respect of the estate. All applications to the court in respect of estates in the hands of a receiver should, as a general rule, be made on behalf of persons beneficially interested in the estate, and not by the receiver. The receiver ought not, generally, to originate any proceedings in the action.[58] The conduct of the action is not nowadays given to a receiver [59] and may be taken from the plaintiff if his interest is adverse to other members of a class, *e.g.* of debenture holders, whom he represents.[60] If, owing to any difficulty, an application to the court becomes necessary, the receiver should apply in the first instance to the party having the carriage of the order,[61] or if necessary, to any other party, to make the necessary application. If, after he has done so, no application

---

[55] Daniell's *Chancery Practice* (8th ed.), p. 1481. The court will not empower a receiver to sue, unless it appears likely that some fruits may be derived from his doing so: *Dacie* v. *John* (1824) M'Clell. 575.

[56] Forms of summons for powers, Atkin's *Court Forms* (2nd ed.), Vol. 33, pp. 203–208; to bring action, p. 203; defend, 204; to carry on business, 207; to pay debts, 204; borrow, 204; repairs, 208; as to the grant of leases, *post*, p. 186.

[57] *Re National Flying Services* [1936] Ch. 271.

[58] *Miller* v. *Elkins* (1825) 3 L.J.(N.S.)Ch. 128; *Parker* v. *Dunn* (1845) 8 Beav. 498; *Ex p. Cooper* (1887) 6 Ch.D. 255. If the receiver of an estate proves without leave against the estate of a bankrupt legatee, a debtor to the estate, he thereby discharges the debt, and entitles the legatee, on the annulment of his bankruptcy, to his legacy: *Armstrong* v. *Armstrong* (1871) L.R. 12 Eq. 614.

[59] *Re Hopkins* (1881) 19 Ch.D. 621.

[60] *Re Services Club Estate Syndicate* [1903] 1 Ch. 78.

[61] *Windschuegel* v. *Irish Polishes Ltd.* [1914] 1 I.R. 33.

is made, and no proper means are taken to relieve the receiver from his difficulty, or if the matter is so urgent that the purpose of the application would be defeated by delay caused in applying to the parties,[62] he may himself apply and would be entitled to his costs.[63] Where a receiver had incurred costs in the execution of his duties, and the parties to the suit had for a long time neglected to provide for them, he may himself apply by summons for payment.[64]

Supervision by plaintiff's solicitor. The solicitor for the party having the conduct of the action should exercise a general supervision over the receiver and protect the estate against irregularities by him; failure to do so may prevent the plaintiff from applying for recoupment out of the fund of expenditure rendered necessary by the irregularity.[65]

Party receiver. Where a party to an action is appointed receiver he is entitled to apply to the court as freely as if he were not holding that office.[66]

Right to sue. A receiver acquires no right of action by virtue of his appointment: he cannot sue in his own name as receiver, *e.g.* for debts to a company, or to parties over whose assets he has been appointed receiver; nor can the court authorise him to do so.[67] In such cases he must maintain the action in the name of the person or persons who would be entitled to sue [68] apart from his appointment.[69] A receiver may, however, acquire a right of action to sue in his own name: for instance, as the holder of a bill of exchange [70]; or the assignee of a debt which has been actually assigned to him; or by virtue of his possession,[71] as, for instance,

---

[62] *Cf. Nangle* v. *Lord Fingal* (1824) 1 Hog. 142.

[63] *Ireland* v. *Eade* (1844) 7 Beav. 55; *Parker* v. *Dunn* (1845) 8 Beav. 498. For a recent example see *Brenner* v. *Rose* [1973] 1 W.L.R. 443, where the receiver applied by summons for directions in relation to an underlease.

[64] *Ireland* v. *Eade* (1844) 7 Beav. 55.

[65] *Craig* v. *Att.-Gen.* [1926] N.I. 218.

[66] *Scott* v. *Plate* (1847) 2 Ph. 229, 230.

[67] *Ex p. Sacker* (1888) 22 Q.B.D. 179; *Rodriguez* v. *Speyer Bros.* [1919] A.C. 59, 75, 112.

[68] It must be remembered in partnership cases that one partner cannot sue or be sued in the name of the firm: *Meyer & Co.* v. *Faber* [1923] 2 Ch. 441.

[69] *Rodriguez* v. *Speyer Bros.* [1919] A.C. 59, where the dicta to the contrary in *Rombach* v. *Gent* (1915) 84 L.J.K.B. 1558, were criticised.

[70] *Ex p. Harris* (1876) 2 Ch.D. 423, explained in *Ex p. Sacker* (1888) 22 Q.B.D. 179.

[71] *Ex p. Sacker* (1888) 22 Q.B.D. 179, 185.

to recover goods which have been in his possession, or to restrain the cutting off of a supply of electric light to an hotel of which he is in possession.[72] In all these cases he acquires a right of action in the course of his receivership, but not in consequence of it alone.[73] So, also, a receiver can sue in his own name on contracts under which he has contracted as principal, *e.g.* in carrying on a business.[74]

Receiver as petitioning creditor in bankruptcy. A receiver is on similar principles a good petitioning creditor in respect of a judgment debt which has been assigned to him, although when received it would fall to be dealt with in the action in which he has been appointed [75]; but not in respect of specific sums ordered to be paid to him as receiver by a defendant, since he could not sue at law or in equity for such sums.[76]

Action by receiver of mortgaged property. After a receiver has been appointed by the court at the instance of a mortgagee the court may direct such proceedings as it considers proper to be commenced or carried on by the receiver at the expense of the mortgaged property: neither the mortgagor nor the mortgagee has an absolute right to insist on or prohibit an action being brought. Thus, in one case a company had commenced an action against its first mortgagees and a purchaser from them to set aside as fraudulent a sale by the former to the latter. The purchaser, having subsequently acquired the interest of a holder of debentures for £10,000 in the company, commenced in his name a debenture holder's action against the company and obtained the appointment of a receiver therein. The court, on the application of the company, ordered the receiver to carry on proceedings in the first action upon the terms that his costs should be a first charge on the company's assets, notwithstanding the protest of the plaintiff in the second action (who was the purchaser's nominee) that assets upon which the purchaser had in effect a first charge would be used to support a claim against him in another capacity.[77]

---

[72] *Husey* v. *London Electric Supply Corp.* [1902] 1 Ch. 411.

[73] *Ex p. Sacker, supra.*

[74] See *Moss S.S. Co.* v. *Whinney* [1912] A.C. 254.

[75] *Re Macoun* [1904] 2 K.B. 700.

[76] *Ex p. Sacker* (1888) 22 Q.B.D. 179; *cf. Re North Bucks Furniture Depositories* [1939] Ch. 690, where a local authority whose only remedy to recover rates was by distress was held competent to petition for winding up.

[77] *Viola* v. *Anglo-American Cold Storage Co.* [1912] 2 Ch. 305.

As has been already pointed out, if the receiver desires to bring an action, leave must be obtained and the application is not made by himself but a party.[78] The application is by summons.[79] Leave to defend,[80] compromise, or discontinue an action must be obtained in the same way. If the cause of action is one vested in the receiver personally, or if an action is brought against him personally, although he can sue or defend without leave, this is at his own risk as to costs; he should therefore obtain leave.

Where it becomes necessary for the receiver to obtain leave to sue in the name of a third person such as a liquidator [81] or a trustee in bankruptcy, he will only be allowed to do so on giving the latter a complete indemnity, not one limited to assets in the hands of the receiver.[82]

Receiver of partnership. When a receiver is appointed to manage a partnership concern, he must be guided by the terms of the order of appointment, keeping in mind the general maxim that, as his authority flows from the court, he must, in every case not covered by the terms of the order appointing him, act under a special order to be obtained from the court.

The court, by appointing a partner to be receiver, protects his operations, and gives him power to have recourse to the court for assistance and advice, but it does not enable him to do that, as against his partner, which the existing conventions or agreements between the parties do not justify.[83] The court has no power to clothe a receiver with an authority which would wholly transcend the nature of the original arrangement between the partners.[84] A partner appointed receiver is, like other receivers, an officer of the court and must act accordingly.[85] It is the duty of a partner to give such information to the receiver as may be necessary to enable him to collect the assets,[86] broadly corresponding to discovery in

---

[78] *Ante*, p. 180; see *Ward* v. *Swift* (1848) 6 Hare 309.

[79] Form, Atkin's *Court Forms* (2nd ed.), Vol. 33, p. 203.

[80] *Ibid.* p. 304.

[81] As to which, see p. 218, *post*.

[82] *Re Grenfell* [1915] H.B.R. 74; *Harrison* v. *St. Etienne Brewery Co.* [1893] W.N. 108; *Re Westminster Syndicate*, 99 L.T. 924.

[83] *Nieman* v. *Nieman* (1889) 43 Ch.D. 198.

[84] *Ibid. per* Bowen L.J. at p. 205.

[85] See *Davy* v. *Scarth* [1906] 1 Ch. 55.

[86] See *Ray* v. *Ellis* (1912) 56 S.J. 724, where the application for a direction to plaintiff to assist in preparing bills of cost due to a solicitor's business was refused in the circumstances. *Parsons* v. *Mather & Platt Ltd.* (1974) Dec. 9, C.A., Appeal Court Judgments (Civil Division) No. 392A.

the action. It is conceived that this duty could not be cut down by any provisions and the arrangements between the partners.

Where there was a conflict of interest between the receiver and the separate estate of a partner, whose trustee in bankruptcy the plaintiff was, it was held that the receiver ought not to be represented by the plaintiff's solicitor, but by the solicitor for the defendant.[87]

Other cases. It is not only in the case of a partnership,[88] that it may become necessary for the receiver to be advised by a separate solicitor in order that he may hold an even hand between the various parties interested.[89] But the mere fact that he consults a solicitor who is also a party, provided the advice is proper, does not necessarily invalidate a transaction with regard to which the advice is given, as against other parties.[90] If the receiver desires to employ a separate solicitor, except in the matter of vouching his own accounts,[91] he should obtain the leave of the court, on his own application if necessary.[92]

That the receiver appointed in an action should be made a party to proceedings in it, is in some cases necessary. Thus, if the receiver pays money in his hands to the solicitors of the plaintiff, who are also his own solicitors, without any previous instructions as to the specific application of the money, it is to be considered to be paid to them as the solicitors not of the plaintiff, but of the receiver, and the receiver must be made a party to an application for payment into court of the money by the solicitors.[93]

Power to lease. At the present day, a direction to set and let is not inserted in an order appointing a receiver over real or leasehold estate,[94] the judge having power to give any direction in chambers as to the management of the estate,[95] though in special circumstances the order may include a direction for the granting of a specific lease or power to grant a class of tenancies.

---

[87] *Bloomer* v. *Curie* (1907) 51 S.J. 277.

[88] See *Bloomer* v. *Curie, supra.*

[89] See, for instance, *Viola* v. *Anglo-American Cold Storage Co.* [1912] 2 Ch. 305.

[90] See *Re Rogerstone Brick, etc., Co.* [1919] 1 Ch. 110.

[91] As to which, see p. 256, *post.*

[92] See p. 181, *ante.*

[93] *Chater* v. *Maclean* (1855) 1 Jur.(N.S.) 175; see, too, *Dixon* v. *Wilkinson* (1859) 4 Drew. 614; 4 D. & J. 501; *Ind, Coope* v. *Kidd* (1894) 63 L.J.Q.B. 726.

[94] Under the former practice a direction to let was included in the order: see *Thornhill* v. *Thornhill* (1845) 14 Sim. 600.

[95] Seton (7th ed.), p. 725.

A receiver cannot, without the sanction of the court, set or let even for a single year.[96] The case of *Shuff* v. *Holdway* [97] was formerly cited as authority for the proposition that a receiver can now, without obtaining the sanction of the court, let for a period not exceeding three years; but the Court of Appeal has now laid it down that no valid lease can be made by a receiver without the sanction of the court; though the court can give a general authority to let or approve any lease which it considers necessary for the protection of, or making fruitful, the property over which a receiver is appointed,[98] and this, if necessary, even after the letting has in fact begun.[99] But even where the receiver is also appointed manager, he should obtain the sanction of the court to a proposed lease.

If a receiver himself grants a lease without sanction, as between him and the person who takes the lease, the lease will be binding by estoppel.[1] As between the lessee, however, and the owner of the legal estate, the lease has, in the absence of special circumstances, no binding force, even though it may have been made with the sanction of the judge.[2] The powers of the receiver are limited to receiving proposals and making arrangements as to the leasing of the property over which he has been appointed receiver.[3] He has no power by a lease made in his own name to transfer the legal estate in the property, nor can such a power be given to him by the judge.[4] Leases should be granted in the name of the estate owner. Leases by a mortgagor or mortgagee, or under the Settled Land Act 1925, or other statute, may be granted in the name of the estate owner, by the person empowered to grant the same, whether the estate owner or not.[5] The lease may be authorised to be executed by the receiver in the name of the proper party.

A receiver should apply for liberty to re-let before an existing

---

[96] *Wynne* v. *Lord Newborough* (1797) 1 Ves. 164.

[97] Seton (7th ed.), p. 769.

[98] *Anon.*, cited *arguendo* in *Stamford, etc., Banking Co.* v. *Keeble* [1913] 2 Ch. 98; *Re Cripps* [1946] Ch. 265; and see *Durnford* v. *Lane* (1806) 2 Madd.Ch.Pr. (3rd ed.) 302. *Quaere* whether a receiver and manager of a land company could properly grant leases without express leave where such grants were in the course of the ordinary business of the company: it is considered that a direction should be obtained.

[99] *Re Cripps, supra.*

[1] *Dancer* v. *Hastings* (1826) 4 Bing. 2; 12 Moo. 34.

[2] See *infra.*

[3] See *Gibbins* v. *Howell* (1818) 3 Madd. 469; *Evans* v. *Mathias* (1857) 7 E. & B. 602.

[4] Though he may be authorised to execute in the name of the estate owner, if a party.

[5] Law of Property Act 1925, s. 8.

lease expires and the property becomes vacant. If he neglects to do so, he may be visited with any loss which may arise.[6]

Where the court directs a receiver to give to any person the option of being tenant of some particular item of property, it generally reserves power to the receiver to inspect the state and condition of the property.[7]

In cases where the estate over which a receiver is appointed is out of the jurisdiction, it is usual to give the receiver more extensive powers of managing and letting than is usual in the case of estates situated in this country,[8] though in the latter case a general direction to avoid numerous applications is given more readily than was formerly the case. A reference to the master may be directed to inquire what should be the term beyond which the receiver should not be permitted to let.[9]

A receiver must let the estate over which he is acting as receiver to the best advantage. He is bound to obtain the best terms.[10] He may not, either in his own name or through the medium of a trustee,[11] become tenant of any part of the estate over which he is acting as receiver.[12] A receiver cannot raise the rents on slight grounds without the leave of the court,[13] nor can he abate the rents, or forgive the tenants their arrears, without leave or the consent of all parties beneficially interested.[14]

Mode in which proposals for leases are dealt with. Applications with reference to property under the management of a receiver are usually made by summons at chambers; proposals for the management and letting of the property may be made by any party interested.

Where a specific lease is to be sanctioned, the proposed tenant enters into a provisional agreement to become tenant or lessee of it upon terms specified in the agreement, subject to the approval of the judge. A summons for an order to carry the agreement into effect is then taken out by the plaintiff's solicitor and served on the

---

[6] *Wilkins* v. *Lynch* (1823) 2 Moll. 499.   [7] *Baylies* v. *Baylies* (1844) 1 Coll. 545.

[8] *Morris* v. *Elme* (1790) 1 Ves.Jun. 139.

[9] *Anon.* v. *Lindsay* (1808) 15 Ves. 91.

[10] *Wynne* v. *Lord Newborough* (1797) 1 Ves.Jun. 164.

[11] See also p. 203, *post.*

[12] *Meagher* v. *O'Shaughnessy* (1826) cit. Fl. & K. 207, 224; see, too, *Anderson* v. *Anderson* (1846) 9 Ir.Eq. 23; *Eyre* v. *M'Donnell* (1864) 15 Ir.Ch. 534. *Cf. King* v. *O'Brien* (1866) 15 L.T. 23.

[13] *Wynne* v. *Lord Newborough* (1797) 1 Ves.Jun. 164; *Alven* v. *Bond* (1841) Fl. & K. 196, 223.

[14] *Evans* v. *Taylor* (1837) Sausse & Sc. 681.

parties interested. The application is supported by the production of the agreement and the affidavit of a land agent, or other competent person, stating the grounds on which, in his judgment, the agreement should be adopted. The power of a party to demise on the terms specified should also be shown by proper evidence. It is convenient to schedule the form of lease to the agreement, in which case no further order is required. Otherwise on approval of the original agreement, either an order is made directing it to be carried into effect, and that the lease to be granted in pursuance thereof be settled by the judge, either absolutely or in case the parties differ; or, to save expense, the master indorses a minute of the approval on the summons, and adjourns the matter until the draft lease has been brought in for approval. Upon the draft lease, or a certified copy of the order (if any) approving the agreement, being left at chambers, a summons is taken out to settle the draft lease [15]; or, if no order has been drawn up, an appointment for this purpose is given. The summons, or notice of the appointment, is then served on the parties interested. The draft lease is then settled by the master, with the assistance, if necessary, of one of the conveyancing counsel. The draft is then engrossed in duplicate, and an affidavit is made, verifying the engrossment of the lease, and that of the counterpart, as being each a true and correct transcript of the draft as settled. A copy of this affidavit is left at chambers, with the engrossments and draft. The master then signs a memorandum of allowance in the margin of each engrossment, and issues his certificate of the result of the proceeding, which is completed in the usual way; or, if an order approving the agreement has been drawn up, an order is made approving the agreement and the lease. Where, as is often the case, the draft lease is settled at chambers before an order approving the agreement has been drawn up, the order may include an approval of the engrossments, thereby saving the expense of a certificate, which, indeed, is often dispensed with, the master's memorandum of allowance, in the margins of the engrossments, being deemed sufficient evidence of the fact of the lease having been settled by the judge.[16]

---

[15] As to forms of summons to approve of agreement to grant a lease, and of affidavits in support, and form of summons to settle a draft lease, see Atkin's *Court Forms* (2nd ed.), Vol. 33, p. 207.

[16] As to form of affidavit verifying engrossments of lease and counterpart, form of certificate of settlement of lease, and minutes of order approving an agreement and the lease to be issued in pursuance thereof, see Atkin's *Court Forms* (2nd ed.), Vol. 33, p. 207; Daniel's *Chancery Practice* (8th ed.), p. 932.

Where, however, the property is shown to be most advantageously let on a number of weekly or quarterly, or even yearly tenancies, a general authority would be given, with limitations as to terms and rent.[17]

Rescission of contract to take lease. If the person who has agreed to take the lease wishes to rescind the contract, his correct course is to apply to the court which sanctioned the contract for release.[18]

Power of receiver to give notice to quit. A receiver appointed by the court over lands, with a general authority to let the lands from year to year, has thereby an implied authority to determine such tenancies by regular notices to quit.[19]

If a tenant holds over after regular notice to quit given to him by a receiver, the court will give the receiver leave to sue the tenant for double the yearly value of the premises, under the Landlord and Tenant Act 1730, s. 1.[20]

Power to insure. A receiver of the rents and profits of real and leasehold estate may with propriety insure the property against damage by fire, either in his own name or in the names of trustees, and he will be allowed in his accounts the premiums which he has paid.[21]

Landlord and Tenant Acts 1927 and 1954. A receiver of leasehold property should, in a proper case, procure an application to be made to the master for directions as to claiming compensation for improvements under Part I of the Landlord and Tenant Act 1927; or a new lease under Part II of the Landlord and Tenant Act 1954. The notice will be given on behalf of the tenant and in his name; an equitable chargee of the tenant such as a debenture holder has a right to enforce the tenant's rights under the statute.[22]

---

[17] See *Anon.* v. *Lindsay* (1808) 15 Ves. 91.

[18] *Grace* v. *Boynton* (1877) 21 S.J. 631.

[19] *Doe* v. *Read* (1810) 12 East 61; *Crosbie* v. *Barry* (1838) Jon. & C. 106; *Wilkinson* v. *Colley* (1771) 5 Burr. 2694; *Jones* v. *Phipps* (1868) L.R. 3 Q.B. 572. As to requirements of notices to quit, see *May* v. *Borup* [1915] 1 K.B. 830; *Queen's Club, etc. Ltd.* v. *Bignell* [1924] 1 K.B. 117; *Dagger* v. *Shepherd* [1946] K.B. 215; *Crate* v. *Miller* [1947] K.B. 946 (date for which notice is given); and, as to agricultural tenancies, Agricultural Holdings Act 1948, ss. 3, 23 and 24; *cf. Edell* v. *Dulieu* [1924] A.C. 38.

[20] *Wilkinson* v. *Colley* (1771) 5 Burr. 2694.

[21] *Re Graham* [1895] 1 Ch. 66, 71; as to employment of policy moneys in rebuilding, see *Sinnot* v. *Bowden* [1912] 2 Ch. 414.

[22] *Gough Garages* v. *Pugsley* [1930] 1 K.B. 615 (a decision under the 1927 Act).

Anything authorised or required by the provisions of the Landlord and Tenant Act 1954, other than those relating to the supplying of information [23] to be done at any time by, to or with the
landlord, or a landlord of a specified description, is, if at that time
the interest of the landlord is subject to a mortgage and a receiver
has been appointed thereunder, authorised or required to be done
by, to or with the mortgagee instead of that landlord.[24]

Miscellaneous notices. Where a receiver of the landlord's interest
has been served with any notices under these or any other Act
(*e.g.* the Town and Country Planning Act 1971 or Housing Acts
1957 to 1975), he should at once cause an application to be made to
the master by the plaintiff for directions.

Power of receiver as to repairs. A receiver appointed by the
court may lay out small sums of money in customary repairs, or
may allow the same to a tenant, but he may not apply money in
repairs to any considerable extent without a previous application
to the judge.[25] It was at one time a rule of the Court of Chancery
that the receiver of an estate could not lay out any money on it
without a previous order of the court.[26] At the present day the rule
of the court is not so strict; a receiver may effect without leave
small repairs estimated to cost not over £150 in any one accounting
period. If the limit is exceeded, the master may allow the excess if
the receiver establishes (if necessary by means of an inquiry) that
he has acted reasonably.[27] If the nature of the property is such that
the normal expenditure is likely to be greater, application should
be made by summons for the limit to be increased in the particular
case.[28] Where the receiver is appointed manager, he can, without
special leave, expend money on such current repairs as are necessary for the purposes of the business. There is no need to stress the
potential liability upon a receiver who allows the premises to
remain out of repair.[29]

If from their extent, or the circumstances under which money
for repairs is claimed, the receiver feels any difficulty in allowing

---

[23] Under s. 40 (2) and (3).
[24] s. 67.
[25] *Waters* v. *Taylor* (1808) 15 Ves. 25; *Ex p. Izard* (1883) 23 Ch.D. 80.
[26] *Tempest* v. *Ord* (1816) 2 Mer. 55, 56.
[27] *Att.-Gen.* v. *Vigor* (1805) 11 Ves. 563; *Tempest* v. *Ord* (1816) 2 Mer. 55; *Ex p.
Izard* (1883) 23 Ch.D. 80. *Cf. Re Langham* (1837) 2 Ph. 299.
[28] Practice Direction [1970] 1 W.L.R. 520.
[29] Consider *Solomons* v. *R. Gertzenstein Ltd.* [1954] 2 Q.B. 243.

them to be done, he should apply to the plaintiff's solicitor to
obtain the sanction of the judge, which is obtained on summons
supported by an affidavit stating the nature and costs of the
repairs and the reasons which lead to their being necessary: an
affidavit by a surveyor may be required if the repairs are extensive.[30]

Power to borrow. If a receiver requires money to enable him to
discharge his duties, the court will give him leave to borrow upon
the security of the property in his hands. This power is most
frequently exercised in the case of a receiver and manager
appointed in the debenture holder's actions.[31]

A receiver appointed under the Mental Health jurisdiction who
was plaintiff in an action relative to certain property of the
patient, upon which were mortgages which the mortgagee was
threatening to call in, was, on application being made in the
action, authorised to borrow upon security of the patient's
property sufficient money to pay a commission to a proposed
transferee of the mortgages as a consideration for his consenting
to take the transfer.[32]

Management of the estate. An order may be obtained in chambers, authorising a receiver to cut and sell timber, and to employ
it, if necessary, in repairs.[33] The court, before giving liberty to cut
timber for repairs, may direct inquiries.[34] Where there is a receiver,
a sale of timber is usually effected under his direction.[35] The receiver
of an estate may obtain an order to grant a licence to win and
get clay and brick earth on the estate, and to manufacture the
same into bricks.[36] But the court has no jurisdiction in a foreclosure action to sanction the grant of a licence to work deposits of
peat, which amounted in effect to a sale of the surface by instalments, nor to sanction mining leases other than such as are
authorised by statute.[37]

An application by a person not a party to the action, for

---

[30] See Seton (7th ed.), p. 770; and, as to order giving the receiver liberty to expend money in repairs, *ibid.* p. 765.
[31] See *post*, p. 239, where the matter is treated at length.
[32] *Chaplin* v. *Barnett* (1911) 28 T.L.R. 256; this order was made under R.S.C., Ord. 29, r. 2.
[33] Seton (7th ed.), p. 766.
[34] Seton (7th ed.), p. 770.
[35] *Ibid.* 766.
[36] *Ibid.* 766.
[37] *Stamford Banking Co.* v. *Keeble* [1913] 2 Ch. 96.

directions as to the management of real property by a receiver, may be made by summons at chambers.[38]

Estate of stranger. Where the estate of a stranger has come into possession of the receiver in an action, and possession of it has been held by him with the acquiescence of such of the parties to the action as are not under disability, and without objection on behalf of any party under disability, the transaction is binding on all those parties; the stranger will be ordered to be compensated out of the fund in court in respect of any rents of the stranger's estate received by the receiver and not paid over to the stranger, and also in regard to any dilapidations during the receiver's possession, since the stranger has a right against the fund by subrogation to the receiver's right of indemnity.[39] This may be ordered on the application of the stranger, although he be not a party to the action.[40]

Lessee committing waste. After a receiver has been appointed an injunction will be granted on motion to restrain a person, in possession under an agreement, from committing waste, though the latter is not a party to the action.[41]

Leaseholds generally. As has already been pointed out, a receiver over leaseholds, though not personally liable,[42] is bound in the first place, out of the sub-rents, to discharge the head-rent and outgoings payable to a lessor, for which the person whose estate is being dealt with by the court is actually liable to that lessor.

If, in consequence of the receiver's default, the head-lessor is compelled to institute proceedings for the recovery of the head-rent, the receiver is held liable for costs, if sub-rents have reached his hands. The sub-rents should be, in the first place, appropriated to the payment of the head-rent. If the receiver pursues a different course, and pays away sub-rents received without providing for the head-rent, choosing to speculate upon obtaining other funds

---

[38] *O'Hagan* v. *North Wingfield Colliery Co.* (1882) 26 S.J. 671; and see *Searle* v. *Choat* (1884) 25 Ch.D. 723.

[39] *Neate* v. *Pink* (1851) 15 Sim. 450; explained in *Hand* v. *Blow* [1901] 2 Ch. 721, 728; *cf. Brocklebank* v. *East London Ry.* (1879) 12 Ch.D. 839. *Quaere,* whether, if the fund remaining in court is insufficient, the stranger could recover from the parties into whose hands the money had come: see *Re Jones's Estates* [1914] 1 I.R. 188.

[40] *Neate* v. *Pink* (1851) 15 Sim. 450.

[41] *Walton* v. *Johnson* (1848) 15 Sim. 352; see, too, *Casamajor* v. *Strode* (1823) 1 Sim. & St. 381.

[42] *Consolidated Entertainments Ltd.* v. *Taylor* [1937] 4 All E.R. 432.

wherewith to pay the latter, he does not act in accordance with the course of the court, and he will be compelled by the court to pay any arrears of the head-rent.[43]

Leaseholds mortgaged by sub-demise. But the above principle does not apply where the receiver has been appointed at the instance of a mortgagee between whom and the lessor or head-lessor there is no such privity as to make the mortgagee liable to pay rent or other outgoings to such lessor or head-lessor, as in the case of a mortgage by sub-demise or by way of legal or equitable charge,[44] the receiver is not, any more than the mortgagee in whose right he was appointed, liable, whether in possession or not, to the lessor or head-lessor for rent or other outgoings. There is no equity entitling the lessor to claim rent, or damages for breach of (for instance) a repairing covenant in the lease, from the receiver by reason of his having occupied the mortgaged premises, even though he has, under an order of the court, sold off the mortgagor's goods and so in effect deprived the lessor of a remedy by distress: there is no principle of honour, honesty or justice requiring the court to interfere in such a case [45]; nor, if the receiver has sold the leaseholds, has the lessor any remedy against the fund in court.[46] And the same principles apply to the use by the receiver of goods on hire to the mortgagor.[47]

But though payment of rent cannot be enforced against the receiver or the fund where the appointment is made on the application of a mortgagee by sub-demise or an equitable incumbrancer, it is often necessary for the receiver to obtain leave to pay the rent in order to avoid distress and safeguard goods on the premises. A receiver who has himself entered into a tenancy

---

[43] *Balfe* v. *Blake* (1850) 1 Ir.Ch.R. 365; *Jacobs* v. *Van Boolen* (1889) 34 S.J. 97. *Cf. Re Mayfair and General Property Trust Ltd.* (1945) 174 L.T. 1.

[44] It must be borne in mind that in the case of sub-terms with a declaration of trust subsisting at the commencement of the Law of Property Act 1925, where the right of redemption was barred or the property had been sold, the head term vests in the mortgagee unless he disclaims it before action: Law of Property Act 1925, Sched. I, Part III, para. 3, and para. 7 (*a*) and (*m*).

[45] *Hand* v. *Blow* [1901] 2 Ch. 721. In *Neate* v. *Pink* (1851) 15 Sim. 450, the court appears to have treated the relationship of landlord and tenant as subsisting in the circumstances between the lessor and the receiver, which thus gave the former a right by subrogation against the fund: see judgment of Stirling L.J. in *Hand* v. *Blow*, *supra*. The receiver is not estopped by having paid one instalment of the rent: *Justice* v. *James* (1898) 15 T.L.R. 181.

[46] *Re J. W. Abbott & Co.* [1913] W.N. 284; but, it is submitted, a reasonable sum in respect of the receiver's occupation would be paid to the lessor: see *Neate* v. *Pink* (1851) 15 Sim. 450. *Cf. Hay* v. *Swedish, etc., Ry.* (1892) 8 T.L.R. 775.

[47] *Hay* v. *Swedish, etc., Ry., supra*.

agreement is personally liable for the rent and the lessor can claim against the fund by subrogation.[48]

If there is uncertainty as to the amount of rent due to the head-lessor, the receiver should cause an application to be made for directions; if he waits until the head-lessor makes an application on the subject, he may appear by his solicitor, state the facts, and have the court's order accordingly.

If the lessor has recovered judgment for possession, rent and mesne profits against the lessee, he cannot recover rent from a person who is actually in possession, such as a receiver for debenture holders of a company entitled in equity to the lease.[49] Inasmuch as the court will in a proper case direct its officer to do what is right and honourable,[50] although it does not profess to cure all the inconveniences caused by the appointment of a receiver,[51] it will, it is submitted, not allow a receiver to retain rents from sub-tenants without paying a head-rent, even though there is no actual liability on the mortgagees to pay such head-rent as between them and the head-lessor, since otherwise the sub-tenants would be exposed to distress and forfeiture: in such a case, it seems, the head-rent would be ordered to be paid out of the funds[52]; and if the receiver has elected to remain in possession and receive a profit rental under a lease in respect of which the company was liable directly to the lessee, *semble* that the receiver will be ordered to pay to the lessor out of moneys in his hands the amount of dilapidations due on the determination of the lease, though the lessor may not be entitled as of right to such payment.[53]

Abandonment of leaseholds. Leave may be given to the receiver of a company to abandon unprofitable leaseholds where neither

---

[48] See p. 238, *post*.

[49] *Re Westminster Motor Garage Co.* (1914) 84 L.J.Ch. 753. Debenture holders or trustees for debenture holders are not necessary parties to an action by the lessor involving forfeiture; they can by leave be added on terms, *Egerton* v. *Jones* [1939] 2 K.B. 702.

[50] As to which, see *Hand* v. *Blow* [1901] 2 Ch. 721; *Re John Griffiths Cycle Corp.* [1902] W.N. 9 (refusal of application by successful appellants to House of Lords for receiver to pay money paid into court by him as security for costs of appeal to the Court of Appeal, and paid out to him, on appeal succeeding in the Court of Appeal); see also *Re Abdy* [1919] 2 K.B. 735; *Re Wigzell* [1921] 2 K.B. 835; *Scranton's Trustee* v. *Pearse* [1922] 2 Ch. 87; *Re Savoy Estate Ltd.* [1949] Ch. 622.

[51] *Per* Collins M.R. in *Hand* v. *Blow, supra.*

[52] See judgment of Stirling L.J. in *Hand* v. *Blow, supra,* and cases cited therein; *Re Levi* [1919] 1 Ch. 416: in most cases the payment would be necessary to prevent forfeiture of a beneficial lease.

[53] *Hand* v. *Blow* [1901] 2 Ch. 736; see *Re Levi* [1919] 1 Ch. 416.

the company nor debenture holders can benefit; the receiver may, however, be ordered to pay rent accrued during possession by him.[54]

Forfeiture of lease. A mortgagee is not a necessary party to an action by a lessor against the lessee involving forfeiture and if the mortgagee wishes to intervene he can be allowed to do so on terms [55]: it may sometimes be necessary for a receiver of leaseholds to obtain a direction as to applying for leave to intervene in such an action in the name of the mortgagee. Leave to serve a counter-notice under the Leasehold Property (Repairs) Act 1938, as amended,[56] may also be necessary.

Rates. As rating authorities normally have an adequate remedy by means of distress, a receiver will not in general be ordered to pay rates, even if he has been receiving inclusive rentals from the tenants of the property.[57]

Income tax. The liability of a receiver to be assessed to tax has already been mentioned.[58] He is presumably also liable to be assessed where he makes any annual payment otherwise than out of profits brought into charge in respect of tax deducted from that payment.[59]

The priority of the Crown in the case of companies is discussed on a later page.[60] In the case of an insolvent estate whether or not an order has been made for administration in bankruptcy under the Bankruptcy Act 1914, s. 130, subject to payment of funeral and testamentary expenses and debts, the same rules as to priority and otherwise apply as in bankruptcy.[61]

It is not within the scope of this work to deal with all the questions as to income tax, capital gains tax, and other taxes which may have to be considered by a receiver over a business or estate; only those matters are attempted to be dealt with which apply to a receiver as distinct from other persons.

---

[54] *Cf. Hay* v. *Swedish, etc. Ry.* (1889) 8 T.L.R. 775.

[55] *Egerton* v. *Jones* [1939] 2 K.B. 702.

[56] See Landlord and Tenant Act 1954, s. 51.

[57] *Re British Fuller's Earth Co.* (1901) 17 T.L.R. 232; *Re Mayfair and General Property Trust Ltd.* (1945) 174 L.T. 1.

[58] p. 132, *ante.*

[59] Income and Corporation Taxes Act 1970, s. 53; Finance Act 1971, ss. 36, 37 and Sched. 6, para. 21. The tax is assessed at the basic rate at date of payment.

[60] p. 209, *post.*

[61] Administration of Estates Act 1925, Sched. I, Part I.

The appointment of a receiver over a business will result in a discontinuance of the trade of the former owner, since the receiver is himself a principal. If he has the direction and control of any property in respect of which income tax is charged in accordance with the provisions of the Income Tax Acts, he will be assessed and charged as if the property were not under the direction and control of the court.[62] And he will be answerable for doing all matters and things required to be done under the Income Tax Acts for the purpose of assessment and payment of income tax.[63]

Subject to any necessary modifications the foregoing provisions apply in relation to capital gains tax as they apply in relation to income tax.[64] They do not, however, affect the question of who is the person to whom chargeable gains accrue, or who is chargeable to the tax, so far as that question is relevant for the purposes of any exemption, or of any provision determining the rate at which capital gains are chargeable.[65]

Purchase tax.[66] For the position in relation to purchase tax, see 14th ed., pp. 188–189.

Value Added Tax. A receiver and manager who makes or intends to make taxable supplies (that is to say, any supply of goods or services other than an exempt supply) [67] for the purpose of the relevant legislation is liable to register under Part I of the Finance Act 1972, and to pay value added tax, in precisely the same circumstances as any individual trader.[68] Since the whole of the business in relation to which he is the receiver and manager will have been transferred to him by the order of the court as a going concern, there will be no charge to this tax on the assets of the business thus transferred to his control on his appointment, nor, conversely, will there be any charge to tax merely on this account on his discharge.[69] The receiver must, however, see to the preservation of any records of the business which under the Act are required to be preserved for any period after the transfer, unless the Commissioners of Customs and Excise otherwise direct.[70]

---

[62] Taxes Management Act 1970, s. 75 (1).
[63] *Ibid.* s. 75 (2).
[64] *Ibid.* s. 77 (1).
[65] *Ibid.* s. 77 (2).
[66] Abolished by the Finance Act 1972, s. 54.
[67] Finance Act 1972, s. 46 (1).
[68] *Ibid.* s. 4 and Sched. 1.
[69] *Ibid.* s. 25 (*a*).
[70] *Ibid.* s. 25 (*b*) and s. 46 (1).

War Damage Act 1943. For the position under this Act see 13th ed., pp. 196–197.

Payment to avoid distress. Where a receiver for debenture holders paid a debt due to the Crown to avoid distraint it was held that he could not claim to be paid a sum, equal to the amount of the discharged debt, out of money, due from the Crown to the company, which had been assigned to third persons.[71]

Duty when tenants interfered with. When the receiver is informed by tenants that defendants have interfered with the rents it is his duty to move for a committal.[72] The interference of the owner of the inheritance with the rents does not exempt the receiver from being charged with the whole amount: in order to discharge himself he must show what the owner of the inheritance received, or hindered him from getting.[73]

Interference between parties. The receiver appointed in an action ought not to interfere in any litigation between the parties to it. If he does, he will not be allowed the costs of a motion for such a purpose.[74]

Interest on incumbrances. If a receiver is appointed at the instance of a puisne mortgagee or judgment creditor, it is no part of his duty without directions to apply any part of the rents in keeping down interest on prior incumbrances.[75] Where, however, he is appointed over a trust estate, or in similar cases, and also where he is directed to keep down the interest on incumbrances, he ought, except under very special circumstances, so far as the rents and profits will go, to pay them on account of the interest of the several incumbrancers in the order of their priority.[76] This rule applies where the receiver has been appointed over the interest of a tenant for life. He must keep down interest on incumbrances on the fee simple out of the rents.

Trade fixtures. Trade machinery and fixtures,[77] a right to remove which belongs to a lessee as against his lessor, pass with the land

---

[71] *Re Ind, Coope & Co.* [1911] 2 Ch. 223; *quaere* whether one debt could have been set off against the other before payment.

[72] *Anon.* (1829) 2 Moll. 499.

[73] *Hamilton* v. *Lighton* (1810) 2 Moll. 499.

[74] *Comyn* v. *Smith* (1823) 1 Hog. 81.

[75] A receiver appointed out of court must keep down interest on prior incumbrances: Law of Property Act 1925, s. 109 (8).

[76] See *Re Kearney* (1890) 25 L.R.Ir. 89.

[77] As to what are fixtures in case of a theatre, see *Vaudeville El. Cinema Ltd.* v. *Muriset* [1923] 2 Ch. 74.

to a mortgagee of the leasehold interest, who can sell them with the land, though he has no right to sever them from the land during the term; if, however, he severs and sells them apart from the land they do not revest in the mortgagor, who has no right to the proceeds of sale, but only a possible claim for damages. Where, therefore, a receiver for debenture holders had consented to a sale of the fixtures by a prior mortgagee the debenture holders had no claim to the proceeds of sale.[78] If the receiver of a business, carried on on leasehold premises during the term, sells machinery and plant, the right of the tenant to which has been negatived by the terms of the lease, the landlord has a right to affirm the sale and recover the proceeds without waiting for the end of the term.[79]

A mortgagee has a reasonable time to remove trade fixtures after the lease has determined. Therefore, where after the appointment of a receiver the lease was determined under a proviso contained in it by the lessee company going into voluntary liquidation, the receiver was entitled to a reasonable time for the sale on the premises and removal of the fixtures, notwithstanding a demand for immediate possession by the lessor.[80]

Statute-barred debts. If a receiver has power to pay debts, he may pay an instalment of a debt, even though the effect of his doing so may be to stop the Limitation Act from running.[81] But a payment made by a receiver, which is not authorised by the order appointing him, will not stop the statute from running[82]; nor will payment by a person administering the estate of a person of unsound mind without an order appointing him receiver.[83] A receiver must not pay statute-barred debts, if not specifically authorised to do so, unless the statute has not run at the date of his appointment. If there is a doubt he should apply for directions.[84]

---

[78] *Re Rogerstone Brick and Stone Co.* [1919] 1 Ch. 110: the prior mortgage had been created with the express assent of the debenture holders, and it was considered that it would have been oppressive for the receiver to refuse his consent.
[79] *Re British Red Ash Collieries Ltd.* [1920] 1 Ch. 327.
[80] *Re Glasdir Copper Works* [1904] 1 Ch. 819.
[81] *Re Hale, Lilley* v. *Foad* [1899] 2 Ch. 107; and see *Wandsworth Union* v. *Worthington* [1906] 1 K.B. 420, where payment to guardians by a receiver under an order in lunacy of the income of the patient's estate (which was insufficient to discharge the sums due for maintenance) was held to take a claim for arrears of maintenance out of the statute.
[82] *Whitley* v. *Lowe* (1858) 25 Beav. 421.
[83] *Re Beavan* [1912] 1 Ch. 196.
[84] See *Re Fleetwood and District Electric Light and Power Syndicate* [1915] 1 Ch. 486; and see *Hibernian Bank* v. *Yourrel* [1919] I.R. 310.

If a receiver directed to keep down interest on a prior incumbrance makes overpayments through a mistake of fact, such as
ignorance of a proviso for a reduction of the rate on punctual payment, the person to whose prejudice the overpayments were
made can recover them from the mortgagee, up to a period of six
years before action.[85]

A receiver appointed on behalf of a mortgagee was the " agent "
of the mortgagor within the Real Property Limitation Act 1833,
s. 40, and a payment of interest by him stopped the running of the
statute [86] and the same is the case under section 24 of the Limitation Act 1939.

Receiver must not defend without leave. It is not proper for a
receiver to defend, without sanction, actions brought against him.[87]
In the case where a receiver had, without the authority of the court,
defended an action arising out of a distress made by him upon a
tenant of the estate for rent, and was unsuccessful, the court
refused to allow him his costs of the action.[88] But if he successfully defends an action brought against him, without putting the
estate to the expense of an application to the court, which he might
have made for his own security, he will stand in the same position
as to indemnity as if he had made that application.[89]

A motion by the tenants of an estate, to restrain a receiver from
doing acts which are within his authority, will be refused with
costs; for they have no sufficient interest to support it.[90]

Sale.[91] A receiver acquires no power of sale by virtue of his
appointment, but in most cases the court has power to direct a
sale of the property over which the receivership extends; for

---

[85] See *Re Jones's Estates* [1914] 1 I.R. 188. Money paid out of court under a mistake of fact may be ordered to be repaid: *Platt* v. *Casey's Brewery* [1912] 1 I.R. 279.

[86] *Chinnery* v. *Evans* (1864) 11 H.L.C. 115; *cf.* Law of Property Act 1925, s. 109 (2).

[87] *Anon.* (1801) 6 Ves. 287; *Swaby* v. *Dickon* (1833) 5 Sim. 629. The receiver should
not wait to apply for leave to defend an action until just before trial: *Anon.* (1801) 6
Ves. 286.

[88] *Swaby* v. *Dickon* (1833) 5 Sim. 629; see *Re Montgomery* (1828) 1 Moll. 419.

[89] *Bristowe* v. *Needham* (1847) 2 Ph. 190, 191. But whether he will, in any particular
case, be indemnified in respect of his costs of defence will depend upon the nature of
the action; see *Re Dunn* [1904] 1 Ch. 648; p. 236, *post.* If the possession of a tenant
under a receiver is disturbed, and no application is made to the court to prevent the
disturbance, the tenant is entitled to the costs of protecting his own possession:
Miller v. *Elkins* (1825) 3 L.J.Ch. 128.

[90] *Wynne* v. *Lord Newborough* (1797) 1 Ves.Jun. 164.

[91] As to capital gains tax, see p. 200, *post.* The receiver will not normally be
directly concerned in any conveyance or transfer of ownership, but if he is he will
be doing so for this purpose as the nominee of the true owner.

instance, where the appointment is made in an action for fore-closure, redemption or sale,[92] including, of course, debenture holders' actions,[93] or in the administration of the estate of a deceased person. The court has power under R.S.C., Ord. 29, r. 4, on the application of any party, to make an order for the sale by any persons and in any manner, of any goods, wares or merchandise which may be of a perishable nature or likely to injure from keeping, or which for any other just and sufficient reason it may be desirable to have sold at once.[94] A sale may be ordered to enforce a charge over land under the Administration of Justice Act 1956, even if a receiver has been appointed thereunder.[95]

In the case of statutory corporations formed to work a public undertaking, a sale of the undertaking cannot be ordered,[96] except where the statute under which the incorporation takes effect authorises a sale.[97]

Although the substance of what was formerly one rule of court [98] has now been split between two rules,[99] in a debenture holder's action, where the debenture holders have a charge and the plaintiff is suing on behalf of himself and other debenture holders, a sale may be ordered before as well as after judgment before all persons interested are ascertained, where the judge is of opinion that there must eventually be a sale.[1] A sale out of court may be directed if all parties are before the court or bound by the order. The sale is frequently ordered to be made by the receiver, and if not directed to be made out of court a conditional contract by him is approved by the judge.[2] The order contains directions as to disposal of the purchase-money.

---

[92] Law of Property Act 1925, ss. 90, 91. Sale cannot be made of part of the surface apart from the rest: see *Stamford, etc., Banking Co.* v. *Keeble* [1913] 2 Ch. 96.

[93] See Palmer's *Company Precedents* (16th ed.), Vol. III, Chap. 60; for an order for sale of a claim against directors, see *Wood* v. *Woodhouse* [1896] W.N. 4.

[94] See notes to this rule in the *Supreme Court Practice* (1976), Vol. 1, p. 474.

[95] Law of Property Act 1925, s. 90.

[96] *Re Woking U.D.C. Act* 1911 [1914] 1 Ch. 300; *Gardner* v. *L.C. & D. Ry.* (1867) 2 Ch. 201.

[97] See *Re Crystal Palace Co.* (1911) 104 L.T. 898; *sub nom. Saunders* v. *Bevan* (1912) 107 L.T. 70.

[98] The former R.S.C., Ord. 51, r. 1 (*b*).

[99] R.S.C., Ord. 29, r. 4 (personalty); Ord. 31, r. 1 (land).

[1] See notes on Debenture Holders' Actions in Vol. II of the *Supreme Court Practice* (1976), paras. 2471–2522, and generally as to sales in debenture holders' actions, Palmer's *Company Precedents* (16th ed.), Vol. III, Chap. 60.

[2] Unless all debenture holders subsequent to the plaintiff are parties, it is usual to direct a sale with the approbation of the judge that absent debenture holders may be brought in on the application to approve the conditional contract: *Re Crigglestone*

Prior and subsequent incumbrancers should not be served with notice of judgment under Ord. 44, r. 3. Subsequent incumbrancers should be added as parties under Ord. 15, r. 6. Where a sale is ordered with the consent of prior incumbrancers in the form used in a creditor's action, informal notice may be given with a view to obtaining such consent.[3]

In cases where the court directs the sale out of court or with the approbation of the judge, the sale is often ordered to be by the receiver, especially in cases where the whole of an undertaking is sold; but, except in the case of the chattels which pass by delivery, the assurance of the property must be executed in the names of those persons in whom the property is vested.[4] The receiver as such has no power in his own name to convey the legal estate which must always where practicable be conveyed by and in the name of the estate owner.[5]

Where the contract is entered into subject to the approval of the court, and the receiver takes no step before the day fixed for completion to obtain such approval, the purchaser is entitled to repudiate the contract and recover his deposit.[6]

A receiver can sell the copyright of a book which had been assigned to the company, free from any author's lien for royalties where such royalties had not, by the original assignment, been charged as an unpaid vendor's lien, but were only secured by the covenant of the company.[7]

Where the receiver is appointed manager he can carry out all such sales as are necessary for the ordinary conduct of the business over which he is appointed, but no sale of the permanent plant or assets should be made without leave of the court.

Capital Gains Tax. As has already been noted, save as regards chattels which pass by delivery, any assurance of property in pursuance of a sale made by a receiver must be executed in the names of the persons in whom the property is vested, or by those who are

---

Coal Co. [1906] 1 Ch. 523. In ordinary cases formal notice of judgment is not served on the debenture holders of the same class but notice is given them by circular letter or advertisement. If a debenture holder served with such notice of the proceedings (without formal notice of the judgment) wishes to attend the proceedings, he must apply for leave: *Re W. Mate & Sons Ltd.* [1920] 1 Ch. 551.

[3] Direction of judges of the Chancery Division, May 12, 1909.

[4] See p. 201, *post.*	[5] See Law of Property Act 1925, ss. 7 (4), 8, 88, 89.

[6] *Re Sandwell Park Colliery Co. Ltd.* [1929] 1 Ch. 277.

[7] *Barker* v. *Stickney* [1919] 1 K.B. 121. As to sale of trade marks and right to use name, *Hart* v. *Thurber Whyland* (1908) 32 R.P.C. 217; *Wood* v. *Hall* (1916) 33 R.P.C. 16.

entitled otherwise to convey it.[8] A receiver is therefore not normally concerned directly with any questions relating to the payment of capital gains tax. Even if he is, for whatever reason, concerned with the disposal of any asset, where he has been appointed for the purpose of enforcing a security, charge, or incumbrance over an asset, he will not be concerned with the incidence of capital gains tax on the disposal of that asset.[9] Where this is not the case, for example where the receiver has been appointed in a partnership dispute, the position is not quite so clear cut, but it is considered that the provisions of section 22 (5) of the Finance Act 1965 produce the result that the basic liability for any capital gains tax arising on the disposal of the asset lies with the person or persons ultimately adjudged to be the true owner or owners thereof. For, although the matter remains doubtful, or may remain doubtful, until the final determination of the action, the receiver will at all times be holding the assets entrusted to him in a fiduciary capacity for those ultimately found to be properly entitled thereto.[10]

Sale through agent. Where the sale is effected through an agent whom the receiver has not obtained the leave of the court to employ, without any binding agreement as to the payment of commission, the court, in its discretion, may award him such compensation for his services as it thinks right.[11]

Conveyance of legal estate. Where the plaintiff or other party is a legal mortgagee, the order for sale may authorise him to convey the fee simple or term, under the powers conferred by the Law of Property Act 1925, s. 92.[12] But where the order merely authorises the sale to be carried into effect, if the contract is entered into by the receiver, the legal mortgagee alone cannot convey the fee simple, or in the case of leaseholds the head-term which remains in the mortgagor.[13] The company or other mortgagor and any other legal mortgagees must concur in the conveyance, unless an order is made under section 91 (7). The concurrence of parties to the action or persons bound by the order with only equitable interests, such as second debenture holders without a fixed legal

---

[8] See p. 200, *ante* and also *infra*.

[9] Finance Act 1965, s. 22 (5), (7): see p. 303, *post*.

[10] Finance Act 1965, s. 22 (5): see p. 130, *ante*, as to the nature of the receiver's possession.

[11] *Re National Flying Services Ltd., Cousins* v. *The Company* [1936] Ch. 271.

[12] See subs. (7) of s. 92 of the Law of Property Act 1925.

[13] s. 104 only applies where the sale is made by a mortgagee.

charge, is not necessary, as they are bound by the order: but unless they are parties or bound by the order their concurrence is necessary. If the plaintiff is an equitable mortgagee or has a charge under the Administration of Justice Act 1956, power to convey the legal estate can be obtained under section 90 or 91.

Dissolved corporations. If a company has been dissolved before the contract for sale has been completed by conveyance, an order must be obtained under the Trustee Act 1925, s. 44 (1) (ii) (c), for vesting in the purchaser any legal interest in land which was vested in the company [14]; or under section 51 (1) (ii) (c) in the case of other property.[15] By section 354 of the Companies Act 1948,[16] all property and rights vested in or held in trust for a dissolved company immediately before its dissolution (including leaseholds, but not including property held by the company on trust for any other person) vest as *bona vacantia* in the Crown or the Duchy of Lancaster or the Duke of Cornwall, as the case may be. Having regard to the exclusion of property held in trust for any person, the section does not apparently apply to property in which a bare legal estate is left in the company after receipt of the purchase-money. A summons for a vesting order under section 44 or section 51 of the Trustee Act can be applied for and should be served on the Solicitor to the Treasury.[17] These sections of the Trustee Act apply in the case of any dissolved corporation, while section 354 of the Companies Act 1948 only applies to companies within the meaning of that Act.[18] By section 181 of the Law of Property Act 1925, where by reason of the dissolution of a corporation before or after the Act, a legal estate in any property has determined,[19] the court

---

[14] As to effect of a vesting order, see Law of Property Act 1925, s. 9 (1) (b). See *Re Strathblaine Estates Ltd.* [1948] Ch. 228.

[15] See also Law of Property Act 1925, s. 3 (5). For a case of a patent, *Re Dutton's Patent* [1923] W.N. 64.

[16] Re-enacting s. 296 of the Companies Act 1929, which, however, was held not to be retrospective; but the doctrine that *bona vacantia* vest in the Crown applies to leaseholds apart from the section; *Re Spencer Wells* [1933] 1 Ch. 29. The Crown has since July 1, 1948, had power to disclaim any property so vesting. See Companies Act 1948, s. 355.

[17] This was not formerly done in all cases: see *Re 9 Bomore Road* [1906] 1 Ch. 359.

[18] *i.e.* companies formed and registered under the Act or the Acts which it replaces, being the Companies Act 1929, the Companies (Consolidation) Act 1908, the Companies Act 1862, and the Joint Stock Companies Acts. It had previously been held that the doctrine of *bona vacantia* did not apply in the case of an unregistered company: *Re Tierney* [1914] 1 I.R. 142. For the power of the court to declare a dissolution void, see s. 352 of the 1948 Act.

[19] For a criticism of the theory upon which this section is apparently based, see *Re Strathblaine Estates Ltd.* [1948] Ch. 228.

may by order create a corresponding estate and vest the same in the person who would have been entitled to the determined estate. Under the present practice, application for a vesting order should be made under the Trustee Act 1925 in all cases where that statute applies, and under section 181 of the Law of Property Act 1925 only where the former Act does not apply. It has been the practice to serve a petition for a vesting order in the case of leaseholds on the reversioner [20]; but having regard to section 354 of the Companies Act 1948 it seems that this is not now necessary in the case of a company within that Act, unless any question of forfeiture arises.

The doubt which had been felt [21] as to whether a debt due to a dissolved corporation vests in the Crown as *bona vacantia* is resolved as regards companies formed and registered under the Companies Acts, by section 354 of the Companies Act 1948. Leaseholds vest in the Crown as *bona vacantia* apart from this section.[22]

Alternatives to sale. Where a sale is impracticable, or is not desired, it may be necessary to obtain the sanction of the court to a scheme of arrangement under section 206 of the Companies Act 1948. It is not necessary that such scheme should be in the nature of a compromise [23]: but if it involves a reduction of capital the provisions of the Act relative thereto must be observed.[24]

An order for sale does not prevent the court from subsequently approving a scheme of realisation involving the disposal of the assets for shares in a new company.[25] The report of the receiver may be an important factor to be considered with regard to the question of whether such scheme should be approved.[26]

Receiver may not purchase. A receiver, being in a fiduciary position, cannot directly or indirectly, without the leave of the court, bid at a sale or purchase any of the property subject to the

[20] *Re Albert Road, Norwood* [1916] 1 Ch. 289.
[21] See *Re Higginson & Dean* [1899] 1 Q.B. 325; *Hastings Corp.* v. *Letton* [1908] 1 K.B. 378; *Re Hills* (1912) 107 L.T. 95 (as to which, see judgments in *Re Spencer Wells, infra*); *Re Henderson's Nigel Co.* (1911) 105 L.T. 370.
[22] *Re Spencer Wells* [1933] 1 Ch. 29 (C.A.).
[23] *Re Guardian Assurance Co.* [1917] 1 Ch. 431.
[24] *Re White Pass Ry.* [1918] W.N. 323. As to practice, see *Supreme Court Practice* (1976), Vol. 1, Ord. 102 and notes.
[25] *Re Buenos Aires Tramways Ltd.* (1920) 123 L.T. 748.
[26] *Ibid.*

receivership, even though the sale is made by a mortgagee selling outside the action.[27]

COMPANIES

Generally. The powers and duties of receivers and managers appointed over the undertaking of a company do not differ in principle from those of receivers for other incumbrancers. In the ensuing pages only those points are discussed which are peculiar to receivers of the property of companies: the earlier portion of the chapter should be referred to in respect of their other powers and duties,[28] and Chapter 9 in respect of their powers and duties as managers.

Statutory duties of receiver. A receiver [29] of the property of a company formed and registered under the Companies Act 1948, or earlier Companies Acts, is under certain statutory obligations.

(a) *Notice of appointment.* If he is appointed receiver or manager of the whole, or substantially the whole, of the property of a company registered in England, on behalf of debenture holders whose security includes a floating charge, he must forthwith, *i.e.* as soon as reasonably practicable,[30] send the company notice of his appointment in the prescribed form.[31]

(b) *Statement of affairs.* Under the circumstances already noted, he comes under a duty to furnish a statement of the affairs of the company to the Registrar of Companies, the court, the trustees for the debenture holders (if any) and the debenture holders themselves.[32] The precise nature and extent of this duty is discussed later.[33]

---

[27] *Nugent* v. *Nugent* [1908] 2 Ch. 546; *Alven* v. *Bond* (1841) 1 Fl. & K. 196. *Cary* v. *Cary* (1804) 2 Sch. & Lef. 173. *Semble,* he could not plead any statute of limitations: *Taylor* v. *Davies* [1920] A.C. 636; and would be liable to account if he resold and re-purchased; see *Gordon* v. *Holland* (1913) 108 L.T. 385.

[28] As to sale, see pp. 198–201, *ante,* and 219, *post.*

[29] See Companies Act 1948, s. 376 (*a*) (p. 107, *ante*) for the meaning of " receiver " in this connection.

[30] *Ex p. Lowe* (1846) 3 Dowl. & L. 737.

[31] Companies Act 1948, s. 372 (1) (*a*), as amended by Companies Act 1976, s. 34 and Sched. 1. The prescribed form is No. 108 in the Schedule to the Companies (Forms) Order 1949 (S.I. 1949 No. 382); Companies Act 1976, s. 34 (2). This sub-section does not apply to the appointment of a receiver or manager to act with an existing receiver or manager or in place of a receiver or manager dying or ceasing to act. *Ibid.* s. 372 (4). The penalty for non-compliance is a fine not exceeding £5 for every day during which the default continues. *Ibid.* s. 372 (7).

[32] *Ibid.* s. 372 (1) (*b*) (*c*), (2).

[33] *Infra,* where the subject is fully dealt with.

(c) *Preferential debts.* He must pay the preferential debts.[34]

(d) *Invoices, etc.* Every invoice, order for goods or business letter issued by or on behalf of the company or the receiver or manager or the liquidator, being a document on or in which the name of the company appears, must contain a statement that a receiver or manager has been appointed.[35]

(e) *Register of debentures.* If the action in which he has been appointed is one to enforce registered debentures or registered debenture stock, the receiver may be directed by the court or a judge to open and keep a register of transfers and other transmissions of such debentures or stock (called " the receiver's register ").[36] The procedure is fully stated in R.S.C., Ord. 87, rr. 1-5.[37] Where the receiver is not directed to keep a register, the debentures must be produced at chambers, when a suitable memorandum will be indorsed thereon.[38]

Enforcement of duties. If any receiver or manager makes default in filing, delivering, or making any return, account, or other document, or in giving any notice, as by law required, after a fourteen-day notice to make good the default the registrar or any member or creditor may, without prejudice to any penalties imposed in respect of such default, apply by summons under R.S.C., Ord. 102, r. 2 (2) (*b*), for an order directing him to make good the default.[39]

Statement of affairs. The statement of affairs must show as at the date of the receiver's appointment the particulars of the company's assets, debts, and liabilities, the names, residences and occupations of its creditors and the securities held by them respectively, the dates when the same were given, and such further or other information as may be prescribed.[40] In the first instance this statement is submitted to the receiver within fourteen days (or such longer period as the court or the receiver may allow) after receipt by the

---

[34] See *post*, pp. 207 *et seq.*, where the subject is fully dealt with.

[35] Companies Act 1948, s. 370. Any officer, liquidator, receiver, or manager who knowingly and wilfully authorises or permits the default, is liable to a fine of £20.

[36] This is ordered only in cases where the debentures are numerous.

[37] For forms, see Chancery Masters' Practice Forms 43–50; *Supreme Court Practice* (1976), Vol. II, paras. 385–392.

[38] Chancery Masters' Practice Form No. 42; *Supreme Court Practice* (1976), Vol. II, para. 384.

[39] Companies Act 1948, s. 375: the receiver may be ordered to pay the costs of the application: *ibid.* subs. (2).

[40] Companies Act 1948, s. 373 (1). The prescribed forms are Nos. 109 and 109A in the Schedule to the Companies (Forms) Order 1949 (S.I. 1949 No. 382); see pp. 394 *et seq., post.*

company of notice of his appointment,[41] in a prescribed form,[42] by, and verified by the affidavit of, one or more of the persons who are at the date of such appointment the directors, and by the person who is at that date the secretary of the company.[43] Alternatively, the receiver, subject always to the directions of the court, may require any of the following persons to submit and verify the statement, namely, persons (a) who are or have been officers of the company; (b) who have taken part in the formation of the company at any time within one year before the date of the receiver's appointment; (c) who are in the employment of the company, or have been in the employment of the company within the said year, and are in the opinion of the receiver capable of giving the information required; or (d) who are or have been within the said year officers of, or in the employment of, a company which is, or within the said year was, an officer of the company to which the statement relates.[44]

Any person making the statement and affidavit must be allowed, and must be paid by the receiver out of his receipts, such costs and expenses incurred in and about the preparation and making of the statement and affidavit as the receiver may consider reasonable.[45]

Comments on statement. Within a period of two months after receipt of the statement, the receiver must send (a) to the Registrar of Companies and to the court, a copy of the statement and of any comments he sees fit to make thereon, and in the case of the registrar also a summary of the statement and of his comments (if any) thereon; (b) to the company, a copy of any such comments, or alternatively notice to the effect that he does not see fit to make any; and (c) to the trustees (if any) for the debenture holders on whose behalf he was appointed, and, so far as he is aware of their addresses, to all such debenture holders, a copy of the summary.[46]

---

[41] Companies Act 1948, s. 372 (1) (b). In a case where a receiver or manager dies or ceases to act before the requirements as to a statement of affairs have been fully complied with, these provisions relate equally to his successor. They do not, however, apply to the appointment of a receiver or manager to act with an existing receiver or manager or (except as stated) to one appointed in place of a receiver or manager dying or ceasing to act. *Ibid.* subs. (4).

[42] See n. 40, p. 205, *ante.*

[43] Companies Act 1948, s. 373 (2).

[44] Companies Act 1948, s. 373 (2). Any person who without reasonable excuse makes default in complying with the requirements of s. 373 is liable to a fine not exceeding £10 for each day during which the default continues. *Ibid.* subs. (5).

[45] *Ibid.* s. 373 (3): subject to an appeal to the court as to quantum.

[46] *Ibid.* s. 372 (1) (c). See also n. 41, *supra.*

Subsequent information. The receiver must also within two months [47] of the expiration of each complete year of office, and also within two months [47] after he ceases to act as receiver or manager, send to the Registrar of Companies, to the trustees (if any) for the debenture holders, to the company, and to all such debenture holders so far as he is aware of their addresses, an abstract in the prescribed form [48] showing his receipts and payments during the year or up to the date of his ceasing to act, as the case may be, and the aggregate amounts of his receipts and payments during all preceding periods since his appointment. [49]

Application of provisions as to statement of affairs, etc. The above provisions apply notwithstanding that the receiver or manager and the liquidator are the same person but with any necessary modifications arising from that fact. [50] They do not prejudice the duty of the receiver to render proper accounts of his receipts and payments apart from their requirements. [51] Default on the part of the receiver renders him liable to a fine not exceeding £5 for every day during which the default continues. [52]

Preferential debts. Section 94 of the Companies Act 1948 provides that where a receiver is appointed on behalf of the holders of any debentures of a company registered in England which are secured by a floating charge, or possession is taken by or on behalf of such debenture holders, then, if the company is not being wound up, the debts which under the provisions of Part V of the Act [53] relating to preferential payments are to be paid in priority to all other debts, shall be paid out of assets coming to the hands of a receiver or other person taking possession in priority to the principal or interest in respect of the debentures. As between themselves they rank equally and if the assets are insufficient to meet them they abate to equal proportions accordingly. [54] The periods of time

---

[47] Or such longer period as the court may allow.

[48] Form No. 57 in the Schedule to the Companies (Forms) Order 1949 (S.I. 1949 No. 382); see p. 390, *post.*

[49] Companies Act 1948, s. 372 (2). The requirements of this subsection are not retrospective, and do not apply to receivers appointed before the Act came into force: *Re Welsh Anthracite Collieries* [1950] Ch. 18.

[50] Companies Act 1948, s. 372 (5).

[51] *Ibid.* subs. (6).

[52] *Ibid.* subs. (7).

[53] ss. 316 *et seq.*, especially ss. 319 and 358. In the case of appointments before July 1, 1948, the provisions of s. 264 of the Companies Act 1929 continue to control the nature of the preferential payments: Companies Act 1948, s. 319 (9).

[54] Companies Act 1948, s. 319 (5) (*a*).

mentioned in Part V are reckoned from the appointment or taking possession. Any payments under the section are to be recouped as far as possible out of the general assets.

Where at the date of the receiver's appointment the company is being wound up, the same debts together with the costs of the winding up are given priority over the claims of debenture holders under a floating charge.[55] These provisions do not appear to apply to statutory companies; they only apply in the case of companies registered in England.

The detailed provisions are mainly contained in section 319 of the Companies Act 1948; certain other debts have been given priority by other statutes.[56]

The preference given by the section is in respect only of property subject to a floating charge and does not extend to property comprised in a specific charge [57]: and where debentures include both a specific and a fixed charge, the preference is limited to the assets not comprised in the fixed charge.[58] Where the floating security has crystallised before the commencement of winding up as regards any property, section 319 does not apply to that property [59]: the same would apply as regards section 94, if the charge had become specific as regards any particular item before the commencement of proceedings in which the receiver is appointed: but this situation can arise only in exceptional cases as the debenture holder with a floating charge must enforce his security against all the property: he cannot select any particular item.[60] But if a secured creditor holds security for both preferential and non-preferential debts, he may appropriate his security as he pleases.[61]

The present practice is not to direct the receiver to pay the preferential debts forthwith, but to direct an inquiry, which is answered if possible before the other inquiries directed by the judgment [62]; when possible the amounts of wage claims should be agreed with the workers' representatives.

---

[55] Companies Act 1948, s. 319 (5) (b) and *Re Barleycorn Enterprises Ltd.* [1970] Ch. 465.

[56] See *infra* and pp. 209–215, *post.* For preferential payments in stannaries cases see Companies Act 1948, s. 358.

[57] See p. 160, *ante,* as to the nature of a floating charge.

[58] *Re Lewis Merthyr Consolidated Collieries* [1929] 1 Ch. 498.

[59] *Re Griffin Hotel* [1941] Ch. 129.

[60] *Evans* v. *Rival Granite Quarries* [1910] 2 K.B. 979.

[61] *Re William Hall (Contractors) Ltd.* [1967] 1 W.L.R. 948.

[62] *Ante,* p. 128; for summons, see Atkin's *Court Forms* (2nd ed.), Vol. 11.

Subject to any of the following express provisions, the Crown has no priority.[63]

Rates. The priority given is in respect of all " local rates " due from the company at the date of the appointment of the receiver and having become due and payable within 12 months next before that date.[64] This expression includes not only general rates but also a Land Drainage Rate payable under a local Act [65]; it does not include water rates.[66] Rates which the receiver is entitled to be recouped by the liquidator [67] include all rates due and payable at the appointment though assessed in respect of a subsequent period.[68] Rates are payable when made and published: an increased rate payable by reason of an amendment in the valuation list, *e.g.* on a successful appeal against de-rating, becomes payable as at the date of the original rate.[69]

Taxes. Priority is here given in respect of (i) all land tax,[70] income tax [71] (including, therein, development land tax),[72] profits tax,[73] excess profits tax,[74] or other assessed taxes assessed on the company up to April 5 next before the date of the appointment, and not exceeding in the whole one year's assessment [75]; (ii) any purchase tax [76] having become due from the company within 12 months before the appointment [77]; (iii) certain estate duty

---

[63] *Food Controller* v. *Cork* [1923] A.C. 647. There is no set-off against the Crown: *Att.-Gen.* v. *Guy Motors* [1928] 2 K.B. 78. As to what are Crown debts, see *Metropolitan Meat Industry Board* v. *Sheedy* [1927] A.C. 899. A fine constitutes a debt due to the Crown: *Re Pascoe* [1944] Ch. 310, but it has no priority under s. 319. As to the inclusion of betterment levy (abolished by Land Commission (Dissolution) Act 1971 with effect from July 22, 1970) as a preferential debt, see Land Commission Act 1967, Sched. 12, paras. 17, 19.

[64] Companies Act 1948, ss. 94 and 319 (1) (*a*) (i).

[65] *Re Ellwood* [1927] 1 Ch. 455, a case under s. 33 (1) (*a*) of the Bankruptcy Act 1914. Rates need not necessarily be demanded in the year of assessment: *Gill* v. *Mellor* [1924] 1 K.B. 97.

[66] *Re Baker* [1954] 1 W.L.R. 1144 (decision under Bankruptcy Act 1914, s. 33).

[67] See p. 208, *ante.*

[68] *Re Mannesman Tube Co.* [1901] 2 Ch. 93.

[69] *Re Airedale Garage* [1933] 2 Ch. 64.

[70] For the provisions as to compulsory redemption of Land Tax, see Finance Act 1949, ss. 37–45 and Sched. 9.

[71] See Income and Corporation Taxes Act 1970, ss. 53 (2)–(4) and 54; Finance Act 1971, s. 37 (1), Sched. 6, paras. 21 (*b*), 22; Finance Act 1972, ss. 104, 111, Sched. 20, paras. 4 (2)–(4), 10, Sched. 24, para. 16.

[72] Development Land Tax Act 1976, s. 42. The reference to one year's assessment is to be construed as a reference to the amount of development land tax the liability for which arose in one financial year: *ibid.* s. 42 (3).

[73] Now spent: Finance Act 1965, s. 46 (3).

[74] Now spent: Finance Act 1953, s. 27.

[75] Companies Act 1948, s. 319 (1) (*a*) (ii).

[76] Now spent: Finance Act 1972, s. 54.

[77] *Ibid.* s. 319 (1) (*a*) (iii).

payable in respect of the assets of the company [78]; and (iv) all income tax which the company has deducted, or should have deducted, under the P.A.Y.E. Scheme, from wages or salaries within one year preceding the appointment. [79]

" Assessed taxes " includes taxes imposed since the Act was passed, [80] and therefore includes corporation tax. [81] It should be noted that where and to the extent to which any interest or other annual payment is not made out of profits or gains brought into charge, income tax is nevertheless deductible by the payer at the basic rate at the date of payment, and the tax is assessed on him. [82]

The assessed taxes which have priority are the taxes assessed for any one year up to April 5 prior to the appointment, whenever the assessment is in fact made. Although only one year's taxes have priority, where more than one year's taxes are unpaid the Crown can select any single year of assessment, [83] and different years for different taxes. [84]

Salaries and wages. Up to a maximum limit of £800 [85] in each individual case, all wages [86] or salary (whether or not wholly or partially earned by way of commission) of any clerk or servant in respect of services rendered during the four months next before the receiver's appointment, and all wages [86] (whether payable for time or piece work) of any workman or labourer [87] in respect of services so rendered, have priority. [88] If the claimant is a labourer in husbandry, there are somewhat different provisions. [89]

---

[78] Companies Act 1948, s. 459 (9) (c); Finance Act 1940, s. 54 (4). Abolished in relation to deaths after November 12, 1974, by the Finance Act 1975, s. 49 (1). Previously, a receiver might here become personally liable under *ibid*. s. 54 (1) (b), if he " disposed of " the assets of the company without first discharging such liability.

[79] Finance Act 1952, s. 30. This provision is to be construed as including any amounts due in respect of deductions required to be made from wages under Finance (No. 2) Act 1975, s. 69 (sub-contracting in the construction industry): *ibid*. ss. 69 (7), 71 (6).

[80] *Re Wingets Ltd.* [1924] 1 Ch. 550.

[81] Imposed by Finance Act 1965: see s. 51 (1).

[82] Income and Corporation Taxes Act 1970, s. 53; Finance Act 1971, ss. 36, 37 and Sched. 6, para. 21.

[83] *Gowers* v. *Walker* [1930] 1 Ch. 262; *Re Pratt* [1950] Ch. 225; *cf. Re Cockell* [1932] W.N. 172.

[84] *I.R.C.* v. *Purvis Industries Ltd.* (1958) 38 T.C. 155.

[85] Companies Act 1948, s. 319 (2); Insolvency Act 1976, s. 1 and Sched. 1. Under s. 264 of the 1929 Act the limit was £50 and, under s. 319 of the 1948 Act, £200.

[86] See *ibid*. s. 319 (8) (a) as to remuneration during holidays and illness.

[87] Under the Act of 1929 the limit in the case of workmen or labourers was £25 in respect of two months' services.

[88] Companies Act 1948, s. 319 (1) (b). See *The British Trade* [1924] P. 104 as to the priority of a seaman's lien for wages.

[89] *Ibid*. s. 319 (2).

This limit is presumably the "gross" and not the "net" amount payable to the employee, since before payment of any salary or wages is effected, the person making the payment must deduct P.A.Y.E. tax [90] and Social Security contributions.[91]

Other debts included in the expression " wages." Various sums statutorily due from an employer to an employee fall to be treated as if they were wages, and so preferential.[92] These are:

(i) a guarantee payment [93];

(ii) remuneration on suspension on medical grounds under section 19 of the Employment Protection (Consolidation) Act 1977 [94];

(iii) any payment for time off for carrying out trade union duties,[95] or looking for work or making arrangements for training pending the expiration of a notice of dismissal on the grounds of redundancy [96];

(iv) remuneration under a protective award, made on a complaint by a trade union to an industrial tribunal on the ground that the employer has dismissed, or is proposing to dismiss, as redundant, one or more employees without having complied with the statutory requirements.[97]

These sums are, of course, also subject to the four-months period already mentioned, and, together with the more orthodox wage items, are subject to the overall £800 limit. In connection with these debts, however, a receiver comes under certain additional duties mentioned above.[98]

Meaning of clerk, etc. It is not possible to give any general definition of the words " clerk or servant " [99]: The existence of

---

[90] Income and Corporation Taxes Act 1970, s. 204; Finance Act 1971, s. 37 (1) and Sched. 6, paras. 1, 25. Income Tax (Employments) Regulations 1973 (S.I. 1973 No. 334), regs. 2, 6.   [91] Social Security Act 1975, s. 1 (4), Sched. 1, para. 5 (1) (a).

[92] Employment Protection (Consolidation) Act 1977, s. 121 (1) (c).

[93] Ibid. s. 121 (2) (a). For definition, see ibid. s. 12.

[94] Ibid. s. 121 (2) (b). For the right to a payment of this nature see ibid. ss. 19–22.

[95] Ibid. s. 121 (2) (c). For the right to time off and the calculation of the remuneration payable see ibid. s. 27.

[96] Ibid. s. 121 (2) (c). For the right of a dismissed employee to such payment see ibid. s. 31.

[97] Ibid. s. 121 (2) (d). For the circumstances in which such an award can be made see s. 101 of the Employment Protection (Consolidation) Act 1977.

[98] See p. 170, ante.

[99] See Simmons v. Heath Laundry [1910] 1 K.B. 543: a contract for service is not necessarily a contract of service so as to constitute a person a servant (ibid.); see also Evans v. Liverpool Corp. [1906] 1 K.B. 160; University of London Press Ltd. v. University Tutorial Press Ltd. [1916] 2 Ch. 601, 610; Smith v. General Motor Cab Co. [1911] A.C. 188.

control by the employer, the degree of independence in the person who renders services, and the place, are all matters to be considered in determining whether there is a contract of service.[1] Where persons are (1) working entirely away from the company's premises: (2) not exclusively employed by the company, but at liberty to take other employment; (3) only bound to render a particular class of service, and (4) might perform the service as they pleased not under the control or subject to the command of the company, they are not within the Act; but one of these circumstances alone, except possibly (4) would not necessarily exclude them.[2] Thus persons contributing articles and reports to a newspaper at a fixed salary and at fixed times, but working away from the office, were excluded [3]; so was an agent who procured the sale of wireless sets and installed them, being paid by commission [4]; but a " dress editress " at a fixed salary, with a seat in the office and a general supervision over illustrations, was held to be a servant.[5]

The managing director of a company is not a " clerk or servant " within the meaning of the Act [6]; nor is a secretary in respect of the salary of a clerk paid by him [7]; but a director may be entitled to preference in respect of salary as a clerk or servant, if also employed in that capacity, and the employment is authorised by the articles.[8] Debts due to the following have been held entitled to priority: workmen paid by way of commission [9]; commercial travellers paid by way of commission [10]; an opera singer paid a certain sum for each performance [11]; a chemist employed for definite hours on three days a week to produce certain formulae, having other employment during the remainder of the week.[12]

Compensation under the Reinstatement in Civil Employment Act 1944. Where an employee of the company was entitled to be reinstated under the provisions of this Act, and the company has made

---

[1] *Re Beeton & Co. Ltd.* [1913] 2 Ch. 279.
[2] *Re Ashley and Smith Ltd.* [1918] 2 Ch. 378.
[3] *Ibid.*
[4] *Re General Radio Co.* [1929] W.N. 172.
[5] *Re Beeton & Co. Ltd.* [1913] 2 Ch. 279.
[6] *Re Newspaper Proprietary Syndicate* [1900] 2 Ch. 349.
[7] *Cairney* v. *Back* [1906] 2 K.B. 746.
[8] *Re Beeton & Co. Ltd., supra.*
[9] *Re Earle's Shipbuilding Co.* [1901] W.N. 78.
[10] *Re Klein* (1906) 22 T.L.R. 664.
[11] *Re Winter German Opera* (1907) 23 T.L.R. 662.
[12] *Re G. H. Morison & Co. Ltd.,* 106 L.T. 731.

default in so doing, then any sum ordered to be paid to him by way of compensation where the default occurred before the appointment of the receiver, whether or not the order was made before that date, has priority [13] up to £800.[14]

Accrued holiday remuneration.[15] All such remuneration becoming payable to any clerk, servant, workman or labourer (or, in the case of his death, of any other person in his right) on the termination of his employment before or by the effect of the appointment of the receiver, is preferential.[16] The phrase includes all sums which, by virtue of a person's contract of employment, or of any enactment (including any order made or direction given under any Act), are payable on account of the remuneration which would in the ordinary course have become payable to him in respect of a period of holiday [17] had his employment with the company continued until he had become entitled to take such holiday.[18]

Social Security contributions. All the debts specified in section 153 (2) of the Social Security Act 1975, Schedule 3 to the Social Security Pensions Act 1975, and any corresponding provision in force in Northern Ireland.[19]

The debts referred to are, shortly stated:

(1) Any sum owed on account of Class 1 contributions [20] (primary or secondary) or Class 2 contributions [20] payable in either case in the period of 12 months immediately preceding the appointment of the receiver [21];

(2) An earner's contributions [22] to an occupational pension scheme,[23] being contributions deducted from earnings paid in the

---

[13] Companies Act 1948, s. 319 (1) (c).

[14] *Ibid.* s. 319 (2), as amended by Insolvency Act 1976, s. 1 and Sched. 1.

[15] As to the precise meaning of these words see *ibid.* s. 319 (8) (b) and (c), as amended by Social Security Act 1973, s. 100 (2) (a) and Sched. 27, para. 9 (b) and Social Security (Consequential Provisions) Act 1975, s. 1 (3) and Sched. 2, Pt. I, para. 7 (b).

[16] Companies Act 1948, ss. 94 (2) and 319 (1) (d).

[17] See n. 15, *supra.*

[18] Companies Act 1948, s. 319 (8) (b).

[19] *Ibid.* s. 319 (1) (e) as substituted by Social Security Act 1973, s. 100 (2) (a) and Sched. 27, para. 9 (a), amended by Social Security (Consequential Provisions) Act 1975, s. 1 (3) and Sched. 2, Pt. I, para. 7 (a) and Social Security Pensions Act 1975, s. 65 and Sched. 4, para. 3. See also Social Security Act 1975, Sched. 18, para. 3.

[20] For definition, see Social Security Act 1975, s. 1 (2).

[21] Social Security Act 1975, s. 153 (2).

[22] See Social Security Pensions Act 1975, s. 40 (1) (b).

[23] For definition, see Social Security Pensions Act 1975, s. 66 (1).

period of four months immediately preceding the appointment or otherwise due in respect of earnings paid or payable in that period [24];

(3) Any sum owed on account of an employer's [25] contributions to a contracted-out scheme,[26] being contributions payable:

(a) in the period of 12 months immediately preceding the date of the appointment; and

(b) in respect of earners in contracted-out employment by reference to the scheme towards the provision for those earners of guaranteed minimum pensions under the scheme [27];

(4) Any sum owed on account of a state scheme premium [28] payable at any time before, or in consequence of the appointment of the receiver [29] but limited to the amount of premium which would have been payable if the service had been confined to the last 12 months taken into account in fixing the actual amount of the premium [30]; and of course all the corresponding provisions in force in Northern Ireland.[31]

Value Added Tax. Priority is given in respect of the amount of any tax due at the date of the receiver's appointment or the debenture holders taking possession and having become due within 12 months next before that date.[32] For the purpose of this provision, the tax having become due within the 12 months' period in respect of any prescribed accounting period falling partly within and partly outside those 12 months is to be taken to be such part of the tax due for the whole of that accounting period as is proportionate to the part of that period falling within those 12 months.[33]

Car tax. Priority is given in respect of any car tax due from the company at the date of the receiver's appointment or the debenture

---

[24] *Ibid.* s. 58 and Sched. 3, para. 1.

[25] For the meaning of " employer " see Social Security Pensions Act 1975, s. 58 and Sched. 3, para. 2 (4).

[26] See *ibid.* Part III as to such schemes.

[27] *Ibid.* s. 58 and Sched. 3, para. 2 (1). Insofar as contributions cannot, from the terms of the scheme, be identified as falling within this provision, the amount of the preferential debt is to be calculated in accordance with *ibid.* para. 2 (2) and (3).

[28] See Social Security Pensions Act 1975, Parts I and II.

[29] *Ibid.* s. 58 and Sched. 3, para. 3 (1).

[30] *Ibid.* para. 3 (2).

[31] See the Social Security (Northern Ireland) Act 1975 and Social Security Pensions Act 1975, s. 58 and Sched. 3, para. 4.

[32] Finance Act 1972, s. 41 (1) (*d*), (2) (*d*).   [33] *Ibid.* s. 41 (2).

holders taking possession and having become due within 12 months next before that date.[34]

Miscellaneous debts. Any excise duty which became due within 12 months before the appointment in respect of general betting duty,[35] gaming licence duty,[36] bingo duty [37] and in certain circumstances where the company has collected the stake on a bet for onward transmission but has in fact not effected the transmission, or pool betting duty,[38] constitutes a preferential debt.

Workmen's compensation. For the position in relation to workmen's compensation, see the 13th ed., pp. 214–215.

Advance to pay preferential debts. There was no provision in the 1908 Act corresponding to subsection (4) of section 319 of the Companies Act 1948 [39] under which preference is given to a debt in respect of an advance made for the purpose of paying wages, salaries or accrued holiday remuneration, and in fact applied for that purpose, to the extent to which the wages or salary or remuneration so paid would have been entitled to priority.[40] Presumably the preference relates to the gross amount advanced, *e.g.* if a Bank advances £200, £175 of which is paid to the workman, £15 being deducted as P.A.Y.E. and £10 as Social Security Contributions,[41] the Bank will be entitled to preference for the full £200. While the 1908 Act was in force, it was held [42] that the effect of section 5 of the Mercantile Law Amendment Act 1856 was to entitle a person who has guaranteed a preferential debt to stand in the shoes of the creditor, and obtain the preference to which the debt so paid would have been entitled on a winding up. This decision appears to be unaffected by subsection (4). It applies to all preferential debts, not merely those to which that subsection applies: but it applies only to payment made under a guarantee, not as in the case of subsection (4) to a simple advance.

[34] *Ibid.* s. 52 (11), Sched. 7, para. 18 (1) (*d*), (2) (*d*).
[35] Betting and Gaming Duties Act 1972, s. 12 (2) and Sched. 1, para. 14 (1) (*c*), (2).
[36] *Ibid.* s. 16 and Sched. 2, para. 11, applying Sched. 1, para. 14.
[37] *Ibid.* s. 20 (1) and Sched. 3, para. 16, applying Sched. 1, para. 14.
[38] *Ibid.* s. 12 (1), (2) and Sched. 1, para. 14 (1) (*c*), (2).
[39] Replacing and extending s. 264 (3) of the Companies Act 1929.
[40] See *Re Primrose (Builders) Ltd.* [1950] Ch. 561 for an unsuccessful attempt to question such priority on special facts, and *Re E. J. Morel (1934) Ltd.* [1962] Ch. 21 (successful); *Re James R. Rutherford & Sons Ltd.* [1964] 1 W.L.R. 1211 (unsuccessful); *Re Rampgill Mill Ltd.* [1967] Ch. 1138 (unsuccessful).
[41] See nn. 90, 91, p. 211, *ante.*
[42] *Re Lamplugh's Iron Ore Co.* [1927] 1 Ch. 308.

Payment of certain Social Security debts by Secretary of State.
As to the subrogation of the Secretary of State for Employment
to certain social security debts paid by him see pp. 169–170,
ante.

Order of application of assets. The effect of subsections (5) and
(6) is to make the costs and expenses of winding up payable out of
the assets not included in the debenture holder's security, in
priority to the preferential debts. If such assets do not suffice for
payment of those debts, the balance is ultimately borne by the
property subject to the floating charge.[43]

The order of application of the assets, where the assets are
deficient, is as follows: (1) costs of realisation, including costs of
an abortive sale; (2) balance due to receiver including remuneration and costs; (3) costs, charges and expenses of the trustees under
the debenture trust deed (if any) including their remuneration; (4)
plaintiff's costs of action; (5) preferential debts; (6) debenture
holders.[44] If the assets are insufficient to discharge the preferential
debts in full, such debts abate in equal proportions.[45]

Distress. Subsection (7) of section 319 relating to the levying of
distress within three months of the date of the winding-up order,
appears to have no application to cases within section 94 where
there is no winding up; for the distrained goods or proceeds of sale
never reach the hands of the receiver.

Where a winding up was in progress and the liquidator stated
that the assets would not suffice for payment in full of the preferential debts, the lessor was restrained from proceeding with a
distress for rent; the fact that the amount due on the debentures
far exceeded the assets was held in the circumstances to be
immaterial.[46]

Failure to pay preferential debts. If money is paid over to debenture holders without providing for preferential debts it may be
recovered: the proper plaintiff is the liquidator in the name of the

---

[43] *Westminster City Council* v. *Chapman* [1916] 1 Ch. 161. As to liquidator's
costs and remuneration, see *Re Beni-Felkai Co.* [1934] 1 Ch. 406; *Re Wm. Adler &
Co.* [1935] 1 Ch. 138.
[44] *Re Glyncorrwg Collieries Co.* [1926] Ch. 951.
[45] Companies Act 1948, s. 319 (5) (*a*).
[46] *Re South Rhondda Colliery Co.* [1928] W.N. 126. The application was made by
originating motion: it would now be made by originating summons. *Semble*, where
there was no winding up, the same principle would apply on the appointment of a
receiver and the receiver might apply either in the name of the company or of a
preferential creditor.

company.[47] The receiver is personally liable to creditors for failure to comply with the provisions of the section and the order directing payment of the preferential debts.[48]

Other rights and duties. The rights and duties of a receiver for incumbrancers with regard to rent [49] and attornment of tenants [50] have already been discussed; also his right to possession.[51]

A receiver for debenture holders has no right to the rents in arrear, as against specific assignees of such arrears, when he goes into possession of property over which the debentures constituted only a floating charge; but the case is otherwise where the arrears of rent claimed by the specific assignees thereof are in respect of property specifically charged by the debentures.[52]

Leaseholds. The liability of a receiver appointed on behalf of equitable incumbrancers for the rent of leaseholds has already been dealt with.[53] A receiver appointed on behalf of debenture holders is in the same position in this respect as a receiver appointed on behalf of a mortgagee by sub-demise: he is therefore under no contractual liability to pay rent under a lease to the company, though he may be in occupation [54]; though he may be compelled to pay arrears to avoid distress. If he enters into a fresh agreement for tenancy or an agreement to pay arrears, he will be personally liable thereon with a right to indemnity.[55]

If the property is onerous and incapable of realisation, the receiver may apply for leave to abandon it, though there may be undertenants. It may be made a term that the receiver shall pay rent in respect of the period of his occupation.[56] Where there are valuable tenant's fixtures such as trade machinery, leave to remove them should be applied for. In such cases if the debentures do not

---

[47] *Semble*, where there is no winding up, the company would be the proper plaintiff: *Westminster City Council* v. *Chapman* [1916] 1 Ch. 161.

[48] *Woods* v. *Winskill* [1913] 2 Ch. 303; *Westminster Corp.* v. *Haste* [1950] Ch. 442; *I.R.C.* v. *Goldblatt* [1972] Ch. 498.

[49] *Ante*, pp. 191–192.

[50] *Ante*, pp. 174–175.

[51] *Ante*, p. 176.

[52] *Re Ind, Coope & Co.* [1911] 2 Ch. 223.

[53] *Ante*, pp. 191–192, to which reference should be made. The power of a liquidator to disclaim under s. 323 is to be considered in this connection: as to which see *Re Katherine et Cie* [1932] 1 Ch. 70. It may become necessary for the plaintiff in a debenture holders' action to apply for a vesting order.

[54] *Re J. W. Abbott & Co.* [1913] W.N. 284; *Hay* v. *Swedish, etc., Ry.* (1892) 8 T.L.R. 775.

[55] *Post*, pp. 224–225.

[56] See n. 53, p. 193, *ante*.

exceed the value of the assets, the liability which the company will incur in damages or breach of covenants in the lease is a factor which will be taken into account.

Debtors to the company. The receiver should at once give notice of his appointment to debtors to the company and require them to pay their debts to him, obtaining where necessary an order for that purpose.[57] If an action to compel payment is necessary it must be brought in the name of the company, or if a winding up has begun, of the liquidator on a complete indemnity to the latter.[58] The debenture holders have no absolute right to insist on or prohibit any action being brought; the court has a discretion to be exercised for the benefit of the parties interested.[59]

Uncalled capital. Where uncalled capital is included in the debenture holders' security, the receiver may be given leave to use the name of the liquidator on a complete indemnity to the latter, in order to recover the calls made by him.[60] It is necessary to apply to the court for directions to the liquidator to make the requisite calls in order to enable the debenture holders to obtain realisation.[61] In such cases it is a usual and convenient practice for the liquidator to be appointed receiver.[62] If the company is not in liquidation, then, if the uncalled capital is included in the security, the plaintiff should apply by summons that the receiver may be authorised to make the call and recover the amount called up, with power if necessary to sue in the company's name. As pointed out,[63] the order appointing a receiver excludes uncalled capital, and therefore special directions are required as to making the call and dealing with the proceeds.[64] If there is a doubt as to whether the uncalled capital is included in the security,[65] it may be necessary to issue a summons to determine the point.[66]

---

[57] *Ante*, p. 179.
[58] See as to extent of the indemnity for costs, p. 183.
[59] *Viola* v. *Anglo-American Cold Storage Co.* [1912] 2 Ch. 305, and *ante*, p. 182.
[60] *Re Westminster Syndicate* (1908) 99 L.T. 924; form of order, Stiebel's *Company Law* (3rd ed.), Vol. I.
[61] *Fowler* v. *Broad's Patent, etc., Co.* [1893] 1 Ch. 724: see as to master's certificate as to unpaid calls, *Madeley* v. *Ross, Sleeman & Co.* [1897] 1 Ch. 505.
[62] *Ante*, p. 108.
[63] *Ante*, p. 100.
[64] Also whether any additional security is to be given.
[65] See *Re Streatham Estates Co.* [1897] 1 Ch. 15; *Re Handyside & Co.* (1909) 131 L.T.J. 125.
[66] See *Re Gregory, Love & Co.* [1916] 1 Ch. 203.

Sale. A sale is often effected by the receiver entering into a conditional contract subject to the approval of the court: a summons is then issued by the plaintiff and an order made conferring the contract and directing it to be carried into effect. A party with power to convey the legal estate may be authorised to convey the fee simple or the term; otherwise the concurrence of the company and legal incumbrancers is required [67]: if any dispute arise as to the form of the conveyance or if any party refuse to concur, a summons is issued for an order that the conveyance be settled by the judge. Where sale by tender is directed, there is under the usual conditions no binding contract until the sale has been confirmed by the order of the master. An offer received after the close of the date for tenders may therefore be accepted.

In the case of disposal of the assets on reconstruction or amalgamation, care should be taken if possible to comply with the requirements of section 55 of the Finance Act 1927; or section 42 of the Finance Act 1930, as amended by section 50 of the Finance Act 1938; or to take advantage of section 252 of the Income and Corporation Taxes Act 1970.

Powers and duties generally. As already stated, the receiver should apply to the court for leave to exercise all powers not implied, or expressly included, in the terms of his appointment,[68] which he considers necessary to preserve the property entrusted to him.

Thus he may be given power to appoint attorneys, to give up possession to prior mortgagees, to give up property generally to prior claimants, to give up tenancies, to close businesses, to compromise claims, to grant leases, to give undertakings not to commit nuisances, to promote a Bill in Parliament, to pay out certain debenture holders, to repair, to pay off prior incumbrances, to go abroad to arrange a sale of assets, and generally to exercise any power or authority which the court can under its statutory or general jurisdiction direct or sanction.[69]

Receivers appointed by mortgagees of a business. It is the duty of a receiver to preserve the property entrusted to him. If, therefore,

---

[67] As to sale generally, and as to conveyance, see pp. 198–200, *ante.* As to Capital Gains Tax, see p. 201, *ante.* After winding up, the seal of the company must be affixed by the liquidator.

[68] See *ante*, pp. 179 *et seq.*

[69] Forms of application, Atkin's *Court Forms* (2nd ed.), Vol. 11. Forms of order, Seton (7th ed.), p. 762; Palmer's *Company Precedents* (16th ed.), Vol. III, Chap. 62.

debenture holders obtain the appointment of a receiver over the actual assets of the business, apart from the goodwill, it is no part of the duty of such receiver to preserve the goodwill: he has to preserve the assets entrusted to him with a view to their most favourable realisation: he need not have regard to contracts entered into by the company,[70] though it may become necessary for him to apply for certain powers of management to preserve the assets which are in his possession. Where, however, the receiver is also appointed manager, the goodwill forms part of the property entrusted to his care, and he must, in order to preserve it, carry out contracts entered into by the mortgagor, unless authorised by the court to disregard them.[71]

A receiver of the property of a foreign company appointed by a foreign court of competent jurisdiction [72] can maintain an action in his own name [73] to recover money due to the company.[74]

---

[70] See *Re Newdigate Colliery Co.* [1912] 1 Ch. 468.
[71] *Ibid.* and see Chap. 9.
[72] See p. 157, *ante.*
[73] *Semble*, the company can be joined as co-plaintiff.
[74] *Macaulay* v. *Guaranty Trust Co.* [1927] W.N. 308: party and party costs were allowed to the defendant and ordered to be deducted. *Semble*, that where the debt and appointment are clearly established, the court may refuse to allow defendants their costs.

CHAPTER 8

LIABILITIES OF A RECEIVER

Liability under general law. In addition to the liabilities of a receiver dealt with in this chapter, there are various statutes and statutory provisions under which a receiver whose duties include the carrying on or winding up of a business may incur liability to penalties, *e.g.* the Factories Acts, the Food and Drugs Acts, the provisions of the Acts relating to income tax, capital gains tax, value added tax, etc.; these have to some extent been indicated in the preceding chapter. Further, he may have to observe agreements with trade unions and other bodies regulating the conditions of employment of workpeople. It is essential for a receiver when concerned in carrying on a business to obtain expert advice from persons experienced in similar businesses.

Liability to account. A receiver is liable to account for all money coming into his hands, in his capacity of receiver, at any time, whether before or after the date of perfecting his security, and even after his appointment has lapsed.[1] The principle, that the appointment is merely conditional until his security is perfected, has no application where the question is as to his own liability, or that of his sureties, in respect of money received or expended by him.[2]

Responsibility for losses. A receiver is responsible for any loss occasioned to the estate over which he is appointed by reason of his wilful default.[3] If he places money received by him in what he knows to be improper hands, he will have to answer the loss out of his own pocket.[4] A receiver, however, is not expected, any more than a trustee or executor, to take more care of property entrusted to him than he would of his own.[5] If he deposits money for safe custody with a banker in good credit, to be placed to his account as receiver, he will not be answerable for the failure of the banker.[6]

---

[1] For the form of the order in this case see *Practice Note* [1943] W.N. 71.
[2] *Smart* v. *Flood* (1883) 49 L.T.(N.S.) 467.
[3] *Re Skerrett's Minor* (1829) 2 Hog. 192.
[4] *Knight* v. *Lord Plymouth* (1747) 3 Atk. 480.
[5] *Massey* v. *Banner* (1820) 1 Ja. & W. 241, *per* Lord Eldon at p. 247. Comp. *White* v. *Baugh* (1835) 9 Bligh 198.
[6] *Knight* v. *Lord Plymouth* (1747) 3 Atk. 480.

The money must, however, be deposited to the account of the receiver in that character, or be otherwise earmarked. If a receiver pays money which comes into his hands as receiver to his private account with a banker, and not to a separate account as receiver, or otherwise mixes up the money which he collects as receiver with his own money, he will be liable for the loss if the banker fails.[7]

Parting with control of fund. If a receiver puts a fund out of his own control so that other persons are able to deal with it, he is answerable for any loss that may ensue.[8] Accordingly, in a case where the receiver, in order to obtain sureties, had agreed that the money to be collected from the property over which he was receiver should be handed over to a partner of one of the sureties, and should be deposited with bankers in the joint names of the sureties, and that all drafts upon the money so deposited should be written by the partner and signed by the receiver, it was held that the receiver was liable for the loss occasioned by the failure of the banking house in which the money had been deposited.[9] If, indeed, a receiver parts with his control over the fund, by introducing the control of an irresponsible person who is unknown to the court, it is conceived that he will be answerable for any loss which may happen to the fund which he has so dealt with, not only where some particular peril in which he has placed the fund can be shown to have been the cause of the loss, but generally where he has not conducted himself as a prudent person would have done.[10]

In a case where a receiver had paid money to the plaintiff's solicitor, with directions to pay it into court, which had not been done, the receiver was held liable for the loss, there being no sufficient evidence to show that the receiver had authority from the plaintiff to pay the money to the solicitor.[11] And where a receiver appointed by way of equitable execution pays money to the judgment creditor's solicitor instead of to the creditor himself, he will be liable if the money never comes to the creditor's hands.[12]

---

[7] *Wren* v. *Kirton* (1805) 11 Ves. 381. As to following money which the receiver has mixed with money of his own, cf. *James Roscoe Ltd.* v. *Winder* [1915] 1 Ch. 62.

[8] *Salway* v. *Salway* (1831) 2 R. & M. 214.

[9] *Salway* v. *Salway, supra; ibid.* in the House of Lords, sub nom. *White* v. *Baugh* (1835) 9 Bligh 181; 3 Cl. & Fin. 44.

[10] *Salway* v. *Salway* (1831) 2 R. & M. 220.

[11] *Delfosse* v. *Crawshay* (1834) 4 L.J.Ch. 32; see, too, *Dixon* v. *Wilkinson* (1859) 4 Drew. 614; 4 A.G. & J. 508.

[12] *Ind, Coope & Co.* v. *Kidd* (1894) 63 L.J.Q.B. 726.

If a receiver is in default for not passing his accounts and paying his balances within the proper time, or if, not being in default, he derives a benefit by accepting interest on the balances which are from time to time in the hands of his banker, he is liable to make good any loss which may be occasioned by the bankruptcy of the banker, although the moneys may have been deposited to a separate account.[13]

A person who, having improperly assumed the character, neglects the duties of a receiver, while the parties interested consider him to be acting as a receiver, makes himself responsible for any property which is lost through his neglect.[14] If a solicitor in an action assumes the character of a receiver, and rents are paid to him in that character, he will be ordered to pay them over to the real receiver, and can claim no lien upon them, either by virtue of an agreement with a party to the action or for costs.[15]

All money which comes to the hands of a receiver by virtue of an order of the court entitling him to receive it, in a sense belongs to the court, and the receiver can only discharge himself by applying it in accordance with an order.[16]

If a receiver has paid money to a wrong person, and is afterwards obliged by that person's mortgagees to pay the amount into court, and after due application thereof a surplus remains, the court will not pay over such surplus to the person to whom the former payment was wrongfully made without satisfying the receiver's demands.[17] If, however, the wrongful payment is made by the receiver's agent, the receiver cannot have the benefit of the payment against the surplus, except subject to any liability of the agent to the person to whom the wrongful payment was made; and the accounts cannot be opened between those persons on application by the executor of the receiver, praying for repayment from the person wrongfully paid, or, in default of such repayment, out of the rents of the estate over which the receiver was appointed.[18]

When ordered to pay costs. A receiver may be ordered personally to pay costs incurred by reason of his misconduct or neglect in the

---

[13] *Drever* v. *Maudsley* (1844) 13 L.J.Ch. 433; 8 Jur. 547; 3 L.T. 157; see, too, *Shaw* v. *Rhodes* (1827) 2 Russ. 539; *Wilkinson* v. *Bewick* (1853) 4 Jur.(N.S.) 1010.
[14] *Wood* v. *Wood* (1828) 4 Russ. 558.
[15] *Wickens* v. *Townsend* (1839) 1 R. & M. 361.
[16] See *de Winton* v. *Mayor of Brecon* (1859) 28 Beav. 200.
[17] *Gurden* v. *Badcock* (1842) 6 Beav. 162.
[18] *Ibid.* p. 157.

discharge of his duties.[19] He will not, however, be held personally responsible if he has honestly done his best and failed. If a receiver has not succeeded in getting in rents, it is his first duty to lay the state of affairs before the court, and to ask for guidance, under circumstances where the incumbrancers on the property can consult with him and advise as to the best course to be pursued for their common interests.[20]

Breach of statutory duty. A receiver is personally liable for breach of a statutory duty; *e.g.* if with notice of a preferential claim he exhausts the assets in making payments to other creditors, he is liable for damages in tort to the preferential creditor [21]: it would be difficult, if not impossible, for a receiver successfully to allege want of notice in such a case, as it would be implied from the circumstances.[22] An inquiry is now ordered as to preferential debts.[23]

Attachment under the Debtors Act. A person who owes money, come to his hands as receiver, is in a fiduciary capacity within the meaning of the third exception to section 4 of the Debtors Act 1869.[24] He is liable to committal for breach of an order to pay such money, made after he has been discharged from being receiver. The mere fact that a defaulting receiver is unable to pay is not sufficient to induce the court to exercise the discretion given by the Debtors Act 1869 Amendment Act 1878, and to refuse leave to issue a committal.[25]

Misconduct in the exercise of duties. Although the court will not allow the possession of its receiver to be disturbed without its leave,[26] it will in its discretion, if the misconduct of the receiver becomes the subject of proceedings in another court, either itself take cognisance of the complaint, or leave the matter to be dealt with in the other proceedings.[27] There is a clear and well-recognised distinction between cases where the jurisdiction of the court,

---

[19] *Ex p. Brown* (1888) 36 W.R. 303.
[20] *Re St. George's Estate* (1887) 19 L.R.Ir. 566.
[21] *Woods* v. *Winskill* [1913] 2 Ch. 303; *Westminster Corporation* v. *Haste* [1950] Ch. 442; and *cf. Argylls Ltd.* v. *Coxeter* (1913) 29 T.L.R. 355.
[22] *Westminster City Council* v. *Chapman* [1916] 1 Ch. 169; see, further, p. 216, *ante.*
[23] *Ante*, p. 208.
[24] Relating to default by a person acting in a fiduciary capacity and ordered to pay any sum in his possession or under his control by a court of equity.
[25] *Re Gent* (1888) 40 Ch.D. 190.
[26] *Ante*, p. 145.
[27] See, further, p. 155, *ante.*

or the validity or propriety of its orders or process, is disputed, and cases where the authority of the court is admitted, but redress is sought against its officer for irregularity or excess in the performance of its orders. In the former case the court has no choice, but must draw the whole matter over to its own cognisance. In the latter case, the court has an indisputable right to assume the exclusive jurisdiction; but it may, if it thinks fit, refuse to interfere and permit another court to proceed for punishment or redress.[28]

Purchase by receiver. As a receiver is in a fiduciary capacity and therefore cannot, without the special leave of the court, purchase either directly, or indirectly in the name of a trustee for himself, any property or interest in property over which he is receiver,[29] he must account for any profit made by him through a purchase or other dealing.[30] A receiver is a trustee for the parties interested of any money due from him as receiver and not accounted for by him, and he could not, as against them, avail himself of any Statute of Limitations, even when his final accounts have been passed and the recognisance vacated.[31] The opinion has been expressed that a receiver was not within the protection of section 19 of the Limitation Act 1939.[32] It appears that a receiver cannot claim relief from personal liability under section 61 of the Trustee Act 1925.[33]

Personal liability and right to indemnity. A receiver appointed by the court is an officer of the court: he is therefore not an agent for any person, but a principal,[34] and as such personally liable to all persons contracting with him, irrespective of the amount of assets in his hands, unless his personal liability is excluded by the express terms of the contract,[35] subject to a correlative right to be indemnified

---

[28] *Aston* v. *Heron* (1834) 2 My. & K. 396; see, too, *Chalie* v. *Pickering* (1837) 1 Keen 749.

[29] *Ante,* p. 203.

[30] See *Nugent* v. *Nugent* [1908] 1 Ch. 546, and notes to *Fox* v. *Mackreth* (1791) 2 White & Tudor, *Cases in Equity.*

[31] *Seagram* v. *Tuck* (1881) 18 Ch.D. 296.

[32] Formerly s. 8 of the Trustee Relief Act 1888: *Re Cornish* [1896] 1 Q.B., *per* Kay L.J. at p. 104.

The actual decision was that the Act did not apply to a trustee in bankruptcy. The observations of Lord Esher on this point appear at variance with those of Lord Sterndale and Warrington L.J. in *Re Richardson* [1920] 1 Ch. 438, 447. See, however, judgment of Younger L.J. at p. 449.

[33] He is a paid trustee: see *Re Windsor Steam Coal Co.* [1929] 1 Ch. 151, *per* Lawrence L.J.

[34] Except receivers of statutory undertakings: see p. 242, *post.*

[35] As to the contrary doctrine evolved by the American courts, see n. 55, p. 235, *post.*

out of the assets in respect of all liabilities properly incurred.[36] He is entitled to this indemnity in priority even to the claims of persons who had advanced money under an order making the repayment of the advance a first charge on all the assets,[37] and in priority to the costs of the action,[38] and subject only to the plaintiff's costs of realisation.[39] Questions as to a receiver's liability and right to indemnity in contract and in tort occur most frequently where he is also appointed manager, and are dealt with fully in Chapter 9. A receiver's right to indemnity does not extend to the costs of an action, successfully defended, charging him with fraud where the acts complained of did not benefit the estate and were not in discharge of his duties.[40]

A receiver appointed by the court at the instance of debenture holders or mortgagees of a company is personally liable as a principal in respect of contracts or engagements entered into by him, but he is not personally liable in respect of breaches of contracts which were entered into by the company before his appointment.[41] A receiver of the assets of a company could not be made personally liable to refund money paid to him in discharge of a debt after he has paid the money into court, though the payment to the receiver was, without his knowledge, void as a fraudulent preference.[42]

If a receiver appointed by the court is liable in trespass, the court has jurisdiction, if it thinks fit, to restrain the action and leave the intending plaintiff to claim in the proceedings in which the receiver was appointed.[43]

The owner made liable by section 38 (4) of the Water Act 1945

---

[36] *Burt, Boulton and Hayward* v. *Bull* [1895] 1 Q.B. 276; *Re Glasdir Copper Mines* [1906] 1 Ch. 365; *Re A. Boynton Ltd.* [1910] 1 Ch. 519; *Moss Steamship Co.* v. *Whinney* [1912] A.C. at p. 271, *per* Lord Mersey; and see *Ex p. Izard* (1883) 23 Ch.D. 75, 79; *Re Brooke* [1894] 2 Ch. 600.

[37] *Strapp* v. *Bull, Sons & Co.* [1895] 2 Ch. 1; *Re Glasdir Copper Mines* [1906] 1 Ch. 365; *Re A. Boynton Ltd.* [1910] 1 Ch. 519.

[38] *Batten* v. *Wedgwood Coal Co.* (1885) 28 Ch.D. 317.

[39] See *Re London United Breweries* [1907] 2 Ch. 511 and *Ramsay* v. *Simpson* [1899] 1 I.R. 194.

[40] *Re Dunn* [1904] 1 Ch. 648.

[41] Cf. *Re Botibol* [1947] 1 All E.R. 26. See Chap. 9 and pp. 191–192, *ante*, as to liability for rent.

[42] See *Re Morant & Co.* [1924] 1 Ch. 79; cf. *Bissill* v. *Ariel Motors* (1910) 27 T.L.R. 73. The same rule would apply even if the debt arose on a contract made by the receiver. Application could be made in the action by the trustee in bankruptcy for payment out of the fund. As to fraudulent preference, see p. 100, *ante*.

[43] See *Aston* v. *Heron* (1834) 2 My. & K. 390; and pp. 224–225, *ante*.

does not include a constructive owner such as a receiver,[44] and
the person liable under paragraph 54 of Schedule 3 to that Act
is the person who actually collects the rents; consequently, where a
mortgagor had appointed a collector who paid them first to the
mortgagor and afterwards to a receiver, the collector and not the
receiver was held liable to pay the water rate.[45]

[44] *Metropolitan Water Board* v. *Brooks* [1911] 1 K.B. 289 (a decision on s. 4 of the
Water Companies (Regulation of Powers) Act 1887). As to liability in respect of gas,
electric light, rates, etc., see pp. 131, 209, *ante.*

[45] *Ibid.* (decided on s. 72 of the Waterworks Clauses Act 1847). References in
Water Act, s. 38, to a water rate include charges payable under Part III of the Water
Act 1973, and those in Sched. 3 include a reference to any such charge for services
which include a supply of water for domestic purposes: Water Act 1973, s. 49 (2) and
Sched. 8, para. 53.

CHAPTER 9

MANAGERS

WHERE a receiver is required for the purpose not only of receiving rents and profits, or of getting in outstanding property, but of carrying on or superintending a trade, business or undertaking, he is called a manager or more usually a receiver and manager. The appointment of a manager implies that he has power to deal with the property over which he is appointed manager and to appropriate the proceeds in a proper manner.[1]

In what cases appointed. Where the court appoints a manager of a business or undertaking, it in effect takes the management of it into its own hands; for the manager is an officer of the court. Managers, when appointed by the court, are responsible to the court, and can have no regard to orders of any of the parties interested in the business. The court will not usually assume the management of a business or undertaking, except with a view to its winding up and sale as a going concern, and with the sale the management ends.[2] The court may, however, appoint a person to manage the business of a testator pursuant to the trusts of his will, although no sale or winding up is contemplated, for instance, where the legatee of the business is an infant.[3] The case of public undertakings is discussed on a later page.[4]

The court has also jurisdiction, upon interlocutory application, to authorise a receiver to exercise such powers of management as are necessary for the preservation of property which is the subject of litigation, and to which the applicant has made out a prima facie title.[5] Thus, where the application was made by a lessor in an action to recover possession of a licensed hotel, the lease of which contained covenants by the lessee to keep the premises continuously

---

[1] *Sheppard* v. *Oxenford* (1855) 1 K. & J. 500; *Re Manchester & Milford Ry.* (1880) 14 Ch.D. 648, 653; *Truman* v. *Redgrave* (1881) 18 Ch.D. 547; *Parsons* v. *Sovereign Bank of Canada* [1913] A.C. 160.

[2] *Gardner* v. *L.C. & D. Ry.* (1867) L.R. 2 Ch.App. 201, 211, 212, *per* Lord Cairns; *Whitley* v. *Challis* [1892] 1 Ch. 64, 69; *Re Newdigate Colliery Co.* [1912] 1 Ch. 468, 472; *Re Newport Construction Co., Barclays Bank* v. *The Company* [1948] Ch. 217, 220.

[3] See *Re Irish* (1888) 40 Ch.D. 49.

[4] p. 242, *post.*

[5] *Leney & Sons Ltd.* v. *Callingham* [1908] 1 K.B. 79. See especially judgment of Farwell L.J.; *Charrington* v. *Camp* [1902] 1 Ch. 386; and see R.S.C., Ord. 29, r. 2.

open as an hotel and not to endanger the licences, the court, being satisfied that the licences were in jeopardy owing to threats by the defendant lessee to close the hotel, appointed a receiver, directed the licences to be handed over to him, and authorised him to keep the premises open as an hotel, and to do all acts necessary to preserve the licences.[6] In such cases the receiver is not given general powers of management, but such powers only as are necessary to preserve the property.

A manager may be appointed to carry on a private trade or business with a view to effecting a sale or winding up for the benefit of the persons interested. Thus, a manager was appointed to carry on the business of an intestate, there being no existing representative of his estate.[7] Where trustees have to manage a business, but are not themselves qualified to do so, and cannot agree in appointing a manager, the court may appoint a receiver and manager of the business [8]; but the more usual course would be to authorise the trustees to appoint a manager at a salary.

Partnership. The court has jurisdiction to appoint a manager of a partnership business, with a view to winding it up or selling it as a going concern,[9] and notwithstanding that the partnership has expired pursuant to a provision contained in the partnership.[10] The appointment is made for the purpose of preserving the assets and nothing more: the court does not intend to throw any liabilities of an onerous nature upon the partners.[11]

Unsoundness of mind. The judge [12] may authorise the receiver of the estate of the patient to carry on his trade or business.[13] The person so authorised is, for the purpose of estimating his liability to persons dealing with him, the agent of the patient.[14]

Bankruptcy. By section 10 of the Bankruptcy Act 1914, the official receiver, while acting as interim receiver of the debtor's estate, may, on the application of any creditor, appoint a special

---

[6] *Leney & Sons Ltd.* v. *Callingham* [1908] 1 K.B. 79, *q.v.* as to form of order.
[7] *Steer* v. *Steer* (1864) 2 Dr. & Sm. 311. See also *Blackett* v. *Blackett* (1871) 19 W.R. 559; *Spencer* v. *Shaw* [1875] W.N. 115; *Re Wright* (1888) 32 S.J. 721. As to manager of a newspaper, see *Chaplin* v. *Young* (1862) 6 L.T.(N.S.) 97.
[8] *Hart* v. *Denham* [1871] W.N. 2, *per* Lord Romilly M.R.
[9] See also pp. 64 *et seq.*, *ante.*
[10] *Taylor* v. *Neate* (1888) 39 Ch.D. 538.
[11] *Per* Chitty J. in *Taylor* v. *Neate* (1888) 39 Ch.D. 538, 545. See also *Boehm* v. *Goodall* [1911] 1 Ch. 155.
[12] See note 34, p. 74, *ante*, as to the meaning of this term in this connection.
[13] Mental Health Act 1959, ss. 100, 103 (1) (*e*), 105 (1), 119 (1).
[14] *Plumpton* v. *Burkinshaw* [1908] 2 K.B. 572.

manager to act until a trustee is appointed.[15] This section enables the official receiver to appoint a special manager while acting as interim receiver under section 8, prior to a receiving order [16]; and if the petition is dismissed the special manager is entitled to be paid his expenses properly incurred and his remuneration out of his receipts; the debtor cannot impugn any acts done by the manager in the proper conduct of the business.[17]

Special manager in winding-up cases. Where the official receiver becomes the liquidator of a company, whether provisionally or otherwise, he may, if satisfied that the nature of the estate or business of the company, or the interests of the creditors or contributories generally, require the appointment of a special manager, other than himself, apply to the court to, and the court may on such application, appoint a special manager thereof, to act during such time as the court may direct, with such powers, including any of the powers of a receiver or manager, as may be entrusted to him by the court.[18]

On application of incumbrancers.[19] The court will appoint a manager upon the application of incumbrancers whose security includes the goodwill [20]; but unless the goodwill is included a receiver only will be appointed [21]; though he may be given such powers of management as are necessary to preserve the property actually comprised in the security.[22] An incumbrancer with a charge upon the goodwill has an option either to have a receiver simply or a receiver and manager.[23]

The legal mortgagees of an hotel, whose security comprised the trade fixtures, goodwill and business, obtained upon interlocutory motion the appointment of a manager of the business of a licensed victualler carried on in it.[24] So a manager has been appointed at

---

[15] As to practice, see Bankruptcy Rules 1952 (S.I. 1952 No. 2113), rr. 319, 353–355. The official receiver has absolute discretion as to whether or not he will make the appointment and no appeal lies: *Re Whittaker* (1884) 1 Morr. 36.

[16] See s. 74 as to powers of interim receiver after receiving order.

[17] *Re A B & Co. (No.* 2) [1900] 2 Q.B. 429; *Re A Bankruptcy Petition* (1900) 7 Mans. 132. Accounts may be enforced under s. 105 (5): see *Re Jones* [1908] 1 K.B. 204.

[18] Companies Act 1948, s. 263.

[19] As to managers appointed under powers of an instrument, see Chap. 16.

[20] *Truman* v. *Redgrave* (1881) 18 Ch.D. 547.

[21] *Whitley* v. *Challis* [1892] 1 Ch. 64; *Re Leas Hotel* [1902] 1 Ch. 332.

[22] Upon the principles illustrated in *Leney & Sons Ltd.* v. *Callingham, ante,* p. 229.

[23] See p. 34, *ante.*

[24] *Truman* v. *Redgrave* (1881) 18 Ch.D. 547; see this case for form of order. See also *Ind, Coope & Co.* v. *Mee* [1895] W.N. 8.

the instance of holders of a registered statutory mortgage of a steamship [25]; of collieries held under a lease containing working covenants [26]; and on the application of the unpaid vendor of the property of a company in liquidation.[27] In order that the goodwill may be included in the security it need not be expressly mentioned: thus, where debentures issued by an hotel company charged " all its property and effects whatsoever," it was held that the goodwill of the business was included.[28]

Companies. The appointment of a manager is very frequently made over the undertaking of an ordinary limited company, on the application of mortgagees or debenture holders whose security includes the goodwill.[29] Formerly the court felt considerable hesitation about appointing a manager of the business of a limited company,[30] but it is now well settled that the court will readily make the appointment in order to enable a beneficial realisation of the property comprised in the security to be effected [31]; for the appointment of a receiver only, without powers of management, must inevitably cause the destruction of the goodwill, which cannot therefore be preserved for the benefit of the persons who have a charge upon it unless a manager is appointed: and even in cases where there is no goodwill of any saleable value, it is often necessary to carry on the business for a time in order to facilitate the sale of the assets as a going concern. Where three sets of debentures had been issued, each of which created a charge on certain specific items in addition to a general floating charge, the court appointed a receiver in each of three actions brought by the different sets of debenture holders, and appointed the receiver for the first debenture holders manager.[32] A manager cannot, except under the express authority of a statute, be appointed of a public undertaking.[33]

[25] *Fairfield, etc., Co.* v. *London and East Coast SS. Co.* [1895] W.N. 64.
[26] *Campbell* v. *Lloyds Bank* (1889) 58 L.J.Ch. 424; *County of Gloucester Bank* v. *Rudry Coal Co.* [1895] 1 Ch. 629.
[27] *Boyle* v. *Bettws Llantwit Co.* (1876) 2 Ch.D. 726.
[28] *Re Leas Hotel Co.* [1902] 1 Ch. 332; but *semble* that a mortgage of land and buildings on which experimental works were carried on would not authorise the appointment of a manager to carry on similar works as a commercial enterprise: *Stamford, etc., Banking Co.* v. *Keeble* [1913] 2 Ch. 96, 102.
[29] See *Re Leas Hotel Co.* [1902] 1 Ch. 332, 334, and *ante*, p. 60.
[30] *Makins* v. *Peter Ibbotson & Co.* [1891] 1 Ch. 133.
[31] See *Edwards* v. *Rolling Stock Syndicate* [1893] 1 Ch. 574; *Re Victoria Steamboats* [1871] 1 Ch. 158; *Re Leas Hotel Co.* [1902] 1 Ch. 332. For form of order, see Seton (7th ed.), p. 735.
[32] *Re Ind, Coope & Co.* [1911] 2 Ch. 223.
[33] See p. 242, *post.*

Practice on appointment. A manager is appointed for a definite period, usually of from one to six months; if a realisation is not likely to be effected at the expiration of that period, application must be made to the court before such expiration to continue the appointment.[34]

A manager must obey strictly the terms of his appointment: he will be disallowed items of expenditure incurred subsequent to the date up to which he was appointed, as well as remuneration for services after that date.[35]

The preceding chapters of this book relative to the practice on the appointment of receivers and to its consequences are equally applicable where the receiver is appointed manager, with the exceptions mentioned below: and many of the topics dealt with in the last two preceding chapters apply to managers. These chapters should therefore be consulted as to any matter not dealt with here.

Effect of appointment of manager. The appointment of a receiver and manager over the assets and business of a company does not dissolve or annihilate the company, any more than the taking possession by the mortgagee of the fee of land let to tenants annihilates the mortgagor. Both continue to exist; but the company is entirely superseded in the conduct of its business, and deprived of all power to enter into contracts in relation to that business, or to sell, pledge or otherwise dispose of the property put into the possession or under the control of the receiver and manager. The powers of the directors in this respect are entirely in abeyance so far as the company is concerned, and the powers of the company are exercised by the receiver under the direction of the court.[36]

Existing contracts. The receiver and manager is the agent of neither the company nor the debenture holders, but owes duties to both. He is appointed to preserve the goodwill of the business and, therefore, subject to any directions made on his appointment, it is his duty to carry into effect contracts entered into by the company before his appointment.[37] Such contracts, unless they

---

[34] By summons in chambers.

[35] *Re Wood Green & Hornsey Laundry Ltd.* [1918] 1 Ch. 423.

[36] *Per* Lord Atkinson in *Moss SS. Co.* v. *Whinney* [1912] A.C. 254, 263; *Parsons* v. *Sovereign Bank of Canada* [1913] A.C. 160. No estate vests in the manager. Any action or assurance is in the name of the company.

[37] See *Re Newdigate Colliery Co.* [1912] 1 Ch. 468; *Parsons* v. *Sovereign Bank of Canada* [1913] A.C. 160; *R.* v. *Board of Trade, ex p. St. Martin's Preserving Co. Ltd.* [1965] 1 Q.B. 603, 614.

are contracts depending on personal relationship, as contracts of employment,[38] remain valid and subsisting notwithstanding the appointment of a receiver and manager. Any breach of them will render the company, not the manager,[39] liable in damages, and will, moreover, destroy the goodwill of the business. In this respect a manager differs from a receiver appointed over the assets without any power to carry on the business, who is under no obligation and has no power to carry out these contracts, nor to have regard to preserving the goodwill, and whose appointment therefore operates to determine the contracts.[40] A manager must not, without leave of the court, disregard contracts in order to benefit the debenture holders, since this course would both destroy the goodwill and render the company liable in damages; nor must he pick and choose which contracts he will carry out as being most profitable.[41] If, however, it can be shown that to fulfil the contracts will benefit neither the company nor the debenture holders, as, for instance, where to disregard them does not affect the value of the goodwill, the court will, on the application of the receiver, allow him to refrain from carrying them into effect.[42] The same principles apply to managers of a business appointed at the instance of mortgagees.

The above principles were illustrated in a case in which the Court of Appeal refused to allow the manager appointed over the undertaking and assets of a colliery company to disregard contracts which had been entered into for the forward supply of coal, although, owing to a rise in price, this course would have enabled the manager to obtain enhanced receipts to the extent of £200 a week.[43] In another case a company had contracted to construct for £60,000 certain ships which were unfinished at the date of the appointment of the receiver and manager, and in respect of which

---

[38] These are discussed *ante*, pp. 165–166.

[39] The manager might however be liable in tort if he himself took steps which effectively prohibited the completion of a contract: see *Re Botibol* [1947] 1 All E.R. 26.

[40] See *ante*, p. 166.

[41] *Re Newdigate Colliery Co.* [1912] 1 Ch. 468; *Moss SS. Co.* v. *Whinney* [1912] A.C. 262.

[42] *Re Thames Ironworks* [1912] W.N. 66; 106 L.T. 674; *Re Great Cobar Ltd.* [1915] 1 Ch. 682. In the latter case it appears to have been considered that the fact that to disregard the contract might have involved a heavy claim for damages was immaterial. See, however, judgment of Buckley L.J. in *Re Newdigate Colliery Co.* [1912] 1 Ch. 478. If the debenture holders will not be substantially prejudiced, it would seem that liability in damages would be an important factor if there is likely to be a surplus after satisfying the debenture holders. *Cf. Airlines Airspares Ltd.* v. *Handley Page Ltd.* [1970] Ch. 193 (receiver and manager appointed out of court), p. 323, *post*.

[43] *Re Newdigate Colliery Co.* [1912] 1 Ch. 468.

£20,000, part of the purchase price, had then been paid on account: the company had given to a bank a charge, which ranked in priority to the debentures, to secure £40,000 on the ships and the unpaid balance of £40,000 to be received under the contract; it was proved that the cost of completing the ships would amount, without profit, to £50,000. In these circumstances, the court refused to sanction a borrowing by the receiver and manager for the purpose of completing the ships, and authorised him to discontinue work upon them, on the ground that no benefit would accrue either to the company or the debenture holders from the completion of the contract, and that in the circumstances it was not shown that the goodwill would be injured.[44]

Contracts: Set-off. Inasmuch as a manager is considered to be carrying out contracts entered into by the company, if he continues to supply goods for which contracts had been entered into by the company before his appointment, the persons to whom the goods are supplied can, in an action by the receiver or by assignees for the price, set off damages for subsequent breach of such contracts by the manager ceasing to carry them out [45]; and unless the receiver and manager has obtained leave to disregard such contracts he will be presumed to have acted thereunder, not on new contracts made by him.[46]

Lien of creditors. Persons contracting with a receiver and manager, carrying on the business of a company, who are cognisant of his appointment,[47] must be taken to know that he is contracting as principal, not as agent for the company, whose powers are paralysed; consequently they could not, under a bill of lading under which goods were expressed to be consigned to the company, and which contained a provision that they were to have a lien on the goods shipped for previously unsatisfied freight due from the shippers or consignees, claim a lien on the goods against the receiver.[48]

---

[44] *Re Thames Ironworks* [1912] W.N. 66; 103 L.T. 674; money had been borrowed to complete other contracts.

[45] *Parsons* v. *Sovereign Bank of Canada* [1913] A.C. 160; *Forster* v. *Nixon's Navigation Co. Ltd.* (1906) 23 T.L.R. 138.

[46] *Parsons* v. *Sovereign Bank of Canada, supra.*

[47] See Companies Act 1948, s. 370, discussed p. 205, *ante.* This section was new in the 1929 Companies Act.

[48] *Moss SS. Co.* v. *Whinney* [1912] A.C. 254. The decision really turned on the construction of the documents. See *Parsons* v. *Sovereign Bank of Canada* [1913] A.C. 160, 167.

A receiver and manager should, subject to any special directions
of the court, carry on the business according to the general course
adopted by the particular trade; he must not speculate,[49] and if he
requires to do anything outside the ordinary course of business he
must obtain the leave of the court.[50] He cannot as a general rule
create any charge or lien without the consent of the court on the
property of the company for debts due from it, though it would
appear that he could create a lien for unsatisfied freight or traffic
charges due from him personally, where such a lien is in the ordinary course of business.[51] But if a receiver for a company purports
to create a lien for unsatisfied freight due from the company, he
cannot himself claim the goods without satisfying the lien, though
the company, or the debenture holders, might do so.[52]

Liability of managers. Receivers and managers appointed by the
court (except the so-called receivers appointed by the Court of
Protection,[53] and probably receivers and managers of statutory
undertakings [54]) are personally liable to persons dealing with them
in respect of liabilities incurred, or contracts entered into by them
in carrying on the business,[55] unless the express terms of the contract exclude, as they may do, any personal liability [56]; but subject
to a correlative right to be indemnified out of the assets in respect
of liabilities properly incurred [57]; for receivers are not agents for
any person but principals,[58] and are therefore assumed to pledge
their personal credit. Their liability will not be displaced by the
fact that in giving orders they sign as " receiver and manager." [59]

This principle, however, does not operate to render the receiver
and manager personally liable in respect of sums which have been

---

[49] *Taylor* v. *Neate* (1888) 39 Ch.D. 544; and see *Re British Power, etc., Co. (No.* 2)
[1907] 1 Ch. 528.

[50] *Ante,* p. 180, as to obtaining leave.

[51] *Moss SS. Co.* v. *Whinney, supra.*

[52] *Ibid., per* Lords Loreburn, Shaw and Mersey.

[53] *Ante,* p. 73 *et seq.*

[54] See p. 240, *post.*

[55] The American courts, starting from the same premises, have evolved a different
doctrine, namely, that actions against the receiver are actions against the receivership,
and that the receiver cannot be held liable beyond assets in his hands. See *Clark on
Receivers,* pp. 839, 844; *cf. Beven on Negligence* (4th ed.), pp. 1468 *et seq.*

[56] *Post,* p. 236.

[57] See pp. 236–237, *post.*

[58] *Burt, Boulton and Hayward* v. *Bull* [1895] 1 Q.B. 276; *Strapp* v. *Bull, Sons & Co.*
[1895] 2 Ch. 1; *Re Glasdir Copper Mines* [1906] 1 Ch. 365; *Moss S.S. Co.* v. *Whinney*
[1912] A.C. 254, 259, 271.

[59] *Burt, Boulton and Hayward* v. *Bull* [1895] 1 Q.B. 276. See *Moss S.S. Co.* v.
Whinney, supra.

advanced pursuant to an order of the court,[60] making repayment of such sums a charge on the assets,[61] whether such sums are advanced by a party to the action or a stranger,[62] nor for breach of contracts entered into by the company.[63]

If the terms of the contract exclude the personal liability of the receiver, and limit the creditor's right to a claim against the assets,[64] then, if the contract is *ultra vires* the receiver, the creditor can have no claim by subrogation against the assets,[65] though it is presumed he could follow money which he could earmark.[66] If the receiver, while negativing his personal liability, falsely represented that he had authority to contract, it is conceived that the creditor might claim damages against him personally for breach of warranty of authority.

Where a receiver in Mental Health is, by an order made by the Court of Protection or nominated judge, authorised to manage the business of the patient, he is not personally liable to creditors in respect of liabilities which he has incurred in carrying on the business, unless he expressly or impliedly pledges his own credit; for he is regarded as agent for the patient.[67]

The position of receivers and managers appointed by debenture holders or mortgagees under the powers of an instrument is discussed in Chapter 16.[68]

Right to indemnity. A receiver and manager appointed by the court is entitled to be indemnified out of the assets against all liabilities properly incurred [69] by him in carrying on the business [70]; he is entitled to this indemnity (in addition to the rest of his costs, charges, expenses and remuneration) in priority to all other claims against the assets (except the plaintiff's costs of realisation),[71]

---

[60] As to time and mode of enforcing the liability, see *Re Ernest Hawkins* (1915) 31 T.L.R. 237.

[61] *Re A. Boynton Ltd.* [1910] 1 Ch. 519.

[62] *Re Glasdir Copper Mines* [1906] 1 Ch. 365, 284; *Re A. Boynton Ltd.* [1910] 1 Ch. 519.

[63] *Ante*, p. 233.   [64] See *Re British Power, etc., Co. (No. 2)* [1907] 1 Ch. 528.

[65] Unless the contract were a beneficial one of which the debenture holders had obtained the benefit. See *Re British Power, etc., Co. (No. 2)* [1907] 1 Ch. 528.

[66] See *Sinclair* v. *Brougham* [1914] A.C. 398.

[67] *Plumpton* v. *Burkinshaw* [1908] 2 K.B. 572.   [68] See *post*, p. 309.

[69] See *Re British Power, etc., Co.* [1906] 1 Ch. 497; *ibid. (No. 2)* [1907] 1 Ch. 528.

[70] *Ex p. Izard* (1883) 23 Ch.D. 75, 79; *Strapp* v. *Bull, Sons & Co.* [1895] 2 Ch. 1; *Re Glasdir Copper Mines* [1906] 1 Ch. 365; *Moss S.S. Co.* v. *Whinney* [1912] A.C. 254, 270; and see *Re Brooke* [1894] 2 Ch. 600.

[71] See *Re London United Breweries* [1907] 2 Ch. 511; *cf. Bertrand* v. *Davies* (1862) 31 Beav. 436; *Fraser* v. *Burgess* (1860) 13 Moo.P.C. 346, but as to priority of an executor's former right of retainer, see *Re Wester-Wemyss* [1940] Ch. 1.

even to the claims of persons who have advanced money to enable
the business to be carried on under an order of the court declaring
the repayment of such advances a first charge on the assets,[72] and
in priority to the costs of the action.[73] The receiver may waive his
rights in this respect, but waiver will not be implied except in a
plain case, [74] nor does the bankruptcy of others affect his rights.[75]
He will still be allowed to apply for a full indemnity even after he has
filed his final account, if the assets are still undistributed.[76]

Even where a receiver and manager has borrowed the whole of a
specified sum which he has been authorised to raise for the general
purposes of the business upon the security of a charge on the assets,
he will be allowed an indemnity in respect of such further liabilities
as he can, in the circumstances, justify as having been properly incurred. It is not, however, enough to show that the additional
liabilities were incurred in the ordinary course of business, for it is
prima facie the duty of the receiver and manager to obtain the leave
of the court before incurring liabilities in excess of the sum specified. Thus a receiver and manager of a motorcar business, who had
exercised to the full extent a power given to him of borrowing a
specified sum, was allowed indemnity in respect of the cost of
supplying bodies of cars which had been ordered, and of the rent of
business premises, but not in respect of the cost of cars for exhibi-
tion at a show, for this was a speculation; nor of an overdraft for
sums employed in carrying on the business, because leave to incur
this liability might and should have been obtained from the court.[77]

The extent of this right to indemnity is limited to the amount of
the assets; if these are insufficient the receiver has no enforceable
claim against the parties to the action in respect of indemnity or
remuneration, even where he has been appointed under a consent
order.[78]

Creditors of receiver who makes default. Where a receiver and
manager has properly incurred liabilities in the discharge of his
duties, his creditors, in the event of his failure to pay them, are

[72] *Strapp* v. *Bull, Sons & Co.* [1895] 2 Ch. 1; *Lathom* v. *Greenwich Ferry* (1895) 72
L.T. 790; *Re Glasdir Copper Mines* [1906] 1 Ch. 365; *Re A. Boynton* [1910] 1 Ch. 519.
The order ought, however, to state whether the charge is to be subject to the receiver's
right of indemnity or not. See *Re Glasdir Copper Mines, supra.*
[73] *Batten* v. *Wedgwood Coal Co.* (1885) 28 Ch.D. 317; *Re London United Breweries*
[1907] 2 Ch. 511.
[74] See *Re Glasdir Copper Mines* [1906] 1 Ch. 365. [75] *Post,* p. 250.
[76] *Levy* v. *Davis* [1900] W.N. 174.
[77] *Re British Power, etc., Co.* (*No.* 2) [1907] 1 Ch. 528.
[78] *Boehm* v. *Goodall* [1911] 1 Ch. 155.

entitled by subrogation to claim against the estate direct,[79] and can resort to funds carried to the separate account of a legatee of the testator in the administration of whose estate the order appointing a receiver was made.[80] If the receiver and manager has become bankrupt, payment will be ordered direct to the creditors, not through the receiver's trustee in bankruptcy.[81] But a creditor could not issue execution against the assets on a judgment obtained against the receiver.[82] The creditors of a receiver and manager appointed by the court to carry on a business authorised by a testator's will to be carried on are entitled by subrogation to be paid out of the assets in priority to the trustees or their creditors.[83]

This right of the creditors to claim against the assets is limited to the amount of the receiver's indemnity; thus where a receiver and manager had properly incurred liabilities to trade creditors to the extent of £900 in respect of which he was entitled to indemnity, and was in default to the estate to the extent of £400, it was held that the creditors could only claim against the assets to the extent of the receiver's net indemnity, *i.e.* £500: and that, therefore, as the estate would suffer no less by the receiver's default, his sureties could not be compelled by the creditors to make good the £400 by which he was in default; the creditors therefore had no remedy, except their claim against the receiver personally, in respect of the £400.[84] In an earlier case [85] the facts were somewhat similar, except that the sureties had paid into court the sum by which the receiver and manager was in default without contesting their liability; the court accordingly directed payment to be made direct to the creditors of the receiver and manager, who had become bankrupt, of the full amount of their debts. The judgment in this case must be read in the light of the fact that the estate would suffer no loss, because the sureties paid the amount of the deficiency; it cannot therefore be considered to conflict with the principles enunciated in the later case above cited.[86]

---

[79] *Re British Power, etc. Co.* [1906] 1 Ch. 497; and *ibid.* (*No.* 2) [1907] 1 Ch. 528; *Re London United Breweries* [1907] 2 Ch. 511.

[80] *O'Neill* v. *M'Grorty* [1915] 1 I.R. 1.

[81] *Re London United Breweries* [1907] 2 Ch. 511.

[82] See *Jennings* v. *Mather* [1902] 1 K.B. 1.

[83] See *Re Healy* [1918] 1 I.R. 366; *Re Oxley* [1914] 1 Ch. 604. Also *Burke* v. *Whelan* [1920] 1 I.R. 200; *Re East* (1914) 111 L.T. 101.

[84] *Re British Power, etc., Co.* (*No.* 3) [1910] 2 Ch. 470. See *Re Johnson* (1880) 15 Ch.D. 548.

[85] *Re London United Breweries* [1907] 2 Ch. 511.

[86] *Re British Power, etc., Co.* (*No.* 3) [1910] 2 Ch. 470.

Borrowing by manager. If a receiver and manager requires money to enable him to carry on the business entrusted to him, the court will give him liberty to borrow upon the security of the property in his control and as a first charge upon the whole undertaking, in priority even to debentures, where the money is required for preservation of the assets and the goodwill [87]; leave will not, however, be given if the borrowing will not benefit either the company or the debenture holders [88]: thus, leave will not be given without a prior incumbrancer's consent where there is a larger amount due on the prior incumbrance than the property is likely to realise. [89]

Where a receiver and manager appointed in a debenture holder's action has been authorised to raise money, this gives him by implication power to create a charge to secure the money in priority to existing debentures. [90] The order ought always to state whether the charge is, or is not, to be subject to the receiver's right of indemnity. [91] In order to secure the money raised the receiver sometimes gives a certificate, sometimes a charge; or the amount may be raised on the security of debentures. [92] In a case where the receiver was authorised to borrow £700 and, not requiring all the money at once, overdrew £500 from the bank and afterwards paid off the overdraft, it was held that he had not exhausted his borrowing powers to the extent of £500, but was still able to borrow the entire £700 without further leave. [93]

The claim of persons who have advanced money to receivers and managers under an order of the court upon security of a charge on the assets, is, unless the order otherwise directs, postponed to the receiver's rights. [94] The receiver is under no personal liability for the sums advanced [95] unless the contract provides otherwise.

Where a manager had contracted in part in excess of an authorised amount, with an express provision that he was not to be

---

[87] *Greenwood* v. *Algeciras Ry.* [1894] 2 Ch. 205.

[88] *Securities and Properties Corp.* v. *Brighton Alhambra* (1893) 62 L.J.Ch. 566. Form of summons, Atkin's *Court Forms* (2nd ed.), Vol. 11.

[89] *Re Thames Ironworks* [1912] W.N. 66; 106 L.T. 674; and *ante*, p. 234.

[90] *Lathom* v. *Greenwich Ferry Co.* [1895] W.N. 77; 72 L.T. 790

[91] See *Re Glasdir Copper Mines* [1906] 1 Ch. 365. Form of order, Seton (7th ed.), p. 764.

[92] See Palmer's *Company Precedents* (16th ed.), Vol. III, Chap. 58.

[93] *Milward* v. *Avill and Smart* [1897] W.N. 162. The order should, however, clearly define the extent of the power to borrow: *e.g.* whether on terms that the outstanding loan or overdraft at any one time should not exceed a specified sum or whether a single limited sum is to be borrowed.

[94] See pp. 236–237, *ante*.

[95] *Re A. Boynton* [1910] 1 Ch. 519.

personally liable, an application by the creditor for payment out of assets, or by the receiver personally, was dismissed as being capable of being dealt with on taking the receiver's accounts.[96]

Torts. As a receiver is a principal he appears to be personally liable, but with a right of indemnity against the assets, to third persons, not parties, in respect of torts committed by him, or by persons in his employment [97] in the ordinary course of their duties [98]; though if the act complained of is done under the express directions of the court, it seems that the person aggrieved should not sue the receiver, but should apply in the action [99]; this is the more convenient course in cases of alleged trespass.[1] If the act complained of is not specifically authorised, but is merely committed in the course of the receiver's duties, *e.g.* where his servant negligently injures a third person, the injured person may sue the receiver, and it seems, without leave of the court,[2] though it can never be improper to apply for such leave.[3] In all such cases the receiver should apply for leave to defend at the cost of the estate.[4]

Statutory undertaking. The case of receivers of statutory undertakings appears to be an exception to the above doctrines, though the question can seldom arise, as the receiver cannot as a rule be appointed manager [5]; if, however, under the authority of a statute, such receiver is given powers of management,[6] it is submitted that he is not personally liable except to the extent of assets in his hands, either in contract or tort. For the company or undertakers derive an exclusive power to carry on a particular undertaking from the statute of incorporation, and it is submitted that the court has no power to authorise a receiver or anyone else to carry on the undertaking except as agent for the undertakers.[7]

---

[96] *Re Ernest Hawkins & Co.* (1915) 31 T.L.R. 247.

[97] *Aston* v. *Heron* (1834) 2 M. & K. 390. The English authorities are scanty. See *Re Dunn* [1904] 1 Ch. 648. The American cases are collected in *Clark on Receivers*, pp. 785 *et seq.*; it must be remembered that the American doctrine of the limitation of the receiver's liability to the assets does not apply in England.

[98] See *Lloyd* v. *Grace, Smith & Co.* [1912] A.C. 716; *Percy* v. *Glasgow Corp.* [1922] 2 A.C. 299.

[99] See p. 145, *ante*; in such a case the court has jurisdiction to restrain a separate action.

[1] See *Re Maidstone Palace of Varieties* [1909] 2 Ch. 283.   [2] See pp. 224–225, *ante*.

[3] *Cf. Re Botibol* [1947] 1 All E.R. 26.

[4] Otherwise he may not be indemnified against costs.   [5] See p. 242, *post*.

[6] *e.g.* Railway Companies Act 1867, s. 4; see p. 52, *ante*.

[7] On similar principles the court cannot authorise a sale of the undertaking where the statute does not do so: *Re Woking U.D.C. (Basingstoke Canal) Act 1911* [1914] 1 Ch. 300.

Liability in general. With regard to parties to the action, the receiver is not liable for defaults of his servants and agents if he has exercised due care.[8]

If an offence against the Food and Drugs Act 1955, or any similar statute, is committed during the receivership by a person in the employment of the receiver, the latter may be liable to prosecution [9]: it seems that the company can be made liable for the receiver's own acts in such a case.[10]

Indemnity. If a receiver becomes liable for damages in tort, or is fined in respect of a criminal act, his right to indemnity depends upon whether the act in respect of which damages were awarded or fine was imposed was done in the course of his duties without any want of due care on his part: for instance, if he is sued or prosecuted in respect of the negligence, fraud or criminality of a person employed by him, he is entitled to be indemnified if he has been reasonably careful in employing that person [11]; but if, for example, he employs a person who is wholly unqualified to do skilled work, it is conceived that he would not be entitled to be indemnified against damages recovered by a third person for negligence on the part of the employee.

Interference with manager. Inasmuch as the property entrusted to him as manager includes the goodwill, the court will restrain deliberate acts calculated to destroy it, either by a party or a stranger: inducing employees to leave a business which is being carried on under the direction of the court, with a view to their employment in another business which is being started in opposition, and attempting to obtain a tenancy of a field which, to the knowledge of the person making the attempt, had been occupied in connection with the business, are such acts of interference and will be restrained by injunction.[12] Deliberate acts of interference are a contempt of court and may be punished as such [13]; it is

---

[8] See p. 221, *ante.*

[9] See *Jarvis* v. *Islington Borough Council* (1909) 73 J.P.J. 323, cited p. 145, *ante. Cf. Booth* v. *Helliwell* [1914] 2 K.B. 252.

[10] *Jarvis* v. *Islington Borough Council, supra. Cf. R.* v. *I.C.R. Haulage Ltd.* [1944] K.B. 551.

[11] See pp. 221, 237, *ante.*

[12] *Dixon* v. *Dixon* [1904] 1 Ch. 161. The acts complained of were done by a defendant to the action. Acts of bona fide trade competition by strangers would not be restrained, although their effect might be to destroy the goodwill. *Cf. Re Bechstein* (1914) 58 S.J. 864 and *Re William Thomas Shipping Co.* [1930] 2 Ch. 368.

[13] *Taylor* v. *Soper* (1890) 62 L.T. 828. See generally as to interference with a receiver, Chap. 6, *ante.*

such an act of interference for one of the partners in the original business to start or conduct a competing business in such a way as improperly to injure the original business when under the control of the court, as, for instance, by representing by circulars that the latter business is no longer carried on.[14]

Interest must not conflict with duty. A receiver and manager, being an officer of the court, must not place himself in a position in which his interest will conflict with his duty: accordingly, where a receiver and manager had been appointed over the undertaking of a railway company, it was held that he must not enter into a partnership with the company and use his own steamboat in conjunction with the company's traffic by issuing through tickets for use on the steamboat and the company's railway.[15]

Public company. Although the court will, in the case of a private trade or business, appoint a manager, the case is different where a company has been incorporated, and empowered by the legislature, acting for the public interest, to construct and maintain an undertaking for a public purpose, and the legislature has imposed powers and duties of an important kind on the company. Inasmuch as these powers and duties have been conferred and imposed on the company and on no other body of persons, the powers must be executed and the duties discharged by the particular company: they cannot be delegated or transferred. Accordingly, although the court may appoint a receiver, it will not appoint a manager of the undertaking of such a company at the instance of a debenture holder; inasmuch as a debenture, in the form scheduled to the Companies Clauses Consolidation Act 1845, gives only a charge on the company's undertaking, not a right to interfere with the carrying on the business of the company, and no right is given to sell the undertaking.[16] Upon this ground the court will not appoint a manager of a tramway company governed by the Tramways Act 1870 [17] and it would not formerly appoint a manager of a railway company.[18]

---

[14] *King* v. *Dopson* (1911) 56 S.J. 51.

[15] *Re Eastern & Midland Ry.* (1890) 90 L.T.J. 20.

[16] *Gardner* v. *London, Chatham & Dover Ry.* (1867) L.R. 2 Ch.App. 201, 212, 215–217, *per* Lord Cairns; *Blaker* v. *Herts and Essex Waterworks Co.* (1889) 41 Ch.D. 399.

[17] *Marshall* v. *South Staffordshire Tramways Co.* [1895] 2 Ch. 36, disapproving *Bartlett* v. *West Metropolitan Tramways Co.* [1893] 3 Ch. 437; [1894] 2 Ch. 286.

[18] *Gardner* v. *London, Chatham & Dover Ry.* (1867) L.R. 2 Ch.App. 201. See now pp. 52, 53, *ante*.

The reasoning upon which these decisions are founded appears not to apply where there is a specific power to sell under the statute which effects the incorporation, as is sometimes the case with statutory companies.[19] If there is a power to sell and therefore to cause the conduct and management to devolve on other persons than those specified by the statute, presumably a manager might be appointed.

Market, etc. Although a receiver may be appointed of the tolls of a market, the court will not appoint a manager of a market belonging to a municipal corporation and regulated by statute, because this would amount to an administration of the affairs of a corporation.[20]

Property abroad. Where an action relates to property in a dominion or colony or in a foreign country, which partakes of the nature of a trade, it is competent for the court to appoint a manager. In a case relating to a West Indian estate, it was said that a manager is appointed, not for the purpose of carrying on the management of the estate, but to enable the court to give relief, when the cause is heard.[21] Persons, for instance, have been appointed to manage landed property, to receive the rents and profits, and to convert, get in, and remit the proceeds of property and assets, in cases in which the property has been situate in India,[22] in the West Indies,[23] in Demerara,[24] and in Brazil.[25] Thus, where the whole undertaking of a limited company is situate abroad, the court may appoint a manager: managers have been appointed of railways in Venezuela,[26] mines in Peru,[27] railway and mines in Chile.[28]

---

[19] See *Re Crystal Palace Co.* (1911) 104 L.T. 251, 898, affd. *sub nom. Saunders* v. *Bevan* (1912) 107 L.T. 70. There is no power to direct a sale unless it is specifically given by the statute; see *Re Woking U.D.C.* (*Basingstoke Canal*) *Act 1911* [1914] 1 Ch. 300.

[20] *De Winton* v. *Mayor, etc., of Brecon* (1859) 26 Beav. 542.

[21] *Waters* v. *Taylor* (1808) 15 Ves. 10, 25, *per* Lord Eldon. See, too, *Sheppard* v. *Oxenford* (1855) 1 K. & J. 500.

[22] *Logan* v. *Princess of Coorg* (1860) Seton (7th ed.), p. 776.

[23] Seton (7th ed.), p. 778. See, too, *Barkley* v. *Lord Reay* (1843) 2 Hare 308.

[24] *Bunbury* v. *Bunbury* (1839) 1 Beav. 336; *Bentinck* v. *Willink* (1842) 2 Hare 1; 67 E.R. 1.

[25] *Sheppard* v. *Oxenford* (1855) 1 K. & J. 500; as to form of order, see *ibid.* p. 501. See, too, *Duder* v. *Amsterdamsch Trustees Kantoor* [1902] 2 Ch. 132, 144, where the same persons were appointed receivers in two actions for enforcing different claims on the same property.

[26] *Re South Western of Venezuela Ry.* [1902] 1 Ch. 701.

[27] *Re Huinac Copper Mines* [1910] W.N. 218.

[28] *Re Arauco Ltd.* (1898) 79 L.T. 336.

A person resident in England may be appointed manager, with authority to appoint an agent abroad in the country where the property is situate [29]; and sometimes a person resident in the country where the estate is situated is appointed manager.[30] Where a receiver and manager, appointed over mines in Peru belonging to a limited company, was unable to obtain possession because the *lex loci* only recognised the title of the company, the court ordered the company to appoint two attorneys to take possession on behalf of the receiver.[31] It is not the practice in such cases to direct the attorneys to give security.[32]

Notice to registrar of companies. A person who obtains an order for the appointment of a receiver or manager of the property of a company, must within seven days give notice to the registrar of companies, who thereupon enters the fact upon the register of mortgages.[33]

Restraint of trade. A purchaser of a business under a contract entered into by a receiver cannot insist upon the insertion in the conveyance of a covenant by the receiver against the carrying on by him of a competing business [34]: and it appears that he will not be entitled to restrain a receiver from carrying on such a business, though the latter must not make use of information obtained as receiver.[35] If a purchaser requires a restriction against carrying on a competing business to be entered into by the receiver, he must procure the insertion in the contract of a stipulation to this effect.

Consignees. In cases where the manager of an estate must necessarily reside in the country where the estate is situated, it was formerly usual to add to the order directing the appointment of a manager an order for the appointment of a consignee or consignees resident in this country, to whom the produce of the property in question might be remitted, and by whom it might be disposed of.[36]

---

[29] Seton (7th ed.), p. 777; Palmer's *Company Precedents* (16th ed.), Vol. III, Chap. 65.
[30] Seton (7th ed.), p. 777.
[31] *Re Huniac Copper Mines* [1910] W.N. 218.
[32] *Per* Warrington J. in chambers, January 18, 1912: though in particular circumstances security may be ordered.
[33] Companies Act 1948, s. 102 (1).
[34] *Re Irish* (1888) 40 Ch.D. 49, commented on in *Boorne* v. *Wicker* [1927] 1 Ch. 667. *Cf. Farey* v. *Cooper* [1927] 2 K.B. 384.
[35] *Re Gent* (1892) 40 W.R. 267; *Re Irish, supra.*
[36] Seton (7th ed.), p. 778.

Under modern commercial practice the appointment of a consignee can be seldom necessary or advisable, the produce being sold *in situ* or consigned to commercial agents. The present practice in such cases is to appoint a receiver in this country with power to appoint attorneys, managers or local agents abroad, with such directions as to disposal of money in the hands of the latter as may be required in any particular case.[37]

The court, in dealing with property overseas, may provide against the inconveniences likely to arise from the death, absence, or incapacity of an existing manager, by appointing another person to act as manager in any of those events.[38]

---

[37] See form of order, Palmer's *Company Precedents* (16th ed.), Vol. III, Chap. 52.

[38] *Rutherford* v. *Wilkinson* (1823) Seton (7th ed.), p. 780; *Forbes* v. *Hammond* (1819) 1 Jac. & W. 88.

CHAPTER 10

SALARY AND ALLOWANCES OF A RECEIVER

Right to salary and allowances. A receiver will, unless it is otherwise ordered, or unless he consents to act without a salary, be allowed a proper salary, or have allowances made to him for his care and pains in the execution of his duties.[1] And, even where he has consented to act without a salary, he may be paid for services which have proved beneficial to the estate, and which it was no part of his duty to perform, *e.g.* working as a mechanic in a business of which he has, by the order appointing him, been constituted manager, though this is an indulgence if the receiver so acts without directions as to payment.[2] Where the order appointing a receiver says nothing about remuneration, this does not amount to a decision that he is to have no remuneration, even though he be a trustee, who as a general rule receives no remuneration.[3] The amount of a receiver's salary or allowance is usually not fixed until the passing of his first account, and often, especially in the case of companies, not till later, when he will be allowed either a percentage upon his receipts, or a gross sum by way of salary.[4] An agreement by a trustee in bankruptcy for pooling his remuneration with the amount recovered in respect of a debt due to his employer or partner is void, as it might result in the creditor obtaining a preference [5]: as receivers must hold an even hand between creditors the same rule appears to apply to them.

A receiver and manager will not be allowed remuneration for any period beyond the term of his appointment, unless an extension is made before it expires.[6]

Formerly, where the court appointed a receiver with a salary he was obliged to pay out of his own pocket any expenses which he

---

[1] R.S.C., Ord. 30, r. 3. The term " receiver " here includes consignee and manager: Ord. 1, r. 4 (1). For the position in relation to receivers appointed by the Court of Protection see Court of Protection Rules 1960 (S.I. 1960 No. 1146), r. 50. A special manager's remuneration is fixed by the court: Companies Act 1948, s. 263 (3).

[2] *Harris* v. *Sleep* [1897] 2 Ch. 80.

[3] *Re Bignell, Bignell* v. *Chapman* [1892] 1 Ch. 59.

[4] Daniell's *Chancery Practice* (8th ed.), 1485. It is usually fixed by the master, but sometimes fixed and allowed by the Taxing Master: *Silkstone, etc., Coal Co.* v. *Edey* [1901] 2 Ch. 652, 655. R.S.C., Ord. 62, does not apply: see *ibid.* r. 9 (2).

[5] *Farmers' Mart Ltd.* v. *Milne* [1915] A.C. 106.

[6] *Re Wood Green and Hornsey Laundry* [1918] 1 Ch. 423.

might incur in giving security, whereas, if he was appointed without salary, he would have been allowed in his accounts expenses reasonably incurred by him for that purpose.[7] Now, in all cases such expenses are normally allowed as a disbursement.[8]

Amount of allowance. There is no settled scale governing the allowance to a receiver. According to a rule laid down by Lord Langdale in *Day* v. *Croft*,[9] the allowance to a receiver of the rents and profits of a freehold or leasehold estate was, at that time, generally 5 per cent. on the amount received. That allowance might, however, be increased if there was any special difficulty in the collection; or it might be diminished; or a fixed salary might be allowed where the rental was considerable.[10] The practice at the present time in the Chancery Division is to allow remuneration on the basis of a *quantum meruit*, according to the time, trouble and degree of responsibility involved. A remuneration statement setting out first a brief description of the work done by the receiver and secondly a time account is required.[11]

A receiver and manager appointed to wind up or carry on a partnership business is, in the absence of express stipulation, entitled to a *quantum meruit*,[12] though he is himself a partner, irrespective of his liabilities to the partnership as a partner [13]; but the scale allowed to liquidators is not a guide.[14]

In the Queen's Bench Division the remuneration of a receiver by way of equitable execution is governed by a Memorandum of the King's Bench Masters of June 1929. This runs as follows:

" Where a receiver is appointed by way of equitable execution, unless the court or a judge otherwise orders, the total amount to be allowed for costs of the receiver (including his remuneration, the costs of obtaining his appointment, of completing his security (if any), of passing his accounts, and of obtaining his discharge), should not exceed 10 per cent. of the amount due under the

---

[7] *Harris* v. *Sleep* [1897] 2 Ch. 80.
[8] See p. 123, *ante*.
[9] (1840) 2 Beav. 491.
[10] Seton (7th ed.), p. 339.
[11] Form, Atkin's *Court Forms* (2nd ed.), Vol. 33, p. 220; Palmer's *Company Precedents* (16th ed), Vol. III, Chap. 68; *ibid.* pp. 696, 697.
[12] *Davy* v. *Scarth* [1906] 1 Ch. 55; and see p. 251, *post*.
[13] *Davy* v. *Scarth, supra.*
[14] See *Prior* v. *Bagster* [1887] W.N. 194. In *Re Carton Ltd.* (1923) 39 T.L.R. 194 remuneration was allowed to a liquidator in a voluntary winding up on the scale applicable to a trustee in bankruptcy.

judgment or the amount recovered by the receiver whichever may be the lesser sum; provided that not less than £5 be allowed unless otherwise ordered, and that where the amount due under the judgment does not exceed £50 the plaintiff or party applying shall be made answerable and the usual security be dispensed with. The amount allowed shall, when required, be apportioned by the Master as between costs and remuneration respectively."

In other cases the practice of the Queen's Bench Division is as follows:

(1) In the case of rent a percentage varying from, say, 2 to 10 per cent. is allowed on the gross rents collected, varying according to the amount of the rent and circumstances as follows:

(a) If the rents are large, say over £100 per annum, and are payable yearly or half yearly and no undue trouble arises owing to the state of repair or otherwise, 2 per cent. or slightly over would be allowed.

(b) If the rents are collected monthly or quarterly, 3 to 5 per cent. would be allowed.

(c) If collected weekly, from 7 to 10 per cent. would be allowed.

In each of the above cases the difficulties, trouble and labour involved would be taken into consideration, and although the percentage as above is taken as a guide, it is not slavishly followed, and is only used as a means to arrive at a *quantum meruit* or proper remuneration.

(2) In the case of dividends a percentage of 1 to 3 per cent. on the gross sums collected would be allowed according to whether the dividends were numerous, or large or small, and in exceptional cases the percentage might be reduced or increased—the percentage being only used to assist in arriving at the proper remuneration.

(3) In other cases a *quantum meruit* allowance is made according to time and trouble involved.

A receiver cannot claim remuneration until he has discharged sums for which he is accountable under his security.[15]

Costs, charges and expenses. A receiver is entitled to have out of the funds collected or realised by him his costs, charges, and expenses properly incurred in the discharge of his ordinary duties, or in the performance of extraordinary services which have been

---

[15] See *Re British Power Traction Co.* [1910] 2 Ch. 470.

sanctioned by the court.[16] Where a receiver has paid sums out of his own pocket in satisfaction of legacies, he will be reimbursed.[17]

It is not generally necessary for a receiver to make any special application to the court for the payment of his costs, charges, and expenses properly incurred in the discharge of his duties.[18]

The payment of the costs, charges, and expenses including the remuneration,[19] of a receiver appointed over an estate is not dependent on the sufficiency of the estate to bear all the costs. This right is not affected by his bankruptcy, but the sum due to him will not be paid out to the trustee in bankruptcy but to the persons entitled by subrogation.[20] A receiver appointed over the assets of a company is entitled to be paid next after payment of the costs of realisation [21] in priority to the plaintiff's costs and costs of trustees of a debenture trust deed and preferential creditors,[22] and even in priority to persons advancing money under an order of the court on the terms that repayment is to be a first charge on the assets.[23] Unless the order otherwise provides, costs of realisation do not include costs of preservation [24] nor of any step in the action.[25] The receiver's claim is, however, limited to the amount of the assets. He has no claim against the parties personally if the assets are deficient even though he may have been appointed under a consent order in a partnership action.[26]

Where the master in an order for payment out of a fund in court in an action for administration of the trusts of a debenture trust

---

[16] *Malcolm* v. *O'Callaghan* (1837) 3 Myl. & C. 52; and see *post*, p. 252. In bankruptcy a receiver is entitled to his costs next after the costs of realising the estate: *Ex p. Royle* (1875) 23 W.R. 908. As to costs of receiverships in the Queen's Bench Division, see 34 S.J. 74, 90.

[17] *Palmer* v. *Wright* (1846) 10 Beav. 236; and see *Morison* v. *Morison* (1855) 7 De G. M. & G. 215.

[18] *Fitzgerald* v. *Fitzgerald* (1843) 5 Ir.Eq. 525; but he may do so personally if it is necessary. Form of summons, Palmer's *Company Precedents* (16th ed.), Vol. III, Chap. 68, p. 698.

[19] *Re Glasdir Copper Mines* [1906] 1 Ch. 365.

[20] *Re London United Breweries, infra.*

[21] *Batten* v. *Wedgwood, etc., Co.* (1885) 28 Ch.D. 323; *Re London United Breweries* [1907] 2 Ch. 511; *Re Glyncorrwg Colliery Co.* [1926] Ch. 951. The plaintiff is entitled to his costs of realisation as between solicitor and client if the estate is deficient for payment of the debentures in full. See *Re A. Boynton Ltd.* [1910] 1 Ch. 519. As to cases where liquidator's costs of realisation have priority to the debentures, *Re Regent's Canal Ironworks* (1876) 3 Ch.D. 411; *Johnstone* v. *Cox* (1882) 19 Ch.D. 17.

[22] *Re Glyncorrwg Colliery Co.* [1926] Ch. 951.

[23] *Strapp* v. *Bull, Sons & Co.* [1895] 2 Ch. 1; *Re Glasdir Copper Mines* [1906] 1 Ch. 365; *Re A. Boynton Ltd.* [1910] 1 Ch. 519.

[24] *Lathom* v. *Greenwich Ferry* (1895) 72 L.T. 790.

[25] *Re Callender's Paper Co., per* Neville J. in chambers, January 18, 1911.

[26] *Boehm* v. *Goodall* [1911] 1 Ch. 155.

deed had by inadvertence omitted an express direction for payment of the trustees' costs in priority to the plaintiff's costs and the receiver's remuneration the order was varied in the winding up of the company by inserting the requisite directions, and the registrar's order to that effect confirmed on appeal: a wrong date in the certificate was also corrected.[27]

Where in a partnership action both partners were adjudicated bankrupt and the fund transferred to the trustee in bankruptcy and possession ordered to be given up by the receiver, it was held that there was no jurisdiction in bankruptcy to reconsider and reassess the receiver's remuneration which had been allowed in passing his accounts in the action, there being no application to vary the certificate.[28]

A receiver appointed over mortgaged property,[29] who goes into possession with a direction to keep down interest on incumbrances and receives the rents of the property with the knowledge of the mortgagee, is entitled to deduct his remuneration and expenses before paying over to a mortgagee the balance of rents in his hands to which the latter is entitled.[30]

It seems that, if a receiver is directed to pay to a successful litigant costs of proceedings to which the receiver is a party, such costs will be payable in priority to his own claim for costs, charges, and expenses.[31] If with leave of the court a liquidator or the company brings, or defends, proceedings for the benefit of the debenture holders, the costs of such proceedings will have priority over the claims of the debenture holders [32]: but where a proceeding is brought by the liquidator of a company on an indemnity from the receiver, the liability to the liquidator for costs paid by him will in default of order to the contrary, have no precedence over other liabilities of the receiver.

Where the court gives a receiver authority to advance money for the benefit of the estate of which he is receiver, interest at 5 per cent. was formerly allowed [33] on the advance; but this is not a fixed rule and a lower rate may be fixed: he is given a charge on the

---

[27] *Re City Housing Trust Ltd.* [1942] Ch. 262. The priority of the remuneration was down to date of the master's order only.

[28] *Re Kay and Lovell* [1941] Ch. 420.

[29] See also p. 192, *ante.*

[30] *Davy* v. *Price* [1883] W.N. 226.

[31] As in the case with a liquidator: *Re Pacific Coast Syndicate* [1913] 2 Ch. 26.

[32] See *Re Wrexham, Mold and Cannah's Quay Co.* [1900] 1 Ch. 261.

[33] *Ex p. Izard* (1883) 23 Ch.D. 80.

assets for that sum and interest. If a receiver advances money without such previous authority, he is entitled only to an indemnity out of the assets.[34]

A receiver has not such a vested right to the collection of money payable in respect of the estate over which he is receiver as to be entitled to prevent such money from being paid into court without passing through his hands, where poundage may be saved by a direct payment into court.[35]

Extraordinary expenses. A receiver may be granted allowances beyond his salary for any extraordinary trouble or expense he may have been put to in the performance of his duties,[36] or in bringing actions, or in defending legal proceedings which have been brought against him,[37] even though defended without leave,[38] though leave should always be obtained as soon as the action against the receiver is commenced.[39] Where, for example, an adverse application had been made against a receiver by a party to the cause, and had been refused with costs, the applicant being wholly unable to pay those costs, it was held that the receiver was entitled to be indemnified, and to have his costs as between solicitor and client out of a fund in hand, although it belonged to incumbrancers.[40]

Again, where one of two partners in a business of agricultural implement makers, being the defendant in an action for dissolution of the partnership, had been appointed receiver and manager of the business without salary, he was allowed in his accounts £2 a week, as wages, for a period of eighteen months during which he had worked as a common workman in the business of which he was receiver. The Court of Appeal, however, pointed out that, in not asking for the wages at the time of his appointment, he had committed a technical irregularity, and had run a great risk of not getting any remuneration for his extraordinary services.[41] The costs of litigation undertaken with the permission of the court to preserve the assets are part of the receiver's costs of administration and ought to be included in his accounts.[42]

---

[34] *Ex p. Izard* (1883) 23 Ch.D. 80.   [35] *Haigh* v. *Grattan* (1839) 1 Beav. 201.
[36] *Potts* v. *Leighton* (1808) 15 Ves. 276; *Harris* v. *Sleep* [1897] 2 Ch. 80.
[37] *Bristowe* v. *Needham* (1847) 2 Ph. 190; *Re W. C. Horne & Sons Ltd.* [1906] 1 Ch. 271. Distinguish *Re Dunn* [1904] 1 Ch. 648, *infra.*
[38] *Bristowe* v. *Needham, supra*: the defence succeeded.
[39] *Anon.* (1801) 6 Ves. 286.
[40] *Courand* v. *Hanmer* (1846) 9 Beav. 3. Distinguish *Re Dunn* [1904] 1 Ch. 648, *infra.*
[41] *Harris* v. *Sleep* [1897] 2 Ch. 80 at pp. 84, 85.
[42] *Re W. C. Horne & Sons Ltd.* [1906] 1 Ch. 271; these costs had been omitted from the receiver's accounts and the solicitor was granted a charging order.

If any extraordinary expenses have been incurred by the receiver without the approbation of the court,[43] allowances for them will not generally be sanctioned, unless the estate has been benefited thereby.[44] Accordingly, where a receiver, without the leave of the court, defended an action arising out of a distress for rent made by him, and compromised it on the terms of the plaintiff abandoning it and each party bearing his own costs, he was not allowed his costs.[45] Nor was he allowed his costs of proceedings improperly taken and abandoned, although he acted bona fide and succeeded in subsequent proceedings.[46]

A receiver appointed and acting in proceedings for the administration of an estate is not entitled to indemnity in respect of the costs of defending a purely personal action against him, having no relation to the estate except so far as the acts complained of were done by him while acting as an officer of the court: for no benefit to the estate can result from his defending such an action.[47] Nor is he entitled to litigate for the profit of his receivership; his only interest is in his remuneration.[48]

The receiver of an estate is not entitled to be reimbursed the expenses of journeys to and residence in a foreign country, for the purpose of prosecuting proceedings before the tribunals of that country for the recovery of property belonging to the estate, unless he has the express sanction and authority of the court for such journeys and residence [49]; though if such proceedings are successful, and it appears that the success has been due to the presence of the receiver, the court may consider it inequitable for the parties to take the benefit of the receiver's exertions without defraying his expenses.[50] The fact that some of the parties interested in the estate may have given the receiver authority furnishes no ground for the allowance by the court of his expenses out of the estate.[51]

If the property involved is small, the court may appoint a receiver without remuneration.[52]

---

[43] *Harris* v. *Sleep, supra*; *Re Ormsby* (1809) 1 Ba. & Be. 189; *Ex p. Izard* (1883) 23 Ch.D. 80. As to allowances to a receiver and manager in respect of liabilities incurred by him, see p. 237, *ante*.
[44] *Bristowe* v. *Needham* (1847) 2 Ph. 190; *Malcolm* v. *O'Callaghan* (1837) 3 My. & C. 52; and see *Viola* v. *Anglo-American Cold Storage Co.* [1912] 2 Ch. 305 at p. 311.
[45] *Swaby* v. *Dikon* (1833) 5 Sim. 629.
[46] *Re Montgomery* (1828) 1 Moll. 419.
[47] *Re Dunn* [1904] 1 Ch. 648, 655, 657.
[48] *Ex p. Cooper* (1887) 6 Ch.D. 255.
[49] *Malcolm* v. *O'Callaghan* (1837) 3 My. & C. 52.   [50] *Ibid.* at p. 58.
[51] *Ibid.* at p. 61.
[52] *Marr* v. *Littlewood* (1837) 2 My. & C. 458.

If a trustee,[53] or party interested, asks leave to propose himself as receiver he will usually be required, if appointed, to act without salary.[54]

Where a receiver in an action is served with a proceeding in it, which makes no personal charge against him, he should not appear, and will get no costs of appearance if he does.[55] In a case under the old practice, in which a receiver had incurred costs which the parties had long neglected to provide for, he was allowed to petition for the payment of them.[56]

If a receiver suffers any costs to accrue which ought to have been prevented, he may have to pay them out of his own pocket.[57]

The costs of drawing out a scheme of an estate over which a receiver has been appointed, and of the holdings of the tenants, are chargeable, if at all, as part of the receiver's costs, and not of the solicitor's; but no allowance will usually be made to the receiver for such an item where he is paid by a percentage, though it may be necessary for the due performance of his duties.[58]

The receiver must obey the terms of orders made in the suit: thus where a receiver was directed by the order appointing him to make a specified payment to a party to the suit, and without leave paid the money to judgment creditors of that party, pursuant to a garnishee order, the creditors were ordered, on motion in the suit by the party aggrieved, to repay the money so paid to them, and a direction was also given that, in default of such repayment, the amount should be disallowed to the receiver on the passing of his account; and the receiver, as well as the creditors, was held liable to pay the costs of the motion.[59]

In a case where the receiver's default in bringing in his accounts on the appointed days was known to the parties, and the accounts had been passed and poundage allowed without objection, no loss having been sustained by the receiver's fault, and no balance being due from him, the court would not afterwards listen to an application to strike out his allowance of poundage and costs at the

---

[53] *Sykes* v. *Hastings* (1805) 11 Ves. 363; *Pilkington* v. *Baker* (1876) 24 W.R. 234; *ante*, p. 103.

[54] *Ante*, p. 104.

[55] *Herman* v. *Dunbar* (1857) 23 Beav. 312. In *General Share Co.* v. *Wetley Brick Co.* (1882) 20 Ch.D. 260, 267, an applicant who had improperly served the receiver was ordered to pay his costs of appearance, but the circumstances were peculiar.

[56] *Ireland* v. *Eade* (1844) 7 Beav. 55; application would now be by summons in the action.

[57] *Cook* v. *Sharman* (1844) 8 Ir.Eq. 515.   [58] See *Re Catlin* (1854) 18 Beav. 511.

[59] *De Winton* v. *Mayor, etc., of Brecon* (1859) 28 Beav. 204.

instance of the parties who had the benefit of his services [60]; but the amount of the allowance made to a receiver may be reconsidered, where, though an objection was originally made to it, the particular circumstances of the case and the nature of the items were not taken into consideration.[61] If a receiver is guilty of a breach of duty he does not necessarily, as is the case with agents,[62] forfeit his remuneration, but the court will usually deprive him of it if any improper profit has been made by him.

Balances in hand. A receiver who passes his accounts and pays his balances regularly, is not entitled on that ground to make interest for his own benefit, out of money which comes into his hands, in his character of receiver, during the intervals between the times of passing his accounts.[63]

Receiver of life interest. If it is necessary, not from the conduct of the parties, but owing to the condition of the estate, to have a receiver appointed over the life interest of a tenant for life of real estate, it is the right of the remainderman to have the ordinary expenses incidental to the appointment paid out of the life interest.[64]

---

[60] *Ward* v. *Swift* (1848) 8 Hare 139.

[61] *Day* v. *Croft* (1840) 2 Beav. 488. See *Re Carton Ltd.* (1923) 39 T.L.R. 194.

[62] See *Andrews* v. *Ramsay* [1903] 2 K.B. 635; *Rhodes* v. *Macalister* (1923) 29 Com. Cas. 19.

[63] *Shaw* v. *Rhodes* (1827) 2 Russ. 539. See, too, *Earl of Lonsdale* v. *Church* (1788) 3 Bro.C.C. 40.

[64] *Shore* v. *Shore* (1859) 4 Drew. 510.

CHAPTER 11

ACCOUNTS

Delivery of accounts.[1] Under the old practice the accounts of a receiver appointed by the court were required to be delivered annually [2]; but under the present practice the master, at his discretion, fixes a longer or shorter period for a receiver to leave and pass his accounts, and also the days on which the receiver shall pay the balances appearing due on the account of such part thereof as shall be certified as proper to be paid by him.[3] A receiver appointed in a creditor's administration action should, if no security is to be given, be ordered to lodge his first account within 14 days after the expiration of his receivership, or three months from the date of the order, whichever period is the shorter, and to lodge his subsequent accounts and pay the balance which may be certified to be due from him as the court may direct.[4] Otherwise, in this type of action, the matter is often overlooked.

The accounts must be delivered at the judge's chambers on or before the days appointed for the purpose. If the receiver should be unable to complete his accounts by the day fixed he may apply for further time by summons in chambers.[5]

Where the receiver is appointed in an action in the Chancery Division commenced in a district registry, other than the Leeds, Liverpool, Manchester, Newcastle upon Tyne, or Preston Registries, the Registrars of which have all the powers of a master in the Chancery Division,[6] the accounts are taken in London, unless the order—as it may do [7]—directs the proceedings to take place in the registry. In Queen's Bench actions proceeding in a district registry the account is passed in the registry.

---

[1] For the complete sequence of the practice of the Chancery Division in taking the receiver's accounts see Atkin's *Court Forms* (2nd ed.), Vol. 33, pp. 169 *et seq.*

[2] See Beames' Ch. Ord. 463.

[3] R.S.C., Ord. 30, rr. 4 (1), 5. Where the expenses of attending and passing a receiver's accounts are large, the court will direct the accounts to be passed once a year only: *Day* v. *Croft* (1851) 20 L.J.Ch. 423.

[4] *Re Sutcliffe* [1942] Ch. 453. In a District Registry case, security, if ordered, should be given in London, but the accounts may be passed in the District Registry: *Re Capper* (1878) 26 W.R. 434.

[5] The application should properly be made by the party with the conduct, but if he refuses the receiver may make it. Form of summons, Atkin's *Court Forms* (2nd ed.), Vol. 33, p. 215.

[6] See R.S.C., Ord. 32, r. 26.   [7] Judicature Act 1925, s. 66.

Form of accounts. No form of accounts is now prescribed by the
R.S.C.; the form normally utilised is Chancery Masters' Practice
Form 40 [8] with such variations as circumstances may require [9];
the title should correspond with that of the order appointing the
receiver. In the first account which he passes, the receiver of an
estate should state, in the column for observations, how each
tenant holds, and every alteration should be noticed in the subsequent accounts. In this column also should be entered any remarks
the receiver may think proper to make as to arrears of rent, state
of repair, or otherwise.[10] If the account is drawn up in an irregular
manner, the receiver may be ordered to draw it up in a proper
form, and to pay the costs occasioned by his irregularity.[11]

Where a receiver appointed by debenture holders out of court is
afterwards appointed receiver in an action to enforce the security,
his accounts as receiver are taken in the action from his first
appointment: if a different person is appointed in the action the
first receiver may apply to have his account taken.[12]

Verification by affidavit. It is the receiver's duty to make out his
account and to verify it by affidavit. The items on each side of the
account ought to be numbered consecutively, and the account to
be referred to by the affidavit as an exhibit.[13] The affidavit of the
receiver verifying his account should be in Chancery Masters'
Practice Form 39 with any necessary variations.[14]

A receiver may employ his own solicitor to carry into chambers
and pass his account and will be allowed the costs, though it is a

---

[8] *Supreme Court Practice* (1976), Vol. II, para. 382.

[9] See Atkin's *Court Forms* (2nd ed.), Vol. 33, pp. 216–218. As to receiver's accounts
in the Queen's Bench Division, see notes to R.S.C., Ord. 51, rr. 1–3 in the *Supreme
Court Practice*. As to separate accounts of real and personal estate, *Hill* v. *Hibbit*
(1868) 18 L.T. 553. As to accounts of a receiver appointed by the Court of Protection,
see Court of Protection Rules 1960 (S.I. 1960 No. 1146), rr. 70–72 and Heywood and
Massey, *Court of Protection Practice* (8th ed.), pp. 674 *et seq.* As to a special manager's
accounts, see Companies Act 1948, s. 263 (2); Companies (Winding-up) Rules 1949
(S.I. 1949, No. 382) r. 51 and Form 21.

[10] Daniell's *Chancery Practice* (8th ed.), p. 1492. If money has been paid to the
receiver under protest, he ought by affidavit to distinguish it from the rest: *Brownhead*
v. *Smith* (1837) 1 Jur. 237.

[11] Daniell's *Chancery Practice* (8th ed.), p. 1492. See, too, *Bertie* v. *Lord Abingdon*
(1845) 8 Beav. 53, 60.

[12] *Practice Note* [1932] W.N. 51; *ante*, p. 108.

[13] R.S.C., Ord. 30, r. 4 (2).

[14] *Supreme Court Practice* (1976) Vol. II, para. 381. See R.S.C., Ord. 30, r. 4 (2).
Unless otherwise directed, it is unnecessary to bespeak office copies: *Practice Directions* [1955] 1 W.L.R. 26.

common practice to employ the solicitor of the party having the conduct for this purpose.[15]

Leaving account in chambers. The receiver leaves his account in the chambers of the judge to whom the action or matter is assigned, together with the affidavit verifying the account. An appointment is thereupon obtained by the plaintiff, or person having the conduct of the action or matter, or by the receiver's solicitor,[16] for the purpose of passing the account.[17]

Passing accounts. Notice of the appointment having been obtained for the purpose of passing the account ought to be served upon the solicitors of such parties as are entitled to attend the passing of the account.[18]

Queen's Bench Division practice. In the Queen's Bench Division the account and verifying affidavit and vouchers are taken to the Master's Secretary's Department (Room 120), and an appointment is made with and notice thereof given to the other side. Fee on the certificate or account is £2.[19] The account is then vouched and approved: the master will, if required, certify that it has been passed. The account is left with the master's secretary for filing, bills of costs being lodged with him and entered with the sitting master. If there are no receipts a nil account is lodged and verified by affidavit.

Chancery Division practice. If numerous parties are entitled to attend the passing of the account at the cost of the estate, a classification order [20] should be obtained.

At the time appointed for passing the account, the receiver's solicitor attends with the vouchers like any other accounting party, and the account is gone through before the junior clerk in the chambers of the judge. Any disputed items will be disposed of by the master at an appointment obtained before him for the

---

[15] Atkin's *Court Forms* (2nd ed.), Vol. 33, p. 159; though the practice has been criticised. See *Dixon* v. *Wilkinson* (1859) 4 Drew. 619; and see also *Bloomer* v. *Curie* (1907) 51 S.J. 277.

[16] See p. 255, *ante.*

[17] R.S.C., Ord. 30, r. 4 (3). On leaving the first account, a copy of the order appointing the receiver, certified by the solicitor, to be a true copy thereof, must be lodged at chambers, if that has not previously been done: Daniell's *Chancery Practice* (8th ed.), 1492, n. (*i*).

[18] Form, Atkin's *Court Forms* (2nd ed.), Vol. 33, p. 221.

[19] S.C.F.O. 1975 (S.I. 1975 No. 1343), Fee No. 28.

[20] See R.S.C., Ord. 44, r. 5; and *cf.* Ord. 15, rr. 12, 13.

purpose. Any person who seeks to charge the receiver beyond
what he has by his account admitted to have received, must give
him notice of his intention, stating, as far as he can, the amount
sought to be charged and the particulars thereof in a short and
succinct manner.[21]

In the Chancery Division, on taking the account a fee is payable
of 20p for every £100 or fraction of £100 up to £1 million of the
amount received on such account (including money borrowed by
the receiver [22]) subject to a minimum fee of £5.[23] If for any reason
the account is not completed, such fee is payable as the master
directs.[24] This is calculated in chambers proportionately to the
work done. Where accounts are referred to an accountant and
adopted by the master the above percentage fee is payable.[25] The
fee is paid by the receiver and allowed in his account, unless otherwise directed. It is paid in cash and the Master's Certificate is
marked by the officer of the court receiving the fee, showing the
amount of the fee and the date of its receipt.[26] Money on which Fee
No. 15 (on sale) or 18 (inquiry as to the estate, or outstanding
estate of any person, property subject to a trust, mortgage or
charge, or partnership assets) under the Supreme Court Fees
Order 1975 has been paid is exempt from this fee.[27]

Costs. The receiver, upon passing his account, brings in also his
bill of costs. The bill is then taxed, and the amount included in his
disbursements. On passing his first account the receiver's costs of
completing his appointment are taxed and allowed.[28] Parties
attending the passing of a receiver's accounts have costs from the
receiver only after a judgment or order disposing of the costs of
the action, and showing who are or is entitled to costs out of the
rents: in other cases the costs of the parties are costs in the action.
Where the parties are entitled to have their costs paid by the
receiver, such costs are taxed at chambers, and paid by the receiver

---

[21] R.S.C., Ord. 43, r. 5.
[22] *Re Crystal Palace Co.* (unrep.), Swinfen Eady J. in chambers, May 25, 1910.
[23] S.C.F.O. 1975, Fee No. 16.
[24] See Art. 8 (1) of the S.C.F.O. 1975 (S.I. 1975 No. 1343) and *Re Crawshay* (1888)
39 Ch.D. 552.
[25] *Re Hutchinson* (1884) 32 W.R. 392.
[26] S.C.F.O. 1975 (S.I. 1975 No. 1343), Art. 7 (1).
[27] Money on which Fee No. 16 (*b*) (account of moneys due to any person); 17 (*b*)
(inquiry as to persons interested in any property) or 18 (inquiry as to estate, property
subject to a trust mortgage or charge or partnership assets) has been paid or is payable
is exempt from Fee No. 15. See proviso (3) to Fee No. 15.
[28] Daniell's *Chancery Practice* (8th ed.), p. 1492, note (*m*).

and included in his account.[29] Sureties are not allowed costs of attending except by order.[30] If a receiver occasions expense and delay by making improper claims he may be disallowed his costs or even ordered to pay the costs of taking the account.[31]

In a case in which an order referred it to the Taxing Master to tax the plaintiff's costs of an action, including the costs and re-muneration of the receivers and managers appointed in the action, and to certify the balance after making a certain deduction, it was held that the Taxing Master had no power to make a separate certificate for the costs alone.[32]

If a receiver includes in his bill of costs charges for work done in another capacity, which he allows the Taxing Master to deal with and strike out without objection, he cannot afterwards recover the amount of the sums so struck out in an action brought for that purpose.[33]

The receiver is usually directed to hand copies of his accounts to such of the parties as are entitled to attend upon the passing thereof, and to charge for the same in his costs.[34] But a plaintiff or a defendant entitled to attend the passing of a receiver's account is not allowed, in the taxation of the receiver's costs, a second copy of the account, if his solicitor is also the solicitor for the receiver, and has a copy in that capacity.[35]

Allowance of accounts. The verified account, with a summary at the foot and a memorandum of allowance thereof, is signed by the master. If any sums are disallowed, they are shown in the summary as deductions.

Certificate of allowance. After the allowance of the account, a certificate [36] of the allowance, stating the balance due from or to the receiver, and the day on which any sum due from him is to be paid into court, is made and signed by the master,[37] and, upon

---

[29] Daniell's *Chancery Practice* (8th ed.), p. 1492.

[30] *Dawson* v. *Raynes* (1826) 2 Russ. 466; *Re Birmingham Brewery* (1883) 31 W.R. 415.

[31] See *Re Holton's Trust* (1919) 88 L.J.Ch. 444 (trustee).

[32] *Silkstone, etc., Coal Co.* v. *Edey* [1901] 2 Ch. 652.

[33] *Terry* v. *Dubois* (1884) 32 W.R. 415.

[34] Daniell's *Chancery Practice* (8th ed.), p. 1492.

[35] *Sharp* v. *Wright* (1866) L.R. 1 Eq. 634.

[36] No fee is payable since S.C.F.O. 1975 (S.I. 1975 No. 1343), Fee No. 21 of £5 payable on a certificate of a Master or District Registrar is not payable (*inter alia*) when Fee No. 16 (see p. 258, *ante*), the fee payable on the taking of the account, has been paid.

[37] R.S.C., Ord. 30, r. 4 (4).

being so signed, is transmitted by the master to the Central Office, to be there filed, and is thereupon binding upon all the parties to the proceedings, unless discharged or varied upon application by summons, to be made before the expiration of two clear days after the filing thereof.[38]

After the certificate has become binding a manifest error may be corrected, as may an accidental omission in the master's order for payment out of a direction as to priority and receiver's remuneration.[39] In a partnership action after the fund had been transferred to a trustee in the bankruptcy of the partners the account was not allowed to be reopened to permit the remuneration allowed to the receiver to be reconsidered.[40] In a proper case the time to apply to vary a certificate may be extended.[41]

Receiver must pay in moneys. An order of the court appointing a receiver usually directs payment into court without a schedule to the order. A lodgment schedule is left in chambers and signed by the master, and is forwarded by him to the Paymaster's Office. The lodgment schedule signed by the master operates in the same manner as a lodgment schedule annexed to an order [42]: there is now no fee.

Although a receiver is only bound by his recognisance to pass his accounts at the periods appointed by the judge, he may at any time apply to the court to pay in money in his hands; and if, in the intervals between passing his accounts, he receives sums of such an amount as to make it worth while to lay them out, he ought to apply for leave to pay them into court, that they may be productive for the benefit of the estate.[43] The receiver prepares a lodgment schedule [44] which is settled by the master's clerk, and then signed by the master: no order is drawn up. If the receiver keep in his hands money which he has been directed to pay into court, it is no excuse for him to say that the circumstances of the estate made it necessary to keep large sums in hand, nor will it prevent the court from directing an inquiry as to what sums might or ought to have

---

[38] R.S.C., Ord. 44, r. 23. For form of certificate of allowance, see Atkin's *Court Forms* (2nd ed.), Vol. 33, p. 222.

[39] See *Re City Housing Trust Ltd.* [1942] Ch. 262, *ante*, p. 250.

[40] See *Re Kay and Lovell* [1941] Ch. 420, *ante*, p. 250.

[41] See *Re Becher* [1944] Ch. 78.

[42] Supreme Court Funds Rules 1975 (S.I. 1975 No. 1803), rr. 6, 18. Where securities are to be lodged, a special direction must be inserted in the order.

[43] *Shaw* v. *Rhodes* (1827) 2 Russ. 539. For practice see Atkin's *Court Forms* (2nd ed.), Vol. 33, p. 145.

[44] For form see Atkin's *Court Forms* (2nd ed.), Vol. 33, p. 224.

been reasonably laid out at interest.[45] Where the order appointing a receiver does not provide for the payment of his balances into court, the receiver will not be allowed to avail himself of the omission, and to keep a balance in his hands without interest, under a pretence of waiting for some party to the action to obtain an order upon him for payment in.[46] He ought to apply by summons, which should be served on the parties to the action, for an order for that purpose, and that the costs be allowed him in his next account; and, unless he does so, the court may charge him with interest.[47]

Default by receiver. If a receiver makes default in leaving any account or affidavit, or in passing his accounts, or in making any payment, or otherwise, the receiver or the parties, or any of them, may be required to attend at chambers to show cause why the account or affidavit has not been left, or the account passed, or the payment made, or any other proper proceeding taken (as the case may be), and all proper directions may thereupon be given at chambers, or upon an adjournment into court, including the discharge of the receiver, the appointment of another, and payment of costs.[48] If, after such delay has taken place, no application is made for this purpose, the master will of his own motion restore the matter to his list for a report. If the receiver brings in his account, but does not attend to pass it, after a summons to show cause why he has not done so has been served on him, the master may allow the sums with which the receiver has charged himself, and disallow such of his payments as he has failed to vouch.[49] In the chambers of some of the judges of the Chancery Division, the practice is to write to the receiver personally, where accounts have not been left. If the receiver neglects to obey the order for an account, a four-day order may be obtained on summons,[50] which must be served on the receiver, and if he does not appear, the order will be made on production of an affidavit of service of the summons, or, if the default consists in not making a payment into

---

[45] *Hicks* v. *Hicks* (1744) 3 Atk. 274.

[46] *Potts* v. *Leighton* (1808) 15 Ves. 273, 274. See, too, 1 Ba. & Be. 230.

[47] Daniell's *Chancery Practice* (8th ed.), p. 1493. As to form of summons, see Atkin's *Court Forms* (2nd ed.), Vol. 33, p. 224.

[48] R.S.C., Ord. 30, r. 6 (i); Daniell's *Chancery Practice* (8th ed.), p. 1493. As to form of order, see Seton (7th ed.), pp. 773, 781.

[49] Daniell's *Chancery Practice* (8th ed.), p. 1493.

[50] Form of summons, Atkin's *Court Forms* (2nd ed.), Vol. 33, p. 61; order, Seton (7th ed.), p. 771.

court, of the order and certificate under which the payment ought to have been made; and the Paymaster General's certificate of the default must be produced in support of the application.[51] The order, which is drawn up by the registrar, must state specifically where the accounts are to be delivered,[52] and an indorsed copy must be served personally on the receiver [53]; or, if personal service of the order cannot be effected, an order for substituted service should be obtained at chambers, on an *ex parte* application by summons, supported by affidavit, and the last mentioned order must be served in conformity with the directions thereby given.[54] If after such original or substituted service the receiver neglects to obey the order, it may be enforced against him by process of contempt. A similar course should be pursued against a receiver who is directed to pay his balance to the parties instead of into court, and neglects to do so. It is irregular to issue a writ of *fi. fa.* for such a balance.[55]

A four-day order requiring a receiver to bring in his accounts may be had by one of several joint receivers against another who is in default. For, even though joint receivers be, by the terms of their appointment, required to account jointly, each of them must bring in his accounts of what he individually receives; and, where the master has certified that one of them is in default, the four-day order is, of course, as long as that certificate stands.[56]

The receiver in an action may be ordered to pass his accounts and pay over the balance, although the action has been dismissed,[57] or the proceedings in it have been ordered to be stayed.[58]

A receiver who does not pay into court money which has been found to be due from him, and which he has been directed to pay, is liable to committal under section 4 (3) of the Debtors Act 1869.[59]

In cases within Order 45, r. 5, a writ of sequestration against the estate and effects of a receiver, for disobedience to an order of the court, may be issued without the leave of the court.[60]

---

[51] Daniell's *Chancery Practice* (8th ed.), p. 1493.

[52] *e.g.* " Room — of chambers of Mr. Justice B., situate at the Royal Courts of Justice, Strand, London." See Practice Note [1923] W.N. 344.

[53] See R.S.C., Ord. 45, r. 7.

[54] *Re Bell's Estate* (1870) L.R. 9 Eq. 172.

[55] *Whitehead* v. *Lynes* (1865) 34 Beav. 161, 165; affd. 12 L.T. 332.

[56] *Scott* v. *Platel* (1847) 2 Ph. 229, 230, 231.

[57] *Pitt* v. *Bonner* (1833) 5 Sim. 577. See, too, *Hutton* v. *Beeton* (1863) 9 Jur.(N.S.) 1339.

[58] *Paynter* v. *Carew* (1854) Kay, App. 36, 44.

[59] *Re Gent* (1888) 40 Ch.D. 190.

[60] *Sprunt* v. *Pugh* (1878) 7 Ch.D. 567.

If the action has abated by reason of the death of the parties or otherwise, *semble* that the receiver may obtain an order for taxation of his costs and payment of the balance into court without reviving the action, where revivor is impracticable.[61] In a proper case a person may be appointed under Order 15, r. 15, to represent the estate of a deceased party in the absence of a personal representative or proceedings may be allowed to continue in the absence of any person representing the estate.[62]

Disallowance of salary and charge of interest on unpaid balances. Where a receiver neglects to leave and pass his accounts, and to pay the balances thereof at the times fixed for that purpose, the judge before whom the receiver has to account may, from time to time, when his subsequent accounts are produced to be examined and passed, disallow the salary therein claimed by such receiver, and may also, if he shall think fit, charge him with interest at the rate of 5 per cent. per annum upon the balances so neglected to be paid by him, during the time the same shall appear to have remained in his hands.[63]

In an old case, in which a receiver of the personal estate of a testator had been appointed, the Court of Chancery declined to charge him with interest on each sum from the time when it was received, but charged him as an executor would be charged, that is by making yearly or half-yearly rests in the accounts.[64] And the present practice is in substantial accordance with that decision.[65]

Remedies after discharge. The remedies which have been indicated remain for the most part available against a receiver even after he has been discharged.[66] Where, however, default had been made by the executors of a deceased receiver, the sureties were only ordered to pay interest at 4 per cent.[67] A receiver may be surcharged on his accounts, notwithstanding he has been discharged.[68]

A receiver may be charged with interest on money improperly kept in his hands, or which he has failed to invest as directed by the order appointing him,[69] although he has passed his accounts, and

---

[61] *Cf. Ballard* v. *Milner* [1895] W.N. 14.
[62] See notes to R.S.C., Ord. 15, r. 15, in *Supreme Court Practice* (1976).
[63] R.S.C., Ord. 30, r. 6 (2).
[64] *Potts* v. *Leighton* (1808) 15 Ves. 273.
[65] See R.S.C., Ord. 30, r. 6 (2) and Daniell's *Chancery Practice* (8th ed.), p. 1494.
[66] *Harrison* v. *Boydell* (1833) 6 Sim. 211.
[67] *Clements* v. *Beresford* (1846) 10 Jur. 771.
[68] *Re Edwards* (1892) 31 L.R.Ir. 242. *Cf. Re Browne* (1886) 19 L.R.Ir. 423.
[69] *Hicks* v. *Hicks* (1744) 3 Atk. 276.

all parties have expressed themselves satisfied; and for this purpose an inquiry what money he has received from time to time, and how long he has kept it in his hands, may be directed.[70] In *Anon.* v. *Jolland,*[71] Lord Eldon intimated that, if such a case should be brought before him, it would at least be a very grave question whether the receiver should be ordered to make good any loss which might have been occasioned from a difference in the price of Government funds between the time when the receiver's balance was paid in, and the time when it ought to have been paid in.

Accounts in foreclosure action. The mortgagor is entitled to credit for rents received by the receiver appointed in a foreclosure action during the period between the date of the master's certificate and the day fixed for redemption. Where a receiver has been appointed an order for foreclosure nisi ought to provide that, in taking the account, the plaintiff should be charged with the amount (if any) paid into court by the receiver, and any sum in the receiver's hands at the date of the certificate, and with such a sum (if any) as the plaintiff shall submit to be charged with in respect of rents and profits come to the receiver's hands before foreclosure absolute.[72] If this form is used the necessity for opening the foreclosure and ordering a fresh account will be avoided. If more is in fact received than the plaintiff submitted to be charged with, a fresh account may be verified by affidavit and vouched without further order; but the plaintiff should be careful to submit to be charged with a sufficient sum to cover all rents and profits. If the balance due from the receiver, after deducting outgoings, is less than the amount with which the plaintiff submitted to be charged, the foreclosure is not opened, the receiver's account being taken at once.[73]

If the order nisi is not made in the above form a fresh account will be directed and a further time, usually one month, given for redemption,[74] though to save the expense of an account, a mortgagee has been allowed to verify the amount due by affidavit after allowing for receipts down to the application.[75] If rents are received

---

[70] *Fletcher* v. *Dodd* (1789) 1 Ves.Jr. 85. See *Hicks* v. *Hicks, supra.*

[71] (1802) 8 Ves. 72, 73.

[72] *Simmons* v. *Blandy* [1897] 1 Ch. 19. This practice also obtains where the receiver has powers of management; *e.g.* of licensed premises. For earlier forms of order, *Smith* v. *Pearman* (1888) 36 W.R. 681; *Cheston* v. *Wells* [1893] 2 Ch. 151.

[73] So decided by Eady J. in an unreported case. See also *Ellenor* v. *Ugle* [1895] W.N. 161.

[74] *Jenner-Fust* v. *Needham* (1886) 32 Ch.D. 582; *Peat* v. *Nicholson* (1886) 34 W.R. 451; but see *Welch* v. *National Cycle Works* (1886) 35 W.R. 137.

[75] *Jenner-Fust* v. *Needham, supra.*

after the date fixed for redemption, the foreclosure is not reopened, but an immediate order absolute made [76]; and where the
order nisi provided that plaintiff might apply for any moneys come
to the hands of the receiver, who received rents after certificate, an
order absolute has been made without further account or extending
the time. [77]

In one case after a receiver appointed in a foreclosure action had
brought in his final account, and the foreclosure had been made
absolute, it subsequently appeared that the receiver had omitted
some rents from his account. It was nevertheless held that, in the
absence of any evidence that the plaintiff in the foreclosure action
had received any of the rents which the receiver had not accounted
for, there was no reason why the foreclosure should be opened
merely because the receiver, who was not the plaintiff's agent but
an officer of the court, had made a mistake which was not dis-
covered before it was too late. [78]

Accounts of deceased receiver. An order may be obtained, on
summons at chambers, that the personal representatives of a
deceased receiver be at liberty to pass his accounts and to lodge
the balance in court. [79] In a case where, on the executor's application, liberty had been given them to pass their accounts, and to pay
in the balance, they were not allowed, after the lapse of many years,
to object to the order on the ground of want of assets. [80]

The order cannot, however, be obtained without the consent of
the personal representatives. If they do not consent, the court has
no jurisdiction to order, in a summary way, that they shall bring in
and pass the deceased receiver's accounts, and pay the balance out
of his assets. [81] The proper course, subject to the remedy against
the surety, is to sue the personal representatives for an account and
administration. [82]

An admission by a receiver's executor of assets to answer what is
due from his testator is sufficient to make the executor liable to pay

---

[76] *National Building Society* v. *Raper* [1892] 1 Ch. 54, following *Constable* v.
Howick (1858) 5 Jur.(N.S.) 331 and not following *Ross Improvement Commissioners* v.
Usborne [1890] W.N. 92.
   [77] *Coleman* v. *Llewellin* (1887) 34 Ch.D. 143.
   [78] *Ingham* v. *Sutherland* (1890) 63 L.T. 614.
   [79] For form of order, see Seton (7th ed.), p. 736. See, too, 15 Sim. 483; and, as to
form of summons, see Atkin's *Court Forms* (2nd ed.), Vol. 33, p. 227.
   [80] *Gurden* v. *Badcock* (1842) 6 Beav. 157.
   [81] *Jenkins* v. *Briant* (1834) 7 Sim. 171.
   [82] *Ludgater* v. *Channell* (1851) 15 Sim. 482; 3 Mac. & G. 180.

such interest as the receiver's estate may be charged with in respect of the rents retained in his hands.[83] But, if there has been laches of the parties, the executor will only be ordered to pay in the principal money and the costs of the application.[84]

Putting recognisance in suit. Where a receiver neglects to bring in his accounts, or, having brought them in, fails to pay the balance certified to be due from him within the time limited, and has been proceeded against for the contempt of court, the party prosecuting the contempt may proceed against the sureties. But he is not at liberty to sue the sureties until he has taken proceedings against the receiver for the contempt, unless the receiver has become bankrupt, or it can be shown that proceedings against him for contempt would be useless.[85]

If proceedings are to be taken against the sureties leave is obtained on summons to be served on the receiver or his personal representatives and the sureties.

Upon the death of a receiver the parties interested may come to the court either against his representatives, or against his sureties, and they should in the first place apply against both, in order to avoid the objection which, if either were omitted, the persons made respondents might raise to the absence of the persons omitted. The court, without deciding whether the representatives or the sureties are primarily liable, can make an order allowing the deceased receiver's guarantee to be enforced against his personal representatives and sureties.[86]

---

[83] *Foster* v. *Foster* (1789) 2 Bro.C.C. 615; *Tew* v. *Lord Winterton* (1792) cit. 4 Ves. 606 on a point not in the ordinary reports of that case.

[84] *Gurden* v. *Badcock* (1842) 6 Beav. 157.

[85] Smith, *Chancery Practice*, p. 1037. See, too, *Ludgater* v. *Channell* (1851) 3 Mac. & G. 176, n. (*a*).

[86] *Ludgater* v. *Channell* (1851) 3 Mac. & G. 175, 179–181.

CHAPTER 12

DISCHARGE OF A RECEIVER

On his own application. Unless the minutes of the order appointing or continuing a receiver, or a receiver and manager, contain a provision for his discharge,[1] an application to the court is generally necessary, in order to divest his possession.[2] The appointment of a receiver made previously to the judgment in an action will not be superseded by it, unless the receiver is appointed only until judgment or further order.[3] But an order to put a purchaser into possession is in itself a discharge of a previous order for a receiver as to the lands mentioned in the subsequent order.[4]

As a general rule, where a receiver has been appointed and has given security, he will not be discharged upon his own application, without showing some reasonable cause why he should put the parties to the expense of a change[5]; otherwise he may have to pay the costs of his removal and of the appointment of his successor. If, however, he can show reasonable cause for his discharge, such as ill-health, he may be discharged and allowed to deduct the costs of and incidental to the application for discharge out of any balance in his hands.[6] As an alternative, if his indisposition be but temporary, he may obtain the leave of the court to appoint an attorney for a limited period.

Under modern conditions a manager may find himself in a situation where, without the wholehearted co-operation of some party to the action, which is not forthcoming and cannot be compelled, he is unable to function effectively as a manager. In these circumstances, it is proper for him to apply in the alternative to be discharged or to have his functions restricted to those which it is possible for him to carry out.[7]

A receiver ought not to make an application for discharge to

---

[1] *Day* v. *Sykes, Walkers & Co.* (1886) 55 L.T. 763; [1886] W.N. 209.
[2] *Thomas* v. *Brigstocke* (1827) 4 Russ. 64.
[3] See *ante*, p. 123.
[4] *Ponsonby* v. *Ponsonby* (1825) 1 Hog. 321; *Anon.* (1847) 2 Ir.Eq. 416.
[5] *Smith* v. *Vaughan* (1744) Ridg.temp.Hard. 251; *cf. Cox* v. *Macnamara* (1839) 11 Ir.Eq. 356.
[6] *Richardson* v. *Ward* (1822) 6 Madd. 266.
[7] *Parsons* v. *Mather & Platt Ltd.* (1974) December 9, unreported C.A. (Appeal Court Judgments (Civil Division) No. 392A) where (in effect) the manager was relieved of his management duties and restricted to those of a pure receivership.

come on with the further consideration of the action; for the court can, on the further consideration, discharge him without such an application. Accordingly, the costs of a separate application for discharge will be refused.[8]

On satisfaction of incumbrance. A receiver is generally continued until judgment in the action in which he has been appointed; but, if the right of the plaintiff ceases before that time, the receiver will be discharged at once.[9] But where the appointment is made in a foreclosure action at the instance of a plaintiff who is subsequently paid off, another incumbrancer may on summons obtain leave to be added as plaintiff, in which case the receiver may be continued.[10] Similarly, if a receiver is appointed for the purpose of satisfying a number of claims, he will not be discharged merely on the application of a satisfied plaintiff if some of the other claims are still outstanding.[11] Proceedings could always be stayed without prejudice to the receivership.[12]

Continuance becoming unnecessary. If, in the course of the proceedings, the continuance of a receiver becomes unnecessary, he will be discharged. Thus, in a case where a receiver had been appointed in consequence of the misconduct and incapacity of trustees under a will, he was ordered to be discharged on the appointment of new trustees.[13] So, where a receiver, who had been appointed in consequence of the executors of a testator's will having refused to act, quitted his place of residence in the vicinity of the estates over which he had been appointed receiver, the court, on the consent of the other parties to the cause, and the executors expressing their willingness to act, made an order that the receiver should pass his accounts.[14] A receiver will be discharged when the object of his appointment has been fully effected,[15] as, for instance, when arrears of annuity, to obtain which he was appointed, have been paid.[16]

---

[8] *Stilwell* v. *Mellersh* (1851) 20 L.J.Ch. 356.
[9] *Davis* v. *Duke of Marlborough* (1818) 2 Sw. 167.
[10] See *Munster, etc., Bank* v. *Mackey* [1917] 1 Ir.R. 49.
[11] *Largan* v. *Bowen* (1803) 1 Sch. & Lef. 297.
[12] *Damer* v. *Lord Portarlington* (1846) 2 Ph. 34; *Paynter* v. *Carew* (1854) 18 Jur. 419; *Murrough* v. *French* (1827) 2 Moll. 498.
[13] *Bainbrigge* v. *Blair* (1841) 3 Beav. 421, 423. *Secus*, if on the appointment of new trustees, there are questions still outstanding: *Reeves* v. *Neville* (1862) 10 W.R. 335.
[14] *Davy* v. *Gronow* (1845) 14 L.J.Ch. 134.
[15] *Tewart* v. *Lawson* (1874) L.R. 18 Eq. 490. See, too, *Hoskins* v. *Campbell* [1869] W.N. 59.
[16] *Braham* v. *Lord Strathmore* (1844) 8 Jur. 567.

Other causes for discharge. A receiver is liable to be discharged for irregularity in carrying on his accounts, for conduct making it necessary to take proceedings to compel him to do so, and for so passing his accounts that the amount of the balance in his hands cannot be ascertained.[17] So if his conduct has been such as to impede the impartial course of justice,[18] or to amount to a gross dereliction of duty,[19] or if his appointment as a receiver has been improper.[20]

It is conceived, however, that a charge of misbehaviour against a receiver, for suffering the owner of an estate over which the receiver was appointed to remain in part possession of it to the prejudice of the estate, will not be regarded by the court as a sufficient reason for discharging the receiver, for in such a case the parties themselves have caused the loss, by not compelling the owner by the authority of the court to deliver up possession to the receiver.[21]

Where a receiver becomes bankrupt, he will be discharged, and another receiver appointed.[22]

If a receiver has been wrongly appointed over property belonging to a person who is not a party to the action, he will be discharged, even though there has been an abatement of the action, by the death of a sole defendant.[23]

The court will discharge a receiver upon the application of a prior mortgagee demanding to go into possession as such by himself or his receiver.[24]

In one case, in which a receiver had been appointed in an administration suit, another person, who was willing to act at a lower salary, was ordered to be substituted for him, as receiver, on the application of a mortgagee of a tenant for life of the property.[25]

Property to be sold. Where estates over which a receiver has been appointed have been ordered to be sold, the receiver will be continued, until completion of the sale, in order that he may collect any arrears of rent.[26]

---

[17] *Bertie* v. *Lord Abingdon* (1845) 8 Beav. 53.
[18] *Mitchell* v. *Condy* [1873] W.N. 232.
[19] *Re St. George's Estate* (1887) 19 L.R.Ir. 566.
[20] *Re Lloyd* (1879) 12 Ch.D. 448; *Nieman* v. *Nieman* (1889) 43 Ch.D. 198; *Re Wells* (1890) 45 Ch.D. 569; *Brenan* v. *Morrissey* (1890) 26 L.R.Ir. 618.
[21] *Griffith* v. *Griffith* (1751) 2 Ves. 400.
[22] Daniell's *Chancery Practice* (8th ed.), p. 1479.
[23] *Lavender* v. *Lavender* (1875) Ir.R. 9 Eq. 593.
[24] *Re Metropolitan Amalgamated Estates* [1912] 2 Ch. 497; *ante*, p. 31.
[25] *Stanley* v. *Coulthurst* [1868] W.N. 305.
[26] See *Quinn* v. *Holland* (1745) Ridg.temp.Hard. 295.

Balance due to receiver. The receiver of an estate will not be discharged until he has received from the estate any balance found due to him on passing his accounts.[27] In administration actions a receiver may be discharged on passing his accounts, and be paid his remuneration and costs, without waiting to see whether the estate is sufficient to pay all costs payable out of it.[28]

Application of one party only. A receiver being appointed for the benefit of all the parties interested, he will not be discharged on the application of that party only at whose instance he was appointed.[29]

Mode of application to discharge. The application to discharge a receiver appointed in an action should be made as a rule by summons [30]; the direction for his discharge may be given in the judgment at the trial, or in the order upon further consideration.[31]

In the Queen's Bench Division, application to discharge a receiver is made to the master on summons, which may be issued before or after passing the receiver's final account. In the former case the order is made subject to the receiver complying with the usual Central Office regulations; in the latter, on production of the master's certificate, and proof that the receiver has complied with the directions therein.

The bond is delivered up on production of the master's order on application at the General Filing Department.

Service and appearance. A summons, or notice of motion, for the discharge of a receiver, should be served on all the parties.[32] The service of it on the receiver should be personal, and such service will not be dispensed with unless an order for substituted service is obtained.[33] But a receiver, though served, is not entitled to appear at the hearing of the application, unless some personal charge is made against him. If he appears he will not be allowed the costs of his appearance,[34] except under special circumstances.[35]

---

[27] *Bertrand* v. *Davies* (1862) 31 Beav. 436.

[28] *Batten* v. *Wedgwood, etc., Co.* (1885) 28 Ch.D. 317.

[29] *Davis* v. *Duke of Marlborough* (1818) 2 Swans. 108; *Bainbrigge* v. *Blair* (1841) 3 Beav. 421, 423.

[30] Form of summons, Atkin's *Court Forms* (2nd ed.), Vol. 33, p. 225; forms of order, Seton (7th ed.), p. 781; also Palmer's *Company Precedents* (16th ed.), Vol. III, Chap. 69.

[31] Seton (7th ed.), pp. 781, 782.

[32] Daniell's *Chancery Practice* (8th ed.), p. 1499.

[33] *Att.-Gen.* v. *Haberdashers' Company* (1838) 2 Jur. 915.

[34] *Herman* v. *Dunbar* (1857) 23 Beav. 312; and see pp. 256–257, *ante*.

[35] *General Share Co.* v. *Wetley Brick Co.* (1882) 20 Ch.D. 260, 267.

Form of order on discharge. If the receiver has not passed his final account and paid over any balance found due from him, the order discharging him directs him to do so.

The order of discharge may be conditional on the performance of some act by the receiver or otherwise contingent on some future event; on proper evidence of compliance or of the happening of the event the master will indorse on the order a direction that the guarantee is to be cancelled. On production of the order in the Filing Department, Central Office, the guarantee is indorsed with the vacating note and delivered to the solicitor on his receipt.[36]

Notice of surety. Under the usual form of guarantee the receiver is bound to give to the surety by post notice of his discharge: and within seven days thereafter send the surety an office copy of the order discharging him.[37]

In an Irish case, in which a receiver was discharged owing to gross dereliction of duty, the order discharging him disallowed his fees and poundage on all accounts not passed within the prescribed time, and directed him to pay interest on the balance (if any) from time to time in his hands, and to pay the costs of the motion to discharge him, of his own discharge, and of the appointment of his successor.[38]

---

[36] Ord. 30, r. 2 (4).

[37] Chancery Masters' Practice Form 37; *Supreme Court Practice* (1976), Vol. II, para. 379.

[38] *Re St. George's Estate* (1887) 19 L.R.Ir. 566.

CHAPTER 13

LIABILITIES AND RIGHTS OF SURETIES

Discharge of sureties. The sureties for a receiver will not be discharged at their own request. Where, therefore, an application was made to discharge a receiver on the ground of misconduct, and the sureties joined in the application, Lord Hardwicke held that no regard was to be had to their application, unless it was for the benefit of the estate, or unless there were special circumstances[1]; as, for instance, where underhand practice can be proved, and the person secured can be shown to have been connected with such practice.[2] In one case a surety was discharged on his own application, where he had become surety in violation of his partnership articles.[3]

Fresh bond required. Where a surety procures his discharge during the continuance of the receivership, the receiver must enter into a fresh covenant with new sureties.[4]

Where one of two sureties dies, or goes abroad, and the receiver is unable to procure another surety, it is not the practice to charge the receiver with the expenses of his discharge, or the appointment of a new receiver.[5]

When a surety becomes bankrupt, or being a company enters into liquidation, the receiver is usually required to procure a fresh guarantee. The order is made on summons.[6]

The amount of security for which the surety is liable may be increased or reduced in a proper case; for example, where part of the assets have been got in and disposed of.[7]

If a yearly premium payable under the guarantee is not paid within 15 days after the expiration of the first year, the surety can under the express terms of the guarantee apply to be relieved from further liability.

---

[1] *Griffith* v. *Griffith* (1751) 2 Ves.Sen. 400; as to application by a surety for his discharge see *O'Keefe* v. *Armstrong* (1852) 2 Ir.Ch. 115.

[2] *Hamilton* v. *Brewster* (1820) 2 Moll. 407, *per* Manners L.C.

[3] *Swain* v. *Smith* (1827) Seton (7th ed.), p. 775.

[4] *Vaughan* v. *Vaughan* (1743) 1 Dick. 90; *Blois* v. *Betts* (1760) *ibid.* 336.

[5] *Lane* v. *Townsend* (1852) 2 Ir.Ch. 120. The surety is usually a single company.

[6] Daniell's *Chancery Practice* (8th ed.), p. 1500. As to form of summons, see Daniell's *Chancery Forms* (7th ed.), p. 788.

[7] The form of guarantee expressly provides for an increase by indorsement.

Order on discharge. In *Shuff* v. *Holdaway*,[8] an order was made on the application of a surety, directing the receiver's accounts down to that time to be passed, and that, on payment into court by the receiver, or by the applicant, of the certified balance (not exceeding the penalty), the applicant should be discharged as surety, and that the applicant should be at liberty to attend the taking of the accounts; but he was ordered to pay the costs of the application.

Attendance at taking of receiver's account. A surety is not entitled without leave to attend at the taking of a receiver's account except at his own expense,[9] but leave will be given in a proper case, as, for instance, where the sureties were likely to be called on to pay a balance [10]; and where a receiver had died in insolvent circumstances, and his personal representative had consented to his final account being taken in the suit to which he was appointed, liberty to attend was given to the personal representative.[11]

Extent of liability of surety. The surety is answerable, to the extent of the amount of the guarantee, for whatever sum of money, whether principal, interest, or costs, the receiver has become liable for to the estate which is being administered, including the costs of his removal and of the appointment of a new receiver in his place.[12] This statement of the law was approved in *Re Graham*,[13] by Chitty J., from whose judgment it may, it is conceived, be concluded that, in ascertaining the liability of sureties the court proceeds on the principle that the surety is liable (to the extent of the amount of the penalty or guarantee) for all sums of money which the receiver himself was properly liable to pay into court or to account for. Consequently, where a receiver of " rents and profits " of real estate had (1) insured some of the farm buildings in his own name and received and misapplied the insurance money; (2) received and not accounted for dividends on consols in court representing

---

[8] September 3, 1857, cited in Daniell's *Chancery Practice* (8th ed.), p. 1500; see, too, *O'Keefe* v. *Armstrong* (1852) 2 Ir.Ch. 115.

[9] *Re Birmingham Brewery Co.* (1883) 31 W.R. 415.

[10] *Dawson* v. *Raynes* (1826) 2 Russ. 467. As to form of summons by surety to attend the passing of a receiver's accounts, see Atkin's *Court Forms* (2nd ed.), Vol. 33, p. 222.

[11] *Simmons* v. *Rose*, November 20, 1860, cited in Daniell's *Chancery Practice* (8th ed.), p. 1501.

[12] *Maunsell* v. *Egan* (1846) 3 Jo. & La.T. p. 251; *Re MacDonaghs* (1876) Ir.R. 10 Eq. 269; *Smart* v. *Flood* (1883) 49 L.T. 467. *Cf. Watters* v. *Watters* (1847) 11 Ir.Eq. 336.

[13] [1895] 1 Ch. 66 at p. 70.

proceeds of sale of real estate; and (3) received under an order of the court money representing personal estate to be spent in repairs, which money he had misappropriated, it was held that the sureties had been properly charged in respect of those three items.[14] In a case, however, where a receiver had been bankrupt with the knowledge of all parties for a considerable time, during which no steps were taken to compel the passing of his accounts, the surety was excused from payment of interest.[15] On taking a defaulting receiver's account, the court does not necessarily exact from his surety the full amount of the sum mentioned in the guarantee.[16]

The liability of the surety under the ordinary bond or guarantee is to make good the net loss, caused by the receiver's default, to the estate which is being administered, not to third persons: where, therefore, a receiver and manager had properly incurred, and was entitled to be indemnified against, trade liabilities to the extent of £900, but was in default to the estate to the extent of £400, it was held that, inasmuch as the trade creditors could only claim against the estate to the net amount of the receiver's indemnity, i.e. £500, the estate had suffered no loss by reason of the receiver's default, and that, consequently, the sureties could not be called upon to pay the £400.[17]

Inasmuch as a receiver of the estate of a patient is not accountable to the Court of Protection in his character of receiver for rents and profits received after the death of the patient, his surety cannot be made liable in respect of the receiver's default as to such rents and profits.[18]

A surety cannot come to the court for protection unless there is an accrued liability enforceable against him or, semble, unless the receiver is threatening an act which will involve the surety in liability.[19]

Indemnity of surety. If a surety has been called on to pay anything on account of the receiver, he is entitled to be indemnified for what he has so paid out of any balance which may be coming to the receiver in the action. Therefore, where a receiver had borrowed money from his surety for the purpose of making sundry

---

[14] Re Graham [1895] 1 Ch. 66.
[15] Dawson v. Raynes (1826) 2 Russ. 466; see, too, Re Herricks (1853) 3 Ir.Ch. 187.
[16] Per Chitty J. in Re Graham [1895] 1 Ch. 66, 70.
[17] Re British Power, etc., Co. (No. 3) [1910] 2 Ch. 470; cited p. 238, ante. Quaere whether this is the case under the modern form of guarantee.
[18] Re Walker [1907] 2 Ch. 120; and see Re Bennett [1913] 2 Ch. 318.
[19] Re Ledgard [1922] W.N. 105.

necessary payments, it was held that the surety was entitled to be repaid the amount which he had lent to the receiver out of a balance in court due to the receiver.[20] Upon the same principle, some shares belonging to a receiver in property which was being administered by the court were applied in making good to his sureties a sum of money which they had been obliged to pay in consequence of his default, although those shares were not included in a security which the receiver had given to the sureties by way of indemnity.[21]

Right against co-surety. A surety who pays the debt of his principal has the same right against a co-surety as he has against the principal, and he will be permitted to claim contribution.[22]

Application for stay, etc. Where an action is brought against a surety upon his guarantee, the proper course for him to pursue is conceived to be to apply to the court by motion or summons, with notice to the parties interested, in the action to which the receiver was appointed, to stay the proceedings against him, offering at the same time to lodge what is due from the receiver, up to the amount of the guarantee in court.[23] The surety must pay the costs of his application, and of the proceedings in consequence of it.[24] If the receiver's account has not been taken, the application should also ask for an inquiry as to what is due from the receiver. The court may, it is conceived, upon an application of this kind, indulge the surety by allowing him to pay the balance due from the receiver by instalments.[25] Payment by a surety to the solicitor prosecuting the proceedings is insufficient.[26]

The practice on discharge of the receiver is dealt with in the preceding chapter.[27]

---

[20] *Glossup* v. *Harrison* (1814) 3 V. & B. 134; Coop. 61.

[21] *Brandon* v. *Brandon* (1859) 3 De G. & J. 524, 530, 531.

[22] *Re Swann's Estate* (1869) Ir.R. 4 Eq. 209.

[23] *Walker* v. *Wild* (1816) 1 Madd. 528; *Re Graham, Graham* v. *Noakes* [1895] 1 Ch. 66, 70; Daniell's *Chancery Practice* (8th ed.), p. 1501.

[24] *Walker* v. *Wild* (1816) 1 Madd. 528.

[25] *Ibid.*

[26] *Mann* v. *Stennett* (1845) 8 Beav. 189.

[27] *Ante*, p. 267.

Part II

RECEIVERS APPOINTED OUT OF COURT

CHAPTER 14

GENERAL PRINCIPLES

When receiver appointed out of court. There are many cases in which the appointment of a receiver, or a receiver and manager, is effected without resort to the courts. Such appointments are made (i) under an agreement between persons interested in the property over which the appointment is made, or (ii) under the provisions of a statute. A receiver so appointed is the agent of the parties or one of them according to the terms of the agreement or statute under which the appointment is made. By statute, however, the receiver may become personally liable to persons contracting with him,[1] and, as is the case with all other agents, he may in certain circumstances in any case become liable as a principal to persons dealing with him.[2]

Advantages. The advantages of the appointment of a receiver out of court are that the costs of an action, and of such formalities as affidavits of fitness and provision of security, are obviated. Additional powers may be conferred, either directly, or by enlargement of the statutory powers, upon a receiver appointed out of court. For example, the right to grant options of purchase may be so conferred. It goes without saying, however, that there is no obligation on the person with the power to make such an appointment to make it: he is fully entitled to resort to such other remedies he may have as he chooses.[3]

Date of appointment. An appointment under hand takes effect when the document of appointment is handed to the receiver by a person having authority so to do in circumstances from which it may fairly be said that he is appointing a receiver, and the receiver accepts the profferred appointment.[4] The date which the document effecting the appointment bears is irrelevant, save as a piece of evidence if the actual date of delivery and acceptance of the appointment is unknown.[5] There is no objection to the appointment

---

[1] See Companies Act 1948, s. 369 (2), and pp. 325–326, *post.*

[2] See p. 326, *post.*

[3] *Reeves* v. *White* (1852) 17 Q.B. 995.

[4] *Cripps (Pharmaceuticals) Ltd.* v. *Wickenden* [1973] 1 W.L.R. 944 at p. 953F–G, *per* Goff J.; *Windsor Refrigerator Co. Ltd.* v. *Branch Nominees Ltd.* [1961] Ch. 375.

[5] *Cripps (Pharmaceuticals) Ltd.* v. *Wickenden, supra,* at p. 954D, *per* Goff J.

being prepared and left until it is required to be brought into effect in the manner indicated above.[6]

Duties of a receiver appointed out of court. Any receiver appointed out of court must, for his own protection, immediately upon being notified of his appointment (assuming that he is willing to accept it), satisfy himself as to (a) the validity of the document (if any) under which the power to appoint him is said to arise[7]; (b) in any case the validity of the appointment itself; (c) who under the terms of the documents in question is his principal; (d) the extent of the powers conferred upon him, and (e) the nature and extent of the property over which he has been appointed.

If there is any flaw in his appointment not only will he be unable to enforce any claims to priority over other parties interested in the property [8] but he may be liable in trespass to any person whose rightful possession he disturbs,[9] though such person will have the option of treating the receiver as either a trespasser or as his agent.[10]

If the validity of his appointment is challenged, it is for the receiver to justify it: the maxim *omnia praesumuntur rite esse acta* does not apply.[11]

If, however, the appointment is made subject to provisions which are not justified by the terms of the power (*e.g.* that all the receiver's cheques are to be countersigned by a designated person) but the owner of the property with knowledge of such provisions allows him to take possession and act as receiver without objection, he will be taken to have assented to and sanctioned such modifications.[12]

Appointment without consent. Nobody can be forced to accept the office of a receiver if he is unwilling so to do. The delivery of the document gives the receiver knowledge or means of knowledge, who the debtor is (if he does not know already) and acceptance

---

[6] *Ibid.* at p. 954D, *per* Goff J.; *Windsor Refrigerator Co. Ltd.* v. *Branch Nominees Ltd., supra*, at p. 395, *per* Lord Evershed M.R. and at p. 397, *per* Harman L.J.

[7] See *A. J. Brush* v. *Ralli Bros.* (*Securities*) (1967) 117 New L.J. 212, where the debenture was attacked as being part of a moneylending transaction.

[8] *Cf. Kasofsky* v. *Kreegars* [1937] 4 All E.R. 374.

[9] *Re Simms* [1934] Ch. 1.

[10] *Ex p. Vaughan* (1884) 14 Q.B.D. 29; *Re Simms, supra.*

[11] *Kasofsky* v. *Kreegars* [1937] 4 All E.R. 374.

[12] *Gosling* v. *Gaskell* [1897] A.C. 575, *per* Lord Herschell at p. 591 and *per* Lord Davey at p. 595.

may, of course, be tacit.[13] Accordingly, if a person has been appointed, or purported to be appointed, to be a receiver, he may, at any time before acceptance of the office,[14] but not after such acceptance,[15] refuse it. Such refusal should be notified to the appointor without delay, and in cases where his appointment has been notified to the registrar of companies,[16] the registrar should forthwith be informed of such refusal.[17] Conversely, a person who assumes the character of a receiver either under an invalid, or without an, appointment may render himself liable to account as such.[18]

Appointments by agreement. The appointment is made wholly under the terms of an agreement in such cases as the appointment of a receiver to wind up a partnership business. Another case is where a person entitled to payment out of a fund not yet in existence, such as gate money to be paid for admission, is given power to appoint a receiver over the receipts.

In all such cases the agreement defines the rights, duties and obligations of the receiver. If the agreement contains no express provision for remuneration, it may be claimed on the basis of a *quantum meruit*, prima facie on the same scale as receivers appointed by the court.[19]

Where the receiver is appointed, whether at the instance of mortgagees or otherwise, to carry on a business, the problems which will confront him are in many respects similar to those which confront a receiver of a company's undertaking, which is dealt with in Chapter 16, although such a receiver is subject to many statutory obligations and entitled to certain statutory privileges which will not apply.[20]

Appointments by mortgagors. In the case of equitable mortgages, the mortgagor may appoint a person to collect and deal with the rents and profits in the same manner as provided in the case of receivers appointed by the mortgagee under the Law of Property Act 1925,[21] or otherwise: the receiver's powers may be defined by

---

[13] *Cripps (Pharmaceuticals) Ltd.* v. *Wickenden* [1973] 1 W.L.R. 944 at p. 954C, *per* Goff J.

[14] *Cf. Robinson* v. *Pett* (1734) 3 P.W. 249.

[15] *Cf. Re Lister* [1926] Ch. 149.

[16] Under Companies Act 1948, s. 102 (1): see p. 316, *post.*

[17] *Cf.* Companies Act 1948, s. 102 (2).

[18] See *Wood* v. *Wood* (1828) 4 Russ. 558.

[19] *Prior* v. *Bagster* [1887] W.N. 194.

[20] See p. 316, *post.*   [21] See Chap. 15, *post.*

reference to the statute: it is usual and advisable in such cases to obtain the approval by the mortgagee of the person appointed. A person so appointed is in all respects the agent of the mortgagor, even though he may have been nominated by the mortgagee.[22] Such an appointment should be made under seal if the person appointed is authorised to take proceedings in the name of the mortgagee or mortgagor. Where a life-tenant appointed a receiver over rents with a direction to the tenants to pay rents to such receiver, to secure payment of an annuity, this was held to create an equitable charge in priority to subsequent incumbrancers with notice.[23]

Appointments by mortgagees. Appointments by mortgagees are normally made under the statutory power,[24] but sometimes a mortgagee in possession of his own authority appoints an agent to collect rents: and a person so appointed is the agent of the mortgagee, who remains accountable as a mortgagee in possession.[25]

Property to which appointment extends. Clearly, the receiver can have no title to property which does not belong to the person over whose property the appointment extends, or which is not comprised in the documents from which his title derives. Thus, no appointment can properly extend to property to which the chargor has no legal or equitable title, nor can it extend to property which is held upon trust by the chargor for third persons.[26] Given the flexibility of the law in relation to the time of transfer of the property in specific or ascertained goods—which is simply such time as the parties to the contract of sale intend it to be transferred [27]—it is possible for a chargor to be in possession of quantities of goods to which he has no title whatsoever.[28] Doubtless, a power of sale, or of otherwise dealing with such goods must be implied if not expressly provided for, but it is then possible for the supplier, by apt provisions in the contract, to provide that the chargor is, as regards such sales or

---

[22] See *Jefferys* v. *Dickson* (1866) L.R. 1 Ch.App. 183, 190; *Law* v. *Glenn* (1867) L.R. 2 Ch.App. 634, 640.

[23] *Cradock* v. *Scottish Provident Institution* [1893] W.N. 146; affirmed [1894] W.N. 88.

[24] See Chap. 15, *post.*

[25] *Leith* v. *Irvine* (1833) 1 My. & K. 277, 286.

[26] *Aluminium Industrie Vaassen B.V.* v. *Romalpa Aluminium Ltd.* [1976] 2 All E.R. 552.

[27] Sale of Goods Act 1893, s. 17.

[28] In the *Romalpa* case title was only to pass when the chargor had met all that was owing to the supplier " no matter on what grounds."

dealings, to stand in a fiduciary position towards him. The result is that the chargor may be a trustee of such proceeds of sale, and possibly of the proceeds of other dealings (*e.g.* sale of a product containing the goods supplied) for the original supplier.[29] Such trust moneys cannot be disposed of in any way so as to affect the supplier's title thereto. The consequences of the combination of these two principles in a suitably drafted contract may, as was the position in the leading case, be very serious from the point of view of an apparently secured creditor.[30]

Protection. The court will if necessary grant an injunction against any person bound by the appointment to prevent interference with a receiver appointed out of court.[31]

Fiduciary position. A receiver clearly stands in a fiduciary position towards those by whom, or on whose behalf, he is appointed.[32] Inasmuch as he will be in control and receipt of assets belonging to a third party, he will also owe a duty not to act negligently to such party as well.[33] He is absolutely disqualified from purchasing the property of those towards whom he stands in such a position [34] withot the uusual safeguards.[35] Further, his appointment to an office of such responsibility presupposes that he will discharge his duties with punctilious rectitude.[36]

Discharge. The receiver obtains his discharge from the person or persons who originally appointed him, or in any other way prescribed in his appointment. Apart from express provision, there are no prescribed formalities, but the receiver usually obtains a release, and frequently a release and indemnity.

[29] Following the principle of *Re Hallett's Estate* (1880) 13 Ch.D. 696, the supplier is allowed to trace the goods supplied into their proceeds.

[30] The consequences of this decision are pointed out by Professor Goode in an article in *The Times* (*Business News*) for May 11, 1977.

[31] *Bayly* v. *Went* (1884) 51 L.T. 764.

[32] *Re Magadi Soda Co. Ltd.* (1925) 94 L.J.Ch. 217 at p. 219, *per* Eve J.

[33] See the judgments in *R.* v. *Board of Trade, ex p. St. Martin's Preserving Co. Ltd.* [1965] 1 Q.B. 603.

[34] *Re Magadi Soda Co. Ltd.* (1925) 94 L.J.Ch. 217 at p. 219, *per* Eve J.

[35] See Snell's *Principles of Equity* (27th ed.), pp. 241–243.

[36] *Re Magadi Soda Co. Ltd.* (1925) 94 L.J.Ch. 217 at p. 219, *per* Eve J.

CHAPTER 15

APPOINTMENTS UNDER STATUTORY POWERS

Law of Property Act 1925, Part III. The principal statutory provisions [1] respecting the appointment of a receiver are contained in Part III of the Law of Property Act 1925 and relate to appointments by mortgagees. There is an express provision [2] enabling the statutory provisions to be varied or extended by the mortgage deed with the like incidents, effects and consequences as if the extension or variation had been contained in the Act.

By section 101 (1) (ii) a mortgagee whose mortgage is by deed [3] has powers to the like extent as if the powers had been expressly conferred by the mortgage, at any time after the mortgage money has become due, to appoint a receiver of the mortgaged property or any part thereof; or, if the mortgaged property consists of an interest in income or a rentcharge or an annual or other periodical sum, a receiver of that property or any part thereof. Apart from express provision in the mortgage deed [4] the appointment cannot be made until the mortgagee has become entitled to exercise the statutory power of sale,[5] that is, unless and until notice has been served on the mortgagor or one of several mortgagors requiring payment of the mortgage money and default in payment of the money or any part thereof has been made for three months after service [6]: or unless and until some interest under the mortgage is in arrear and unpaid for two months after becoming due, or there has been a breach of some provision contained in the mortgage deed or in the Act (other than the covenant for payment of the mortgage money or interest), on the part of the mortgagee or some other person concurring in the mortgage.[7] The further restrictions imposed by the Rent Acts are discussed on a later page.[8]

---

[1] For other statutory provisions, see p. 304, *post.*

[2] s. 101 (3).

[3] Charges registrable under Class A (other than a land improvement charge registered after December 31, 1969) and Class B of the Land Charges Act 1972, s. 2 (1), (2), (3), if for securing money, take effect as if they were legal mortgages created by deed, and Law of Property Act 1925, s. 101, applies accordingly: see Land Charges Act 1972, s. 4 (1).

[4] See s. 101 (4).

[5] s. 109 (1).

[6] s. 103 (1): the notice cannot be served until the principal money has become due.

[7] s. 103 (ii) and (iii).

[8] *Post*, p. 305.

The statutory power of appointment applies only to mortgages executed after 1881, and only if and so far as a contrary provision is not contained in the mortgage deed, and has effect subject to the provisions of that deed.[9]

The statutory provisions apply to all mortgages or charges by deed whether legal or equitable.[10] Apart from express provision, an equitable mortgagee has no right to possession and can therefore only obtain the rents and profits by means of a receiver [11]: but a second or subsequent mortgagee under a legal mortgage has now a legal estate; and, subject to the rights of the prior mortgagees, has a right to possession. An express power is conferred by section 102 upon a mortgagee of an undivided share in land under a mortgage made before 1926 to appoint a receiver to receive the share of the rents and profits arising under the statutory trusts imposed by the Act, from the trustees in whom the land is vested.[12] Where the charge is under hand, application must be made to the court if the appointment of a receiver is required unless the mortgagor concurs in the appointment.[13]

Method of appointment. Where there is a pending action in existence between the mortgagee and mortgagor relating to the mortgage, it is preferable that the court shall be asked to appoint the receiver, rather than that the mortgagee should exercise his undoubted right to effect the appointment out of court.[14]

Time for appointment. In many cases the mortgage deed provides that the appointment of a receiver may be made at an earlier date than is provided by the statute. In the case of debentures [15] and other commercial charges it is usual to provide that the appointment may be made as soon as the principal money has become payable or if interest is more than a specified number of days in arrear or as soon as payment of principal or interest has been demanded and default has been made for a specified number of days.

---

[9] s. 101 (4) and (5).

[10] See s. 205 (xvi).

[11] *Vacuum Oil Co.* v. *Ellis* [1914] 1 K.B. 693. The court may apparently let an equitable mortgagee into possession: *Barclays Bank Ltd.* v. *Bird* [1954] Ch. 274.

[12] Not the position where all the undivided shares are vested in the same mortgagee to secure the same debt. See Sched. I, Part IV, para. 1 (7).

[13] See p. 281, *ante*.

[14] *Tibbett* v. *Nixon* (1883) 25 Ch.D. 238.

[15] See Chap. 16, *post*.

In some cases a receiver is appointed on the execution of the mortgage [16]: for example, where the mortgage is of short lease-holds or other property held or existing for a limited period, or where the principal is to be repaid by short-dated instalments. In such cases it was formerly the practice to make the appointment by a separate deed which could be produced to tenants: but as mortgage deeds are now short, it seems simpler to execute the mortgage in duplicate, in order that a counterpart may be handed to the receiver.

In the case of mortgages made after 1925, a power to appoint a receiver, or of sale, expressed to be exercisable by reason of the mortgagor committing an act of bankruptcy, or entering into liquidation by arrangement or being a company being wound up, cannot be exercised solely on the ground of the happening of any of those events without the leave of the court.[17] If any other event has occurred which renders the power exercisable, leave is not required, though bankruptcy or winding up has supervened.

The appointment under the statutory power may be made by a mortgagee in possession [18]: and it may be submitted that the appointment determines his liability to account as mortgagee in possession as regards such part of the property as is let [19]: but not where he retains actual possession.

Who may be appointed. The statute empowers the mortgagee to appoint " such person as he thinks fit " to be receiver.[20] In exercising his power of appointment the mortgagee is acting in a fiduciary relation to the mortgagor. He should not, therefore, appoint any person who is incompetent or unable to act with responsibility. The statutory power is apparently wide enough to authorise the mortgagee to appoint himself.[21] In a case where the appointment was made under an express power the mortgagee himself was not allowed remuneration.[22] But it is difficult to see how if he can appoint himself he could be deprived of the 5 per

---

[16] As in *United Realisation Co. Ltd.* v. *C.I.R.* [1899] 1 Q.B. 361.

[17] Law of Property Act 1925, ss. 110 and 205 (1) (i).

[18] *Tillett* v. *Nixon* (1883) 25 Ch.D. 238; *County of Gloucester Bank* v. *Rudry* [1895] 2 Ch. 629.

[19] Notwithstanding dicta to the contrary in *Re Prytherch* (1889) 42 Ch.D. 590: see *Anchor Trust* v. *Bell* [1926] Ch. 805, 817, where, however, the mortgagee's possession was wrongful.

[20] Law of Property Act 1925, s. 109 (1).

[21] *Sed quaere* whether such an appointment would not conflict with the principle that a mortgagee is entitled to nothing more than principal, interest and costs.

[22] *Nicholson* v. *Tutin* (1857) 3 K. & J. 159: including one of several mortgagees.

cent. commission to which he is entitled under the express provisions of section 109 (6). Where the mortgagee was a company and extended powers of management were conferred, it was held that there was no such fiduciary relation between its directors and the mortgagor as to disentitle one of such directors to remuneration for his services as receiver.[23]

Mode of appointment. A receiver under the statute is appointed by writing [24] under the hand of the mortgagee [25]: and the receiver may in like manner be removed by the mortgagee and a new receiver appointed in his place.[26] The instrument of appointment (and presumably also of removal and fresh appointment) may be prepared in advance and left until required.[27] An appointment can be made in like manner on the death of a receiver.[28]

The appointment takes effect when the instrument of appointment is handed to the receiver in such circumstances that the part of the appointment is communicated to him and he accepts the appointment.[29] The date of the instrument of appointment is irrelevant.[29]

The instrument of appointment may include a delegation by the mortgagee to the receiver of the powers of leasing and accepting surrenders of leases or any specified lease exercisable by the mortgagee [30]: a direction to insure the mortgaged property or any part thereof [31]: and a direction to apply the balance of any money remaining after providing for the payments referred to in sub-paragraphs (i) to (iv) or section 109 (8) in or towards discharge of the principal money owing to the mortgagee.[32] These matters or any of them can, however, be dealt with by separate directions after the appointment. Where extended powers are conferred by the mortgage, it may be desirable to deal with them in the appointment.

---

[23] *Per* Cozens-Hardy M.R. and Buckley L.J. in *Bath* v. *Standard Land Co.* [1911] 1 Ch. 618, 626, 646, disapproving *Kavanagh* v. *Workingman's Benefit Building Society* [1896] 1 Ir.R. 56. It is not unusual for a building society mortgage to contain an express provision authorising an official of the society to be appointed receiver: but, *semble*, this power exists without express provision.

[24] As to a possibly invalid deed taking effect as an appointment in writing see *Windsor Refrigerator Co. Ltd.* v. *Branch Nominees Ltd.* [1961] Ch. 375.

[25] s. 109 (1).   [26] s. 109 (5).

[27] *Windsor Refrigerator Co. Ltd.* v. *Branch Nominees Ltd.* [1961] Ch. 375.

[28] *Re Hill* [1920] W.N. 386.

[29] *Cripps (Pharmaceuticals) Ltd.* v. *Wickenden* [1973] 1 W.L.R. 944 at p. 953, *per* Goff J.

[30] ss. 99 (19), 100 (13).

[31] Under s. 108 (7).   [32] s. 109 (8) (v).

In the case of a transfer of a registered charge of registered land by the original mortgagee, the power of appointment remains in him until the transferee is registered. Any person ostensibly appointed receiver by the transferee prior to such registration is merely his own agent.[33]

If it is considered necessary to appoint the receiver attorney, *e.g.* to execute a conveyance in the name of the mortgagee, his appointment as receiver must be under seal if his appointment as attorney is included therein.[34] But where the mortgage contains an express delegation to a receiver of a power to sell and convey in the name of the mortgagor, the appointment can be made under hand; the execution under seal by the mortgagor of the mortgage containing such a provision is sufficient.

Priorities. If made by a second or subsequent mortgagee the appointment remains effective until a receiver is appointed by a prior incumbrancer upon which the receiver appointed by the subsequent incumbrancer is displaced. If a receiver has been appointed by the court or judgment creditor at the instance of a puisne incumbrancer, a prior incumbrancer can appoint a receiver under the statute: but unless the order appointing a receiver expressly reserves the rights of subsequent incumbrancers, application must be made to the court for discharge of its receiver[35]: and the statutory receiver is entitled only to rents unpaid at date of service of the notice of motion for discharge.[36]

Effect of appointment. A receiver appointed under the statutory power is deemed to be the agent of the mortgagor who is liable for his acts and defaults unless the mortgage deed otherwise expressly provides, which it seldom, if ever, does.[37] He has power to demand and recover all the income of which he is appointed receiver in the name of the mortgagor or the mortgagee to the full extent of the interest which the mortgagor could dispose of and to give effectual receipts and to exercise any powers delegated to him by

---

[33] *Lever Finance Ltd.* v. *Needleman's Trustee* [1956] Ch. 375.

[34] As the mortgagee's power of sale is not fiduciary (see *Kennedy* v. *de Trafford* [1897] A.C. 180) *semble* it can be delegated; but as to building societies see *Reliance P.B. Society* v. *Harwood-Stamper* [1944] Ch. 362. See also *Cuckmere Brick Co.* v. *Mutual Finance* [1971] Ch. 949 as to the duty not to exercise the power negligently.

[35] See *Re Metropolitan Amalgamated Estates* [1912] 2 Ch. 497; *Underhay* v. *Read* (1887) 20 Q.B.D. 209.

[36] *Thomas* v. *Brigstocke* (1827) 4 Russ. 64; *Preston* v. *Tunbridge Wells Opera House Ltd.* [1903] 2 Ch. 323, 325; *Re Metropolitan Amalgamated Estates, supra.*

[37] s. 109 (2): see *post*, p. 291.

the mortgagee pursuant to the Act.[38] The appointment does not prevent the mortgagee from suing for the mortgage debt.[39]

The effect of the appointment is to determine the interest in possession of the mortgagor. The title of the receiver therefore prevails over that of a receiver for a judgment creditor whether such receiver be appointed with or without the creation of a charge, which would of course be a subsequent charge only [40]: thus a landlord who under the old practice [41] had obtained possession under an *elegit* on a judgment for the rent, was entitled after a receiver had been appointed by a mortgagee to distrain for rent accrued due thereafter on the ground that his interest by *elegit* determined by the appointment.[42]

As the receiver is agent for the mortgagor, there is no change of occupation if the receiver obtains possession to enable the receiver to insist on entering into a new agreement for supply of water, gas or electric light without payment of arrears.[43]

But where the mortgagor is in occupation, a receiver appointed under the statute has no power to recover possession against him by force of his own title: he has only a right to recover the rents: though if he can recover possession he can let, if the power to do so has been delegated to him.[44] If the mortgage deed confers on the receiver a right to take possession, presumably he can maintain ejectment against the mortgagor: but if it does not the mortgagee must either himself proceed in ejectment,[45] and thus assume the liability of a mortgagee in possession, or commence foreclosure proceedings and obtain the appointment of a receiver and apply for an order for possession to be given to the receiver: or that the mortgagor attorn tenant at a rent.[46]

After the appointment the mortgagor cannot distrain without

---

[38] *Ibid.* subs. (3).

[39] *Lynde* v. *Waithman* [1895] 2 Q.B. 180, 184, 188; *Poulett* v. *Hill* [1893] 1 Ch. 277.

[40] See p. 96, *ante.* Of course the leave of the court will be required for the receiver appointed out of court to displace the possession of the receiver appointed by the court, unless the order otherwise so provides.

[41] See now Administration of Justice Act 1956, ss. 34–36.

[42] *Johns* v. *Pink* [1900] 1 Ch. 296.

[43] *Cf.* p. 131, *ante.*

[44] Under s. 99 (19).

[45] Under R.S.C., Ord. 88, r. 1. But note the exclusive jurisdiction of the county court in all cases where it has jurisdiction: Administration of Justice Act 1970, s. 37 and the impossibility of escape merely by adding a formal claim for foreclosure or sale: *Trustees of Manchester Unity Life Insurance Collecting Society* v. *Sadler* [1974] 1 W.L.R. 770.

[46] See p. 173, *ante.* It is submitted that if the receiver after delegation of the power to him creates a tenancy, the tenant could maintain ejectment against the mortgagor.

the receiver's authority even if the receiver neglects or refuses to do so.[47] If the receiver sues in the name of the mortgagor, the tenant can maintain a counterclaim against the mortgagor, *e.g.* on covenants by the mortgagor in the lease.

Powers which can be delegated. As already indicated, the powers which can be delegated to the receiver by the mortgagee include:

(i) Power where the mortgage has been made after 1881 to create leases or tenancies which may in the case of agricultural or occupation leases be for a term not exceeding 21 years, or where the mortgage has been made after 1925 not exceeding 50 years, and in the case of building leases not exceeding 99 years, or where the mortgage has been made after 1925, 999 years; all leases must take effect in possession within 12 months: the best rent must be reserved and no fine taken.[48] Leases must contain a covenant for payment of rent and proviso for re-entry if rent is in arrear for any period not exceeding 30 days: a counterpart must be executed by the lessee.[49]

The lease should usually be granted in the name of the mortgagee, though it can be granted in the name of the mortgagor [50]: for if covenants, other than the usual qualified covenant for quiet enjoyment, are entered into by the lessor, there is no power without express authority to bind the mortgagor by such covenants. In general the mortgagee's power to lease only applies to legal mortgages: for, apart from express provision in the mortgage, an equitable mortgagee is not entitled to possession [51] and is therefore not within subsection (2) of section 99. It follows that a receiver appointed by an equitable mortgagee cannot usually create a lease, for he can do so only in the same manner as if the mortgagee his appointor were in possession.[52]

(ii) Power to accept surrenders for the purpose of enabling new leases to be granted.[53]

(iii) Power to insure up to two-thirds of the sum required to rebuild unless there is a provision in the mortgage deed that no

---

[47] *Bayly* v. *Went* (1884) 51 L.T. 654; *Woolston* v. *Ross* [1900] 1 Ch. 788.

[48] In the case of a building lease a peppercorn rent for any period up to five years is permissible.

[49] s. 99. The section applies to tenancy agreements, subs. (17).

[50] See Law of Property Act 1925, ss. 7 (4) and 8. After the death of the mortgagor until a personal representative is constituted, or after bankruptcy, the lease should be made in the name of the mortgagee.

[51] *Cf.* n. 11, p. 285, *ante.*

[52] s. 99 (19).   [53] s. 100, *q.v.* as to conditions to be observed.

insurance is required or unless an insurance is kept up by the mortgagor in accordance with the mortgage deed or under an agreement with the mortgagee up to the full amount specified above.[54]

Agency for mortgagor. The agency of the receiver for the mortgagor is a statutory recognition of the old conveyancing practice of making the mortgagee's appointee the agent of the mortgagor.[55] The agency is, however, a real one: " [The receiver] must be faithful to [the mortgagor]; he must act in his interest; he must protect him against claims which are not sustainable; he must not assume liabilities which cannot be enforced against his principal." [56] The receiver is agent of the mortgagor, however, only so long as his appointment by the mortgagee is effective, and, accordingly, he ceases to be such agent when that appointment is superseded by one made by the court. Thus, where a receiver was appointed by a mortgagee of leaseholds, and subsequently appointed by the court, the ground landlord could not claim to be paid ground rent out of money in the hands of the receiver representing the property of the mortgagor.[57] The effect of his being agent of the mortgagor is that the mortgagee is not liable in respect of money paid away improperly by the receiver, the mortgagee being liable only for money which reaches his hands.[58] Nor does receipt of rent by the receiver necessarily create a tenancy by estoppel as between the tenant and the mortgagee.[59] The mortgagee may however create, by virtue of his legal estate in the land, the relationship of landlord and tenant between himself and a tenant of the mortgagor whose tenancy is not binding upon him without previously terminating the receivership.[60] The mortgagor may recover from the mortgagee sums paid to the latter by the receiver, under a mistake of fact, in excess of the sums due, for a period of six years before action.[61]

---

[54] s. 109 (7) and s. 108, *q.v.* as to application of insurance money.

[55] *Jefferys* v. *Dickson* (1866) L.R. 1 Ch. 183; *Gosling* v. *Gaskell* [1897] A.C. 575.

[56] *Hibernian Bank* v. *Yourell* (*No. 2*) [1919] 1 I.R. 310 at p. 312, *per* O'Connor M.R.

[57] *Hand* v. *Blow* [1901] 2 Ch. 736.

[58] *Re della Rocella's Estate* (1892) 29 L.R.Ir. 464.

[59] *Serjeant* v. *Nash* [1903] 2 K.B. 304. *Lever Finance Ltd.* v. *Needleman's Trustee* [1956] Ch. 375; *Stroud Building Society* v. *Delamont* [1960] 1 W.L.R. 431; *Chatsworth Properties Ltd.* v. *Effiom* [1971] 1 W.L.R. 144. *Quaere* whether it ever does. But if a mortgagee appoints a receiver in respect of rent due under tenancies not otherwise binding upon him, he may thereby waive all right to treat the tenants as trespassers.

[60] *Stroud Building Society* v. *Delamont, supra*; *Chatsworth Properties Ltd.* v. *Effiom, supra*.

[61] *Re Jones' Estate* [1914] 1 Ir.R. 188.

Where the statutory powers are extended the mortgage should expressly provide that the receiver is to be regarded as agent for the mortgagor: in the absence of an express provision he may be held to be agent for the mortgagee. It is a question of construction in each case.[62]

The death or bankruptcy or winding up [63] of the mortgagor does not affect the statutory powers: the receiver becomes agent for the mortgagor's successor in title so far as to enable him to exercise the statutory powers.[64] But the bankruptcy or winding up of the mortgagor determines the power of the receiver to impose any personal liability on the mortgagor or his estate. The receiver can still carry on the business but he becomes personally liable to persons dealing with him subject to any right of indemnity against the mortgagee.[65]

The receiver being agent for the mortgagor, it appears that as long as the receiver is in receipt of the rents, time cannot run against the mortgagor under the Limitation Act 1939, although the rents are insufficient for payment in full of the interest on the mortgage. Equally, payments made by the receiver will prevent the Limitation Act 1939 running in favour of the mortgagor.[66]

Liability to the mortgagor. The mortgagor can maintain an action for an account against the receiver as his agent.[67] Notwithstanding the relationship of principal and agent, however, the mortgagor cannot dismiss the receiver, since, for valuable consideration he has committed the management of his property to an attorney whose appointment he cannot interfere with.[68]

Nevertheless, as regards negligence a receiver cannot be in any better position than a mortgagee in possession.[69] Hence, he must be liable to the mortgagor in respect of gross or wilful negligence in respect of his acts whilst in possession of the mortgaged property or its produce. Similarly, if he is proposing to exercise any of his powers negligently—e.g. a sale at one price when a better offer is available for acceptance—of if he is causing unnecessary injury to

---

[62] *Post*, p. 351.
[63] See p. 350, *post*, as to the necessity of obtaining the leave of the court to take possession in this case.
[64] *Re Hale* [1899] 2 Ch. 107, 117.
[65] See *post*, p. 351.
[66] *Portman Building Society* v. *Gallwey* [1955] 1 All E.R. 227.
[67] *Jefferys* v. *Dickson* (1866) L.R. 1 Ch. 183 at p. 190.
[68] *Gaskell* v. *Gosling* (1896) 1 Q.B. 669 at p. 692, *per* Rigby L.J.
[69] See Fisher & Lightwood, *Law of Mortgages* (8th ed.), p. 297.

the property he may be restrained from such exercise by the court.[70]

Receipt of rents, etc. The receiver has power to demand and recover all the income of which he is appointed receiver. This includes the income arising from trust property, where the interest therein of the mortgagor is included in the mortgage, to the extent of the income to which the mortgagor is entitled in possession: and includes income arising under the statutory trusts from an undivided share to which the mortgagor is entitled: but the receiver has no effective title to this income until notice has been given by him or the mortgagee to the trustees requiring payment.[71] If the mortgagor has leased land together with chattels (*e.g.* furniture) and the mortgage only extends to the land, the rent must be apportioned between the land and the chattels.[72] The receiver may proceed by action, distress, or otherwise, in the name either of the mortgagor or of the mortgagee, to the full extent of the estate or interest which the mortgagor could dispose of.[73] He can give effectual receipts for such income.[73a] Generally, he may exercise any powers which may have been delegated to him by the mortgagee pursuant to the Law of Property Act 1925 [74]: these do not include a power to forfeit a lease for non-payment of rent.

Notice to tenants. The receiver must give the tenants notice to pay their rents to him. Until he does so, they can, though aware of the appointment, obtain a valid receipt from the mortgagor.[75] If a receiver has been appointed by the court at the instance of a subsequent incumbrancer, the receiver appointed by a prior incumbrancer cannot claim the future rents until the leave of the court has been obtained unless the order, as it usually does and should do, expressly reserves his rights to do so.[76]

As long as the receivership is in force, and the receiver's notice to the tenants of his appointment has not been withdrawn, no valid distress can be levied except by the receiver, or by some person, including the mortgagor, authorised by him.[77] In the absence of such authority, the mortgagor will be restrained by injunction from

---

[70] *Hanson* v. *Derby* (1700) 2 Vern. 392. *Cf. Kernohan Estates* v. *Boyd* [1967] N.I. 27.
[71] See *Re Pawson's Settlement* [1917] 1 Ch. 541.
[72] See *Salmon* v. *Matthews* (1841) 8 M. & W. 827; *C. Hoare & Co.* v. *Hove Bungalows* (1912) 56 S.J. 686.
[73] Law of Property Act 1925, s. 109 (3).   [73a] See n. 65, *ante*.
[74] *Ibid.*
[75] *Vacuum Oil Co.* v. *Ellis* [1914] 1 K.B. 693.
[76] *Ante*, pp. 143–144.   [77] *Woolston* v. *Ross* [1900] 1 Ch. 788.

distraining for rent due from a tenant of part of the mortgaged property, even though the receiver may have been negligent in collecting the rents.[78] The fact that rent is payable in advance does not prevent a distress, nor will distress be restrained on this ground after a winding-up order.[79] If a receiver, appointed by mortgagees, distrains under the statutory power after the title of the mortgagees has come to an end, he may be sued by the tenant, and be made personally liable in damages, on the ground of wrongful distress.[80]

Subsection (2) of section 141 of the Law of Property Act 1925, which provides that any rent, covenant or possession reserved by or contained in a lease is capable of being recovered, enforced and taken advantage of by the person from time to time entitled, subject to the term, to the income of the land leased, deals with procedure only and means that a person entitled to the rent to the exclusion of all others may sue: this does not entitle a beneficiary to sue without joinder of the trustee or to distrain.[81] Where, therefore, the mortgagor is a beneficiary under a trust for him the receiver cannot distrain in his name.

A person paying money to the receiver is not concerned to inquire whether any case has happened to authorise the receiver to act.[82]

Notices, etc. under the Landlord and Tenant Act 1954. See p. 321, *post.*

Liability under the London Building Acts. See p. 321, *post.*

Death or removal of receiver. The receiver may be removed, and a new receiver may be appointed, from time to time, by the mortgagee by writing under his hand.[83] By analogy with the time of appointment,[84] removal presumably dates from the time of communication of the removal to the receiver.

If money stands to the credit of a receiver at a bank as agent for a mortgagor, it is doubtful whether the bank is bound to transfer the account to a new receiver on the demand of the latter.[85]

---

[78] *Bayly* v. *Went* (1884) 51 L.T. 764.
[79] *Venner's Appliances Ltd.* v. *Thorpe* [1915] 2 Ch. 404.
[80] *Serjeant* v. *Nash, Field & Co.* [1903] 2 K.B. 304.
[81] *Schalit* v. *Nadler Ltd.* [1933] 2 K.B. 79.
[82] Law of Property Act 1925, s. 109 (4).
[83] s. 109 (5).
[84] See p. 279, *ante.*
[85] See *Société Coloniale Anversoise* v. *London and Brazilian Bank* [1911] 2 K.B. 1031n. In a proper case an injunction and an order for transfer could be obtained in an action against the first receiver, the company or other mortgagor with or without the mortgagee being plaintiffs.

If the receiver is discharged or dies and a new receiver is appointed in his place without undue delay, the receivership is regarded as continuous.[86] If after the death of a receiver the mortgagor attempts to collect rent before the mortgagee has had an opportunity of appointing a new receiver, he might be restrained by injunction: and a tenant would be well advised to withhold the rent in such circumstances: it is doubtful whether he would obtain a valid receipt from the mortgagor.

Application of moneys received. The statutory provisions as to the application by the receiver of money in his hands (Law of Property Act 1925, s. 109 (8)) define the rights as between the mortgagor and the mortgagee, and the mortgagee and puisne incumbrancers.[87] They do not enable third persons, *e.g.* a local authority, to maintain, under subsection (8) (i), an action against the receiver for rates.[88] They impose a statutory duty upon the receiver pursuant to which the mortgagee can maintain an action against the receiver for an account of the money come to his hands and its application.[89] The mortgagor could also do so as the receiver is his agent, at his own risk as to costs. In an Irish case where the receiver had given a bond to the mortgagee the mortgagor was held entitled to maintain an action against the surety, joining the mortgagee as obligee of the bond as co-plaintiff, to recover a sum equal to that which the receiver had failed to pay to the mortgagee and which had in consequence been raised by sale of part of the mortgaged property; and it is considered that where a receiver with money in his hands negligently omits to make payments, *e.g.* for rates, with the consequence of distress, the mortgagor might sue for damage thereby caused.

The statutory mode of application directed by section 109 (8) [90] of money come to the receiver's hands is as follows:

(i) " In discharge of all rents, taxes, rates, and outgoings whatever affecting the mortgaged property."

This includes arrears of rents, taxes,[91] and rates assessed upon the property, water rate, and payments for gas and electric light. As already stated, it does not enable the persons or incorporated

---

[86] *Re White's Mortgage* [1943] Ch. 166. No fresh leave would be required under the Reserve and Auxiliary Forces, etc., Act 1951.

[87] *Yourell* v. *Hibernian Bank* [1918] A.C. 372 at pp. 386, 387, *per* Lord Atkinson.

[88] *Liverpool Corp.* v. *Hope* [1938] 1 K.B. 751.

[89] *Leicester P.B. Soc.* v. *Butt* [1943] Ch. 308.

[90] See *Yourell* v. *Hibernian Bank* [1918] A.C. 372.

[91] As to income tax, see pp. 298–299, *post.*

bodies entitled to these payments to maintain an action against the receiver.[92] The receiver is usually bound to pay arrears for gas, water and electric light if the supply is to be continued.

The statutory provisions may be varied by agreement between the mortgagee and the mortgagor but not by a direction given by the mortgagee alone.[93]

Neither paragraph (i) nor paragraph (iii) authorises the receiver to pay an unsecured debt of the mortgagor though incurred, *e.g.* for repairs executed before the receiver's appointment [94]: any such payment apart from agreement could only be justified if the payment were made on the direction of the mortgagee out of money payable to him under paragraph (v) of subsection (8).

Where, however, the mortgage conferred wide powers to carry on a business and pay outgoings, the payment by the receiver of an instalment of a trade debt of the mortgagor was sufficient to raise an implied promise by the executrix of the mortgagor, who was dead at the date of the appointment,[95] to pay the balance and thus prevent the debt from becoming statute-barred.[96]

(ii) " In keeping down all annual sums or other payments and the interest on all principal sums, having priority to the mortgage in right whereof he is receiver."

In a case decided under the corresponding provisions of the Conveyancing Act 1881, the receiver was held not entitled to justify a payment in reduction of principal [97]: but now a direction in writing by the mortgagee under paragraph (v) would justify such a payment.

Statute-barred interest cannot be paid either by the receiver or by the mortgagee out of money paid to him by the receiver.[98]

(iii) " In payment of his commission, and of the premium on fire, life, or other insurances, if any, properly payable under the mortgage deed, or under the Act, and the cost of executing necessary or proper repairs directed in writing by the mortgagee."

The rate of commission (which includes remuneration and all

---

[92] *Liverpool Corp.* v. *Hope* [1938] 1 K.B. 751. The local authority has no remedy by action for rates, *ibid.*

[93] *Yourell* v. *Hibernian Bank* [1918] A.C. 372.

[94] See *White* v. *Metcalf* [1903] 2 Ch. 567.

[95] See definition of mortgagor in s. 205 (1) (xvi).

[96] *Re Hale* [1899] 2 Ch. 107.

[97] *Yourell* v. *Hibernian Bank* [1918] A.C. 372. This defect was, however, cured by the assent of both parties.

[98] *Hibernian Bank* v. *Yourell* (*No.* 2) [1919] 1 Ir.R. 310.

costs, charges, and expenses incurred by the receiver [99]) is such rate (not exceeding 5 per cent. on the gross amount of all moneys received [1]) as is specified in his appointment, and if no rate is specified then at that rate on such amount or at such other rate as the court thinks fit to allow on an application by the receiver made for that purpose.[2] If the mortgage fixes the rate, it cannot be varied by the appointment. The rate will only be varied by the court in exceptional circumstances, as for example where the expense and difficulty of collecting the rents has been seriously increased. The application by the receiver can be made in foreclosure or redemption proceedings.[3]

Premiums include premiums on insurances of the mortgaged property subsisting at the date of the appointment or effected under section 108, and on life or other policies comprised in the mortgage.

Repairs include any necessary or proper repairs though the mortgagee could not execute them without making himself liable as receiver in possession.[4] The cost of repairs executed by the receiver will not be allowed him, in his accounts as against the mortgagee, unless the same were so executed on the written instructions of the mortgagee. If verbally directed by the mortgagee the expenditure by the receiver might be justified against the mortgagee but not against the mortgagor; nor can they be justified against the mortgagee if paid on the mortgagor's direction.

(iv) " In payment of the interest accruing due in respect of any principal money due under the mortgage."

In virtue of this direction a receiver appointed by mortgagees is bound to pay any arrears of interest due to the mortgagees at the date of his appointment, as well as interest accruing due subsequently,[5] but not statute-barred arrears.[6]

Save in certain special cases,[7] income tax is no longer deductible

---

[99] This does not include the mortgagee's costs of the appointment.

[1] It would appear from this that if a power of sale is conferred by the mortgage upon a receiver, and he exercises such power, he will be entitled to a percentage of the sale price; *aliter* if a sale is effected by the mortgagee under the statutory power.

[2] See s. 109 (6).

[3] *Semble*, in the absence of such proceedings it could be made by originating summons (see Law of Property Act 1925, s. 203 (2) (*a*)) to which the mortgagor and mortgagee would be respondents.

[4] *White* v. *Metcalf* [1903] 2 Ch. 567, 573 in which case the statutory position of a receiver was discussed at some length: the alteration effected in the receiver's powers by s. 109 must be borne in mind.

[5] *National Bank* v. *Kenny* [1898] 1 Ir.R. 197.

[6] *Hibernian Bank* v. *Yourell* [1919] 1 Ir.R. 310.

[7] Income and Corporation Taxes Act 1970, s. 54.

from payments of mortgage interest.[8] Tax is still, however, deductible where interest is payable (otherwise than in a fiduciary or representative capacity) by a company or local authority; by or on behalf of a partnership of which a company is a member; or by any person to another person whose usual place of abode is outside the United Kingdom.[9] In these exceptional cases, income tax thereon for the year in which the payment is made[10] is to be deducted at the time of payment, including cases where the interest is paid as a lump sum.[11] In these cases, where interest is added to the principal, it is not treated as paid where so added, and tax should not be deducted; it should only be deducted when payment is actually made.[12] Similarly in such cases a mortgagee or receiver who receives proceeds of sale of mortgaged property can apply an adequate part of the proceeds in payment of tax on the amount received as interest.[13]

(v) " In or towards the discharge of the principal money if so directed in writing by the mortgagee."

This direction may be given in the instrument of appointment, or at any time while the receiver retains money in his hands. This provision was not contained in the Conveyancing Act 1881 and the cases before 1926 must be read accordingly: it is thought that before 1926 the mortgagee might have given such a direction but would have become liable as mortgagee in possession. Many mortgages made before 1926 contain an express power to the same effect as this direction.

Position of moneys pending payment. The moneys in the hands of the receiver do not, until payment over by him to the mortgagee, cease to belong to the mortgagor. So that, if the receiver disappears together with the rents and profits which he has collected, even if those rents and profits exceed the amount of the interest payable the mortgagor is still liable on his covenants to the mortgagee.[14]

Income Tax/Corporation Tax. Where the mortgagor is an individual, the situation is simply that the receiver will be receiving

---

[8] For the former practice see *Kerr on Receivers* (13th ed.), p. 298.

[9] Income and Corporation Taxes Act 1970, s. 54 (1); Finance Act 1971, s. 37 (1) and Sched. 6, Pt. I, para. 22. For the corresponding obligation on the receiver to furnish a certificate of deduction see *ibid.* s. 55.

[10] *i.e.* At the basic rate then prevailing; Finance Act 1971, s. 36.

[11] *Re Craven's Mortgage* [1907] 2 Ch. 448.

[12] *I.R.C.* v. *Oswald* [1945] A.C. 360.

[13] *Hollis* v. *Wingfield* [1940] Ch. 337; see *Howell* v. *I.R.C.* [1939] 2 K.B. 597.

[14] *White* v. *Metcalf* [1903] 2 Ch. 567 at p. 571; *Re Della Rocella's Estate* (1892) 29 L.R. Ir. 464 at p. 468.

part of that individual's income, and there are provisions in the Income and Corporation Taxes Act 1970, relating separately to each schedule likely to be relevant whereunder income tax under that schedule will be charged on and paid by the person actually receiving the profits or gains in respect of which tax under that schedule is charged.[15]

However, these provisions, apart from that relating to Schedule B, in terms apply only to income tax, and not to corporation tax.[16] Hence, if the mortgagor is any body corporate, or unincorporated association,[17] these provisions do not apply. For a discussion of the position in such cases, see p. 320, *post*.

The interest due under the mortgage or other charge will not, of course, in the usual case form part of the income of the mortgagee unless and until the receiver pays it to him.[18] Prior to payment over, he normally has no title to the moneys in the hands of the receiver. However, there may be special cases where the arrangements made by the receiver put the moneys collected by him under the direct control of the mortgagee or debenture holder. In such cases the mortgagee will be regarded, to the extent in each year of the interest which he is entitled to be paid thereout, as having actually received it.[19]

Application of residue. The residue of the money received by the receiver is payable to the person who, but for the possession of the receiver, would have been entitled to receive the income of which the receiver was appointed, or who is otherwise entitled to the mortgaged property. A mortgagee must pay any balance in his hands after satisfaction of his claim to the person entitled to receive it. He cannot set up the Statute of Limitations, and claim to pay the second mortgagee only six years' interest, on behalf of a third mortgagee, though such third mortgagee is himself.[20]

The person to whom the surplus is payable is usually the mortgagor [21] or his personal representatives or his or their assigns

---

[15] ss. 68 (1) (Sched. A); 92 (1) (Sched. B); 114 (1) (Sched. D).

[16] ss. 68 (2); 114 (4).

[17] Income and Corporation Taxes Act 1970, ss. 238 and 526 (5).

[18] See note 15, *supra*.

[19] *Visbond* v. *The Federal Commissioner of Taxation* (1943) 68 C.L.R. 354.

[20] *Re Thompson's Mortgage Trusts* [1920] 1 Ch. 508.

[21] It has in consequence been held in Ireland that a fidelity bond taken out by a mortgagee concerning the statutory application of his receipts by a receiver enures for the benefit of the mortgagor: *Kenny* v. *Employers Liability Association* [1901] 1 Ir.R. 301.

if he or they retain the right to possession,[22] or, if a subsequent incumbrancer has appointed a receiver or become mortgagee in possession, such receiver or incumbrancer. If the mortgagee who appointed the receiver holding a surplus is himself mortgagee in possession the surplus would be payable to him without an express direction under subsection (8) (v): but it is advisable to give an express direction and it is essential if such mortgagee is not in possession.

In certain cases such as a mortgage of a life or other determinable interest, part of the money, not only the surplus in the hands of the receiver, on the death of the mortgagor may represent money to which neither the mortgagor's personal representatives nor his incumbrancers are entitled, *e.g.* money representing rents paid in advance in respect of a period which determined only after the death of the mortgagor. Where the tenant for life was tenant for life under the Settled Land Act 1925, it seems that a valid receipt for the proportion attributable to the period after his death might be obtained from his personal representatives as his receipt for the rents was a discharge to the tenants: but in the case of land subject to a trust for sale, or personalty, the apportioned part should be paid to the trustees of the settlement.

If the receiver is in doubt as to whom the surplus should be paid to, or if the mortgagor cannot be found, and there is no action pending, the receiver might have the point determined under Order 85, r. 2 (1) or (2), or might, perhaps, pay the money into court under section 63 of the Trustee Act 1925: but only in exceptional circumstances where the persons prima facie entitled cannot be traced.

Timber. The statutory power to cut and sell timber and other trees which is conferred by section 101 (1) (iv) on a mortgagee in possession [23] does not, apart from express provision in the mortgage, become exercisable on the appointment of a receiver nor can it be delegated to a receiver if exercisable. If the power has been exercised by the mortgagee, it is thought that the proceeds of the timber become applicable as rents and profits; and having regard

---

[22] *White* v. *Metcalf* [1903] 2 Ch. 572; *Turner* v. *Walsh* [1909] 2 K.B. 496, explained *Schalit* v. *Nadler Ltd.* [1933] 2 K.B. 79. As to what are costs, charges and expenses of the mortgage, see *Re Smith's Mortgage* [1931] 2 Ch. 163, where costs of successful defence of an action by the mortgagor claiming to have purchased at an auction were disallowed against a second mortgagee.

[23] See *Re Yates* (1888) 38 Ch.D. 112, 117, 129.

to the definition of income in section 205 (1) (xix) read with sections 101 (1) (iii) and 109 (3), are payable to the receiver, whether the contract is made before or after his appointment, as regards money unpaid at the date of the appointment. But the purchaser of the timber will require an express direction from the mortgagee before paying the receiver.

Business and book debts. In some cases book debts are included in a mortgage made by an individual and power is conferred on a receiver to carry on a business, *e.g.* the business of a licensed victualler. In all cases where book debts are included and power is conferred on the receiver to collect the debts, or to get in other money in the nature of capital which is included in the mortgage, notice should be given forthwith to the debtors or other persons liable to the mortgagor, or holding the property in trust for him, requiring the debt or other money to be paid to the receiver, such notice is required to take the debt out of the order and disposition of the mortgagor.[24] The title of the mortgagee and the receiver prevails over that of a garnishor where the assignment to the mortgagee was before the date of the judgment or after judgment before service of the order nisi.[25]

In such cases where the goodwill of the business is expressly or impliedly included in the security (*e.g.* in the case of a mortgage of licensed premises), but the stock in trade and chattels are not included, the latter must be acquired by purchase from the mortgagor or third persons: but this will be done by the mortgagee not the receiver. In such cases it is usually convenient to apply to the court for a receiver in order to obtain directions which will protect the mortgagee.

In the case of licensed property the primary necessity is to preserve the licences and obtain any necessary transfers. Where the mortgage confers an express power on the receiver to take possession and carry on the business, it usually appoints the mortgagee, or his substitutes, attorneys, to do everything necessary to obtain a transfer: but if it does not, application for the appointment of a receiver should be made to the court.[26]

---

[24] See *Rutter* v. *Everett* [1895] 2 Ch. 872 and pp. 140–141, *ante*; *Re Pawson's Settlement* [1917] 1 Ch. 541.

[25] See *Hirsch* v. *Coates* (1856) 25 L.J.C.P. 315; *Wise* v. *Birkenshaw* (1860) 29 L.J.Ex. 240; *Glegg* v. *Bromley* [1912] 3 K.B. 474.

[26] See p. 229, *ante*.

Where a mortgage authorised the mortgagee to appoint a receiver with power to carry on a business as agent for the mortgagor, it was held that the payment by the receiver of an instalment of a trade debt of the mortgagor operated to raise an implied promise to pay the balance and so prevent the debt from becoming statute-barred.[27]

Foreign property. In the case of property out of the jurisdiction, the statutory powers to collect rents are ineffective. In such cases the mortgage usually contains provisions for the appointment of the receiver as attorney or confers power on him to appoint attorneys to take all necessary steps for collection of rents or recovery of the mortgaged premises. The method by which those steps are taken in any particular case depends upon the law of the country in which the property is situated: here again in the absence of such provisions it is necessary to apply to the court.[28]

Sale. Apart from express provisions in the mortgage, the receiver has no power to sell or convey; nor can an equitable mortgagee convey the legal estate. But in an action brought for realisation of the security, or for redemption or foreclosure, the court may order or direct a sale, and may make a vesting order in favour of the purchaser, or alternatively create and vest in the mortgagee a mortgage term sufficient to enable him to carry out the sale.[29] Debentures and other equitable mortgages often confer on a receiver power to sell the mortgaged property and convey the legal estate in the name of the mortgagor or mortgagee: and usually exclude the restriction imposed by section 103 as to the time for exercise of such power. An irrevocable power of attorney so conferred is unaffected by the death, disability, bankruptcy, or winding up of the mortgagor.[30]

Upon a sale of freehold or leasehold property the mortgagee cannot convey the legal estate in the fee or term of years under the Law of Property Act 1925, s. 104, unless the contract is entered into by him. Where the contract has been entered into by the receiver the concurrence of the mortgagee is essential unless the receiver has

---

[27] *Re Hale* [1899] 2 Ch. 107. The death of the mortgagor did not affect the power of appointment and the payment by the receiver operated as if made by his principal the executrix.

[28] See p. 91, *ante*.   [29] Law of Property Act 1925, ss. 90 and 91.

[30] Powers of Attorney Act 1971, s. 4. As to the former necessity of filing at the Central Office or Land Registry see Law of Property Act 1925, s. 125. It is still possible to search for, inspect and copy or obtain an office copy of any such document filed before the commencement of the Act of 1971: *ibid.* s. 2 (2).

express power to convey in his name, as well as in the name of the mortgagor. On a sale by the receiver upon whom the statutory powers of a mortgagee are by reference conferred, minerals may be severed and conveyed; or reserved easements may be granted and restrictions imposed on land retained or the land sold.[31]

Capital gains tax. A receiver is not concerned with the payment of capital gains tax arising as a result of any such sale. There is an express provision in section 22 (7) of the Finance Act 1965 to the effect that where a person entitled to an asset by way of security, or to the benefit of a charge or an incumbrance on an asset, deals with it for the purpose of giving effect to his security, charge or incumbrance, his dealings with it are to be treated as if they were done through him as a nominee for the true owner. It is further provided that this assumption is to extend to the dealings of any person, such as a receiver, appointed to enforce the security, charge or incumbrance. In the case of such a nominee, section 22 (5) further provides that his acts are to be taken as if they are the acts of the person or persons for whom he is the nominee or trustee, and as if the asset were vested in such person. Combining these two provisions, it follows that liability for any capital gains tax rests with the person or persons who own the property subject to the security, charge or incumbrance to enforce which the receiver has been appointed, and not with the receiver.

Other statutory provisions. In addition to the statutory power conferred on mortgagees by the Law of Property Act 1925, other powers to appoint a receiver are conferred by statute.

By section 122 of the same Act power is conferred on a person entitled to a rentcharge or other annual sum (not being rent incident to a reversion) [32] charged on or issuing out of another rentcharge or other annual sum charged on land or payable out of the income of land, to appoint a receiver over the rentcharge or annual sum on which his rentcharge is charged if any instalment of the latter is in arrear and unpaid for 21 days: the provisions of the Act relating to the appointment, powers, remuneration, and duties of a receiver appointed by a mortgagee apply to such a receiver.[33]

---

[31] These provisions only apply to mortgages made after 1911: Law of Property Act 1925, s. 101 (2); but in the case of other mortgages an order can be obtained under s. 92 of the Law of Property Act 1925.

[32] *i.e.* payable under a sub-lease.

[33] These provisions are in substitution for the remedies conferred on the holder of a rentcharge by s. 121, which include powers to distrain and enter into possession: they are given because the holder of a sub-rentcharge has no power to distrain.

The remedies of a person entitled to a rentcharge created under the Improvement of Land Act 1864 or any special Improvement Act are limited to the remedies given by section 121 of the Law of Property Act 1925 [34]: he cannot appoint a receiver but after a legal mortgage has been created under subsection (4) the mortgagee could do so.

Charges under statutes. Powers of appointing a receiver to enforce certain statutory charges [35] are conferred on local authorities by section 181 (3) of the Highways Act 1959, and other statutes. A local authority has all the remedies, including a power of appointing a receiver, conferred by the Law of Property Act 1925, on mortgagees by deed, to recover sums charged under the Public Health Act 1936, s. 291.[36] There is a similar provision in respect of sums charged under the Housing Act 1957, s. 10 (7).[37] It is presumed that a person in whose favour an annual sum was charged under the Public Health Act 1936, s. 295 (repealed by the Local Government (Miscellaneous Provisions) Act 1976, s. 27 (3)), had only the remedies conferred by the Law of Property Act 1925, s. 121. This section was expressly applied to charges created under the Housing Act 1957, s. 14, in favour of an owner.[38]

Extension of statutory powers. As already indicated [39] the statutory powers given to a receiver which are limited to the collection and application of income arising from the mortgaged property are inappropriate where property such as book debts or a business is included in the security. In such cases the mortgage or debenture usually confers an express power on the receiver to collect and get in the book debts and to carry on the business. In the absence of such an express power application should be made to the court for the appointment of a receiver, for an appointment out of court is useless. The cases relating to the carrying on by a receiver appointed by a mortgagee of a business are almost invariably cases where the mortgagor is a company and are dealt

---

[34] See Improvement of Land Act 1899, s. 3, and Law of Property Act 1925, s. 207 (c).
[35] As to the priority over all other charges, see *Paddington Council* v. *Finucane* [1928] Ch. 567.
[36] See subs. (4) of s. 291; as to limit in case of lessees and power to deduct from rent, s. 294.
[37] See as to the time for appointment *ibid.* s. 10 (8).
[38] See s. 15 (3): and as to other charges having priority over this charge, see subs. (1) of s. 15.
[39] p. 301, *ante.*

with in the next chapter [40]: in other cases the provisions of the Bills of Sale Acts usually render such charges inappropriate or invalid.

Restriction on appointment of a receiver. Under the provisions of the Reserve and Auxiliary Forces (Protection of Civil Interests) Act 1951, a person is not entitled in the cases to which that Act applies,[41] without leave of the appropriate court to exercise any remedy which is available to him by way of (among other things) the taking possession or appointment of a receiver of any property or re-entry upon any land or the realisation of any security [42]: the restriction does not affect the mortgagee's power of sale of land or an interest therein where the mortgagee is in possession at the relevant date,[43] or has appointed a receiver who is in possession or receipt of the rents and profits at that date.[44] Where a receiver who has been appointed and is in possession or receipt of the rents and profits on the relevant date, dies or is removed after that date, leave is not required to appoint another in his place if the appointment is made with reasonable promptness: if there is a substantial interval the appointment will be regarded as a new one and leave will be required.[45]

Where, as was formerly a common practice, a receiver approved by the mortgagee is appointed by the mortgage itself or contemporaneous deed, the case is outside the Act: even if the receiver is not to act until interest is in arrear: at all events if no notice or requirement by the mortgagee is necessary before he could act: for in such cases no step is taken by the mortgagee to exercise any remedy.[46]

Rent Restriction Acts. Certain restrictions on the enforcement of a mortgagee's remedies are imposed by the Rent Act 1977.[47] The mortgages with which that Act is concerned are divided into four classes, there being in respect of each class a fixed date, such

---

[40] p. 309, *post*.

[41] See Reserve and Auxiliary Forces, etc. Act 1951, s. 3.

[42] *Ibid*. s. 2 (2) (*a*).

[43] See *ibid*. s. 3 (10).

[44] *Ibid*. s. 2 (2), proviso.

[45] *Re White's Mortgage* [1943] Ch. 166.

[46] But if the receiver's power is conferred by reference to Law of Property Act 1925, it is thought that leave might be required before giving a direction under s. 109 (8) (v): the mortgage deed or contemporaneous deed can, however, make express provision for the application of the surplus.

[47] Rent Act 1977, ss. 129–136 and Sched. 19.

that mortgages of that class made subsequent to that date are subject to no such restriction.[48]

These respective dates are:

  (i) if the tenancy was then subject to the Rent Acts, December 8, 1965 [48];

  (ii) where on November 28, 1967, land consisting of or including a dwelling-house was subject to a long tenancy which became a regulated tenancy on that date under the Leasehold Reform Act 1967, that date [49];

  (iii) if the tenancy only became a regulated tenancy by virtue of section 14 of the Counter-Inflation Act 1973 (which, broadly speaking, raised the limits of rateable values controlled by the Rent Acts from £400 in Greater London and £200 elsewhere to £1,500 in Greater London and £750 elsewhere [50]), the date is March 22, 1973, the date on which the 1973 Act was passed [51];

  (iv) if the tenancy was a furnished one which only became a regulated one by virtue of section 1 of the Rent Act 1974, the date is August 14, 1974, the date of commencement of the 1974 Act.[52]

Mortgages in the first class may either be " controlled " or " regulated "; all others are " regulated."

A " controlled " mortgage is one which would have been subject to the Rent Act 1920 (whether or not as amended by the 1939 Act) [53] had neither the Act of 1968 nor the Act of 1977 been

---

[48] Rent Act 1977, s. 129 (2) (d).   [49] *Ibid.* s. 129 (2) (a).

[50] Counter-Inflation Act 1973, s. 14 (1). The full provision is that where the date on which a value for the dwelling-house is first shown in the valuation list (the appropriate day: see Rent Act 1968, s. 6 (3))

  (a) fell before March 22, 1973

    (i) the rateable value on the appropriate day exceeded £400 in Greater London or £200 elsewhere;

    (ii) the rateable value on March 22, 1973, exceeded £600 in Greater London or £300 elsewhere; and

    (iii) the rateable value on April 1, 1973, exceeded £1,500 in Greater London or £750 elsewhere;

  (b) fell between March 22, 1973, and April 1, 1973

    (i) the rateable value on the appropriate day exceeded £600 in Greater London or £300 elsewhere; and

    (ii) the rateable value on April 1, 1973, exceeded £1,500 in Greater London or £750 elsewhere;

  (c) falls on, or after, April 1, 1973, the rateable value on that date exceeded £1,500 in Greater London or £750 elsewhere.

[51] Rent Act 1977, s. 129 (2) (b).   [52] Rent Act 1977, s. 129 (2) (c).

[53] See the Increase of Rent and Mortgage Interest (Restrictions) Act 1920, ss. 7, 12 (4); Rent and Mortgage Interest Restrictions (Amendment) Act 1933, s. 9; Rent and Mortgage Interest Restrictions Act 1939; Rent Act 1957, s. 11.

passed.[54] That is to say, it is a legal [55] mortgage, where the security consists of or comprises one or more dwelling-houses let as separate dwellings with rateable values in London, the Metropolitan Police District, or the City of London up to £40, in Scotland up to £40, and elsewhere up to £30, provided that the rateable value of the houses so let [56] was not less than one-tenth of that of the whole property comprised in the mortgage.[57]

A " regulated " mortgage is one which is not controlled but is a legal mortgage of land consisting of or including a dwelling-house subject to a regulated tenancy [58] which is binding on the mortgagee.[59] There is the same " one-tenth " test as in the case of controlled mortgages.[60] A mortgage ceases to be regulated if the mortgagor is in breach of covenant, other than the covenant for repayment of the principal in a lump sum: if he is in breach of a covenant to pay by instalments the mortgage ceases to be regulated.[61]

In the case of controlled mortgages, the mortgagee is unable to call in his mortgage, or take any steps for exercising any right of foreclosure or sale, or for otherwise enforcing his security or recovering the principal money, so long as no interest is more than 21 days in arrear, and the covenants by the mortgagor (except the covenant for payment) are performed, and the property is kept in repair and instalments of principal and interest due under prior securities are paid.[62] As the power of sale is thus not exercisable, except in certain specified events, the statutory power of appointing a receiver is in like manner exercisable only on the happening of such events.[63] If the proceedings are commenced while interest is

---

[54] Rent Act 1977, s. 130.

[55] Rent Act 1920, s. 12 (4) (*b*); see *London County and Westminster Bank Ltd.* v. *Tompkins* [1918] 1 K.B. 515; *Jones* v. *Woodward* [1917] W.N. 61.

[56] *Re Dunn's Application* (1920) 149 L.T.Jour. 215, *sed quaere*. See as to apportionment between property within and without the Rent Acts, s. 12 (5) of the 1920 Act and *Coutts & Co.* v. *Duntroon Investment Corp. Ltd.* [1958] 1 W.L.R. 116.

[57] Rent Act 1920, s. 12 (4) (*a*).

[58] Prior to the Counter-Inflation Act 1973, a regulated tenancy was one of a dwelling-house whose rateable value is not in excess of £400 in Greater London or £200 elsewhere and which was not a controlled tenancy: Rent Act 1968, ss. 1 (1), 7 (2).

[59] Rent Act 1977, s. 131 (1).

[60] *Ibid*. s. 131 (2) (*a*). In the case of mortgages of the second class above, the rateable values are for this purpose ascertained as at March 7, 1973, and not the appropriate day: *ibid*. s. 131 (3).

[61] *Ibid*. s. 131 (2) (*b*).

[62] *Ibid*. Sched. 19, para. 6 (1).

[63] These provisions do not restrict the power of the court to appoint a receiver over the estate of the mortgagor or direct a sale in an administration action, where the mortgagee sues on behalf of himself and all other creditors.

more than 21 days in arrear, subsequent payment does not revive the statutory protection.[64]

As regards regulated mortgages, the mortgagee's right to exercise his remedies is not directly controlled, but in certain circumstances, which include the mortgagee's demanding repayment or taking any steps for exercising any right of foreclosure or sale or for otherwise enforcing his security, the mortgagor is entitled to apply to the court [65] for relief.[66] On any such application the court,[67] if satisfied that by reason of the circumstances and of the operation of the 1977 Act the mortgagor would suffer severe financial hardship, may make such order extending the time for the repayment of the principal money or otherwise varying the terms of the mortgage or imposing any limitation or condition on the exercise of any right or remedy as the court [67] thinks appropriate.[68] The court [69] may revoke or vary any such order by a subsequent order.[70]

These restrictions in relation to controlled mortgages are seldom material with regard to the appointment of a receiver by a mortgagee as the power is not usually exercisable until the interest is so far in arrear as to cause the restrictions to cease to apply. But the restrictions on increasing rents or determining tenancies protected by the Acts have to be considered by receivers in dealing with tenants of the mortgaged property. It is not within the scope of this work to discuss in detail these provisions: a textbook dealing with these Acts should be consulted.

Discharge of receiver. A receiver is entitled to a discharge on the termination of his receivership, and as a practical matter it may often be necessary for the mortgagee, or other the appointor, to give the receiver an indemnity against all claims which might be made against him arising out of the receivership.

---

[64] *Evans* v. *Horner* [1925] 1 Ch. 177.

[65] The court is the county court, except that where an application is made in pursuance of any step taken by the mortgagee in the High Court it is that court: Rent Act 1977, s. 132 (6).

[66] *Ibid.* s. 132 (1).

[67] See n. 65, *supra.*

[68] *Ibid.* s. 132 (2). Where an order is made the court can, if appropriate, on the application of the mortgagee, apportion the mortgage money between dwelling-houses and other land, in which case the mortgage will take effect as if it were two separate mortgages: *ibid.* s. 132 (3), (4).

[69] See n. 65, *supra.*

[70] *Ibid.* s. 132 (5).

CHAPTER 16

APPOINTMENTS OVER THE PROPERTY OF A COMPANY[1]

Legal mortgages. In the case of legal mortgages created by a company,[1] the statutory power of appointing a receiver applies, as in the case of any other mortgage.[2] But in general, though the powers of such a receiver are the same as in any other case, he will be subject to additional statutory duties and liabilities.[3] In all cases the mortgage and appointment must be registered.[4] If the mortgage is not registered, though it will be valid as between the company and the mortgagee, and any appointment of a receiver will be good as between them,[5] neither the mortgage nor the appointment will hold good against the liquidator or other creditors of the company.[6]

Debentures. A debenture is defined by section 455 of the Companies Act 1948, as including " debenture stock, bonds and any other securities of a company whether constituting a charge on the assets of the company or not." [7] But where there is no charge a receiver cannot be appointed by the debenture holders, who, in such a case, have merely the rights of unsecured creditors.[8] Debentures of this class, termed naked debentures or notes, might, however, expressly confer upon the holders an express power to appoint a receiver of the property of the company, but such a receiver would have no rights, beyond those of the company itself, against execution creditors or the liquidator, unless on the construction of the debenture a charge could be implied.[9]

Where the company has issued debentures creating a charge under its seal, even in the absence of any express provision, the debenture holder can rely upon the statutory power and appoint

---

[1] The word " company " is used throughout this and the following chapters as meaning a company formed and registered under the Companies Act 1948 or under any previous Joint Stock Companies Act. See Companies Act 1948, s. 455 (1). For the meaning of the phrase " property of a company " see p. 310, *post.*

[2] See Chap. 15, *ante.*

[3] See pp. 316 *et seq., post.*

[4] See ss. 95 and 102 of the Companies Act 1948 and pp. 58, 61, *ante.*

[5] *Burston Finance Ltd.* v. *Speirway* [1974] 1 W.L.R. 1648, *per* Walton J. at p. 1657E.

[6] Companies Act 1948, s. 95 (1). See *Re Monolithic Building Co.* [1915] 1 Ch. 643.

[7] As to the general validity of debentures, see Chap. 2, pp. 57–58, *ante.*

[8] *Cf. Wylie* v. *Carlyon* [1922] 1 Ch. 51.

[9] Income stock certificates giving a charge on the net profits though not under seal are debentures: *Re Austin Friars Investment Co.* [1926] Ch. 1.

a receiver at any time after the security has crystallised, if all the debenture holders concur in the appointment.[10] But unless the powers of the receiver are extended, such an appointment is of little value, and application should be made to the court to appoint a receiver.

For this reason, debentures and debenture stock trust deeds almost invariably confer in express terms upon the debenture holders or their trustees power to appoint a receiver, or a receiver and manager, sometimes by reference to the relevant sections of the Law of Property Act 1925, but more usually with wide extensions and variations of these provisions.[11] The power to appoint is usually made exercisable as soon as the principal money becomes payable or the interest is in arrear for a specified number of days: or so soon as interest in arrear is demanded. If the principal money is made payable on demand, this means what it says: the company is not entitled to any more time for raising the money than is required to fetch it from a secure place, such as a vault or bank.[12] If made exercisable by reason of the company being wound up, it cannot be exercised solely upon this ground without the leave of the court.[13]

Where the power is conferred upon trustees, or one or more of the holders of a class of debentures all ranking *pari passu*, such a power is a fiduciary power, to be exercised by the appointor bona fide in the interests of all the debenture holders.[14]

Position of receivers of the property of a company. The position and powers of such receivers are derived from and depend upon the contract between the parties expressed by the authorising instrument, as modified by statute.[15] Except where the context of the statute otherwise requires, the statutory provisions contained in the Companies Act 1948 relating to receivers and managers of the property of a company apply to a receiver or manager of part only of that property, and to a receiver only of the income arising from that property or from part of it.[16] Further, any reference in that

---

[10] The opinion expressed by Kay J. to the contrary in *Blaker* v. *Herts and Essex Waterworks* (1889) 41 Ch.D. 405, 406, it is submitted, without justification. The dicta relate to a power of sale; the case under discussion was one of a public undertaking, where no power of sale could be implied. See also *Deyes* v. *Wood* [1911] 1 K.B. 806.

[11] See Palmer's *Company Precedents* (16th ed.), Vol. III, Chap. 28.

[12] *Cripps (Pharmaceuticals) Ltd.* v. *Wickenden* [1973] 1 W.L.R. 944.

[13] Law of Property Act 1925, s. 110.

[14] *Re Maskelyne British Typewriter Co.* [1898] 1 Ch. 133.

[15] See especially Companies Act 1948, ss. 366 to 376.

[16] Companies Act 1948, s. 376 (*a*).

Act to the appointment of a receiver or manager under powers contained in an instrument includes a reference to an appointment made under powers which, by virtue of any enactment (such as the Law of Property Act 1925) are implied in and have effect as if contained in an instrument.[17]

But a person so appointed is not a " manager " of the company (as distinct from the property of the company) within the definition section [18] of the Companies Act 1948. Hence he cannot be made liable for misfeasance under section 333 of the Act by unsecured creditors or contributories, to whom in any event he owes no duty.[19] This does not mean that, in properly constituted proceedings, he can never be liable to the company.[20]

Conditions for appointment. Clearly, the conditions specified in the debenture, or otherwise imposed by statute, should be complied with before any appointment of a receiver can be made.[21] It sometimes happens, however, that the company by its board invites the debenture holders to appoint a receiver even though the specified conditions have not been fulfilled. In such cases, the invitation and appointment are together thought to constitute *pro tanto* a contractual variation in the terms of the debenture. Similarly, if the company acquiesces in the appointment although the specified conditions have not been fulfilled, it may be held to have accepted the validity of the appointment.[22]

Who may be appointed. A body corporate may not be appointed receiver of the property of a company. Such a body acting as receiver is liable to a fine of £100.[23] Any such purported appointment is a nullity.[24] Though there is no prohibition as such against his appointment, an undischarged bankrupt who acts as receiver or manager of the property of a company on behalf of debenture holders commits a criminal offence,[25] though this does not apply where the appointment under which he acts and the bankruptcy

[17] Companies Act 1948, s. 376 (*b*).
[18] s. 455 (1).
[19] *Re B. Johnson & Co.* (*Builders*) *Ltd.* [1955] Ch. 634. It would appear to follow that if an auditor is appointed as such, he will still be qualified for reappointment as such in spite of *ibid.* s. 161 (2) (*a*).
[20] See p. 292, *ante*.
[21] As to the common case where the money received is payable on demand and a receiver may be appointed as soon as default is made, see text to n. 12, p. 310, *ante*.
[22] *Cf.* n. 12, p. 310, *ante*.
[23] Companies Act 1948, s. 366.
[24] *Portman Building Society* v. *Gallwey* [1955] 1 All E.R. 227.
[25] Companies Act 1948, s. 367 (1).

were both before July 1, 1948.[26] Subject to these special provisions, the general principles as to appointments already discussed [27] will be applicable.

Method of appointment. The method of appointment must comply with any formalities required by the debentures or the trust deed. If none is specified, the receiver may be appointed under hand,[28] except in a case where he has power to execute a deed [29] in the name of the debenture holders, when like any other agent appointed for this purpose he must be appointed by deed. There is no objection to the appointment being prepared in advance since it will only take effect when communicated to the receiver.[30]

Effect of appointment. The effect of the appointment out of court is as regards the crystallisation of the floating charge into a fixed charge [31] and the consequences as regards judgment creditors [32] the same as in the case of an appointment by the court.[33] The powers of the company and its directors to deal with the property comprised in the appointment [34] (both property subject to a floating charge and property subject to a fixed charge), except subject to the charge, are paralysed; for though under debentures or a trust deed in the usual form the receiver is agent for the company, the company's powers are delegated to the receiver so far as regards carrying on the business or collecting the assets; and frequently so as to enable the receiver as attorney to convey a legal estate. The actual powers, however, depend on the terms of the instrument; if they are defective, as, for example, if they give no sufficient power to carry on the business, it is often necessary to apply to the court to make the appointment, or for a vesting order to vest the legal estate in a purchaser.[35]

---

[26] Companies Act 1948, s. 367 (2).

[27] p. 286, *ante.*

[28] For a precedent, see Palmer's *Company Precedents* (16th ed.), Vol. III, Chap. 35, and as to a possibly invalid deed taking effect as an appointment in writing see *Windsor Refrigerator Co. Ltd.* v. *Branch Nominees Ltd.* [1961] Ch. 375.

[29] *Berkeley* v. *Hardy* (1826) 5 B. & C. 355.

[30] *Windsor Refrigerator Co. Ltd.* v. *Branch Nominees Ltd., supra.*

[31] See *Kasofsky* v. *Kreegars* [1937] 4 All E.R. 374 and pp. 161, 162, *ante.*

[32] See *Cairney* v. *Back* [1906] 2 K.B. 746 and p. 162, *ante.*

[33] p. 161, *ante.*

[34] Property held by the company upon trust for third parties is not comprised in the appointment. *Aluminium Industrie Vaassen B.V.* v. *Romalpa Aluminium Ltd.* [1976] 2 All E.R. 552. See p. 282, *ante.*

[35] Law of Property Act 1925, ss. 91, 92; Trustee Act 1925, s. 44 (ii) (*b*), where a corporation has been dissolved.

The right of the receiver against execution creditors is governed by the same principles as in the case of an appointment by the court.[36]

In other respects the effect of the appointment differs from that of an appointment by the court; persons with paramount rights, such as prior incumbrancers, can exercise those rights without leave; for the receiver appointed out of court is not an officer of the court but an agent of the company or of the debenture holders.[37]

Property in the United Kingdom comprised in a floating charge. A receiver appointed under the law of any part of the United Kingdom in respect of the whole or part of any property or undertaking of a company and in consequence of the company having created a charge which, as created, was a floating charge, may exercise his powers in any other part of the United Kingdom so far as their exercise is not inconsistent with the law applicable there.[38] In Scotland, subject to due registration, a floating charge will comprise any heritable property there to which it relates notwithstanding that the instrument creating it is not recorded in the Register of Sasines.[39]

Having regard to the wide powers which are conferred by statute upon receivers appointed whether in or out of court in Scotland,[40] it is extremely unlikely that the debenture would contain any powers which would not be valid under Scots law. However, the appointment will be subject:

(i) to the rights of persons who have effectually executed diligence (*i.e.* levied execution) on all or any part of the property of the company prior to the appointment of the receiver; and

(ii) to the rights of any person who holds over all or any part of the property of the company a fixed security or floating charge having priority over, or ranking *pari passu* with, the floating charge by virtue of which the receiver was appointed.[41]

A person transacting with a receiver appointed pursuant to a

---

[36] pp. 47 *et seq., ante.*   [37] pp. 321–322, *post.*

[38] Administration of Justice Act 1977, s. 7 (1). The 1977 Act repeals Companies (Floating Charges and Receivers) (Scotland) Act 1972, s. 15 (4). In the above provision, " receiver " includes a receiver and manager: 1977 Act, s. 7 (2).

[39] Companies (Floating Charges and Receivers) (Scotland) Act 1972, s. 3. This does not appear to be restricted to a floating charge created by a Scottish company. *Cf.* s. 2, which lays down the formalities requisite for the creating of such a charge by such a company, and which clearly does not apply to the case being considered in the text.

[40] *Ibid.* s. 15 (1).   [41] *Ibid.* s. 15 (2).

floating charge granted by a company which the Court of Sessions has power to wind up is not concerned to inquire whether any event has happened to authorise the receiver to act.[42] It is not clear to what extent this provision applies in relation to receivers of the property of a company incorporated in England with property in Scotland.

There should be no particular problem so far as property in Northern Ireland is concerned.

Property comprised in appointment. It is, of course, purely a matter of construction of the instrument of charge as to what property of the company [43] is comprised in that charge, and of the appointment as to what property is included therein. Under all forms of floating charge, however, the company is at liberty to create charges and other similar rights, at least in the ordinary course of business, ranking in priority to the floating charge, even after it has crystallised. If the receiver nevertheless obtains possession of such property, he must account for it to the prior incumbrancer.[44]

It is also important to bear in mind that there may well be statutory rights under modern legislation—*e.g.* the right to detain an aircraft for unpaid fees and charges—which are exercisable against the chattel concerned irrespective of the existence of a fixed charge, and which a receiver is therefore powerless to prevent.[45]

Limited appointment. In some cases on an application by holders of a floating charge for the appointment of a receiver the court has excluded from the appointment property which is valueless to the holders of that charge, such as property mortgaged up to its full value to specific mortgagees. It appears to follow that on an appointment by debenture holders out of court any particular items of property may be excluded, with the result that the charge is not crystallised but continues to float as regards that property; but this can only be done where the power to appoint a receiver expressly authorises the appointment to be made over a part, as is the case with the statutory power.[46] The point has however not been expressly determined [47]; and it is suggested that if the

---

[42] *Ibid.* s. 15 (3). *Cf.* Law of Property Act 1925, s. 109 (4).

[43] See *ante*, p. 282, as to property held in trust.

[44] *Re Aranco Co.* (1898) 79 L.T. 336.

[45] *Channel Airways Ltd.* v. *Manchester Corporation* [1974] 1 Lloyd's Rep. 456.

[46] See Law of Property Act 1925, s. 101 (1) (iii).

[47] The decision in *Evans* v. *Rival Granite Quarries Ltd.* [1910] 2 K.B. 799 is not to the contrary, but only negatived the right of the holder of a floating charge to claim any particular item against, *e.g.* a judgment creditor, until the security had been crystallised into a fixed charge by the accepted method.

debenture holders elect to exclude from the appointment any particular item of property, this may preclude them from afterwards extending the appointment to that item.

Regularity of appointment. A receiver appointed by debenture holders should before accepting the appointment satisfy himself that the appointment is properly made in accordance with the provisions of the debentures or trust deed, and where there is more than one debenture holder that the requisite majority has concurred. If there is any flaw in his appointment, or if the debentures under which he is appointed do not constitute a valid charge, he may find himself liable as a trespasser to the liquidator in a subsequent winding up, or to the trustee in bankruptcy of a vendor to the company [48]; although as an alternative the liquidator or trustee may elect to treat him as their agent. [49] If the floating charge contained in the debentures becomes invalid on the liquidation of the company under section 322 of the Companies Act 1948 as being issued by the company, when insolvent, otherwise than for cash within 12 months of the winding up, the appointment is not void *ab initio* and the receiver will be fully entitled to act in the normal way until liquidation. [50] But on the winding up he will be accountable to the liquidator for all property in his hands, [51] and he cannot properly act after its commencement. The receiver may also be liable as a trespasser where the company has no title to property included in the security, *e.g.* where a sale to it is set aside as a fraud on the creditors of the vendor. [52]

Relationship with board of directors. Although as regards the outside world the receiver is the sole person in charge of the company's operations, nevertheless the corporate structure of the company still subsists. The directors are not thereby relieved of their normal statutory duties, although the discharge of those duties may well be rendered extremely difficult or even impossible without the co-operation of the receiver, which they are in no position to require. Moreover, the directors are entitled to use the name of the company for the purposes of litigating the validity of the security under which the appointment has taken place, [53] and

---

[48] See *Re Goldburg* [1912] 1 K.B. 606; *cf. Re Simms* [1934] 1 Ch. 1.

[49] *Ex p. Vaughan* (1884) 14 Q.B.D. 29; *Re Simms, supra.*

[50] *Burston Finance Ltd.* v. *Speirway* [1974] 1 W.L.R. 1648, *per* Walton J. at p. 1657E.

[51] As in *Re Destone Fabrics Ltd.* [1941] Ch. 319.   [52] *Re Simms* [1934] Ch. 1.

[53] *Hawkesbury Development Co. Ltd.* v. *Landmark Finance Pty. Ltd.* (1969) 92 W.N.(N.S.W.) 199 (Australia).

presumably also for bringing the kind of actions for damages for gross negligence which, in an ordinary mortgage situation could be brought by the mortgagor against a receiver.[54]

Notice of appointment. Notice of the appointment must be given by the person making the same to the registrar of companies within seven days of the appointment; the notice is then entered in the charges register.[55]

Notice on letters, etc. Notice of the appointment must be given on every invoice, order, or business letter issued by or on behalf of a receiver, manager, or liquidator, in which the name of the company appears.[56]

Receiver's statutory obligations. The receiver's duties in connection with invoices, orders and business letters have just been considered. In addition the receiver is under a large number of other statutory duties.

(a) *Notice to the company.* If he is appointed receiver or manager of the whole, or substantially the whole, of the property of a company registered in England, on behalf of debenture holders whose security includes a floating charge, he must forthwith (*i.e.* as soon as reasonably practicable) send to the company notice of his appointment in the prescribed form.[57]

(b) *Statement of affairs.* With certain necessary and appropriate modifications, the provisions of sections 372 and 373 of the Companies Act 1948 relating to the obtaining and furnishing of a statement of affairs by a receiver or manager of the whole, or substantially the whole, of the property of a company registered in England, on behalf of debenture holders whose security includes a floating charge, apply to such a receiver appointed out of court.[58] The modifications are:

(i) the deletion of references to the court in subsection (1) of section 372 [59];

---

[54] See pp. 292–293, *ante.*

[55] Companies Act 1948, s. 102 (1) as amended by Companies Act 1976, s. 42 (2) and Sched. 3. Even prior to the amendment no fee was prescribed by the Companies (Fees) Regulations 1967 (S.I. 1967 No. 1557).

[56] Companies Act 1948, s. 370 (1). See as to the effect of failure to make such disclosure *Moon Workshops* v. *Wallace* (1950) C.L.C. 1752. The penalty for default is £20: *ibid.* s. 370 (2).

[57] *Ibid.* s. 372 (1) (*a*) as amended by Companies Act 1976, s. 34 and Sched. 1. The prescribed form is No. 108 in the Schedule to the Companies (Forms) Order 1949 (S.I. 1949 No. 382): Companies Act 1976, s. 34 (2).

[58] See pp. 204 *et seq., ante.*

[59] Companies Act 1948, s. 372 (3): see p. 206, *ante.*

(ii) the substitution in sections 372 (2) and 373 of references to the Board of Trade for references to the court [60]; and

(iii) the substitution in section 373 (2) of references to a statutory declaration for references to an affidavit.[61]

(c) *Preferential debts.* The obligation of a receiver to discharge the preferential debts out of property subject to a floating charge in priority to the claims of the debenture holders is the same as in the case of a receiver appointed by the court.[62] The relevant date for determining whether the charge is fixed or floating is the date of the appointment; there is therefore no obligation to discharge preferential debts incurred by the company after the appointment in respect of property excluded from the appointment, and upon which the charge continues to float, out of the property on which the charge becomes fixed by virtue of the appointment.[63] If the receiver fails to comply with the statutory obligation, he becomes personally liable in damages to the disappointed preferential creditors.[64]

The right of recoupment out of the general assets not subject to the debenture holders' charge [65] would, it seems, be enforceable by the receiver on summons in the winding up.

(d) *Accounts.* Except where he is under an obligation to furnish the accounts required by section 372 (2) of the Companies Act 1948,[66] *viz.* where he has been appointed over the whole, or substantially the whole of the property of a company registered in England on behalf of debenture holders whose security comprises a floating charge,[67] a receiver appointed under the powers contained in any instrument [68] must deliver to the registrar of companies for registration an abstract in the prescribed form [69] showing his receipts and payments during the period of the first six months of his appointment. Thereafter, an abstract is to be delivered in respect of each successive period of six months, in each case within

---

[60] Companies Act 1948, ss. 372 (3) and 373 (4): see p. 207, *ante.*

[61] Companies Act 1948, s. 373 (4).

[62] See pp. 207 *et seq., ante.*

[63] *Re Griffin Hotel Co. Ltd.* [1941] Ch. 129.

[64] *Woods* v. *Winskill* [1913] 2 Ch. 303; *Westminster Corporation* v. *Haste* [1950] Ch. 442.

[65] Under Companies Act 1948, s. 94 (5). See, *e.g. Re Yagerphone* [1935] Ch. 392 (money recovered in respect of a fraudulent preference).

[66] See p. 316, *ante.*

[67] Companies Act 1948, s. 372 (1).

[68] See note 79, p. 319, *post.*

[69] Form No. 57 in the Schedule to the Companies (Forms) Order 1949 (S.I. 1949 No. 382): see pp. 390 and 391, *post.*

one month, or such longer period as the registrar may allow, after the expiration of that period. On ceasing to act, the abstract must be delivered within one month, and should include the figures from the last abstract up to the date of so ceasing. Each abstract after the first must also show the aggregate amount of his receipts and of his payments during all preceding periods since his appointment.[70] A penalty of £5 is incurred for every day of default.[71]

The receiver is not a debtor to the company in respect of such sums as may ultimately prove to be the balance in his hands due to it after discharge of the debenture holders' claims, preferential debts, and any other proper payments, even though his accounts show that something will probably be due. Consequently, such sums cannot be the subject of a garnishee order.[72]

Where a receiver is appointed out of court, and subsequently the same person is appointed in a debenture holders' action, his accounts are taken in the action: if a different person is appointed, the first receiver may apply by summons to have his account taken in the action.[73]

Enforcement of duties under the Companies Act. If any receiver or manager of a company makes default in filing, delivering, or making any return, account, or other document, or in giving any notice as by law required from a receiver [74] after a 14-day notice to make good the default, the registrar or any member or creditor may apply for an order directing the receiver or manager to make good the default within such time as may be specified in the order,[75] without prejudice to any penalties incurred in respect of such default.[76] The application is by originating summons.[77]

Other statutory obligations. There are other statutory obligations according to the nature of the trade or business which is carried on, and which it is impossible to specify in detail. Thus, for example, a receiver carrying on a business is liable as occupier to penalties under section 155 of the Factories Act 1961.[78]

It is essential for a person appointed to be receiver and manager of a business to obtain advice from persons skilled in the conduct of that business.

---

[70] Companies Act 1948, s. 374 (1).
[71] *Ibid.* s. 374 (2).
[72] *Seabrook Estate Co. Ltd.* v. *Ford* [1949] 2 All E.R. 94.
[73] *Practice Note* [1932] W.N. 79.
[74] See p. 316, *ante.*
[75] Companies Act 1948, s. 375 (1) and (2).   [76] *Ibid.* s. 375 (3).
[77] R.S.C., Ord. 102, r. 2 (1).   [78] *Meigh* v. *Wickenden* [1942] 2 K.B. 160.

Application for directions. A receiver or manager of the property of a company appointed under the powers contained in any instrument [79] may now apply to the court [80] for directions in relation to any particular matter arising in connection with the performance of his functions, and on such an application the court may give such directions, or may make such order declaring the rights of persons before the court or otherwise, as the court thinks just. [81]

Liability in respect of property. A receiver will incur many liabilities in respect of the property comprised in the security, more especially as regards the supply of gas, water and electricity, rates and income tax.

(a) *Gas, water and electricity.* Where the receiver is agent for the company, there is no change in the occupier of the premises and consequently he is as a rule not entitled to enter into a fresh agreement for any such supply, but is bound to discharge any arrears if he requires the supply to be continued. [82] Where he is agent for the debenture holders, the position is exactly the same as if he were appointed by the court. [83]

(b) *Rates.* Debentures and debenture trust deeds usually make provision for the payment of rates, taxes and other outgoings by the receiver: but as in the case of the similar provisions in section 109 (8) of the Law of Property Act 1925, this provision only defines the position between the company and the debenture holders; it does not enable a local authority to sue the receiver for rates. [84] The receiver may become personally liable to assessment if he personally takes such possession as constitutes rateable occupation. [85]

---

[79] This includes a reference to an appointment made under powers which, by virtue of any enactment, are implied in and have effect as if contained in an instrument: Companies Act 1948, s. 376 (*b*).

[80] *i.e.* the court having jurisdiction to wind the company up: Companies Act 1948, s. 455 (1).

[81] Companies Act 1948, s. 369 (1).

[82] See *Re Marriage, Neave & Co.* [1896] 2 Ch. 663; *Paterson* v. *Gas Light & Coke Co.* [1896] 2 Ch. 482.

[83] See p. 131, *ante.*

[84] *Liverpool Corp.* v. *Hope* [1938] 1 K.B. 751, and p. 296, *ante.*

[85] *Richards* v. *Kidderminster Overseas* [1896] 2 Ch. 212 (where the debenture expressly provided that on appointment the possession of the company should cease and that the receiver should take possession); *Re Marriage, Neave & Co.* [1896] 2 Ch. 663. As to what possession constitutes rateable occupation, see *Westminster Council* v. *Southern Ry.* [1936] A.C. 511, *per* Lord Russell at p. 529. *Cf.* Companies Act 1948, ss. 94 and 319.

(c) *Corporation Tax.* If, as is usually the case, the receiver is the agent of the company, and so long as he remains such agent, the corporation tax position remains unchanged: no fresh accounting period will have commenced with his appointment, and the company will be chargeable to tax on all the profits he makes as on any other part of its profits.[86] Normally, of course, there will be losses against which any profits made by the receiver can be set, so that the actual payment of the tax will not often arise. It is provided that everything to be done by a company under the Taxes Acts is to be done by the company acting through the proper officer of the company, and similarly that any documents under those Acts which require to be served on the company may be served on such proper officer.[87] The expression " proper officer " is then defined as the secretary, or person acting as the secretary of the company, or, if the company is in liquidation, the liquidator.[88] Where there is no such proper officer, then the responsible person is the treasurer, or person acting as treasurer, of the company.[89]

Since the word " treasurer " in relation to a company is clearly not in any sense a term of art, and it is postulated that there will be such a person when there is no person acting as secretary of the company, it would appear to be likely that a receiver will be comprised within this term.

In this case also it is clear that there will not be a change in the persons engaged in carrying on the trade of the company within the meaning of section 154 of the Income and Corporation Taxes Act 1970, so that losses can be carried forward. Similarly, there would be no succession where a receiver was appointed by prior incumbrancers after an appointment by subsequent incumbrancers: each receiver would be accountable as being entitled to the income during the receivership.

If, alternatively, the receiver is the agent of the debenture holders, and thus cannot under any circumstances be regarded as the " treasurer " of the company, it would appear that resort must be had to the fiduciary character of a receiver, and to have regard to the company—the company which created the debenture or the company (or individuals) having the benefit thereof. For a company is chargeable to corporation tax on profits accruing for

---

[86] Income and Corporation Taxes Act 1970, s. 243 (1).
[87] Taxes Management Act 1970, s. 108 (1).
[88] *Ibid.* s. 108 (3) (*a*).   [89] *Ibid.* s. 108 (3) (*b*).

its benefit under any trust, in any case in which it would be so chargeable if the profits accrued to it directly.[90]

If this is the correct way of looking at the matter, then so long, at any rate, as it remains uncertain whether or not the trade or business of the mortgagor company will revert to it at some future date, the profits would form part of those of the mortgagor company, and, once again, be available for setting off against past losses. But, once it became clear (as it might well do either upon the appointment of the receiver, or upon later liquidation) that there was no prospect of any return to the company, then the business would be carried on for the benefit of the debenture holders, and the profits would belong to them, and form part of their income, accordingly. There would also simultaneously be a fresh accounting period and a cessation of the company's former trade.

(d) *Landlord and Tenant Act* 1954. Anything authorised or required by the provisions of this Act, other than those relating to the supplying of information,[91] to be done at any time by, with, or to the landlord, or a landlord of a specified description, is, after the appointment of a receiver, authorised or required to be done by, to, or with the mortgagee instead of that landlord.[92] It follows also that if a mortgagee goes into possession, or appoints a receiver, between the making of an application by the tenant for a new lease and the hearing of such application, the mortgagee must be added as a respondent. If this step is not taken, the court has no jurisdiction.[93]

(e) *London Building Acts*. A receiver would appear to be an " owner " for the purposes of Part V but not Part XII of the 1939 Act.[94]

Receiver agent for the company. Debentures and debenture trust deeds usually provide in express terms that the receiver is to be agent for the company, as in the case of the statutory power. Sometimes this provision is omitted and in such cases it may be inferred from the terms of the instrument that the receiver is agent for the debenture holders, as, for instance, where he is given power

---

[90] Income and Corporation Taxes Act 1970, s. 243 (2). *Cf. C.I.R.* v. *Thompson* [1937] 1 K.B. 290 which was decided on Rules under Sched. D which no longer form part of the Code. As to an alternative view so far as Sched. B is concerned, see p. 299, *ante*.

[91] Under s. 40 (2), (3).

[92] s. 67. See *Meah* v. *Mouskos* [1964] 2 Q.B. 23.   [93] *Meah* v. *Mouskos, supra*.

[94] *Solomons* v. *Gertzenstein Ltd.* [1954] 2 Q.B. 243.

to carry on the business or other powers largely in excess of those conferred on receivers by statute.[95] When this is the case, the debenture holders will be themselves personally liable to persons dealing with the receiver, and also to the receiver for his remuneration.[96] Where debentures specifically incorporated certain of the provisions relating to receivers contained in the Conveyancing Act 1881, but conferred also large additional powers, including the power to carry on the business and to sell, the Court of Appeal held that there was sufficient contrary intention within section 24 (2) of the Conveyancing Act 1881 (now s. 109 (2) of the Law of Property Act 1925) to prevent the receiver being agent for the company, and that he was agent for the debenture holders, and therefore entitled to recover his remuneration from them.[97] But the omission to state in the debenture in express terms that the receiver is to be the agent of the company does not necessarily prevent him from being so. The question is one of construction in each case.[98]

The receiver's agency for the company is, of course, one with very peculiar incidents. Thus the principal may not dismiss the agent,[99] and his possession of his principal's assets is really that of the mortgagee who appointed him. He owes no higher duty to the principal than that of a mortgagee in possession.[1]

Effect of appointment on contracts. The appointment of a receiver with powers of management does not normally affect or determine contracts other than certain contracts of employment, as to which see generally Chapter 17, *post.*

In the case of contracts current at the date of his appointment which he elects to cause the company to fulfil, in default of provision to the contrary he will, like a receiver appointed by the court, be deemed to be carrying out contracts already entered into by the company: if he supplies goods in pursuance of them, persons to whom he supplies such goods can set off damages for subsequent breach against the price.[2]

---

[95] *Re Vimbos* [1900] 1 Ch. 470; *Robinson Printing Co.* v. *Chic Ltd.* [1905] 2 Ch. 123; *Deyes* v. *Wood* [1911] 1 K.B. 806.

[96] *Robinson Printing Co.* v. *Chic Ltd., supra.*

[97] *Deyes* v. *Wood* [1911] 1 K.B. 806.

[98] *Cully* v. *Parsons* [1923] 2 Ch. 512; dist. *Deyes* v. *Wood, supra; Central London Electricity* v. *Berners* (1945) 172 L.T. 289.

[99] *Per* Rigby L.J. in *Gosling* v. *Gaskell* [1896] 1 Q.B. 669, 692; his dissenting judgment in that case was upheld [1897] A.C. 575.

[1] *Re B. Johnson & Co. (Builders) Ltd.* [1955] Ch. 634, 644–645, 662.

[2] See p. 234, *ante.*

This is commonly and conveniently, if inaccurately, spoken of as the receiver " adopting " the contract; certainly merely by causing the company to carry it out he does not render himself personally liable thereon, as would be the case with a contract *de novo*. At any rate, unless to disregard the contract would adversely affect the realisation of the assets, or seriously affect the trading prospects of the company in a case where it will probably continue to trade, the receiver is not under the smallest obligation to " adopt " the contract: he may safely disregard it.[3] Specific performance of such a contract will never be ordered against the company.[4]

Generally the powers and duties of a receiver depend on the instrument under which he is appointed and the terms of his appointment. Prima facie it is his duty to preserve the goodwill, where he is authorised to carry on the business, although he owes no duty to the unsecured creditors or contributories of the company to preserve either the business or the goodwill of the company[5]: and it is thought that, provided the preferential debts are provided for, he would be justified in paying an unsecured debt due before his appointment, where payment is necessary to ensure a continuation of a supply of goods essential to the company's business.[6] But he must not pay statute-barred debts.[7] If, as is sometimes the case, he is appointed receiver without any powers of management his duty is to close down the business and collect the assets.

Liability of receiver to third persons in tort. If the receiver interferes with the rights of third parties,[8] however innocently, he is personally liable as a trespasser, and the company (or debenture holders, as the case may be) are in the same position as if he had acted within the scope of his authority. Thus, where a receiver and manager of the undertaking of a company had been appointed by debenture holders, and subsequently the assignment by the vendor to the company of the whole of the assets was set aside as

---

[3] *Airlines Airspares Ltd.* v. *Handley Page Ltd.* [1970] Ch. 193. In any event the receiver would appear to owe no duty *to the other contracting party* to " adopt " the contract. See *Ardmore Studios (Ireland) Ltd.* v. *Lynch* [1965] I.R. 1.
[4] *Macleod* v. *Alexander Sutherland Ltd.*, 1977 S.L.T. (Notes of Recent Decisions) 44.
[5] *Re B. Johnson & Co. (Builders) Ltd.* [1955] Ch. 634; *Kernohan Estates* v. *Boyd* [1967] N.I. 27.
[6] *Cf. Re Hale* [1899] 2 Ch. 107.   [7] See p. 197, *ante*.
[8] *Cf. Re Botibol* [1947] 1 All E.R. 26 and *Said* v. *Butt* [1920] 3 K.B. 497.

fraudulent within the Fraudulent Conveyances Act 1571 (now section 172 of the Law of Property Act 1925), in such circumstances that the title of the trustee in bankruptcy of the vendor related back, the receiver and the debenture holders were held liable as trespassers in respect of all such parts of the property in question as had come into the hands of the receiver, and an inquiry was directed as to the amount thereof: they were, however, only liable in respect of the actual property which had belonged to the bankrupt, not in respect of assets into which it had by sale been converted.[9]

In a similar case, where the trustee in bankruptcy again elected to treat the receiver as a trespasser,[10] he was not allowed to claim an account of profits against the receiver in respect of contracts completed by him.[11] A receiver who had been managing director of the company, sued with the company, was held not entitled to refuse to produce material documents in an action in which fraudulent conspiracy between the defendants was alleged, though he asserted that he now held the documents as agent for the debenture holders.[12]

Vicarious liability to third persons in tort. Since all employees engaged by a manager for the purpose of continuing the company's business will be employees of his principal (whether company, debenture holders, or their trustees) and not employees of the manager himself,[13] it is apprehended that a manager will only be liable in tort to third parties vicariously in the same classes of cases as directors would be.[14] That is to say, only where he has either (i) directly or by necessary implication authorised the tort committed or (ii) has been otherwise privy thereto.[15] Apart from these classes of cases, the principal of the tortious employee and such employee himself will alone be liable.

Liability of receiver's principal. Assuming the receiver has a principal (*i.e.* the company of the debenture holders, as the case

---

[9] *Re Goldburg* [1912] 1 K.B. 606; *cf. Re Gunsbourg* [1920] 2 K.B. 426; *Re Herman* [1915] H.B.R. 41; *Re Dombrowski* (1923) 92 L.J.Ch. 415.

[10] See p. 280, *ante.*

[11] *Re Simms* [1934] 1 Ch. 1.

[12] *Fenton Textile Assocn.* v. *Lodge* [1928] 1 K.B. 1.

[13] *Owen* v. *Cronk* [1895] 1 Q.B. 265, *per* Lord Esher at p. 272.

[14] See *Cargil* v. *Bower* (1878) 10 Ch.D. 502; *Rainham Chemical Works* v. *Belvedere Fish Guano Co.* [1921] 2 A.C. 465, *per* Lord Buckmaster at pp. 475, 476; *Performing Right Society Ltd.* v. *Ciryl Theatrical Syndicate Ltd.* [1924] 1 K.B. 1; *British Thomson-Houston Co.* v. *Sterling Accessories Ltd.* [1924] 2 Ch. 33.

[15] *Stone* v. *Cartwright* (1795) 6 T.R. 411.

may be) such principal is liable to third persons in respect of frauds, deceits, concealments, misrepresentations, torts, negligences, or other malfeasances, misfeasances, or omissions of duty in the course of the performance of the receiver's duties, but not for acts done outside the agency, unless ratified or subsequently adopted.[16]

Liability to third persons in contract. The powers of the receiver as regards the making of contracts will be governed by the terms of the debenture under which he is appointed and the terms of his appointment, subject always to the fact that, as agent of the company he cannot of course exceed the company's own powers. Section 369 (2) and (3) of the Companies Act 1948 provides that a receiver or manager appointed out of court will, irrespective of the date of his appointment, to the same extent as if he had been appointed by order of the court,[17] be personally liable on any contract entered into by him in the performance of his functions after July 1, 1948,[18] except in so far as the contract otherwise provides, and entitled in respect of that liability to indemnity out of the assets. This provision does not limit any right of indemnity which he would have had apart from it, nor does it limit his liability in respect of contracts entered into without authority, or confer upon him any indemnity in respect of such liability.[19]

If a receiver ratifies a contract ostensibly made on behalf of the company by a person acting without the receiver's authority, such a ratification does not result in a novation of the contract (which would entail his becoming personally liable thereon); since the receiver is never a party to the contract, the provisions of section 369 (2) have no operation.[20] Ratification will have the normal result of relating back to the date of the contract.[20]

This statutory provision assimilating the position of a receiver appointed out of court to that of one appointed by the court makes a radical departure in the law, since before it a receiver was not in general [21] personally liable in contract, such liability being the liability of his principal, whether company or debenture holders.

---

[16] See *Lloyd* v. *Grace, Smith & Co.* [1912] A.C. 716; *Percy* v. *Glasgow Corp.* [1922] 2 A.C. 299.

[17] As to which see p. 225, *ante.*

[18] For an example of personal liability see *Re Mack Trucks (Britain) Ltd.* [1967] 1 W.L.R. 780.

[19] See pp. 225–226, *ante.*

[20] *Lawson* v. *Hosemaster Machine Co. Ltd.* [1966] 1 W.L.R. 1300.

[21] *Cf. Thomas* v. *Todd* [1926] 2 K.B. 511.

There is, however, nothing in the section to exclude the liability of the receiver's principal, and accordingly the third party would seem to have a choice of defendants.

If the receiver is an agent for the company, neither the trustees for the debenture holders who appointed him, nor the debenture holders themselves, are under any personal liability for debts incurred in carrying on the business.[22] If the receiver continues to carry on the business after his agency for the company has determined, he does not in a normal case [23] become an agent for the debenture holders,[24] but becomes a principal.[25]

Where the receiver has incurred personal liability in respect of which he is entitled to indemnity, his creditor cannot on a judgment against him issue execution against the company's assets,[26] but he can apply for payment out of the assets of the company by way of subrogation.[27] Although the receiver is not personally liable in respect of the contracts of the company made before his appointment, like any other agent he may be liable to repay money received by him under a mistake of fact, or a voidable contract, unless before action brought he has accounted to his principal, which he may do by payment into his receivership account.[28]

Contractual liens. If, under a contract made in the ordinary course of business [29] before the appointment of a receiver, who is the agent of the company, under a floating charge, the other contracting party obtains the right to a general lien over goods belonging to the company, that right may be exercised after the appointment of the receiver over any goods of the company which come properly [30] into the hands of such other party thereafter.[31] It is immaterial that the lien so conferred had not become exercisable before the appointment of the receiver, since the right to the lien antedated the appointment.[32] The only way in which,

---

[22] *Gosling* v. *Gaskell* [1897] A.C. 575; *Cully* v. *Parsons* [1923] 2 Ch. 512.
[23] See *Re Brown & Sons (General Warehousemen) Ltd.* [1940] Ch. 961; but note the comments thereon in *Re Wood* [1941] Ch. 112.
[24] *Gosling* v. *Gaskell* [1897] A.C. 575.
[25] *Thomas* v. *Todd* [1926] 2 K.B. 511. For a case where on special facts the receiver was held to be the agent of the company in liquidation, see *Re Northern Garage Ltd.* [1946] Ch. 188.
[26] See *Jennings* v. *Mather* [1902] 1 K.B. 1.
[27] *Re Rylands Glass Co.* (1905) 118 L.T.J. 87; the report in 49 S.J. is not to be relied upon.
[28] *Bissell* v. *Ariel Motors* (1910) 27 T.L.R. 73.
[29] See *Robson* v. *Smith* [1895] 2 Ch. 118 at p. 124.
[30] *George Barker Ltd.* v. *Eynon* [1974] 1 W.L.R. 462 at p. 466F.
[31] *Ibid.*   [32] *Ibid.* at pp. 473B–C and 475G.

otherwise than by agreement, the receiver could prevent the lien from attaching would be by ensuring that no goods of the company available to satisfy the lien fell into the hands of such party.[33]

Contracts: Set off. The position in relation to set off is in general the same whether the receiver is appointed in or out of court.[34] The principles applicable are those relating to the right of set off as against an equitable assignee.[35] For either the debenture contains a fixed charge upon all the future property of the company, thus assigning in equity the benefit of any contractual debt due to the company to the debenture holders immediately upon its coming into existence, or else the debenture contains a floating charge upon all the future property of the company, in which case the crystallisation of the floating charge produces the same equitable assignment by way of charge in favour of the debenture holders.

Obviously, in either case if at the date of the assignment the debtor holds a cross-claim against the company of such a nature that it can be set off no matter how such claim originated, set off is permissible in the absence of an express agreement to the contrary.[36] Nor will knowledge or notice of the existence of an uncrystallised floating charge alter the position.[37] Further, if subsequently the debtor becomes entitled to cross claims arising out of the same contract as the assigned claim, which may happen whether the receiver " adopts " the contract or elects not to cause the company to carry it out, these will afford a valid set off, no matter when they arise.[38]

In the case however, where the claims arise under one contract, and the cross-claim which it is sought to set off arises subsequent to the appointment of the receiver and under a different contract, the position is more complex. The general rule is undoubtedly that set

---

[33] *Ibid. per* Stamp L.J. at p. 471H.

[34] See *per* Russell L.J. in *N. W. Robbie & Co. Ltd.* v. *Witney Warehouse Co. Ltd.* [1963] 1 W.L.R. 1324 at p. 1340 and p. 234, *ante.*

[35] *Ibid.*; *Rother Iron Works Ltd.* v. *Canterbury Precision Engineers Ltd.* [1974] Q.B. 1; *Security Trust Co.* v. *The Royal Bank of Canada* [1976] A.C. 503.

[36] *Phoenix Assurance Co. Ltd.* v. *Earls Court Ltd.*, 30 T.L.R. 50, C.A.; *Rother Iron Works Ltd.* v. *Canterbury Precision Engineers Ltd., supra.*

[37] *Biggerstaff* v. *Rowatt's Wharf Ltd.* [1896] 2 Ch. 93; *Re Roundwood Colliery Co. Ltd.* [1897] 1 Ch. 373, C.A.

[38] *Young* v. *Kitchin* (1878) 3 Ex.D. 127; *Government of Newfoundland* v. *Newfoundland Ry. Co.* (1888) 13 App.Cas. 199; *Parsons* v. *Sovereign Bank of Canada* [1913] A.C. 160; *Lawrence* v. *Hayes* [1927] 2 K.B. 111.

off is not, in general, possible.[39] And this is so even although the receiver, in order to recover the claim, will have to sue in the name of the company, against which the cross claim lies.[40] This, however, is not an inflexible rule; and where the two contracts under which the claim and cross-claim respectively are both between the debtor and the company, and the second contract is intimately connected with the first, set off will be allowed notwithstanding that the claim under the second contract arises only after the equitable assignment.[41] And, although the limits of the doctrine are not easy to discern, in general set off will be allowed if the debtor can show some equitable ground for being protected against the receiver's demands.[42]

A receiver cannot claim to set off damages for breach of contract against moneys validly assigned absolutely to a person in contractual relationship with the company: his only remedy is by way of damages for breach of contract.[43]

Third-party insurance. The principles applicable are the same as in the case of a receiver appointed by the court.[44]

Extent of receiver's indemnity. If the receiver becomes liable to third persons in respect of acts done or contracts entered into by him in the course of his duties as receiver, he is entitled to indemnity out of the assets subject to the charge, unless he has forfeited such right by improper conduct, such indemnity extending to his costs as between solicitor and client.[45]

If the receiver is placed in a position in which he is liable to pay money to a third person, he is entitled to be indemnified by his principal, though the latter is not relieved from liability.[46]

Leasehold property. After the appointment of a receiver out of court, remedies of the landlord of leasehold properties belonging

---

[39] *Biggerstaff* v. *Rowatt's Wharf Ltd.* [1896] 2 Ch. 93; *Lynch* v. *Ardmore Studios (Ireland) Ltd.* [1966] I.R. 133; *Business Computers Ltd.* v. *Anglo-African Leasing Ltd.* [1977] 1 W.L.R. 578.

[40] *Watson* v. *Mid-Wales Ry. Co.* (1867) L.R. 2 C.P. 593; *Re Pinto Leite and Nephews* [1929] 1 Ch. 221, 233; *N. W. Robbie & Co. Ltd.* v. *Witney Warehouse Co. Ltd.*, *supra.*

[41] As in *Collins* v. *Jones* (1830) 10 B. & C. 777; *McKinnon* v. *Armstrong Bros. & Co.* (1877) 2 App.Cas. 531.

[42] *Rawson* v. *Samuel* (1841) Cr. & Ph. 161; *Barretts Case (No. 2)* (1865) 4 De G.J. & S. 756; *Handley Page Ltd.* v. *Commissioners of Customs and Excise* [1970] 2 Lloyd's Rep. 459.

[43] *Ashby Warner & Co. Ltd.* v. *Simmons* [1936] 2 All E.R. 697 (interpleader proceedings by the fund-holder).

[44] See p. 171, ante.

[45] *Williams* v. *Lister & Co.* (1914) 109 L.T. 699.

[46] *Adams* v. *Morgan* [1924] 1 K.B. 751.

to the company are unaffected: he can distrain or re-enter, if the rent is not paid by the receiver. He can also sue the company for the rent: but this remedy is generally useless, as the judgment cannot be enforced against the property of the company which is subject to the debenture holders' charge. It may therefore be to the advantage of the debenture holders for the receiver to abandon leasehold property which is burdensome and of no value.[47] The receiver cannot safely adopt this course unless it is clear that the assets are insufficient to discharge the debentures: and in all cases the approval of the debenture holders should be obtained. Apart from this the power of sale conferred on mortgagees authorises surrender of a lease for proper consideration. It is considered that a receiver with power to carry on the business can accept surrenders of leases and tenancies apart from the power conferred by section 100 of the Law of Property Act 1925 on mortgagees.

The receiver can in the name of the company exercise the right to claim renewal of a lease under Part II of the Landlord and Tenant Act 1954.[48]

Realisation.[49] As the duty of the receiver is to get in the assets, he can for this purpose sue in the company's name without the company's consent. Thus, where a contract for sale of land has been entered into by the company, he may sue for rescission and return of the deposit or alternatively for specific performance.[50]

Debentures as a rule confer upon the receiver a power to sell the property comprised in the security. In the absence of such a power the receiver has no power to sell: the sale must be effected by the debenture holders' under the statutory power.[51] The statement of the statutory powers of mortgagees under ordinary mortgages in Chapter 15 should be consulted.[52]

A mere power to sell does not enable the receiver to convey the legal estate: but express power to do so in the name of the company or in the case of specific legal mortgages of the mortgagee is usually conferred: this power is not affected by a winding up.[53]

---

[47] The receiver has no right of disclaimer, such as is now vested in the liquidator with leave of the court under s. 323 of the Companies Act 1948, as to which, see *Re Katherine et Cie* [1932] 1 Ch. 70.

[48] *Gough's Garages* v. *Pugsley* [1930] 1 K.B. 615 (a decision under the Landlord and Tenant Act 1927).

[49] As to capital gains tax, see p. 303, *ante*.

[50] *M. Wheeler & Co.* v. *Warren* [1928] Ch. 840.

[51] He can only convey the legal estate where the debenture constitutes a legal mortgage, and then only after the statutory power has become exercisable.

[52] See p. 284, *ante*.   [53] Law of Property Act 1925, ss. 126 (1), 205 (1).

Where the charge created by the debentures is only equitable, *e.g.* where there is a floating charge, the company must concur to convey the legal estate, the seal being affixed in accordance with the provisions of the articles, or, where there is a winding up, by the liquidator; unless in either case the debenture confers an express power on the receiver to convey in the name of the company. If it does, he can convey in the name of the company and affix his own seal.[54]

Where the debenture [55] or trust deed creates a legal mortgage the conveyance can be made by the debenture holder or trustees: but in that case the contract for sale should be entered into by them and not by the receiver in his own name: for the power conferred by section 104 of the Law of Property Act 1925 upon a mortgagee to convey the whole legal estate on sale applies where the mortgagee exercises the power of sale, and not when the receiver as agent for the company has sold. Where the conveyance is in the name of the company the debenture holder with a legal mortgage must concur to surrender his term or release his charge. For like reasons a second mortgagee must concur if the sale is expressed to be made by the company.

If the receiver or debenture holder attempts to sell before the power of sale has become exercisable, an injunction can be obtained [56]; so, if the sale is at such a gross undervalue as to be fraudulent.[57] But a sale by a mortgagee will not be restrained on mere proof that it is at an undervalue [58]; this is of course without prejudice to the right of the company to claim damages in respect of a negligent sale.[59]

A clause protecting a purchaser against irregularities may be effective.[60]

---

[54] Law of Property Act 1925, s. 74 (3). The purchase-money is expressed to be paid to the receiver.

[55] Debentures seldom do (and never should) purport to create a legal mortgage where they are more than one in number.

[56] *Hickson* v. *Darlow* (1883) 23 Ch.D. 690; Seton (7th ed.), p. 719.

[57] As to set-off where a sale is improperly made, see *Ellis' Trustee* v. *Dixon-Johnson* [1924] 2 Ch. 451; [1925] A.C. 48.

[58] See *Waring* v. *Manchester Ass. Co.* [1924] 1 Ch. 310, and see *Reliance P.B.S.* v. *Harwood-Stamper* [1944] Ch. 362 (a building society case where the provisions are reviewed) and *Leon* v. *York-o-Matic Ltd.* [1966] 1 W.L.R. 1450.

[59] *Cuckmere Brick Co.* v. *Mutual Finance* [1971] Ch. 949, C.A.

[60] See *Dicker* v. *Angerstein* (1876) 3 Ch.D. 600; *Selwyn* v. *Garfit* (1888) 38 Ch.D. 273. As to inquiries with regard to notices, see *Life, etc., Corp.* v. *Hand in Hand Society* [1898] 2 Ch. 230.

Power to carry on business. Power to carry on the business is usually conferred on a receiver, but he has no such power apart from express provision.[61] His powers are limited by the powers of the company as stated in the memorandum of association. But he will usually have sufficient powers to carry out tax saving schemes, and indeed it may (where the saving is certain) be his duty so to do.[62]

Power to borrow. It seems that a power to carry on a business implies a power to borrow [63] and to give creditors the benefit of his right to indemnity out of the assets, and that the receiver may pledge the assets as security for loans made to him, at all events if he has a power to sell.[64] It is a question of construction in each particular case whether he is authorised to borrow money on the security of the assets in priority to the debenture holders. Thus where he was authorised " to make such arrangements as he might think expedient," he was held to have such a power.[65] For his own protection he should see that the terms of his appointment give him express powers to borrow and create charges for loans. If they do not, and it is imperative that he should raise money, he should apply to the court for directions.[66]

Although a receiver may be the agent of the debenture holders, he is for some purposes to be treated as agent for the company, for instance, to enable him to sell or borrow on the security of the assets.[67] And in other cases the acts of the receiver may bind the debenture holders; thus, where the receiver consents to a prior mortgage of leaseholds including certain fixed plant in a sale of chattels over which the debenture holders' security extends, it is difficult, if not impossible, for the debenture holders to assert any claim to damages for severance, as the consent of the receiver was in their own interests.[68]

Calls. If the company is not in liquidation,[69] the receiver must

[61] See *Bompas* v. *King* (1886) 33 Ch.D. 279 as to his powers and indemnity.
[62] *Lawson* v. *Hosemaster Machine Co. Ltd.* [1966] 1 W.L.R. 1300.
[63] See *Ex p. City Bank* (1868) L.R. 3 Ch.App. 758; *General Auction Co.* v. *Smith* [1891] 3 Ch. 432.
[64] *Robinson Printing Co.* v. *Chic Ltd.* [1905] 2 Ch. 123; *Deyes* v. *Wood* [1911] 1 Ch. 806. In the former case it was held that the power to charge did not extend to debts accruing due after discharge.
[65] *Robinson Printing Co.* v. *Chic Ltd., supra.*
[66] Under Companies Act 1948, s. 369 (1); see p. 319, *ante.*
[67] *Robinson Printing Co.* v. *Chic Ltd., supra; Deyes* v. *Wood, supra.*
[68] See *Re Rogerstone Brick and Stone Co.* [1919] 1 Ch. 110; and p. 197, *ante.*
[69] See Chap. 19, *post,* for the position when it is.

apply to the court for directions,[70] which will presumably be
given as in the corresponding case of a receiver appointed by the
court.[71]

Remuneration. The remuneration payable to the receiver is
usually fixed by the debentures or debenture trust deed by reference
to and incorporating section 109 (6) of the Law of Property Act
1925. This section will normally apply without express mention.

[70] Under Companies Act 1948, s. 369 (1); see p. 319, *ante*.
[71] See p. 218, *ante*.

CHAPTER 17

APPOINTMENTS OVER THE PROPERTY OF A COMPANY [1]—CONTRACTS OF EMPLOYMENT

General. This chapter makes no attempt to deal with the general law of employment, which is now a specialist subject in itself, but solely with those aspects of such law which bear peculiarly upon receivers and managers.

Directors and other officers of the company. The appointment of a receiver by debenture holders has no effect whatsoever upon the position of the main officers of the company, the directors and the secretary, and that, whether the receiver is the agent of the debenture holders, or of the company, or (as would be the case where an appointment was made after the company was in liquidation) [2] himself a principal. The corporate structure of the company remains unimpaired, [3] and although the management and control of the assets comprised in the appointment is thereby taken completely out of the hands of the officers of the company, they remain as such officers, with all the usual statutory duties to discharge. There is nothing to prevent the Board from convening a general meeting of the company to put it into voluntary liquidation. [4]

The Board of Directors of the company may also, in some situations, still have active duties to perform. This will be obvious enough if the security under which the receiver is appointed does not extend to the entirety of the assets of the company. In any event, property which is held by the company in trust for third parties is obviously not caught by the terms of the security. [5] Its control therefore remains with the directors, upon whom falls the active duty of ensuring that the company carries out its duties as trustee.

Deemed insolvency for benefit of employees. Just as the appointment of a receiver by the court at the instance of the holders of

---

[1] As to the meaning of " company " see n. 1, p. 309, *ante.*

[2] See Chap. 19, *post.*

[3] *Hawkesbury Development Co. Ltd.* v. *Landmark Finance Pty. Ltd.* (1969) 92 W.N. (N.S.W.) 199, 209, *per* Street J.

[4] See p. 349, *post.*

[5] *Aluminium Industrie Vaassen B.V.* v. *Romalpa Aluminium Ltd.* [1976] 2 All E.R. 552.

debentures constituting a floating charge on the company's assets produces a deemed insolvency conferring certain rights on its employees,[6] so also does the appointment of a receiver or manager by or on behalf of the holders of such debentures of any property comprised in the charge.[7] If the receiver, when appointed, is the agent of the debenture holders, the situation will in all respects be precisely the same for this purpose as in the case of the appointment by the court.[8] If, on the other hand, the receiver is, as is the normal case, the agent of the company,[9] then the company will continue to be the employer of the employees, until liquidation.

Position where the receiver is the agent of the company. The general rule in this case is that the appointment has no effect whatsoever upon the contract of service, which continues as before the appointment.[10] It has already been noticed that, as is the case with the appointment of a receiver by the court, the appointment of a receiver out of court produces a deemed insolvency of the company, which event has certain consequences as regards the discharge of various claims by employees by the Secretary of State for Employment, and the vesting of the employees' rights in the Secretary of State accordingly.[11] Subject to this possibility, and the necessity of ensuring that all preferential payments [12] are properly made, the receiver is not personally involved in employment matters. He might, however, become personally so involved if he failed to procure the company to give an employee the minimum period of notice required under the Employment Protection (Consolidation) Act 1977,[13] or caused the company to dismiss the employee unfairly.[14] In these cases it could well be said that the receiver had caused the company to break the terms of the contract.

However, the appointment of the receiver must, of necessity, terminate the employment of a person occupying a management position which is of such a nature as to impinge upon the rights

---

[6] See generally pp. 167–171, *ante*.
[7] Employment Protection (Consolidation) Act 1977, s. 127 (1) (*c*).
[8] See pp. 167–171, *ante*.
[9] See p. 321, *post*.
[10] *Re Foster Clark Ltd.'s Indenture Trusts* [1966] 1 W.L.R. 125; *Re Mack Trucks (Britain) Ltd.* [1967] 1 W.L.R. 780; *Griffiths* v. *Social Services Secretary* [1974] Q.B. 468.
[11] See *supra*.
[12] See pp. 207–215, *ante*.
[13] s. 1.
[14] Following *Re Botibol* [1947] 1 All E.R. 26.

of the receiver to manage the company as he thinks fit. Where the contract of employment cannot subsist together with the receiver's appointment, the employment will be automatically terminated, and once again, apart from the question of discharge of any preferential claims, the receiver will not be further concerned.[15] However, such discharge will not necessarily follow automatically from the mere description of the appointment held.[15] In all cases it is necessary to scrutinise carefully the terms of the relevant contract to ascertain whether there is, in reality, any inconsistency between the terms of that contract and the functions and duties of the receiver. Thus, in one case it was held that the mere labelling of the position as that of " managing director " did not prevent the contract of service from continuing after the appointment, since, upon a close analysis, his position was no more than that of a closely supervised employee.[16]

The position of additional staff. If the receiver engages additional staff, including the dismissal and re-engagement of existing staff, or, indeed, if he causes the company to enter into any fresh contract with existing staff, he will be personally liable, in addition of course to the liability of his principal, the company, on that contract as if he were the direct employer.[17]

Position where the receiver is not the agent of the company. If the receiver is not the agent of the company when appointed (either because the debenture does not provide for him to become the agent of the company, or because it does but he is nevertheless appointed after the liquidation of the company)[18] or subsequently ceases to be such agent only because the company has gone into liquidation,[19] then his appointment, or such liquidation, produces the result that all the employees of the company are discharged, as in the case of the appointment of a receiver by the court. For the purposes of redundancy pay, as well as the general law of employment, such discharge is the act of the company, not of the receiver.[20]

---

[15] *Griffiths* v. *Social Services Secretary* [1974] Q.B. 468.
[16] *Ibid.*
[17] Companies Act 1948, s. 369 (2). Theoretically, the contract may " otherwise provide " (*ibid.*) but this rarely happens in practice. *Re Mack Trucks (Britain) Ltd.* [1967] 1 W.L.R. 780.
[18] See p. 350, *post.*
[19] See p. 350, *post.*
[20] Employment Protection (Consolidation) Act 1977, s. 93 (1).

If the receiver then re-engages any of the employees, he will do so either on behalf of the debenture holders as his principal, or on his own behalf as principal. Such re-engagement will normally be effective both to extinguish any claim against the company for damages for wrongful dismissal,[21] and to extinguish any immediate claim in respect of a redundancy payment.[22]

Sale of the business of the company. If the receiver sells the business of the company as a going concern, then quite clearly all the contracts of service with the company, or with the receiver (depending upon his status in the matter) will be automatically terminated.[23] It may not be practicable to give the statutory period of notice to the employees of the business, and in any event it is as well to avoid, where possible, any question of damages for breach of contract at common law or any claims for redundancy pay. In this connection the device, subsequently mentioned,[24] formerly adopted mainly for taxation purposes, of the receiver transferring the business of the company to a subsidiary formed specially for this purpose, is a useful device for these purposes also. For the dismissed employee can and will be offered immediate continued employment in the same job with the subsidiary company, which of course is controlled by the receiver, thus extinguishing any claims for breach of contract at common law,[25] and also ensuring that the employee, if he refuses the offer of continued employment in the same job in the same place, with only the employer changed, will lose his right to redundancy pay.[26] Further, when the receiver sells the shares in the subsidiary company, there will be no further problems. The receiver, even if an agent of the subsidiary company, is not personally liable in respect of its contracts, so that all personal liability will have come to an end on the transfer of the employee to the subsidiary company, and, as the receiver is in a position at the stage of transfer to control the activities of the subsidiary company, he can ensure that the steps necessary to secure that a proper offer of continued employment is made to each employee are taken. It is superfluous to add that on a sale off of the

---

[21] *Cf. Reid* v. *Explosives Co.* (1887) 19 Q.B.D. 264 (receiver appointed by the court re-engaging an employee: no damages against company for breach of contract).

[22] See p. 337, *post.*

[23] *Brace* v. *Calder* [1895] 2 Q.B. 253; *Re Foster Clark Ltd.'s Indenture Trusts* [1966] 1 W.L.R. 125.

[24] See p. 353, *post.*

[25] *Reid* v. *Explosives Co., supra.*

[26] See p. 338, *post.*

shares there is no change in the employer, and hence no difficulties with the rights of the employees.

Statutory minimum period of notice to determine employment. The Employment Protection (Consolidation) Act 1977,[27] lays down minimum periods of notice to determine contracts of employment, basically by reference to the length of continuous service of the employee concerned. Where there is a succession to the trade, business, or undertaking, of one employer, employment with such employer is regarded for this purpose as if it were employment with the successor.[28] Accordingly, for this purpose employment with the company and the receiver, whether as agent for the company, as agent for the debenture holders, or as principal, or any succession of these capacities, counts as one continuous period of employment. And it does not matter that the employment is under a succession of contracts.[29]

Although the receiver will not normally be concerned with the position which arises where he causes the trade, business, or undertaking of the company to be transferred to a subsidiary company, such company will be an " associated company " of the original company, and the continuity of employment will for this purpose continue unbroken by this change of employers.[30]

Redundancy pay. Redundancy pay is also basically calculated by reference to continuous periods of employment, on the same pattern.[31] A contract of employment is treated as terminated by the employer for the purposes of such payments when any rule of law operates so as to terminate the contract under which the employee is employed.[32] Accordingly, prima facie if any contract of service is terminated by the appointment of the receiver, or by the liquidation of the company, or by the sale of the business of the company, a redundancy payment will fall to be made by the employer.

However, in such a situation if, by agreement with the employee, the person who immediately after the change is the owner of the business (the receiver; the debenture holders acting through the

---

[27] s. 49.
[28] Employment Protection (Consolidation) Act 1977, Sched. 13, para. 17 (2).
[29] *Re Mack Trucks (Britain) Ltd.* [1967] 1 W.L.R. 780. *Cf. Deaway Trading* v. *Calverley* [1973] I.C.R. 546.
[30] Employment Protection (Consolidation) Act 1977, Sched. 13, para. 18.
[31] Employment Protection (Consolidation) Act 1977, s. 81 and Sched. 4.
[32] *Ibid.* s. 93 (1).

receiver as their agent; or the purchaser of the business) renews the employee's contract of employment, with the substitution of the new owner for the previous owner, or re-engages him under a new contract of employment, those provisions of the 1977 Act which apply in the case of a dismissal and re-engagement by a current employer will also apply. The result will be that the employee will not be regarded as dismissed for the purpose of the 1977 Act.[33]

Further, if the present owner of the business offers to renew the employee's contract of employment with the substitution of the present owner as employer in the place of the previous owner, or to re-engage him under a new contract of employment,[34] the relevant provisions of the Employment Protection (Consolidation) Act 1977,[35] will have effect in relation to that offer as they would have had effect in relation to the like offer made by the previous owner. The effect is that if the contract is offered to be continued without any change apart from the identity of the employer, or otherwise that the offer constitutes an offer of suitable employment in relation to the employee, and in either case the employee refuses that offer, he will lose his right to a redundancy payment.

---

[33] *Ibid.* s. 94 (2).
[34] *Ibid.* s. 94 (3), (4).
[35] *Ibid.* s. 82 (3)–(6).

CHAPTER 18

APPOINTMENTS OVER THE PROPERTY OF A COMPANY: EXTRA-TERRITORIALITY OF FLOATING CHARGES AND OF RECEIVERSHIPS

By the term " extra-territoriality " is here meant the recognition by, and the enforceability in, foreign jurisdictions of a floating charge created in the United Kingdom, and specifically under the laws of England, and of receivers appointed to enforce them, normally out of court, although many of the relevant principles are equally applicable to an appointment by the court. These questions become relevant only if the following circumstances are present:

(1) the charge charges property physically or juridically situate within that foreign jurisdiction and subject to its laws;

(2) the charge does not of itself constitute a charge created and possessing " territorial validity " according to those laws;

(3) the property charged is adversely claimed within that juris-diction either (a) by one or more individual creditors of the chargor, or (b) by a liquidator (or a person performing analogous functions) of the chargor or of its assets within that jurisdiction and subject to its laws.

Only in cases where a conflict arises between the chargee and an adverse claimant under paragraph (3) does it become necessary to consider the extent to which the claim of one party prevails over the other; in all but the most exceptional cases, the charge is effective and enforceable against the chargor itself in all jurisdictions in accordance with the comity of nations, subject to necessary compliance with the formal requirements of the *lex loci rei sitae*, *e.g.* the local mortgage law.[1]

This problem has already been briefly noticed in Chapter 6, *ante*,[2] in relation to the circumstances in which, and subject to what restrictions, the court will appoint a receiver over property in foreign parts; such an appointment will not be made by the court where it would be useless, and any order made can take

---

[1] See *Re Anchor Line (Henderson Brothers) Ltd.* [1937] Ch. 483, and further see *Carse* v. *Coppen*, 1951 S.C. 233 (Inner House), *infra*, p. 343.

[2] pp. 146–147, *ante*.

effect and be enforced only in accordance with the laws of the country where the property is situate. Where the property in question consists of immovable property, *i.e.* land, the primary title thereto is established in accordance with the local laws relating to such property. Since in the case of land that title almost invariably depends on, and is proved by, registration in the appropriate register, the person there registered as owner will be the chargor. Unless therefore the charge can be, and has been, registered against the land, the title vested in the chargor will in general be available to be claimed, attached or executed against by creditors of the chargor (whether local or themselves foreigners) or by a liquidator; indeed, the loan secured on such land may itself be governed by the law of the place where the land is situated.[3]

The main question here being considered, however, concerns not immovables, but movables, which are, of course, the principal class of assets which it is the purpose of a floating charge to charge. Such movable assets will include stock-in-trade, raw materials, book-debts (receivables), royalties and licence fees, but the precise classification of such items of property as movables depends upon the *lex situs*, that is to say, the law of the place where they are situate. It is, however, generally agreed that the location of a debt or other chose of action is the place where it is recoverable or enforceable [4]; unless it be a debt not due for payment, which appears to have no location.[5]

The attitudes of foreign jurisdictions to a floating charge in the general United Kingdom form will depend to a very large extent on whether the jurisdiction in question recognises the concept of the floating charge or does not recognise it at all. Having regard to the wide differences between the many possible jurisdictions, it is impossible to give more than a general indication of the principles likely to be applied in any particular case, and of those jurisdictions where such recognition will be or may be obtainable.

As already explained, the concept of the floating charge was " invented " by the English judiciary, based upon our system of equity law. That system of law was exported to the " old " British Dominions and to the former colonies, now the " new " Dominions, and forms part of their laws. Accordingly, the floating

---

[3] *B.S.A. Co.* v. *De Beers* [1910] 1 Ch. 354. Dicey & Morris (9th ed.), r. 155.
[4] Dicey & Morris (9th ed.), rr. 78, 81. *Arab Bank* v. *Barclays Bank* (*D.C.O.*) [1954] A.C. 495.
[5] *Re Helbert Wagg & Co. Ltd.'s Claim* [1956] Ch. 323.

charge is recognised, very much in the English form, in all the
" Anglo-Saxon " jurisdictions; it has also been directly introduced
into Canadian law by statutes which not only codified the law
relating thereto for the common law provinces, but also introduced
it *de novo* into the French-based law of Quebec,[6] and in the
Republic of South Africa, and in Rhodesia (strictly Southern
Rhodesia), which are still governed by Roman-Dutch law. In all
those jurisdictions, the English floating charge will, subject to
local requirements or variations, be enforced.

In the United States of America, the position is now regulated by
the Uniform Commercial Code (U.C.C.), which has been adopted
by all the States and Territories except the State of Louisiana, and
has accordingly replaced their original individual state laws; the
U.C.C. is almost, but not entirely, uniform, for there are local
variations affecting the State of New York and other states. The
U.C.C., by Article 9, establishes a class of " security interests,"
which is the name given to any charge given by a debtor to his
creditor over all or any of his assets to secure payment. Such
security interests are unenforceable unless duly " filed," either in
their entirety or as summarised in a " financing statement," in
the appropriate registers maintained by the state or states in which
the relevant assets are situated or (if they be mobile) are situated
for the time being.

The class of security interests recognised by Article 9 of the
U.C.C. necessarily includes what is known in United States law
as a " floating lien " [7]; neither that term nor the term " floating
charge " [7] are used in the Code itself, but they appear in the official
commentary to Articles 9–204, 9–205. Subject to due " filing,"
which corresponds approximately to the requirements of section 95
of the Companies Act 1948 (as amended), with respect to charges
created in England and Wales, and now Scotland, the policy of the
U.C.C. is to give the widest recognition to security interests, including floating liens; accordingly, United Kingdom floating
charges will, if filed in the relevant state or states where the assets
charged or to be charged are located, be fully enforceable in each
of those states. On the other hand, if such a charge be not so filed,
it will be invalid as against other creditors claiming those assets
adversely to the chargee.

---

[6] See *e.g.* the Special Corporate Powers Act (Revised Statutes of Quebec 1964, c.
275), s. 22 (a bi-lingual statute).
[7] Also known as a " continuing general lien " or a " lien on a shifting stock."

When one turns to countries other than those already referred to, where the concept of the floating charge is not juridically recognised at all, or only in extremely modified or limited forms, considerable difficulties are likely to arise. In the first place, in the absence of any system of local registration or " filing " of charges over assets (other than charges over land of which it is thought that registration is almost invariably provided), it is impossible for the " foreign " (i.e. United Kingdom) chargee to comply with any equivalent to the requirements of section 95, whereby priority of title and notice to other creditors are conferred.

In the second place, since the essence of a floating charge is that it may, or must, charge assets other than those which, at the time of its creation, are the property of, or in the possession of, the chargor, any such charge—of which ex hypothesi no public notice can be given—must operate to the detriment of existing or subsequent creditors. Such a charge may therefore, in the " civil law " jurisdictions, be impeached by means of " the Paulian action " (actio Pauliana) as a "fraud upon creditors." That form of action has a considerably wider ambit, and imports a good deal less in the way of express fraud, than does the English "fraudulent conveyance " under section 172 of the Law of Property Act 1925.[8] [See Appendix VII, post, on the Paulian action in relation to the Draft Bankruptcy Convention of the E.E.C.]

Even without the aid of a Paulian action to set the charge aside, creditors in a foreign jurisdiction may be held entitled to execute upon or to attach assets there situate, notwithstanding that they are charged by an ostensibly valid English floating charge.[9]

The situation with respect to such a jurisdiction is well illustrated by that which obtained in Scotland, itself in origin a " civil law jurisdiction," prior to the introduction of the English floating charge into Scots law by statute in 1961. Prior to that date, the Scottish courts had consistently refused to recognise or give effect to anything in the nature of a floating charge; for Scots law required delivery of property to the acquirer or to the recipient of it by way of security, either by actual delivery or its legal equivalent, e.g. in the case of the assignment of an incorporeal moveable such as a book debt, an actual assignment together with " intimation " (i.e. notice) to the book debtor, none of which could happen under

---

[8] See Re Eichholz (deceased) [1959] Ch. 708 and Lloyds Bank Ltd. v. Marcan [1973] 1 W.L.R. 1387.
[9] As in Re Maudslay Sons & Field [1900] 1 Ch. 602.

the English floating charge. The concept of a " floating charge "
was therefore " absolutely unmeaning." [10]

The approach of a jurisdiction which does not recognise a
floating charge is well illustrated by *Carse* v. *Coppen* (1951) S.C.
233, where there was a liquidation of a company registered in
Scotland, over the whole of whose assets (situated partly in Scotland and partly in England) a floating charge had been created in
England. The chargee conceded that he could not enforce his
charge over the Scottish-based assets, but he was even denied
enforcement over the English-based assets, for the Scottish court
declined to recognise the floating charge for any purpose. However
valid such a charge may be in its own home court of the English
Chancery Division, it had no extra-territorial validity.

This, and other analogous decisions, contributed to the Scottish
Law Reform Committee reporting [11] that the general need for a
floating charge to contribute to successful economic activity
required its recognition in Scotland as a security; but they declined
to go further than such recognition, and refused to recommend the
introduction of the institution of receivership; accordingly, such a
charge could only crystallise on the liquidation of the company.
Thus was conceived the Companies (Floating Charges) (Scotland)
Act 1961; in its operation, however, the absence of any provision
for the appointment of a receiver proved so disadvantageous that
the Act was largely repealed and re-enacted by the Companies
(Floating Charges and Receivers) Act 1972.[12]

Those Acts, in so far as they constitute, for the United Kingdom,
the first codification of the institution of the floating charge and of
receivership, are discussed elsewhere in this work.[13] What is here
significant is the refusal of the Scottish courts, until compelled so
to do by statute, to recognise these concepts at all.

Another illustration of the problems presented in the enforcement in a foreign, non-recognising, jurisdiction of an English
floating charge was provided by the facts of the litigation (in
1970–71) between *Rolls-Royce Ltd. (In Receivership)* and some
American creditors of that company. Having obtained judgments in
the English courts for the price of goods sold and delivered to Rolls-
Royce Ltd., they were baulked of any opportunity of executing

[10] *Ballachulish Slate Quarries Co.* v. *Bruce*, 1908 16 S.L.T. 48, *per* Lord Dunedin at
p. 51, cited in *Carse* v. *Coppen, infra.*
[11] Eighth Report, Cmnd 1017 (1960).
[12] Following a Report by the Scottish Law Commission, Cmnd. 4336 (1970).
[13] See pp. 162–163 and pp. 313–314, *ante.*

those judgments over the assets of that company in the United Kingdom, by reason of the prior claims of the receiver, under a floating charge which had crystallised. Accordingly, the creditors took steps to levy execution over the assets of Rolls-Royce Ltd., whether movable or immovable, in other countries, and in particular France, West Germany and the United States.

Since they had duly registered their judgments as required in each jurisdiction, the receiver was compelled to contend that his title was paramount to theirs, so as to enable him to have those executions set aside as levied on assets which no longer " belonged " to Rolls-Royce Ltd. The principal litigation took place in the French High Court (*Tribunal de Grande Instance*), and was (unfortunately for the clarification of the questions of private international law arising) settled by a compromise of the respective claims; but not before a considerable area of controversy had been demarcated between the parties.

The creditors, having duly registered English judgments, were entitled under French law and the application of the Franco-British Convention of 1934 on the Reciprocal Enforcement of Judgments,[14] to obtain *saisies-arrêts* on the Rolls-Royce assets in France. The receiver was compelled to concede and to contend:

(1) that the assets in question " belonged " to the legal person entitled " Rolls-Royce Ltd.";

(2) that, other things being equal, the creditors were entitled to levy execution on them; but

(3) that those assets had come, by virtue of the previous appointment of the receiver and the crystallisation of the floating charge, to " belong " to the trustees for the debenture holders, in whom the floating charge was vested.

Apart from the absence from French law at that time of any recognition of the concept of the floating charge, at least so as to postpone to its holder creditors lawfully levying execution, and the apparent lack of any French case-law to support the extra-territorial enforceability of the charge, great difficulty also arose from the peculiar characteristics of the office of receivership as practised then and now as the standard method of enforcing a floating charge by realisation of the assets of the chargor.

As discussed elsewhere in this work,[15] for historical and practical

---

[14] Cmd. 4717 (1933–34), enacted as S.R. & O. 1936 No. 609.
[15] See pp. 288 and 321–322, *ante*.

reasons, the receiver by the debenture or the trust deed is declared, and by section 109 (2) of the Law of Property Act 1925 is deemed, to be the agent of the company, as opposed to the agent of the debenture holder *qua* mortgagee. Accordingly, the " persona " of the company remains juridically unchanged, the only ostensible change being in the personality of its agents; the receiver is substituted for the Board of Directors and manages the company as they did. Indeed, in this very capacity, the receiver had, in the *Rolls-Royce* case, consented, on behalf of the company, to judgment being entered in the English High Court for the creditors, no doubt on the hypothesis that such judgment could not compete with the charge in favour of the debenture holders.

Such United Kingdom case-law as was placed before the French court in the sworn opinions delivered by each of the contestant parties principally comprised the decisions in *Liverpool Marine Credit Co.* v. *Hunter* [16]; *Re Maudslay Sons & Field* [17] (where the former case was discussed); *Re Vocalion (Foreign) Ltd.*[18] and *Galbraith* v. *Grimshaw*.[19] They did not touch the actual question at issue, whether the French court could, and should, prefer the execution creditors to the receiver for debenture holders or vice versa, but are of some assistance in illustrating the principles involved in the problem.

Liverpool Marine Credit Co. v. *Hunter* concerned an English ship-mortgage (*i.e.* a fixed charge) over a British ship granted by the owner to English lenders; the ship sailed to New Orleans, Louisiana, where it was attached by creditors of the owner to secure payment of their debts. All the attaching creditors were British subjects, trading both in England and at New Orleans. It was proved that by the law of Louisiana transfers of property in chattels (*i.e.* including a ship) without delivery of possession was not recognised, and accordingly the title of the English mortgagees was not regarded as precluding the New Orleans courts from attaching the ship as security for the debts of local creditors.

It was in the opinion of both courts plain that they could not deny to an English creditor of the debtor company the right, enjoyed by every creditor of the company, to enforce his debt against his debtor's property situate in Louisiana, and the courts'

[16] (1867) L.R. 4 Eq. 62, *affirmed on appeal* (1868) L.R. 3 Ch. 479, L.C.
[17] [1900] 1 Ch. 602. See p. 147, *ante*.
[18] [1932] 2 Ch. 196.
[19] [1910] A.C. 511. See p. 162, *ante*.

power to enjoin that creditor from that course could not, or at least should not, be exercised by way of discrimination against him as opposed to local creditors or to those of other nations,[20] even when that creditor was physically within the court's jurisdiction. Having regard to the fact that the charge in question was a fixed charge on an existing and tangible asset, the dicta must be applicable *a fortiori* to the case of a floating charge.

In *Re Maudslay Sons & Field*,[21] an English company had charged all its assets wheresoever situate to an English debenture holder, which had obtained the appointment of a receiver by the court; English creditors of the company thereafter attached debts due to the company from its French book debtor. It was established by expert evidence of French law that the English debenture was ineffective to convey to its holder any title to the debt, which could only be assigned under French law by an instrument in writing, duly registered and served on the book debtor in one of the recognised modes. In the absence of such an assignment, the debenture holder acquired no right valid as against third parties, including the company's creditors, who were entitled to attach the debt in the hands of the book debtor. It was held that " that assignment which alone is recognised by the law of France ought to prevail. . . . In other words, the receiver is not put in possession of foreign property by the mere order of the court. Something else has to be done, and until that has been done in accordance with the foreign law, any person, not a party to the suit, who takes proceedings in the foreign country, is not guilty of a contempt either on the ground of interfering with the receiver's possession or otherwise. For this purpose no distinction can be drawn between a foreigner and a British subject."

Applying comparable principles in *Re Vocalion (Foreign) Ltd.*[22] the English court refused to restrain a foreign corporation from enforcing its debt against an English company in the courts of its own country, notwithstanding that the company was in liquidation in England. Similarly, in *Re Suidair International Airways Ltd.*[23] the English court, which had made an " ancillary " winding-up

---

[20] Distinguishing *Simpson* v. *Fogo* (1863) 32 L.J. 249 and other cases where the foreign court had acted in defiance of natural justice and the comity of nations: *cf.* *Lord Cranstown* v. *Johnston* (1796) 3 Ves. 170.
[21] [1900] 1 Ch. 602: see at pp. 610–612, applying *Liverpool Marine Credit Co.* v. *Hunter, supra.*
[22] [1932] 1 Ch. 196: *cf.* Dicey & Morris (9th ed.) notes to r. 144 at pp. 714–715.
[23] [1951] Ch. 165.

order against a South African company carrying on business in England, upheld the claim of an English execution creditor levying on the company's assets in England against the claim of the South African liquidator.

Finally, in *Galbraith* v. *Grimshaw* [24] an English creditor's attachment in England of a debt due to a Scottish bankrupt was held to prevail against the title of the Scottish trustee in bankruptcy.

Applying all the foregoing principles, it would seem probable that the French court would have refused the claim of the English receiver in Rolls-Royce Ltd., that the executions over Rolls-Royce Ltd.'s assets in France should be lifted, on the ground that by French law neither the debenture holders nor their receiver had acquired any title to those assets, whether tangible or incorporeal, which could prevail over executions valid under French law.

If, however, a possible test of the probability of recognition by a foreign jurisdiction of the " civil law " type of an United Kingdom floating charge is based upon the existence of the concept of a floating charge, or its absence, in their jurisprudence, the position among such jurisdictions is by no means uniform. Japan, for example, possesses not merely one but two systems of floating charge, the one of indigenous origin, the other an importation from (seemingly) the Anglo-Saxon world.

In Federal Germany, the creation of some forms of security which somewhat resemble floating charges is steadily proceeding, partly by the expansion of simpler forms through the use of legal fictions. In France and Belgium, on the other hand, the position has advanced little beyond a charge on the goodwill of a business and a charge on manufacturing plant, machinery and tools. The position in Scandinavia and Holland somewhat resembles that in Federal Germany.

In none of these jurisdictions, however, can it reasonably be anticipated that the existence of some local species of floating charge, or its equivalent, will do more than to facilitate the creation by the English chargee of a comparable charge under local law and procedure, and, it may be, to render the local courts more sympathetic to the concept of security without dispossession of existing or future assets. Some details of analogous charges in other commercial countries are set out in Appendix VI.[25]

---

[24] [1910] A.C. 511.
[25] See p. 406, *post*.

Even in those jurisdictions where what we may now (since the Scottish statutes were enacted) call " the United Kingdom form " of floating charge may receive some degree of recognition, problems may arise in the field of preferential debts. In certain countries, such debts constitute preferential claims *per se* over the assets of the debtor, ahead of any other security, and *a fortiori* over any security of foreign origin, on grounds of *ordre public* (public policy). Such preferential claims are generally in the process of abatement in foreign countries (in contrast with the United Kingdom, where they tend to proliferate in number and in value); in France, for example, the super-preferential claims of the French Treasury (*le privilège du fisc*) have been made, to a limited extent, subject to public registration for the information of creditors. In the field, however, of the rights of the employees of insolvent businesses, the tendency may be regarded as in the opposite direction, and the aspect of *ordre public*, above referred to, may be becoming more pronounced.

This subject of the impact of preferential debts upon the rights of the floating chargee, which arises by reason of the provisions of sections 94 and 319 of the Companies Act 1948 (as amended) is dealt with elsewhere in this work,[26] where the question is considered, to what classes of preferential claim (whether arising abroad or at home) priority is conferred by those sections to the detriment of a United Kingdom chargee enforcing his rights by the appointment of a receiver in the United Kingdom.

---

[26] See pp. 207–215, *ante*.

CHAPTER 19

APPOINTMENTS OVER THE PROPERTY OF A
COMPANY [1]—THE EFFECT OF LIQUIDATION

Appointment of receiver no bar to winding up. A winding-up order must not be refused on the ground only that the assets of the company have been mortgaged to an amount equal to or in excess of their value, or that the company has no assets.[2] It follows that the court can make a winding-up order even though a receiver is in possession and although no benefit accrues to the creditors by the order. Thus a winding-up order was made where the receiver was incurring large liabilities [3]; and again where the business was being carried on in the interests of the debenture holders, and though the majority of the unsecured creditors opposed.[4] Conversely, if the debenture holder who has appointed the receiver can show any benefit to himself which might arise as the result of liquidation, he may himself petition for an order.[5] There is also no legal impediment to the company going into voluntary liquidation.[6]

Effect of winding up on appointment of receiver. Lack of registration under section 95 of the Companies Act 1948 is not a matter of which the company, whilst a going concern, can complain, but an unregistered charge is made void (so far as any security is concerned) not only against other creditors but also the liquidator of the company. For this reason no person will normally accept appointment as receiver under an unregistered charge,[7] although if he does so he may safely act until liquidation,[8] when he must account to the liquidators for all the assets then in his hands.

An order or resolution for winding up may, as a result of the application of section 320 of the Companies Act 1948, relating to

---

[1] As to the meaning of " company " see n. 1, p. 309, *ante*.

[2] Companies Act 1948, s. 225 (1).

[3] *Re Chic Ltd.* [1905] 2 Ch. 345.

[4] *Re Clandown Colliery* [1915] 1 Ch. 369.

[5] *Borough of Portsmouth Tramways Co.* [1892] 2 Ch. 362.

[6] Companies Act 1948, s. 278.

[7] Debenture holders who have actually seized chattels under an unregistered charge may be in a better position than a receiver who does not seize them as their agent: see *Re Toomer* (1883) 23 Ch.D. 254; *Wrightson* v *McArthur and Hutchisons* (1919) *Ltd.* [1921] 2 K.B. 807; *Mercantile Bank of India Ltd.* v. *Chartered Bank of India, Australia and China* [1937] 1 All E.R. 231.

[8] *Burston Finance Ltd.* v. *Speirway* [1974] 1 W.L.R. 1648, *per* Walton J. at p. 1657E.

fraudulent preference, or section 322 of that Act, relating to the possible invalidity of floating charges, have the effect of invalidating either the whole, or a portion of, the charges in respect of which the receiver has been appointed, and hence, either *pro tanto* or wholly, his appointment. Since section 320 relates to charges given within six months, and section 322 relates to floating charges given within 12 months, of the commencement of the liquidation,[9] no receiver who is appointed within such period of 12 months (in relation to a floating charge) or six months (whatever the nature of the charge) will usually be willing to act before such time limits have expired without either the most searching inquiry into the circumstances surrounding the giving of the charge, or more usually, an indemnity from the debenture holder.

Subject to the foregoing, neither the making of a winding-up order—nor, still less, the passing of a resolution to wind up—displaces the receiver appointed by the debenture holders,[10] or in any way terminates his powers.[11] Nor does it prevent the debenture holders from appointing a receiver if one has not already been appointed [12]; but after the making of a winding-up order the receiver must apply to the liquidator or the court in the winding up for liberty to take possession of any property of which he is not then in possession.[13] A receiver or manager must also, at any time whether during or after his tenure of office, when so required by the liquidator, render proper accounts of his receipts to the liquidator, vouch the same, and pay over to the latter the amount properly payable to him.[14] In default, the court may make an order, on the application of the liquidator, for this to be done within a specified time, and may order that all costs of and incidental to the application should be borne by the receiver or manager, as the case may be.[15]

Agency of receiver for company. On the commencement of the liquidation, the agency of the receiver for the company determines.[16] If he continues to carry on business after such determination,

---

[9] If the winding up is compulsory, this means the date of presentation of the petition: Companies Act 1948, s. 229; if voluntary, the date of the passing of the special resolution to wind up: *ibid.* s. 280.

[10] This topic is discussed *ante*, p. 108.

[11] *Gough's Garages Ltd.* v. *Pugsley* [1930] 1 K.B. 615, *per* Romer L.J. at p. 626.

[12] *Ante*, p. 109.

[13] *Ante*, p. 109.

[14] Companies Act 1948, s. 375 (1) (*b*).

[15] *Ibid.* s. 375 (1) (*b*) and (2); R.S.C., Ord. 102.

[16] *Gosling* v. *Gaskell* [1897] A.C. 575.

he does not in a normal case [17] become an agent for the debenture holders [18]; he becomes a principal.[19] Thus he will become personally liable on all contracts into which he enters, to the exclusion of the company. He will of course be entitled to a right of indemnity out of the assets in his hands.[20] After the commencement of a winding up he should if possible obtain authority from the debenture holders to continue to carry on business as their agent.

This determination of his agency entails that he can no longer convey property in the name of the company, even if the debenture so provides: this will have to be done by the debenture holder as mortgagee under the statutory powers,[21] or effected by the liquidator on behalf of the company with the debenture holder concurring. Alternatively, an application will have to be made to the court for a vesting order. The provisions of section 227 of the Companies Act 1948, which avoid any disposition of the property of a company after the commencement of the winding up, do not apply: the relevant " disposition " is of course the original charge under which the receiver has been appointed.[22]

If, however, part of the assets of the company over which the receiver is appointed consists of shares in a subsidiary company which is put into compulsory liquidation, the provision of this section will apply to any disposition of the assets of the subsidiary.[23]

As regards the property of the company charged to the debenture holder, including (if charged) its undertaking, this remains in the control of the receiver, who will continue to manage and deal with it as a principal.[24] Although the precise legal theory applicable has not been fully elucidated, it would appear that the receiver is entitled not merely to possession of all the physical assets of the company (as regards which he would be in the same position as debenture holders who had validly seized their security) but also solely entitled to all choses in action, such as the benefit of

---

[17] See *Re Brown & Son (General Warehousemen) Ltd.* [1940] Ch. 961; but note the comments thereon in *Re Wood* [1941] Ch. 112.

[18] *Gosling* v. *Gaskell* [1897] A.C. 575.

[19] *Thomas* v. *Todd* [1926] 2 K.B. 511. For a case where on special facts the receiver was held to be the agent of the company in liquidation, see *Re Northern Garage Ltd.* [1946] Ch. 188.

[20] Companies Act 1948, s. 369 (2).

[21] See pp. 284 *et seq., ante.*

[22] *Cf.* the position under ss. 320 and 322, pp. 349, 350, *ante.*

[23] See *Re Clifton Place Garage Ltd.* [1970] Ch. 477.

[24] See *Gosling* v. *Gaskell* [1897] A.C. 575.

contracts with the company existing at the date of the winding up.[25] And for enforcing such rights he may if required sue in the name of the company.[26]

Nature of receiver's status. Although the receiver is technically the principal, yet of course he is not acting on his own behalf. He is still acting as receiver of the company, and his possession and control is throughout for the benefit of the debenture holders and the company to the extent of their respective interests in the assets he holds. It has been held that in consequence, for the purposes of legislation governing employment, if the receiver transfers the business of the company to a third party, that transfer may be regarded as a transfer from the company, and not from the receiver himself personally, thus ensuring technical continuity of the employment.[27]

Effect of termination of agency

(a) *Contracts.* The receiver will be entitled to the benefit of all contracts entered into by the company as well before as after his appointment, and entitled to enforce the same. For this purpose he may if necessary use the name of the company in litigation.[28] It is not considered that liquidation has any effect on rights of set-off.

However, all contracts of personal service with the company will be terminated, as if the appointment was one made by the court.[29] Moreover, for the purposes of the Redundancy Payments Act 1965, such termination is treated as a termination by the company.[30]

(b) *Corporation tax.* Although the matter does not appear ever to have been considered by the court, it would appear that (if this has not already taken place) the winding-up order causes an immediate cessation of the company's trade or business, which (if

---

[25] *Gough's Garages Ltd.* v. *Pugsley* [1930] 1 K.B. 615 (right to apply for new lease under Landlord and Tenant Act 1927, s. 5, a right charged by company; receiver accordingly entitled to enforce that right in name of company notwithstanding liquidation).

[26] *Ibid.*

[27] *Deaway Trading Ltd.* v. *Calverley* [1973] I.C.R. 546 (a decision of the N.I.R.C. under the Contracts of Employment Act 1963, Sched. 1, para. 10 (2) (now Employment Protection (Consolidation) Act 1977, Sched. 13, para. 17 (2)), and the Employment Protection (Consolidation) Act 1977, s. 151. It is not, however, clear why the court did not simply regard the appointment of the receiver in that case as effecting a transfer of the business to him. See pp. 336–338, *ante.*   [28] See n. 25, *ante.*

[29] See *Reid* v. *Explosives Co. Ltd.* (1887) 19 Q.B.D. 264 and pp. 165–166, *ante.*

[30] Employment Protection Act 1975, s. 93 (1) (*b*). See generally Chap. 17, *ante.*

thereafter carried on at all) is carried on by the receiver for the benefit of the debenture holders.

For this reason, it is customary for receivers who have the necessary powers to do so to take advantage of the provisions of section 252 of the Income and Corporation Taxes Act 1970 by selling, shortly after their appointment, the whole of the assets over which they have been appointed to another company in exchange for shares. The new company thus becomes a wholly owned subsidiary of the original company and entitled to take advantage of any unutilised tax losses suffered by the original company.[31] There are additional practical advantages in that the receiver will cause the shares to be vested in his nominees (although of course in trust for the company as part of its assets) and will thus be in a position to make title to the whole of the assets without difficulty (via a sale of the shares) even if a winding up supervenes.

(c) *Tort of employees.* The maxim *respondeat superior* will now apply in its full force to the receiver.

Calls. The proper person to get in uncalled capital charged by a debenture is the liquidator,[32] and if he does not do so the receiver may apply in the liquidation for an order directing him to do so.[33]

Fraudulent preference. Where money has been recovered by the liquidator from a creditor on the ground of fraudulent preference made within six months [34] of the winding up, the receiver for debenture holders has no title to the money, which belongs to the general body of creditors.[35] But moneys recovered in misfeasance proceedings are included in the debenture holders' security.[36]

Variation of remuneration. The remuneration payable to the receiver is usually fixed by the debentures or debenture trust deed by reference to and incorporating section 109 (6) of the Law of Property Act 1925. This section would normally apply without express mention. By section 371 of the Companies Act 1948 the court may, upon the application of the liquidator, fix the amount to be paid by way of remuneration; and may vary or amend the

---

[31] Income and Corporation Taxes Act 1970, s. 252 (3). See for an example of this technique *Airlines Airspares Ltd.* v. *Handley Page Ltd.* [1970] Ch. 193.

[32] *Fowler* v. *Broad's Patent, etc., Co.* [1893] 1 Ch. 724.

[33] *Re Westminster Syndicate Ltd.* (1908) 99 L.T. 924.

[34] Formerly three: see now Companies Act 1948, s. 320 (1).

[35] *Re Yagerphone* [1935] Ch. 392.

[36] *Re Anglo-Austrian Printing, etc., Union* [1895] 2 Ch. 891.

order upon the application of the liquidator or the receiver. Where no previous order has been made under this section, the power of the court extends to fixing such remuneration for a period before the making of the order or the application therefor [37]; is exercisable notwithstanding that the receiver has died or ceased to act before the making of the order or the application therefor; and, if in the opinion of the court there are special circumstances which render it proper for this power to be exercised, extends to requiring the receiver or his personal representative to account for the whole or any part of any remuneration paid to or retained by him in respect of any period before the making of the order in excess of the sum so fixed by the court.[38]

The amount allowed depends upon the circumstances of each case. There is no hard-and-fast rule as to the amount to be allowed either to a receiver or a liquidator.

The application by the liquidator where a compulsory winding up is in progress is by summons in the winding up, and where the winding up is voluntary by originating summons; in each case it must be served upon the receiver.

Books and papers. The liquidator will be entitled to the custody of such books and documents of the company as relate to its management of the statutory books of the company, and of all other books and documents of the company as relate to the management and business of the company and are not necessary to support the title of the debenture holders. It is thought that, by analogy with the position which obtains where a receiver is appointed by the court, the liquidator must produce such books to the receiver when requested.[39]

---

[37] Companies Act 1948, s. 371 (2) (*a*), reversing the effect of *Re Greycaine Ltd.* [1946] Ch. 269.

[38] *Ibid.* s. 371 (2).

[39] See p. 100, *ante.*

CHAPTER 20

APPOINTMENTS OVER THE PROPERTY OF A
COMPANY [1]—TERMINATION OF RECEIVERSHIP

Displacement of the receiver. A receiver appointed by the debenture holders may, if the court thinks fit, be displaced by the court, on the application of other debenture holders, or of the appointors, in favour of its own receiver.[2] A receiver appointed by or on behalf of subsequent debenture holders will be displaced by the appointment of a receiver by or on behalf of prior debenture holders.[3]

Removal. Just as the appointment takes effect only when communicated to the receiver, so also (in the absence of any special provision) notice of removal under a power to remove is effective only when received by him.[4] To the extent to which it is his duty to have paid preferential debts,[5] a receiver who is removed from office must ensure that these are discharged, or that he retains sufficient assets in his hands to meet them, before he parts with the assets. Alternatively (see below) his removal may be accompanied by another appointment under such circumstances that the receivership may properly be regarded as continuous, in which case he will be justified in transferring the whole of the assets in his hands, save as mentioned below, to the new receiver. If he does not either ensure the payment of the preferential debts or else that the receivership may properly be regarded as continuous, he will be personally liable to any disappointed preferential creditor whose debt he ought to have discharged.[6]

Having regard to the personal liability imposed upon all receivers by statute in respect of their own contracts (save in so far as such contracts may provide, which is unusual, to the contrary) a receiver who has been removed will, like any other agent who

---

[1] As to the meaning of " company " see n. 1, p. 309, *ante.*

[2] *Re Maskelyne British Typewriter Co.* [1898] 1 Ch. 133; *Re Slogger Automatic Feeder Co.* [1915] 1 Ch. 478. See p. 109, *ante.*

[3] See p. 288, *ante.*

[4] *Windsor Refrigerator Co. Ltd.* v. *Branch Nominees Ltd.* [1961] Ch. 375, *per* Donovan L.J. at p. 398.

[5] See p. 317, *ante.*

[6] *I.R.C.* v. *Goldblatt* [1972] Ch. 498. The debenture holder who procured the removal of the receiver was also held liable.

has properly made himself liable in respect of his principal's contracts, have a lien on the assets in his hands against all such liabilities personally incurred by him.[7]

Duty to cease to act. If, at any stage of his management of the company, the receiver has in his hands sufficient monies to discharge all the debts of the company which he is bound to discharge, all possible claims which could be made against him and in respect of which he is entitled to an indemnity, his own remuneration, and all monies secured by the instrument pursuant to which he was appointed, it will be his duty to cease to act forthwith. If he refrains from taking this course, any accounts will be taken against him thereafter with annual rests from the date when he has sufficient monies in his hands to cover all such amounts.[8] It is also possible that his continuance in possession of the company's assets thereafter would be regarded by the courts as wrongful, since his appointment is for the purpose, and only for the purpose, of enabling the encumbrancers entitled to the benefit of the instrument under which he was appointed to recover their debt, and, once this purpose has been achieved, there is no ground for his continuance in office. The effect would be that thereafter he would be in the position of a trespasser.[9]

It may well be that, for many reasons, although he has sufficient monies in his hands for the above purpose, the receiver is not in a position to settle all possible claims which could be made against him and in respect of which he is entitled to an indemnity. In such cases it is thought that his duty is to obtain his discharge from the person appointing him, retain sufficient monies to answer his indemnity, and account at once for any balance to the company. Alternatively, he may (but cannot be forced to) accept an indemnity from the company which may (but cannot be compelled to) offer such indemnity.

Death. If, after the death of a receiver, the company attempted to deal with its assets before the debenture holders had an opportunity of appointing a new receiver, the company could clearly be restrained by injunction from so acting. In the normal case an appointment will be promptly made in replacement, and the

---

[7] *Foxcraft* v. *Wood* (1828) 4 Russ. 487.
[8] *Cf. Ashworth* v. *Lord* (1887) 36 Ch.D. 545. As to the taking of accounts see p. 357, *post.*
[9] *Cf.* p. 315, *ante.*

receivership can then be regarded as continuous,[10] but provision will of course have to be made to ensure the indemnification of the receiver's estate against all liabilities personally incurred by him.

Continuity of receivership. Although the only direct decision relates to a special statutory situation,[11] it is considered that if a fresh receiver is appointed in the place of a receiver who has died or been removed without undue delay, the receivership may be regarded as continuous. This is particularly important as regards any undischarged statutory duties, such as the duty to discharge preferential debts. If these have not been discharged prior to the death or removal, then the personal representatives or the receiver himself, as the case may be, will, if the receivership can be regarded as being continuous, but not otherwise, be justified in accounting to the new receiver in respect of the entirety of the assets in his hand (save for such portion thereof as is required for his protection against contractual claims) leaving it to the new receiver to complete the statutory obligations in this regard.

If, however, the receivership cannot be regarded as continuous,[12] he cannot safely take this course. Nor, if no further receiver is to be appointed, can he simply take the course of accounting to the company without first discharging all preferential debts.

Ceasing to act. Upon ceasing to act as such, a receiver or manager is required to render accounts, as set out below, and is also, on so ceasing, required to give to the registrar of companies notice thereof.[13] This notice is entered by the registrar in the register of charges. A penalty of £5 is incurred in respect of every day during which default in giving such notice continues.[14]

Accounts upon ceasing to act. On ceasing to act, the receiver must deliver the usual abstract within one month, and must include the figures from the last abstract [15] up to the date of so ceasing.[16]

---

[10] See *infra.*

[11] *Re White's Mortgage* [1943] Ch. 166 (appointment of receiver requiring leave under the Courts (Emergency Powers) Act 1939.

[12] In *Re White's Mortgage, supra,* a delay of 10 months was held to break the continuity of the receivership.

[13] Companies Act 1948, s. 102 (2).

[14] *Ibid.* s. 102 (3). All notices under this section must be in the prescribed form: Companies Act 1976, s. 34 and Sched. 1, adding a new subsection (3A) to this effect. The appropriate form is No. 57A in the Schedule to the Companies (Forms) Order 1949 (S.I. 1949 No. 382): Companies Act 1976, s. 34 (2).

[15] For prescribed form, see p. 392, *post.*

[16] Companies Act 1948, s. 374 (1).

It will, as in the case of all other abstracts, show the aggregate amount of his receipts and of his payments during all preceding periods since his appointment.[16] A penalty of £5 is incurred for every day of default.[17]

Where a receiver is appointed out of court, and subsequently the same person is appointed in a debenture holders' action, his accounts are taken in the action: if a different person is appointed, the first receiver may apply by summons to have his accounts taken in the action.[18]

Balance in accounts due to company. Whereas the receiver is not a debtor to the company in respect of any intermediate balance which might appear from his accounts to be due to the company, it must correspondingly follow that he will be a debtor to the company in respect of the final balance, after discharging all preferential debts and so forth, shown by his accounts to be due to the company, and that therefore, this balance could be the proper subject of a garnishee order.[19]

Withdrawal of receiver before payment off of debenture holders in full. If a receiver is withdrawn by consent before the debenture holders have been paid off in full, any floating charge comprised in their security, having once crystallised,[20] will not refloat automatically and can only be made so to do by express agreement. A more difficult question is whether after the withdrawal of a receiver the debenture holders are still entitled to a fixed equitable charge on the assets so released to the company; in principle there appears to be no reason why this charge should not continue to attach to any assets which belonged to the company at the date of crystallisation and which have not been disposed of during the receivership. The charge would not attach to assets of the company acquired subsequent to the date of crystallisation.[21] The practical results of this position are so inconvenient that it is thought that an intention to waive the fixed charge will readily be implied.

---

[17] Companies Act, 1948, s. 374 (2).

[18] Practice Note [1932] W.N. 79.

[19] As envisaged by the judgment in *Seabrook Estate Co. Ltd.* v. *Ford* [1949] 2 All E.R. 94, 97.

[20] See p. 312, *ante.*

[21] *Re Yagerphone* [1935] Ch. 392. The passage in the text was criticised by Russell L.J. in *N. W. Robbie & Co. Ltd.* v. *Witney Warehouse Co. Ltd.* [1963] 1 W.L.R. 1324 at p. 1338, but he omitted to observe that it is dealing with the position of future assets acquired after (i) a crystallisation of the charge and (ii) a subsequent withdrawal of the receiver. It is still submitted that future assets fall within the scope of the floating charge only.

APPENDICES

I. Law of Property Act 1925
s. 99. Leasing powers of mortgagor and mortgagee in possession.
s. 100. Powers of mortgagor and mortgagee in possession to accept surrenders of leases.
s. 101. Powers incident to estate or interest of a mortgagee.
s. 102. Provision as to mortgages of undivided shares in land.
s. 109. Appointment, powers, remuneration and duties of receiver.
s. 110. Effect of bankruptcy of the mortgagor on the power to sell or appoint a receiver.
s. 122. Creation of rentcharges charged on another rentcharge and remedies for recovery thereof.

II. Companies Act 1948
s. 94. Payment of certain debts out of assets subject to floating charge in priority to claims under the charge.
s. 102. Registration of enforcement of security.
s. 319. Preferential payments.
s. 322. Effect of floating charge.
s. 358. Preferential payments in stannaries cases.
s. 366. Disqualification of body corporate for appointment as receiver.
s. 367. Disqualification of undischarged bankrupt from acting as receiver or manager.
s. 368. Power in England to appoint official receiver as receiver for debenture holders or creditors.
s. 369. Receivers and managers appointed out of court.
s. 370. Notification that receiver or manager appointed.
s. 371. Power of court to fix remuneration on application of liquidator.
s. 372. Provisions as to information where receiver or manager appointed.
s. 373. Special provisions as to statement submitted to receiver.
s. 374. Delivery to registrar of accounts of receivers and managers.
s. 375. Enforcement of duty of receivers and managers to make returns, etc.
s. 376. Construction of references to receivers and managers.

III. Administration of Justice Act 1956
s. 34. Abolition of writs of elegit, etc.
s. 35. Power of courts to impose charges on land of judgment debtor.
s. 36. Receivers.

IV. Rules of the Supreme Court
Order 30: Receivers
r. 1. Application for receiver and injunction.
r. 2. Giving of security by receiver.
r. 3. Remuneration of receiver.
r. 4. Receiver's accounts.
r. 5. Payment of balance, etc., by receiver.
r. 6. Default by receiver.
Order 51: Receivers: Equitable Execution
r. 1. Appointment of receiver by way of equitable execution.
r. 2. Masters and registrars may appoint receiver, etc.
r. 3. Application of rules as to appointment of receiver, etc.
Order 87: Debenture Holders' Actions: Receiver's Register
r. 1. Receiver's register.
r. 2. Registration of transfers, etc.

r. 3. Application for rectification of receiver's register.
r. 4. Receiver's register evidence of transfers, etc.
r. 5. Proof of title of holder of bearer debenture, etc.
r. 6. Requirements in connection with payments.

V. Companies (Forms) Order 1949 (S.I. No. 382 of 1949)
Form 53. Notice of appointment of a Receiver or Manager.
Form 57. Receiver or Manager's Abstract of Receipts and Payments.
Form 57A. Notice of ceasing to act as Receiver or Manager.
Form 108. Notice of Appointment of Receiver or Manager.
Form 109. Statement as to the Affairs of [a Company].
Form 109A. Statement as to the Affairs of [a Company].
Statement of Affairs and Lists to be annexed to Forms 109 and 109A.

VI. Securities Comparable to Floating Charges in Other Jurisdictions

VII. Effect of Draft EEC Bankruptcy Convention, if adopted

Law of Property Act 1925

Leasing powers of mortgagor and mortgagee in possession

99.—(1) A mortgagor of land while in possession shall, as against every incumbrancer, have power to make from time to time any such lease of the mortgaged land, or any part thereof, as is by this section authorised.

(2) A mortgagee of land while in possession shall, as against all prior incumbrancers, if any, and as against the mortgagor, have power to make from time to time any such lease as aforesaid.

(3) The leases which this section authorises are—
- (i) agricultural or occupation leases for any term not exceeding twenty-one years, or, in the case of a mortgage made after the commencement of this Act, fifty years; and
- (ii) building leases for any term not exceeding ninety-nine years, or, in the case of a mortgage made after the commencement of this Act, nine hundred and ninety-nine years.

(4) Every person making a lease under this section may execute and do all assurances and things necessary or proper in that behalf.

(5) Every such lease shall be made to take effect in possession not later than twelve months after its date.

(6) Every such lease shall reserve the best rent that can reasonably be obtained, regard being had to the circumstances of the case, but without any fine being taken.

(7) Every such lease shall contain a covenant by the lessee for payment of the rent, and a condition of re-entry on the rent not being paid within a time therein specified not exceeding thirty days.

(8) A counterpart of every such lease shall be executed by the lessee and delivered to the lessor, of which execution and delivery the execution of the lease by the lessor shall, in favour of the lessee and all persons deriving title under him, be sufficient evidence.

(9) Every such building lease shall be made in consideration of the lessee, or some person by whose direction the lease is granted, having erected, or agreeing to erect within not more than five years from the date of the lease, buildings, new or additional, or having improved or repaired buildings, or agreeing to improve or repair buildings within that time, or having executed, or agreeing to execute within that time, on the land leased, an improvement for or in connection with building purposes.

(10) In any such building lease a peppercorn rent, or a nominal or other rent less than the rent ultimately payable, may be made payable for the first five years, or any less part of the term.

(11) In case of a lease by the mortgagor, he shall, within one month after making the lease, deliver to the mortgagee, or, where there are

more than one, to the mortgagee first in priority, a counterpart of the lease duly executed by the lessee, but the lessee shall not be concerned to see that this provision is complied with.

(12) A contract to make or accept a lease under this section may be enforced by or against every person on whom the lease if granted would be binding.

(13) This section applies only if and as far as a contrary intention is not expressed by the mortgagor and mortgagee in the mortgage deed, or otherwise in writing, and has effect subject to the terms of the mortgage deed or of any such writing and to the provisions therein contained.

(14) The mortgagor and mortgagee may, by agreement in writing, whether or not contained in the mortgage deed, reserve to or confer on the mortgagor or the mortgagee, or both, any further or other powers of leasing or having reference to leasing; and any further or other powers so reserved or conferred shall be exercisable, as far as may be, as if they were conferred by this Act, and with all the like incidents, effects, and consequences:

Provided that the powers so reserved or conferred shall not prejudicially affect the rights of any mortgagee interested under any other mortgage subsisting at the date of the agreement, unless that mortgagee joins in or adopts the agreement.

(15) Nothing in this Act shall be construed to enable a mortgagor or mortgagee to make a lease for any longer term or on any other conditions than such as could have been granted or imposed by the mortgagor, with the concurrence of all the incumbrancers, if this Act and the enactments replaced by this section had not been passed:

Provided that, in the case of a mortgage of leasehold land, a lease granted under this section shall reserve a reversion of not less than one day.

(16) Subject as aforesaid, this section applies to any mortgage made after the thirty-first day of December, eighteen hundred and eighty-one, but the provisions thereof, or any of them, may, by agreement in writing made after that date between mortgagor and mortgagee, be applied to a mortgage made before that date, so nevertheless that any such agreement shall not prejudicially affect any right or interest of any mortgagee not joining in or adopting the agreement.

(17) The provisions of this section referring to a lease shall be construed to extend and apply, as far as circumstances admit, to any letting, and to an agreement, whether in writing or not, for leasing or letting.

(18) For the purposes of this section " mortgagor " does not include an incumbrancer deriving title under the original mortgagor.

(19) The powers of leasing conferred by this section shall, after a receiver of the income of the mortgaged property or any part thereof has been appointed by a mortgagee under his statutory power, and so long as the receiver acts, be exercisable by such mortgagee instead of by the mortgagor, as respects any land affected by the receivership, in like manner as if such mortgagee were in possession of the land, and the mortgagee may, by writing, delegate any of such powers to the receiver.

Powers of mortgagor and mortgagee in possession to accept surrenders of leases

100.—(1) For the purpose of only enabling a lease authorised under the last preceding section, or under any agreement made pursuant to that section, or by the mortgage deed (in this section referred to as an authorised lease) to be granted, a mortgagor of land while in possession shall, as against every incumbrancer, have, by virtue of this Act, power to accept from time to time a surrender of any lease of the mortgaged land or any part thereof comprised in the lease, with or without an exception of or in respect of all or any of the mines and minerals therein, and, on a surrender of the lease so far as it comprises part only of the land or mines and minerals leased, the rent may be apportioned.

(2) For the same purpose, a mortgagee of land while in possession shall, as against all prior or other incumbrancers, if any, and as against the mortgagor, have, by virtue of this Act, power to accept from time to time any such surrender as aforesaid.

(3) On a surrender of part only of the land or mines and minerals leased, the original lease may be varied, provided that the lease when varied would have been valid as an authorised lease if granted by the person accepting the surrender; and, on a surrender and the making of a new or other lease, whether for the same or for any extended or other term, and whether subject or not to the same or to any other covenants, provisions, or conditions, the value of the lessee's interest in the lease surrendered may, subject to the provisions of this section, be taken into account in the determination of the amount of the rent to be reserved, and of the nature of the covenants, provisions, and conditions to be inserted in the new or other lease.

(4) Where any consideration for the surrender, other than an agreement to accept an authorised lease, is given by or on behalf of the lessee to or on behalf of the person accepting the surrender, nothing in this section authorises a surrender to a mortgagor without the consent of the incumbrancers, or authorises a surrender to a second or subsequent incumbrancer without the consent of every prior incumbrancer.

(5) No surrender shall, by virtue of this section, be rendered valid unless:—

   (a) An authorised lease is granted of the whole of the land or mines and minerals comprised in the surrender to take effect in possession immediately or within one month after the date of the surrender; and

   (b) The term certain or other interest granted by the new lease is not less in duration than the unexpired term or interest which would have been subsisting under the original lease if that lease had not been surrendered; and

   (c) Where the whole of the land or mines and minerals originally leased has been surrendered, the rent reserved by the new lease is not less than the rent which would have been payable under the original lease if it had not been surrendered; or where part only of the land or mines and minerals has been surrendered, the aggregate rents respectively remaining payable or reserved under the original lease and new lease are not less than the rent which would have been payable under the original lease if no partial surrender had been accepted.

(6) A contract to make or accept a surrender under this section may be enforced by or against every person on whom the surrender, if completed, would be binding.

(7) This section applies only if and as far as a contrary intention is not expressed by the mortgagor and mortgagee in the mortgage deed, or otherwise in writing, and shall have effect subject to the terms of the mortgage deed or of any such writing and to the provisions therein contained.

(8) This section applies to a mortgage made after the thirty-first day of December, nineteen hundred and eleven, but the provisions of this section, or any of them, may, by agreement in writing made after that date, between mortgagor and mortgagee, be applied to a mortgage made before that date, so nevertheless that any such agreement shall not prejudicially affect any right or interest of any mortgagee not joining in or adopting the agreement.

(9) The provisions of this section referring to a lease shall be construed to extend and apply, as far as circumstances admit, to any letting, and to an agreement, whether in writing, or not, for leasing or letting.

(10) The mortgagor and mortgagee may, by agreement in writing, whether or not contained in the mortgage deed, reserve or confer on the mortgagor or mortgagee, or both, any further or other powers relating to the surrender of leases; and any further or other powers so conferred or reserved shall be exercisable, as far as may be, as if they were conferred by this Act, and with all the like incidents, effects and consequences:

Provided that the powers so reserved or conferred shall not prejudicially affect the rights of any mortgagee interested under any other mortgage subsisting at the date of the agreement, unless that mortgagee joins in or adopts the agreement.

(11) Nothing in this section operates to enable a mortgagor or mortgagee to accept a surrender which could not have been accepted by the mortgagor with the concurrence of all the incumbrancers if this Act and the enactments replaced by this section had not been passed.

(12) For the purposes of this section " mortgagor " does not include an incumbrancer deriving title under the original mortgagor.

(13) The powers of accepting surrenders conferred by this section shall, after a receiver of the income of the mortgaged property or any part thereof has been appointed by the mortgagee, under the statutory power, and so long as the receiver acts, be exercisable by such mortgagee instead of by the mortgagor, as respects any land affected by the receivership, in like manner as if such mortgagee were in possession of the land; and the mortgagee may, by writing, delegate any of such powers to the receiver.

Powers incident to estate or interest of mortgage

101.—(1) A mortgagee, where the mortgage is made by deed, shall, by virtue of this Act, have the following powers, to the like extent as if they had been in terms conferred by the mortgage deed, but not further (namely):

(i) A power, when the mortgage money has become due, to sell, or to concur with any other person in selling, the mortgaged property, or any part thereof, either subject to prior charges or not, and either together or in lots, by public auction or by private contract, subject to such conditions respecting title, or evidence of title, or other matter, as the mortgagee thinks fit, with power to vary any contract for sale, and to buy in at an auction, or to rescind any contract for sale, and to re-sell, without being answerable for any loss occasioned thereby; and

(ii) A power, at any time after the date of the mortgage deed, to insure and keep insured against loss or damage by fire any building, or any effects or property of an insurable nature, whether affixed to the freehold or not, being or forming part of the property which or an estate or interest wherein is mortgaged, and the premiums paid for any such insurance shall be a charge on the mortgaged property or estate or interest, in addition to the mortgage money, and with the same priority, and with interest at the same rate, as the mortgage money; and

(iii) A power, when the mortgage money has become due, to appoint a receiver of the income of the mortgaged property, or any part thereof; or, if the mortgaged property consists of an interest in income, or of a rentcharge or an annual or other periodical sum, a receiver of that property or any part thereof; and

(iv) A power, while the mortgagee is in possession, to cut and sell timber and other trees ripe for cutting, and not planted or left standing for shelter or ornament, or to contract for any such cutting and sale, to be completed within any time not exceeding twelve months from the making of the contract.

(2) Where the mortgage deed is executed after the thirty-first day of December, nineteen hundred and eleven, the power of sale aforesaid includes the following powers as incident thereto (namely):—

(i) A power to impose or reserve or make binding, as far as the law permits, by covenant, condition, or otherwise, on the unsold part of the mortgaged property or any part thereof, or on the purchaser and any property sold, any restriction or reservation with respect to building on or other user of land, or with respect to mines and minerals, or for the purpose of the more beneficial working thereof, or with respect to any other thing:

(ii) A power to sell the mortgaged property, or any part thereof, or all or any mines and minerals apart from the surface:—

(*a*) With or without a grant or reservation of rights of way, rights of water, easements, rights, and privileges for or connected with building or other purposes in relation to the property remaining in mortgage or any part thereof, or to any property sold: and

(*b*) With or without an exception or reservation of all or any of the mines and minerals in or under the mortgaged property, and with or without a grant or reservation of powers of working, wayleaves, or rights of way, rights of water and drainage and other powers, easements, rights, and privileges for or connected with mining purposes in relation to the property remaining unsold or any part thereof, or to any property sold: and

(*c*) With or without covenants by the purchaser to expend money on the land sold.

(3) The provisions of this Act relating to the foregoing powers, comprised either in this section, or in any other section regulating the exercise of those powers, may be varied or extended by the mortgage deed, and, as so varied or extended, shall, as far as may be, operate in the like manner and with all the like incidents, effects, and consequences, as if such variations or extensions were contained in this Act.

(4) This section applies only if and as far as a contrary intention is not expressed in the mortgage deed, and has effect subject to the terms of the mortgage deed and to the provisions therein contained.

(5) Save as otherwise provided, this section applies where the mortgage deed is executed after the thirty-first day of December, eighteen hundred and eighty-one.

(6) The power of sale conferred by this section includes such power of selling the estate in fee simple or any leasehold reversion as is conferred by the provisions of this Act relating to the realisation of mortgages.

Provision as to mortgages of undivided shares in land

102.—(1) A person who was before the commencement of this Act a mortgagee of an undivided share in land shall have the same power to sell his share in the proceeds of sale of the land and in the rents and profits thereof until sale, as, independently of this Act, he would have had in regard to the share in the land; and shall also have a right to require the trustees for sale in whom the land is vested to account to him for the income attributable to that share or to appoint a receiver to receive the same from such trustees corresponding to the right which, independently of this Act, he would have had to take possession or to appoint a receiver of the rents and profits attributable to the same share.

(2) The powers conferred by this section are exercisable by the persons deriving title under such mortgage.

. . . .

Appointment, powers, remuneration and duties of receiver

109.—(1) A mortgagee entitled to appoint a receiver under the power in that behalf conferred by this Act shall not appoint a receiver until he has become entitled to exercise the power of sale conferred by this Act, but may then, by writing under his hand, appoint such person as he thinks fit to be receiver.

(2) A receiver appointed under the powers conferred by this Act, or any enactment replaced by this Act, shall be deemed to be the agent of the mortgagor; and the mortgagor shall be solely responsible for the receiver's acts or defaults unless the mortgage deed otherwise provides.

(3) The receiver shall have power to demand and recover all the income of which he is appointed receiver, by action, distress, or otherwise, in the name either of the mortgagor or of the mortgagee, to the full extent of the estate or interest which the mortgagor could dispose of, and to give effectual receipts accordingly for the same, and to exercise any powers which may have been delegated to him by the mortgagee pursuant to this Act.

(4) A person paying money to the receiver shall not be concerned to inquire whether any case has happened to authorise the receiver to act.

(5) The receiver may be removed, and a new receiver may be appointed, from time to time by the mortgagee in writing under his hand.

(6) The receiver shall be entitled to retain out of any money received by him, for his remuneration, and in satisfaction of all costs, charges, and expenses incurred by him as receiver, a commission at such rate, not exceeding five per centum on the gross amount of all money received, as is specified in his appointment, and if no rate is so specified, then at the rate of five per centum on that gross amount, or at such other rate as the court thinks fit to allow, on application made by him for that purpose.

(7) The receiver shall, if so directed in writing by the mortgagee, insure to the extent, if any, to which the mortgagee might have insured and keep insured against loss or damage by fire, out of the money received by him, any building, effects or property comprised in the mortgage, whether affixed to the freehold or not, being of an insurable nature.

(8) Subject to the provisions of this Act as to the application of insurance money, the receiver shall apply all money received by him as follows, namely:

  (i) In discharge of all rents, taxes, rates, and outgoings whatever affecting the mortgaged property; and

  (ii) In keeping down all annual sums or other payments, and the interest on all principal sums, having priority to the mortgage in right whereof he is receiver; and

  (iii) In payment of his commission, and of the premiums on fire, life, or other insurances, if any, properly payable under the mortgage deed or under this Act, and the cost of executing necessary or proper repairs directed in writing by the mortgagee; and

  (iv) In payment of the interest accruing due in respect of any principal money due under the mortgage; and

  (v) In or towards discharge of the principal money if so directed in writing by the mortgagee;

and shall pay the residue, if any, of the money received by him to the person who, but for the possession of the receiver, would have been entitled to receive the income of which he is appointed receiver, or who is otherwise entitled to the mortgaged property.

Effect of bankruptcy of the mortgagor on the power to sell or appoint a receiver

110.—(1) Where the statutory or express power for a mortgagee either to sell or to appoint a receiver is made exercisable by reason of the mortgagor committing an act of bankruptcy or being adjudged a bankrupt, such power shall not be exercised only on account of the act of bankruptcy or adjudication, without the leave of the court.

(2) This section applies only where the mortgage deed is executed after the commencement of this Act; and in this section " act of bankruptcy " has the same meaning as in the Bankruptcy Act 1914.

.   .   .   .   .   .

Creation of rentcharges charged on another rentcharge and remedies for recovery thereof

122.—(1) A rentcharge or other annual sum (not being rent incident to a reversion) payable half yearly or otherwise may be granted, reserved, charged or created out of or on another rentcharge or annual sum (not being rent incident to a reversion) charged on or payable out of land or on or out of the income of land, in like manner as the same could have been made to issue out of land.

(2) If at any time the annual sum so created or any part thereof is unpaid for twenty-one days next after the time appointed for any payment in respect thereof, the person entitled to receive the annual sum shall (without prejudice to any prior interest or charge) have power to appoint a receiver of the annual sum charged or any part thereof, and the provisions of this Act relating to the appointment, powers, remuneration and duties of a receiver, shall apply in like manner as if such person were a mortgagee entitled to exercise the power of sale conferred by this Act, and the annual sum charged were the mortgaged property and the person entitled thereto were the mortgagor.

(3) The power to appoint a receiver conferred by this section shall (where the annual sum is charged on a rentcharge) take effect in substitution for the remedies conferred, in the case of annual sums charged on land, by the last preceding section, but sub section (6) of that section shall apply and have effect as if herein re-enacted and in terms made applicable to the powers conferred by this section.

(4) This section applies to annual sums expressed to be created before as well as after the commencement of this Act, and, but without prejudice to any order of the court made before the commencement of this Act, operates to confirm any annual sum which would have been validly created if this section had been in force.

II

Companies Act 1948

Payment of certain debts out of assets subject to floating charge in priority to claims under the charge

94.—(1) Where, in the case of a company registered in England, either a receiver is appointed on behalf of the holders of any debentures of the company secured by a floating charge, or possession is taken by or on behalf of those debenture holders of any property comprised in or subject to the charge, then, if the company is not at the time in course of being wound up, the debts which in every winding up are under the provisions of Part V of this Act relating to preferential payments to be paid in priority to all other debts, shall be paid out of any assets coming to the hands of the receiver or other person taking possession as aforesaid in priority to any claim for principal or interest in respect of the debentures.

(2) In the application of the said provisions, section three hundred and nineteen of this Act shall be construed as if the provision for payment of accrued holiday remuneration becoming payable on the termination of employment before or by the effect of the winding-up order or resolution were a provision for payment of such remuneration becoming payable on the termination of employment before or by the effect of the appointment of the receiver or possession being taken as aforesaid.

(3) The periods of time mentioned in the said provisions of Part V of this Act shall be reckoned from the date of the appointment of the receiver or of possession being taken as aforesaid, as the case may be.

(4) Where the date referred to in the last foregoing subsection occurred before the commencement of this Act, subsections (1) and (3) of this section shall have effect with the substitution, for references to the said provisions of Part V of this Act, of references to the provisions which, by virtue of subsection (9) of the said section three hundred and nineteen are deemed to remain in force in the case therein mentioned, and subsection (2) shall not apply.

(5) Any payments made under this section shall be recouped as far as may be out of the assets of the company available for payment of general creditors.

. . . .

Registration of enforcement of security

102.—(1) If any person obtains an order for the appointment of a receiver or manager of the property of a company, or appoints such a receiver or manager under any powers contained in any instrument, he shall, within seven days from the date of the order or of the appointment under the said powers, give notice of the fact to the registrar of companies, and the registrar shall, [on payment of such fee as may be specified by regulations made by the Board of Trade],[1] enter the fact in the register of charges.

---

[1] Words in square brackets repealed by Companies Act 1976, s. 42 (2) and Sched. 3.

(2) Where any person appointed receiver or manager of the property of a company under the powers contained in any instrument ceases to act as such receiver or manager, he shall, on so ceasing, give the registrar of companies notice to that effect, and the registrar shall enter the notice in the register of charges.

(3) If any person makes default in complying with the requirements of this section, he shall be liable to a fine not exceeding five pounds for every day during which the default continues.

(3A)² Any notice under this section shall be in the prescribed form.

[(4) The power conferred by this section on the Board of Trade shall be exercisable by statutory instrument which shall be subject to annulment in pursuance of a resolution of either House of Parliament.]³

. . . .

Preferential payments

319.—(1) In a winding up there shall be paid in priority to all other debts—

    (*a*) the following rates and taxes,—

            (i) all local rates due from the company at the relevant date, and having become due and payable within twelve months next before that date;

            (ii) all [land tax,]⁴ income tax, profits tax, excess profits tax or other assessed taxes assessed on the company up to the fifth day of April next before that date, and not exceeding in the whole one year's assessment;

            [(iii) the amount of any purchase tax due from the company at the relevant date, and having become due within twelve months next before that date;]⁵

    (*b*) all wages or salary (whether or not earned wholly or in part by way of commission) of any clerk or servant in respect of services rendered to the company during four months next before the relevant date and all wages (whether payable for time or for piece work) of any workman or labourer in respect of services so rendered;

    (*c*) any sum ordered under the Reinstatement in Civil Employment Act 1944, to be paid by way of compensation where the default by reason of which the order for compensation was made occurred before the relevant date, whether or not the order was made before that date;

    (*d*) all accrued holiday remuneration becoming payable to any clerk, servant, workman or labourer (or in the case of his death to any

---

² Subsection added by Companies Act 1976, s. 34 and Sched. 1.

³ See n. 1, *ante.*

⁴ Words in square brackets repealed by Statute Law (Repeals) Act 1975, s. 1 and Sched. I, Pt. I.

⁵ Words in square brackets repealed by Finance Act 1972, s. 134 and Sched. 28, Pt. II.

other person in his right) on the termination of his employment
before or by the effect of the winding-up order or resolution;

(e) [unless the company is being wound up voluntarily merely for
the purpose of reconstruction or of amalgamation with another
company, all the debts specified in section 153 (2) of the Social
Security Act 1975, Schedule 3 to the Social Security Pensions
Act 1975, and any corresponding provisions in force in Northern
Ireland;][6]

(f) unless the company is being wound up voluntarily merely for
the purposes of reconstruction or of amalgamation with another
company, or unless the company has, at the commencement of
the winding up, under such a contract with insurers as is mentioned in section seven of the Workmen's Compensation Act
1925, rights capable of being transferred to and vested in the
workman, all amounts due in respect of any compensation or
liability for compensation under the said Act, being amounts
which have accrued before the relevant date in satisfaction of a
right which arises or has arisen in respect of employment before
the fifth day of July, nineteen hundred and forty-eight (that is to
say, the day appointed for the purposes of the National Insurance (Industrial Injuries) Act 1946);

(g) the amount of any debt which, by virtue of subsection (5) of
section three of the Workmen's Compensation (Coal Mines) Act
1934, is due from the company to an insurer in respect of a
liability in respect of the satisfaction of a right falling within the
last foregoing paragraph.

(2) Notwithstanding anything in paragraphs (b) and (c) of the foregoing subsection, the sum to which priority is to be given under those
paragraphs respectively shall not, in the case of any one claimant,
exceed [£800][7]:

Provided that where a claimant under the said paragraph (b) is a
labourer in husbandry who has entered into a contract for the payment
of a portion of his wages in a lump sum at the end of the year of hiring,
he shall have priority in respect of the whole of such sum, or a part
thereof, as the court may decide to be due under the contract, proportionate to the time of service up to the relevant date.

(3) Where any compensation under the Workmen's Compensation
Act 1925 is a weekly payment, the amount due in respect thereof shall
for the purposes of paragraph (f) of subsection (1) of this section be
taken to be the amount of the lump sum for which the weekly payment
could, if redeemable, be redeemed if the employer made an application
for that purpose under the said Act.

(4) Where any payment has been made—

(a) to any clerk, servant, workman or labourer in the employment
of a company, on account of wages or salary; or

---

[6] Words in brackets substituted by Social Security Act 1973, s. 100 (2) (a) and
Sched. 27, para. 9 (a) and Social Security Pensions Act 1975, s. 65 and Sched. 4,
para. 3.   [7] Maximum limit was raised by the Insolvency Act 1976, Sched. 1.

(b) to any such clerk, servant, workman or labourer or, in the case of his death, to any other person in his right, on account of accrued holiday remuneration;

out of money advanced by some person for that purpose, the person by whom the money was advanced shall in a winding up have a right of priority in respect of the money so advanced and paid up to the amount by which the sum in respect of which the clerk, servant, workman or labourer, or other person in his right, would have been entitled to priority in the winding up has been diminished by reason of the payment having been made.

(5) The foregoing debts shall—

(a) rank equally among themselves and be paid in full, unless the assets are insufficient to meet them, in which case they shall abate in equal proportions; and

(b) in the case of a company registered in England or Scotland so far as the assets of the company available for payment of general creditors are insufficient to meet them, have priority over the claims of holders of debentures under any floating charge created by the company, and be paid accordingly out of any property comprised in or subject to that charge.

(6) Subject to the retention of such sums as may be necessary for the costs and expenses of the winding up, the foregoing debts shall be discharged forthwith so far as the assets are sufficient to meet them, and in the case of the debts to which priority is given by paragraph (e) of subsection (1) of this section formal proof thereof shall not be required except in so far as is otherwise provided by general rules.

(7) In the event of a landlord or other person distraining or having distrained on any goods or effects of the company within three months next before the date of the winding-up order, the debts to which priority is given by this section shall be a first charge on the goods or effects so distrained on, or the proceeds of the sale thereof:

Provided that, in respect of any money paid under any such charge, the landlord or other person shall have the same rights of priority as the person to whom the payment is made.

(8) For the purposes of this section—

(a) any remuneration in respect of a period of holiday or of absence from work through sickness or other good cause shall be deemed to be wages in respect of services rendered to the company during that period;

(b) the expression " accrued holiday remuneration " includes, in relation to any person, all sums which, by virtue either of his contract of employment or of any enactment (including any order made or direction given under any Act), are payable on account of the remuneration which would, in the ordinary course, have become payable to him in respect of a period of holiday had his employment with the company continued until he became entitled to be allowed the holiday;

(c) references to remuneration in respect of a period of holiday include any sums which, if they had been paid, would have been treated for the purposes of the [Social Security Act 1975 or the Social Security (Northern Ireland) Act 1975, as earnings paid in that period and] [8]

(d) the expression " the relevant date " means—

(i) in the case of a company ordered to be wound up compulsorily, the date of the appointment (or first appointment) of a provisional liquidator, or, if no such appointment was made, the date of the winding-up order, unless in either case the company had commenced to be wound up voluntarily before that date; and

(ii) in any case where the foregoing sub-paragraph does not apply, means the date of the passing of the resolution for the winding up of the company.

(9) This section shall not apply in the case of a winding up where the relevant date as defined in subsection (7) of section two hundred and sixty-four of the Companies Act 1929, as originally enacted, occurred before the commencement of this Act, and in such a case the provisions relating to preferential payments which would have applied if this Act had not passed shall be deemed to remain in full force.

. . . . . .

Effect of floating charge

322.—(1) Where a company is being wound up, a floating charge on the undertaking or property of the company created within twelve months of the commencement of the winding up shall, unless it is proved that the company immediately after the creation of the charge was solvent, be invalid, except to the amount of any cash paid to the company at the time of or subsequently to the creation of, and in consideration for, the charge, together with interest on that amount at the rate of five per cent. per annum or such other rate as may for the time being be prescribed by order of the Treasury:

Provided that, in relation to a charge created more than six months before the commencement of this Act, this section shall have effect with the substitution, for the words " twelve months ", of the words " six months ".

(2) The power conferred by this section on the Treasury shall be exercisable by statutory instrument which shall be subject to annulment in pursuance of a resolution of either House of Parliament.

. . . . . .

Preferential payments in stannaries cases

358.—(1) In the application to companies within the stannaries of the

---

[8] Words in brackets substituted by the Social Security Act 1973, s. 100 (2) (a) and Sched. 27, para. 9 (b) as amended by the Social Security (Consequential Provisions) Act 1975, s. 1 (3) and Sched. 2, para. 7 (b).

provisions of this Act with respect to preferential payments, the following modifications shall be made:—

    (*a*) in the case of a clerk or servant of such a company, the priority with respect to wages and salary given by this Act shall not extend to the principal agent, manager, purser or secretary;

    (*b*) all wages in relation to the mine of a miner, artisan, or labourer employed in or about the mine, including all earnings by a miner arising from any description of piece or other work, or as a tributer or otherwise, but not exceeding an amount equal to four months' wages, shall be included amongst the payments which are, under this Act, to be made in priority to other debts;

    (*c*) the following debts, that is to say:—

        (i) wages of any miner, artisan or labourer and accrued holiday remuneration becoming payable to or in right of any miner, artisan or labourer as mentioned in paragraph (*d*) of subsection (1) of section three hundred and nineteen of this Act, being wages or remuneration unpaid at the commencement of the winding up;

        (ii) all such amounts due in respect of contributions payable in respect of a miner under the enactments mentioned in paragraph (*e*) of the said subsection (1) as are given priority by that paragraph; and

        (iii) all such amounts due in respect of any compensation or liability for compensation under the Workmen's Compensation Act 1925 payable to a miner or the dependants of a miner as are given priority by paragraph (*f*) of the said subsection (1); shall be paid by the liquidator forthwith in priority to all costs, except (in the case of a winding up by the court) such costs of and incidental to the making of the winding-up order as in the opinion of the court have been properly incurred, and to all claims by mortgagees, execution creditors, or any other persons, except the claims of clerks and servants in respect of their wages or salary or accrued holiday remuneration due to them;

    (*d*) subject as aforesaid, the court may, by order, charge the whole or any part of the assets of the company, in priority to all claims and to all existing mortgages or charges thereon, with the payment of a sum sufficient to discharge the debts to be paid in priority under the last foregoing paragraph, together with interest thereon at a rate not exceeding five per cent. per annum, and this charge may be made in favour of any person who is willing to advance the requisite amount or any part thereof, and as soon as the said sum has been so advanced, the said debts shall be paid without delay so far as the amount advanced extends, and in such order of payment as the court directs;

    (*e*) the provision giving a right of priority to a person who has advanced money for the making of payments on account of wages, salary or accrued holiday remuneration shall have effect subject to the modifications contained in this section.

(2) References in the foregoing subsection to wages shall be construed as including references to such remuneration in respect of a period of holiday or absence from work as is deemed for the purposes of section three hundred and nineteen of this Act to be wages, and for the purposes of that subsection the expression " accrued holiday remuneration " has the same meaning as it has for the purposes of that section.

(3) The foregoing provisions of this section shall not apply in the case of such a winding up as is mentioned in subsection (9) of the said section three hundred and nineteen, and in such a case the provisions which, by virtue of that subsection, are deemed to remain in force shall have effect in their application to companies within the stannaries subject to the modifications subject to which they would have had effect if this Act had not passed.

Disqualification of body corporate for appointment as receiver

366. A body corporate shall not be qualified for appointment as receiver of the property of a company, and any body corporate which acts as such a receiver shall be liable to a fine not exceeding one hundred pounds.

Disqualification of undischarged bankrupt from acting as receiver or manager

367.—(1) If any person being an undischarged bankrupt acts as receiver or manager of the property of a company on behalf of debenture holders, he shall, subject to the following subsection, be liable on conviction on indictment to imprisonment for a term not exceeding two years, or on summary conviction to imprisonment not exceeding six months or to a fine not exceeding five hundred pounds or to both.

(2) The foregoing subsection shall not apply to a receiver or manager where—

(a) the appointment under which he acts and the bankruptcy were both before the commencement of this Act; or

(b) he acts under an appointment made by order of a court.

Power in England to appoint official receiver as receiver for debenture holders or creditors

368. Where an application is made to the court to appoint a receiver on behalf of the debenture holders or other creditors of a company which is being wound up by the court in England, the official receiver may be so appointed.

Receivers and managers appointed out of court

369.—(1) A receiver or manager of the property of a company appointed under the powers contained in any instrument may apply to the court for directions in relation to any particular matter arising in connection with the performance of his functions, and on any such application the court may give such directions, or may make such order declaring the rights of persons before the court or otherwise, as the court thinks just.

(2) A receiver or manager of the property of a company appointed as aforesaid shall, to the same extent as if he had been appointed by order of a court, be personally liable on any contract entered into by him in the performance of his functions, except in so far as the contract otherwise provides, and entitled in respect of that liability to indemnity out of the assets; but nothing in this subsection shall be taken as limiting any right to indemnity which he would have apart from this subsection, or as limiting his liability on contracts entered into without authority or as conferring any right to indemnity in respect of that liability.

(3) This section shall apply whether the receiver or manager was appointed before or after the commencement of this Act but subsection (2) thereof shall not apply to contracts entered into before the commencement of this Act.

Notification that receiver or manager appointed

370.—(1) Where a receiver or manager of the property of a company has been appointed, every invoice, order for goods or business letter issued by or on behalf of the company or the receiver or manager or the liquidator of the company, being a document on or in which the name of the company appears, shall contain a statement that a receiver or manager has been appointed.

(2) If default is made in complying with the requirements of this section, the company and any of the following persons who knowingly and wilfully authorises or permits the default, namely, any officer of the company, any liquidator of the company and any receiver or manager, shall be liable to a fine of twenty pounds.

Power of court to fix remuneration on application of liquidator

371.—(1) The court may, on an application made to the court by the liquidator of a company, by order fix the amount to be paid by way of remuneration to any person who, under the powers contained in any instrument, has been appointed as receiver or manager of the property of the company.

(2) The power of the court under the foregoing subsection shall' where no previous order has been made with respect thereto under that subsection,—

(a) extend to fixing the remuneration for any period before the making of the order or the application therefor; and

(b) be exercisable notwithstanding that the receiver or manager has died or ceased to act before the making of the order or the application therefor; and

(c) where the receiver or manager has been paid or has retained for his remuneration for any period before the making of the order any amount in excess of that so fixed for that period, extend to requiring him or his personal representatives to account for the excess or such part thereof as may be specified in the order:

Provided that the power conferred by paragraph (c) of this subsection shall not be exercised as respects any period before the making of the application for the order unless in the opinion of the court there are special circumstances making it proper for the power to be so exercised.

(3) The court may from time to time on an application made either by the liquidator or by the receiver or manager, vary or amend an order made under subsection (1) of this section.

(4) This section shall apply whether the receiver or manager was appointed before or after the commencement of this Act, and to periods before, as well as to periods after, the commencement of this Act.

Provisions as to information where receiver or manager appointed

372.—(1) Where, in the case of a company registered in England, a receiver or manager of the whole or substantially the whole of the property of the company (hereafter in this section and in the next following section referred to as " the receiver ") is appointed on behalf of the holders of any debentures of the company secured by a floating charge, then subject to the provisions of this and the next following section—

(a) the receiver shall forthwith send to the company notice of his appointment in the prescribed form[9]; and

(b) there shall, within fourteen days after receipt of the notice, or such longer period as may be allowed by the court or by the receiver, be made out and submitted to the receiver in accordance with the next following section a statement in the prescribed form as to the affairs of the company; and

(c) the receiver shall within two months after receipt of the said statement send—

(i) to the registrar of companies and to the court, a copy of the statement and of any comments he sees fit to make thereon and in the case of the registrar of companies also a summary of the statement and of his comments (if any) thereon; and

(ii) to the company, a copy of any such comments as aforesaid or, if he does not see fit to make any comment, a notice to that effect; and

(iii) to any trustees for the debenture holders on whose behalf he was appointed and, so far as he is aware of their addresses, to all such debenture holders a copy of the said summary.

(2) The receiver shall within two months, or such longer periods as the court may allow after the expiration of the period of twelve months from the date of his appointment and of every subsequent period of twelve months, and within two months or such longer period as the court may allow after he ceases to act as receiver or manager of the

---

[9] As amended by the Companies Act 1976, s. 34 and Sched. 1.

property of the company, send to the registrar of companies, to any trustees for the debenture holders of the company on whose behalf he was appointed, to the company and (so far as he is aware of their addresses) to all such debenture holders an abstract in the prescribed form showing his receipts and payments during that period of twelve months or, where he ceases to act as aforesaid, during the period from the end of the period to which the last preceding abstract related up to the date of his so ceasing, and the aggregate amounts of his receipts and of his payments during all preceding periods since his appointment.

(3) Where the receiver is appointed under the powers contained in any instrument, this section shall have effect—

(*a*) with the omission of the references to the court in subsection (1); and

(*b*) with the substitution for the references to the court in subsection (2) of references to the Board of Trade;

and in any other case references to the court shall be taken as referring to the court by which the receiver was appointed.

(4) Subsection (1) of this section shall not apply in relation to the appointment of a receiver or manager to act with an existing receiver or manager or in place of a receiver or manager dying or ceasing to act, except that, where that subsection applies to a receiver or manager who dies or ceases to act before it has been fully complied with, the references in paragraphs (*b*) and (*c*) thereof to the receiver shall (subject to the next following subsection) include references to his successor and to any continuing receiver or manager.

Nothing in this subsection shall be taken as limiting the meaning of the expression "the receiver" where used in, or in relation to, subsection (2) of this section.

(5) This and the next following section, where the company is being wound up, shall apply notwithstanding that the receiver or manager and the liquidator are the same person, but with any necessary modifications arising from that fact.

(6) Nothing in subsection (2) of this section shall be taken to prejudice the duty of the receiver to render proper accounts of his receipts and payments to the persons to whom, and at the times at which, he may be required to do so apart from that subsection.

(7) If the receiver makes default in complying with the requirements of this section, he shall be liable to a fine not exceeding five pounds for every day during which the default continues.

Special provisions as to statement submitted to receiver

373.—(1) The statement as to the affairs of a company required by the last foregoing section to be submitted to the receiver (or his successor) shall show as at the date of the receiver's appointment the particulars of the company's assets, debts and liabilities, the names, residences and occupations of its creditors, the securities held by them respectively, the dates when the securities were respectively given and such further or other information as may be prescribed.

(2) The said statement shall be submitted by, and be verified by affidavit of, one or more of the persons who are at the date of the receiver's appointment the directors and by the person who is at that date the secretary of the company, or by such of the persons hereafter in this subsection mentioned as the receiver (or his successor), subject to the direction of the court, may require to submit and verify the statement, that is to say, persons—

(a) who are or have been officers of the company;

(b) who have taken part in the formation of the company at any time within one year before the date of the receiver's appointment;

(c) who are in the employment of the company, or have been in the employment of the company within the said year, and are in the opinion of the receiver capable of giving the information required;

(d) who are or have been within the said year officers of or in the employment of a company which is, or within the said year was, an officer of the company to which the statement relates.

(3) Any person making the statement and affidavit shall be allowed, and shall be paid by the receiver (or his successor) out of his receipts, such costs and expenses incurred in and about the preparation and making of the statement and affidavit as the receiver (or his successor) may consider reasonable, subject to an appeal to the court.

(4) Where the receiver is appointed under the powers contained in any instrument, this section shall have effect with the substitution for references to the court of references to the Board of Trade and for references to an affidavit of references to a statutory declaration; and in any other case references to the court shall be taken as referring to the court by which the receiver was appointed.

(5) If any person without reasonable excuse makes default in complying with the requirements of this section, he shall be liable to a fine not exceeding ten pounds for every day during which the default continues.

(6) References in this section to the receiver's successor shall include a continuing receiver or manager.

Delivery to registrar of accounts of receivers and managers

374.—(1) Except where subsection (2) of section three hundred and seventy-two of this Act applies, every receiver or manager of the property of a company who has been appointed under the powers contained in any instrument shall, within one month, or such longer period as the registrar of companies may allow, after the expiration of the period of six months from the date of his appointment and of every subsequent period of six months, and within one month after he ceases to act as receiver or manager, deliver to the registrar of companies for registration an abstract in the prescribed form showing his receipts and his payments during that period of six months, or, where he ceases to act as aforesaid, during the period from the end of the period to which the last preceding abstract related up to the date of his so ceasing, and the aggregate amount of his receipts and of his payments during all preceding periods since his appointment.

(2) Every receiver or manager who makes default in complying with the provisions of this section shall be liable to a fine not exceeding five pounds for every day during which the default continues.

Enforcement of duty of receivers and managers to make returns, etc.
375.—(1) If any receiver or manager of the property of a company—

(a) having made default in filing, delivering or making any return, account or other document, or in giving any notice, which a receiver or manager is by law required to file, deliver, make or give, fails to make good the default within fourteen days after the service on him of a notice requiring him to do so; or

(b) having been appointed under the powers contained in any instrument, has, after being required at any time by the liquidator of the company so to do, failed to render proper accounts of his receipts and payments and to vouch the same and to pay over to the liquidator the amount properly payable to him;

the court may, on an application made for the purpose, make an order directing the receiver or manager, as the case may be, to make good the default within such time as may be specified in the order.

(2) In the case of any such default as is mentioned in paragraph (a) of the foregoing subsection, an application for the purposes of this section may be made by any member or creditor of the company or by the registrar of companies, and in the case of any such default as is mentioned in paragraph (b) of that subsection, the application shall be made by the liquidator, and in either case the order may provide that all costs of and incidental to the application shall be borne by the receiver or manager, as the case may be.

(3) Nothing in this section shall be taken to prejudice the operation of any enactments imposing penalties on receivers in respect of any such default as is mentioned in subsection (1) of this section.

Construction of references to receivers and managers
376. It is hereby declared that, except where the context otherwise requires,—

(a) any reference in this Act to a receiver or manager of the property of a company, or to a receiver thereof, includes a reference to a receiver or manager, or (as the case may be) to a receiver, of part only of that property and to a receiver only of the income arising from that property or from part thereof; and

(b) any reference in this Act to the appointment of a receiver or manager under powers contained in any instrument includes a reference to an appointment made under powers which, by virtue of any enactment, are implied in and have effect as if contained in an instrument.

III

Administration of Justice Act 1956

PART IV

GENERAL PROVISIONS AS TO ENFORCEMENT OF JUDGMENTS AND ORDERS

Abolition of writs of elegit and repeal of enactments imposing charges on land, etc.

34.—(1) No writ of elegit shall be issued after the coming into operation of this section.

(2) Subsections (1) to (3) and (5) of section one hundred and ninety-five of the Law of Property Act 1925 (which provide that judgments entered up in the Supreme Court operate, subject to the provisions of those subsections, as charges on land of the judgment debtor) shall cease to have effect.

(3) Section one hundred and thirty-six of the County Courts Act 1934 (which relates to the removal to the High Court of a county court judgment where the judgment debtor has no goods or chattels which can be conveniently seized to satisfy the judgment) shall cease to have effect.

Power of courts to impose charges on land of judgment debtor

35.—(1) The High Court may, for the purpose of enforcing a judgment or order of those courts respectively for the payment of money to a person, by order impose on any such land or interest in land of the debtor as may be specified in the order a charge for securing the payment of any moneys due or to become due under the judgment or order.

(2) An order under subsection (1) of this section may be made either absolutely or subject to conditions as to notifying the debtor or as to the time when the charge is to become enforceable or as to other matters.

(3) The Land Charges Act 1925 and the Land Registration Act 1925 shall apply in relation to orders under subsection (1) of this section as they apply in relation to other writs or orders affecting land issued or made for the purpose of enforcing judgments, but, save as aforesaid, a charge imposed under the said subsection (1) shall have the like effect and shall be enforceable in the same courts and in the same manner as an equitable charge created by the debtor by writing under his hand.

(4) The preceding provisions of this section shall apply in relation to a judgment, order, decree or award (however called) of any court or arbitrator (including any foreign court or foreign arbitrator) which is or has become enforceable (whether wholly or to a limited extent) as if it were a judgment or order of the High Court as they apply in relation to a judgment or order of the High Court.

Receivers

36.—(1) The power of the High Court to appoint a receiver by way of equitable execution shall be extended so as to operate in relation to all legal estates and interests in land.

(2) The said power may be exercised in relation to an estate or interest in land whether or not a charge has been imposed on that land under the last preceding section for the purpose of enforcing the judgment, decree, order or award in question, and the said power shall be in addition to and not in derogation of any power of any court to appoint a receiver in proceedings for enforcing such a charge.

(3) Where an order under the last preceding section imposing a charge for the purpose of enforcing a judgment, decree, order or award has been registered under section six of the Land Charges Act 1925, subsection (1) of section seven of that Act (which provides that, amongst other things, an order appointing a receiver and any proceedings pursuant to the order or in obedience thereto shall be void against a purchaser unless the order is for the time being registered under section six of that Act) shall not apply to an order appointing a receiver made either in proceedings for enforcing the charge or by way of equitable execution of the judgment, decree, order or award or, as the case may be, of so much thereof as requires payment of moneys secured by the charge.

(4) Consequentially on the provisions of subsection (1) of this section, in subsection (2) of section forty of the Bankruptcy Act 1914, for the words " or, in the case of an equitable interest," and in subsection (2) of section three hundred and twenty-five of the Companies Act 1948, for the words " and, in the case of an equitable interest," the word " or " shall be substituted.

IV

Rules of the Supreme Court

ORDER 30

RECEIVERS

Application for receiver and injunction

1.—(1) An application for the appointment of a receiver may be made by summons or motion.

(2) An application for an injunction ancillary or incidental to an order appointing a receiver may be joined with the application for such order.

(3) Where the applicant wishes to apply for the immediate grant of such an injunction, he may do so ex parte on affidavit.

(4) The Court hearing an application under paragraph (3) may grant an injunction restraining the party beneficially entitled to any interest in the property of which a receiver is sought from assigning, charging or otherwise dealing with that property until after the hearing of a summons for the appointment of the receiver and may require such a summons, returnable on such date as the Court may direct, to be issued.

Giving of security by receiver

2.—(1) Where a judgment is given, or order made, directing the appointment of a receiver, then, unless the judgment or order otherwise directs, a person shall not be appointed receiver in accordance with the judgment or order until he has given security in accordance with this rule.

(2) Where by virtue of paragraph (1), or of any judgment or order appointing a person named therein to be receiver, a person is required to give security in accordance with this rule he must give security approved by the Court duly to account for what he receives as receiver and to deal with it as the Court directs.

(3) Unless the Court otherwise directs, the security shall be by guarantee or, if the amount for which the security is to be given does not exceed £1,000, by an undertaking.

(4) The guarantee or undertaking must be filed in the Central Office unless the cause or matter in which the receiver in question is appointed is proceeding in the Admiralty Registry, the principal registry of the Family Division or a district registry, in which case it must be filed in that registry, and it shall be kept as of record until duly vacated.

Remuneration of receiver

3. A person appointed receiver shall be allowed such proper remuneration, if any, as may be fixed by the Court.

Receiver's accounts

4.—(1) A receiver must submit accounts to the Court at such intervals or on such dates as the Court may direct in order that they may be passed.

(2) Unless the Court otherwise directs, each account submitted by a receiver must be accompanied by an affidavit verifying it.

(3) The receiver's account and affidavit (if any) must be left at the appropriate office, and the plaintiff or party having the conduct of the cause or matter must thereupon obtain an appointment for the purpose of passing such account.

(4) The passing of a receiver's account must be certified by a master, the Admiralty Registrar, a registrar of the Family Division or a district registrar, as the case may be.

Payment of balance, etc. by receiver

5. The days on which a receiver must pay into court the amounts shown by his account as due from him, or such part thereof as the Court may certify as proper to be paid in by him, shall be fixed by the Court.

Default by receiver

6.—(1) Where a receiver fails to attend for the passing of any account of his, or fails to submit any account, make any affidavit or do any other thing which he is required to submit, make or do, he and any or all of the parties to the cause or matter in which he was appointed may be required to attend in chambers to show cause for the failure, and the Court may, either in chambers or after adjournment into court, give such directions as it thinks proper including, if necessary, directions for the discharge of the receiver and the appointment of another and the payment of costs.

(2) Without prejudice to paragraph (1), where a receiver fails to attend for the passing of any account of his or fails to submit any account or fails to pay into court on the date fixed by the Court any sum shown by his account as due from him, the Court may disallow any remuneration claimed by the receiver in any subsequent account and may, where he has failed to pay any such sum into court, charge him with interest at the rate of £5 per cent. per annum on that sum while in his possession as receiver.

ORDER 51

RECEIVERS: EQUITABLE EXECUTION

Appointment of receiver by way of equitable execution

1.—(1) Where an application is made for the appointment of a receiver by way of equitable execution, the Court in determining whether it is just or convenient that the appointment should be made shall have regard to the amount claimed by the judgment creditor, to the amount likely to be obtained by the receiver and to the probable costs of his appointment and may direct an inquiry on any of these matters or any other matter before making the appointment.

(2) Where on an application for the appointment of a receiver by way of equitable execution it appears to the Court that the judgment creditor is resident outside the scheduled territories, or is acting by order or on behalf of a person so resident, then, unless the permission of the Treasury required by the Exchange Control Act 1947 has been given unconditionally or on conditions that have been complied with, any order for the appointment of a receiver shall direct that the receiver shall pay into court to the credit of the cause or matter in which he is appointed any balance due from him after deduction of his proper remuneration.

Masters and registrars may appoint receiver, etc.

2. Subject, in the Chancery Division, to any directions given by the judges of that Division under Order 32, rule 14, a master and the Admiralty Registrar and a registrar of the Family Division shall have power to make an order for the appointment of a receiver by way of equitable execution and to grant an injunction if, and only so far as, the injunction is ancillary or incidental to such an order.

Application of rules as to appointment of receiver, etc.

3. An application for the appointment of a receiver by way of equitable execution may be made in accordance with Order 30, rule 1,

and rules 2 to 6 of that Order shall apply in relation to a receiver appointed by way of equitable execution as they apply in relation to a receiver appointed for any other purpose.

ORDER 87

DEBENTURE HOLDERS' ACTIONS: RECEIVER'S REGISTER

Receiver's register

1. Every receiver appointed by the Court in an action to enforce registered debentures or registered debenture stock shall, if so directed by the Court, keep a register of transfers of, and other transmissions of title to, such debentures or stock (in this Order referred to as " the receiver's register ").

Registration of transfers, etc.

2.—(1) Where a receiver is required by rule 1 to keep a receiver's register, then, on the application of any person entitled to any debentures or debenture stock by virtue of any transfer or other transmission of title, and on production of such evidence of identity and title as the receiver may reasonably require, the receiver shall, subject to the following provisions of this rule, register the transfer or other transmission of title in that register.

(2) Before registering a transfer the receiver must, unless the due execution of the transfer is proved by affidavit, send by post to the registered holder of the debentures or debenture stock transferred at his registered address a notice stating—

   (a) that an application for the registration of the transfer has been made, and

   (b) that the transfer will be registered unless within the period specified in the notice the holder informs the receiver that he objects to the registration,

and no transfer shall be registered until the period so specified has elapsed.

The period to be specified in the notice shall in no case be less than 7 days after a reply from the registered holder would in the ordinary course of post reach the receiver if the holder had replied to the notice on the day following the day when in the ordinary course of post the notice would have been delivered at the place to which it was addressed.

(3) On registering a transfer or other transmission of title under this rule the receiver must indorse a memorandum thereof on the debenture or certificate of debenture stock, as the case may be, transferred or transmitted, containing a reference to the action and to the order appointing him receiver.

Application for rectification of receiver's register

3.—(1) Any person aggrieved by any thing done or omission made by a receiver under rule 2 may apply to the Court for rectification of the receiver's register, the application to be made by summons in the action in which the receiver was appointed.

(2) The summons shall in the first instance be served only on the plaintiff or other party having the conduct of the action but the Court may direct the summons or notice of the application to be served on any other person appearing to be interested.

(3) The Court hearing an application under this rule may decide any question relating to the title of any person who is party to the application to have his name entered in or omitted from the receiver's register and generally may decide any question necessary or expedient to be decided for the rectification of that register.

Receiver's register evidence of transfers, etc.

4. Any entry made in the receiver's register, if verified by an affidavit made by the receiver or by such other person as the Court may direct, shall in all proceedings in the action in which the receiver was appointed be evidence of the transfer or transmission of title to which the entry relates and, in particular, shall be accepted as evidence thereof for the purpose of any distribution of assets, notwithstanding that the transfer or transmission has taken place after the making of a certificate in the action certifying the holders of the debentures or debenture stock certificates.

Proof of title of holder of bearer debenture, etc.

5.—(1) This rule applies in relation to an action to enforce bearer debentures or to enforce debenture stock in respect of which the company has issued debenture stock bearer certificates.

(2) Notwithstanding that judgment has been given in the action and that a certificate has been made therein certifying the holders of such debentures or certificates as are referred to in paragraph (1), the title of any person claiming to be such a holder shall (in the absence of notice of any defect in the title) be sufficiently proved by the production of the debenture or debenture stock certificate, as the case may be, together with a certificate of identification signed by the person producing the debenture or certificate identifying the debenture or certificate produced and certifying the person (giving his name and address) who is the holder thereof.

(3) Where such a debenture or certificate as is referred to in paragraph (1) is produced in the chambers of the judge, the solicitor of the plaintiff in the action must cause to be indorsed thereon a notice stating—

　(a) that the person whose name and address is specified in the notice (being the person named as the holder of the debenture or certificate in the certificate of identification produced under paragraph (2)) has been recorded in the chambers of the judge as the holder of the debenture or debenture stock certificate, as the case may be, and

(b) that that person will, on producing the debenture or debenture stock certificate, as the case may be, be entitled to receive payment of any dividend in respect of that debenture or stock unless before payment a new holder proves his title in accordance with paragraph (2), and

(c) that if a new holder neglects to prove his title as aforesaid he may incur additional delay, trouble and expense in obtaining payment.

(4) The solicitor of the plaintiff in the action must preserve any certificates of identification produced under paragraph (2) and must keep a record of the debentures and debenture stock certificates so produced and of the names and addresses of the persons producing them and of the holders thereof, and, if the Court requires it, must verify the record by affidavit.

Requirements in connection with payments

6.—(1) Where in an action to enforce any debentures or debenture stock an order is made for payment in respect of the debentures or stock, the Accountant-General shall not make a payment in respect of any such debenture or stock unless either there is produced to him the certificate for which paragraph (2) provides or the Court has in the case in question for special reason dispensed with the need for the certificate and directed payment to be made without it.

(2) For the purpose of obtaining any such payment the debenture or debenture stock certificate must be produced to the solicitor of the plaintiff in the action or to such other person as the Court may direct, and that solicitor or person must indorse thereon a memorandum of payment and must make and sign a certificate certifying that the statement set out in the certificate has been indorsed on the debenture or debenture stock certificate, as the case may be, and send the certificate to the Accountant-General.

V

The Companies (Forms) Order 1949

No. of Company........   Form No. 53

(No
Registration
Fee payable)

THE COMPANIES ACT 1948

NOTICE OF APPOINTMENT OF A RECEIVER OR MANAGER

Pursuant to Section 102 (1)

Name of Company......................................Limited

Presented by

....

....

....

To the Registrar of Companies

I,..

of ....

with reference to ....

.... Limited

hereby give notice that:—

(*a*) I have obtained an Order of the (*b*)........................

dated the .... day of .... 19 ...... for the appointment of

....

of ....

as (*c*)

*(1) of the whole or substantially the whole of the property of this company.

*(2) of part of the property of this company.

*(3) of the income arising from the property or part of the property of this company,

on behalf of the holders of (*d*) ....

(*a*) On the .... day of .... 19 .... I appointed

.... of ....

as (*c*) ....

*(1) of the whole or substantially the whole of the property of this company.

*(2) of part of the property of this company.

*(3) of the income arising from the property or part of the property of this company,

on behalf of the holders of (*d*) ....

under the powers contained in that instrument.

(*Signature*)...........................

Dated the .... day of .... 19 ....

(*a*) *Of these two paragraphs strike out that which does not apply.*

(*b*) *Name of Court making the order.*

(*c*) " Receiver " *or* " Manager " *or* " Receiver and Manager " *as the case may be.*

(*d*) *Describe fully the instrument under which appointment is made, and state whether it is a debenture secured by a floating charge.*

* *Delete as necessary.*

No. of Company......   Form No. 57

(No
Registration
Fee payable)

THE COMPANIES ACT 1948

RECEIVER OF MANAGER'S ABSTRACT OF RECEIPTS
AND PAYMENTS

Pursuant to Sections 372 (2) and 374 (1)

Name of Company .... *Limited* ..

*Name and
address of
Receiver or
Manager.*   ....
                   ....

*Date and
description
of security
containing
the powers
under which
Receiver or
Manager is
appointed.*   ....
                   ....
                   ....
                   ....
                   ....

*Period
covered by
the Abstract.*   From
                   ....
                   To
                   ....

Presented by

          ....
          ....
          ....

ABSTRACT

Receipts			Payments	
Brought forward ..	£	p	Brought forward ..	£ p
			The receipts and payments must severally be added up at the foot of each sheet and the totals carried forward from one abstract to another without any intermediate balance, so that the gross totals shall represent the total amounts received and paid by the Receiver or Manager since the date of appointment.	
Carried forward ..			Carried forward ..	

(*Signature*).........................

Dated the .... day of .... 19 ....

No. of Company......   Form No. 57A

THE COMPANIES ACT 1948

(No
Registration
Fee payable)

NOTICE OF CEASING TO ACT AS RECEIVER OR MANAGER

Pursuant to Section 102 (2)

Name of Company .... Limited

Presented by

....

....

....

_____

To the Registrar of Companies.

   I,...

of ....

hereby give you notice that I ceased to act as Receiver and/or Manager

of ....

.... Limited,

on the .... day of .... 19 ......

                (*Signature*).........................

Dated the .... day of .... 19 ....

THE COMPANIES ACT 1948
NOTICE OF APPOINTMENT OF RECEIVER OR MANAGER

Pursuant to Section 372 (1) (a)

To (a)...

....

I, ... of .... hereby give notice that:—

(b) Under an Order of the (c)................................

dated the .... day of .... 19 .... in the matter of (d) ....

I was appointed (e) .... of (f) ....
of the property of your company.

(b) On the .... day of .... 19 .... I was appointed (e) .... of (g) ....
of the property of your company under the powers contained in an instrument dated (h)   ....

(*Signature*).......................

Dated the .... day of .... 19 ....

(a) *Name of company.*
(b) *Of these two paragraphs strike out that which does not apply.*
(c) *Name of Court making Order.*
(d) *Short title of action.*
(e) " Receiver " *or* " Manager " *or* " Receiver and Manager " *as the case may be.*
(f) *Short recital from the Order of the property over which appointed.*
(g) *Short description of the property over which appointed.*
(h) *Describe fully the instrument under which the appointment is made.*

No. of Company........   Form No. 109

THE COMPANIES ACT 1948

STATEMENT AS TO THE AFFAIRS OF * .... LIMITED

Submitted in pursuance of Sections 372 (1) (*b*) and 373 (2) of the
Companies Act 1948

IN THE MATTER OF A DEBENTURE (SERIES OF DEBENTURES)

REGISTERED......................19......

Statement as at the .... day of .... 19 .... the date
of the appointment of the Receiver.

We, ... of ....

a director of .... Limited

and .... of

.... the secretary thereof

do solemnly and sincerely declare that the statement made overleaf and

the several lists hereunto annexed marked ...... are to the best of our

knowledge and belief a full, true and complete statement as to the

affairs of the above-named company on the .... day of ....

19 .... the date of the appointment of the Receiver.

Declared at .... ⎤
this ...... day of ...... 19 .... | *Signatures* ....
Before me .... | ....
A Commissioner of Oaths. ⎦

The Commissioner is particularly requested, before accepting the
Declaration, to ascertain that the full name, address and description of
each Declarant are stated, and to initial all crossings-out or other
alterations on the printed form. A deficiency in the Declaration in any
of the above respects will entail its refusal, and will necessitate its being
re-declared.

NOTE.—The several lists annexed are not exhibits to the Declaration.

---

* *Insert full name of company.*

No. of Company......   Form No. 109A

THE COMPANIES ACT 1948

STATEMENT AS TO THE AFFAIRS OF *.......... LIMITED
Submitted in pursuance of Sections 372 (1) (*b*) and 373 (2) of the
Companies Act 1948

IN THE HIGH COURT OF JUSTICE

Chancery Division

IN THE MATTER OF †............

Statement as at the .... day of .... 19 ...., the date of
the appointment of the Receiver.

We, ... of ....
a director of .... Limited
and..
of .... the secretary thereof
make oath and say that the statement made overleaf and the several
lists hereunto annexed marked .... are to the best of our
knowledge and belief a full, true and complete statement as to the
affairs of the above-named company, on the .... day of ......
19 ...., the date of the appointment of the Receiver.

Sworn at ....
this ...... day of ...... 19 ....   } *Signatures*..................
Before me ....
A Commissioner of Oaths.

The Commissioner is particularly requested, before swearing the
Affidavit, to ascertain that the full name, address and description of
each Deponent are stated, and to initial any crossings-out or other
alterations in the printed form. A deficiency in the Affidavit in any of
the above respects will entail its refusal by the Court, and will necessitate
its being re-sworn.

NOTE.—The several lists annexed are not exhibits to the Affidavit.

---

* *Insert full name of company.*
†*Insert title of action.*

STATEMEN'
TO BE ANNE

STATEMENT AS TO THE AFFAIRS OF

....LIMITED

ON THE ....19.., THE DATE OF THE APPOINTMENT OF THE RECEIVER, SHOWING ASSETS AT ESTIMATED REALISABLE VALUES AND LIABILITIES EXPECTED TO RANK

Estim
Realis
Val
£

ASSETS NOT SPECIFICALLY PLEDGED (as per List "A")

Balance at Bank	.. ..
Cash in Hand ..	.. ..
Marketable Securities ..	.. ..
Bills Receivable ..	.. ..
Trade Debtors ..	.. ..
Loans and Advances ..	.. ..
Unpaid Calls ..	.. ..
Stock in Trade ..	.. ..
Work in Progress	.. ..
....	.. ..
Freehold Property ..	.. ..
Leasehold Property ..	.. ..
Plant and Machinery ..	.. ..
Furniture, Fittings, Utensils, etc.	.. ..
Patents, Trade Marks, etc.	.. ..
Investments other than marketable securities ..	.. .. ..
Other property, viz.:—	
....	.. ..
....	.. ..

	(a) Estimated Realisable Values	(b) Due to Secured Creditors	(c) Deficiency ranking as Unsecured (see next page)	Surplus carried to last column
ASSETS SPECIFICALLY PLEDGED (as per List " B ") Freehold Property	£	£	£	£
	£	£	£	£

Estimated surplus from Assets specifically pledged .. .. ..

ESTIMATED TOTAL ASSETS AVAILABLE FOR PREFERENTIAL CREDITORS, DEBENTURE HOLDERS SECURED BY A FLOATING CHARGE, AND UNSECURED CREDITORS * (carried forward to next page) .. .. £

SUMMARY OF GROSS ASSETS

(d)
£

Gross realisable value of assets specifically pledged   .. ..

Other assets   .. ..

GROSS ASSETS   .. .. £

AIRS AND LISTS
ORMS 109 AND 109A

TED TOTAL ASSETS AVAILABLE FOR PREFERENTIAL CREDITORS, DEBENTURE
DERS SECURED BY A FLOATING CHARGE, AND UNSECURED CREDITORS *   £
ught forward from preceding page).

e)   LIABILITIES
oss   (to be deducted from surplus or added to
lities   deficiency as the case may be)
£
          SECURED CREDITORS (as per List " B ") to extent to which claims
             are estimated to be covered by Assets specifically pledged
             (item (a) or (b) on preceding page, whichever is the less)   ..
             [Insert in " Gross Liabilities " column only.]
          PREFERENTIAL CREDITORS (as per List " C ")   ..   ..   ..

          Estimated balance of assets available for Debenture Holders
             secured by a floating charge, and Unsecured Creditors *   .. £
          DEBENTURE HOLDERS secured by a floating charge (as per List
             " D ")   ..   ..

          Estimated SURPLUS/DEFICIENCY as regards Debenture Holders *   £

          UNSECURED CREDITORS (as per List " E "):—   £
             Estimated unsecured balance of claims of
                Creditors partly secured on specific assets,
                brought from preceding page (c).
             Trade Accounts   ..   ..
             Bills Payable   ..   ..
             Outstanding Expenses   ..   ..
             ....
             ....
             Contingent Liabilities (State nature):—
             ....

          ESTIMATED   SURPLUS/DEFICIENCY   AS   REGARDS
             CREDITORS *
                being difference between: £
                GROSS ASSETS brought from preceding
                   page (d)   ..   ..
                and GROSS LIABILITIES as per column (e)

          ISSUED AND CALLED-UP CAPITAL:
             ....preference shares of .... each   £
             .... called-up   ..   ..
             ....ordinary shares of .... each
             ....called-up   ..   ..
             ....
             ....

          ESTIMATED   SURPLUS/DEFICIENCY   AS   REGARDS
             MEMBERS * (as per List " F ")   £

ese figures must be read subject to the following notes:—
1) (f) There is no unpaid capital liable to be called-up, or   Strike out
    (g) The nominal amount of unpaid capital liable to be   (f) or (g)
         called-up is £   estimated to produce £   which
         is/is not charged in favour of Debenture Holders.
2) The estimates are subject to costs of the Receivership and
    to any surplus or deficiency on trading pending realisation
    of the Assets.

Statement of affairs
List " A "

LIST " A "—ASSETS NOT SPECIFICALLY PLEDGED

Full particulars of every description of property not specifically pledged and not included in any other list are to be set forth in this list

Full statement and nature of property	Book value £	Estimated to produce £	p
Balance at bank .. .. *(State name of bankers)*	:		
Cash in hand	:		
Marketable securities, viz.:—	:		
Bills receivable (as per Schedule I)	:		
Trade debtors (as per Schedule II)	:		
Loans and advances, viz.:—	:		
Unpaid calls (as per Schedule III)	:		
Stock in Trade .. .. *(State nature)*	:		
Work in progress .. .. *(State nature)*	:		
Freehold property, viz.:—	:		
Leasehold property, viz.:—	:		
Plant and machinery, viz.:—	:		
Furniture, fittings, utensils, etc.	:		
Patents, trade marks, etc., viz.:—	:		
Investments other than marketable securities, viz.:—	:		
Other property, viz.:—	:		

Dated 19 .

Signature

SCHEDULE I.—BILLS OF EXCHANGE, PROMISSORY NOTES, ETC., ON HAND AVAILABLE AS ASSETS
The names to be arranged in alphabetical order and numbered consecutively

Statement of Affairs
Schedule I to List " A "

No.	Name of acceptor of Bill or Note	Address, etc.	Amount of Bill or Note		Date when due	Estimated to produce		Particulars of any property held as security for payment of Bill or Note
			£	p		£	p	

Dated   19 .

Signature

SCHEDULE II.—TRADE DEBTORS

The names to be arranged in alphabetical order and numbered consecutively

NOTE:—If the debtor to the company is also a creditor, but for a less amount than his indebtedness, the gross amount due to the company and the amount of the contra account should be shown in the third column, and the balance only be inserted under the heading " Amount of Debt " thus:—

£   p.

Due to company   ..   ..   ..
Less: Contra account   ..   ..   ..
No such claim should be included in List " E "

Statement of Affairs
Schedule II to List " A "

No.	Name	Residence and Occupation	Amount of Debt						Folio of Ledger or other book where particulars are to be found	When contracted		Estimated to produce		Particulars of any securities held for debt
			Good		Doubtful		Bad			Month	Year			
			£	p	£	0	£	p				£	p	

Dated   19 .

Signature

SCHEDULE III—UNPAID CALLS

Statement of Affairs

Schedule III to List "A"   The names to be arranged in alphabetical order and numbered consecutively

Consecutive No.	No. in share register	Name of Shareholder	Address	No. of shares held	Amount of call per share unpaid £ p	Total amount due £ p	Estimated to realize £ p

Signature   Dated   19 .

LIST "B".—ASSETS SPECIFICALLY PLEDGED AND CREDITORS FULLY OR PARTLY SECURED
(NOT INCLUDING DEBENTURE HOLDERS SECURED BY A FLOATING CHARGE)

Statement of Affairs

List "B"   The names of the secured creditors are to be shown against the assets on which their claims are secured, numbered consecutively, and arranged in alphabetical order as far as possible

Particulars of assets specifically pledged	Date when security given	Estimated value of security £ p	No.	Name of Creditor	Address and Occupation	Amount of debt £ p	Date when contracted — Month	Date when contracted — Year	Consideration	Balance of debt unsecured carried to List "E" £ p	Estimated surplus from security £ p

Signature   Dated   19 .

Statement of Affairs
List "C"

LIST "C"—PREFERENTIAL CREDITORS FOR RATES, TAXES, SALARIES, WAGES AND OTHERWISE

The names to be arranged in alphabetical order and numbered consecutively

No.	Name of Creditor	Address and Occupation	Nature of Claim	Period during which claim accrued due	Date when due	Amount of Claim		Amount payable in full		Balance not preferential carried to List "E"	
						£	p	£	p	£	p

Signature Dated 19 .

Statement of Affairs
List "D"

LIST "D"—LIST OF DEBENTURE HOLDERS SECURED BY A FLOATING CHARGE

The names to be arranged in alphabetical order and numbered consecutively
Separate Lists must be furnished of holders of each issue of Debentures, should more than one issue have been made

No.	Name of Holder	Address	Amount		Description of assets over which security extends
			£	p	

Signature Dated 19 .

Statement of Affairs

LIST " E "—UNSECURED CREDITORS

List " E "

NOTES,—1.   The names to be arranged in alphabetical order and numbered consecutively

When there is a contra account against the creditor less than his claim against the company, the amount of the creditor's claim and the amount of the contra account should be shown in the third column and the balance only be inserted under the heading " Amount of Debt " thus:—

	£	p
Total amount of claim	..	..	..	..
Less: Contra account	..	..	..	..

No such set-off should be included in Schedule I attached to List "A".

2.   The particulars of any Bills of Exchange and Promissory Notes held by a creditor should be inserted immediately below the name and address of such creditor.

No.	Name	Address and Occupation	Amount of Debt		Date when contracted		Consideration
			£	p	Month	Year	
		Unsecured balance of creditors partly secured—brought from List " B "					
		Balance not preferential of preferential creditors—brought from List " C "					

Signature   Dated   19 .

Statement of Affairs

List " F "

LIST " F "—DEFICIENCY OR SURPLUS ACCOUNT

The period covered by this Account must commence on a date not less than three years before the appointment of the Receiver, or, if the company has not been incorporated for the whole of that period, the date of formation of the company, unless the Receiver otherwise agrees.

ITEMS CONTRIBUTING TO DEFICIENCY (OR REDUCING SURPLUS):

£

1. Excess (if any) of Capital and Liabilities over Assets on the ....19....as shown by Balance Sheet (copy annexed)   :   :   :   :   :

2. Net dividends and bonuses declared during the period from ....19.... to the date of the Statement   :   :

3. Net trading losses (after charging items shown in note below) for the same period.   :   :   :

4. Losses other than trading losses written off for which provision has been made in the books during the same period (give particulars or annex schedule)   :   :   :

5. Estimated losses now written off for which provision has been made for the purpose of preparing the Statement (give particulars or annex schedule)   :   :   :

6. Other items contributing to Deficiency or reducing Surplus:
....

£

ITEMS REDUCING DEFICIENCY (OR CONTRIBUTING TO SURPLUS):

£

7. Excess (if any) of Assets over Capital and Liabilities on the ....19.... as shown on the Balance Sheet (copy annexed)   :   :

8. Net trading profits (after charging items shown in note below) for the period from the ....19.... to the date of the Statement   :   :   :

9. Profits and income other than trading profits during the same period (give particulars or annex schedule)   :   :

10. Other items reducing Deficiency or contributing to Surplus: :   :
....

DEFICIENCY/SURPLUS as shown by Statement

£

LIST " F ".—DEFICIENCY OR SURPLUS ACCOUNT—*continued*

NOTE AS TO NET TRADING PROFITS AND LOSSES:

Particulars are to be inserted here (so far as applicable) of the items mentioned below, which are to be taken into account in arriving at the amount of net trading profit or losses shown in this Account:—

	£
Provisions for depreciation, renewals or diminution in value of fixed assets	
Charges for United Kingdom income tax and other United Kingdom taxation on profits	
Interest on debentures and other fixed loans	
Payments to directors made by the company and required by law to be disclosed in the accounts	
Exceptional or non-recurring expenditure:—	
....	£
Less:—Exceptional or non-recurring receipts:—	
....	£
Balance, being other trading profits or losses	£
Net trading profits or losses as shown in Deficiency or Surplus Accounts above	

Signature ... ... Dated ... ... 19 .

Statement of Affairs
List "G"

LIST "G"

In substitution for such of the lists "A" to "F" as will have to be returned blank

List	Particulars	Remarks
		Where no entries are made on any one or more of the Lists "A" to "F" the word "Nil" should be inserted in this column opposite the List or Lists thus left blank
A	Assets not specifically pledged	
B	Assets specifically pledged and creditors fully or partly secured (not including debenture holders secured by a floating charge).	
C	Preferential creditors for Rates, Taxes, Salaries, Wages and otherwise	
D	Debenture holders secured by floating charge	
E	Unsecured creditors	
F	Deficiency or Surplus Account	

Signature

Dated   19

VI

Securities Comparable to Floating Charges in Other Jurisdictions

United States of America. A " floating lien " may be validly conferred by the creation of a " security interest " under Article 9 of the Uniform Commercial Code, comprising a " financing statement " in writing, which refers to the assets or categories of assets charged, and is " filed " (*i.e.* registered) in each State where those assets are situated.

Japan. The two systems of floating charge, " Fuyu Tampo " (non-statutory) and " Kigyō Tampo " (statutory) differ widely in respect of their form, the assets chargeable thereby, the giving of notice, and the need for registration and the modes of enforcement.

West Germany. The forms in current use (which are steadily developing) include (1) the " Raumsicherungsvertrag " (analogous to a warehousekeeper's lien which has been expanded into a charge over the varying contents of an industrial or commercial building, somewhat resembling the United States system of " field warehousing ") which is itself a species of the class of " Sicherungsübereignung," and (2) the " Globalzessionsvertrag," a species of general assignment of book-debts or classes of book-debts, present and/or future. The chargee must not take a charge on the *whole* of his debtor's assets, on pain of making himself liable *pro tanto* for his debtor's debts. German jurisprudence also regards the practice or doctrine of " Eigentumsvorbehalt " (the reservation by the vendor of goods of the title thereto until he is paid) as resembling a floating charge, having regard to the extensive rights thereby conferred on the vendor to secure payment of the price: this is particularly the case with the " extended " form, known as the " erlängerter Eigentumsvorbehalt " and other yet more complex devices extending the charge over the goods when worked upon, mixed or combined, or over the whole of the purchases of goods by a group of companies, jointly and severally. None are registrable. Reference may be made to the *Romalpa* case (p. 282, *ante*). Considerable problems of conflict arise between the charges described above and the doctrine of reservation of title.

France. The only legal forms are the " Nantissement de fonds de commerce " (a charge on the goodwill of a business, defined as the totality of the commercial undertaking) and the " Nantissement d'outillage et du matériel d'Equipement " (a charge over plant and machinery). Neither include raw materials, work in progress or finished goods. Both are registrable in statutory form.

Belgium. Resembles France, above.

The Netherlands. There is a species of charge entitled " Eigendomsverdracht tot zekerheid " (transfer of property for security purposes) which covers practically all categories of assets, and is not registrable. The observations on reservation of title under " West Germany " above apply in considerable part also to the Netherlands.

Sweden. There is a " Företagsinteckning " (business mortgage), which appears capable of charging practically all classes of business assets. It is registrable.

Norway. There is a " Forlagspant " (a charge over the inventory, including raw materials, work in progress and finished goods) and a " Tilbehørspant " (or " Industripant ") (a charge on plant, transport, fixtures and fittings), limited to undertakings above a certain size. All are registrable.

VII
Effect of Draft EEC Bankruptcy Convention, if Adopted

Since 1970, there has been in currency a " Preliminary Draft Convention on Bankruptcy, Winding-up, Arrangements, Compositions and Similar Proceedings," prepared under the auspices of the Commission of the European Economic Communities. The Draft Convention was originally prepared on the basis of the original Six Member States of the EEC (" the Six "), but with the enlargement of the Communities in 1972 by the accession of the United Kingdom, Eire and Denmark to comprise now " the Nine " Member States, the draft is is under further review.[1]

In August 1976 the Department of Trade published the Report of the Advisory Committee on the Draft Convention, in which the probable effects of a Convention in such terms upon the United Kingdom law and business practice were examined; among the subjects discussed in that Report were Floating Charges and Receiverships.[2] It was the opinion of the Committee that a floating charge in the current United Kingdom form might, in Member States where the concept of such a charge was not a recognised and accepted part of their legislation or jurisprudence (*i.e.* in principle all Member States except Eire) be attacked either as (1) conferring no effective charge upon the assets of the grantor of the floating charge within the relevant Member State, or (2) as constituting a " fraud upon creditors," in the special sense expressed by " the Paulian action," or (3) in any event as a transaction falling within one of the provisions of the Uniform Law intended to be imposed on the Member States by Annex 1, Article 4.

The first and second categories of invalidity are of course common to all countries (whether Members of the EEC or not) where floating charges are not recognised or the Paulian action forms part of their jurisprudence; the Draft Convention would however institutionalise these grounds of impeachment and would, if and when the Draft

---

[1] The current revised draft is numbered CEE Doc.XI/449/1/75-E dated December 15, 1976 (original drafted in French dated October 1, 1975). The Report of the Advisory Committee (Cmnd. 6602 (1976)) was based on an earlier draft, the French version of which was numbered CEE Doc.3.327/1/XIV/70F and dated February 16, 1970, and the English version of which was dated August 1974. Some of the revisions were of substance: see n. 6, p. 408, *post.*

[2] The relevant paragraphs are 59 and 60, and 361 to 367; the latter are printed, *infra.*

Convention is adopted and ratified, become, through Article 4, part of the legislation of the United Kingdom.[3]

Article 35 of the Draft Convention is entitled " Suspect periods, actions to set aside frauds on creditors [4] and set off " and provides " (1) The invalidity as against the general body of creditors of transactions effected by the debtor before the opening of the bankruptcy shall be governed by Article 4 of Annex 1. (2) The law applicable to the proceedings referred to in Article 4 (F) of Annex 1 shall be that of the State in which the bankruptcy is opened. . . ." In connection with Article 35 (2), it must be noted first that jurisdiction to open " bankruptcy proceedings " (which by the terminology of the Convention includes winding-up proceedings) is exclusively conferred on the courts of the Member State within which the debtor has his (or its) " centre of administration," namely the place where he (or it) " usually administers his main interests "; this place will generally be presumed to be his (or its) registered office (*ibid*. Art. 3) and, secondly, that the like exclusive jurisdiction is conferred by Article 17 (1) (2) and (3) on those courts to entertain proceedings to invalidate transactions carried out by the debtor during " the suspect period " or in fraud of the rights of his creditors.

Article 4 of Annex 1, referred to in Article 35 (the heading of which is " Suspect period and action to set aside frauds on creditors " [4]), provides by paragraph (A) that " the following acts shall, if done by the debtor less than one year before the opening of the bankruptcy, be void as against the general body of creditors. . . . (B) . . . (2) All securities whether contractual, arising by operation of law or created by court order or administrative regulation [5] after the date of cessation of payments and less than one year before the opening of the bankruptcy to secure debts existing prior to the creation of the security. (C) (1) All other payments made voluntarily by the debtor in respect of debts which have become due by the date of the opening of the bankruptcy, and all other acts done for valuable consideration by the debtor after the date of cessation of payments and less than one year before the opening of the bankruptcy, shall be void as against the general body of creditors, if they have prejudiced the latter, and if the persons who received the payments from the debtor or were parties to the transactions with him knew of the cessation of payments. However, for reasons of equity and by special reasoned judgment the judge may decline to declare such acts void." [6]

---

[3] As would be required, after ratification, under Art. 76 of the Convention.

[4] These words are the English " translation " of the French original text " action paulienne." " Suspect period " is also a direct " translation " of " période suspecte," the approximate equivalent of " period of relation back."

[5] As originally translated from the then French text, this sub-paragraph began: " Any security conferred under contract, by court order or by operation of law." The word " created " (French: " constituées ") must presumably still be taken to apply to each category of security.

[6] The last sentence of this paragraph, conferring a discretion on the court not to avoid the transaction, was added in the revised (1975) draft, and did not appear in

It will have been noted that in the official translation of the headings to Article 35 and Article 4 of the Uniform Law, the French term " action paulienne " has been reproduced as " actions to set aside frauds on creditors "; as already stated (*supra*, p. 408), the " Paulian action " has a considerably wider ambit than would be suggested to an English lawyer by that term, which naturally relates to " fraudulent conveyances " in English law, *i.e.* a conveyance of property with intent to defraud creditors.[7]

The concept of fraud on creditors to which the Paulian action is directed is of a more objective and less pejorative character, and is conveniently summarised in the following paragraphs from the Report of the Advisory Committee [8]:

" **The Paulian action**
361. Article 35 of the Convention and Article 4F of the Uniform Law envisage the retention in the laws of Member States of the ' Paulian action ' (see paragraph 346). This action was available in Roman Law to a creditor where (a) the debtor had impoverished himself to the detriment of his creditors, and (b) he did so in the knowledge that he was insolvent or would be made so by the act. Its effect was to annul the transaction challenged and to restore the property to the general body of creditors. It was incorporated into the French Civil Code by Article 1167 which declares that the creditors ' may also, in their personal name, attack transactions of the debtor in fraud of their rights '. As interpreted by the French courts, this article covers every species of transaction, whether done with or without valuable consideration, which creates or aggravates the debtor's state of insolvency. It may include not merely a fraudulent transfer but even a failure to accept a succession or gift. Though the text refers to the ' fraud ' of the debtor, it is not necessary in every case to establish actual fraud. When the debtor knows that a transaction into which he is entering will make him insolvent or increase his insolvency, he is presumed to intend to injure his creditors. The nature of the action implies that the creditor seeking to set the transaction aside had prior rights which the transaction prejudiced. The action is directed against the person who profited by the debtor's act and not against the debtor himself. Where that person received the debtor's property as a gift, he is liable to restore the property, whether or not he was aware of the debtor's fraud. Where he gave valuable consideration, he is liable only where he was aware of the debtor's fraud. Where the property has been transferred by that person to another person, the former

---

the 1970/1974 drafts as critically considered by the Advisory Committee at paragraphs 351 to 358.

[7] See ss. 172, 173 of the Law of Property Act 1925, replacing the Statutes of Elizabeth I.

[8] Reproduced with the authority of the Secretary of State for Trade and with the permission of H.M. Stationery Office.

is liable in damages. The latter is liable to restore the property only when he received it as a gift or was himself acting in bad faith.

362. There are analogues to the Paulian action in the legal systems of the United Kingdom. The Scots Act of 1621, c. 18, still in force, which strikes at gratuitous alienations and preferences in fraud of creditors, was modelled on the Paulian action, and the preamble refers to the intention ' to follow and practice the good and commendable laws, civil and canon, made against fraudful alienations in prejudice of creditors '. In England, the Acts of Elizabeth I impeaching fraudulent conveyances and purchases, now largely reproduced in sections 172 and 173 of the Law of Property Act 1925, have a similar purpose; but the requirement of affirmative proof of a fraudulent, or at least a dishonest, intention renders it narrower in scope than, for example, Article 1167 of the French Civil Code. These provisions of the 1925 Act give individual rights, which anyone can enforce to set aside fraudulent transactions. However, it has been held that the right to take such proceedings against a bankrupt is vested in the trustee, and this would seem to be in line with the intention in Article 4F of the Uniform Law. . . .

Floating Charges

364. Jurisdiction in actions to set aside acts done by the debtor in fraud of his creditors is exclusively conceded by Article 17 (3) to the courts of the State of the bankruptcy, and the law of that State is applicable by virtue of Article 35 (2). Unless, therefore, there is a measure of harmonisation of the principles adopted by Member States in setting aside transactions not covered by a specific period of relation-back, there is a serious risk of prejudice to persons who might have had reason to believe that a transaction entered into by them with a person who later becomes bankrupt was legally unassailable. In this respect, too, the Convention, despite the terms of Articles 75 and 76, will operate retrospectively.

365. A special problem arises in the context of floating charges (see paragraphs 59 and 60) which, though an important security device in the legal systems of the United Kingdom, are only known in other Member States in very limited forms. Section 322 of the Companies Act 1948, section 290 of the Companies Act (Northern Ireland) 1960 and section 1 (2) of the Companies (Floating Charges) (Scotland) Act 1961 provide that, where a company is being wound up, a floating charge created within the previous 12 months shall, unless it is proved that immediately after the creation of the charge the company was solvent, be invalid, except to the amount of cash paid then or thereafter to the company and interest thereon. There was some doubt, however, whether this provision superseded the Scottish rules relating to fraudulent preferences, which may be challenged without limitation as to date. The Com-

panies (Floating Charges and Receivers) (Scotland) Act 1972 removes this doubt by adding a new subsection to section 322 of the 1948 Act:

'(3) Where a company is being wound up in Scotland, a floating charge over all or any part of its property shall not be held to be an alienation or preference voidable by statute (other than by the provisions of this Act) or at common law on the ground of insolvency or notour bankruptcy .'

It may be, however, that some Community systems would regard certain forms of floating charge as alienations or preferences voidable by virtue of the Paulian action. Where, therefore, a foreign court finds that the centre of administration of a United Kingdom company is situated within its own territory and opens bankruptcy proceedings in relation to the company there, it might hold that a floating charge, even in relation to the company's assets in the United Kingdom, is invalid under the Paulian action as a ' fraudulent ' disposition.

366. We recognise the great importance of floating charges to the commercial community in the United Kingdom, and we would consider it undesirable if the Convention in any way prejudiced their validity. We recommend that a special provision should be included in the Convention (not in the Uniform Law) to afford them, and the powers of receivers and managers appointed under them, recognition throughout the Community. The provisions of the Uniform Law should then expressly include them as a security for the purposes of the law. To achieve acceptance of the United Kingdom form of floating charge within the Community, we envisage that a number of concessions, and/or protective provisions for the benefit of non-United Kingdom creditors within the Community, will need to be made, such as compulsory registration, invalidity within a period of relation-back (as under section 322 of the 1948 Act) and the prior rights of local preferential creditors; but we consider that these would be worth conceding for the obtaining of recognition of the floating charge.

367. In this connection, as we observed in paragraph 60, there is currently in preparation by the Commission of the European Communities a draft Directive on the Recognition of Non-Possessory Securities over Moveables (Reference XI/466/73-E), the text of which, and in particular the footnotes thereto, seem to go a long way towards preparing the ground for such recognition." [9]

The concept of the creation of a floating charge operating, when enforced, to the prejudice of the unsecured creditors (whether preferential or not) of a limited company has, of course, received a degree of recognition in the United Kingdom company legislation. By section 322 of the 1948 Act such charges, if created within 12 months before its

---

[9] See " Projet de Directive des sûretés mobilières sans dessaisissement et des clauses de réserve de propriété dans les ventes mobiliéres " (CEE Doc.XI/466/73-F (English version) -E).

winding up by an insolvent company, are void except to the amount of
any cash paid to the company at the time of or subsequently to the
creation of, and in consideration for the charge; by sections 94 and 319, the
proceeds of the realisation of the assets charged by any floating charge,
whether by the receiver appointed thereunder or by the debenture
holder, are applicable first in payment of debts which are or would be
preferential in the winding up of a company: and by section 320, the
charge if created within six months before the winding up of the
company at a time when it was unable to pay its debts as they fell due,
may be declared a fraudulent preference and invalid accordingly.

It would, however, seem to be arguable that, whether under the
general mantle of the Paulian action or under the express words of
Article 4 of the Uniform Law, a floating charge in the United Kingdom
form might be impeachable on grounds other than those already
prescribed by our own legislation, however imprecisely they may so far
have been adumbrated. A case where such impeachment might be
feasible is perhaps exemplified by the facts in *Re Yeovil Glove Co. Ltd.*[10]
In that case, a floating charge although created by the company, within
12 months before its winding up, in favour of its bankers to secure an
existing overdraft was held not to be invalid, since the charge had ceased
to be impeachable as a fraudulent preference and the original overdraft
had been paid off by the application of *Clayton's* case [11] leaving the
bank's subsequent advances secured by the charge.

There is a further problem presented in the application of Article 4
B2 and C1 both generally and in relation to floating charges, by the
concept of the " cessation of payments," which constitutes both an
objective test under B (1), and a subjective test, of actual notice, under
C (1). Space does not permit of a detailed examination of the scope of
this concept, again comprising a direct " translation " of the French
term " la cessation des paiements "; briefly, it connotes a state of insolvency of the debtor, whether actual, notional or imputed, to which
the " suspect period " relates back, during which period the debtor's
transactions with others are impeachable by the trustee or liquidator.
The facts of *Re Yeovil Glove Co. Ltd.*, *supra*, would, it is thought, have
satisfied a court exercising a jurisdiction founded upon such a term, both
as to proof of a requisite state of insolvency, and as to the bankers
having notice of it; indeed, both points were admitted by the bankers at
the trial.

In conclusion, therefore, it may need to be envisaged that if and when
the Draft Convention is concluded and ratified in terms such as have
been discussed above, a floating charge created in the United Kingdom,
and duly registered in accordance with our laws, might be attacked
either (1) in a " foreign " EEC bankruptcy of the chargor, if the company's " centre of administration " was then situated in a jurisdiction
not recognising or not sympathetic to a charge in such a form, or (2)

---

[10] [1965] Ch. 148, C.A.
[11] (1816) Mer. 572.

in a United Kingdom bankruptcy, in so far as it charged assets situated in such a foreign jurisdiction, to the detriment of local creditors, or (3) in a United Kingdom bankruptcy in relation to assets situated here, in so far as the laws of the United Kingdom had been amended so as to incorporate Article 4 of the Uniform Law and perhaps the Paulian action itself.

INDEX

(References to Part II: " Receivers Appointed out of Court " are in bold type.)

415

CHARGE—*cont.*
  invention of concept, **340–341**
  nature of, 160–161
  Paulian action, **342**
  payment of certain debts, and, **369**
  preferential debts, and, **348**
  Scotland, in, **342–343**
  securities comparable in other jurisdictions, **406–407**
    Belgium, **406**
    France, **406**
    Japan, **406**
    Netherlands, **406**
    Norway, **407**
    Sweden, **407**
    U.S.A., **406**
    West Germany, **406**
  test of probability of recognition by foreign jurisdiction, 347
  United States of America, **341**
  interest in land, over, 137
  interests in personalty, 137–138
  land, on, 137
  power of court to impose, **381**
  statute, under, **304**
CHARGING ORDER, 139, 142, 149
CHATTELS, 46
  delivery of possession, 174
  right of judgment creditor, 52–53
CLAIMS,
  paramount, 138
COMMITTAL,
  disturbance of receiver, 155–156
COMPANIES, 55–61, 99–101, 125–128, 160 *et seq.*, 204 *et seq.*
  accrued holiday remunerations, 213
  advance to pay preferential debts, 215
  agency of receiver for, **350–352**
  appointment of receiver, 107–110
  appointment over property of, **309** *et seq.*
    conditions for, **311**
    effect of, **312–313**
    method of, **312**
    who may be appointed, **311–312**
  assignment, 99
  board of directors, **315–316**
  books and papers, 100–101
  calls, **331–332**
  car tax, 214–215
  chattels
    right of judgment creditor, 52–53
  clerk or servant, 211–212
  contracts, and, 165
    effect of appointment on, **322** *et seq.*
    set-off, **327–328**
  contracts of service, 165–167
  contractual liens, **326–327**
  Corporation Tax, 320
  debenture holders, 56–57
  debentures, **309–310**
  debtors to, 218
  deemed insolvency, 167 *et seq.*
  directors and other officers, **333**
  distress, 216

COMPANIES—*cont.*
  enforcement of duties, 205
    Companies Act, **318**
  extra-territoriality of floating charges and receiverships, **339–348**
  failure to pay preferential debts, 216–217
  floating charge,
    crystallisation, 161–162
    nature of, 160–161
  form of application, 125–127
  forms, **388** *et seq. See also* FORMS
  fraudulent assignment, 164–165
  indemnity, extent of, **328**
  invoices, 205
  Landlord and Tenant Act 1954, **321**
  leaseholds, 217–218, **328–329**
  legal mortgages created by, **309**
  liability of receiver's principal, **324–325**
  liability to third persons in contract, **325–326**
  limited appointment, **314–315**
  liquidation, **349** *et seq. See also* LIQUIDATION
  London Building Acts, **321**
  manager, appointment of, 231
  miscellaneous debts, 215
  mortgagees, 56–57
  notice of appointment, 204, **316**
  notice on letters, **316**
  order of application of assets, 216
  order over, 127–128
  payment of Social Security debts by Secretary of State, 216
  petition to wind up, 171–172
  position of receivers of property of, **310–311**
  powers and duties generally, 219
  preferential debts, 205, 207–209
  preferential payments, **370–373**
    stannaries, **373–375**
  property comprised in appointment, **314**
  property in Scotland comprised in floating charge, **313–314**
  powers to borrow, **331**
  power to carry on business, **331**
  public,
    receiver and manager, 242–243
    rates, 209
  realisation of assets, **329–330**
  receiver agent for, **321–322**
    contract of employment, and **334–335**
  receiver's statutory obligations, **316–318**
    accounts, **317–318**
    notice to company, **316**
    preferential debts, **317**
    statement of affairs, **316–317**
  register of debentures, 205
  registration of enforcement of security **369–370**
  regularity of appointment, **315**